THE WORKER IN "POST-INDUSTRIAL" CAPITALISM

THE WORKER IN "POST-INDUSTRIAL" CAPITALISM

Liberal and Radical Responses

EDITED AND WITH INTRODUCTION BY

Bertram Silverman
Murray Yanowitch

THE FREE PRESS

A Division of Macmillan Publishing Co., Inc.

NEW YORK

The Free Press
A Division of Macmillan Publishing Co., Inc.
866 Third Avenue, New York, N.Y. 10022

Library of Congress Catalog Card Number: 73–14431

Printed in the United States of America

printing number
1 2 3 4 5 6 7 8 9 10

Library of Congress Cataloging in Publication Data

Silverman, Bertram, comp.
    The worker in "post—industrial" capitalism.

    Includes bibliographical references.
    1. Labor and laboring classes--Addresses, essays,
lectures. 2. Labor economics--Addresses, essays,
lectures. I. Yanowitch, Murray, joint comp.
II. Title.
HD4854.S55   331   73-14431
ISBN 0-02-928780-4

ACKNOWLEDGMENTS

Reinhard Bendix and Seymour Martin Lipset, "Karl Marx's Theory of Social Class," from *Class, Status and Power*, pp. 7–11. Copyright © 1966 by The Free Press, a Division of Macmillan Publishing Co., Inc. See page 27.

Selig Perlman, excerpts from *Toward a Theory of the Labor Movement*, New York: A. M. Kelley, 1949, pp. 3–10. Reprinted by permission of Mrs. Selig Perlman. See page 51.

Edward P. Thompson, "The Meaning of Class," from *The Making of the English Working Class*, pp. 9–11. Copyright © 1963 by Edward P. Thompson. Reprinted by permission of Pantheon Books, A Division of Random House, Inc. See page 55.

Paul M. Sweezy, excerpts from "Marx and the Proletariat," from *Monthly Review*, December 1967, pp. 28–29, 31–42. Copyright © 1967 by Monthly Review, Inc. Reprinted by permission of Monthly Review Press. See page 61.

Clark Kerr, John T. Dunlop, Frederick Harbison, Charles A. Myers, excerpts from *Industrialism and Industrial Man*, pp. 33–39, 40–44. Copyright ©1960 by The President and Fellows of Harvard College. Reprinted by permission of The Harvard University Press, Cambridge, Massachusetts. See page 70.

John H. Goldthorpe, "Social Stratification in Industrial Society," from *The Sociological Review*, Monograph No. 8, 1964, pp. 97–110. Reprinted by permission of the author and the publisher. See page 78.

Daniel Bell, excerpts from *The Coming of Post-Industrial Society*, pp. 123–129. Copyright © 1973 by Daniel Bell. Reprinted by permission of the author and Basic Books, Inc., New York. See page 91.

Robert L. Heilbroner, "Economic Problems of a "Post-Industrial Society," from *Dissent*, Spring 1973, pp. 163–176. Copyright © 1973 by Dissent Publishing Corporation. Reprinted by permission of *Dissent* and the author. See page 96.

Kurt B. Mayer, "The Changing Shape of the American Class Structure," from *Social Research*, Vol. 30, No. 4, Winter 1963, pp. 460–468. Copyright © 1963 by the New School for Social Research. See page 117.

Michael Harrington, excerpts from "Old Working Class, New Working Class," from *Dissent*, Winter 1972, pp. 146–158. Copyright © 1972 by Dissent Publishing Corporation. Reprinted by permission of *Dissent* and the author. See page 123.

Robert Blauner, "Alienation and Freedom in Perspective," from *Alienation and Freedom: the Factory Worker and His Industry*, pp. 169–182. Copyright © 1964 by The University of Chicago. Reprinted by permission of the author and The University of Chicago Press. See page 137.

André Gorz, excerpts from *A Strategy for Labor: A Radical Proposal*, pp. 35–40, 41–43, 46–47, 48–54, 70–73. Copyright © 1964 by Editions du Seuil; English translation copyright © 1967 by Beacon Press. Reprinted by permission of Beacon Press. See pages 148, 459.

John H. Goldthorpe, et al., "Affluence and the Workers' Work World," from *The Affluent Worker in the Class Structure*, pp. 82–84, 179–187. Copyright © 1969 by Cambridge University Press. Reprinted by permission of the author and Cambridge University Press. See page 151.

Seymour M. Lipset, excerpts from *The Political Man*, pp. 87, 89–92, 114–116. Copyright © 1959, 1960 by Seymour Martin Lipset. Reprinted by permission of Doubleday & Company, Inc. See page 160.

Seymour Michael Miller and Frank Riessman, excerpts from "Working-Class Authoritarianism: A Critique," pp. 264–267, 269–272, from *British Journal of Sociology*, September 1961. Reprinted by permission of the publisher and the authors. See page 165.

Bogdan Denitch, "Is There A New Working Class?" from *Dissent*, July–August 1970, pp. 351–355. Reprinted by permission of the author and *Dissent*. Copyright © 1970 by Dissent Publishing Corporation. See page 175.

Alain Touraine, trans. by Leonard F. X. Mayhew, excerpts from *The Post Industrial Society—Tomorrow's Social History: Classes, Conflicts, and Culture in the Programmed Society*, pp. 27–28, 51–69. Copyright © 1971 by Random House, Inc. See page 180.

Stanley Aronowitz, "Does the United States Have a New Working Class?" in *The Revival of American Socialism*, George Fischer, ed., Oxford University Press, pp. 199–216. Copyright © by Stanley Aronowitz. Reprinted by permission of the author. See page 195.

Ivar Berg, excerpts from *Education and Jobs: The Great Training Robbery*, pp. 185–194. Copyright © 1970 by Praeger Publishers, Inc. Published 1970 by Praeger Publishers, Inc., New York. Excerpted and reprinted by permission of the publisher. See page 213.

Christopher C. Lasch and Eugene D. Genovese, "The Education and the University We Need Now," from *The New York Review of Books*, October 9, 1969, pp. 21–24. Reprinted with permission of *The New York Review of Books*. Copyright © 1969 by Nyrev, Inc. See page 219.

Samuel Bowles, "Unequal Education and the Reproduction of the Hierarchical Division of Labor," from *The Capitalist System*, Richard C. Edwards, Michael Reich, Thomas E. Weisshopf, eds., pp. 219–299. Copyright © 1971 by Samuel Bowles. Reprinted by permission of the authors. See page 225.

Christopher Jencks and David Riesman, excerpts from *The Academic Revolution*, pp. 146–154. Copyright © 1968 by Christopher Jencks and David Riesman. Reprinted by permission of Doubleday and Company, Inc. See page 237.

Richard H. Leftwich, excerpts from *The Price System and Resource Allocation*, Fourth Edition, pp. 307–309, 311, 313–317, 322–325. Copyright © 1970 by the Dryden Press, Inc. Copyright © 1966 by Holt, Rinehart and Winston, Inc. Copyright © 1955, 1960 by Richard H. Leftwich. Reprinted by permission of the Dryden Press, Inc. See page 249.

James Tobin, "On Improving the Status of the American Negro," from *Daedalus*, Fall, 1965, pp. 485–493, 497–498. Reprinted by permission of *Daedalus*, Journal of The American Academy of Arts and Sciences, Boston, Massachusetts. See page 257.

Bennett Harrison, excerpts from *The Political Economy of Public Service Employment*, Harold L. Sheppard, Bennett Harrison, and William J. Spring, eds., pp. 41–57, 61–63. Copyright © 1972 by D. C. Heath and Company. See page 269.

Howard M. Wachtel, "Capitalism and Poverty in America: Paradox or Contradiction?" from *Monthly Review*, June 1972, pp. 51–61. Copyright © 1972 by Monthly Review, Inc. Reprinted by permission of the editors of *Monthly Review*. See page 288.

William K. Tabb, "Race Relations Models and Social Change," from *Social Problems*, Spring 1971, Vol. 18, No. 4, pp. 433–441. Copyright © 1971 by The Society for the Study of Social Problems. Reprinted by permission of the author. See page 300.

Karl W. Deutsch and Thomas Edsall, "The Meritocracy Scare," from *Society*, September–October 1972, Vol. 9, pp. 71–73, 77–79. Copyright © 1972 by Transaction, Inc. Reprinted by permission of Transaction, Inc. See page 315.

R. J. Herrnstein, Karl W. Deutsch, Thomas B. Edsall, "I.Q.: Measurement of Race and Class?" from *Transaction/Society*, Vol. 10, No. 4, pp. 5–6. Copyright © 1973 by Transaction, Inc. See page 323.

CONTENTS

X. THE TURN TO WORKER CONTROL: REFORM OR REVOLUTION?

CONTRIBUTORS

Stanley Aronowitz has been a labor organizer and is currently associated with Staten Island Community College. His book, *False Promises: The Shaping of American Working Class Consciousness,* has been recently published.

Frank Bechhofer is a British sociologist at the University of Edinburgh. He has been associated with John Goldthorpe, David Lockwood and Jennifer Platt in their affluent worker studies.

Daniel Bell is a sociologist presently associated with Harvard University. He is the author of numerous studies including *The End of Ideology,* and *The Coming of Post-Industrial Society.*

Reinhard Bendix is a professor of sociology at the University of California at Berkeley. He has written numerous books including *Work and Authority in Industry,* and *Social Mobility in Industrial Society* (with S. M. Lipset).

Margaret Benston teaches chemistry at Simon Frazier University. She is co-author of a forthcoming book on women in society, to be published by Monthly Review Press.

Ivar Berg has taught at the Columbia University Graduate School of Business. His book, *Education and Jobs: The Great Training Robbery,* has focused on the issue of "credentialism" in the operation of labor markets.

Barbara Bergmann teaches economics at the University of Maryland and is Director of the Project on the Economics of Discrimination. She has written extensively on women in the United States economy.

Eduard Bernstein was one of the leaders of pre-World War I Social Democracy and became the leading theoretical spokesman for evolutionary socialism.

Robert Blauner is a sociologist associated with the University of California at Berkeley. He is the author of *Alienation and Freedom: The Factory Worker and his Industry,* and *Racial Oppression in America.*

Samuel Bowles has taught economics at Harvard University where he was associated with the Center For Educational Policy Research. He is the author of numerous studies on education, including *Planning Educational Systems for Economic Growth.*

Robert A. Dahl is a political scientist at Yale University. He is the author of many books including *Polyarchy: Participation and Opposition,* and *Politics, Economics and Welfare* (with Charles E. Lindblom).

xiii

Bogdan Denitch is a sociologist who has been associated with the Bureau of Applied Social Research at Columbia University. He has written on the sociology of Eastern Europe and is one of the editors of *Opinion-Making Elites in Yugoslavia.*

Karl W. Deutsch is Stanfield Professor at Harvard University and a Fellow of the American Academy of Arts and Sciences. He is editor of *Behavioral Science* and has written extensively on government and international relations.

John T. Dunlop is a labor economist associated with Harvard University. He is currently Director of the Cost of Living Council of the United States government. Among his published works are *Industrial Relations Systems,* and *Labor and the American Community* (with Derek Bok).

Thomas Edsall, a former VISTA volunteer, has been a political reporter for the *Baltimore Evening Sun.*

John K. Galbraith is an economist at Harvard University. He has written many books including *The New Industrial State,* and most recently *Economics and the Public Purpose.*

Eugene Genovese, a historian, has written extensively on the economy and society of the slave South. One of his major works is *The Political Economy of Slavery.* He is currently teaching at the University of Rochester.

Herbert Gintis has taught economics at Harvard University where he was associated with the Center for Educational Policy Research. He has been working with Samuel Bowles on the relation between schooling and class structure.

John H. Goldthorpe is a British sociologist associated with the University of Cambridge. He is co-author with David Lockwood, Frank Bechhofer and Jennifer Platt of a number of studies dealing with the affluent British worker.

André Gorz is a prominent French Marxist and a member of the editorial board of *Les Temps Modernes.* Among other studies, he is the author of *A Strategy For Labor.*

Frederick H. Harbison is a labor economist working at Princeton University. He is the author of numerous studies including *Education, Manpower and Economic Growth* (with Charles Myers).

Michael Harrington is the leader of a newly formed Democratic Socialist Organizing Committee in the United States. He is the author of many books including *The Other America,* and *Socialism.*

Alice Harris is a labor historian currently teaching at Hofstra University. She is co-editor with Blanche Cook and Ronald Radosh of *Past Imperfect: Alternative Essays in American History.*

Bennett Harrison teaches economics and urban studies at MIT and has specialized in the study of ghetto labor markets. He is the author of *Education, Training,* *and the Urban Ghetto,* and co-author (with Thomas Vietorisz) of *The Economic Development of Harlem.*

Robert L. Heilbroner is a professor of economics at the New School for Social Research. He has written many books on economic history and ideas including *Between Capitalism and Socialism,* and *The Future as History.*

Richard Herrnstein is a psychologist associated with Harvard University. His recent writings on the social significance of I.Q. (*I.Q. in the Meritocracy*) have stirred considerable controversy.

Christopher Jencks teaches at the Harvard Graduate School of Education and is associated with the Center for Educational Policy Research at Harvard University. His latest book is *Inequality: A Reassessment of the Effect of Family and Schooling in America.*

David Jenkins is a journalist and author residing in Europe. He has written a number of books including *Sweden and the Price of Progress,* and *Job Power: Blue and White Collar Democracy.*

Clark Kerr, a labor economist and former president of the University of California at Berkeley, has been recently associated with the Carnegie Commission on Higher Education. He is the author of numerous studies including *Higher Education in the United States.*

Christopher C. Lasch is a social historian currently teaching at the University of Rochester. He is the author of numerous books including *The New Radicalism In America,* and *The Agony of the American Left.*

Richard Leftwich is an economist who has taught at Oklahoma State University. His *The Price System and Resource Allocation* is one of the leading texts in micro-economics.

Vladimir I. Lenin was the leader of the Bolshevik wing of the Russian Social Democratic Party. His role in the Russian Revolution needs little introduction. His ideas still have a profound influence on revolutionary movements throughout the world.

Seymour M. Lipset is a political sociologist presently associated with Harvard University. He is the author of numerous books including *Political Man,* and *The First New Nation.*

David Lockwood is a British sociologist associated with the University of Essex. He has worked with John Goldthorpe, Frank Bechhofer and Jennifer Platt on their affluent worker studies.

Kurt B. Mayer is a sociologist currently associated with the University of Bern in Switzerland. He is the co-author with Walter Buckley of *Class and Society.*

Seymour M. Miller is a sociologist currently associated with Boston University. He has written extensively on social mobility and problems of inequality. His recent book (co-authored with Pamela Roby) is *The Future of Inequality.*

Charles A. Myers is a professor of industrial relations at the Massachusetts Institute of Technology. He is the author of *The Impact of Computers on Management*, and *Industrial Relations in India* (with Subbiah Kannappan).

James O'Connor is a political economist at San Jose College. He is the author of *The Origins of Cuban Socialism*, and *The Fiscal Crisis of the State*.

Selig Perlman was a labor historian and economist and one of the leading members of the influential "Wisconsin School" of labor studies. He is the author of numerous studies including *The History of Trade Unionism in the United States*.

Jennifer Platt is a British sociologist at the University of Sussex. She has worked with John Goldthorpe, David Lockwood and Frank Bechhofer on their affluent worker studies.

David Riesman is a sociologist associated with Harvard University. He is the author of numerous studies including *The Lonely Crowd*, and *Abundance For What?*

Frank Riessman has written extensively on issues of social class and education. He is editor of the journal *Social Policy* and co-author (with S. M. Miller) of the book *Social Class and Social Policy*.

John and Mickey Rountree have taught at universities in Buffalo and Toronto. John is an economist and Mickey a political scientist. Both are currently doing research and writing in San Francisco.

Bertram Silverman is an economist teaching at Hofstra University. He is the editor of *Man and Socialism in Cuba: The Great Debate*.

Paul Sweezy is a prominent Marxist economist and co-editor of the socialist journal *Monthly Review*. He is the author of many books including *The Theory of Capitalist Development*, and *Monopoly Capitalism* (with Paul Baran).

William K. Tabb is an economist currently teaching at Queens College of the City University of New York. He is the author of *The Political Economy of the Black Ghetto*.

Edward P. Thompson is a British labor historian associated with the University of Warwick. He has helped stimulate interest in the culture of the working class and is best known for his book *The Making of the English Working Class*.

James Tobin is a former President of the American Economic Association, currently associated with Yale University. One of his more recent books is *Essays in Economics*.

Alaine Touraine is director of the Laboratory of Industrial Sociology at Ecole Pratique des Hautes-Etudes. He is author of numerous studies including *The May Movement: Revolt and Reform*, and *The Post Industrial Society*.

Howard Wachtel teaches economics at American University and has served on the editorial board of the *Review of Radical Political Economics*. He has conducted economic research in Yugoslavia and has presented his results in *Workers' Management and Workers' Wages in Yugoslavia*.

James Weinstein is editor of the journal *Socialist Revolution* and author of *The Decline of Socialism in America, 1912–1925*, and *The Corporate Ideal in the Liberal State, 1900–1918*.

Murray Yanowitch teaches economics at Hofstra University and is co-editor of a volume of essays on Soviet social structure, *Social Stratification and Mobility in the USSR*.

PREFACE

This reader exposes students of labor economics, industrial sociology, and social stratification to alternative ways of understanding recent transformations in the economic and social structure of advanced industrial societies. More specifically, it introduces various constructs of "postindustrial" capitalism as a framework for examining the current position of the "old" and "new" working class and the strategies and implications for social change evolved from liberal and radical interpretations of recent social conflicts.

Since these problems have transcended the limits of a single discipline, our approach focuses simultaneously on the economic, political, sociological, and ideological aspects of the labor problem. Thus the approach is in the tradition of classical political economy rather than of "pure" economics. The contributions are drawn from all the social sciences and most contributors employ an interdisciplinary approach to the study of labor problems. The reader also consciously brings together interpretations from a variety of political perspectives. The purpose is to isolate the major concepts, issues, and interpretations that divide "liberal" and "radical" analyses of the working class and the political and policy implications flowing from them. The book is also designed to stimulate a dialogue on the strengths and weaknesses of current theories and to stimulate research on the working class.

These problems are part of the great debate on the working class originating in the works of Marx and in the responses of his critics. This reader is part of the revival of the central themes of that debate and reflects an increasing interest in Marxist analysis by liberals and radicals spurred by the heightened instability and conflict characterizing both capitalist and socialist societies in the past decade. The "rediscovery" of inequality, power, alienation, and economic irrationality as products of class society in the process of economic development has reopened the Marxist theme of the working class as a potential agency for social transformation. This general theme encompasses many underlying questions currently debated by liberal and radical social scientists. For example:

Is class analysis in the traditional Marxist sense still relevant?

Is the "old" working class disappearing via embourgeoisement?

What is meant by the "new" working class? Does its emergence serve to stabilize the system or is it potentially an agency of revolutionary transformation?

What is the relationship between the "old" and the "new" working class?

How is the educational system adapted to the new technology of a postindustrial society? Is the extension of education a source of class integration or cleavage?

What is the relationship of race and sex to changes in class structure?

What are the implications of regulation of conflict under the corporate state for trade unionism and labor-capital relations?

Our reader presents both "liberal" and "radical" responses to these and other questions which help explain their divergent political strategies.

The qualitative changes of advanced industrialization have stimulated a search for more adequate paradigms for interpreting contemporary labor problems. Thomas Kuhn (*The Structure of Scientific Revolutions*) has argued that the questions science asks are largely determined by its underlying conception of reality and a particular paradigm may hinder rather than advance knowledge.

In the social sciences, an underlying paradigm may become the property of some conventional wisdom that serves as an ideological rationalization for an existing social order. Keynes illustrated this tendency in his attempt to break out of traditional conceptions about economic crisis, which denied for more than one hundred years the capitalist tendency to overproduction:

> The great puzzle of Effective Demand (overproduction) with which Malthus had wrestled vanished from economic literature. . . . It could only live on furtively, below the surface in the underworlds of Karl Marx, Silvio Gesell or Major Douglas.
>
> The completeness of the Ricardian victory is something of a curiosity and a mystery. It must have been due to a complex of suitabilities in the doctrine to the environment into which it was projected. That it reached conclusions quite different from what the ordinary uninstructed person would expect, added, I suppose, to its intellectual prestige. That its teaching translated into practice, was austere and often unpalatable, lent it virtue. That it was adapted to carry a vast and consistent logical superstructure, gave it beauty. That it could explain much social injustice and apparent cruelty as an inevitable incident in the scheme of progress, and the attempt to change such things as likely on the whole to do more harm than good, commended it to authority. That it afforded a measure of justification to the free activities of the individual capitalist, attracted to it the support of the dominant social forces behind authority (J. M. Keynes, *The General Theory*, pp. 32–33).

The same criticism can be applied to the neoclassical conception of the labor problem reflected in most labor economics textbooks. Labor is analyzed in its fetish-like form—as a commodity, and in instrumental and operational terms. The focus is on determination of the price and allocation of labor within the labor market. In its more ideological form, Clark's dictum that labor receives exactly what it contributes to production is demonstrated with mathematical precision. Indeed, the greater the precision and rigor of the model, the further removed it becomes from reality. It is here that Keynes' comments are so appropriate.

In order to provide greater realism, most texts differ from each other chiefly in the relative weight that they attach to analysis of the labor market mechanism, on the one hand, versus descriptions of trade unionism, collective bargaining, and labor legislation, on the other. Recently, some texts have included chapters on poverty, unemployment, and inflation. But these additions do not represent any significant modification of the central theoretical framework. Nor is there recognition in the standard texts or readings on labor of the debate over the working class that has recently undergone a vigorous and exciting revival among social scientists. As a result, many relevant labor problems included in recent texts seem to hang as intriguing descriptive additions remote from and in contradiction to the underlying assumptions of the neoclassical model.

This book offers an alternative framework with origins in the Marxist model. Instead of focusing primarily on allocation and pricing of labor within the labor market, as the central aspect of the labor problem, the emphasis shifts to explore the impact of economic development on the working class. One way social scientists define the stage of economic development is to look at the structure of the labor force—that is, the characteristics of the social division of labor. How the social division of labor is determined, directed, and controlled is another way of examining the locus of power, authority, class relationships, and ownership of resources, thus explaining (and distinguishing between) types of social systems. Broadly defined, the study of labor—its unfolding social and economic characteristics—provides insights into essential features of the institutional process of modernization in capitalist society.

The revival of this approach to the labor problem has been stimulated by the work of labor economists such as Kerr, Dunlop, Harbison, and Myers, as well as sociologists such as Lipset and Bell. But our reader also attempts to contrast their approach (liberal) with Marxist (radical) interpretations. Liberal analysis emphasizes the impact of technology on the social division of labor and social stratification. Radicals stress economic and social control over technology and its consequences for class analysis. Liberals have been more interested in integrative tendencies and therefore in prescriptions for easing social conflict. Radicals have been more concerned with isolating sources of social and class conflict as means of identifying the forces for revolutionary transformation.

There is no presumption in our distinctions between "liberal" and "radical" that these orientations encompass homogeneous positions. In fact, considerable divergence and evidence of conflicting viewpoints may be found within each of these categories. Moreover, there is occasional overlap between the radical and liberal approaches. Our selections provide a number of illustrations of this. Nonetheless, these two orientations seem sufficiently distinct to organize the volume around them.

By presenting an alternative framework, our reader helps to stimulate renewed interest in the labor problem as a means of understanding underlying economic and social forces influencing contemporary society. In contrasting liberal and radical approaches, we hope to stimulate student interest in these issues, to broaden their perspectives, and to remove prevailing stigmas concerning alternative interpretations of social reality.

A final note on the structure of the volume. Our introduction provides an overview of the intellectual sources of liberal and radical interpretations of the working class and the changing course of the debate. The first selections (Part II) present Marx's theory of the working class and early responses both within and outside the socialist movement to the original Marxian formulations. Parts III and IV introduce the modern debate. At issue are the following questions: Do the conditions of advanced industrialism so transform the working class that it is no longer an agent of revolutionary change? Is there a "logic of industrialization" in which high rates of social mobility and increasing equality operate to defuse capital-labor conflict? How useful is the concept of the "post-industrial society" for understanding the class relations and conflicts of advanced capitalism? What are the chief characteristics of and relationships between the traditional working class, on the one hand, and the increasingly important categories of professional, technical, and skilled employees, on the other? Part V focuses on the educational institutions in which the modern working class is trained, with special emphasis on their role in reproducing inequality and the tensions which result. Conflicting interpretations of the functioning of labor markets are presented in Part VI, particularly as they bear on problems of poverty, race, and working-class segmentation. The selections in Part VII focus on the relationship between class position and genetic endowment, an issue revived in the current "meritocracy" debate. Do the skill requirements of advanced capitalism make class inequalities largely a consequence of differences in original genetic endowment? To what extent is the concept of a "meritocracy" a rationalization for existing hierarchical forms of economic organization? The selections in Part VIII reflect the increasingly important role of women in the working class of advanced capitalism. They provide various interpretations of the sources of women's unequal social and economic position, and of their discontent at work and at home. Part IX examines, from both liberal and radical perspectives, the importance of the state as a mechanism for regulating and institutionalizing class conflict and worker discontent. Finally, Part X reveals the turn to worker control by both liberals and radicals. It includes selections which explore the possibility for reforming or transforming capitalist institutions through the strategy of worker control.

The readings have been selected and organized so that the volume may serve a variety of purposes. It may be used as the main text for a course designed to compare liberal and radical approaches to the labor problem. Alternatively, it may be used as a source of supplementary materials in courses relying on the more traditional textbook expositions in the areas of labor economics, industrial sociology, and social stratification. We have used both approaches with success; this would have been impossible without the constant help and stimulation of our students and colleagues at Hofstra University and elsewhere.

I.   INTRODUCTION

THE DEBATE ON THE WORKING CLASS: RADICAL AND LIBERAL PERSPECTIVES

Bertram Silverman

Murray Yanowitch

ORIGINS OF THE RADICAL PERSPECTIVES

The debate on the working class begins with the writings of Karl Marx, whose theory has been the focal point of both radical and liberal perspectives. Marx did not discover the proletariat; its existence was already well known to others who acknowledged its arrival on the historical landscape. For Marx, however, the proletariat dominated the center of the stage of capitalist society. Understanding its significance was equivalent to revealing the social and economic processes directing capitalism.[1] His legacy was to formulate an intellectual framework for a newly emerging social class that not only justified its struggles but predicted its ultimate victory.[2]

But his abstract ideas and reasoning, hardly more accessible to the general public than those of David Ricardo and other classical economists, would not have become perhaps the most widely debated intellectual endeavor of the modern period had not his theory been so closely connected with revolutionary praxis.[3] Marx's dissection of the symptoms of capitalist ills in combination with a guide to action helped stimulate both the movements for revolutionary change and the responses of his critics.

Why did the work process and its organization play such an important role in Marx's conception of evolving social systems? For Marx, man was first and foremost *homo faber* (man, the producer). Unlike other living forms, human beings consciously created their tools and organized their work activities to meet their needs for collective survival, and in this process created their own social existence. The tools, skills, knowledge, work habits, and so on (forces of production) used by humanity, and the social relationships emerging out of the organization of production, were the critical elements in understanding a particular social order. The differing position of groups in the production process defined class relationships and therefore, the locus of power and authority.[4]

While Marx focused his chief attention on the economic structure (productive forces and production relations) of modern societies, he was not unaware of the influence of superstructural institutions.[5] But the state, religious, and educational institutions were superstructural forms concerned primarily with providing social control, modes of legitimization, and moral justification for class positions within an economic structure. It was necessary to see behind the rationalizations of a particular social system to understand its class relationships.[6]

3

A crucial element in the Marxian analysis of class and its role in a particular economic system is the concept of economic surplus or surplus labor. In Maurice Dobb's formulation:[7]

> ... A class does not necessarily consist of people on the same income level, nor are people at, or near, a given income level necessarily united by identity of aims. Nor is it sufficient to say simply that a class consists of those who derive their income from a common source; although it is source rather than size of income that is here important. In this context one must be referring to something quite fundamental concerning the roots which a social group has in a particular society: namely to the relationship in which the group as a whole stands to the process of production and hence to other sections of society. In other words, the relationship from which in one case a common interest in preserving and extending a particular economic system and in the other case an antagonism of interest on this issue can alone derive must be a relationship with a particular mode of extracting and distributing the fruits of surplus labour, over and above the labour which goes to supply the consumption of the actual producer. Since this surplus labour constitutes its Life-blood, any ruling class will of necessity treat its particular relationship to the labour process as crucial to its own survival; and any rising class that aspires to live without labour is bound to regard its own future career, prosperity and influence as dependent on the acquisition of some claim upon the surplus labour of others.

The creation and capitalization of surplus value (i.e., the absorption by the capitalist of income generated by workers above the cost of their labor power) is an essential feature of capitalist dynamics. The surplus, for Marx, is created by the laboring activity of the proletariat, a "class of wage workers who own no means of production and can live only by the sale of their labor power."[8]

The treatment of workers as primarily means to the expansion of capital results in alienated labor in various forms. Not only is a portion of the workers' product alienated from him and used for the capitalist's private accumulation,[9] but human labor itself is transformed into a commodity, an object (like any other) to be bought and sold. The social relations between human beings assume, according to Marx, "the fantastic form of a relationship between things."[10] As a consequence, the worker becomes increasingly alienated from his work, from his product, from his fellow man, and ultimately from himself.[11]

But the process of capital accumulation and the continuing growth of the proletariat produce the eventual downfall of capitalism. Recurring economic crises and the alienation and exploitation of the worker create a *class for itself,* that is, a class in opposition to capitalist domination and acting consciously in its own class interest. The insurgent proletariat represents "in the midst of degraduation, the revolt against degradation"[12] and the vision of a new communist society. Hence the concluding sentences of the opening section of the *Communist Manifesto:* "What the bourgeoisie therefore produces above all are its own grave-diggers. Its fall and the victory of the proletariat are equally inevitable."[13] Thus the theory of a revolutionary proletariat is central to the radical Marxist tradition and is intimately connected with the theory of capitalist development. The downfall of capitalism, however, is not only the result of an oppressed class' revolt against inhuman conditions, but is rooted in a growing contradiction between the increasingly social nature of the productive forces and their continued private ownership and control.

But the revolutionary potential of the working class is not automatically realized. It depends on development of a revolutionary consciousness through the struggle to transform the social relations of production, a process in which the proletariat also changes itself.[14] Marx never explored the implications of this theory of class consciousness, but in various forms it has become central to the debate on the working class. How far have Marx's expectations concerning the evolution and political mission of the working class been borne out by the course of events? Does the apparent failure of the proletariat to assume a revolutionary role in advanced capitalism reflect serious flaws in his analysis of capitalism? Does the proletariat still play a central role in the transformation of advance societies? Has capitalism escaped the transformation predicted for it?

The first phase of the debate concerned the perplexing problem of working class embourgeoisement, particularly in relation tó the British worker in the last decades of the nineteenth century. Instead of developing a revolutionary consciousness, the working class of the most developed capitalist economy appeared preoccupied with limited economic issues and had apparently accepted the social values, life styles, and political ideas of the bourgeoisie. The explanation offered by Marx's collaborator Engels reflected what was to become a standard argument among orthodox Marxists: The circumstances surrounding the British case (and subsequently other cases) were exceptional. The country's predominance in international trade and colonial exploitation enabled some sectors of the working class to enjoy living standards temporarily undermining revolutionary consciousness. But the development of capitalism as a world system would eventually rekindle class conflict and a revolutionary working class would emerge to assume its historic mission.[15]

For other Marxists, however, the issues associated with working class embourgeoisement remained unresolved. In the late 1890s, a major controversy erupted in the socialist movement around these questions. A group of German socialists, led by Eduard Bernstein, began to question the vision of a revolutionary culmination to capitalist development. Bernstein rejected the theory of increasing polarization of society into two sharply divided and antagonistic classes.[16] In his view the distribution of wealth was becoming more rather than less equal. Given the existence of democratic institutions, the working class could continue to improve its economic status and extend its participation in society. Therefore, for Bernstein, "the ultimate aim of socialism is nothing, but the movement is everything."[17] Thus the evolutionary road to socialism was proclaimed, a road that could not be traveled by an impoverished, backward proletariat. "We cannot demand from a class, the great majority of whose members live under crowded conditions, are badly educated, and have an uncertain and insufficient income, the high intellectual and moral standard which the organization and existence of socialist community presupposes."[18] However, Bernstein did not examine how, in the daily struggle to improve his socioeconomic position, the worker developed a socialist consciousness (e.g., solidarity, cooperativeness, egalitarianism, etc.) differing substantially from his capitalist counterpart. Nor did he fully explore the implications of a theory of capitalist development that questioned the revolutionary potential of the working class. This orientation was to be more fully developed within the liberal, rather than the radical, tradition.[19]

The response to Bernstein came from many of the major figures who had inherited the Marxist tradition—such as Kautsky, Mehring, Bebel, Plekhanov, and particularly Rosa Luxemburg, who led the attack on Bernstein's revisionism. With respect to Bernstein's theory of the working class, Rosa Luxemburg countered:[20]

1. Political democracy and the possibility of reforms did not rule out the necessity for revolution, since the laws regulating exploitation were not matters of legislative statute but required changes in class relationships of production. "The extra-legal nature of bourgeois domination was precisely the reason why revolution rather than reform was logically necessary."[21]

2. Trade union activity was necessary to protect workers but could not significantly alter the relative shares of profits and wages. Narrow trade union activity by itself was like a labor of Sisyphus.

3. For socialists, the main purpose of trade union and political activity should be development of the class consciousness and class organization required for ultimate seizure of power. "The great socialist importance of the trade union and political struggle consists in *socializing the knowledge, the consciousness of the proletariat*, in organizing it as a class."[22]

Thus Rosa Luxemburg,, in contrast to Bernstein's stress on the objective factors inhibiting revolution, emphasized the subjective factor: revolutionary practice. For Rosa Luxemburg, class consciousness emerged out of the confrontations and conflicts workers experienced in both trade union and political activity.

A new element in the theory of working-class consciousness was introduced during this period by Lenin, who responded sharply to the emphasis on what he called "economism" and "reformism" in both Russia and West European working class movements. Lenin emphasized the distinction between trade union consciousness and socialist class consciousness. The working class by itself, he contended, could only develop a limited narrow reformist awareness. "The history of all countries shows," he wrote, "that the working class, exclusively by its own efforts, is able to develop only trade union consciousness, i.e., the conviction that it is necessary to combine in unions, fight the employers and strive to compel the government to pass necessary labor legislation, etc."[23] Socialist ideology and theory, on the other hand, do not arise "spontaneously" out of workers' day-to-day economic struggles. They emerge originally out of the economic and philosophical ideas of revolutionary intellectuals basing themselves on the development of modern science. In this sense, socialist consciousness must be introduced among workers "from without."

For Lenin, a critical aspect of this process was the need for a political party of professional revolutionaries (including both workers and intellectuals) to instill socialist consciousness and "guide" the working class in the struggle against autocracy and capitalism.

In part, this was consistent with Luxemburg's thesis that not capitalism *per se* but the revolutionary struggle to overthrow capitalism created the conditions for socialist class consciousness. Like Luxemburg, Lenin stressed the volitional element in the development of class consciousness. But the idea that imparting socialist consciousness was a function of professional revolutionaries organized in a "vanguard" party was a significant, if subtle, addition to the radical tradition.[24] Lenin's proposition raised important conceptual issues which are beyond the scope of this introduction. For example, if there were many competing revolutionary groups, which was the real vanguard? Even more troublesome was the implication of professional revolutionaries in a vanguard party already imbued with revolutionary consciousness, standing above the working class. It was, in fact, Rosa Luxemburg who led the attack on the implicit elitism and antidemocratic possibilities of Lenin's formulation—a criticism, for many, submerged by the triumph of the Soviet revolution, but whose implication would continue to influence the history of communist and socialist parties.[25]

Equally important was the seed Lenin planted regarding the significance of the periphery (the underdeveloped and colonial areas) in overthrowing the world capitalist system. Imperialism, Lenin argued, spawned a labor aristocracy in the advanced capitalist countries, but also helped mobilize new revolutionary allies. This suggested a new strategy: in the imperialist stage the proletariat must look for new allegiances outside its class—in particular, the peasantry and the exploited colonial peoples.[26] Of course, for Lenin, the proletariat in the advanced capitalist countries remained the primary agency for the overthrow of the world capitalist system; and he vainly waited for its predicted occurrence after the Russian Revolution. At the same time, the example of the first socialist revolution in a relatively backward country led by a party of professional revolutionaries became for many radicals a model for its achievement in the more developed Western capitalist countries.

For several decades after the Soviet revolution, there was a general tendency among radicals to shun detailed analysis of new developments in the working class of the more advanced capitalist countries. As two prominent Marxists wrote recently, "Marxists have too often been content to repeat familiar formulations, as though nothing really new had happened since the days of Marx and Engels—or of Lenin at the latest."[27] Orthodox interpretations dominated the radical theory of the working class, removed from the significant transformations occurring in the forces of production and their organization. The primary debates among radicals were over questions of strategies and tactics. But these issues did not initially lead to new directions in the theory of the working class.

Consequently, radical analyses through the 1950s were frequently responses to an emerging alternative theory of the working class and capitalism, mainly from liberal quarters. This alternative approach not only predicted embourgeoisement of the working class, but its progressive disappearance in a newly emerging postcapitalist society. It is necessary, therefore, to break off this discussion of the radical Marxist heritage and turn our attention to the liberal tradition and its counterpart to the Marxian theory of the working class.

ORIGINS OF THE LIBERAL PERSPECTIVES

Liberal analysis of the working class reflects a set of assumptions in sharp contrast with most aspects of the Marxian tradition.

First, Marx's economics was questioned—in particular, his concept of working class exploitation. Capitalism did not lead to increased class conflict and polarization but contained the promise of class harmony and improved living standards as a result of increased labor productivity. At the turn of the 20th century liberal thought found intellectual support in J. B. Clark's theory of marginal productivity. Unlike Marx, who regarded working-class exploitation as a normal feature of capitalism, Clark's theory suggested that a natural law controlled the distribution of income so that under static ideal assumptions "every agent of production receives the amount of wealth that agent creates. . . ."[28] If, he argued, "every man receives all that he creates, then the different classes of men who combine their forces in industry have no grievances against each other."[29]

The implications of Clark's theory for liberal thought followed: Workers' incomes depended on their productivity; that is, on the amount of capital available, on the one hand, and on workers' skills and education, on the other.[30] Poverty could be substantially reduced by improving workers' positions in the market for their skills. Thus increased education became a major liberal demand, but also equality of opportunity for each worker in the competitive struggle.

Second, liberals rejected the conception of the working class as a revolutionary agency. The major intellectual inspiration came from John Commons, Selig Perlman, and their associates in the so-called Wisconsin school. Perlman, unlike Lenin, explicitly identified revolutionary intellectuals as a negative force in the development of a labor movement. Assuming the relative stability of capitalism and the "effective will to power" of capitalists, he argued that improvement of workers' conditions and democratization of the workplace depended on the stability and development of trade union organization. An essential condition for trade union growth was the noninterference of intellectuals or revolutionaries who "pictured 'labor' as an abstract mass in the grip of an abstract force," distorting the real purpose of workers' organizations. Trade union or job consciousness, far from being a lower order of worker awareness, was based on the natural social psychology of workers and the possibilities open to them. Consciousness of scarcity of opportunity led unions to restrict competition among workers and to establish "job control" and "union rules" to gain greater parity with capitalists. This differed from socialism or communism that would "communize" not only job opportunity but also production and distribution. For Perlman revolutionary intellectuals, rather than raising working-class consciousness, distorted it, undermining real possibilities for reform.[31]

However, the actual condition of inequality of opportunity between labor and capital led most liberals initially to actively support the emerging trade union movement as a source of social justice and industrial democracy. Increasingly, liberals turned to study of trade union institutions—their function, structure, and bargaining relations with employers—as a dominant aspect of working-class experience. This interest in and support for trade unions was part of the liberal commitment to policies designed to create conditions of equality of opportunity within the framework of a capitalist society.[32]

Third, Marx's sociology was questioned. Liberals argued that Marx had exaggerated the importance of property as a source of social cleavage. Critics maintained that social stratification was multidimensional, depending on a variety of factors in addition to property, such as education, income, occupation, religion, ethnicity and so on.[33] The origins of this approach are found in Max Weber's conception of stratification, particularly in his distinction between class and status. *Status,* as distinct from class, was largely determined by criteria frequently diverging from a group's objective position in the economic order. According to Weber, "Status honor need not necessarily be linked with a class situation. On the contrary, it normally stands in sharp opposition to the pretensions of sheer property."[34] Some liberals extended Weber's conceptions so that class no longer plays a dominant role in the distribution of power and rewards, despite the fact that Weber, like Marx, made class position a major focus of his analysis. The appeal to Weber, as Frank Parkin suggests, is not unrelated "to recent scholarly attempts to refute the materialist [Marxist] argument"—that is, to reduce the significance of the economic order in analyzing stratification.[35]

Finally, liberal analysts questioned Marx's political theory, particularly his theory of the state. In ways analogous to sociologists, political theorists argued that state policies were determined by a plurality of group interests rather than solely, or even predominantly by objective class factors. Workers' loyalties were divided among competing interest groups. Therefore, public policy was a function of specific issues, not of conflicting class interests.[36] The latter were indeterminate because group interests shifted from issue to issue. The gradual integration of the working class through collective bargaining and protective labor legislation reflected a movement away from class politics to group interest or "veto group" politics. According to Arthur Bentley, to whom liberal theorists turned, Marx's theory of classes "was poorly representative of what was happening because he made his classes too 'hard and fast,' or, in other words, because the particular groups which he called classes were abstractions; because his theory merely indicated a connection but did not attempt to work out the position of the discussion groups among others, and because the economic basis of grouping was overemphasized in too crude a form."[37] Therefore, Marx's view of the state was fundamentally mistaken. Rather than being primarily an agency of class domination, the state could play an independent role of limiting the power of property, guaranteeing civil liberties, and conciliating between the multidimensional group interests composing the complexities of advanced industrial democracy.

The idea of the state as a regulator, a "gyroscope," capable of reducing the tensions of industrial capitalist society, was given powerful support by Keynesian political economic theory.[38] Through enlightened government economic policies, capitalism could be stabilized without serious economic crisis. In one sense, Keynesian theory was a vindication of Marxism, suggesting a natural tendency toward unemployment and stagnation in capitalist development. Nevertheless, Keynesian economics reinforced the conviction that reform, not revolution, could solve the serious economic crisis which in the 1930s shook the foundations of the capitalist edifice.

Most significantly for our discussion, the Keynesian theory symbolically proclaimed a new era that would also influence radical analysis. For Marx, capital accumulation implied extraction of the surplus product through the limited consumption of the masses of workers. For Keynes, the major problem of capitalism was no longer surplus extraction but rather finding outlets for a growing economic surplus (surplus absorption). Unless outlets were found for the potential surplus product the growing productive capacity would lead to unemployment and the threat of secular stagnation. Under these circumstances, rising incomes for some strata of the working class were not inconsistent with capitalist development but a means of maintaining adequate demand. The era of "high mass consumption" and the coming of the "affluent society" were thus wholly compatible with the economic requirements of the new era.

The liberal arguments, while not systematized into a general theory, had all the components of an alternative to the Marxist theory of capitalism and the working class. Clearly, they suggested not the tendency toward transformation of a *class in itself* into a *class for itself* leading to the revolutionary transfer of power but, rather, progressive integration of the working class into the institutional structure of capitalism; in effect, an alternative conception of capitalist development challenged the notion of the revolutionary potential of the working class. This, then, was the stage of the debate about the early 1950s. In recent years, a new phase in the debate emerged, markedly changing liberal conceptions and rekindling new strands of Marxist analylsis of the working class.

THE MODERN DEBATE: LIBERAL PERSPECTIVES

In the 1960s there was a significant shift in the debate on the working class. Fundamental changes seemed to have occurred within the advanced capitalist orbit. Among the factors stressed by liberals were the following:

1. Economic growth could continue without major cyclical interruptions, an unprecedented achievement.

2. An era of high mass consumption had been attained, blurring differences that had previously separated social classes.

3. In the work world a second industrial revolution with automated, electronically controlled production units was replacing the older repressive factory. New work conditions were accompanied by the development of "human relations" approaches as a means of easing work tensions and increasing worker productivity.

4. There was an increasing separation of ownership from the management and direction of the day-to-day productive process. Salaried managers (Galbraith's techno-structure[39]) were now in control of the more advanced sectors of the economy.

5. The high cost of investment in capital and labor in the more technologically advanced economic sectors was no longer compatible with the instability and uncertainty of unregulated markets. Thus planning and market control were central to the new industrial system.

6. Corresponding to the changes in production was a shift in the structure of the labor force. Of particular significance was the movement away from blue-collar employment and a growth in the relative importance of service, professional, and white-collar jobs.

7. Of equal importance, the movement from farm to city continued at a high rate. In the United States large numbers of black and low-income workers moved into urban slums and low-paid service occupations or into the ranks of the unemployed and onto welfare rolls. Many of the higher income strata of the working class had begun to leave urban centers, disrupting old communities, leaving the city to the poor and establishing new suburban communities with their distinctive middle-class styles of life.

Under these changing circumstances some liberal analysts began to develop a theory of industrial development that changed the nature of the debate on the working class. A new paradigm was formulated questioning the usefulness of the very concept of capitalism.

Instead of seeing economic development as moving along an axis that defined various types of class societies (e.g., feudalism, capitalism, socialism), they argued that it could best be analyzed in terms of stages of industrialization— preindustrial (traditional or agricultural), industrial, and postindustrial. Societies such as the United States were at the threshold of a postindustrial era in which labor-capital conflict was no longer a dominant feature of the society's dynamics.

Under the impact of the changes outlined above, it was not simply the revolutionary potential of the proletariat that was questioned; this had already been rejected. Rather, it was now argued that the working class had entered a period of incipient decline and decomposition. Instead of the process of proletarianization engulfing the middle class, it was suggested that the proletariat would be absorbed into a middle-class society in which the sharp class divisions of earlier industrialism would no longer be visible. In place of a theory of working-class revolution as a culmination of the process of capitalist development, a theory of the progressive disappearance of workers as a distinct social class was proposed as part of the inherent "logic of industrialization." These changes implied an end to ideology in the sense of an end to radical (socialist) politics.[40]

Paradoxically, the liberal theory revived the developmental perspective of Marxism to support the theory of the working class in decline. As Goldthorpe suggests, "The Marxist claim that the development of the forces of production is the ultimate determinant of the pattern of stratification and of the balance of cohesive and disruptive forces within society was generally accepted, but a radically different view was taken of the consequences of this relationship in the past and for the future.[41] According to Lipset, "History has validated a basic premise of Marxist sociology, at the expense of Marxist politics."[42]

The first extensive formulation of this approach was presented by four prominent United States labor economists: Clark Kerr, John Dunlop, Frederic Harbison, and Charles Myers.[43] The logic of industrialization, they suggested, leads to increasing differentiation in the occupational structure of the labor force. Advanced industrial society requires complex rules and bureaucratic forms of organization, with responsibility increasingly shared by employers, organized labor, and the state. The new technology creates a highly mobile society. The worker is constantly shifting his location and occupation. Moreover, as skills increase and workers assume greater responsibility for complex and expensive equipment, old paternalistic relationships break down. Especially in the more advanced sectors of industry the distinction between staff and line is blurred. A greater sense of professionalism develops among workers, resulting in greater identification with their enterprise.

These trends have wide-ranging implications. In an advanced industrial society, education becomes a leading activity and—at least in the Kerr et al. version— leads to increased equality. First, it pulls workers out of unskilled occupations and reduces the scarcity of skilled workers, thus reducing wage differentials. Second, it raises labor productivity generally (with advanced technology) and thus income levels; and "middle incomes make for a middle class."[44]

The counterpart to integration of workers into the productive process is the increased homogeneity in the consumption patterns and life styles of working- and middle-class strata. The mass culture in commodities, entertainment, dress, and place of residence blurs economic and social distinctions. Thus, a distinct working-class culture disappears into a more integrated middle-class society.

The imperatives of industrialism lead all societies, whatever their underlying ideological convictions, down this path. There are no other realistic possibilities. According to Kerr:[45]

> The age of ideology fades. When man first entered the irreversible journey into industrialization, there were innumerable views about the best way to organize the society. Some of them have largely disappeared from the scene: anarchism, syndicalism, communalism, cooperativism. Others of them have been blunted and revised from their original form, particularly capitalism and socialism. The age of utopia is past. An age of realism has taken its place.

These changing conceptions of the working class, particularly with the intensification of the cold war, produced a striking reversal in some liberals' perceptions of the worker as an agency of social reform. The growth of large-scale bureaucratic labor organizations led some to consider the working class as another special interest group with considerable privileges and power, with certain strata of the underclass—particularly the uban poor—as harbingers not of progressive reform but of antidemocratic movements. These workers were viewed as potential sources of authoritarianism for both left-wing and right-wing political movements.[46]

Recently, a more sophisticated version of the logic of the industrialization thesis has appeared in the various conceptions of a postindustrial society, developed most fully in the work of Daniel Bell.[47] For Bell, the significance of physical capital declines in relative importance while knowledge and organization become the most strategic productive factors of advanced or postindustrial society.

The social conflicts and tensions of a postindustrial society are therefore quite different than those associated with the earlier industrial period. Two central problems are particularly important. First, there is the problem of the "meritocracy." If knowledge (especially of a scientific and technical nature) is essential, the university and schooling play increasingly important roles in the distribution of income and occupational status.

But, as Bell suggests, if access to managerial, professional, and technical positions depends on acquired skills, "the post-industrial society, in its logic, is a meritocracy."[48] The issue of the meritocracy has produced considerable consternation and confusion within liberal quarters, particularly since some psychologists have related the skills of a meritocracy to inherited I.Q. Thus, according to Harvard psychologist Richard Hernstein,[49] if the liberal ideal of equality of opportunity is realized, social standing will to a great extent be based on inherited mental capacities. An individual's standing in the stratification system will be virtually determined at birth. This has rekindled the nature versus nurture argument once thought buried by liberals, reopening the debate over equality. Bell suggests a confusion between equality of opportunity and equality of result. Equality of result, he argues, may be impossible and he suggests the notion of a "just meritocracy" where mutual respect for differences is tempered by a policy of social justice.[50]

The second major problem of postindustrial society, what Weber called rational bureaucracy, emerges from the impersonality of modern organizations. Increasingly, those with skills and greater education resent the "organizational harness" in which they are forced to work. The student revolt was in part a reaction of a counterculture against growth of the science-based society. But in greater "measure it was a reaction against bureaucracy." According to Bell:[51]

> The most besetting dilemma confronting all modern society is bureau-
> cratization, or the rule of rules. Historically, bureaucratization was in
> part an advance of freedom. Against the arbitrary and capricious power,
> say of a foreman, the adoption of impersonal rules was a guarantee of
> right. But when an entire world becomes impersonal, and bureaucratic
> organizations are run by mechanical rules (and often for the benefit and
> convenience of the bureaucratic staff) then inevitably the principle
> has swung too far.

In response to recent rumblings in workshops calling into question established patterns of industrial relations and managerial prerogatives, some liberals have turned their attention once again to the problems of the worker and his work world. This has led to a renewal of interest in the concept of worker participation in management.

The sources of liberals' support for worker participation flow logically from their conception of industrial society. First, the growth of large-scale economic units with considerable power vested in management is seen as incompatible with industrial democracy.[52] The absence of effective decision-making authority for increasingly more educated employees in enterprises not managed by their owners, is no longer seen as justified. Second, increased evidence of worker discontent is linked to the impersonality of large-scale bureaucratic organization. Thus the renewed interest in the theme of worker alienation. But liberals' concern with alienation is often connected with the development of human relations techniques to overcome worker discontent.[53] In this sense, the readiness to accept worker participation represents a new version of earlier experiments designed primarily to increase worker productivity. Therefore, worker participation is basically a part of the liberal perspective of reforming modern industrial society by extending democracy to the workplace and simultaneously maintaining high levels of productivity. Power to the workers, for the liberal, means reform, not revolution.[54]

THE MODERN DEBATE: RADICAL RESPONSES

Radical analysis has also been affected by the recent development of contemporary capitalism. Indeed, except for orthodox Marxists, radicals did not disagree fundamentally with many descriptions offered by liberals of changes in the *appearances* of capitalist society. Most agreed that new technology, changes in the structure of the labor force, rising incomes of certain strata of the working class, growth of large-scale economic organization, containment of cylical economic fluctuations, and so on had produced important qualitative changes, in advanced capitalism. But, despite these significant modifications, the radical view was that capitalism as a social system had not altered its fundamental characteristics. It was certainly premature to talk about the postcapitalist society.

The private control of the means of production (and therefore of the control and use of the economic surplus) was still intact. Consequently, the production process was still guided primarily by private profit considerations, although now more predominantly within monopolistic rather than competitive markets. The distribution of income from production was still determined primarily by control over property.[55] The inequality of income, wealth, and ultimately power was still related functionally to the way the means of production and the economic surplus were owned, controlled, and directed. The emperor may wear new clothes, but it was still capitalism, "neo" or otherwise.

Nevertheless, it was also undeniable that large segments of the labor force, particularly in the more advanced or better organized sectors, had benefited from the rise in labor productivity. They were more integrated into the economic system and deradicalization was freely admitted, with its implications discussed and evaluated.

But the concept of the decomposition and ultimate disappearance of the proletariat was rejected. On the contrary, it was argued that the process of proletarianization was continuing unabated, bringing large numbers of professional and technical workers into the ranks of wage earners.[56] Here, of course, the radical and liberal definition of class diverge sharply. For radicals, class position was primarily a function of a group's relation to the production process. A group's place in production as wage earners within the structure of authority and control ultimately determined social relationships and consciousness. Liberal analysis had confused appearances—income, clothes, cars, homes—with class relationships and behavior. The traditional worker, despite his frequently middle-class appearance, was still socialized within families and schools that reproduced the existing relations of production and through these his membership in the working class.[57]

For most radicals, however, leadership of the struggle against capitalism had shifted from the traditional working class to new strata within and outside the advanced capitalist orbit. It was now generally conceded that the integration of segments of the old working class was rooted in the dynamics of late capitalism.[58] Therefore, it was necessary to explore the tensions and contradictions in advanced capitalist societies to isolate those sectors of the working class with the greatest potential for radicalization. As a consequence, radicals renewed their analysis of basic capitalist institutions and processes (e.g., the accumulation process, the impact of changes in the forces of production, the labor market, modes of social control and legitimization).

Two distinct strands in radical thought emerged, identifying different sectors of the working class as potential agencies of radical transformation. The first approach, associated mainly with the work of Herbert Marcuse, Paul Baran, and Paul Sweezy, concluded that the traditional working class in advanced capitalist societies could no longer be expected to provide the revolutionary initiative against capitalism. This initiative was more likely to come from the impoverished masses in the "periphery" and the "dispossessed" at home. In contrast, the second approach stressed the revolutionary potential of growing numbers of the more educated and skilled sectors of the working class, which reflected new tensions arising out of modern technology. This view is associated with the work of European writers such as Alaine Touraine, Serge Mallet and Andre Gorz.

The first strand in the radical revival (particularly evident in the work of Marcuse) reflected a profound pessimism about the working class in the advanced metropolitan centers. He accepted the view that technological change—and, in particular, the growth of labor productivity—had reduced class conflict. But this had not led to a more rational social system. The most problematic feature of advanced capitalism has been the manner in which ideological mystifications was used to obscure its irrational nature. Thus, while accepting some chief assumptions of the postindustrial construct, his conclusions were in sharp contrast to those of his liberal counterparts:[59]

> We are again confronted with one of the most vexing aspects of the advanced industrial civilization: the rational character of its irrationality. Its productivity and efficiency, its capacity to increase and spread comforts, to turn waste into need, and, destruction into construction, the extent to which this civilization transforms the object world into an extension of man's mind and body makes the very notion of alienation questionable. The people recognize themselves in their commodities; . . . the very mechanism which ties the individual to his society has changed, and social control is anchored in the new needs which it has produced.

Thus advanced industrial society fostered new modes of social control which gave the appearance of rationality. In fact, mystification and alienation, rather than ending, were extended to all spheres of human activity. Extension of alienation to all spheres of life (that is, the manipulation of the worker as both producer and consumer) led to systematic suffocation of workers' self-realization and perpetuation of false needs by the dominant social class. Power was retained by this class not only through control over the means of production and violence but "in fact over the entire set of means of creating social consciousness."[60] Therefore, only those groups outside the "one dimensional" universe could offer effective opposition—"the substratum of the outcasts and outsiders, the exploited and persecuted of other races and colors, the unemployed and unemployable."[61]

The analytical basis for the turn to an external proletariat was more fully developed by Paul Sweezy and Paul Baran. In their view:

> The class struggle in our times has been thoroughly internationalized. The revolutionary initiative against capitalism, which in Marx's day belonged to the proletariat in the advanced countries, has passed into the hands of the impoverished masses in the underdeveloped countries who are struggling to free themselves from imperialist domination and exploitation.

In part, this conception flows from the central thesis of their study: the tendency of economic surplus to rise under conditions of monopoly capitalism.[63] By stressing the problems associated with absorption of the economic surplus, they have shifted their analysis away from labor-capital relations as the central feature of advanced capitalism, a turn which we have also observed among liberal theorists of postindustrial society.

Under monopoly capitalism, according to Baran and Sweezy, competition to reduce the cost of production replaces price competition as a means of obtaining larger profits and competitive advantage. Increasing labor productivity through innovation and technological change leads to declining costs and potentially widening profit margins. Therefore, the major problem of monopoly capitalism is that of absorbing the expanding economic surplus to contain the tendency toward secular stagnation. The production of waste, militarism, and the irrational commodity culture become primary means of surplus absorption. These activities provide income and employment at home and, by implication, reduce workers' resistance to their economic and social status. Moreover, the large-scale corporation, with its complex technology, creates an increasingly differentiated and hierarchical labor force that recreates the "craft mentality" of an earlier era.[64]

But the picture is quite different in the periphery or in the colonized regions of the capitalist world. A significant portion of the economic surplus, particularly of the United States, is used for military purposes in order to contain socialist advances in the Third World. Economic imperialism in the periphery, providing substantial profits for many leading corporations, requires military support and aid to the most conservative governments. The United States, especially during the post–World War II period, has become the most counterrevolutionary force in the world; consequently, the class struggle has shifted from the metropolis to the periphery. Thus, despite sharply contrasting conceptions of capitalism, some prominent radicals have accepted the conclusion of their liberal counterparts that the working class has been integrated into the mainstream of capitalist society.

But the renewal of social conflict in the advanced capitalist countries symbolized by the May 1968 demonstrations in France, worker militancy (particularly in France and Italy), the student movement, and so on have heightened interest in the second major strand of radical theory: that of a "new working class."[65] This approach stresses that changes in technology are increasing the significance of educated labor, particularly of technical and professional workers. Moreover, changes in the nature of production are making white-collar, technical, and public service employment more like traditional blue-collar work. If there is a tendency toward convergence, it is in the direction of absorption of educated labor into the working class. For some radicals, the process of proletarianization stimulated by changes in production and mass culture represents a progressive step in breaking down working-class divisions based on neighborhood, kinship, ethnicity, and between mental and manual labor, thus creating a greater potential for development of class consciousness.[66] Moreover, working-class "prosperity," although seemingly an anodyne influence, could lead to discontent and protest resulting from new social needs that remain unfulfilled because of capitalism's continued focus on private consumption and accumulation.[67]

This approach differs from the postcapitalist interpretation of these developments, arguing that it is not technology *per se* that creates conflicts in postindustrial society but, rather, the way technology is used in both capitalist and state socialist society. The continued struggle for reduced costs and efficiency and the need for a hierarchy of control has transformed modern enterprises into massive bureaucracies. This has reduced old-style professionals to paid employees who in some ways increasingly resemble the traditional working class. Their sense of discontent is heightened by the disparity between their relatively high educational and skill attainments, on the one hand, and their lack of power in the enterprise, on the other. Consequently, rather than identifying with the enterprise, (as many liberal analysts suggest), these workers find the bureaucratic harness intolerable and are more likely to demand greater control and participation in the decision-making process. Thus the "new working class' theory has become a principal source of the revival of "worker control" as a radical strategy. It has also provided a framework for interpreting the significance of student discontent as (in B. Denitch's words) "an inchoate early struggle of a class in the process of becoming," a response to the university "as a rite of passage designed to prepare technicians and white-collar workers for a bureaucratized economy."[68]

Thus the two main strands of radical thought have shifted focus away from the traditional working class as the primary agency for the socialist transition. The realization that this working class is a highly segmented social group has been promoted by the recent emergence of empirically based radical studies showing promise of contributing to development of a viable radical theory of the modern working class. These studies have provided new insights into functionality of labor force segmentation for containment of class conflict and class consciousness. Studies by Sam Bowles, Herbert Gintis, David Gordon, Richard Edwards, Michael Reich among others, have begun to explore how schools, labor markets, and industrial structures interact to produce distinctive social strata within the working class.[69] These divisions cut across the usual breakdowns between white-collar and blue-collar workers. This analysis has been stimulated by several studies noting the emergence over the past half century of a "dual labor market," and by recent poverty studies of ghetto markets.[70]

The primary labor market, basically an internal market regulated by large corporations, is characterized by relatively high wages, good working conditions, employment stability, job security, and so on; the secondary market is characterized by low wages, poor working conditions, employment instability, harsh and arbitrary discipline. These are distinct, separate markets regulated by the labor requirements of different economic sectors with particular organizational structures. Each job environment, therefore, requires workers with distinct work habits and social-psychological profiles.

Segmentation within the working class is reinforced at various stages of an individual's life process. Bowles and Gintis explore the way in which socialization patterns operating through the family and schooling mirror differences in the position of classes and strata. These patterns set limits on the range of labor force opportunities reinforced by the existence of distinct labor markets and the particular social relations of production in the firm. This mode of analysis attempts to demonstrate how class divisions and working-class stratification are reproduced by system-reinforcing institutions and are therefore outside an individual's control. The liberal solution of equality of opportunity will not resolve problems of poverty and economic, social, and political inequality. Only replacement of capitalist class relationships by cooperative, non-hierarchical forms of organization can resolve these problems.

But it is difficult to escape the pessimistic conclusion that powerful institutional forces stand in the way of forming an effective working-class coalition to implement these structural changes. While these studies provide a positive corrective to some earlier orthodox radical conceptions of a homogeneous working class, they focus on the functionality rather than the conflict-producing elements of capitalist institutions.[71]

It is clear from the discussion of the main trends in recent radical thought that Marx's original conception of the revolutionary mission of a unified working class has become problematic. This has made it all the more necessary for radicals to evolve a new strategy that would reflect the actual social relations of production in advanced capitalist society. One major theme dominating such a newly evolving strategy is "worker control." This approach recognizes that the evolving industrial relations system of advanced capitalism has stifled worker initiative by fostering divisions within the working class, and between work and nonwork experience.

These ideas have been developed most fully in the work of Andre Gorz, who has sought to relate working-class consciousness to revolutionary practice, to "link the struggle for socialism to the everyday demands of the workers."[72] According to this strategy, workers' organizations must go beyond the immediate concern with the paycheck and their integration within the collective bargaining process to issues concerning greater effective control in the decision-making process of the work center (in particular, how labor is used, to what end, and finally the environment in which the worker can satisfy his material, professional, and human needs). These types of reforms are particularly attractive to younger, more educated workers and are seen as touching upon issues that begin to challenge the basic structure and processes of capitalist institutions. The radical strategy for workers' control differs basically from the liberal approach, linking workers' alienation to the basic structure of *capitalist* (rather than *industrial*) institutions. Thus far, the strategy of worker control has received greater attention in Europe than in the United States. Recent reports of the discontent of young workers and spontaneous protests and wildcat strikes in both Europe and the United States, however, have provoked growing interest in the working class. There is a growing air of excitement around the theme of workers and their potential as an agency for social transformation.

It is clear from this review of liberal and radical perspectives that there is as yet no comprehensive or unifying theory on the working class.[73] But we are in a period of creative work which can bring new advances in our understanding of the labor process and its impact on social relationships and human consciousness.

NOTES

1. For a recent discussion of this issue, see Shlomo Avineri, *The Social and Political Thought of Karl Marx* (Cambridge: Cambridge University Press, 1968), pp. 52–64.
2. In Marx's words, "The proletariat finds its intellectual weapons in philosophy" but "philosophy finds its material weapons in the proletariat." Cited in John H. Goldthorpe et al., *The Affluent Worker in the Class Structure* (Cambridge: Cambridge University Press, 1969), p. 2.
3. The relationship between theory and practice was expressed in Marx's often cited eleventh thesis on Feuerbach, "Philosophers have only interpreted the world in various

ways, the point however, is to change it." Karl Marx, *Thesis on Feuerbach,* cited in Lewis Feuer (ed.), *Basic Writings on Politics and Philosophy* (New York: Doubleday Anchor Books, 1959), p. 245.

4. See Avineri, *Social and Political Thought,* pp. 65–77.

5. See Reinhard Bendix and Seymour M. Lipset, "Karl Marx's Theory of Social Classes," in Part II of this book. Engels' correspondence reveals his concern about this issue. "Marx and I are ourselves to blame for the fact that the younger people sometimes lay more stress on the economic side than is due to it. We had to emphasize the main principle vis-à-vis our adversaries, who denied it, and we had not always the time, the place, or the opportunity to give their due to the other elements involved in the interaction."

And in another context he wrote: "While the materialist mode of existence is the *primum agens* this does not preclude the ideological spheres from reacting upon it in their turn, though with a secondary effect. . . . The materialist conception of history, has a lot of them nowadays, to whom it serves as an excuse for not studying history. Just as Marx used to say, commenting on the French 'Marxists' of the late seventies, 'All I know is that I am not a Marxist.' " Cited in Feuer (ed.), *Basic Writings,* pp. 397–400.

6. Cf. Karl Marx, Preface to the *Contribution to the Critique of Political Economy* (Chicago: Kerr, 1904), pp. 10–15. See also Bertram Silverman, "Ideology and Mystification in the Transition to Socialism," mimeographed, 1973.

7. Maurice Dobb, *Studies in the Development of Capitalism* (New York: International Publishers, 1947), pp. 14–15. Dobb's analysis suggests an important aspect of Marx's methodology. His interest is in long-term historical periods and entire social systems. Such a macroscopic approach requires a methodology that would reduce non-essential details to a minimum and rely heavily on ideal types and abstractions. See Paul Sweezy, *The Theory of Capitalist Development* (New York: Monthly Review Press, 1968), chap. 1.

8. For an elaboration of this view and its implication, see Paul Sweezy, "The Transition to Socialism," *Monthly Review,* May 1971, pp. 3–16.

9. Of course, part of the surplus is used by the capitalist for his personal consumption.

10. Karl Marx, *Capital,* vol. I, Modern Library, p. 83. See also Georg Lukacs, *History and Class Consciousness* (Cambridge: MIT Press, 1971), pp. 83–92, and Sweezy, *Theory of Capitalist Development,* pp. 33–40.

11. Karl Marx, "Alienated Labor," in Economic and Philosophical Manuscripts, First Manuscript, of *Karl Marx Early Writings,* translated and edited by T. B. Bottomore (New York: McGraw-Hill, 1964), pp. 120–134.

12. Cited in Goldthorpe et al., *Affluent Worker,* p. 2.

13. Cited in Paul Sweezy, "Transition to Socialism," p. 5.

14. In opposition to a minority group within the Communist League, Marx wrote: "While we say to the workers: you have to undergo fifteen, twenty, fifty years of civil wars and popular struggles not only to change the relations but to change yourselves and prepare yourself for political mastery, they tell them on the contrary, 'WE must come to power immediately, or we can forget about it.' While we make a special point of emphasizing to the German worker the underdeveloped state of the German pro-letariat, they flatter his national feeling and the craft prejudice of the German artisan, which to be sure is more popular." Cited in Sweezy, "Transition to Socialism," p. 10. See also Avineri, *Social and Political Thought,* p. 195.

15. Cf. Marx and Engels, *On Britain* (Moscow, 1962), and in particular in this book the Preface to the 1892 edition of Engels, *The Condition of the Working-Class in England,* pp. 17–33.

16. Cf. Karl Marx, *Capital*, chap. 32.
17. Eduard Bernstein, *Evolutionary Socialism* (New York: Schocken Books, 1961), p. 221. See also pp. 36–43 of this book.
18. *Ibid.,* p. 221.
19. Cf. Michael Harrington, *Socialism* (New York: Saturday Review Press, 1971), chap. 11, 12.
20. Peter Nettl, *Rosa Luxemburg* (New York: Oxford University Press, 1969). The following discussion is based on Nettl's interpretation, especially chap. 6.
21. *Ibid.,* p. 134.
22. Cited in *Ibid.,* p. 136.
23. V. I. Lenin, *What Is To Be Done?* (Peking: Foreign Languages Press, 1973). See Lenin, Part II of this book.
24. It should be clear, however, that Lenin's discussion of revolutionary organizations relates explicitly to the conditions prevailing under the czarist autocracy.
25. Rosa Luxemburg, *The Russian Revolution, Leninism or Marxism?* (Ann Arbor Paperbacks, 1961).
26. V. I. Lenin, *Imperialism, The Highest Stage of Capitalism*, chap. 8; see also Eric Hobsbaum, "Lenin and the Aristocracy of Labor," *Monthly Review*, April 1970.
27. Paul Baran and Paul Sweezy, *Monopoly Capitalism* (New York: Monthly Review Press, 1968), p. 3.
28. John Bates Clark, *The Distribution of Wealth* (New York: Macmillan, 1924), p. 3.
29. *Ibid.,* p. 8.
30. In strictly technical terms for Clark, labor's income (as well as that of capital and land) depended on the value of its marginal product. In perfect competition, workers (or any factor of production) will be hired until the product of the last unit is equal to the cost of that unit. Variations in the marginal product of labor are due to the variation in the amount of capital employed with labor. The more recent emphasis on education and skills reflects greater concern with the determination of the supply of labor and the factors influencing its productivity.
31. Selig Perlman, *A Theory of the Labor Movement* (New York: A. M. Kelley, 1949); see Part II of this book.
32. For a recent criticism of this focus, see Herbert Gutman, "Work, Culture and Society in Industrializing America, 1815–1919," *American Historical Review*, June 1973, pp. 531–588. His analysis has been influenced by the work of E. P. Thompson; see Part II of this book.
33. For a critical evaluation of this position, see Frank Parkins, *Class, Inequality, and the Political Order* (New York: Praeger, 1971).
34. H. H. Gerth and C. Wright Mills, *From Max Weber* (London, 1948), p. 187, cited in *ibid.* Weber's analysis was particularly fruitful in incorporating racial and ethnic factors in stratification and in the analysis of preindustrial societies where ownership of land, ritual or religious knowledge, commercial skills, etc., have provided a distinct basis for status and reward.
35. *Ibid.,* p. 40.
36. David Riesman et al. expressed this view as follows: "Power in America seems to me situational and mercurial; it resists attempts to locate it the way a molecule, under the Heisenberg principle, resists attempts simultaneously to locate and time its velocity." *The Lonely Crowd* (New Haven: Yale University Press, 1962, p. 223.
37. Arthur F. Bentley, *The Process of Government* (Bloomington: Principia Press, 1949), pp. 467–468.
38. John Maynard Keynes, *The General Theory of Employment, Interest and Money* (New York: Harbinger Edition, 1964).

39. John Kenneth Galbraith, *The New Industrial State* (Boston: Houghton Mifflin, 1967).
40. Cf. Daniel Bell, *The End of Ideology* (New York: Collier, 1960), S. M. Lipset, *Political Man* New York: Anchor, 1963), chap. 13.
41. Goldthorpe et al., *Affluent Workers*, p. 6.
42. S. M. Lipset, "The Changing Conception of Contemporary European Politics," *Daedalus,* vol. 63, No. 1 (1964), cited in ibid., p. 7.
43. Clark Kerr et al., *Industrialism and Industrial Man* (New York: Oxford University Press, 1964). See Part III of this book.
44. *Ibid.,* p. 230.
45. *Ibid.,* p. 227.
46. Lipset, *Political Man*, chap. 4, see Part IV A of this book.
47. Various versions and aspects of the theme have appeared, recently culminating in a book, *The Coming of Post-Industrial Society* (New York: Basic Books, 1973). See Part III of our book. For an evaluation of the postindustrial theme, see Heilbroner, Part III of our book.
48. Daniel Bell, "On Meritocracy and Equality," *The Public Interest,* Fall 1972, p. 30.
49. Richard Herrnstein, "IQ," *Atlantic Monthly,* September 1971, pp. 43–64; see Part VII of this book.
50. Bell, "On Meritocracy and Equality," pp. 64–68.
51. Daniel Bell, "The Post-Industrial Society: The Evolution of an Idea," *Survey,* Spring 1971, p. 164.
52. Robert A. Dahl, *After the Revolution?* (New Haven: Yale University Press, 1970), chap. 3.
53. Paul Blumberg, *Industrial Democracy* (New York: Schocken Books, 1969), chap. 2.
54. For an analysis of these earlier experiments, see Daniel Bell, "Work and Its Discontents," in *End of Ideology,* pp. 227–272.
55. Cf. F. Ackerman, H. Birnbaum, J. Wetzler, and A. Zimbalist, "Income Distribution in the United States," *Review of Radical Political Economics,* Summer 1971, pp. 20–43. Gabriel Kolko, *Wealth and Power in America* (New York: Praeger, 1962).
56. Michael Reich, "The Evolution of the United States Labor Force," in Richard Edward et al., *The Capitalist System* (Englewood Cliffs, N.J.: Prentice-Hall, 1972), pp. 174–183.
57. David Cohen and Marvin Lazerson, "Education and the Corporate Order," *Socialist Revolution,* May/June 1971, also Samuel Bowles, Part VII of this book.
58. Michael Harrington seems to be an outstanding exception, cf. *Socialism,* chap. eleven. In his view the platform of organized labor in the United States already contains the major elements for the evolutionary road to a democratic socialist society.
59. Herbert Marcuse, *One Dimensional Man* (Boston: Beacon Press, 1964), p. 9.
60. For a discussion of the containment of class conflict and its implications for social consciousness, see *ibid.,* pp. 19–38.
61. *Ibid.,* p. 256.
62. Baran and Sweezy, *Monopoly Capitalism,* p. 9.
63. For a discussion of the concept of economic surplus as used by Baran and Sweezy, see Paul Baran, *The Political Economy of Growth* (New York: Monthly Review Press, 1967), chap. 2.
64. Paul Sweezy, "Marx and the Proletariat," *Monthly Review,* December 1967, pp. 25–42; see Part III of this book.
65. Cf. Serge Mallet, *La Nouvelle Classe Ouviere* (Paris, 1963); Andre Gorz, *A*

Strategy for Labor (Boston: Beacon Press, 1967; Alaine Touraine, *The Post- Indus- trial Society,* (New York; Random House, 1971). For interpretations by United States analysts, see Herbert Gintis, "The New Working Class and Revolutionary Youth," *Socialist Revolution,* May/June 1970, pp. 13–43, Bogdan Denitch, "Is There a New Working Class?" *Dissent,* July/August 1970, pp. 351–355, see Part IV B of this book.

66. Cf. Perry Anderson, "Problems of Socialist Strategy," and John Westergaard, "The Withering Away of Class," in Perry Anderson and Robin Blackburn (eds.), *Toward Socialism* (London, 1965).

67. A liberal version of the conflict between social versus private consumption can be found in John Kenneth Galbraith, *The Affluent Society* (Boston: Houghton Mifflin, 1958). For its radical implications, cf. Baran and Sweezy, *Monopoly Capitalism,* and Gintis, "New Working Class."

68. Denitch, "New Working Class?" p. 352 (see chap. Part IV B of this book).

69. Cf. David Gordon, *Theories of Poverty and Underemployment* (Lexington, Mass.: Lexington Books, 1972), and David Gordon, Richard Edward, and Michael Reich, "Labor Market Segmentation in American Capitalism," presented at the Conference on Labor Market Segmentation, Harvard University, March 16–17, 1973, pp. 1–90. See also Howard Wachtel and Bennett Harrison, Part VI of this book, Samuel Bowles, Part V of this book.

70. The original analysis of segmentation can be found in Clark Kerr, "The Balkaniza- tion of Labor Markets," in E. Wright Bakke et al., *Labor Mobility and Economic Opportunity* (Cambridge: M.I.T. Press, 1954); see also Peter Doeringer and Michael Peore, *The Internal Labor Market* (Lexington, Mass.: D. C. Heath, 1971), and Gordon, *Theories of Poverty and Underemployment.*

71. One example of radical thought which deals more explicitly with the tensions in capitalist institutions arising from the differential economic position and power of various working-class strata is James O'Connor's work on the sources of the state's fiscal crisis. While O'Connor is concerned only incidentally with working-class segmentation, in part his analysis of the state rests on certain contradictions asso- ciated with class and intraclass divisions. In his analysis, the power of employers and organized workers in the more advanced monopolistic sectors to shift the cost of their income gains on to other strata—particularly to low-income workers in the more backward competitive sectors and the poor generally—has helped produce the state's recent fiscal crisis. James O'Connor, *The Fiscal Crisis of the State* (New York: St. Marin's Press, 1973). See O'Connor, Part IX of our volume.

72. Gorz, *Strategy for Labor,* chap. 1; see also Part X of our volume.

73. Any such comprehensive theory would have to take account of the important issues raised in the recent "Cambridge Controversy" centering on a critique of the neo-classical theory of production and distribution. This critique has questioned the major assumptions underlying the orthodox theory of the determinants of labor's income and the nature of capital's share. This controversy signifies a revival of the classical and Marxian analytical framework in economic theory. While this controversy is related to the issues raised in our book, much of the literature is thus far too technical for inclusion in our volume. For a more popular presentation of this issue see Edward J. Nell, "Property and the Means of Production," *Journal of Radical Political Economics,* Vol. IV, No. 2, 1971, pp. 1–27. See also Maurice Dobb, *Theories of Value and Distribution Since Adam Smith* (Cambridge: Cam- bridge University Press, 1973), chaps. 8, 9.

II. EARLY DEBATES: THE WORKING CLASS AND CLASS CONSCIOUSNESS

INTRODUCTION

The historic debate on the working class begins with the ideas of Karl Marx. His revolutionary conception of the working class and its role in the development and revolutionary transformation of capitalism sparked a controversy between and among his adversaries and supporters which has touched on the central issues of contemporary industrial society. Marx's concept of class was intimately connected with those issues which have continued to dominate all serious discussions of the dynamics of advanced capitalism: namely, technology, class inequality and conflict, poverty, economic power, alienation, and so on.

Therefore, we begin by presenting an exposition of Marx's concepts of class and class consciousness which marked the first phase of the debate on the working class. Since Marx's ideas of social class are dispersed throughout his works, we open the selections with an overview by Bendix and Lipset which seeks to identify the main strands of Marx's class theory. Bendix and Lipset distinguish between the objective determinants of class position (common location in the productive process) and the class's subjective perception of that position through the development of class consciousness. This provides the basis for Marx's distinction between a class "in itself" and a class "for itself." Revolutionary class consciousness embodies the values of solidarity, egalitarianism, and cooperation, providing the impetus for revolutionary transformation and implicitly the seeds for the communist society of the future.

The early phase of the debate on the working class focused on the theme of working-class consciousness. The failure of the working class to spontaneously develop revolutionary class consciousness raised questions about this crucial element in the Marxian framework. The problem had been discussed by Engels during the 1860s and 1870s, particularly in response to the development within the British working class of middle-class rather than working-class values and attitudes. Almost all followers of the Marxist tradition thought the so-called embourgeoisment of workers a temporary phenomenon influenced by the special position of Britain as a colonial power. The first major dissent among radicals came from Eduard Bernstein, a German socialist who had been residing in England at the turn of the nineteenth century. In the selection from *Evolutionary Socialism,* Bernstein rejects the interpretation of an inevitable revolutionary confrontation between working and capitalist classes. In the absence of revolutionary prerequisites, a reformist rather than revolutionary strategy was necessary to improve the

24

worker's economic conditions and to develop the skills and education essential for the working-class assumption of power.

But for revolutionaries such as Rosa Luxemburg and V. I. Lenin, class consciousness was intimately connected with revolutionary practice. Socialist, as opposed to bourgeois, values could emerge only from the development of a revolutionary rather than narrow economic or job consciousness. In *What Is to Be Done?*, Lenin distinguished between *trade union consciousness,* which develops spontaneously among workers, and *socialist class consciousness,* which can be introduced into the working class only by the leadership of a revolutionary political party.

These views were vigorously disputed by the dominant liberal interpretation of trade unionism in the United States—the so-called Wisconsin School. One of its leading spokesmen, Selig Perlman, an immigrant who participated in these debates in Russia, presents a sharply contrasting view of trade unionism. In *Toward a Theory of the Labor Movement,* Perlman identifies the revolutionary intellectual as a major force in undermining trade union development and distorting the limited but realistic social democratic functions of unions.

A more recent labor historian, E. P. Thompson, continues the debate on the working class in the light of British labor history. He argues against conceptions which would assign a predetermined mission to this class, but also against the view that class consciousness is an invention of "displaced intellectuals." He insists that the study of the working class should rest on the actual historical experience of working class behavior in all its manifestations.

KARL MARX'S THEORY OF SOCIAL CLASS

Reinhard Bendix
Seymour Martin Lipset

A social class in Marx's terms is any aggregate of persons who perform the same function in the organization of production. "Freeman and slave, patrician and plebeian, lord and serf, guild-master and journeyman, in a word, oppressor and oppressed" (*Communist Manifesto*) are the names of social classes in different historical periods. These classes are distinguished from each other by the difference of their respective positions in the economy. Since a social class is constituted by the function, which its members perform in the process of production, the question arises why the organization of production is the basic determinant of social class. Marx's answer is contained in his early writings on philosophy, especially in his theory of the division of labor.

Fundamental to this theory is Marx's belief that work is man's basic form of self-realization. Man cannot live without work; hence the way in which man works in society is a clue to human nature. Man provides for his subsistence by the use of tools; these facilitate his labor and make it more productive. He has, therefore, an interest in, and he has also a capacity for, elaborating and refining these tools, and in so doing he expresses himself, controls nature and makes history. *If* human labor makes history, then an understanding of the conditions of production is essential for an understanding of history. There are four aspects of production, according to Marx, which explain why man's efforts to provide for his subsistence underlie all change in history.

> a. . . . life involves before everything else eating, and drinking, a habitation, clothing and many other things. The first historical act is thus the production of the means to satisfy these needs, the production of material life itself.[1]

> b. The second fundamental point is that as soon as a need is satisfied (which implies the action of satisfying, and the acquisition of an instrument), new needs are made.[2]

> c. The third circumstance which, from the very first, enters into historical development, is that men, who daily remake their own life, begin to make other men, to propagate their kind: the relation between

SOURCE: *Class, Status, and Power* (New York: The Free Press, 1966), pp. 7–11.

man and wife, parents and children, the FAMILY. The family which to begin with is the only social relationship, becomes later, when increased needs create new social relations and the increased population (creates) new needs, a subordinate one. . . .[3]

d. The production of life, both of one's own in labor and of fresh life in procreation, now appears as a double relationship: on the one hand as a natural, on the other as a social relationship. By social we understand the cooperation of several individuals, no matter under what conditions, in what manner and to what end. It follows from this that a certain mode of production, or industrial stage, is always combined with a certain mode of cooperation, or social stage, and this mode of cooperation is itself a "productive force." Further, that the multitude of productive forces accessible to men determines the nature of society, hence that the "history of humanity" must always be studied and treated in relation to the history of industry and exchange.[4]

There is a logical connection between these four aspects. The satisfaction of man's basic needs makes work a fundamental fact of human life, but it also creates new needs. The more needs are created the more important is it that the "instruments" of production be improved. The more needs are created and the more the technique of production is improved, the more important is it that men cooperate, first within the family, then also outside it. Cooperation implies the division of labor and the organization of production (or in Marx's phrase "the mode of cooperation" as a "productive force") over and above the techniques of production which are employed. It is, therefore, the position which the individual occupies in the social organization of production, that indicates to which social class he belongs. The fundamental determinant of class is the way in which the individual cooperates with others in the satisfaction of his basic needs of food, clothing, and shelter. Other indexes such as income, consumption patterns, educational attainment, or occupation are so many clues to the distribution of material goods and of prestige-symbols. This distribution is a more or less revealing consequence of the organization of production; it is not identical with it. Hence, the income or occupation of an individual is *not,* according to Marx, an indication of his class-position, i.e., of his position in the production process. For example, if two men are carpenters, they belong to the same occupation, but one may run a small shop of his own, while another works in a plant manufacturing pre-fabricated housing; the two men belong to the same occupation, but to different social classes.

Marx believed that a man's position in the production process provided the crucial life experience, which would determine, either now or eventually, the beliefs and the actions of that individual. The experience gained in the effort of making a living, but especially the experience of economic conflict, would prompt the members of a social class to develop common beliefs and common actions. In analyzing the emergence of these beliefs and actions Marx specified a number of variables which would facilitate this process:

1. Conflicts over the distribution of economic rewards between the classes;
2. Easy communication between the individuals in the same class-position so that ideas and action-programs are readily disseminated;

3. Growth of class-consciousness in the sense that the members of the class have a feeling of solidarity and understanding of their historic role;

4. Profound dissatisfaction of the lower class over its inability to control the economic structure of which it feels itself to be the exploited victim;

5. Establishment of a political organization resulting from the economic structure, the historical situation and maturation of class-consciousness.

Thus, the organization of production provides the necessary but not a sufficient basis for the existence of social classes. Repeated conflicts over economic rewards, ready communication of ideas between members of a class, the growth of class-consciousness, and the growing dissatisfaction with exploitation which causes suffering in psychological as much as in material terms: these are the conditions which will help to overcome the differences and conflicts between individuals and groups within the class and which will encourage the formation of a class-conscious political organization.

Marx's discussions of the development of the bourgeoisie and of the proletariat give good illustrations of the manner in which he envisages the emergence of a social class.

> In the Middle Ages the citizens in each town were compelled to unite against the landed nobility to save their skins. The extension of trade, the establishment of communications, led the separate towns to get to know other towns, which had asserted the same interests in the struggle with the same antagonist. Out of the many local corporations of burghers there arose only gradually the burgher *class*. The conditions of life of the individual burghers became, on account of their antagonism to the existing relationships and of the mode of labour determined by these, conditions which were common to them all and independent of each individual. The burghers had created the conditions in so far as they had torn themselves free from feudal ties, and were created by them in so far as they were determined by their antagonism to the feudal system which they found in existence. When the individual towns began to enter into associations, these common conditions developed into class conditions. The same conditions, the same antagonism, the same interests necessarily called forth on the whole similar customs everywhere. The bourgeoisie itself, with its conditions, develops only gradually, splits according to the division of labour into various fractions and finally absorbs all earlier possessing classes (while it develops the majority of the earlier non-possessing, and a part of the earlier possessing, class into a new class, the proletariat) in the measure to which all earlier property is transformed into industrial or commercial capital.

> The separate individuals form a class only in so far as they have to carry on a common battle against another class; otherwise they are on hostile terms with each other as competitors. On the other hand, the class in its turn achieves an independent existence over against the individuals, so that the latter find their conditions of existence predestined, and hence have their position in life and their personal development assigned to them by their class, become subsumed under it.

> This is the same phenomenon as the subjection of the separate indi-
> viduals to the division of labour and can only be removed by the
> abolition of private property and of labour itself. . . .[5]

This passage makes it apparent that Marx thought of social class as a condition of group-life which was constantly generated (rather than simply given) by the organization of production. Essential to this formation of a class was the existence of a common "class enemy," because without it competition between individuals would prevail. Also, this is a gradual process, which depends for its success upon the development of "common conditions" and upon the subsequent realization of common interests. But the existence of common conditions and the realization of common interests are in turn only the necessary, not the sufficient bases for the development of a social class. Only when the members of a "potential" class enter into an association for the organized pursuit of their common aims, does a class in Marx's sense exist.

In discussing the development of the proletariat under capitalism Marx described a process which was essentially similar to that which he had described for the development of the modern bourgeoise.

> The first attempts of the workers to *associate* among themselves always
> take place in the form of combinations (unions).

> Large-scale industry concentrates in one place a crowd of people un-
> known to one another. Competition divides their interests. But the
> maintenance of wages, this common interest which they have against
> their boss, unites them in a common thought of resistance—combina-
> tion. Thus combination always has a double aim, that of stopping the
> competition among themselves, in order to bring about a general com-
> petition with the capitalist. If the first aim of the general resistance was
> merely the maintenance of wages, combinations, at first isolated, con-
> stitute themselves into groups as the capitalists in their turn unite in the
> idea of repression, and in the face of always united capital, the main-
> tenance of the association becomes more necessary to them than that
> of wages. This is so true that the English economists are amazed to see
> the workers sacrifice a good part of their wages in favor of associations,
> which in the eyes of the economists are established solely in favor of
> wages. In this struggle—a veritable civil war—are united and developed
> all the elements necessary for the coming battle. Once it has reached
> this point association takes on a political character.

> Economic conditions had first transformed the mass of the people of
> the country into workers. The domination of capital has created for
> this mass a common situation, common interests. This mass is thus
> already a class as against capital, *but not yet for itself*. In this struggle,
> of which we have noted only a few phases, this mass becomes united,
> and constitutes itself as a class for itself. The interests it defends be-
> come class interests. But the struggle of class against class is a political
> struggle.[6]

Thus in the case of the proletariat, as in the case of the bourgeoisie, Marx cited several conditions which were essential for the development of a social class: conflict over economic rewards, physical concentration of masses of people and easy communication among them, the development of solidarity and political organization (in place of competition between individuals and organization for purely economic ends).

The antagonism of the workers to the capitalist class and to the prevailing economic system was to Marx not simply a consequence of the struggle for economic advantage. In addition to the conditions mentioned he laid great stress on the human consequences of machine production under capitalism. The social relations which capitalist industry imposed deprived the workers of all opportunities to obtain psychological satisfaction from their work. This complete want of satisfaction Marx called the alienation of human labor. He attributed it to the division of labor in modern industry, which turned human beings into the appendages of the machine.

> The knowledge, the judgment and the will, which though in ever so small a degree, are practiced by the independent peasant or handicraftsman, in the same way as the savage makes the whole art of war consist in the exercise of his personal cunning—these faculties(?) are now required only for the workshop as a whole. Intelligence in production expands in one direction, because it vanishes in many others. What is lost by the detail laborer, is concentrated in the capital that employs them. It is a result of the division of labor in manufactures, that the laborer is brought face to face with the intellectual potencies of the material process of production, as the property of another, and as a ruling power. This separation begins in simple cooperation, where the capitalist represents to the single workman, the oneness and the will of the associated labor. It is developed in manufacture which cuts down the laborer into a detail laborer. It is completed in modern industry, which makes science a productive force distinct from labor and presses it into the service of capital.

> In manufacture, in order to make the collective laborer, and through him capital, rich in social productive power, each laborer must be made poor in individual productive powers. [According to A. L. Ferguson] "Ignorance is the mother of industry as well as of superstition. Reflection and fancy are subject to err; but a habit of moving the hand or the foot is independent of either. Manufactures, accordingly, prosper most where the mind is least consulted, and where the workshop may . . . be considered as an engine, the parts of which are men."[7]

> . . . within the capitalist system all methods for raising the social productiveness of labor are brought about at the cost of the individual laborer; all means for the development of production transform themselves into means of domination over, and exploitation of the producers; they mutilate the laborer into a fragment of a man, degrade him to the level of an appendage of a machine, destroy every remnant of charm in his work and turn it into a hated toil; they estrange from him the

intellectual potentialities of the labor-process in the same proportion as science is incorporated in it as an independent power; they distort the conditions under which he works, subject him during the labor-process to a despotism the more hateful for its meanness; they transform his life time into working-time and drag his wife and child under the wheels of the Juggernaut of capital. But all methods for the accumulation of surplus value are at the same time methods of accumulation; *and every extension of accumulation becomes again a means for the development of those methods. It follows therefore that in proportion as capital accumulates, the lot of the laborer, be his payments high or low, must grow worse.*[8]

Marx believed that the alienation of labor was inherent in capitalism and that it was a major psychological deprivation, which would lead eventually to the proletarian revolution. This theory of why men under capitalism would revolt, was based on an assumption of what prompts men to be satisfied or dissatisfied with their work. Marx contrasted the modern industrial worker with the medieval craftsman, and—along with many other writers of the period—observed that under modern conditions of production the workers had lost all opportunity to exercise his "knowledge, judgment and will" in the manufacture of his product. To Marx this psychological deprivation seemed more significant even than the economic pauperism to which capitalism subjected the masses of workers. At any rate, two somewhat conflicting statements can be found in his work. In one he declared that the physical misery of the working classes would increase with the development of capitalism.

> Accumulation of wealth at one pole is, therefore, at the same time ac-
> cumulation of misery, agony of toil, slavery, ignorance, brutality, mental
> degradation, at the opposite pole. . . .[9]

But in the other he maintained that capitalism could result in an absolute increase of the standard of living for the workers, but that it would result nevertheless in the experience of mounting personal deprivation.

> When capital is increasing fast, wages may rise, but the profit of capital
> will rise much faster. The material position of the laborer has improved,
> but it is at the expense of his social position. The social gulf which
> separates him from the capitalist has widened.[10]

And, as we have seen, Marx summarized his analysis of the oppressive effects of capitalism with a long list of striking phrases, only to conclude this eloquent recital with the sentence: "It follows therefore that in proportion as capital ac-cumulates, the lot of the labourer, *be his payment high or low,* must grow worse."

It will be apparent from the preceding discussion that Marx did not simply identify a social class with the fact that a large group of people occupied the same objective position in the economic structure of a society. Instead, he laid great stress on the importance of subjective awareness as a precondition of orga-nizing the class successfully for the economic and the political struggle. Marx felt

certain that the pressures engendered by capitalism would determine its development in the future. And he believed it to be inevitable that the masses of individual workers would come to a conscious realization of their class interests. Subjective awareness of class interests was in his view an indispensable element in
the development of a social class, but he believed that this awareness would inevitably arise along with the growing contradictions inherent in capitalism. In the
preceding discussion we have cited two of the conditions which made Marx feel
sure of this prediction: the concentration of workers in towns and the resulting
ease of communication between them, and the psychological suffering engendered
by the alienation of labor. By way of summarizing Marx's theory of class we cite
his views on the French peasants who occupy a similar position in the economic
structure but do not thereby provide the basis for the formation of a social class.

> The small peasants form a vast mass, the members of which live in
> similar conditions, but without entering into manifold relations with one
> another. Their mode of production isolates them from one another, in-
> stead of bringing them into mutual intercourse. . . . In so far as millions
> of families live under economic conditions of existence that divide their
> mode of life, their interests and their culture from those of other classes,
> and put them into hostile contrast to the latter, they form a class. In so
> far as there is merely a local interconnection among these small peas-
> ants, and the identity of their interests begets no unity, no national
> union, and no political organization, they do not form a class.[11]

That is to say, the peasants occupy the same position in the economic structure
of their society. But in their case this fact itself will *not* create similar attitudes
and common actions. The peasants do not form a social class in Marx's sense,
because they make their living on individual farms in isolation from one another.
There is no objective basis for ready communication between them.

In the case of the industrial workers, however, such an objective basis for ready
communication existed. They were concentrated in the large industrial towns, and
the conditions of factory production brought them into close physical contact with
one another. Yet, even then Marx did not believe that the political organization
of the working class and the development of class-consciousness in thought and
action would be the automatic result of these objective conditions. In this view
these objective conditions provided a favorable setting for the development of
political agitation. And this agitation was in good part the function of men, who
were not themselves workers, but who had acquired a correct understanding of
historical change, and who were willing to identify themselves with the movement
of those who were destined to bring it about.

> . . . in times when the class struggle nears the decisive hour, the process
> of dissolution going on within the ruling class, in fact within the whole
> range of old society, assumes such a violent, glaring character, that a
> small section of the ruling class cuts itself adrift and joins the revolu-
> tionary class, the class that holds the future in its hands. Just as, there-
> fore, at an earlier period, a section of the nobility went over to the
> bourgeoisie, so now a portion of the bourgeoisie goes over to the
> proletariat, and in particular, a portion of the bourgeois ideologists, who

have raised themselves to the level of comprehending theoretically the historical movement as a whole.[12]

There is little question that Marx conceived of his own work as an example of this process. The scientific analysis of the capitalist economy, as he conceived of it, was itself an important instrument by means of which the class consciousness and the political organization of the workers could be furthered. And because Marx conceived of his own work in these terms, he declared that the detachment of other scholars was spurious, was merely a screen thrown up to disguise the class-interests which their work served. Hence he denied the possibility of a social science in the modern sense of that word. The "proof" of his theory was contained in the actions of the proletariat.

It is apparent that Marx's theory of social classes, along with other parts of his doctrine, involved a basic ambiguity which has bedevilled his interpreters ever since. For, on the one hand, he felt quite certain that the contradictions engendered by capitalism would inevitably lead to a class conscious proletariat and hence to a proletarian revolution. But on the other hand, he assigned to class-consciousness, to political action, and to his scientific theory of history a major role in bringing about this result. In his own eyes this difficulty was resolved because such subjective elements as class-consciousness or a scientific theory were themselves a by-product of the contradictions inherent in capitalism. The preceding discussion has sought to elucidate the meaning of this assertion by specifying the general philosophical assumptions and the specific environmental and psychological conditions on the basis of which Marx felt able to predict the *inevitable* development of class-consciousness.[13] To the critics this claim to predict an inevitable future on the basis of assumptions and conditions, which may or may not be valid, has always seemed the major flaw in Marxian theory.

NOTES

1. Karl Marx and Friedrich Engels, *The German Ideology* (New York: International Publishers, 1939), p. 16.
2. *Ibid.*, pp. 16–17.
3. *Ibid.*
4. *Ibid.*, p. 18.
5. Marx and Engels, *German Ideology,* pp. 48–49.
6. Karl Marx, *The Poverty of Philosophy* (New York: International Publishers, n.d.), pp. 145–146.
7. Karl Marx, *Capital* (New York: Modern Library, 1936), pp. 396–397.
8. Marx, *op. cit.,* pp. 708–709 (our emphasis).
9. *Ibid.*, p. 709.
10. Karl Marx, "Wage, Labor and Capital," in *Selected Works* (Moscow: Cooperative Publishing Society of Foreign Workers in the U.S.S.R., 1936), I, p. 273.
11. Karl Marx, *The Eighteenth Brumaire of Louis Bonaparte* (New York: International Publishers, n.d.), p. 109.
12. Karl Marx and Friedrich Engels, *Manifesto of the Communist Party* (New York: International Publishers, 1932), p. 19.
13. On a few occasions Marx allowed for the possibility that the development from

capitalism to socialism might occur without a proletarian revolution, especially in England, Holland, and the United States. Properly understood the statement to this effect did not mean that this development was a mere possibility, but that it might take several forms, depending upon the historical situation of each country. By his analysis of the capitalist economy Marx sought to predict major changes, not specific occurrences; but while he allowed for the latter he did not expect them to alter the central tendency of the former.

EVOLUTIONARY SOCIALISM

Eduard Bernstein

For a party which has to keep up with a real evolution, criticism is indispensable and tradition can become an oppressive burden, a restraining fetter.

But men in very few cases willingly and fully account for the importance of the changes which take place in their traditional assumptions. Usually they prefer to take into account only such changes as are concerned with undeniable facts and to bring them into unison as far as can be with the traditional catchwords. The method is called pettifogging, and the apologies and explanations for it are called cant.

Cant—the word is English, and is said to have been first used in the sixteenth century as a description of the saintly sing-song of the Puritans. In its more general meaning it denotes an unreal manner of speech, thoughtlessly imitative, or used with the consciousness of its untruth, to attain any kind of object, whether it be in religion, politics, or be concerned with theory or actuality. In this wider meaning cant is very ancient—there were no worse "canters," for example, than the Greeks of the past classic period—and it permeates in countless forms the whole of our civilised life. Every nation, every class and every group united by theory or interest has its own cant. It has partly become such a mere matter of convention, of pure form, that no one is any longer deceived by its emptiness, and a fight against it would be shooting idly at sparrows. But this does not apply to the cant that appears in the guise of science and the cant which has become a political battle cry.

My proposition, "To me that which is generally called the ultimate aim of socialism is nothing, but the movement is everything," has often been conceived as a denial of every definite aim of the socialist movement, and Mr. George Plecha-now* has even discovered that I have quoted this "famous sentence" from the book *To Social Peace,* by Gerhard von Schulze-Gävernitz. There, indeed, a passage reads that it is certainly indispensable for revolutionary socialism to take as its ultimate aim the nationalisation of all the means of production, but not for practical political socialism which places near aims in front of distant ones. Because an ultimate aim is here regarded as being dispensable for practical objects, and as I also have professed but little interest for ultimate aims, I am an "indiscriminating follower" of Schulze-Gävernitz. One must confess that such demonstration bears witness to a striking wealth of thought.

When eight years ago I reviewed the Schulze-Gävernitz book in *Neue Zeit,* although my criticism was strongly influenced by assumptions which I now no

SOURCE: *Evolutionary Socialism* (New York: Schocken Books, 1963) (originally published in 1909), pp. 201–213, 215–222.

longer hold, yet I put on one side as immaterial that opposition of ultimate aim and practical activity in reform, and admitted—without encountering a protest— that for England a further peaceful development, such as Schulze-Gävernitz places in prospect before her was not improbable. I expressed the conviction that with the continuance of free development, the English working classes would certainly increase their demands, but would desire nothing that could not be shown each time to be necessary and attainable beyond all doubt. That is at the bottom nothing else than what I say to-day. And if anyone wishes to bring up against me the advances in social democracy made since then in England, I answer that with this extension a development of the English social democracy has gone hand in hand from the Utopian, revolutionary sect, as Engels repeatedly represented it to be, to the party of political reform which we now know.[1] No socialist capable of thinking, dreams to-day in England of an imminent victory for socialism by means of a violent revolution—none dreams of a quick conquest of Parliament by a revolutionary proletariat. But they rely more and more on work in the municipalities and other self-governing bodies. The early contempt for the trade union movement has been given up; a closer sympathy has been won for it and, here and there also, for the co-operative movement.

And the ultimate aim? Well, that just remains an ultimate aim. "The working classes have no fixed and perfect Utopias to introduce by means of a vote of the nation. They know that in order to work out their own emancipation—and with it that higher form of life which the present form of society irresistibly makes for by its own economic development—they, the working classes, have to pass through long struggles, a whole series of historical processes, by means of which men and circumstances will be completely transformed. They have no ideals to realize, they have only to set at liberty the elements of the new society which have already been developed in the womb of the collapsing bourgeois society." So writes Marx in *Civil War in France*. I was thinking of this utterance, not in every point, but in its fundamental thought in writing down the sentence about the ultimate aim. For after all what does it say but that the movement, the series of processes, is everything, whilst every aim fixed beforehand in its details is immaterial to it. I have declared already that I willingly abandon the form of the sentence about the ultimate aim as far as it admits the interpretation that every general aim of the working class movement formulated as a principle should be declared valueless. But the preconceived theories about the drift of the movement which go beyond such a generally expressed aim, which try to determine the direction of the movement and its character without an ever-vigilant eye upon facts and experience, must necessarily always pass into Utopianism, and at some time or other stand in the way, and hinder the real theoretical and practical progress of the movement.

Whoever knows even but a little of the history of German social democracy also knows that the party has become important by continued action in contravention of such theories and of infringing resolutions founded on them. What Engels says in the preface to the new edition of *Civil War* with regard to the Blanquists and Proudhonists in the Paris Commune of 1871, namely that they both had been obliged in practice to act against their own theory, has often been repeated in another form. A theory or declaration of principle which does not allow attention being paid at every stage of development to the actual interests of the working classes, will always be set aside just as all foreswearing of reforming detail work and of the support of neighbouring middle class parties has again and again been forgotten; and again and again at the congresses of the party will the complaint be heard that here and there in the electoral contest the ultimate aim of socialism has not been put sufficiently in the foreground.

In the quotation from Schulze-Gävernitz which Plechanow flings at me, it runs that by giving up the dictum that the condition of the worker in modern society is hopeless, socialism would lose its revolutionary point and would be absorbed in carrying out legislative demands. From this contrast it is clearly inferred that Schulze-Gävernitz always used the concept "revolutionary" in the sense of a struggle having revolution by violence in view. Plechanow turns the thing round, and because I have not maintained the condition of the worker to be hopeless, because I acknowledge its capability of improvement and many other facts which bourgeois economists have upheld, he carts me over to the "opponents of scientific socialism."

Unfortunately for the scientific socialism of Plechanow, the Marxist propositions on the hopelessness of the position of the worker have been upset in a book which bears the title, *Capital: A Criticism of Political Economy*. There we read of the "physical and moral regeneration" of the textile workers in Lancashire through the Factory Law of 1847, which "struck the feeblest eye." A bourgeois republic was not even necessary to bring about a certain improvement in the situation of a large section of workers! In the same book we read that the society of to-day is no firm crystal, but an organism capable of change and constantly engaged in a process of change, that also in the treatment of economic questions on the part of the official representatives of this society an "improvement was unmistakable." Further that the author had devoted so large a space in his book to the results of the English Factory Laws in order to spur the Continent to imitate them and thus to work so that the process of transforming society may be accomplished in ever more humane forms. All of which signifies not hopelessness but capability of improvement in the condition of the worker. And, as since 1866, when this was written, the legislation depicted has not grown weaker but has been improved, made more general, and has been supplemented by laws and organisations working in the same direction, there can be no more doubt to-day than formerly of the hopefulness of the position of the worker. If to state such facts means following the "immortal Bastiat," then among the first ranks of these followers is—Karl Marx.

Now, it can be asserted against me that Marx certainly recognised those improvements, but that the chapter on the historical tendency of capitalist accumulation at the end of the first volume of *Capital* shows how little these details influenced his fundamental mode of viewing things. To which I answer that as far as that is correct it speaks against that chapter and not against me.

One can interpret this chapter in very different kinds of ways. I believe I was the first to point out, and indeed repeatedly, that it was a summary characterisation of the tendency of a development which is found in capitalist accumulation, but which in practice is not carried out completely and which therefore need not be driven to the critical point of the antagonism there depicted. Engels has never expressed himself against this interpretation of mine, never, either verbally or in print, declared it to be wrong. Nor did he say a word against me when I wrote, in 1891, in an essay on a work of Schulze-Gävernitz on the questions referred to: "It is clear that where legislation, this systematic and conscious action of society, interferes in an appropriate way, the working of the tendencies of economic development is thwarted, under some circumstances can even be annihilated. Marx and Engels have not only never denied this, but, on the contrary, have always emphasised it." If one reads the chapter mentioned with this idea, one will also, in a few sentences, silently place the word "tendency" and thus be spared the need of bringing this chapter into accord with reality by distorting arts of interpretation. But then the chapter itself would become of less value the more progress is made in actual evolution. For its theoretic importance does not lie in the argument of the general tendency to capitalistic centralisation and accumulation which had been affirmed long before Marx by bourgeois economists and socialists, but in the presentation, peculiar to Marx, of circumstances and forms under which it would work at a more advanced stage of evolution, and of the results to which it would lead. But in this respect actual evolution is really always bringing forth new arrangements, forces, facts, in face of which the presentation seems insufficient and loses to a corresponding extent the capability of serving as a sketch of the coming evolution. That is how I understand it.

One can, however, understand this chapter differently. One can conceive it in this way, that all the improvements mentioned there, and some possibly ensuing, only create temporary remedies against the oppressive tendencies of capitalism, that they signify unimportant modifications which cannot in the long run effect anything substantially against the critical point of antagonisms laid down by Marx, that this will finally appear—if not literally yet substantially—in the manner depicted, and will lead to catastrophic change by violence. This interpretation can be founded on the categoric wording of the last sentences of the chapter, and receives a certain confirmation because at the end reference is again made to the *Communist Manifesto,* whilst Hegel also appeared shortly before with his negation of the negation—the restoration on a new foundation of individual property negatived by the capitalist manner of production.

According to my view, it is impossible simply to declare the one conception right and the other absolutely wrong. To me the chapter illustrates a dualism which runs through the whole monumental work of Marx, and which also finds expression in a less pregnant fashion in other passages—a dualism which consists in this, that the work aims at being a scientific inquiry and also at proving a theory laid down long before its drafting; a formula lies at the basis of it in which the result to which the exposition should lead is fixed beforehand. The return to the *Communist Manifesto* points here to a real residue of Utopianism in the Marxist system. Marx had accepted the solution of the Utopians in essentials, but had recognised their means and proofs as inadequate. He therefore undertook a revision of them, and this with the zeal, the critical acuteness, and love of truth of a scientific genius. He suppressed no important fact, he also forebore belittling artificially the importance of these facts as long as the object of the inquiry had no immediate reference to the final aim of the formula to be proved. To that point his work is free of every tendency necessarily interfering with the scientific method.[2]

For the general sympathy with the strivings for emancipation of the working classes does not in itself stand in the way of the scientific method. But, as Marx approaches a point when that final aim enters seriously into the question, he becomes uncertain and unreliable. Such contradictions then appear as were shown in the book under consideration, for instance, in the section on the movement of incomes in modern society. It thus appears that this great scientific spirit was, in the end, a slave to a doctrine. To express it figuratively, he has raised a mighty building within the framework of a scaffolding he found existing, and in its erection he kept strictly to the laws of scientific architecture as long as they did not collide with the conditions which the construction of the scaffolding prescribed, but he neglected or evaded them when the scaffolding did not allow of their observance. Where the scaffolding put limits in the way of the building, instead of destroying the scaffolding, he changed the building itself at the cost of its right proportions and so made it all the more dependent on the scaffolding. Was it the consciousness of this irrational relation which caused him continually to pass from completing his work to amending special parts of it? However that may be, my conviction is that wherever that dualism shows itself the scaffolding must fall if the building is to grow in its right proportions. In the latter, and not in the former, is found what is worthy to live in Marx.

Nothing confirms me more in this conception than the anxiety with which some persons seek to maintain certain statements in *Capital,* which are falsified by facts. It is just some of the more deeply devoted followers of Marx who have not been able to separate themselves from the dialectical form of the work—that is the scaffolding alluded to—who do this. At least, that is only how I can explain the words of a man, otherwise so amenable to facts as Kautsky, who, when I observed in Stuttgart that the number of wealthy people for many years had increased, not decreased, answered:

> "If that were true then the date of our victory would not only be very long postponed, but we should never attain our goal. If it be capitalists who increase and not those with no possessions, then we are going ever further from our goal the more evolution progresses, then capitalism grows stronger, not socialism."

That the number of the wealthy increases and does not diminish is not an invention of bourgeois "harmony economists," but a fact established by the boards of assessment for taxes, often to the chagrin of those concerned, a fact which can no longer be disputed. But what is the significance of this fact as regards the victory of socialism? Why should the realisation of socialism depend on its refutation? Well, simply for this reason: because the dialectical scheme seems so to prescribe it; because a post threatens to fall out of the scaffolding if one admits that the social surplus product is appropriated by an increasing instead of a decreasing number of possessors. But it is only the speculative theory that is affected by this matter; it does not at all affect the actual movement. Neither the struggle of the workers for democracy in politics nor their struggle for democracy in industry is touched by it. The prospects of this struggle do not depend on the theory of concentration of capital in the hands of a diminishing number of magnates, nor on the whole dialectical scaffolding of which this is a plank, but on the growth of social wealth and of the social productive forces, in conjunction with general social progress, and, particularly, in conjunction with the intellectual and moral advance of the working classes themselves. . . .

Similar conflicts exist with regard to the estimate of the relation of economics and force in history, and they find their counterpart in the criticism on the practical tasks and possibilities of the working class movement which has already been discussed in another place. This is, however, a point to which it is necessary to recur. But the question to be investigated is not how far originally, and in the further course of history, force determined economy and *vice versa*, but what is the creative power of force in a given society.

Now it would be absurd to go back to the prejudices of former generations with regard to the capabilities of political power, for such a thing would mean that we would have to go still further back to explain those prejudices. The prejudices which the Utopians, for example, cherished rested on good grounds; indeed, one can scarcely say that they were prejudices, for they rested on the real immaturity of the working classes of the period as a result of which, only a transitory mob rule on the one side or a return to the class oligarchy on the other was the only possible outcome of the political power of the masses. Under these circumstances a reference to politics could appear only to be a turning aside from more pressing duties. To-day these conditions have been to some extent removed, and therefore no person capable of reflecting will think of criticising political action with the arguments of that period.

Marxism first turned the thing round, as we have seen, and preached (in view of the potential capacity of the industrial proletariat) political action as the most important duty of the movement. But it was thereby involved in great contradictions. It also recognised, and separated itself thereby from the demagogic parties, that the working classes had not yet attained the required maturity for their emancipation, and also that the economic preliminary conditions for such were not present. But in spite of that it turned again and again to tactics which supposed both preliminary conditions as almost fulfilled. We come across passages in its publications where the immaturity of the workers is emphasised with an acuteness which differs very little from the doctrinairism of the early Utopian socialists, and soon afterwards we come across passages according to which we should assume that all culture, all intelligence, all virtue, is only to be found among the working classes—passages which make it incomprehensible why the most extreme social revolutionaries and physical force anarchists should not be right. Corresponding with that, political action is ever directed towards a revolutionary convulsion expected in an imminent future, in the face of which legislative work for a long time appears only as a *pis aller*—a merely temporary device. And we look in vain for any systematic investigation of the question of what can be expected from legal, and what from revolutionary action.

It is evident at the first glance that great differences exist in the latter respect. But they are usually found to be this: that law, or the path of legislative reform, is the slower way, and revolutionary force the quicker and more radical.[3] But that only is true in a restricted sense. Whether the legislative or the revolutionary method is the more promising depends entirely on the nature of the measures and on their relation to different classes and customs of the people.

In general, one may say here that the revolutionary way (always in the sense of revolution by violence) does quicker work as far as it deals with removal of obstacles which a privileged minority places in the path of social progress: that its strength lies on its negative side.

Constitutional legislation works more slowly in this respect as a rule. Its path is usually that of compromise, not the prohibition, but the buying out of acquired rights. But it is stronger than the revolution scheme where prejudice and the limited horizon of the great mass of the people appear as hindrances to social progress, and it offers greater advantages where it is a question of the creation of permanent economic arrangements capable of lasting; in other words, it is best adapted to positive social-political work.

In legislation, intellect dominates over emotion in quiet times; during a revolution emotion dominates over intellect. But if emotion is often an imperfect leader, the intellect is a slow motive force. Where a revolution sins by over haste, the every-day legislator sins by procrastination. Legislation works as a systematic force, revolution as an elementary force.

As soon as a nation has attained a position where the rights of the propertied minority have ceased to be a serious obstacle to social progress, where the negative tasks of political action are less pressing than the positive, then the appeal to a revolution by force becomes a meaningless phrase.[4] One can overturn a government or a privileged minority, but not a nation. When the working classes do not possess very strong economic organisations of their own, and have not attained, by means of education on self-governing bodies, a high degree of mental independence, the dictatorship of the proletariat means the dictatorship of club orators and writers. I would not wish that those who see in the oppression and tricking of the working men's organisations and in the exclusion of working men from the legislature and government the highest point of the art of political policy should experience their error in practice. Just as little would I desire it for the working class movement itself.

One has not overcome Utopianism if one assumes that there is in the present, or ascribes to the present, what is to be in the future. We have to take working men as they are. And they are neither so universally pauperised as was set out in the *Communist Manifesto*, nor so free from prejudices and weaknesses as their courtiers wish to make us believe. They have the virtues and failings of the economic and social conditions under which they live. And neither these conditions nor their effects can be put on one side from one day to another.

Have we attained the required degree of development of the productive forces for the abolition of classes? In face of the fantastic figures which were formerly set up in proof of this and which rested on generalisations based on the development of particularly favoured industries, socialist writers in modern times have endeavoured to reach by carefully detailed calculations, appropriate estimates of the possibilities of production in a socialist society, and their results are very different from those figures. Of a general reduction of hours of labour to five, four, or even three or two hours, such as was formerly accepted, there can be no hope at any time within sight, unless the general standard of life is much reduced. Even under a collective organisation of work, labour must begin very young and only cease at a rather advanced age [if] it is to be reduced considerably below an eight-hours' day. Those persons ought to understand this first of all who indulge in the most extreme exaggerations regarding the ratio of the number of the nonpropertied classes to that of the propertied. But he who thinks irrationally on one point does so usually on another. And, therefore, I am not surprised if the same Plechanow, who is angered to see the position of working men represented as not hopeless, has only the annihilating verdict, "Philistine," for my conclusions on the impossibility at any period within sight of abandoning the principle of the economic self-responsibility of those capable of working. It is not for nothing that one is the philosopher of irresponsibility.

But he who surveys the actual workers' movement will also find that the freedom from those qualities which appeared Philistine to a person born in the bourgeoisie, is very little valued by the workers, that they in no way support the morale of proletarianism, but, on the contrary, tend to make a "Philistine" out of a proletarian. With the roving proletarian without a family and home, no lasting, firm trade union movement would be possible. It is no bourgeois prejudice, but a conviction gained through decades of labour organisation, which has made so many of the English labour leaders—socialists and non-socialists—into zealous adherents of the temperance movement. The working class socialists know the faults of their class, and the most conscientious among them, far from glorifying these faults, seek to overcome them with all their power.

We cannot demand from a class, the great majority of whose members live under crowded conditions, are badly educated, and have an uncertain and insufficient income, the high intellectual and moral standard which the organisation and existence of a socialist community presupposes. We will, therefore, not ascribe it to them by way of fiction. Let us rejoice at the great stock of intelligence, renunciation, and energy which the modern working class movement has partly revealed, partly produced; but we must not assign, without discrimination to the masses, the millions, what holds good, say, of hundreds of thousands. I will not repeat the declarations which have been made to me on this point by working men verbally and in writing; I do not need to defend myself before reasonable persons against the suspicion of Pharisaism and the conceit of pedantry. But I confess willingly that I measure here with two kinds of measures. Just because I expect much of the working classes I censure much more everything that tends to corrupt their moral judgment than I do similar habits of the higher classes, and I see with the greatest regret that a tone of literary decadence is spreading here and there in the working class press which can only have a confusing and corrupting effect. A class which is aspiring needs a sound morale and must suffer no deterioration. Whether it sets out for itself an ideal ultimate aim is of secondary importance if it pursues with energy its proximate aims. The important point is that these aims are inspired by a definite principle which expresses a higher degree of economy and of social life, that they are an embodiment of a social conception which means in the evolution of civilisation a higher view of morals and of legal rights.

NOTES

* Plekhanov

1. I use the words "social democracy" here in the wider sense of the whole independent socialist movement.
2. I take no account of that tendency which finds expression in the treatment of persons and the representation of occurrences, and which has no necessary connection with the analysis of the economic evolution.
3. In this sense Marx speaks in *Capital,* in the chapter about the working day, of the "peculiar advantages of the French revolutionary method" which had been made manifest in the French twelve hours' law of 1848. It dictates for all workers and all factories without distinction the same working day. That is right. But it has been ascertained that this radical law remained a dead letter for a whole generation.
4. "Fortunately, 'revolution' in this country has ceased to be anything more than an affected phrase."—The monthly *News* of the Independent Labour Party in England, January 1899.

THE SPONTANEITY OF THE MASSES AND THE CONSCIOUSNESS OF SOCIAL-DEMOCRATS

Vladimir I. Lenin

. . . Social-Democracy must change from a party of the social revolution into a democratic party of social reforms. Bernstein has surrounded this political demand with a whole battery of symmetrically arranged "new" arguments and reasonings. The possibility of putting Socialism on a scientific basis and of proving from the point of view of the materialist conception of history that it is necessary and inevitable was denied, as was also the growing impoverishment, proletarianization and the intensification of capitalist contradictions. The very conception, *"ultimate aim,"* was declared to be unsound, and the idea of the dictatorship of the proletariat was absolutely rejected. It was denied that there is any counterdistinction in principle between liberalism and Socialism. *The theory of the class struggle* was rejected on the grounds that it could not be applied to a strictly democratic society, governed according to the will of the majority, etc.

Thus, the demand for a resolute turn from revolutionary Social-Democracy to bourgeois social-reformism was accompanied by a no less resolute turn towards bourgeois criticism of all the fundamental ideas of Marxism. As this criticism of Marxism has been going on for a long time now, from the political platform, from university chairs, in numerous pamphlets and in a number of learned treatises, as the entire younger generation of the educated classes has been systematically trained for decades on this criticism, it is not surprising that the "new, critical" trend in Social-Democracy should spring up, all complete, like Minerva from the head of Jupiter.[1] The content of this new trend did not have to grow and take shape, it was transferred bodily from bourgeois literature to socialist literature.

To proceed. If Bernstein's theoretical criticism and political yearnings are still unclear to anyone, the French have taken the trouble graphically to demonstrate the "new method." In this instance, too, France has justified its old reputation of being the country in which "more than anywhere else, the historical class struggles were each time fought out to a decision. . . ." (Engels, in his introduction[2] to Marx's *The Eighteenth Brumaire.*[3]) The French Socialists have begun, not to theorize, but to act. The democratically more highly developed political conditions in France have permitted them to put "Bernsteinism into practice" immediately, with all its consequences. Millerand has provided an excellent example of practical Bernsteinism; not without reason did Bernstein and Vollmar rush so zealously to defend and praise him! Indeed, if Social-Democracy, in essence, is merely a

SOURCE: *What Is to Be Done?* (Peking: Foreign Languages Press, 1973), pp. 7–10, 35–37, 46–52.

party of reform, and must be bold enough to admit this openly, then not only has a Socialist the right to join a bourgeois cabinet, but must always strive to do so. If democracy, in essence, means the abolition of class domination, then why should not a Socialist minister charm the whole bourgeois world by orations on class collaboration? Why should he not remain in the cabinet even after the shooting down of workers by gendarmes has exposed, for the hundredth and thousandth time, the real nature of the democratic collaboration of classes? Why should he not personally take part in greeting the tsar, for whom the French Socialists now have no other name than hero of the gallows, knout and exile (knouteur, pendeur et déportateur)? And the reward for this utter humiliation and self-degradation of Socialism in the face of the whole world, for the corruption of the socialist consciousness of the worker masses—the only basis that can guarantee our victory—the reward for this is pompous *plans* for niggardly reforms, so niggardly in fact that much more has been obtained from bourgeois governments!

He who does not deliberately close his eyes cannot fail to see that the new "critical" trend in Socialism is nothing more nor less than a new variety of *opportunism*. And if we judge people not by the brilliant uniforms they don, not by the high-sounding appellations they give themselves, but by their actions, and by what they actually advocate, it will be clear that "freedom of criticism" means freedom for an opportunistic trend in Social-Democracy, the freedom to convert Social-Democracy into a democratic party of reform, the freedom to introduce bourgeois ideas and bourgeois elements into Socialism.

"Freedom" is a grand word, but under the banner of free trade the most predatory wars were conducted; under the banner of free labour, the toilers were robbed. The modern use of the term "freedom of criticism" contains the same inherent falsehood. Those who are really convinced that they have advanced science would demand, not freedom for the new views to continue side by side with the old, but the substitution of the new views for the old. The cry "Long live freedom of criticism," that is heard today, too strongly calls to mind the fable of the empty barrel.[4]

We are marching in a compact group along a precipitous and difficult path, firmly holding each other by the hand. We are surrounded on all sides by enemies, and we have to advance under their almost constant fire. We have combined voluntarily, precisely for the purpose of fighting the enemy, and not to retreat into the adjacent marsh, the inhabitants of which, from the very outset, have reproached us with having separated ourselves into an exclusive group and with having chosen the path of struggle instead of the path of conciliation. And now several among us begin to cry out: let us go into this marsh! And when we begin to shame them, they retort: how conservative you are! Are you not ashamed to deny us the liberty to invite you to take a better road! Oh, yes, gentlemen! You are free not only to invite us, but to go yourselves wherever you will, even into the marsh. In fact, we think that the marsh is your proper place, and we are prepared to render *you* every assistance to get there. Only let go of our hands, don't clutch at us and don't besmirch the grand word "freedom," for we too are "free" to go where we please, free to fight not only against the marsh, but also against those who are turning towards the marsh! . . .

. . . [Previously] we pointed out how *universally* absorbed the educated youth of Russia was in the theories of Marxism in the middle of the 'nineties. The strikes that followed the famous St. Petersburg industrial war of 1896 assumed a similar wholesale character. The fact that these strikes spread over the whole of Russia clearly showed how deep the newly awakening popular movement was, and if we are to speak of the "spontaneous element" then, of course, it is this movement which, first and foremost, must be regarded as spontaneous. But there is spontaneity and spontaneity. Strikes occurred in Russia in the 'seventies and 'sixties (and even in the first half of the nineteenth century), and were accompanied by the "spontaneous" destruction of machinery, etc. Compared with these "riots" the strikes of the 'nineties might even be described as "conscious," to such an extent do they mark the progress which the working-class movement had made in that period. This shows that the "spontaneous element," in essence, represents nothing more nor less than consciouness in an *embryonic form*. Even the primitive riots expressed the awakening of consciousness to a certain extent: the workers were losing their agelong faith in the permanence of the system which oppressed them. They began . . . I shall not say to understand, but to sense the necessity for collective resistance, and definitely abandoned their slavish submission to their superiors. But this was, nevertheless, more in the nature of outbursts of desperation and vengeance than of *struggle*. The strikes of the 'nineties revealed far greater flashes of consciouness: definite demands were advanced, the strike was carefully timed, known cases and examples in other places were discussed, etc. While the riots were simply revolts of the oppressed, the systematic strikes represented the class struggle in embryo, but only in embryo. Taken by themelves, these strikes were simply trade union struggles, but not yet Social-Democratic struggles. They testified to the awakening antagonisms between workers and employers, but the workers were not, and could not be, conscious of the irreconcilable antagonism of their interests to the whole of the modern political and social system, i.e., theirs was not yet Social-Democratic consciousness. In this sense, the strikes of the 'nineties, in spite of the enormous progress they represented as compared with the "riots," remained a purely spontaneous movement.

We have said that *there could not yet be* Social-Democratic consciousness among the workers. It could only be brought to them from without. The history of all countries shows that the working class, exclusively by its own effort, is able to develop only trade union consciousness, i.e., the conviction that it is necessary to combine in unions, fight the employers and strive to compel the government to pass necessary labour legislation, etc.[5] The theory of Socialism, however, grew out of the philosophilc, historical and economic theories that were elaborated by the educated representatives of the propertied classes, the intellectuals. According to their social status, the founders of modern scientific Socialism, Marx and Engels, themselves belonged to the bourgeois intelligentsia. In the very same way, in Russia, the theoretical doctrine of Social-Democracy arose quite independently of the spontaneous growth of the working-class movement, it arose as a natural and inevitable outcome of the development of ideas among the revolutionary socialist intelligentsia. At the time of which we are speaking, i.e., the middle of the 'nineties, this doctrine not only represented the completely formulated program of the Emanicpation of Labour group, but had already won over to its side the majority of the revolutionary youth in Russia. . . .

To supplement what has been said above, we shall quote the following profoundly just and important utterances by Karl Kautsky on the new draft program of the Austrian Social-Democratic Party:[6]

Many of our revisionist critics believe that Marx asserted that economic development and the class struggle create not only the conditions for socialist production, but also, and directly, the *consciousness* (K. K.'s italics) of its necessity. And these critics aver that England, the country most highly developed capitalistically, is more remote than any other from this consciousness. Judging from the draft, one might assume that this allegedly orthodox-Marxist view, which is thus refuted, was shared by the committee that drafted the Austrian program. In the draft program it is stated: 'The more capitalist development increases the numbers of the proletariat, the more the proletariat is compelled and becomes fit to fight against capitalism. The proletariat becomes conscious' of the possibility and of the necessity for Socialism. In this connection socialist consciousness appears to be a necessary and direct result of the proletarian class struggle. But this is absolutely untrue. Of course, Socialism, as a doctrine, has its roots in modern economic relationships just as the class struggle of the proletariat has, and, just as the latter, emerges from the struggle against the capitalist-created poverty and misery of the masses. But Socialism and the class struggle arise side by side and not one out of the other; each arises under different conditions. Modern socialist consciousness can arise only on the basis of profound scientific knowledge. Indeed, modern economic science is as much a condition for socialist production as, say, modern technology, and the proletariat can create neither the one nor the other, no matter how much it may desire to do so; both arise out of the modern social process. The vehicle of science is not the proletariat, but the *bourgeois intelligentsia* (K. K.'s italics): it was in the minds of individual members of this stratum that modern Socialism originated, and it was they who communicated it to the more intellectually developed proletarians who, in their turn, introduce it into the proletarian class struggle where conditions allow that to be done. Thus, socialist consciousness is something introduced into the proletarian class struggle from without (von Aussen Hineingetragenes) and not something that arose within it spontaneously (urwüchsig). Accordingly, the old Hainfeld program quite rightly stated that the task of Social-Democracy is to imbue the proletariat (literally: saturate the proletariat) with the *consciousness* of its position and the consciousness of its task. There would be no need for this if consciousness arose of itself from the class struggle. The new draft copied this proposition from the old program, and attached it to the proposition mentioned above. But this completely broke the line of thought. . . .

Since there can be no talk of an independent ideology being developed by the masses of the workers themselves in the process of their movement[7] the *only* choice is: either the bourgeois or the socialist ideology. There is no middle course (for humanity has not created a "third" ideology, and, moreover, in a society torn by class antagonisms there can never be a non-class or above-class ideology). Hence, to belittle the socialist ideology *in any way, to turn away from it in the slightest degree* means to strengthen bourgeois ideology. There is a lot of talk about spontaneity, but the *spontaneous* development of the working-class movement leads to its becoming subordinated to the bourgeois ideology, *leads to its developing according to the program* of the *Credo,* for the spontaneous working-class movement is trade unionism, is Nur-Gewerkschaftlerei, and trade unionism means the ideological enslavement of the workers by the bourgeoisie. Hence, our task, the task of Social-Democracy, is to *combat spontaneity,* to *divert* the working-class movement from this spontaneous, trade-unionist striving to come under the wing of the bourgeoisie, and to bring it under the wing of revolutionary Social-Democracy. The phrase employed by the authors of the "economic" letter in the *Iskra,* No. 12, about the efforts of the most inspired ideologists not being able to divert the working-class movement from the path that is determined by the interaction of the material elements and the material environment, *is absolutely tantamount* therefore *to the abandonment of Socialism,* and if only the authors of this letter were capable of fearlessly, consistently and thoroughly considering what they say, as everyone who enters the arena of literary and public activity should do, there would be nothing left for them but to "fold their useless arms over their empty breasts" and . . . leave the field of action to Messrs. the Struves and Prokopoviches who are dragging the working-class movement "along the line of least resistance," i.e., along the line of bourgeois trade unionism, or to the Zubatovs, who are dragging it along the line of clerical and gendarme "ideology."

Recall the example of Germany. What was the historical service Lassalle rendered to the German working-class movement? It was that he *diverted* that movement from the path of trade unionism and cooperation preached by the Progressives along which it had been travelling spontaneously (*with the benign assistance of Schulze-Delitzsch and those like him*). To fulfil a task like that it was necessary to do something altogether different from indulging in talk about underrating the spontaneous element, about tactics-as-a-process, about the interaction between elements and environment, etc. *A fierce struggle against spontaneity* was necessary, and only after such a struggle, extending over many years, was it possible, for instance, to convert the working population of Berlin from a bulwark of the Progressive Party into one of the finest strongholds of Social-Democracy. This fight is by no means finished even now (as might seem to those who learn the history of the German movement from Prokopovich, and its philosophy from Struve). Even now the German working class is, so to speak, broken up among a number of ideologies. A section of the workers is organized in Catholic and monarchist labour unions; another section is organized in the Hirsch-Duncker unions,[8] founded by the bourgeois worshippers of English trade unionism, while a third section is organized in Social-Democratic trade unions. The last is immeasurably more numerous than all the rest, but the Social-Democratic ideology was able to achieve this superiority, and will be able to maintain it, only by unswervingly fighting against all other ideologies.

But why, the reader will ask, does the spontaneous movement, the movement along the line of the least resistance, lead to the domination of the bourgeois ideology? For the simple reason that the bourgeois ideology is far older in origin than the socialist ideology; because it is more fully developed and because it possesses *immeasurably* more opportunity for being spread.[9] And the younger the socialist movement is in any given country, the more vigorously must it fight against all attempts to entrench non-socialist ideology, and the more strongly must the workers be warned against those bad counsellors who shout against "overrating the conscious element," etc. The authors of the economic letter, in

unison with the *Rabocheye Dyelo,* declaim against the intolerance that is characteristic of the infancy of the movement. To this we reply: yes, our movement is
indeed in its infancy, and in order that it may grow up the more quickly, it must
become infected with intolerance against those who retard its growth by their
subservience to spontaneity. Nothing is so ridiculous and harmful as pretending
that we are "old hands" who have long ago experienced all the decisive episodes
of the struggle.

Thirdly, the first number of the *Rabochaya Mysl* shows that the term "Economism" (which, of course, we do not propose to abandon because, however it
may be, this appellation has already established itself) does not adequately convey
the real character of the new trend. The *Rabochaya Mysl* does not altogether
repudiate the political struggle: the rules for a workers' benefit fund published
in the *Rabochaya Mysl,* No. 1, contain a reference to combating the government.
The *Rabochaya Mysl* believes, however, that "politics always obediently follows
economics" (and the *Rabocheye Dyelo* gives a variation of this thesis when, in its
program, it asserts that "in Russia more than in any other country, the economic
struggle is *inseparable* from the political struggle"). *If by politics is meant Social-
Democratic politics,* then the postulates advanced by the *Rabochaya Mysl* and
the *Rabocheye Dyelo* are absolutely wrong. The economic struggle of the workers
is very often connected (although not inseparably) with bourgeois politics, clerical
politics, etc., as we have already seen. The *Rabocheye Dyelo's* postulates are
correct if by politics is meant trade union politics, i.e., the common striving of
all workers to secure from the government measures for the alleviation of the
distress characteristic of their position, but which do not abolish that position,
i.e., which do not remove the subjection of labour to capital. That striving indeed
is common to the British trade unionists who are hostile to Socialism, to the
Catholic workers, to the "Zubatov" workers, etc. There are politics and politics.
Thus, we see that the *Rabochaya Mysl* does not so much deny the political struggle as bow to its *spontaneity,* to its lack of consciousness. While fully recognizing
the political struggle (it would be more correct to say the political desires and
demands of the workers), which arises spontaneously from the working-class
movement itself, it absolutely refuses *independently to work out* a specifically
Social-Democratic policy corresponding to the general tasks of Socialism and to
contemporary conditions in Russia. . . .

NOTES

1. According to the Roman mythology, Jupiter was the chief of the gods, while Min-
   erva was guardian goddess of handicrafts, science and art, of teachers and doctors.
   Minerva was said to have sprung in helmet and armour, sword in hand, from
   Jupiter's head. Her mode of birth was popularly used to illustrate a person or
   phenomenon as being complete from the very beginning.
2. Lenin quotes a passage from Engels' "Preface to the Third German Edition of
   The Eighteenth Brumaire of Louis Bonaparte," Karl Marx and Frederick Engels,
   Selected Works, Eng. ed., FLPH, Moscow, 1951, Vol. I, p. 223.
3. Karl Marx, *The Eighteenth Brumaire of Louis Bonaparte.*
4. From Ivan Andreyevich Krylov's fable "Two Barrels." One barrel was empty and

rattled on the cart with such deafening noise that passersby all tried to keep out of the way.

5. Trade unionism does not exclude "politics" altogether, as some imagine. Trade unions have always conducted some political (but not Social-Democratic) agitation and struggle. We shall deal with the difference between trade union politics and Social-Democratic politics in the next chapter.

6. *Neue Zeit,* 1901–02, XX, I, No. 3, p. 79. The committee's draft to which Kautsky refers was adopted by the Vienna Congress (at the end of last year) in a slightly amended form.

7. This does not mean, of course, that the workers have no part in creating such an ideology. But they take part not as workers, but as socialist theoreticians, as Proudhons and Weitlings; in other words, they take part only when, and to the extent that they are able, more or less, to acquire the knowledge of their age and advance that knowledge. And in order that workingmen *may be able to do this more often,* every effort must be made to raise the level of the consciousness of the workers generally; the workers must not confine themselves to the artificially restricted limits of "*literature for workers*" but should learn to master *general literature* to an increasing degree. It would be even more true to say "are not confined," instead of "must not confine themselves," because the workers themselves wish to read and do read all that is written for the intelligentsia and it is only a few (bad) intellectuals who believe that it is sufficient "for the workers" to be told a few things about factory conditions, and to have repeated to them over and over again what has long been known.

8. *The Hirsch-Duncker unions* — founded by the bourgeois liberals Hirsch and Duncker in 1868 in Germany. Hirsch and Duncker advocated "harmony of class interests," drew the workers away from the revolutionary class struggle against the bourgeoisie, reduced the tasks and role of trade union organizations to those of benefit societies and cultural and educational clubs.

9. It is often said: the working class *spontaneously* gravitates towards Socialism. This is perfectly true in the sense that socialist theory defines the causes of the misery of the working class more profoundly and more correctly than any other theory, and for that reason the workers are able to assimilate it so easily, *provided, however,* that this theory does not itself yield to spontaneity, *provided* it subordinates spontaneity to itself. Usually this is taken for granted, but it is precisely this which the *Rabocheye Dyelo* forgets or distorts. The working class spontaneously gravitates towards Socialism, but the more widespread (and continuously revived in the most diverse forms) bourgeois ideology nevertheless spontaneously imposes itself upon the working class still more.

TOWARD A THEORY OF THE
LABOR MOVEMENT

Selig Perlman

. . . The present time offers a unique opportunity for stock taking [with respect to the theory of the labor movement]. First, because during the throbbing dozen years just past, filled to the brim with war and revolution, both capitalism and the labor movement have undergone a testing heretofore undreamed of. At no other time in modern history has society shown itself so nearly "with the lid off" as since the Russian Revolution. Nor has the labor movement ever before been made to render so strict an account to the outside world, as well as to itself, of what its deep-lying purposes truly are, as during the crowded decade which witnessed the successful Bolshevist Revolution, the decisive defeat of Communism in Germany (largely with the aid of the organized labor movement itself), the class war in Britain culminating in the general strike, the progressive metamorphosis of American capitalism into a "welfare capitalism," with the arrest of the growth of American unionism, notwithstanding the economic prosperity—to say nothing of the eclipse of French unionism and of the destruction of any independent labor movement in Fascist Italy. Second, the present appears an opportune time for a reëxamination of the theory of the labor movement, since, even in the eyes of the Communists, the revolutionary era has been succeeded by a "temporary" stabilization of capitalism.

Three dominant factors are emerging from the seeming medley of contradictory turns and events in recent labor history. The first factor is the demonstrated capacity, as in Germany, Austria, and Hungary, or else incapacity, as in Russia, of the capitalist group to survive as a ruling group and to withstand revolutionary attack when the protective hand of government has been withdrawn. In this sense "capitalism" is not only, nor even primarily, a material or governmental arrangement whereby one class, the capitalist class, owns the means of production, exchange, and distribution, while the other class, labor, is employed for wages. Capitalism is rather a social organization presided over by a class with an "effective will to power," implying the ability to defend its power against all comers—to defend it, not necessarily by physical force, since such force, however important at a crisis, might crumble after all—but to defend it, as it has done in Germany, through having convinced the other classes that they alone, the capitalists, know how to operate the complex economic apparatus of modern society upon which the material welfare of all depends.

SOURCE: *A Theory of The Labor Movement,* (New York: A. M. Kelley, 1949), pp. 3–10.

The second factor which stands out clearly in the world-wide social situation is the rôle of the so-called "intellectual," the "intelligentsia," in the labor movement and in society at large. It was from the intellectual that the anti-capitalist influences in modern society emanated. It was he who impressed upon the labor movement tenets characteristic of his own mentality: the "nationalization" or "socialization" of industry, and political action, whether "constitutional" or "unconstitutional," on behalf of the "new social order." He, too, has been busily indoctrinating the middle classes with the same views, thus helping to undermine an important prop of capitalism and to some extent even the spirit of resistance of the capitalists themselves.

The third and the most vital factor in the labor situation is the trade union movement. Trade unionism, which is essentially pragmatic, struggles constantly, not only against the employers for an enlarged opportunity measured in income, security, and liberty in the shop and industry, but struggles also, whether consciously or unconsciously, actively or merely passively, against the intellectual who would frame its programs and shape its policies. In this struggle by "organic" labor[1] against dominance by the intellectuals, we perceive a clash of an ideology which holds the concrete workingmen in the center of its vision with a rival ideology which envisages labor merely as an "abstract mass in the grip of an abstract force."[2]

Labor's own "home grown" ideology is disclosed only through a study of the "working rules" of labor's own "institutions." The trade unions are the institutions of labor today, but much can be learned also from labor's institutions in the past, notably the gilds.

It is the author's contention that manual groups, whether peasants in Russia, modern wage earners, or medieval master workmen, have had their economic attitudes basically determined by a consciousness of scarcity of opportunity, which is characteristic of these groups, and stands out in contrast with the business men's "abundance consciousness," or consciousness of unlimited opportunity. Starting with this consciousness of scarcity, the "manualist" groups have been led to practising solidarity, to an insistence upon an "ownership" by the group as a whole of the totality of economic opportunity extant, to a "rationing" by the group of such opportunity among the individuals constituting it, to a control by the group over its members in relation to the conditions upon which they as individuals are permitted to occupy a portion of that opportunity—in brief, to a "communism of opportunity." This differs fundamentally from socialism or communism, which would "communize" not only "opportunity," but also production and distribution—just as it is far removed from "capitalism." Capitalism started from the premise of unlimited opportunity, and arrived, in its classical formulation, at "laissez faire" for the individual all along the line—in regard to the "quantity" of opportunity he may appropriate, the price or wage he may charge, and in regard to the ownership of the means of production. "Communism of opportunity" in the sense here employed existed in the medieval gilds before the merchant capitalists had subverted them to the purposes of a protected business men's oligarchy; in Russian peasant land communities with their periodic redivisions, among the several families, of the collectively owned land, the embodiment of the economic opportunity of a peasant group; and exists today in trade unions enforcing a "job control" through union "working rules."

But, in this country, due to the fact that here the "manualist" had found at hand an abundance of opportunity, in unoccupied land and in a pioneer social condition, his economic thinking had therefore issued, not from the scarcity premise but from the premise of abundance. It thus resulted in a social philosophy which was more akin to the business men's than to the trade unionists' or gildsmen's. Accordingly, the American labor movement, which long remained unaware of any distinction between itself and the "producing classes" in general,—which included also farmers, small manufacturers, and small business men,—continued for many decades to worship at the shrine of individualistic "anti-monopoly." "Anti-monopoly" was a program of reform, through politics and legislation, whereby the "producing classes" would apply a corrective to the American social order so that economic individualism might become "safe" for the producers rather than for land speculators, merchant capitalists, and bankers. Unionism, on the contrary, first became a stabilized movement in America only when the abundance consciousness of the pioneer days had been replaced in the mind of labor by a scarcity consciousness—the consciousness of job scarcity. Only then did the American wage earner become willing to envisage a future in which his union would go on indefinitely controlling his relation to his job rather than endeavoring to afford him, as during the anti-monopoly stage of the labor movement, an escape into free and unregulated self-employment, by winning for him a competitive equality with the "monopolist."

In America, the historical struggle waged by labor for an undivided expression of its own mentality in its own movement was directed against the ideology of "anti-monopoly." But in Europe the antithesis to the labor mentality has been the mentality of the intellectual.

Twenty-five years ago, Nicolai Lenin[3] clearly recognized the divergence which exists between the intellectual and the trade unionist, although not in terms of an inevitable mutual antagonism, when he hurled his unusual polemical powers against those in the Social-Democratic Party, his own party at the time, who would confine their own and the party's agitational activities to playing upon labor's economic grievances. He then said that if it had not been for the "bourgeois intellectuals" Marx and Engels, labor would never have got beyond mere "trifling,"—going after an increase in wage here and after a labor law there. Lenin, of course, saw labor and the trade union movement, not as an aggregation of concrete individuals sharing among themselves their collective job opportunity, as well as trying to enlarge it and improve it by joint effort and step by step, but rather as an abstract mass which history had predetermined to hurl itself against the capitalist social order and demolish it. Lenin therefore could never have seen in a non-revolutionary unionism anything more than a blind groping after a purpose only vaguely grasped, rather than a completely self-conscious movement with a full-blown ideology of its own. But to see "labor" solely as an abstract mass and the concrete individual reduced to a mere mathematical point, as against the trade unionists' striving for job security for the individual and concrete freedom on the job, has not been solely the prerogative of "determinist-revolutionaries" like Lenin and the Communists. The other types of intellectuals in and close to the labor movement, the "ethical" type, the heirs of Owen and the Christian Socialists, and the "social efficiency" type, best represented by the Fabians—to mention but English examples,—have equally with the orthodox Marxians reduced labor to a mere abstraction, although each has done so in his own way and has pictured "labor" as an abstract mass in the grip of an abstract force, existing, however, only in his own intellectual imagination, and not in the emotional imagination of the manual worker himself. . . .

NOTES

1. Trade unionists and intellectuals use alike the term "labor," which has an abstract connotation. But, to the trade unionists, "labor" means nothing more abstract or mystical than the millions of concrete human beings with their concrete wants and aspirations.
2. I use frequently the term "ideology" in imitation of the usage of socialist intellectuals taken over from Napoleon's term applied by him in contempt to the idealists of his day. I find, however, that the term has quite the same meaning as that which scientists call "ideas" and "theory," philosophers call "idealism" or "ethics," and business men and working men call "philosophy." Unionists speak of "the philosophy of trade unionism." If they were "intellectuals," they would call it "theory," "ideology," "ideas," or "idealism," or "ethics," all of which I sometimes include in the term "mentality."
3. "The history of all countries attests to the fact that, left to its own forces, the working class can only attain to trade union consciousness,—that is, the conviction that it is necessary to unite in unions, wage the struggle against the bosses, obtain from the government such or such labor reforms, etc. As to the socialist doctrines, they came from philosophic, historic and economic theories elaborated by certain educated representatives of the possessing classes, the Intellectuals. In their social situation, the founders of contemporary scientific socialism, Marx and Engels, were bourgeois intellectuals." Lenin in *What Is to Be Done?*

THE MEANING OF CLASS

Edward P. Thompson

. . . By class I understand an historical phenomenon, unifying a number of disparate and seemingly unconnected events, both in the raw material of experience and in consciousness. I emphasise that it is an *historical* phenomenon. I do not see class as a "structure," nor even as a "category," but as something which in fact happens (and can be shown to have happened) in human relationships.

More than this, the notion of class entails the notion of historical relationship. Like any other relationship, it is a fluency which evades analysis if we attempt to stop it dead at any given moment and anatomise its structure. The finest-meshed sociological net cannot give us a pure specimen of class, any more than it can give us one of deference or of love. The relationship must always be embodied in real people and in a real context. Moreover, we cannot have two distinct classes, each with an independent being, and then bring them *into* relationship with each other. We cannot have love without lovers, nor deference without squires and labourers. And class happens when some men, as a result of common experiences (inherited or shared), feel and articulate the identity of their interests as between themselves, and as against other men whose interests are different from (and usually opposed to) theirs. The class experience is largely determined by the productive relations into which men are born—or enter involuntarily. Class-consciousness is the way in which these experiences are handled in cultural terms: embodied in traditions, value-systems, ideas, and institutional forms. If the experience appears as determined, class-consciousness does not. We can see a *logic* in the responses of similar occupational groups undergoing similar experiences, but we cannot predicate any *law*. Consciousness of class arises in the same way in different times and places, but never in *just* the same way.

There is today an ever-present temptation to suppose that class is a thing. This was not Marx's meaning, in his own historical writing, yet the error vitiates much latter-day "Marxist" writing. "It," the working class, is assumed to have a real existence, which can be defined almost mathematically—so many men who stand in a certain relation to the means of production. Once this is assumed it becomes possible to deduce the class-consciousness which "it" ought to have (but seldom does have) if "it" was properly aware of its own position and real interests. There is a cultural superstructure, through which this recognition dawns in inefficient ways. These cultural "lags" and distortions are a nuisance, so that it is easy to pass from this to some theory of substitution: the party, sect, or theorist, who disclose class-consciousness, not as it is, but as it ought to be.

SOURCE: *The Making of the English Working Class* (New York: Vintage Books, 1963), pp. 9–11.

But a similar error is committed daily on the other side of the ideological divide. In one form, this is a plain negative. Since the crude notion of class attributed to Marx can be faulted without difficulty, it is assumed that any notion of class is a pejorative theoretical construct, imposed upon the evidence. It is denied that class has happened at all. In another form, and by a curious inversion, it is possible to pass from a dynamic to a static view of class. "It"—the working class— exists, and can be defined with some accuracy as a component of the social structure. Class-consciousness, however, is a bad thing, invented by displaced intellectuals, since everything which disturbs the harmonious co-existence of groups performing different "social rôles" (and which thereby retards economic growth) is to be deplored as an "unjustified disturbance-symptom"[1] The problem is to determine how best "it" can be conditioned to accept its social rôle, and how its grievances may best be "handled and channelled."

If we remember that class is a relationship, and not a thing, we can not think in this way. "It" does not exist, either to have an ideal interest or consciousness, or to lie as a patient on the Adjustor's table. Nor can we turn matters upon their heads, as has been done by one authority who (in a study of class obsessively concerned with methodology, to the exclusion of the examination of a single class situation in a real historical context) has informed us:

> Classes are based on the differences in legitimate power associated with certain positions, i.e. on the structure of social rôles with respect to their authority expectations. . . . An individual becomes a member of a class by playing a social rôle relevant from the point of view of authority. . . . He belongs to a class because he occupies a position in a social orga- nisation; i.e. class membership is derived from the incumbency of a social rôle.[2]

The question, of course, is how the individual got to be in this "social rôle," and how the particular social organisation (with its property-rights and structure of authority) got to be there. And these are historical questions. If we stop history at a given point, then there are no classes but simply a multitude of individuals with a multitude of experiences. But if we watch these men over an adequate period of social change, we observe patterns in their relationships, their ideas, and their institutions. Class is defined by men as they live their own history, and, in the end, this is its only definition. . . .

NOTES

1. An example of this approach, covering the period of this book, is to be found in the work of a colleague of Professor Talcott Parsons: N.J. Smelser, *Social Change in the Industrial Revolution* (1959).
2. R. Dahrendorf, *Class and Class Conflict in Industry Society* (Stanford: Stanford University Press, 1959), pp. 148–149.

III. THE MODERN DEBATE: WORKERS AND INDUSTRIALIZATION

INTRODUCTION

The industrial societies of Western Europe and the United States have continued to mature and evolve without undergoing the kind of systemic transformation led by the working class which Marx had expected. Radicals have thus been forced to confront the challenge of reconciling their revolutionary perspective with the apparent quiescence of the working class. For some, this has stimulated the search for an alternative revolutionary agent inherent in capitalism as a global system. For nonradicals, the application of science and technology under conditions of mature industrialism (or "post-industrialism") creates "dynamic" societies in which issues of revolutionary transformation of property relationships recede into the background.

Writing from a radical perspective, Paul Sweezy (in "Marx and the Proletariat") concedes that modern technology produces a proletariat "which is less rather than more revolutionary" than the working class of the past. Rising living standards and the proliferation of new occupational groupings tend to undermine class consciousness and to heighten occupational and status consciousness in the industrialized nations. But if capitalism is treated as a world system, the role of revolutionary agent is now assumed by the proletariat of the "dependent" nations. "These masses now become an agent of revolutionary change in precisely the sense that Marx believed the industrial proletariat of the mid-19th century to be."

A nonrevolutionary perspective on the theme of industrialization and the working class is developed in the selection by Kerr and his colleagues ("The Logic of Industrialism"). They accept the view that the development of modern science and technology is the ultimate determinant of the pattern of social stratification and requires the hierarchical organization of the work process. But constantly changing production methods, products, and technology also create an "open society" with high rates of mobility and an ethos antithetical to status based upon class and race. The logic of industrialization also creates a consensus around an accepted "web of rules" dominated by middle-class values and ideology. All these "imperatives" of the industrialization process submerge the prospects for capitalism's revolutionary transformation by a class-conscious working class.

Some aspects of the Kerr et al. vision of modern industrialism are challenged by Goldthorpe in "Social Stratification in Industrial Society." In particular, he argues that social and economic equality and mobility have been exaggerated. Significant class distinctions continue to characterize capitalist societies and predictions of their disappearance based on the "requirements" of modern industrialism are not convincing.

A more recent variant of the logic of industrialization theme has centered on the concept of a "post-industrial" society, most fully developed in the writings of Daniel Bell. This concept has become a way of characterizing a new "stage" which advanced industrial societies are presumably entering. Among the dominant features of "post-industrialism" are a significant shift of labor to service occupations, the increased role of "knowledge inputs," and increased reliance on "theoretical knowledge" for the solution of both economic and social problems. While conflict does not disappear, class antagonisms become subordinate to the conflict between professionalism and participation. In an important sense, therefore, the "post-industrial" society in Bell's formulation emerges also as a "post-capitalist" society.

Some of the empirical and theoretical underpinning of this concept comes under critical scrutiny in Heilbroner's selection, "Economic Problems of a 'Post-industrial' Society." The shift to service occupations in recent decades has not been accompanied by any significant decline in the relative importance of industrial factory work. Moreover, some of the rise in service employment represents a shift to the labor market of work previously performed in the household. Perhaps more important, Heilbroner sees the dominant features and problems of "post-industrialism" in the West as reflecting the continuation of the capitalist mode of organization rather than a stage "beyond" capitalism. The extreme concentration of capital and wealth, the stability of income shares, a "massive misallocation of resources," and emergence of the inflation problem all reflect "the failure of the market mechanism and the special constraints of private ownership." Although the bitter class antagonisms characteristic of earlier capitalism appear to have diminished, the prospect of a "redundancy" of labor and the increased psychological strains of work also imply that "postindustrialism," like earlier capitalism, has not solved the "labor problem." Thus, continuities with the traditional problems of a capitalist order may be as important as the departures implied by the concept of "postindustrialism."

MARX AND THE PROLETARIAT

Paul Sweezy

Marx's theory of capitalism, which was sketched with broad and sweeping strokes in the *Communist Manifesto* and achieved its most comprehensive and polished form in the first volume of *Capital,* published just a hundred years ago, holds that capitalism is a self-contradictory system which generates increasingly severe difficulties and crises as it develops. But this is only half the story: equally characteristic of capitalism is that it generates not only difficulties and crises but also its own grave-diggers in the shape of the modern proletariat. A social system can be ever so self-contradictory and still be without a revolutionary potential: the outcome can be, and in fact history shows many examples where it has been, stagnation, misery, starvation, subjugation by a stronger and more vigorous society. In Marx's view capitalism was not such a society; it was headed not for slow death or subjugation but for a thorough-going revolutionary transformation. And the reason was precisely because by its very nature it had to produce the agent which would revolutionize it. This is the crucially important role which the proletariat plays in the Marxian theoretical schema.

In the eyes of many people, including not a few who consider themselves to be essentially Marxists, this theory of the revolutionary agency of the proletariat is the weakest point of the whole system. They point to the fact that the English and other Western European proletariats, which Marx considered to be the vanguard of the international revolutionary movement, have actually developed into reformist forces which, by accepting the basic assumptions of capitalism, in fact strengthen it. And they note that the proletariat of what has become the most advanced and powerful capitalist country, the United States of America, has never developed a significant revolutionary leadership or movement, and shows fewer signs of doing so today than at any time in its history.

I do not believe that the empirical observations which support this type of criticism of Marx's theory can be seriously challenged. And yet it certainly will not do to jump from there to the conclusion that Marx's theory is "refuted" and must be abandoned. A more legitimate procedure, I suggest, is to inquire into the inner logic of the theory to discover *why* Marx assigned the role of revolutionary agent to the proletariat. In this way I believe we shall find that it is not the theory itself which is at fault so much as its misinterpretation and misapplication.

First, we must be quite clear that Marx's theory of the revolutionary agency of the proletariat has nothing to do with an emotional attachment to, or blind faith in, the working class as such. He believed that objective forces, generated by the capitalist system, were inexorably molding a revolutionary class, i.e. one which

SOURCE: *Monthly Review,* December, 1967, pp. 28–29, 31–42.

would have both the ability and the will to overthrow the existing order. The ability stemmed from its numerical strength and its indispensable role in the capitalist production process, the will from its being deprived not only of material possessions but of its essential and ultimately irrepressible humanity . . . the proletariat was *not* a revolutionary force from its birth but on the contrary acquired this quality in the course of its capitalistic development.

In this connection it is necessary to recall an aspect of Marx's theory of capitalism which is of course known to all students of the subject but which, I believe, is generally considered to have mostly historical interest. This is his division of the capitalist epoch into what Engels, in his editor's preface to the first English edition of the first volume of *Capital,* called "two great and essentially different periods of economic history: the period of manufacture proper, based on the division of manual labor, and the period of modern industry based on machinery." What separated the two periods was the Industrial Revolution, a term much used by Marx, the beginning of which he dated from Wyatt's spinning machine of 1735, and which had worked its transforming effects by 1825, a year of economic crisis in which "modern industry . . . for the first time opens the periodic cycle of its modern life."

From our present point of view there are two fundamental differences between these phases of capitalist development. One relates to the dynamics of the production process itself, the other to the changed character of the proletariat brought about by the transition from the earlier phase to the later. (It should be noted in passing that the formal concepts of Marxian economic theory—constant and variable capital, surplus value, expanded reproduction, etc.—are equally applicable to both phases. At the level of abstraction implied by this conceptual apparatus, there is therefore no difference between the two phases, which is perhaps why many Marxist economists have failed to appreciate the importance of distinguishing between them.)

Manufacture is an extension and adaptation of age-old handicraft methods of production. The chief innovation is the assembling of many craftsmen in a single enterprise, which permits forms and degrees of specialization unthinkable under the medieval guild system. This specialization of crafts—or division or labor, as it was called by Adam Smith, the theorist *par excellence* of the manufacture phase— results in an enormous increase in labor productivity and in this sense marks a great stride forward in human progress. However, it is important to recognize that, technologically, manufacture is still an essentially conservative mode of production. The increase of productivity for which it is responsible stems from the more rational utilization of existing technologies, not from the introduction of new technologies. The latter process, often called invention, is no part of the logic of manufacture. Hence, in Marx's words, "History shows how the division of labor peculiar to manufacture, strictly so called, acquires the best adapted form at first by experience, as it were behind the backs of the actors, and then, like the guild handicrafts, strives to hold fast that form when once found, and here and there succeeds in keeping it for centuries." This naturally does not mean that invention was absent or that the culture and ideology of this phase of capitalism did not favor the inventive arts. If such had been the case, there would have been no industrial revolution at the time and in the place where it actually occurred. What it does mean is that invention was not an integral part of the process of production and indeed was often strongly resisted by the practitioners of existing methods of production. This special combination of circumstances, both favoring and inhibiting the progress of invention, found an interesting reflection in Adam Smith who, as Nathan Rosenberg has shown,[1] regarded major inventions as the work of neither laborers nor capitalists but rather of "philosophers" who are totally separated from the productive process.

The labor force of the manufacturing phase corresponded to the requirements of this particular mode of production. It consisted of a multitude of craftsmen possessing a great variety of specialized skills which were characteristically passed on from father to son. Craft consciousness rather than class consciousness was the hallmark of a proletariat so composed. The skilled handworker tended to be bigoted, proud, undisciplined, contentious, capable of waging a bitter and often violent struggle against the constraints of capitalist production and the employer who imposed them upon him. But his vision was necessarily limited: he could not see the system as a whole nor understand his place in it, and he was therefore incapable of sustained revolutionary activity to change it. Capitalism in its manufacturing phase, in addition to being technologically conservative was also highly resistant to political and social change.

. . . Whereas capitalism in its manufacturing phase was technologically conservative and immune to the threat of revolutionary change, modern industry based on machinery is the opposite in both respects. Technological progress no longer depends on the ingenuity of the skilled worker or on the genius of the great inventor; it now becomes the province of the rational sciences. This is one of the major themes of Marx's masterful chapter entitled "Machinery and Modern Industry" which alone would be enough to mark the first volume of *Capital* as an epoch-making work. Here we must be content with a couple of brief quotations which convey the gist of his thought:

> The principle, carried out in the factory system, of analyzing the process of production into its constituent phases, and of solving the problems thus proposed by the application of mechanics, of chemistry, and of the whole range of the natural sciences, becomes the determining principle everywhere.

> Modern Industry rent the veil that concealed from men their own social process of production, and that turned the various spontaneously divided branches of production into so many riddles, not only to outsiders but even to the initiated. The principle which it pursued of resolving each into its constituent parts without any regard to their possible execution by the hand of man, created the new modern science of technology. The varied, apparently unconnected, and petrified forms of the production process now resolved themselves into so many conscious and systematic applications of natural science to the attainment of given useful effects.

From this the conclusion flowed logically: "Modern Industry never looks upon and treats the existing form of a process as final. The technical base of that industry is therefore revolutionary, while all earlier modes of production were essentially conservative."

With respect to its social base, Marx regarded modern industrial capitalism as no less revolutionary—once again in sharp contrast to capitalism in its manufacturing phase. Machinery progressively abolishes the crafts which are the basis of manufacture and thereby renders obsolete the multitudinous special skills of the craftsmen. In this way it cheapens the labor power of adult males by obviating the need for prolonged and expensive training programs. At the same time, by putting a premium on dexterity and quickness it opens the door to the mass employment of women and children. There followed a vast expansion of the labor supply which was augmented and supplemented by two further factors: (1) Once solidly entrenched in the basic industries, machinery invades ever new branches of the economy, undercutting the old handworkers and casting them onto the labor market. And (2) the progressive improvement of machinery in industries already conquered continuously eliminates existing jobs and reduces the employment-creating power of a given rate of capital accumulation.

The effects of machinery, in short, are on the one hand to extend, homogenize, and reduce the costs of production of the labor force; on the other, to slow down the rate of increase of the demand for labor power. This means a fundamental change in the economic power relation between capital and labor, to the enormous advantage of the former. Wages are driven down to, and often below, the barest subsistence minimum; hours of work are increased beyond anything known before; the intensity of labor is stepped up to match the ever increasing speed of the machinery. Machinery thus completes the process, begun in the period of primitive accumulation, of subjecting labor to the sway of capital. It is the capitalistic employment of machinery, and not merely capitalism in general, which generates the modern proletariat as Marx conceived it.

But the coin has two sides. Economically, the power of the proletariat under modern industry is much reduced compared to that of its predecessor in the period of manufacture. But politically, its potential power is infinitely greater. Old craft and geographical divisions and jealousies are eliminated or minimized. The nature of work in the modern factory requires the organization and disciplining of the workers, thereby preparing them for organized and disciplined action in other fields. The extreme of exploitation to which they are subjected deprives them of any interest in the existing social order, forces them to live in conditions in which morality is meaningless and family life impossible, and ends by totally alienating them from their work, their products, their society, and even themselves. Unlike the skilled craftsmen of the period of manufacture, these workers form a proletariat which is both capable of, and has every interest in, revolutionary action to overthrow the existing social order. These are the ones of whom Marx and Engels had already declared in the *Communist Manifesto:* "The proletarians have nothing to lose but their chains. They have a world to win." In the first volume of *Capital* this bold generalization is supported by a painstaking analysis of the immanent features and tendencies of capitalist "modern industry" as it emerged from the industrial revolution.

So far I have tried to show that Marx's theory of capitalism encompasses two quite distinct phases, separated by the industrial revolution, which can be characterized as follows:

	Manufacture		*Modern Industry*
Technology	Conservative	Technology	Revolutionary
Proletariat	Non-revolutionary	Proletariat	Revolutionary

It must be immediately added, however, that the word "revolutionary" applied to technology has a somewhat different meaning from what it does when applied to the proletariat. A revolutionary technology is one which by its very nature changes continuously and rapidly; a revolutionary proletariat, on the other hand, is one which has the *potential* to make a revolution but which can actually make it only once under favorable conditions (the so-called revolutionary situation). Here a question obviously arises: If, for whatever reason, the emergence of a revolutionary situation is long delayed, what will be the effect in the meantime of modern industry's revolutionary technology on the composition and capabilities of the proletariat?

Marx never asked this question, perhaps because it never occurred to him that the revolution might be long delayed. And yet it is a question which arises quite naturally within the framework of his theory. He had explicitly recognized that modern industry "is continually causing changes not only in the technical basis of production, but also in the functions of the laborer and in the labor-process"; and no one knew better than he that it is the functions of the laborer and the nature of the labor process which determine the character of the proletariat. In the absence of a revolutionary situation, would the proletariat tend to become more or less revolutionary? It would have been a perfectly logical question for Marx to ask when he was writing *Capital;* a hundred years later it seems to be not only a logical but an inescapable question for Marx's followers.

This is obviously not the occasion to attempt a comprehensive answer, and I have to admit that my knowledge of the interrelation between technology and the labor process is far too limited to permit me to speak as an expert on the subject. I will therefore restrict myself to indicating in a very general way why it seems to me that the advance of modern technology must tend to shape a proletariat which is less rather than more revolutionary than that which emerged from the industrial revolution in the middle of the 19th century.

I would not put the main emphasis on the consequences of technological change for the workers who actually mind the machines and do functionally similar work, much of it virtually unknown in Marx's time, such as manning assembly lines. These are still for the most part dehumanizing jobs requiring little skill; and speed-up of machinery and increasing work loads certainly do not make them more bearable, not to say attractive. A proletariat dominated by operatives of this general description might well have as great a revolutionary potential as its mid-19th-century predecessor. The point is that relative to the total work force there are so many fewer jobs of this kind than there used to be. Progressive mechanization of particular processes, and more recently the perfection of generally applicable methods of partial or full automation, have reduced this traditional blue-collar segment of the proletariat from what was once a large majority to what is today in the most industrialized societies a small minority. Since the output of this minority has at the same time enormously increased, it is clear that modern technology has multiplied the productivity of labor many times over and put within society's grasp a potential surplus of vast proportions.

The obverse of this development is that a great variety of new categories of jobs has been created. Some of these are integrally related to the new technology—scientists, researchers, engineers, technicians, highly skilled maintenance and repair men, etc.—but many more (both absolutely and relatively) are concerned in one way or another with the manipulation and absorption of the surplus made possible by the increased productivity of the underlying production workers. Under this heading one could list government workers of all kinds, including teachers; those employed in the many branches of the sales apparatus, including most of the personnel of the mass communication media; workers and salaried personnel in finance, insurance, and real estate; and the providers of many different kinds of personal services from beauty treatment to sports spectacles. In the United States today these job categories, taken all together, probably account for close to three quarters of the employed non-agricultural labor force.

In terms of the occupational composition of the labor force, then, the two chief consequences of modern industry's revolutionary technology have been (1) a drastic (and continuing) reduction in the production-worker component, and (2) a vast proliferation of job categories in the distribution and service sectors of the economy. At the same time there has taken place a slow but cumulatively substantial increase in the real wages of both production and non-production workers. In part this reflects an increase in the cost of production of labor power as the educational and training requirements of the new employment categories have risen. And in part it reflects the fact that the workers—and here we mean primarily production workers—have been able through non-revolutionary class struggle to wrest from the capitalists a part of the fruits of increasing productivity.

To sum up: The revolutionary technology of modern industry, correctly described and analyzed by Marx,[2] has had the effect of multiplying by many times the productivity of basic production workers. This in turn has resulted in a sharp reduction in their relative importance in the labor force, in the proliferation of new job categories, and in a gradually rising standard of living for employed workers. In short, the first effects of the introduction of machinery—expansion and homogenization of the labor force and reduction in the costs of production (value) or labor power—have been largely reversed. Once again, as in the period of manufacture, the proletariat is highly differentiated; and once again occupational and status consciousness has tended to submerge class consciousness.

It might be thought that despite these changes the blue-collar proletariat would remain a revolutionary element within the working class as a whole. No doubt there is a tendency for this to happen, and it would be short-sighted in the extreme to overlook the revolutionary potential still remaining in this large body of workers. But one must not go too far in isolating them from the rest of the labor force. As James Bogg says: "Today most workers in the plant [i.e. blue-collar workers] have been to high school and quite a few have even been to college. All either plan or wish to send their sons and daughters to college—their sons so they won't have to work in the factory on what they call a dull and automated job; their daughters . . . so they won't have to marry some bum but can make their own living and be free to decide whether they want to marry or not marry. . . ." In other words, blue-collar workers, being a diminishing minority of the whole working class, do not think of their families as permanently stuck in the stratum which they occupy. As long as this is so, their attitudes and ideology are not likely to be radically different from those of the non-revolutionary majority of the working class which surrounds them.

If we accept these general propositions about the direct and indirect effects of modern technology on the composition and character of the working class, must we conclude that Marx's theory of the proletariat has been refuted? I do not think so. His theory in fact dealt with the early impact of machinery on the proletariat, not with the longer-run consequences of the machine technology for the proletariat. One might perhaps complain that Marx did not attempt to develop a more comprehensive theory; and one could argue, I think persuasively, that he certainly could have done so. Indeed from many remarks scattered throughout his writings, it would probably be possible for a follower of Marx to construct a more or less systematic theory of what the future held in store for the proletariat if capitalism should survive the revolutionary threat inherent in the early period of modern industry. But this is not the occasion for such an effort, and the fact that Marx himself did not make it provides no justification for denying the validity of the theory he did put forward within the limits of it applicability.

In this connection I would go further and argue that the Russian Revolution of 1917 provides extremely strong empirical evidence for the validity of Marx's theory. This revolution occurred in a capitalist country where modern industry was in the process of establishing itself and where it had already created a large and highly revolutionary urban proletariat. Under these circumstances, when the revolutionary situation matured (as it had not done in the Western European countries at a comparable stage of development), the proletariat played precisely the role attributed to it in Marx's theory. In the social sciences, a theory rarely receives a more striking confirmation.

Here, however, a much more serious question arises: Does the fact that capitalism in Western Europe and North America survived the initial period of modern industry and that its new technology then went on progressively to reduce the revolutionary potential of the proletariat, mean that as of the second half of the 20th century we have to abandon the whole idea of a revolutionary agent destined to overthrow the capitalist order? Again, I do not think so.

The belief that the *industrial* proletariat is the only possible revolutionary agent under capitalism stems from focusing attention too exclusively on the advanced capitalist countries where modern industry got its start and where the new technology has had a chance to develop under favorable conditions. But capitalism as a social order has never consisted only of industrialized countries. In fact, as Marx explicitly recognized, the industrialization of some countries had as its counterpart from the outset the non-industrialization of others, with the two sets of countries being integrally tied together in a single system.

> So soon . . . as the general conditions requisite for production by the modern industrial system have been established, this mode of production acquires an elasticity, a capacity for sudden extension by leaps and bounds that finds no hindrance except in the supply of raw material and in the disposal of the produce. On the one hand, the immediate effect of machinery is to increase the supply of raw material in the same way, for example, as the cotton gin augmented the production of cotton. On the other hand, the cheapness of the articles produced by machinery, and the improved means of transport and communications furnish the weapons for conquering foreign markets. By ruining handicraft production in other countries, machinery forcibly converts them into fields for the supply of its raw material. In this way East India was compelled to produce cotton, wool, hemp, jute, and indigo for Great Britain. . . . A new and international division of labor, a division

suited to the requirements of the chief centers of modern industry springs up, and converts one part of the globe into a chiefly agricultural field of production for supplying the other part which remains a chiefly industrial field.

Once it is recognized that capitalism is not and never has been confined to one or more industrializing countries, but is rather a global system embracing both the (relatively few) industrializing countries and their (relatively numerous) satellites and dependencies, it becomes quite clear that the future of the system cannot be adequately analyzed in terms of the forces at work in any part of the system but must take full account of the *modus operandi* of the system as a whole.

Lenin was the first Marxist to see this and to begin work on the theoretical extensions and reformulations which it made necessary. His major contribution was his little book *Imperialism: the Highest Stage of Capitalism* which, having been published in 1917, is exactly half as old as the first volume of *Capital*. There he argued that "Capitalism has grown into a world system of colonial oppression and of the financial strangulation of the overwhelming majority of the people of the world by a handful of 'advanced' countries. And this 'booty' is shared between two or three powerful world pirates armed to the teeth. . . ." He also argued that the capitalists of the imperialist countries could and do use a part of their "booty" to bribe and win over to their side an aristocracy of labor. As far as the logic of the argument is concerned, it could be extended to a majority or even all the workers in the industrialized countries. In any case it is clear that taking account of the global character of the capitalist system provides strong additional reasons for believing that the tendency in this stage of capitalist development will be to generate a less rather than a more revolutionary proletariat.

But once again the coin has two sides. If imperialist exploitation brings wealth to the industrialized countries and enables them to raise further the standard of living of their working classes, it brings poverty and misery to the great mass of the working people—agricultural as well as industrial—in the dependencies. These masses now become an agent of revolutionary change in precisely the sense that Marx believed the industrial proletariat of the mid-19th century to be. Let me quote again what he wrote in the *Holy Family:* "Because the abstraction of all humanity, even the appearance of humanity, is practically complete in the fully developed proletariat, because the living conditions of the proletariat represent the focal point of all inhuman conditions in contemporary society, because the human being is lost in the proletariat, but has won a theoretical consciousness of loss and is compelled by unavoidable and absolutely compulsory need . . . to revolt against this inhumanity—all these are the reasons why the proletariat can and must emancipate itself."

These words certainly do not apply to the working classes of the United States and Western Europe today. But do they not apply all the more obviously and forcefully to the masses in the much more numerous and populous underdeveloped dependencies of the global capitalist system? And does not the pattern of successful socialist revolutions since the Second World War—highlighted by Vietnam, China, and Cuba—demonstrate beyond any doubt that these masses do indeed constitute a revolutionary agent capable of challenging and defeating capitalism?

Allow me in conclusion to present a very brief summary of my thesis: In

Marx's theory of capitalism, the proletariat is not always and necessarily revolutionary. It was not revolutionary in the period of manufacture, becoming so only as a consequence of the introduction of machinery in the industrial revolution. The long-run effects of machinery, however, are different from the immediate effects. If the revolutionary opportunities of the early period of modern industry are missed, the proletariat of an industrializing country tends to become less and less revolutionary. This does not mean, however, that Marx's contention that capitalism produces its own gravediggers is wrong. If we consider capitalism as a global system, which is the only correct procedure, we see that it is divided into a handful of exploiting countries and a much more numerous and populous group of exploited countries. The masses in these exploited dependencies constitute a force in the global capitalist system which is revolutionary in the same sense and for the same reasons that Marx considered the proletariat of the early period of modern industry to be revolutionary. And finally, world history since the Second World War proves that this revolutionary force is really capable of waging successful revolutionary struggles against capitalist domination.

NOTES

1. Nathan Rosenberg, "Adam Smith on the Division of Labor: Two Views or One?", *Economics*, May 1965.
2. As a matter of fact Marx's treatment of the relations among industry, technology, and science was far ahead of his time and has only become fully realistic and applicable a hundred years later.

THE LOGIC OF INDUSTRIALISM

Clark Kerr
John T. Dunlop
Frederick H. Harbison
Charles A. Myers

Industrialization refers to the actual course of transition from the traditional society toward industrialism. Industrialism is an abstraction, a limit approached through historical industrialization. Industrialism is the concept of the fully industrialized society, that which the industrialization process inherently tends to create. Even the most economically advanced countries today are to some degree and in some respects underdeveloped. They contain features derived from earlier stages of development which obscure the pure logic of the industrialization process.

The central purpose of this chapter is to state the imperatives intrinsic in the industrialization process; the logic of the process taken as a whole constitutes industrialism. The present purpose is not to predict the actual course of the future, or to approximate the most probable industrial society of 1984, 2060, or 2460. Neither is the task to extrapolate the course of development of any contemporary society, now highly or slightly industrialized, through the long transition period to the fully industrialized society.

The present objective is rather analytical and deductive. Given the character of science and technology and the requirements inherent in modern methods of production and distribution, what may be deduced as to the necessary or the likely characteristics of workers and managers and their interrelations, in societies that continue to industrialize? What are the inherent tendencies and implications of industrialization for the work place—factory, office, laboratory, site, transport, or mine—and the larger community? Assuming the transition stage of industrialization to have passed, what would be the principal features of the new society?

In the actual course of history the inherent tendencies of the industrial process are not likely, at least for a very long time, to be fully realized. Industrialization ordinarily develops in an existing and established society; even in an "empty country" immigrants bring along many traits of an old society. The existing societies shape and constrain the full implications and inherent features of the industrialization process. The leaders of economic development influence the directions and the rate of industrial growth, and the existing resources and the contemporaneous developments in other countries are also likely to affect actual

SOURCE: *Industrialism and Industrial Man* (Cambridge: Harvard University Press, 1960), pp. 33–39, 40–44.

events in an industrialization. These influences do not vitiate the significance of the underlying tendencies within industrialization generally. Indeed, an understanding of the logic of the industrialization process (industrialism) is requisite to an appreciation of the full measure of the influence of historical, cultural, and economic factors on the actual course of industrialization.

THE INDUSTRIAL WORK FORCE

The industrialization process utilizes a level of technology far in advance of that of earlier societies. Moreover, the associated scientific revolution generates continual and rapid changes in production methods, products, and in technology. The continuing changes in science and the technology and production methods inherent in industrialization have a number of decisive consequences for workers, managers, the state, and their interrelation.

The science and technology of industrialization is based upon research organizations: universities, research institutes, laboratories, and specialized departments of enterprises. The methods and procedures of scientific research are likewise applied to a variety of economic and social problems. It is an axiom of scientific inquiry that the frontiers of knowledge are virtually limitless, and research experience shows that accretions to knowledge yield further unsuspected relations and conclusions in unending vistas. While individual research projects or fields of inquiry may be played out, the totality of research appears to defy any diminishing returns. A dynamic science creates changes in technology which defy prediction and appear to stretch without limit into the future.

The industrial system requires a wide range of skills and professional competency broadly distributed throughout the work force. These specialized human resources are indispensable to the science, technology, and production methods of industrialism. Indeed, the creation of such a highly skilled and professional labor force is one of the major problems of a society in transition to industrialism. The absence of a specialized and highly qualified labor force is no less serious an impediment to industrial growth than a shortage of capital goods. The professional, technical, and managerial component of the labor force, private and public, is particularly strategic since it largely carries the responsibility of developing and ordering the manual and clerical labor force.

Mobility and the Open Society

The science and technology of the industrial society is never static; it generates continual, rapid, widespread changes in production methods and products, which in turn create frequent changes in the skills, responsibilities and occupations of the work force. Some are made redundant and new ones are created. Both insecurities of obsolescence and gains from new and expanding fields reflect the highly dynamic qualities of jobs and occupations. The work force is confronted with repeated object lessons of the general futility of fighting these changes, and in the industrial society the work force comes to be reconciled, by and large, to adaptations required by the repeated changes in ways of earning a living generated by technology and science. But there may be continuing conflict over the timing of change and the division of the gains. The industrial society requires continual training and retraining of the work force; the content of an occupation or job classification is seldom set for life, as in the traditional society. Its occupational mobility is associated with a high degree of geographical movement in a work force and with social mobility in the larger community both upwards and downwards.

The industrial society tends to be an open society, inconsistent with the assignment of managers or workers to occupations or to jobs by traditional caste, racial groups, by sex or by family status. There is no place for the extended family in the industrial society; it is on balance an impediment to requisite mobility. The primary family constitutes a larger and more mobile labor force. The function of the family under industrialism is constricted: it engages in very little production; it provides little, if any, formal education and occupational training; the family business is substantially displaced by professional management. ". . . economic growth and a transference of women's work from the household to the market go closely hand in hand."[1] In the industrial society the primary family is largely a source of labor supply, a unit of decision-making for household expenditures, and a unit of cultural activity.

This society is always in flux and in motion as a result of its science and technology. It is continuously rearranging what people do for a living, where they work and where they live, and on what they spend their incomes. Their children come to expect to live different lives from their parents, so rapid and extensive are the changes. But mobility in the industrial society is not random; it comes to be organized and governed by a complex of rules of the work community.

Education—The Handmaiden of Industrialism

Industrialization requires an educational system functionally related to the skills and professions imperative to its technology. Such an educational system is not primarily concerned with conserving traditional values or perpetuating the classics; it does not adopt a static view of society, and it does not place great emphasis on training in the traditional law. The higher educational system of the industrial society stresses the natural sciences, engineering, medicine, managerial training, whether private or public, and administrative law. It must steadily adapt to new disciplines and fields of specialization. There is a relatively smaller place for the humanities and arts, and the social sciences are strongly related to the training of managerial groups and technicians for the enterprise and the government. The increased leisure time of industrialism, however, can afford a broader public appreciation of the humanities and the arts.

In the industrial order, as in all societies, there is debate over the curriculum in higher education and over what the youth is to be taught, at least on the narrow grounds of selecting the programs that provide most effectively for the range of careers. The largest part of the higher educational system tends to be specialized and designed to produce the very large volume of the professionals, technicians, and managers required in the industrial society. There is a case for some degree of generality in the educational system because of the rapidity of change and growth of knowledge during the course of a career. A technically trained work force needs to be able to follow and adapt to changes in its specialities and to learn to shift to new fields. Generality is also requisite for those coordinating and leading the specialists.

The industrial society tends to create an increasing level of general education for all citizens, not only because it facilitates training and flexibility in the work force, but also because as incomes rise natural curiosity increases the demand for formal education, and education becomes one of the principal means of vertical social mobility in a technical world. "This demand for a certain minimum of culture is created by the conditions of the capitalist mode of production itself, with its high technique, complexity, flexibility, mobility, rapidity of development of world competition, and so forth."[2] It will be observed that the industrial society tends to transform drastically the educational system of the pre-industrial society. Further, the high level of technical and general education requisite to the industrial society cannot but have significant consequences for political life. The means of mass communication play a significant role both in raising standards of general education and in conditioning political activity and shaping political control.

Research organizations develop scientific, professional, technical, and managerial specialists indispensable to the operation and administration of the industrial society. The industrial society requires increasing numbers of this high-level manpower, and the areas of specialization continue to multiply. The relations of workers, managers, and governments even develop into a field of significant specialization, and a discipline of industrial relations emerges. Technicians in industrial relations are formally trained for a place in all organizations participating in the labor market.

The Structure of the Labor Force

The labor force of the industrial society is highly differentiated by occupations and job classifications, by rates of compensation, and by a variety of relative rights and duties in the work place community. The labor force is not a homogeneous mass of workers and managers freely substituable for each other. It is impossible to consider the individual worker or manager in isolation from his place in the complex of responsibilities, relative compensation, and differentiated rights in the work community.[3] The labor force in industrialism has form and structure vastly different from the traditional society.

The variety of skills, responsibilities, and working conditions at the work place of enterprises requires an ordering or a hierarchy. There are successive levels of authority of managers and the managed, as well as considerable specialization of function at each level of the hierarchy of the work place. There is a related differentiation according to compensation; enterprises establish a wage and salary schedule which differentiates groups of workers and managers. Job evaluation and salary plans symbolize the ordering of the industrial work force by function and compensation.

The work force in the industrial society is also structured in the sense that movement within the work community is subjected to a set of rules; hiring, temporary layoffs, permanent redundance, promotions, shift changes, transfers, and retirement are applied to individual workers and managers according to their position, station, seniority, technical competency, or some other measure of status in a group rather than in random fashion. Not all jobs are open at all times to all bidders except in the structureless market. The ports of entry from outside into an enterprise are limited, and priorities in selection are established. Movement tends to be relatively easier within certain groupings of jobs than among these job families in an enterprise. Job families may be defined differently according as movement is promotion, layoff, or transfer. The relative rights of workers and their protection in particular jobs constitute a complex structuring of job relationships at their work places. . . .

Large Role for Government

The industrial society is necessarily characterized by a substantial range and scale of activities by the government. In a society of advanced technology there are, by virtue of this technology, a larger number of activities for government; for instance, the need for roads and highways, the provision for airports, the regulation of traffic, radio and television, a result of modern means of communication. Urban development has the same consequences. Technology also creates a more complex problem for a military establishment, extending in many directions the activities of government. The more integrated character of the world increases the activities significant to international relations and hence typically the scope of governmental activities. The scale of some scientific applications and the capital needs of new technologies tend to increase the scope of public agencies. As income rises, the demand of consumers may be for services largely provided by governments, such as education, parks, roads and health services.

The industrial society and individual freedom, however, are not necessarily to be regarded as antagonists. A high degree of discipline in the work place imposed by a web of rules and a large range of governmental activities is fully consistent with a larger freedom for the individual in greater leisure, a greater range of choice in occupations and place of residence, a greater range of alternatives in goods and services on which to use income, and a very wide range of subgroups or associations in which to choose participation. It is a mistake to regard the industrial society as antithetical to individual freedom by citing ways in which the scope of public and private governments has increased without also noting ways in which the industrial society expands individual freedom.

The role of government in countries entering upon industrialization, regardless of political form, may therefore be expected to be greater than before. There is wisdom in the observation: ". . . it is extremely unlikely that the highly modernized systems of the world today could have developed indigenously on the basis of any system other than ones that relied very heavily indeed on private individual operations, and it is extremely unlikely that latecomers can carry out such development without relying very heavily on public operations."[4]

The Web of Rules

The production of goods and services in the industrial society is largely in the hands of large-scale organizations. They consist of hierarchies of those with authority to direct, including staff advisers, and those with the function of following such directions. There are relatively few managers, and there are a great many to be managed. The managers and the managed are connected by an elaborate web of rules that is made the more intricate and complex by technology, specialization, and the large-scale operations.

A network of relationships between managers and the managed and a complex of substantive rules is required to make the industrial system operative at the work place, quite apart from the issues concerned with who formulates or promulgates these rules. At any one time, the rights and duties of workers and of managers, indeed of all those in the hierarchy, must be established and understood by all those involved in the hierarchy. Answers must be provided to the many questions that arise in the course of operating a complex organization with managers and workers, and procedures are required to provide promptly such answers. The web of rules of the work place concerns compensation, discipline, layoffs, transfers and promotions, grievances, and a vast array of matters, some common to all work places and others specialized for the type of activity—factory, airline, railroad, mine, or office—and to the specific establishment. The rules also establish norms of output, pace, and performance. Moreover, the web of rules is never static, and procedures arise for the orderly change of these rules. The industrial system creates an elaborate "government" at the work place and work community. It is often said that primitive societies have extensive rules, customs, and taboos, but a study of the industrial society reflects an even greater complex and a different set of detailed rules.

The web of rules established at a work place may be viewed partially as the consequence of the technological features and market or budgetary constraints of the work place, which are in a large measure common to all types of industrializing countries, and also partially the consequence of the particular resources, political and economic forms of the country, and its path to industrialism. The relative strength of these factors, and their mode of interaction, is significant to an understanding of any particular industrial society. The industrial system tends to develop a common set of rules under common technological and economic conditions. Cultural and national differences are less significant to the web of rules, the further a country is along the road toward industrialism.

Governments tend to have a significant role in determining the substantive rules of the work community or in establishing the procedures and responsibilities of those with this power. In the fully industrialized society, regardless of the relative balance and roles of enterprise managers, workers, and the government in the transition, all three tend to have a significant part in the establishment, adaptation, and administration of the rules of the work place and work community. The industrial relations system of the industrial society is genuinely tripartite.

CONSENSUS IN SOCIETY

The industrial society, as any established society, develops a distinctive consensus which relates individuals and groups to each other and provides a common body of ideas, beliefs, and value judgments integrated into a whole. There must be a consensus to permit the industrial society to function. Various forms of the industrial society may create some distinctive features of an ideology, but all industrialized societies have common values. In the pure industrial society science and technical knowledge have high values, and those engaged in advancing science and in applying it to industrial processes have high prestige and receive high rewards in the society. The pure industrial society eliminates taboos against technical change, and it places high values on being "modern," "up-to-date," and in "progress" for their own sake.

Education also has a high value in the industrial society because of the fundamental importance of science and the utility of education as a means of social mobility. The industrial society is an open community encouraging occupational and geographic mobility and social mobility. In this sense industrialism must be flexible and competitive; it is against tradition and status based upon family, class, religion, race, or caste. The industrial society is pluralistic, with a great variety of associations and groups and of large-scale operations; the individual is attached to a variety of such groups and organizations.

The pure industrial society places a high value on output of goods and services, and the "demonstration effect" is very strong on the part of individuals and groups seeking to imitate the standards of those with higher income levels.

In the industrial society the work force at the work place is dedicated to hard work, to maintain a high pace of work and a keen sense of individual responsibility for performance of assigned norms and tasks. The ethic of hard work and a rapid work pace at the work place is required by the logic of industrialization. Industrial countries may differ with respect to the ideals and drives which underlie the devotion to duty and responsibility for performance, but industrialism requires an ideology and ethic which motivate and command individual members of the work force at the work place. Strict supervision and exacting management imposed on a lethargic work force will not suffice; the personal responsibility for performance and the achievement of norms of quantity and quality of output must be implanted within workers, front-line supervisors, and top managers to be truly effective.[5]

It is not by accident that the leaders of industrializing countries today exhort their peoples to hard work. "This generation is sentenced to hard labor" (Nehru). "We shall march forward as one people who have vowed to work and to proceed on a holy march of industrializing . . ." (Nasser). "The chief preoccupation of every Communist regime between the Elbe and the China Sea is how to make people work; how to induce them to sow, harvest, mine, build, manufacture and so forth. It is the most vital problem which confronts them day in, day out, and it shapes their domestic policies and to a considerable extent their attitude toward the outside world."[6] There are many substitutes and counterparts for the Protestant ethic.

The Western tradition has been to harness the drive of individualism; the Communist method combines in varying proportions at varying times money incentives, devotion to a revolutionary creed, and the compulsion of terror. Regardless of the means that are used in the industrializing process, the industrial society achieves at the work place a pace of work and a personal responsibility exercised by individual workers and managers seldom known in economic activity in traditional societies.

The function of making explicit a consensus and of combining discrete beliefs and convictions into a reasonably consistent body of ideas is the task of intellectuals in every society. Industrial society does not uniquely create intellectuals; they exist in all societies in some degree. There are probably more intellectuals, at least potentially, in the industrial society on account of the higher levels of general education, higher income levels, and greater leisure. There are also new patrons to the intellectuals as compared to pre-industrial society. A diversity of markets for intellectuals—the university, enterprise, labor organization, voluntary association, government, and self-employment—tends to displace the old aristocratic patrons. The function of formulating and restating the major values, premises, and consensus of a society from time to time, of sweeping away the old and adopting the new or reconciling the industrial processes with the old order, plays a significant role in industrialization. The intellectuals accordingly are an influential group in the process of the creation and molding of the new industrial society....

N O T E S

1. W. Arthur Lewis, *The Theory of Economic Growth* (London: George Allen and Unwin Ltd., 1955), p. 116.
2. V. I. Lenin, "Differences in the European Labour Movement" (December 1910), *Selected Works,* XI (London: Lawrence and Wishart Ltd., 1939), p. 741.
3. "The general conditions of an unstructured market, then, are five-fold: (1) there must be no unions with their usual accompaniment of seniority, preference of employment, and other limitations upon access to the labor market; (2) there must be an impersonal relationship between employer and employee, lest informal obligations and various types of moral tenure develop; (3) the productive employment must be largely unskilled so that it becomes accessible to a large and unspecialized labor force. . . ; (4) the method of compensation must be by unit of product rather than by unit of time; (5) the operation must employ little or no capital or machinery." Lloyd H. Fisher, *The Harvest Labor Market in California* (Cambridge, Massachusetts: Harvard University Press, 1953), p. 9.
4. Marion J. Levy, Jr., "Some Social Obstacles to 'Capital Formation' in 'Underdeveloped Areas,' " in *Capital Formation and Economic Growth,* A Conference of the Universities—National Bureau Committee for Economic Research (New Jersey: Princeton University Press, 1955), p. 461.
5. Daniel Bell, *Work and Its Discontents* (Boston: Beacon Press, 1956). "Although religion declined, the significance of work was that it could still mobilize emotional energies into creative challenges" (p. 56).
6. Eric Hoffer, "Readiness to Work" (unpublished manuscript).

SOCIAL STRATIFICATION IN INDUSTRIAL SOCIETY

John H. Goldthorpe

For a decade or so now, a growing interest has been apparent, chiefly among American sociologists, in the pattern of long-term social change within relatively mature industrial societies. This interest appears to derive from two main sources.

In the first place, it can be seen as resulting from broadly based studies of the sociology of industrialisation, concentrating originally on the underdeveloped or developing countries of the world. For example, work conducted as part of the Inter University Study of Labour Problems in Economic Development led up to the theoretical statement on the "logic" of industrialism attempted by Clark Kerr and his associates in their book, *Industrialism and Industrial Man*.[1] Secondly, this interest has undoubtedly been stimulated by the revival in comparative studies of social structure and social processes in economically advanced countries. Important here, for example, has been the work of Professor Lipset and a number of other members of the Berkeley campus of the University of California; and even more so, perhaps, studies which have chiefly involved comparisons between Western and Communist societies, such as those produced in connection with the Harvard Project on the Soviet Social System by Professor Inkeles and his colleagues.[2]

However, it is notable that in spite of possibly different origins, current American interpretations of the development of industrial societies often reveal marked similarities. Basically, it may be said, they tend to be alike in stressing the standardising effects upon social structures of the exigencies of modern technology and of an advanced economy. These factors which make for uniformity in industrial societies are seen as largely overriding other factors which may make for possible diversity, such as different national cultures or different political systems. Thus, the overall pattern of development which is suggested is one in which, once countries enter into the advanced stages of industrialisation, they tend to become increasingly comparable in their major institutional arrangements and in their social systems generally. In brief, a *convergent* pattern of development is hypothesised.

Kerr and his associates have been the most explicit in this connection—and also in the matter of specifying the type of society on which the process of convergence is focussed. In their conception, "the road ahead" for all advanced societies leads in the direction of what they call "pluralistic" industrialism. By this they mean a form of industrial society in which the distribution of power is neither "atomistic" nor "monistic," nor yet radically disputed by warring classes; but rather a social order in which an "omnipresent State" regulates competition

SOURCE: *Sociological Review Monograph*, No. 8 (1964), pp. 97–110.

and conflict between a multiplicity of interest groups on the basis of an accepted "web of rules," and at the same time provides the means through which a degree of democratic control can be exercised over the working of the economy and over other key social processes such as the provision of welfare and public services, education and so on.[3] Other theorists have usually been a good deal more guarded than this in their formulations; but it would nonetheless be fair to say that, in the main, they have adopted views which have been broadly consistent with the Kerr thesis. In general, the "logic" of industrialism has been regarded as powerfully encouraging, even if not compelling, the emergence of a new type of society from out of former "class" and "mass" societies alike.[4]

Clearly, then, a central theme in the interpretations in question concerns the development in advanced societies of systems of social stratification. And it is perhaps indicative of the importance of this theme that it has on several occasions been singled out for special discussion. In this paper[5] my main purpose will be to consider this particular aspect of current theories of industrialism and, further, to raise certain doubts and objections which seem to me to be of a serious kind and to have negative implications for these theories *in toto*. But at the outset I should say that I in no way intend to criticise the *kind* of sociological endeavour which is here represented. On the contrary, we are, I believe, much indebted to the authors of these theories for showing us a way to escape from the cramped quarters of trivialised empiricism without falling victim to highly speculative building with "empty boxes."

The arguments concerning the development of social stratification which form a core element in American interpretations of industrialism can be usefully stated under three main heads: differentiation, consistency and mobility.[6] To begin with, I would like to consider these three sets of arguments in turn.

DIFFERENTIATION

In regard to differentiation, the major proposition that is put forward is that, in course of industrial advance, there is a decrease in the degree of differentiation in all stratification subsystems or orders. In other words, to follow Inkeles' formulation: "a process of relative homogenisation takes place, reducing the gap or range separating the top and bottom of the scale"—in income and wealth, in status formal and informal, and in political power.[7] As a result of this process, a marked increase occurs within each stratification order in the proportion of the total population falling into the middle ranges of the distribution. The "shape" of the stratification hierarchy thus ceases to be pyramidal and approximates, rather, to that of a pentagon or even of a diamond.

This trend is related to the "logic" of industrialism in several different ways. But, primarily, the connection is seen as being through the changing division of labour. An advancing technology and economy continually repattern the occupational structure, and in ways which progressively increase the number of higher level occupational rôles; that is to say, rôles requiring relatively high standards of education and training and at the same time commanding relatively high economic rewards and social status. Thus, the middle of the stratification hierarchy becomes considerably expanded.

So far as Western societies are concerned, a further factor in this homogenising process is also recognised in the growing intervention of the state in economic affairs; particularly in governmental policies which lead to the redistribution and control of economic power. For example, it is observed that policies of progressive taxation and of social welfare in various ways modify for the benefit of the less privileged the division of income and balance of social advantage which would have resulted from the free operation of market mechanisms. However, in this case great stress is placed on the close relationship that exists between this expansion in the regulatory functions of government and the direct requirements of the industrialisation process. The state, it is argued *must* be the key regulatory organisation in any advanced society: the complexity of its technology and economy demand this. At minimum, the state must be responsible for the general rate of economic progress, and thus ultimately, for the overall allocation of resources between uses and individuals, for the quality of the national labour force, for the economic and social security of individuals and so on.[8]

In other words, even where greater social equality results directly from the purposive action of governments, the tendency is to see behind this action not a particular complex of socio-political beliefs, values or interests but rather the inherent compulsions of "industrialism" itself.[9] For example, on the subject of the development of education and its consequences, Kerr and his associates write as follows:

> Education is intended to reduce the scarcity of skilled persons and this after a time reduces the wage and salary differentials they receive; it also pulls people out of the least skilled and most disagreeable occupations and raises wage levels there. *It conduces to a new equality which has nothing to do with ideology.* . . .[10]

Furthermore, one should note, a similar viewpoint is taken in arguing that greater equality in political power—in the form of a pluralistic system—will tend to emerge in societies which now have totalitarian (or autocratic) regimes. In the first place, it is held, the production technology of an industrial society is such that any regime must become increasingly interested in the consent of the mass of the labour force; for the efficient use of this technology requires responsible initiative and freely given co-operation on the part of those who operate it. Secondly, the growing complexity of technical problems arising in the process of government itself necessitates the greater involvement in decision-making of experts and professionals, and in this way the latter come to acquire some independent authority. Thus, a monolithic structure gives way to one in which there are a number of "strategic" elites and of different foci of power. In brief, industrialism is regarded as being ultimately inimical to any form of monistic political order.[11]

CONSISTENCY

In this respect, the central argument is that as societies become increasingly industrial, there is a growing tendency within the stratification system towards what Inkeles terms "equilibration"; that is, a tendency for the relative position of an individual or group in any one stratification order to be the same as, or similar to, their position in other orders.[12] In traditional societies, it is observed, inconsistencies in the stratification system may have been contrary to the prevailing ideology but were nonetheless frequent because of the rigidity of the levels within the different subsystems and the relatively low degree of interaction between them. For example, a merchant might become extremely wealthy yet be debarred from "noble" status; in fact, legally, he could be of peasant status and might be treated as such in certain circumstances in spite of his wealth. In industrial societies, by contrast, there are far fewer difficulties in the way of "adjustments" which serve to bring the position of individuals and groups more or less into line from one stratification order to another. Moreover, there is also a shift away from the relative diversity of the bases of stratification which is characteristic of traditional society. With industrialism, the occupational structure takes on overwhelming primacy in this respect. The occupational rôle of the individual is in general in close correlation with most other of his attributes which are relevant to his position in the stratification hierarchy as a whole: his economic situation, his educational level, his prestige in the local community and so on.[13]

In the same way as the trend towards greater equality, the trend towards greater consistency in stratification systems is also treated as an integral part of the industrialisation process and as being directly linked to technological and economic advance. In industrial society, it is argued, the distribution of both economic rewards and prestige must come into a close relationship with occupational performance since this type of society in fact presupposes an overriding emphasis upon achievement, as opposed to ascription, as the basis of social position—and specifically upon achievement in the sphere of production. At the same time, though, as a result of technological progress, occupational achievement becomes increasingly dependent upon education, and in this way closer ties are formed between economic standing on the one hand and life-styles and subculture on the other. The ignorant and vulgar tycoon and the poor scholar are seen alike as figures of declining importance. In other words, the argument is that inevitably in modern societies, the various determinants of an individual's placing in the overall stratification hierarchy come to form a tight nexus; and that in this nexus occupation can be regarded as the central element—providing as it does the main link between the "objective" and "subjective" aspects of social inequality.

Implicit, then, in this interpretation is the view that in industrial societies stratification systems tend to become relatively highly integrated, in the sense that specifically class differences (i.e. those stemming from inequalities in the economic order) are generally paralleled by status differences (i.e. those based on inequalities in social evaluation); and, thus, that changes in the pattern of the former will automatically result in changes in the pattern of the latter. For example, Kerr and his associates see the growth of "middle incomes" as making for a "middle class society"; that is, a society in which middle class values are widely accepted, both among manual workers and elite groups, and in which the bulk of the population share in "middle class" status.[14]

MOBILITY

In regard to mobility, the central proposition that is made is one which complements the previous arguments concerning differentiation and consistency. It is that once societies have reached a certain level of industrialisation, their overall rates of social mobility tend to become relatively high—higher, that is, than is typical in preindustrial or traditional societies. The increasing number of intermediate positions in the stratification hierarchy widens the opportunity for movement upward from the lower levels, while the emphasis upon occupational achievement rather than on the ascription of social positions means that intergenerationally the talented will tend to rise at the expense of those whose talent is unequal to their birth. In this respect, the educational system is seen as the crucial allocative mechanism, sieving ability and matching capacity to the demands and responsibilities of occupational rôles.[15]

In other words, then, industrial society is regarded as being essentially "open" and "meritocratic." And once more, one should note, the interpretation derives from a conception of the structural and functional imperatives of this type of social order. The high level of mobility is taken as an inevitable consequence of the technologically and economically determined division of labour and of the necessary pressure within a highly dynamic form of society for the increasingly efficient use of talent. To quote again from the authors of *Industrialism and Industrial Man:*

> The industrial society is an open community encouraging occupational and geographic mobility and social mobility. In this sense industrialism *must* be flexible and competitive; it is against tradition and status based upon family, class, religion, race or caste.[16]

In this approach, thus, there is little room for consideration of institutional variations or of value differences between industrial societies which might be associated with *differing* patterns of mobility. It is taken that the overall similarities in this respect are, or at any rate are certainly becoming, the feature of major significance.

These, then, in a necessarily abbreviated form, are the main arguments concerning the development of stratification systems which figure, with varying degrees of refinement or crudity, in current American theories of industrialism. I would now like to turn to what I have to say by way of criticism of these arguments and, to begin with, I would like to comment on each of the three themes on which I based the foregoing exposition. My main purpose here will be to indicate that the views which I have outlined are not always in entire accord with empirical data, and in this connection I shall refer primarily to the industrial societies of the West. Subsequently, however, I shall offer certain more basic, theoretical criticisms which are suggested by a consideration of social stratification in modern Communist society. [not included in this volume]

On the question of reduced differentiation—or greater equality—in stratification systems, my remarks at this stage will be largely confined to the economic order. This is because it is chiefly in this regard that we have data which will permit, at least in principle, some test of the arguments involved; that is, data on the distributions of income and wealth.[17]

At the outset it may be said that, although the evidence is often very patchy, a broad trend towards greater economic equality *does* seem to be discernible in the case of all those societies which have so far progressed from a traditional to an industrial form. Myths of "golden ages" of economic equality in pre-industrial times are now little heeded, and, as a rough generalisation, it would, I think, be widely accepted that the poorer the society, the greater the "skew" one may expect in its distributions of income and wealth alike.[18] With this view I would not wish to quarrel—provided that it is taken merely as a formula summing up historical experience, and as one which is subject to exceptions. But there are no grounds at all, in my view, for regarding the regularity in question as manifesting the operation of some process inherent in industrialism—of some general economic law—which will necessarily persist in the future and ensure a continuing egalitarian trend. Rather, the possibility must be left quite open that where such a trend exists, it may at some point be checked—and at a point, moreover, at which considerable economic *in*equality remains. In fact, in my assessment, the relevant data suggest that such a check may already be occurring in some of the more advanced societies of the West; or, at any rate, I would say that on present evidence *this* conclusion is indicated as much as any other.

For the distributions of income and wealth alike, it is true that figures exist to show a movement towards greater equality in most western industrial societies over the years for which adequate time-series are available; that is, from the late inter-war or early post-war period onwards.[19] However, it is now becoming increasingly clear that these figures, which are largely based on tax returns, are not always to be taken at their face value. And, in general, their defects appear to be such that they tend on balance to underestimate the income and wealth which accrue to the economically more favoured groups and in this and other ways to give a somewhat exaggerated idea of the degree of "levelling" that has taken place. In fact, for some western societies at least, there are now grounds for believing that during the last twenty years or so, overall economic inequality has in reality declined only very little, if at all. And particularly so far as wealth is concerned, it is likely that such changes as have occurred have been virtually negligible in their implications for social stratification.[20] Such conclusions have been suggested for the United Kingdom, for example, in Professor Titmuss' recent study, *Income Distribution and Social Change*. It must, of course, be admitted that the whole matter remains a highly controversial one,[21] and it is not possible here to enter into all its complexities. But what is, I think, justified by the evidence, and what is certainly most relevant to my general argument, is Titmuss' contention that "we should be much more hesitant in suggesting that any equalising forces at work in Britain since 1938 can be promoted to the status of a 'natural law' and projected into the future . . . There are other forces, deeply rooted in the social structure and fed by many complex institutional factors inherent in large-scale economies, operating in reverse directions."[22]

A similar point of view is maintained, with reference to the United States, in Gabriel Kolko's somewhat neglected book, *Wealth and Power in America*. This study involves not only a critique of previous findings on the distribution of income and wealth in the USA but also a positive reappraisal of the situation. This is particularly important in regard to income. Kolko supplements material from official sources with generally more reliable survey data, and on this basis suggests that over as long a period as 1910 to 1959 there has been no significant *general* trend in the USA towards greater income equality.[23]

Kolko's study prompts one to note the often overlooked point that simply because there may be some levelling of incomes going on in *certain ranges* of the total income distribution, this does not necessarily mean that *overall* equality is increasing; for in other ranges inegalitarian trends may simultaneously be operating. For example, there may be a tendency towards greater equality in that the number of middle-range incomes is growing; but at the same time the position of the lower income groups, relative to the upper and middle groups alike, may be worsening.

In fact, it seems more than possible that a pattern of change of this kind is now going on in the United States. This is indicated by a good deal of recent investigation, apart from that of Kolko, and particularly by the growing volume of work on the extent of poverty. Gunnar Myrdal, for example, has argued in his book, *Challenge to Affluence,* that while many Americans in the intermediate social strata may well be benefiting from a levelling upwards of living standards, at the base of the stratification hierarchy there is increasing inequality, manifested in the emergence of an "underclass" of unemployed and unemployable persons and families. In other words, the middle ranks of the income distribution may be swelling, but the gap between the bottom and the higher levels is, if anything, tending to widen.[24]

Moreover, what is also significant in Myrdal's study for present purposes is the way in which he brings out the *political* aspects of the problem. Myrdal observes that structural unemployment, resulting from technological innovation in industry, is a basic, and increasingly serious, cause of poverty in America, whereas, in a country like Sweden, in which technological advance is also proceeding rapidly, full employment has been steadily maintained. Again, he notes the relative failure of the United States, compared with most western European countries, to stabilise aggregate demand in its economy on a high and rising level.[25] The explanation of these differences, Myrdal then argues, while not of course entirely political, must nonetheless be regarded as being significantly so. In particular, he stresses the inadequate achievement of government in America in long-range economic planning, in redistributional reforms, and in the provision of public services and advanced social welfare schemes. And the sources of this governmental inadequacy he traces back to certain basic American socio-political dispositions and also to a relative lack of "democratic balance" in the institutional infrastructure of the American policy. On the one hand, Myrdal claims, there is among the powerful business community and within government itself a reluctance to take the long view and to envisage more central direction and control of the economy; also "a serious and irrational bias against public investment and consumption." On the other hand, among the lower strata of American society there is an unusual degree of political apathy and passivity which is most clearly seen in the general failure of the poorer sections of the population to organise themselves effectively and to press for the fundamental social reforms that would be in their interest. In this way an imbalance in organised power is brought about within the "plural society" which makes the need for initiative on the part of government all the more pressing—at the same time as it seems to paralyse this.[26]

If, then, Mydral's analysis has any general validity—and it has yet, I think, to be seriously disputed—it follows that we should look somewhat doubtfully on arguments about a new equality which "has nothing to do with ideology" but which is the direct outcome of technological and economic advance. Such new equality there may be for some. But for those at the base of stratification hierarchies at least—how "equal" they are likely to become seems to have a good deal to do with ideology, or at any rate with purposive social action, or lack of this, stemming from specific social values and political creeds as well as from interests.[27] And differences between some industrial societies in these respects may well be giving rise to divergent, rather than convergent, patterns of change in their stratification systems.

On the second set of arguments—those concerning growing consistency between different stratification orders—I shall have relatively little to say for the good reason that there is little empirical data which directly bears on the crucial issue here; that is, the issue of whether there really is a *continuing* increase in the degree of integration of the stratification systems of *advanced* societies. About the long-term historical trend, one would not wish to argue; but again it is a question of whether such a trend is a reliable guide to the present and the future.

My main comment is that such evidence as does appear relevant to this issue indicates that in some industrial societies, at least, ongoing economic progress is resulting in stratification systems becoming, if anything, somewhat *less* well integrated in certain respects. This evidence refers to what has become known as the "new working class." It suggests that the appreciable gains in income and in general living standards recently achieved by certain sections of the manual labour force have not for the most part been accompanied by changes in their life-styles of such a kind that their *status* position has been enhanced commensurately with their *economic* position. In other words, there is evidence of cultural and, in particular, of "social" barriers still widely existing between "working class" and "middle class" even in cases where immediate material differences have now disappeared.[28] Thus it seems that, contrary to the expectations of Kerr and his associates, "middle incomes" have not resulted, as yet at least, in the generalisation of "middle class" ways of life or of "middle class" status.

Moreover, there are grounds for believing that notable discrepancies in stratification will persist in industrial societies. As Kerr himself recognises, there will still exist in the forseeable future in such societies a division between "managers" and "managed"—between those who are in some way associated with the exercise of authority in productive and administrative organisations and those who are not. And this division, one would suggest, will remain associated with differences in prestige, as well as in power, while at the same time managers and managed overlap to some extent in terms of living standards. One would agree that in an economically advanced society a broad stratum of workers, performing skilled or, one would add particularly arduous or irksome jobs, are likely to earn middle-range incomes. But there are no grounds for automatically assuming that they will thereby become socially accepted and assimilated into even the lower levels of what Renner has usefully termed the "service class."[29] After all, it must be recognized that groups which have some serious basis for claiming superior status generally take advantage of this. And further, it should be borne in mind that, increasingly, the members of this "service class" will be selected through their educational attainments rather than being recruited from the rank and file. Thus, if anything, they are likely to become more set apart from the latter in terms of culture and life-styles than they are at present.

In sum, one might suggest that the "increasing consistency" argument is flawed because it fails to take into account first, that occupational rôles with similar economic rewards may in some instances be quite differently related to the exercise of authority; and secondly, that relatively high income may serve as recompense for work of otherwise high "disutility" to the operative as well as for work involving expertise and responsibility.

Lastly, then, we come to the matter of social mobility. In this case, the first question which arises is that of whether it is in fact valid to regard industrial societies as having regularly higher rates of mobility than pre-industrial societies. Several writers, one should note, have recently argued that this view should not be too readily taken and have produced evidence to suggest that certain pre-industrial societies were far less rigidly stratified than seems generally to have been supposed.[30] Nevertheless, I would not wish to argue here against the more orthodox view, except to make the point that an increased rate of *inter*generational mobility in advanced societies is likely to be associated with some limitation of *intra*generational or "career" mobility. To the extent that education becomes a key determinant of occupational achievement, the chances of "getting ahead" for those who start in a lowly position are inevitably diminished. This fact is most clearly demonstrated in recent studies of the recruitment of industrial managers. These show that as the educational standards of managers have risen, the likelihood of shop floor workers being promoted above supervisory level has been reduced.[31] Furthermore, in an advanced society, increasingly dominated by large scale organisations, the possibilities for the "little man" of starting up a successful business of his own also tend to be more limited than they were at an earlier phase in the industrialisation process. Thus, for that large proportion of the population at least, with rank-and-file jobs and "ordinary" educational qualifications, industrial society appears to be growing significantly *less* "open" than it once was.

However, other, and perhaps more basic, issues arise from the arguments concerning mobility which I earlier outlined; in particular issues relating to the determinants of mobility patterns and rates. What are the grounds, one might ask, for believing that in advanced societies the crucial factor here is the occupational distribution, and thus that from one such society to another social mobility will tend to be much the same? Support for this view can be found in the well-known Lipset and Zetterberg study which led in fact, to the conclusion that western industrial societies have broadly similar rates of intergenerational mobility, and which produced no evidence to suggest that factors other than the "standardising" one of the occupational structure were of major significance.[32] Their data, the authors claim, give no backing for the idea that differences in social ideologies, religious beliefs or other aspects of national cultures exercise a decisive influence on mobility. But it has to be noted that, as Lipset and Zetterberg themselves make quite clear, their findings in this respect refer only to "mass" mobility; that is, simply to movements across the manual-nonmanual line. And indeed they point out that the investigation of some aspects of "élite" mobility—for example, the recruitment of higher civil servants—has indicated some important national variations.[33]

Moreover, we have more recently the outstanding study of comparative social mobility made by Professor S. M. Miller.[34] This covers a still greater amount of data than Lipset and Zetterberg's work and demonstrates fairly conclusively that when *range* as well as frequency of mobility is taken into consideration, industrial societies do reveal quite sizeable differences in their mobility patterns. Such differences tend to be most evident in the case of long-range mobility. This is generally low—another reason for querying just how "open" and "meritocratic" industrial societies have so far become—but certain countries, the USA and USSR, for example, appear to have attained quite significantly higher rates of "élite" mobility than do others, such as many in western Europe. Further, though,

Miller shows that countries with low long-range mobility may still have relatively high short-range mobility—as, for instance, does Great Britain: there is no correlation between rates of mobility of differing distance. Thus, industrial societies have quite various "mobility profiles"; the overall similarity indicated by the study of "mass" mobility turns out to be somewhat spurious.

On this basis, then, Miller is able to argue very strongly that patterns of social mobility in advanced societies cannot be understood *simply* in terms of occupational structure[35]—or, one would add, in terms of any "inherent" features of industrialism. Their diversity precludes this. It appears necessary, rather, to consider also the effects on mobility of other, and more variable, aspects of social structure—educational institutions, for example, and their articulation with the stratification hierarchy itself—and further, possibly, *pace* Lipset and Zetterberg, the part played by cultural values.[36] As Miller points out, what is perhaps most surprising about his data is the *lack* of convergence in mobility patterns that is indicated between societies at broadly comparable levels of economic development. The "logic" of industrialism, it appears, is often confused by "extraneous" factors. . . .

NOTES

1. Clerk Kerr, J. T. Dunlop, F. H. Harbison and C. A. Myers, *Industrialism and Industrial Man*, 1960.
2. See, e.g., Raymond A. Bauer, Alex Inkeles and Clyde Kluckhohn, *How the Soviet System Works*, 1956; Inkeles and Bauer, *The Soviet Citizen*, 1959.
3. Op. cit., Chaps. 1, 2 and 10 especially.
4. The issue on which, of course, there has been greatest doubt and discussion is that of whether totalitarian régimes will *inevitably* become less 'monistic' with continuing industrial advance. As emerges later in this paper (not included in this selection), Inkeles appears somewhat uncertain on this point. Another leading American theorist of industrialism, W. E. Moore, has expressly rejected the idea that industrialisation necessarily engenders increased political participation and more representative government. See his section, 'Industrialisation and Social Change,' in B. F. Hoselitz and W. E. Moore (eds.), *Industrialisation and Society*, 1963, pp. 357–359 especially. Nevertheless, the greater part of this section is written in terms of the social exigencies of an industrial technology and economy.
5. I am indebted to my friend M. Alfred Willener for his criticisms of an earlier draft of this paper and also to colleagues in the Faculty of Economics and Politics of the University of Cambridge who have discussed many specific points with me.
6. The following exposition is derived chiefly from Kerr et al., op. cit.; Inkeles, 'Social Stratification in the Modernisation of Russia' in Cyril E. Black (ed.), *The Transformation of Russian Society*, 1960; and Moore, pp. 318–322, 353–359 especially. It is, however, important to note the very marked differences in tone and style between these contributions. Kerr and his colleagues are most dogmatic and 'prophetic', but also the most diffuse in their arguments; Inkeles, on the other hand, is the most explicit yet is clearly writing, as he says, 'not to settle a point but to open a discussion'; while Moore, aiming at the summing-up of a body of research data, puts forward by far the most cautious and qualified statements.
7. Loc. cit., p 341. Cf. Kerr et al., *Industrialism*, pp. 286–294. Moore, (p. 354) claims that during early industrialisation 'differences in social origin, education and power of

managers and workers are likely to be widest' and the following paragraph appears to support the 'relative homogenisation' thesis. It is not clear, however, how far Moore is prepared to regard the trend towards reduced differentiation as one which has so far continued progressively with industrial advance.

8. Cf. Kerr et al., *Industrialism,* pp. 31, 40–41, 273–274, 290–292; Moore, pp. 357–359.

9. For a discussion of the strengths and weaknesses of attempts to apply this approach to the explanation of the development of social policy in 19th century England, see John H. Goldthorpe, 'Le développment de la politique sociale en Angleterre de 1800 à 1914', *Sociologie du Travail,* No. 2 (1963). (English version forthcoming in *Transactions of the Vth World Congress of Sociology,* vol. 4, 1964.)

10. *Op. cit.,* p. 286 (my italics). The theme of 'the end of ideology'—in the West at least— runs strongly throughout *Industrialism and Industrial Man.* Moore, by contrast, is sufficiently detached and sophisticated to recognise 'the ideology of a pluralistic society.'

11. Cf. Kerr et al., pp. 274–276, 288–290; Inkeles, *Social Stratification,* p. 346. As earlier noted, Moore diverges here. He notes (p. 359) the empirical probability of increased political participation as societies become industrial, but argues that so far there is no evidence of a *necessary* incompatibility between industrialism and totalitarianism.

12. Inkeles' 'equilibration' (following E. Benoit-Smullyan, 'Status Types and Status Interrelations', *Am. Soc. Rev.,* vol. 9, 1944) thus largely corresponds to what Lenski and Landecker have referred to as 'crystallisation' and Adams and Homans as 'congruence." See Gerhard E. Lenski, 'Status Crystallisation: a Non-Vertical Dimension of Social Status', *Am. Soc. Rev.,* vol. 19, 1954; Werner S. Landecker, 'Class Crystallisation and Class Consciousness', *Am. Soc. Rev.,* vol. 28, 1963; Stuart Adams, 'Social Climate and Productivity in Small Military Groups,' *Am. Soc. Rev.,* vol. 19, 1954; G. C. Homans, 'Status Congruence' in *Sentiments and Activities,* 1962. Moore refers simply to 'consistency' or 'coalescence.'

13. Cf. Kerr et al., pp. 272–273, 284, 292–293; Inkeles, pp. 341–342; Moore, pp. 356–7

14. Op. cit., pp. 272–273, 286.

15. Cf. Kerr et al., pp. 35–37; Moore, pp. 319–321, 343–344. Inkeles does not include the factor of increased mobility as a separate element in his model of the 'modernisation' of stratification systems. It is, however, incorporated in his discussion of both decreasing differentiation and growing consistency. E.g, in modern societies, 'Movement from one to another position on the scale . . . will not be sharply proscribed. Fluidity will characterise the [stratification] system as a whole . . .' Loc. cit., p. 341.

16. P. 35 (my italics).

17. It should be acknowledged, however, that for the West, at least, there is clear evidence on one other important point; that is, on the reduction, indeed virtual elimination, of *formal* inequalities of status. This has been the concomitant of the growth of 'citizenship' through which all members of national communities have been granted equal civil, political and social rights. Cf. T. H. Marshall, 'Citizenship and Social Class', in *Sociology at the Crossroads,* 1963.

18. Cf. United Nations, *Preliminary Report on the World Social Situation,* 1952, pp. 132–134; and *Report on the World Social Situation,* 1961, pp. 58–61.

19. See, e.g., United Nations, *Economic Survey of Europe in 1956,* 1957, chap. 7; R. M. Solow, 'Income Inequality since the War', in Ralph E. Freeman (ed.), *Postwar Economic Trends in the United States,* 1960. Recent studies relating specifically to Great Britain are H. F. Lydall, 'The Long-term Trend in the Size Distribution of Income', *Journ. Royal Stat. Soc.,* vol. 122, Part I, 1959, and H. F. Lydall and D. C. Tipping, 'The Distribution of Personal Wealth in Britain', *Oxford Inst. Stat. Bull.,* vol. 23, 1961.

20. Chiefly, this is because much levelling which appears to have gone on at the top of the distribution has in fact taken place simply *within* families—particularly between parents and children and generally as a means of avoiding taxation. E.g., Lydall and Tipping (op. cit.,) note the 'growing tendency for owners of large properties to distribute their assets amongst the members of their families well in advance of death.' (p. 85). However, it is, of course, the family, not the individual, that must be regarded as the basic unit of stratification

21. See, e.g., the critical review of Titmuss' book by A. R. Prest, and Titmuss' reply, in *British Tax Review,* March–April 1963.

22. *Income Distribution and Social Change,* 1962, p. 198. In this connection it should also be remembered that certain major developments which have made for greater equality in incomes in the recent past are of a non-repeatable kind—notably, the ending of large scale unemployment and the considerable expansion in the number of working class wives in gainful employment.

23. *Wealth and Power in America,* 1962, chap. 1. The data in question refer to pre-tax incomes, but Kolko is prepared to argue (chap. 2) that 'Taxation has not mitigated the fundamentally unequal distribution of income . . .'

24. *Challenge to Affluence,* 1963, chap. 3. The data assembled by the Conference on Economic Progress, *Poverty and Deprivation in the United States,* 1962, suggest that there was real improvement in the income position of low-income groups during World War II but that since then the economy has not greatly enhanced the living standards of the low-income population. In regard to the distribution of wealth, Robert J. Lampman, *The Share of Top Wealth-Holders in National Wealth,* 1962, has produced data to show that the share of personal sector wealth held by the wealthiest 1% of adults in the USA has steadily increased from 1949 to 1956.

25. Op. cit., pp. 13–15, 27–30.

26. Ibid., chaps. 4, 6, 7. A basically similar view is presented in Michael Harrington, *The Other America,* 1962. On the organisational, and thus political, weakness of the poor, see pp. 13–17; on the past failure and present responsibility of the Federal Government, pp. 163–170. Cf. also Stephen W. Rousseas and James Farganis, 'American Politics and the End of Ideology, *Brit. Journ. Soc.,* vol. 14, No. 4, 1963.

27. Cf. Harrington's emphasis on the fact that 'If there is to be a way out (of poverty) it will come from human action, from political change, not from automatic processes' (p. 162). Similarly, Raymond Aron has observed that the present problem of poverty in the USA is not that of the 'pauperisation' envisaged by Marx but that 'Il n'en existe pas moins et il rappele opportunément, à ceux qui seraient enclins à oublier, que la croissance économique ou les progrès techniques ne sont pas des recettes miraculeuses de paix sociale ou de relations authentiquement humaines'; and further that '. . . ni la croissance economique livrée à elle-même, ni le progrès technique, emporté par son dynamisme, ne garantissent un ordre juste ni, moins encore, des conditions de vie conformes aux aspirations d'une humanité qui a transformé le monde plus qu'elle ne c'est transformé elle-même.' *La Lutte des Classes,* 1964, pp. 15–16.

28. See, e.g., for Great Britain, John H. Goldthorpe and David Lockwood, 'Affluence and the British Class Structure', *Soc. Rev.,* vol. 11, No. 2, 1963; for the USA, Bennet Berger, *Working Class Suburb: A Study of Auto Workers in Suburbia,* 1960; for France, A. Andrieux and J. Lignon, *L'Ouvrier D'Aujourd'hui,* 1960. In all these contributions a common emphasis is that on the growing *disparity* between the situation of the manual worker as *producer* and *consumer.*

29. Karl Renner, *Wandlungen der modernen Gesellschaft; zwei Abhandlungen über die Probleme der Nachkriegzeit,* 1953.

30. See, e.g., for China, Robert M. Marsh, *The Mandarins: the Circulation of Elites in*

China, 1600–1900, 1961, and 'Values, Demand and Social Mobility', *Am. Soc. Rev.,* vol. 28 (1963), also, Ping-ti Ho, *The Ladder of Success in Imperial China: Aspects of Social Mobility, 1368–1911,* 1963.

31. For Great Britain, see Action Society Trust, *Management Succession,* 1956, and R. V. Clements, *Managers: A Study of Their Careers in Industry,* 1958. For the USA see W. Lloyd Warner and James C. Abegglen, *Occupational Mobility in American Business and Industry,* 1955.

32. See S. M. Lipset and Hans L. Zetterberg, 'A Theory of Social Mobility', *Transactions of the Third World Congress of Sociology,* 1956, vol. 3, pp. 155–177, and chap. 2, 'Social Mobility in Industrial Society,' in S. M. Lipset and R. Bendix, *Social Mobility in Industrial Society,* 1959.

33. Ibid., pp. 38–42.

34. S. M. Miller, 'Comparative Social Mobility', *Current Sociology,* vol. 9, No. 1, 1960.

35. Ibid., pp. 22–23, 57–58.

36. As an example of the kind of study which would seem particularly relevant and valuable, see Ralph H. Turner, 'Modes of Social Ascent through Education: Sponsored and Contest Mobility', in A. H. Halsey, Jean Floud and C. Arnold Anderson (eds.), *Education, Economy and Society,* 1961. This paper is concerned with the relation between differences in the American and English educational systems and differences in the prevailing norms in the two societies pertaining to upward mobility. More specifically, the aim is to investigate how the *accepted mode* of upward mobility shapes the pattern of educational institutions.

LABOR IN THE POST-INDUSTRIAL SOCIETY

Daniel Bell

In *The Communist Manifesto,* which was completed in February 1848, Marx and Engels envisaged a society in which there would be only two classes, capitalist and worker—the few who owned the means of production and the many who lived by selling their labor power—as the last two great antagonistic classes of social history, locked in final conflict. In many ways this was a remarkable prediction, if only because at that time the vast majority of persons in Europe and the United States were neither capitalist nor worker but farmer and peasant, and the tenor of life in these countries was overwhelmingly agrarian and artisan.

England was the evident model for industrialization, but despite Manchester, Leeds, Birmingham, and Sheffield, Great Britain at the mid-century mark was not at all industrial, a fact which is clearly demonstrated in the occupational statistics. As David Landes writes:

> The British census of 1851—for all its inaccuracies—shows a country in which agriculture and domestic service were far and away the most important occupations; in which most of the labour force was engaged in industries of the old type: building trades, tailoring, shoemaking, unskilled work of all sorts. Even in the cotton manufacture, with over three-fifths of its working force of over half a million (of a total of almost sixteen millions) in mills, two-thirds of the units making returns employed less than fifty men; the average mill in England employed less than 200; and tens of thousands of hand looms were still at work in rural cottages.[1]

If Britain was barely advanced, at mid-century, continental Europe was about a generation behind her in industrial development. In Belgium, the most industrialized nation on the continent, about half the labor force was engaged in agriculture (in Britain it was only one-fourth). Germany took another twenty-five years just to reach that 50 percent industrial mark; indeed, as late as 1895 there were more people engaged in agriculture than in industry. And in France the number of persons in industry was outnumbered by those in agriculture until the Second World War! To return to Marx's day, in the Prussia of 1852, which in this respect was representative of all of Germany, 72 percent of the population was Classified as rural. As Sir John Clapham comments: "German industry in general could in no sense be called capitalistic; and before 1840 large enterprises of the factory

SOURCE: *The Coming of Post-Industrial Society* (New York: Basic Books, 1973), pp. 123–129.

type were extraordinarily rare." In France in 1851, only 10½ percent of the population lived in towns and, writes Clapham, "the number of concerns employing more than a hundred people in 1848 was so small that they could not much affect the average for the whole country; outside mining and metallurgy they hardly existed [and] true factory conditions were exceptional in the France of 1848." In the United States in 1850, of a population of 23 million persons, 19.6 million lived in rural territory (defined as places with under 2,500 persons), and of a labor force of 7.7 million, 4.9 were engaged in agriculture, 1.2 in manufacturing and construction combined (it was only in 1870 that the two figures were separated), and almost one million in domestic service.[2]

Marx's vision of the inexorable rise of industrial society was thus a bold one. But the most important social change in Western society of the last hundred years has been not simply the diffusion of industrial work but the concomitant disappearance of the farmer—and in a Ricardian world of diminishing returns in land, the idea that agricultural productivity would be two or three times that of industry (which it has been in the United States for the last thirty years) was completely undreamed of.

The transformation of agrarian life (whose habits had marked civilization for four thousand years) has been the signal fact of the time. In beholding the application of steam power to a textile mill, one could venture predictions about the spread of mechanization and the extension of factory work. But who would, with equal confidence, have made similar predictions following the invention by Cyrus McCormick of the reaper in 1832 and its exhibition at the Crystal Palace in London in 1851? Yet in the United States today, only 4 percent of the labor force is engaged in agriculture; the work of little more than three million persons (as against more than twice that number two decades ago) feeds 207 million persons, and if all crop restraints were released, they could probably feed fifty million more.

In place of the farmer came the industrial worker, and for the last hundred years or so the vicissitudes of the industrial worker—his claims to dignity and status, his demand for a rising share of industrial returns, his desire for a voice in the conditions which affected his work and conditions of employment—have marked the social struggles of the century. But beyond that, in the utopian visions of Marx and the socialist movement, the working class, made conscious of its fate by the conditions of struggle, was seen as the agency not only of industrial but of human emancipation; the last great brakes on production and abundance would be removed when the working class took over control of the means of production and ushered in the socialist millennium.

Yet if one takes the industrial worker as the instrument of the future, or, more specifically, the factory worker as the symbol of the proletariat, then this vision is warped. For the paradoxical fact is that as one goes along the trajectory of industrialization—the increasing replacement of men by machines—one comes logically to the erosion of the industrial worker himself.[3] In fact by the end of the century the proportion of factory workers in the labor force may be as small as the proportion of farmers today; indeed, the entire area of blue-collar work may have diminished so greatly that the term will lose its sociological meaning as new categories, more appropriate to the divisions of the new labor force, are established. Instead of the industrial worker, we see the dominance of the professional and technical class in the labor force—so much so that by 1980 it will be the second largest occupational group in the society, and by the end of the century the largest. This is the new dual revolution taking place in the structure of occupations and, to the extent that occupation determines other modes of behavior (but this, too, is diminishing), it is a revolution in the class structure of society as well. This change in the character of production and of occupations is one aspect of the emergence of the "post-industrial" society.

The concept of a post-industrial society gains meaning by comparing its attributes with those of an industrial society and pre-industrial society.

In pre-industrial societies—still the condition of most of the world today—the labor force is engaged overwhelmingly in the extractive industries: mining, fishing, forestry, agriculture. Life is primarily a game against nature. One works with raw muscle power, in inherited ways, and one's sense of the world is conditioned by dependence on the elements— the seasons, the nature of the soil, the amount of water. The rhythm of life is shaped by these contingencies. The sense of time is one of *durée*, of long and short moments, and the pace of work varies with the seasons and the storms. Because it is a game against nature, productivity is low, and the economy is subject to the vicissitudes of tangible nature and to capricious fluctuations of raw-material prices in the world economy. The unit of social life is the extended household. Welfare consists of taking in the extra mouths when necessary—which is almost always. Because of low productivity and large population, there is a high percentage of underemployment, which is usually distributed throughout the agricultural and domestic-service sectors. Thus there is a high service component, but of the personal or household sort. Since individuals often seek only enough to feed themselves, domestic service is cheap and plentiful. (In England, up to the mid-Victorian period, the single largest occupational class in the society was the domestic servant. In *Vanity Fair,* Becky Sharp and Captain Rawdon Crawley are penniless, but they have a servant; Karl Marx and his large family lived in two rooms in Soho in the 1850s and were sometimes evicted for failing to pay rent, but they had a faithful servant, Lenchen, sometimes two.) Pre-industrial societies are agarian societies structured in traditional ways of routine and authority.

Industrial societies—principally those around the North Atlantic littoral plus the Soviet Union and Japan—are goods-producing societies. Life is a game against fabricated nature. The world has become technical and rationalized. The machine predominates, and the rhythms of life are mechanically paced: time is chronological, methodical, evenly spaced. Energy has replaced raw muscle and provides the power that is the basis of productivity—the art of making more with less—and is responsible for the mass output of goods which characterizes industrial society. Energy and machines transform the nature of work. Skills are broken down into simpler components, and the artisan of the past is replaced by two new figures —the engineer, who is responsible for the layout and flow of work, and the semi-skilled worker, the human cog between machines—until the technical ingenuity of the engineer creates a new machine which replaces him as well. It is a world of coordination in which men, materials, and markets are dovetailed for the production and distribution of goods. It is a world of scheduling and programming in which the components of goods are bought together at the right time and in the right proportions so as to speed the flow of goods. It is a world of organization—of hierarchy and bureaucracy—in which men are treated as "things" because one can more easily coordinate things than men. Thus a necessary distinction is introduced between the role and the person, and this is formalized on the organization chart of the enterprise. Organizations deal with the requirements of roles, not persons. The criterion of *techne* is efficiency, and the modes of life is modeled on economics: how does one extract the greatest amount of energy from a given unit of embedded nature (coal, oil, gas, water power) with the best machine at what comparative price? The watchwords are maximization and optimization, in a cosmology derived from utility and the felicific calculus of Jeremy Bentham. The unit is the individual, and the free society is the sum total of individual decisions as aggregated by the demands registered, eventually, in a market. In actual fact, life is never as "one-dimensional" as those who convert every tendency into an ontological absolute make it out to be. Traditional elements remain. Work groups intervene to impose their own rhythms and "bogeys" (or output restrictions) when they can. Waste runs high. Particularism and politics abound. These soften the unrelenting quality of industrial life. Yet the essential, technical features remain.

A post-industrial society is based on services. Hence, it is a game between persons. What counts is not raw muscle power, or energy, but information. The central person is the professional, for he is equipped, by his education and training, to provide the kinds of skill which are increasingly demanded in the post-industrial society. If an industrial society is defined by the quantity of goods as marking a standard of living, the post-industrial society is defined by the quality of life as measured by the services and amenities—health, education, recreation, and the arts—which are now deemed desirable and possible for everyone.

The word "services" disguises different things, and in the transformation of industrial to post-industrial society there are several different stages. First, in the very development of industry there is a necessary expansion of transportation and of public utilities as auxiliary services in the movement of goods and the increasing use of energy, and an increase in the non-manufacturing but still blue-collar force. Second in the mass consumption of goods and the growth of populations there is an increase in distribution (wholesale and retail), and finance, real estate, and insurance, the traditional centers of white-collar employment. Third, as national incomes rise, one finds, as in the theorem of Christian Engel, a German statistician of the latter half of the nineteenth century, that the proportion of money devoted to food at home begins to drop, and the marginal increments are used first for durables (clothing, housing, automobiles) and then for luxury items, recreation, and the like. Thus, a third sector, that of personal services, begins to grow: restaurants, hotels, auto services, travel, entertainment, sports, as people's horizons expand and new wants and tastes develop. But here a new consciousness begins to intervene. The claims to the good life which the society has promised become centered on the two areas that are fundamental to that life—health and education. The elimination of disease and the increasing numbers of people who can live out a full life, plus the efforts to expand the span of life, make health services a crucial feature of modern society; and the growth of technical requirements and professional skills makes education, and access to higher education, the condition of entry into the post-industrial society itself. So we have the growth of a new intelligentsia, particularly of teachers. Finally, the claims for more services and the inadequacy of the market in meeting people's needs for a decent environment as well as better health and education lead to the growth of government, particularly at the state and local level, where such needs have to be met.

The post-industrial society, thus, is also a "communal" society in which the social unit is the community rather than the individual, and one has to achieve a "social decision" as against, simply, the sum total of individual decisions which, when aggregated, end up as nightmares, on the model of the individual automobile and collective traffic congestion. But cooperation between men is more difficult than the management of things. Participation becomes a condition of community, but when many different groups want too many different things and are not prepared for bargaining or trade-off, then increased conflict or deadlocks result. Either there is a politics of consensus or a politics of stymie.

As a game between persons, social life becomes more difficult because political claims and social rights multiply, the rapidity of social change and shifting cultural fashion bewilders the old, and the orientation to the future erodes the traditional guides and moralities of the past. Information becomes a central resource, and within organizations a source of power. Professionalism thus becomes a criterion of position, but it clashes, too, with the populism which is generated by the claims for more rights and greater participation in the society. If the struggle between capitalist and worker, in the locus of the factory, was the hallmark of industrial society, the clash between the professional and the populace, in the organization and in the community, is the hallmark of conflict in the post-industrial society.

This, then, is the sociological canvas of the scheme of social development leading to the post-industrial society. . . .

NOTES

1. David Landes, *The Unbounded Prometheus: Technological Change and Industrial Development in Western Europe from 1750 to the Present* (Cambridge, England, 1969), pp. 119–120.
2. Sources for the above are Landes, op. cit., p. 187; J. H. Clapham, *The Economic Development of France and Germany, 1815–1914* (Cambridge, England, 1945; original edition, 1921), pp. 82, 84, 54, 70–71; *Historical Statistics of the United States* (Washington, D.C., 1960), pp. 14, 74.
3. In Marx's writings, there are many contradictory views of this situation. In the *Grundrisse,* the outline sketch for the master work which preceded *Capital,* and which was never published by Marx, he envisaged a time when almost all work would be replaced by the machine, and science, not labor power, would be considered the main productive force. In *Capital,* when he is working out the logic of the changing organic composition of capital, Marx describes a dual process resulting, on the one hand, in an increasing concentration of firms, and, on the other, an increase in the "industrial reserve army," i.e. the unemployed. Yet Marx could never escape the power of his own rhetoric, and in the penultimate chapter of *Capital,* when he is describing, nay sounding, the death-knell of capitalism, he writes: "Along with the constantly diminishing number of the magnates of capital . . . grows the revolt of the working-class, a class always increasing in numbers. . . . Centralization of the means of production and socialization of labor at last reach a point where they become incompatible with their capitalist integument. This integument is burst asunder." (*Capital,* vol. 1, p. 837.)

ECONOMIC PROBLEMS OF A "POSTINDUSTRIAL" SOCIETY

Robert Heilbroner

I think I should begin by expressing a certain caution with respect to the premise of my paper, a caution indicated by the quotation marks I have placed around the critical word *postindustrial* in my title. The premise is that we are moving rapidly into a new framework of socioeconomic relationships, a framework sufficiently different from that of the recent past to warrant designation as a new "stage" of our historical development. As this paper will make clear, I do not quarrel with the argument that deepseated changes in structure, institutions, and behavior are indeed surfacing within the economic sphere, whence they spread out to affect social and political life;[1] but unfortunately a certain voguish quality has come to surround the word "postindustrial" by which we describe this phenomenon.[2] Accordingly, it may be helpful to commence by specifying as clearly as possible what we mean by the "postindustrial" transformation, both to clarify its relationship to the "industrial" era now presumably on the wane, and to highlight those aspects of the coming era that are genuinely new.

Let me therefore start by exploring rather skeptically three different means that are commonly advanced with regard to the idea of a "postindustrial" society:

1. *A postindustrial society is one in which a preponderance of economic activity is located in the "tertiary" sector of the economy.*

This definition of postindustrialism calls attention to the shift in occupational locus whose beginnings can be discerned far back in the 19th century. As the history of every industrialized country indicates, the proportion of the labor force employed in agriculture shrinks to a very small fraction of the total work force: in the United States only 4 percent of the civilian labor force is to be found on the farm and this includes a considerable residue of subsistence farmers. Meanwhile, the industrial "core," Comprising manufacturing, mining, transportation, construction, and utilities, has stabilized at roughly a third of the work force. The remainder of the population—over 60 percent of the work force in the United States today—is employed in the congeries of occupations that produce "final" services.

From one industrial nation to another the magnitude of these proportions varies, but the "drift" is visible in all, as the table below clearly indicates:

SOURCE: *Dissent*, Spring 1973, pp. 163–176.

Percentage Distribution of Employed Workers

	AGRICULTURE	INDUSTRY	SERVICE
U.S., 1900	38	38	24
1970	4	34	61
France, 1950	35	45	20
1970	17	39	44
West Germany, 1950	24	48	28
1968	10	48	42
U.K., 1950	6	56	39
1970	4	45	50

SOURCE: *U.S. Historical Statistics*, p. 74; *Economic Indicators* (1972), European countries: OECD, *Basic Statistics of the Community* (1970).

Thus the definition of a postindustrial society that rests on a marked shift in the locus of employments can be amply demonstrated by statistical data. Nonetheless, a few cautionary remarks are in order. First, let us note that the industrial sector has not been the source of the main change in the profile of sectoral employment. Although it has declined slightly in France and England during the last 20 years, in Germany the percentage is unchanged; and in the United States *over a period of 70 years* the decline has been minuscule. The great sectoral transformation of our times, in other words, has not been so much a shift from "industry" to "service" as a shift from agricultural to service tasks. In addition, we must note that some part of the rise in service employment represents the transfer of certain kinds of work from the nonmonetized household sector to the monetized commercial world. The well-known rise in female labor participation (from 18 percent of all females of working age to 37 percent, in the years 1890 to 1969 in the United States) has brought as a consequence the illusion of a rise in service "employment," as tasks that were formerly carried out within the home, where they remained invisible to the eye of the statistician, emerged onto the marketplace. The growth of the laundry industry, the restaurant industry, the professional care of the aged, even "welfare," represent instances of this semispurious inflation of the growth of "employment" in service occupations.

These caveats and distinctions are important to bear in mind when we use the shift in employment locus as the basis for speculations about the implications of the postindustrial era. Let me briefly summarize what these cautionary thoughts might be.

Presumably the importance of the employment shift for a postindustrial system is that a change in occupational habitat brings new social experiences and needs. Without in any way challenging that supposition, let me warn against the misconception of that change as a massive emigration from industrial work. Nothing of that kind is visible. Instead, the primary "experiential" fact of the employment shift has been the decisive decline of agricultural (farm) employment and a corresponding growth of market-located, service-connected tasks. The industrial "core" remains roughly constant. Put differently, the industrial factory worker— the key *dramatis persona* of the Marxian drama—continues to account for approximately the same proportion of the total work experience of the community: unskilled, semiskilled, and skilled workers—the blue-collar group—constituted 25.5 percent of the labor force in 1900 and 34.9 percent in 1968, the main shift taking place *within* this group as most unskilled labor rose to semiskilled levels.

Thus, if postindustrial society in fact represents a new stage of socioeconomic relationships, the cause must be sought elsewhere than in the disappearance of the industrial sector as a milieu for work.

2. *A postindustrial society may refer to a change in the nature of growth-producing inputs from quantitative to qualitative factors.*

Here the primary meaning of "postindustrial" calls our attention to numerous studies of growth within industrial countries, and to the more or less common conclusions that "knowledge" has played a steadily rising role in promoting growth, compared with increases in the size of the labor force or the quantity of (unchanged) capital.[3] Drawing on Denison's work we may generalize for the United States that for the two decades prior to 1929 increases in the stock of capital goods and in labor supply together accounted for about two-thirds of our increase in outputs, whereas in the decades 1929–59 increases in these quantitative factors accounted for only 44 percent of growth. Conversely, improved education and training, which were credited with only 13 percent of growth in the earlier period, were presumed to be the source of more than twice that proportion of growth in the later period. Finally, improved technology—which is, after all, only the concrete application of knowledge—rose from 12 percent of the causes of growth to 20 percent in the same two periods.[4]

These proportions also differ from nation to nation, as Denison has shown in a study of the sources of growth in Western European nations, but the direction of change—as in the case of the migration of labor—is the same throughout. In sum, there is little doubt that statistical examination of growth patterns among industrialized nations shows a steadily increasing importance of "knowledge-related" inputs, and a corresponding decline in increases in brute "labor power" or sheer quantities of unchanged capital (for example, the addition of more railroad tracks).

As in the case of the definition of postindustrialism that emphasizes the shift in the locus of employment, I do not want to denigrate the importance that has been attached to human "capital."[5] Nonetheless it is important, as before, that we scrutinize this characterization of postindustrialism with a certain reserve. For when we do so, we encounter some disconcerting considerations.

First, as we have all come to realize, the meaning of growth is both ill-specified and elusive. Between that collection of often arbitrarily defined outputs called "Gross National Product" and any operational concept of "welfare" is a wide and perhaps unbridgeable chasm. Hence much of the "growth" to which modern knowledge seems to contribute so strikingly may be of little or no welfare significance: armaments, space exploration, and pollution-generating production at one extreme; frivolous gadgetry, style changes, and pollution-absorbing technology at the other —the one extreme producing deleterious or dangerous growth, the other illusory or "defensive" growth. In a word, the *quality* of the growth of a "postindustrial" society must be compared with that of an "industrial" society, before we can discuss the rise of knowledge-inputs as a cause for celebration, as well as a simple fact.

Second, before looking for the implications of the shift toward a knowledge-input economy, it behooves us to inquire further into the "fact" of the increase in knowledge input itself. This brings us to the ways in which knowledge input is *measured*. One of these ways—research and development (R & D)—is certainly grossly inflated. Government statistics show a rise in R & D expenditures from roughly $1 billion at the end of World War I to a level of $28 billion in the early 1970s. This enormous increase has led many observers to conclude that we have now "institutionalized" the process of scientific discovery and application, thereby radically changing the nature of the propulsive forces within the economy. More skeptical observers have noted that (inflation aside) the R & D figures in the later years are swollen by the growing tendency to include routine testing or marketing procedures within the category of "research." The actual amount going for basic research in new industrial products for 1966 was estimated to be not $20 billion, but $1 billion.[6]

In addition, a study of Jewkes, Sawers, and Stillerman throws considerable doubt on the effectiveness of "institutional" invention, citing evidence that the preponderance of the important inventions or innovations of the last third of a century have been made by individuals or small firms.[7] Thus there is some reason to regard the institutionalized knowledge-input of the postindustrial society as much less sharply differentiated from that of "industrial" society than might at first appear.

A further caveat with respect to the supposed information revolution applies to the rise in the "stock" of education embodied in the work force. Measured by the conventional criteria of man-years of schooling, there is no doubt that this stock has increased markedly: whereas only 6 percent of the population aged 17 were high school graduates in 1900, nearly 80 percent had completed high school in 1970. Equally dramatic, whereas those enrolled in college in 1900 constituted only 4 percent of the population aged 18–21, today well over half of this age group is in college.

No one can gainsay this change which, like the change in the sectoral location of labor, surely augurs new outlooks, experiences, and expectations for the labor force. To this matter we will return. But it would be hasty to jump from the fact of a higher stock of embodied education to the conclusion that the stock of "knowledge" of the society has increased *pari passu*. For along with the increased training undergone by the labor force has come an increase in the compartmentalization and specialization of its skills, best exemplified by comparing the wide-ranging capabilities of the farmer with the much more narrowly defined work capabilities of the office clerk. To put the matter differently, we cannot assume that a post-industrial society is one in which the general level of "know-how" is raised along with the general level of formal education. Insofar as formal education is devoted to exposing the student to the broadest vistas of history, the social and natural sciences, etc., one kind of "knowledge" is undoubtedly increased. In that sense, the average citizen of the post-industrial society is not only "better educated" but really knows more, with regard to the natural sciences, human behavior, etc., *considered as abstractions*, than did his counterpart in industrial or preindustrial society. At a less abstract level, however, the gain is much less. And within that very important branch of social knowledge concerned with the operation of the socioeconomic mechanism, what seems to mark the education-intensive postindustrial society is a marked *decrease* in the ability of the individual to perform work outside his trained specialty—witness our helplessness in the face of a broken utensil, vehicle, electrical system, or plumbing fixture, compared with the versatility of the farmer (or industrial artisan), proverbially jack of all trades, even if master of none.

To raise these cautions against a simplistic view of the postindustrial society as one characterized by a "knowledge explosion" is not to deny that profound alterations are visible within contemporary society as a result of greater educational inputs—alterations that are likely to become even more pronounced in the society of the future.

The first, whose implications we will examine again subsequently, is a change in the expected life-styles of a postindustrial population. Whatever else its effects may be, the exposure to prolonged schooling seems to encourage an expectation of careers in white-collar, as opposed to blue-collar, tasks; and this may indeed militate against the willingness of the "educated" population to consider many manual tasks as appropriate ways of making a livelihood, regardless of the relative incomes to be had from goods-handling, rather than paper-handling, work. Needless to say, this change in expectations accords very well with the actual displacement of labor from agricultural tasks and from the unskilled categories of industrial work, and its increasing deployment in service occupations.

Second and perhaps more important—although necessarily more conjectural—is the educationally based evolution of a "subclass" of highly skilled technicians, scientists, and experts who seem to be moving gradually toward a position of greater influence within the socioeconomic system as a whole. The rise of this "knowledge elite" has been remarked by many.[8] The actual power possessed by the new elite, as well as its degree of sub- or superordination to older elites, is as yet unclear. Nonetheless, there seems little doubt that a new education-based stratification has been created at the apex of the system, and that a new mystique surrounds "the scientist," symbol of the knowledge-oriented postindustrial system, comparable to that which formerly adhered to "the captain of industry."[9] Thus the emphasis on "knowledge" as the *differentia specifica* of a postindustrial system is not misplaced, although the precise nature of this difference requires to be spelled out a good deal more carefully than is often the case.

3. *A postindustrial society can be regarded as a "postcapitalist" society—that is, as a socioeconomic formation in which the traditional problems of capitalism will give way before the new organizational modes of a postindustrial system.*

As with the previous "visions" of a postindustrial system, I think there is a core of truth in this view. The bitter class divisions endemic to capitalism in the late 19th and early 20th centuries seem to be yielding to a society of much greater economic (if not necessarily social or political) consensus. The "welfare" state, however inadequate in actuality, is now a generally accepted model for all industrial societies, and brings with it a considerable degree of "socialism" in the form of guaranteed incomes, family allowances, public health assurance, educational subsidization of lower income groups, and the like. The extreme vulnerability of the system to failures of aggregate demand has been tempered by the growth of a public sector. As a result of these and still other changes, the "revolutionary" proletariat has failed to materialize; moreover, as we have seen above, the size of the industrial proletariat has remained approximately constant.

Thus there *are* cogent reasons for thinking of the postindustrial society as one that differs in significant ways from the economic performance of the industrial capitalism to which it is a successor. Nonetheless, as before, it is wise to look for continuities as well as differences in seeking to delineate the nature of the new socioeconomic environment.

The first of these is the continuance of a trend whose origins can be traced back at least to the third quarter of the 19th century. This is the slow, irregular, but apparently irreversible trend toward the concentration of capital. The figures are well known: in manufacturing, the assets of the top 100 firms in 1968 were as large a share (roughly 49 percent) of all corporate manufacturing assets as the share of the 200 largest industrial firms in 1950. Similarly the top 200 firms in 1968 controlled as large a fraction of total assets as the top 1,000 firms in 1941.[10] Economic society today is strikingly characterized by what Robert Averitt has called a Center—a small number of very large and powerful industrial units— and a Periphery—a very large number of generally small and weak firms.[11]

It should be noted that we are far from understanding the dynamics of this two-sector division with regard to the performance of the system as a whole. The oligopolistic Center has been shown to be the source of much economic ineffi- ciency and perhaps of inflationary pressures;[12] the sprawling Periphery has been identified by at least one student as the main source of business instability.[13] More important, but even less well understood, are the extent and nature of the linkages that bind the Center and political power structure. That linkages exist has been amply demonstrated, but the direction in which power flows (*from* the economic *to* the political structure, or vice versa) is unclear or perhaps unstable.[14] That is not a problem for this paper. What I rather wish to stress is the existence of an economic concentrate allied in some fashion with a political concentrate— a state of affairs that is not basically different from that which existed under "industrial" society, and which can, incidentally, be seen as well in the economic- political ententes of Japan, France, Germany, and other candidates for entry into the postindustrial realm.[15]

The development of a "postindustrial" configuration of employment or educa- tion does not seem likely to undo this characteristic of economic concentration. Rather, it seems probable that the concentration process will now proceed rapidly in the burgeoning service sector, where significant inroads have already been made (as is also the case in agriculture, still by far the least concentrated sector). We tend to picture the service sector as comprised of large numbers of indepen- dent proprietorships (lawyers, self-employed, one-man enterprises); but in fact a considerable proportion of employment in this sector is already provided by monopolistic or oligopolistic units. Of roughly 44 million employed in the service sector in 1970 (not including utilities or transportation), 13 million were in government, 15 million in trade, 4 million in finance (banking, insurance, broker- age, real estate). By comparison with the manufacturing sector, these are all relatively unconcentrated industries, but in terms of *absolute size of units,* the large firm, with it bureaucratic organization, is increasingly evident. A mere 29 retail chains, for instance, control a fifth of all assets in trade; the predominance and growth of large banks and insurance companies is well-known (the top 50 banks account for a third of all banking employment; the top 50 insurance com- panies for almost half of all employment in that field). *Thus the organizational character of industrial capitalism, with its hierarchies, bureaucracies, and above all its trend toward concentration, seems likely to continue in the postindustrial society.*

Next, we find the distribution of wealth and income little if at all disturbed by the types of changes we have discussed. Many studies have shown the extraordi- nary stability of income-shares accruing to the top and bottom deciles in the United States;[16] the top 10 percent of family units receiving about 30 percent of income, the bottom 30 percent less than one-tenth of income. These shares have remained roughly constant, or have inclined slightly toward inequality during the late decade, in which the effects of the postindustrial changes might have been expected to reveal their influence.

More significant is the stubborn continuation and defense of the extreme concentration of wealth in the top 1 or 2 percent of family units who collectively own about a third of *all* wealth. Control of corporate wealth—by far the most strategic item of wealth—is much more tightly centered, with about two-thirds of such wealth in the hands of 0.2 percent of all families.[17] In passing, it might be remarked that this extreme concentration of control is not peculiar to capitalism— it could no doubt be found under feudalism and (insofar as power can be used as a proxy for wealth) under existing forms of socialism. What is specifically capitalist about the phenomenon is the focus of control on corporate enterprise; and there is no sign that this concentration or its focus will diminish appreciably in a postindustrial setting, although the wealth-holding elites may recruit newcomers from the scientific-technological community.

Finally, we pass from structure to function. We have already noted that the more extreme destabilizing tendencies of capitalism now seem to be faced with rough-and-ready remedies. Let us only add that the specific features of postindustrialism that we have heretofore discussed—the sectoral shift and the increased education input—are not in themselves the source of any stabilizing tendencies (although one might claim that the defensive weaponry of macroeconomics is itself in part a product of the knowledge input of our time). However successfully we may have obviated the threat of mass unemployment and catastrophic income decline, there is scant evidence as yet that postindustrial society has solved problems that reflect the capitalist *modus operandi*. Inflation has replaced deflation, but the one, like the other, is surely a market phenomenon. A massive misallocation of resources, visible especially in the decay of the cities, has taken public priority over mass unemployment; but once again the fault lies with the failure of the market mechanism and the special constraints of private ownership. Specifically "capitalist" relations with the underdeveloped world seem to have worsened in the most recent period, or perhaps we should simply say that the capitalist problem of "imperialism" has reemerged to a central position.

All these elements suggest that whatever else we may say about the postindustrial future, *we should consider it as a stage of capitalism and not as a step "beyond" capitalism.* The stage may display new endemic characteristics and problems—indeed, I shall next turn to an exploration of what these may be—but it must also be expected to manifest many of the structural attributes of industrial capitalism, including concentrated economic power and wealth, a highly unequal distribution of pre (and probably post) tax income, and macro-malfunctions and misallocations of resources that arise from the predominance of the market as the principal allocatory mechanism.

Shall we then dismiss the idea of a "postindustrial" society as a chimera? That is not my intention. Just as late industrial capitalism differs in striking and significant ways from the small-scale capitalism of Adam Smith's day, so it is probable that the "postindustrial" trends within contemporary capitalism are pushing in directions that also portend substantial change.

Let me therefore turn the coin over and review the evidence I have just marshalled in order to factor out those elements that seem to me particularly freighted with change. The first of these, we will remember, had to do with the sectoral relocation of the work force away from the farm through the factory and into the office. Is it possible to generalize about the effects of such a massive relocation, particularly when one takes into account the extraordinary heterogeneity of tasks contained within the service sector?[18]

One such generalization is self-evident, but none the easier to interpret. It is a farreaching change in the character of what we call, or think of, as "work." Like industrial man, postindustrial man is divorced from knowledge of the most fundamental provisioning activities of society: the seasons affect him only insofar as they determine his vacation time, the weather only as it upsets his travel plans or conditions his choice of clothing. Unlike industrial man, however, who also shares in this complete ignorance of the fundamental provisioning tasks, postindustrial man is no longer even familiar with the environment in which the great bulk of our industrial products originate. The bleak expanse of the factory wasteland, surrounded with its high, electrified fence; the clangor of the industrial shed, the dirty work clothes, the lunch pail, the grease, the grime, the dust that we find in most places of industrial work are missing from the store and the office. Changed, too, is the character of work supervision, away from factory whistles, check-ins, foremen. Service work, in all (or most) of its varieties is characterized by trim surroundings, neat dress or a prestigious uniform, constant exposure to a "clientele," coffee breaks, telephone calls. This is by no means all gain, although some of it is. The physical dangers of work are less; the psychological strains may be greater. The expenditure of physical effort is greatly reduced; that of psychic energies may be greatly increased.

It is difficult to know what conclusions follow from this impressionistically drawn change in work milieu. For example, whether "alienation" is exacerbated or alleviated is a matter about which we cannot even make informed guesses, not least because of the variety of tasks embraced within the service sector. Yet, in full awareness of the frailty of such "sociologizing," let me hazard one conjecture that combines the changed work experience mentioned above with a second characteristic of the postindustrial world—namely, the lengthened and broadened exposure of its work force to formal education. The conjecture (it is perhaps too untestable to be dignified with the name of "hypothesis") is that the lengthened exposure to the "white-collar" atmosphere of the classroom tends to identify the expected characteristics of "work." That is, college prepares one not only intellectually, but experientially, for the store and the office rather than for the factory or the farm. I am aware, of course, of exceptions: agronomists, engineers, and a few similar professions. But in the main I think I am on firm ground in holding that education nurtures the association of "work" with reading, writing, and calculation, rather than with handling things. Thus the postindustrial society encourages what Veblen called a "trained incapacity" for "dirty work" among that ever-growing fraction of the population that pursues formal education through the college level. In passing, I should note that the smooth running of postindustrial society may hinge, even more than that of industrial society, on the presence of that "secondary" labor force (the drop-outs, casual labor-market participants, or exploited minorities) who continue to be available for the picking of fruit, the digging of ditches, the sweeping of floors, the washing of dishes.

Along with the new sense of what "work" means there comes, I think, a growing expectation of security in the world of work. A man or woman who has been relieved of virtually all economic necessity until the age of 21 or even 25 is reared in an environment in which some sort of economic provision, even if at a frugal level, is taken for granted. It would not be surprising if the graduates of the postindustrial educational institutions bring with them strong expectations that "work" is not a scarce privilege to be competed for, but a basic right—the normal reward for having completed the long training that society has enjoined. Guarantees of employment, security of tenure in work, the "right" to expect an uninterrupted flow of income are thus plausible consequences of the transition to a postindustrial occupational and educational framework. Perhaps this is nothing more than the diffusion among the great bulk of the population of attitudes that were formerly evident mainly among the upper decile.

Let me turn finally to another new attribute of the postindustrial world which also follows from the characteristics we have examined in our previous section. This concerns the problems of economic function and malfunction that a postindustrial society can expect to inherit from its precursor.

Here one major trend seems likely to be reinforced by the postindustrial system. This is the growth of business-state coordination at an overt rather than covert level. Business-state cooperation is, of course, as old as capitalism itself; it is the mythology rather than the reality of "laissez-faire," which has dominated the past century. Many forces within the postindustrial framework seem likely to diminish the strength of that mythology, and to strengthen the tendencies toward open coordination. The importance of maintaining an adequate level of aggregate demand in the face of widespread expectations of "guaranteed white-collar work," of remedying the disruptive effects of the misallocation of resources, and of dealing with the problems of an economic system increasingly polarized between a Center and a Periphery all seem likely to increase the need for, and the political acceptibility of, some kind of "planning." No doubt the form and functions of this planning will display differing reaches and effectiveness in various societies with their particular ideological, traditional, and structural differences. But in all postindustrial systems I would anticipate something that might be described as a "corporate state"—that is, a state in which the activities of the Center and the state are brought into compatible paths, in which the risks and instabilities of the Periphery are offset, or at least partially underwritten, and in which acceptable resource allocation is attacked by coordinated action between the public and private sectors.

In suggesting that the changeful elements of the postindustrial trend will encourage overt planning, I do not mean to imply that the politicoeconomic problems of this stage of capitalism will necessarily be easier to solve than those of industrial capitalism. The difficulties of controlling inflation may well be greater than those of overcoming depression, both to diagnose and to cope with politically. The power of the moderately affluent middle classes, and of the service-sector located work force may prove more troublesome for a viable "incomes policy" than the wage-determination in an industrial setting (the recent experience in the municipal sectors is a case in point).[19] No less of a difficult problem for the macromanagement of the postindustrial system may be that of persuading the majority of income recipients, whose incomes lie in the fourth income decile and up, to relinquish substantial sums for the benefit of the poor who are to be found in the bottom three deciles. All these problems seem likely to add further impetus to the overall drift toward business-state planning to which we have already pointed.

Heretofore I have been discussing the postindustrial society from two points of view: first, analyzing the inadequacies of certain views concerning the term; second, suggesting the kernel of truth that resides in these views. Now I wish to proceed in a somewhat different direction. First, I wish to inquire into two structural or transformational stresses to which postindustrial society will be subject, beyond those that we have already identified. Finally, I will ask the much more difficult question as to the social consequences we can anticipate as following from these changes.

What further *economic* changes can be expected from the trajectory out of agrarian, through industrial, into the service-centered, education-intensive system we call "postindustrial"? Two such changes appear integrally connected with this trajectory, although as we shall see, the connections are not the same in each case.

The first change has to do with the progressive mechanization of work—that is, with the further development of the very force that lies behind the trajectory of economic transformation itself. There is no doubt that technology is the major element in bringing about the sectoral migration of the labor force, for it has been the widening "technicization" of rural and then factory work that has released the manpower that has flowed into the tertiary areas of the economy.[20] We do not fully understand the reason for the particular sequence of technology that has given us this shift and cannot therefore make firm predictions with respect to the future. But every indication is that invention and innovation will be proportionately more concentrated on the tasks performed in the service sector. This seems likely for three reasons: (1) we are reaching the limits of labor displacement in agriculture (although there remains a small group that can still be dispossessed from their jobs in that sector); (2) almost three-quarters of a century of invention and innovation within the industrial core has left the proportion of the labor force relatively unchanged, as we have seen, and we can therefore assume that if the same general forces of technology and demand continue, there will not be significant labor displacement from this sector; and (3) the most "attractive" sector for the introduction of machinery lies in the heretofore technically "neglected" service area.[21] In this sector labor costs are high, productivity low, and a new level of technological capability begins to bring many heretofore "unmechanizable" tasks within the reach of machinery: as a result we have the vending machine for the counter man; the self-service store for the clerk; the programmed lathe, the automatic check-reader, the omnipresent computer.

What will be the effect of this further mechanization? The answer hinges entirely on the elasticity of demand for the services produced in this sector. If demand swells *pari passu* with the increased productivity per service worker that will result from "automation," then the service sector may continue to absorb its present 60–65 percent of the labor force. If demand swells more rapidly, or if technology enters more slowly, employment in this sector may rise still further in both absolute and percentage terms. It is also possible that the demand for "services," like that for "manufactures," will ultimately reach "satiety." In more concrete terms, there may be a limit as to the amount of government services, retail-trade services, education, recreation, financial advice, etc., that a man wants at a given income level; and that the "amount" of services (measured in the dollars we spend for them) may not rise as rapidly as income rises.

In that case, where will the displaced labor go? Several possibilities for adjustment are available. One is the creation of a public employment sector designed to create employment for those displaced from the service area. This sector need not itself be within the tertiary sector, but might embrace subsidized small farming, labor-intensive subsidized handicraft, labor-intensive public construction, etc. A second possibility is the deliberate steady reduction in the work force, achieved partly by further extending the compulsory years of schooling, partly by reducing retirement ages, partly by shortening the work week. A third possibility is the extension of the transfer mechanism to permit a certain proportion of the young working-age population to live without work, at socially determined subsistence levels, if it so chooses.

All these adjustments—the need for which hinges, let me repeat, on the unpredictable rate of technological displacement and the shift in the demand for various services—portend considerable strains on the "traditional" capitalist mechanism. They imply as well new strains on the macroprocesses of a system in which the historic underpinning identified by both Marx and Weber—a propertyless class of workers—has been replaced by a class of workers which, however "propertyless," are not *forced* to sell their labor power at the prevailing market rate. It would be foolhardy to assert that an economic system operating under the constraints of "capitalist" ideologies and institutions cannot make these adjustments—one has but to consider the very great degree of social adaptation displayed by the capitalist nations of Scandinavia. But the basic nature of the challenge of mechanization is nonetheless clear. The postindustrial society is likely to be faced with a "redundancy" of labor owing to the progressive incursion of mechanization into the service sector; and this redundancy—if it is not absorbed by a spontaneous growth of private demand for "services"—will require intervention into the market process on a far-reaching scale.

A second dimension of the mechanization problem has already engaged our attention. This is the effect of "automation" on the psychophysical process of "work" itself. We have already seen that the displacement of "muscular" by "intellectual" labor is one of the main attributes of postindustrialization. Even at the simplest level—the man behind the tractor wheel instead of behind the hoe, behind the adding machine instead of behind the ledger, behind the computerized lathe instead of behind the chuck lathe—the nature of human effort in postindustrial society is given a supervisory, rather than directly "active," aspect. This change in the existential and experiential character of labor offers rich ground for speculation, but little substantial basis for extraeconomic prediction. We return at the conclusion to this problem of social forecasting.

A second structural challenge to be faced by the postindustrial world is the problem of ecological adjustment that must be faced over the coming decades—a problem that will steadily grow in intensity as population densities rise, pollution accumulates, and resources become depleted.

The dimensions of the ecological problem are ultimately very great and its restrictive implications severe. What is at question is the time scale during which adjustment can be made and the degree of technological adaptation that can be achieved.[22] At stake is the level of qualitative well-being, the rate of tolerable growth, and in the end the viability of the planet itself as a human habitat. It need hardly be said that the ecological threat affects not just the "postindustrial" world, but all nations, albeit in different fashions and at varying time schedules.

In terms of the immediate impact on the quality of life, it may well be the most developed nations, with their high rate of pollution and their voracious consumption of resources, that stand to be the first affected.

When the ecological problem arrives "in earnest," it will pose an acute problem for postindustrial societies. We have already called attention to the presence and the undoubted continuing importance of the industrial core which, together with the agricultural sector, supports the tertiary activities of the postindustrial world. The problem, then, is the extent to which the expansive drive of a capitalist mechanism, expressed through the acquisitive and accumulatory behavior of its corporations, can be given an appropriate area in which to manifest itself, if unrestricted growth within the industrial sector becomes impermissible for environmental reasons.

Of the many new sources of tension and malfunction within the postindustrial world, this looming constriction of the expansive drive within the industrial sector seems among the most difficult of solution. The export of capital, a major means of venting the expansive drive in the past, becomes less open, owing to environmental problems of pollution in the other developed countries (which are currently most attractive to capital), and to political problems in the underdeveloped world. To what extent the expansive international momentum of capitalism can be diverted to the areas of services is an uncertain question, but not one that seems especially promising, as the various "service" occupations are now defined.

There is no point in attempting to guess to what degree industrial companies will be able to move into such fields as entertainment, travel, personal services and the like. What is important to bear in mind is that some form of "growth," with all its money illusions and its mixture of "goods" and "bads," is an indispensable means of lessening the tensions generated by the need to divide the total product between wages and property income. In a postindustrial society in which industrial expansion were necessarily constrained because of ecological hazards, and in which the large corporation had not found a satisfactory means of penetrating the service occupations, we could expect serious stresses to manifest themselves—a fall in profit rates and/or a much more acrimonious struggle over the division of the social product. Whether "capitalism" could adjust to such a situation is moot—in the opinion of economists as different in orientation as Marx and Keynes it could not—but in all likelihood such a trend would accelerate the tendency toward the "managerialization" of the public-private corporate state to which other tendencies, discussed above, now point.

We have already indulged in sufficient speculation with regard to the socioeconomic characteristics of the postindustrial world, and the temptation is to conclude on a note of solid empiricism. Yet I shall resist this temptation in order to explore one last highly conjectural area that seems inescapable in any consideration of what the future may be like.

This is the classic problem of the economic "base" and the noneconomic "superstructure"—a problem that finds its starkest expression in Marx, but that can be traced back to the Scottish Historical School. For a fact that must be admitted in all our conjecturings about the shape of things to come is that we reveal ourselves, wittingly or otherwise, to be economic determinists—indeed, even technological determinists. To put it differently, all speculation about postindustrialism assumes that the causal line of inference runs *from* the economic changes *to* the political and social changes, and although feedbacks may be discussed (such as the drive toward plannification) the *primum mobile* of "prediction" is the economic dynamic of social evolution.

This primacy of economic dynamics has nothing to do with ideology. It arises because we can discern "lawlike" motions within the economic sphere that have no counterparts in the political and social realms. However indistinct and blurred, these motions can nonetheless be described and, moreover, within broad limits their interactions can be deduced. One of these lawlike motions is the drive for profits characteristic of a capitalist system. Although this drive does not produce the determinate "equilibrium" solutions of neoclassical economics,[23] it nonetheless permits us to anticipate with a fair degree of certainty such types of behavior as the search for cost-reducing technology, the concentration of business enterprise (whether for reasons of efficiency or profitable financial manipulation), the probable advent of economies of scale in industries that have not yet been "invaded" by technology, the crucial role to be played by autonomous public and private expenditures magnified by a "multiplier" of reasonably known dimensions, and still other regularities.

I hasten to stress the extreme tenuousness of our knowledge in all these fields. Short-run economic prediction, based on presumptively "known" behavioral functions and technical constraints, has been shown to be egregiously faulty. But this constraint does not apply with quite the same force to the longer run, when the persistent trends of economic life assert themselves over their short-term vagaries.[24] Hence to whatever extent we dare to predict the contours of postindustrial society, it is perforce on the basis of these economic projections. For what "lawlike" statements can we apply to the organization of political affairs, to social organization, to changes in cultural life-style, and the like? Apart from a few descriptive generalizations—Michels' "iron law" of oligarchy, Weber's description of bureaucratic organization, Freud's or Erikson's outline of the topography of the psyche and its developmental stages—what do the other social sciences have to offer by way of predictive theory? The answer I fear is, discouragingly little. Thus, however inaccurate or inadequate the economic determinist view may be, it is foisted upon us as an initial mode of viewing the future for lack of any alternative "positive" approach.

This raises very grave problems for social scientists. Not only are the "laws of motion" of economics extremely imprecise, but the linkages between any given economic structure and its interlocked political and social accouterments are even more difficult to describe with any degree of assurance. I must confess to a suspicion that if postindustrial society follows the general economic trajectory I have described, it will be accompanied by a more authoritarian political structure, by more anomic groups in the undereducated, by increasing restlessness and boredom among the educated "middle classes" still subject to the stimuli of a competitive, acquisitive culture. But this is only conjecture; perhaps one can draw equally or more convincing scenarios of greater stability, communal morale, individual fulfillment.

In this situation of extreme indeterminacy a key may be provided by what Adolph Lowe has identified as the mood of the times—certainly of the postindustrial age. He calls this "the end of social fatalism."[25] By this he means the end of an age in which not only the events of nature but the events of society are taken as "givens," to be mutely accepted by the uncomplaining masses or explained away in terms of a theological or a political religion.

If this identification of a profound change in mood is true—and I believe that it is—perhaps our view of the future as something to be "predicted" is fundamentally at variance with the realities of the age. In an era that has rejected social fatalism, the future will no longer "arrive," but it will be *made,* however crudely, cruelly, or well by the harnessing of political wills and their focusing on deliberately chosen goals. It may therefore be quite mistaken to search, within economics or in its sister disciplines, for "positive" perspectives on a future that will not come into being by the workings of "lawlike" mechanisms (although it may be influenced by their residual influence), but by the political selection of social goals whose means of attainment then become the subject for social scientific investigation.[26]

This leaves open, of course, the choice of goals. About this all-important question the social scientist has nothing to say, either as counselor or as expert "prognosticator." Perforce he relinquishes his place to the moral philosopher—his historical godfather—whose task it is to raise the consciousness of men to the alternatives open to them. The goals once chosen, the social scientist again comes into his own in the more modest, but nonetheless important, role of social "engineer." If there is one ultimate definition for postindustrial society, then, I would suggest, it is that stage of socioeconomic organization in which men gradually escape from the thralldom of blind mechanisms to enter the perilous, but potentially liberating, terrain in which human beings finally assert themselves, for better or worse, as the masters of their fate.

NOTES

1. This statement implies a certain economic determinism. I will deal specifically with this issue at the end of this essay.
2. A great amount of literature too long for a footnote—now deals with "postindustrial society." The most sophisticated version of the concept is to be found in Daniel Bell's work: see especially the symposium, including his essay, in *Survey,* Winter 1971; see also "The Post-Industrial Society: The Evolution of an Idea," *Survey,* Spring 1971, and *The Coming of Post-Industrial Society* (New York: Basic Books, 1973). Reference should also be made to Zbigniew Brzezinski's *Between Two Ages: America's Role in the Technotronic Era* (New York: Viking, 1970). A more simplistic and quantitative exploration of the term is to be found in Herman Kahn's and Anthony Wiener's *The Year Two Thousand* (New York: Macmillan, 1967). Numerous books have popularized the idea, of which the currently most widely quoted is Alvin Toffler's *Future Shock* (New York: Random House, 1970).
3. The literature again is too large to be reviewed. Key statements are those of M. Abramovitz, *Resource and Output Trends in the United States Since 1870* (New York: National Bureau of Economic Research, 1956); Robert Solow, "Technical Change and the Aggregate Production Function," *Review of Economics and Statistics,* August 1957; and Edward Denison, *Sources of Economic Growth in the United States* (New York: Committee for Economic Development, 1962).
4. Denison, op. cit.
5. Ferenc Janossy, *The End of the Economic Miracle* (White Plains, N.Y.: International Arts and Sciences Press, 1971), has a dramatic imaginative illustration of the respective importance of knowledge versus "labor power" or "capital." He asks us to imagine the instantaneous transfer of the populations of two nations, one developed and one

underdeveloped—say, England and Pakistan (before its civil war). Is there any doubt, he asks, that the growth curve of "Pakistan" would rapidly turn upward, while that of "England" would soon turn sharply down?

6. John M. Blair, *Economic Concentration* (New York: Harcourt Brace Jovanovich, 1972), p. 15, citing estimate by David Novick of the Rand Corporation.

7. *The Sources of Invention* (New York: St. Martin's Press, 1958 2nd rev. ed., Norton, 1970). See also Blair, *Economic Concentration*, pp. 215–27.

8. See among others, Bell, op. cit., Brzezinski, op. cit., J. K. Gailbraith, *The New Industrial State* (Boston: Houghton Mifflin, 1967), and R. Heilbroner, *The Limits of American Capitalism* (New York: Harper & Row, 1966).

9. Perhaps it is to be noted in passing that the same ambivalence also attaches to this new figure who is viewed, as was the older entrepreneur, both as a heroic personage capable of building a great society and as a demonic force capable of destroying it.

10. Blair, op. cit., chap. 4.

11. Robert T. Averitt, *The Dual Economy* (New York: Norton, 1968).

12. Blair, *Economic Concentration*, p. 152, ff., and *passim*.

13. Howard Sherman, *Radical Political Economy* (New York: Basic Books, 1972), pp. 110, 113–114.

14. For a few studies of these linkages see: AEA *Proceedings*, 1972, pp. 279–318, esp. articles by Kaufman and Melman; Robert Engler, *The Politics of Oil* (New York: Macmillan, 1971); G. Kolko, *The Triumph of Conservatism* (Glencoe, Ill., and New York: Free Press, 1963); H. Kariel, *The Decline of American Pluralism* (Stanford: Stanford University Press, 1961).

15. See A. Shonfield, *Modern Capitalism* (London and New York: Oxford University Press, 1965).

16. See G. Kolko, *Wealth and Power in America* (New York: Praeger, 1962). Also Ackerman, Birnbaum, Wetzler, and Zimbalist, "The Extent of Income Inequality in the United States" in R. Edwards, M. Reich, and T. Weisskopf (eds.), *The Capitalist System* (Englewood Cliffs, N.J.: Prentice-Hall, 1972).

17. R. Lampman, *The Share of Top Wealth Holders in National Wealth 1922–56* (Princeton: Princeton University Press, 1962), p. 24.

18. Let me simply remind the reader that this sector includes the most highly bureaucratized elements of American life—the federal government—and the least bureaucratized—the individual proprietor or professional in the service trades or professions; very highly skilled tasks (surgeons) and very low-skilled (filing clerks); the very highly paid (entertainers) and the very poorly paid (servants).

19. Joan Robinson has suggested (in *Economic Heresies* [New York: Basic Books, 1971], p. 93) that control over the price level ultimately depends on the acquiescence of the population in a "traditional" set of hierarchical gradations, so that the determination of a few key wage bargains in fact settles the aggregate wage bill. The increasing "white collar" nature of work and the greater educational exposure of the majority may lessen this means of internalized control, unleashing a "free-for-all" race which no mechanism other than outright controls will be able to restrain.

20. A brief technical footnote seems necessary here. Technology releases the manpower, but its migration into another sector thereafter depends on the demand for commodities originating in the various sectors. Had the demand for agricultural output been extremely elastic, the release of labor through mechanization would have resulted only in a much vaster increase in total farm output than we have in fact experienced. The same applies to manufacturing. It is not only technology, but the inelasticity of demand for "food" (Engels's Law) and the approximately unitary elasticity for manufactured goods that have resulted in the precipitous fall in rural employment and the secular steadiness of manufacturing employment.

21. See J. Schmookler, *Invention and Economic Growth* (Cambridge: Harvard University Press, 1966) for evidence of the role of demand in directing the course of technological discovery and application.
22. See, Robert Heilbroner, "Growth and Survival," *Foreign Affairs,* October 1972, and (with J. Allentuck) "Ecological Balance and the Stationary State," *Journal of Land Economics,* October 1972.
23. On this point see especially the discussion by Adolph Lowe, *On Economic Knowledge* (New York: Harper & Row, 1965, 1970).
24. See Robert Heilbroner, "On the Limits of Economic Prediction," *Between Capitalism and Socialism* (New York: Random House, 1970).
25. Adolph Lowe, "Is Present Day Higher Education 'Relevant'?," *Social Research,* Fall 1971.
26. See again the work of Lowe, *op. cit.,* and my essay "On the Possibility of a Political Economics," *Journal of Economic Issues,* December 1970.

IV. THE MODERN DEBATE: WORKERS OLD AND NEW

A. The Old Worker: Bourgeois, Authoritarian or Radical?

INTRODUCTION

What has been the impact of recent changes in technology, occupational structure, and living standards on the traditional blue-collar worker? A crucial aspect of the modern debate on the working class has centered on the extent to which the rise in manual workers' incomes and consequent changes in their consumption patterns and life styles have blurred the distinction between them and those strata traditionally ranked above them in earlier periods of capitalism. This debate has been particularly lively in England, where it has focused on the concept of the embourgeoisement of the working class, but it has also had its counterpart in the United States.

An American version of the embourgeoisement thesis is presented in Mayer's selection, "The Changing Shape of the American Class Structure." Mayer contends that a significant proportion of the working class has been absorbed into middle-class life styles and values. He suggests that in the middle range of the class structure "we are witnessing the beginning of a classless society in a modern industrial economy." The clear implication of Mayer's position is that the working class, or at least its blue-collar stratum, is in the process of disappearing as a distinct social group with a common life situation.

Harrington sharply disputes this version of the embourgeoisement thesis in "The Old Working Class." He argues that, despite significant shifts in social structure, the worker's subordinate position in the production process and in the labor market is still the ultimate determinant of his distinctive class status and behavior.

Although most recent discussions have focused on the consequences of "affluence" for workers' consumption behavior, a modest literature has developed

115

about their work world. The theory of the integration of the working class re-appears in the contention that in the most progressive branches of industry the distinction between the manual and white-collar worker breaks down and workers increasingly tend to identify with their enterprise.

In "Alienation and Freedom in Perspective," Blauner presents a version of this theory. For Blauner, the Marxian concept of alienation applies to the manufacturing stage of industrial development. Automated industries produce more meaningful work in a more cohesive and integrated industrial setting. Goldthorpe et al. reject this version of the embourgeoisement theory. In the selection from *The Affluent Worker in the Class Structure,* they contend that there has been little qualitative change in the worker's position "in the social organization of production and the constraints and life-chances that he consequently experiences." But at the same time they reject the theory that "consumerism" is a response to alienation at work. They argue that the worker's instrumental attitude toward work stems from the importance that he assigns to consumption. In "Alienated Worker, Alienated Consumer" Gorz presents a radical position suggesting alienated labor produces the "false needs" of a manipulated consumer escaping from work.

For some liberals under the conditions of the cold war, the theory of the revolutionary potential of the working class was transformed into a theory of working-class authoritarianism. In "Working-Class Authoritarianism," Lipset argues that unstable family relationships, economic insecurity, poverty, and inadequate education make the marginal worker more likely to identify with and support antidemocratic movements. A leftist intellectual, he contends, should not be upset to learn that poverty, insecurity, and ignorance do not produce "as 'decent' people as do wealth, security and knowledge."

In "Working-Class Authoritarianism: A Critique," Miller and Riessman contend that Lipset's definition of democracy provides the basis for an emphasis on the authoritarian potential of workers. If other characteristics of democracy such as "the equalitarian, antielitist, cooperative connotations" were stressed, working-class authoritarianism would not be so ominous.

THE CHANGING SHAPE OF THE
AMERICAN CLASS STRUCTURE

Kurt Mayer

. . . The concepts necessary to discern the current shape of the class structure and its probable future changes are not new but it seems to this writer that they are sometimes inadequately handled if not needlessly confused. Certain conceptual distinctions are *not* merely terminological questions and matters of arbitrary definition but are essential for a useful analysis of contemporary social reality.

The first of these distinctions is that between social differentiation and social stratification.[1] Social differentiation refers to the hierarchical ordering of *social positions.* Evidently this is a universal characteristic of all societies since a division of specialized functions and roles is essential for their survival. Inherent in this functional differentiation of roles is a process of evaluation and ranking. Every society not only develops a division of labor but also judges and evaluates the importance of different functions and thereby ranks the positions in its social structure in importance.

Social stratification, on the other hand, refers to the fact that in many, though *not* in all, societies certain *collectivities of people* continue to occupy the same positions through several generations. In other words, *if* societies are stratified there exist groupings of people, social strata, who manage to monopolize access to certain positions on an *hereditary, permanent* basis. Now, some of the conceptual confusion in the field of social stratification arises from the fact that certain theorists of the structural-functional persuasion do not make this distinction but instead define social stratification as "a structure of regularized inequality in which men are ranked higher or lower according to the value accorded to their various *roles and activities.*"[2] Note that this definition refers to stratification as a hierarchy of social *positions,* whereas this writer holds that social strata are collectivities of people who occupy hierarchical positions hereditarily.

To be sure, definitions depend upon one's purpose, but if one uses the functionalist definition of stratification one cannot investigate the relationship between the existence of hierarchies of differentiated positions and the existence—or the absence—of groupings of people who monopolize access to such positions for several generations. This is unfortunate, for the fact is that there do exist societies which are socially diffe.entiated, that is, one finds a division of labor and of functions and roles, with corresponding rank differences and prestige differentials, but where the incumbency of such roles and positions is not hereditary. These are classless societies.

SOURCE: *Social Research,* Winter 1963, pp. 460–468.

It is true that such classless societies are found only among relatively small, non-literate societies which live close to the level of subsistence and in a few types of agricultural communities, such as the Israeli kibbutzim. This poses the fascinating question whether a classless society would be possible in a complex, highly developed industrial society. We shall argue that the answer is yes, and indeed that American society is currently travelling along this road at least part of the way, but we will defer this discussion until later since we must first be concerned with some further conceptual distinctions before the point can be made.

If we want to apprehend the nature of modern societies we cannot perceive their hierarchies of positions as unidimensional. Instead, we must follow the lead of Max Weber and distinguish at least three different rank orders: an economic hierarchy, a prestige hierarchy, and a power hierarchy. Note that these are hierarchies of positions, not of people. But they are interrelated because individuals who hold positions in one order can often, though by no means always, employ this as a basis for also holding corresponding positions in one or both of the other hierarchies. For example, a high position in the economic hierarchy may also support a high position in the prestige hierarchy and in the power hierarchy—but not automatically so, and here lies an important difference between modern industrial societies and earlier social structures.

Certainly, when one looks at the history of Western societies one is impressed with the fact that pre-industrial social structures were all characterized by clear-cut, highly visible and relatively unambiguous divisions not only of social positions but also of social strata. Despite many concrete differences in time and place, the various classes of people were then clearly demarcated and sharply set off from each other because they occupied congruent positions in each of the separate rank orders and because their positions were also hereditary. In feudal society, for example, a man's estate was not only hereditary and legally fixed but also generally implied well-matched positions in the economic, prestige, and power hierachies. Differing sharply in wealth, honor, prestige, and political power, each class was characterized by distinctive patterns of conduct, by a sharp sense of social distance, and by outward symbols of a distinct way of life which placed narrow limits on inter-marriage and social intercourse. At the same time, the prevailing ideologies and religious creeds explained and justified the existing hierarchical arrangements.

The situation is quite different, however, in modern industrial societies where social classes are no longer set apart by tangible, legal boundaries. Of course, the three rank orders of positions exist here, too, and if anything they have become considerably more differentiated and more complex. But in the absence of legal restrictions, dynamic economic, technological and demographic forces have greatly increased the social mobility of individuals and families and of entire groups. This has been accompanied by a democratization of behavior patterns and a change in ideology toward equalitarianism. The result of these massive changes has been two-fold: many indviduals now move up or down the separate rank orders at different rates of speed, thereby creating sizeable proportions of the total population who find themselves at noticeably different levels of the three hierarchies of social position at any given time, a fact which bedevils all unidimensional conceptual schemes of social stratification. At the same time, the increased mobility has also greatly weakened the inheritance of positions, particularly in the middle ranges of the economic, prestige, and power orders. In modern, industrial societies, therefore, social classes still clearly inhabit both the top and the bottom of the rank hierarchies, but they are now beginning to dissolve in the middle. Moreover, since the middle ranges have been greatly expanding, this portends major changes in the shape of the social structure.

If we now focus specifically on American society, we note that impressive changes have taken place during the last quarter century in the positional hierarchies. The most obvious transformation has occurred in the economic hierarchy which no longer represents a pyramid with a broad base, a smaller middle and a narrow top. The pyramid diagram was indeed applicable before World War II, but during the past two decades major shifts have occurred in the occupational structure and in the distribution of incomes. The unskilled occupations and the farm jobs have contracted sharply while the proportion of the labor force working in white collar jobs and in the skilled manual categories has expanded. Well over half of the labor force today is employed in white collar and skilled manual jobs.

The shifts in the distribution of income which have accompanied these changes in the occupational structure have been even more dramatic. In terms of constant (1959) dollars, median family incomes rose 50 per cent during the 1950's alone.[3] Underlying this increase in median family incomes has been a major shift of families upward along the entire income scale. The proportion of families with incomes of less than $5,000 declined from 80 per cent in 1949 to 42 per cent in 1959, while the proportion receiving incomes between $5,000 and $10,000 increased from 17 per cent to 43 per cent during the decade, and families with incomes of $10,000 and over rose from 3 per cent to 15 per cent. Note, however, that despite the remarkable overall rise in income, somewhat more than one-fifth of all American families still had incomes of less than $3,000 in 1959. Despite this very significant lag, to which we shall return later, it is no exaggeration to conclude that the economic rank order of American society has changed its shape from the traditional pyramid to a diamond bulging at the middle and somewhat flat at the bottom.

The transformation of the economic structure has also significantly affected the shape of the prestige hierarchy. The time-honored invidious distinctions between the style of white collar employees and of manual workers have become blurred to a considerable extent. The rising standard of living has made many elements of a middle class style of life, such as home ownership, suburban living, paid vacations, and highly valued consumer goods, available not only to white collar employees but also to large numbers of manual wage earners. Nor has this trend been confined to material status symbols. The economic leveling has been accompanied by a visible "democratization" of behavior patterns. The gap in formal education which has traditionally set the wage worker sharply apart from the white collar employee has been reduced considerably as the median number of school years completed by the American population twenty-five years of age and over rose from 8.6 in 1940 to 10.6 in 1960.[4] The rise in educational achievements, combined with the increasing exposure to the mass media of communication, has induced large numbers of people at the lower social levels to adopt behavior patterns which differ little from those of the higher status circles who, quite significantly, seem to have relaxed stiff etiquette and elaborate social rituals in favor of greater informality, partly because domestic servants have become a vanishing breed.

Most visible, perhaps, has been the diminishing difference in wearing apparel: as the factories have installed lockers and cafeterias, the traditional blue shirts and lunch boxes of the workers have largely disappeared. The sports shirts and slacks they now wear to and from work resemble the increasingly informal attire of the supervisory personnel. Indeed, in growing numbers workers now wear the sports shirts on the job, as automation reduces the number of "dirty" jobs. Similarly, "correct speech" patterns are being diffused more widely by schools and mass media at the same time that standards of English usage are constantly becoming more lax among the well-educated.

To be sure, this assimilation of life styles has not obliterated all status differentials. There remain important differences in food habits, reading tastes, leisure time pursuits, participation in formal and informal associations, church attendance, and so forth, which all serve as badges of belonging to separate status groups. In fact, there is reason to believe that emphasis on subtle prestige differences is increasing precisely because crude and highly visible status differences have become blurred. But the heightening emphasis on symbolic minutiae counts little as compared to the growing proportion of Americans whose style of life is becoming steadily more similar.

Unfortunately, we have much less information about what is happening in the power dimension. This is an area where empirical research has barely begun to penetrate the surface, especially at the national level. Until we get the urgently needed information, it would appear that this hierarchy still retains its pyramid shape. The great mass of the population is apathetic and participates little in the decision-making process. This leaves the field to the relatively small minorities of policy makers and the somewhat larger groups who execute the policies. At the present time it is far from clear whether the national structure of power is monolithic or pluralistic, but there is no doubt that both access to and exercise of power remain more concentrated than the distribution of positions in the economic and prestige rank orders.

Finally, the crucial question of the effects which structural changes in the various hierarchies of roles and positions have had on the collectivities of people who occupy these roles must be raised. How have these changes affected the intergenerational transmission of positions, or the opportunities to attain them? It would appear that we still find rather clearly delimited classes both at the top and the bottom of the positional hierarchies. Here there are segments of the population whose position in all three rank orders is congruent and continues to be transmitted by ascription.

At the top is a numerically small but influential upper class of big businessmen, top corporation officials, independently wealthy men and women, and some professionals who originate from this class or are associated with it. It is difficult to estimate their numbers but one may hazard a guess that they comprise about one half of one per cent of the total population. These people are our economic elite, and most though not all of them move in top prestige circles. Many of them also belong to the power elite, although not all of them avail themselves of the opportunities to exercise power, nor are all men in top power positions necessarily members of the upper class. It is true that this class is not really homogeneous; there are status differences between old upper class families who have been wealthy for generations and whose hallmark is inconspicuousness, and the newer, flashy cafe society circles and Texas billionaires. Still, their way of life, their attitudes, values and tastes differ from those of the rest in many respects and they successfully endeavor to pass on their positions on a hereditary basis.

At the other end of the scale there is a lower class of impoverished people. It comes as something of a shock that in our affluent society there is still a great mass of people who are literally poor and underprivileged in every respect. Who are they? They are the unskilled workers, migrant farm workers, unemployed workers who have been displaced by automation, and many of the nonwhites. How many of them are there? This depends upon the statistical standards used, but even the most conservative yardstick indicates well over thirty million people. This is "the other America" as Michael Harrington has so poignantly described it in a recent book,[5] a submerged fifth of our total population, literally forgotten and invisible to the rest of society. For them poverty is a permanent way of life. Here, too, the three dimensions coincide and the positions at the bottom are also transmitted from father to son. Particularly dismaying is the fact that the prospects for improving their lot and reducing their numbers are not at all bright.

Who is in between these two classes? There are first of all the skilled and semi-skilled urban manual workers, the core of what has been traditionally the working class. They account for about a third of the population, but the traditional dividing line between manual workers and white collar employees no longer holds, because large segments of the working class now share a "white collar" style of life and many also accept middle class values and beliefs. To be sure, we still have a sizeable segment of workers who are not socially mobile, who live in a separate working class culture, emphasizing a philosophy of "getting by" rather than "getting ahead." They, too, form a stable class with congruent, hereditary positions. But one of the great gaps in our current knowledge in the field of social stratification is that we have no reliable information about the size of this group as compared to those manual workers who are mobile or are at least encouraging and urging, successfully for the most part, their children to move out of the working class. These latter form an important segment of the population, of indeterminate size, which is quite literally in transition, with positions no longer congruent and no longer hereditary.

Immediately beyond them is the white collar world, a truly heterogeneous aggregate of salaried employees, independent enterprisers, and professionals. They comprise well over two-fifths of the population. It has been customary to call them middle class and to distinguish between an upper and a lower middle class. It seems to this writer, however, that these designations are losing their validity. Here we have so much mobility that many people hold different positions in the various rank orders and the situation is becoming so fluid that one can no longer truly speak of classes in the middle ranges of positional hierarchies. We therefore boldly conclude that what we have been accustomed to calling the middle class or middle classes is well on the way to losing its class character altogether. What is emerging here is social differentiation without stratification. More and more the bulk of white collar positions are opened up to competition through achievement and ability. They are less and less passed on from generation to generation on the basis of monopolistic pre-emption. Increasingly, there is free upward and downward mobility all the way up and down the widening middle ranges of the economic and prestige hierarchies.

To sum it up, America's social structure today and in the proximate future can be perceived as a diamond where the top and bottom are still pretty rigidly fixed, inhabited by upper and lower classes. A working class of the traditional sort also persists but comprises nowadays only a part of the manual workers. Between the extremes, however, classes are disappearing. To be sure, prestige, power and economic differentials persist here too, of course, and prestige differentials tend even to become accentuated as crude economic differences diminish and lose their visibility. But these differentials are no longer the hallmarks of social classes. In the middle ranges of the various rank orders we are witnessing the beginnings of a classless society in a modern industrial economy. It already involves roughly one-half of our population and may well involve more than that in the future although there are no signs that the top and bottom classes are likely to disappear altogether. This is a somewhat different classless society from that envisaged by Marx a century ago, but it is at least a partially classless society nevertheless.

NOTES

1. Cf. the lucid treatment of this point by Walter Buckley, "Social Stratification and Social Differentiation," *American Sociological Review*, 23 (August 1958), pp. 369–375. See also Dennis H. Wrong, "The Functional Theory of Stratification: Some Neglected Considerations," *American Sociological Review*, 24 (December 1959), pp. 777–782.
2. Bernard Barber, *Social Stratification* (New York: Harcourt, Brace, 1957), p. 7. Italics mine.
3. U.S. Bureau of the Census, *U.S. Census of Population: 1960, General and Economic Characteristics, United States Summary*. Final Report PC (1)–1C (Washington, D.C.: U.S. Government Printing Office, 1962), p. xxix.
4. *Ibid.*, p. xxi.
5. Michael Harrington, *The Other America: Poverty in the United States* (New York: Macmillan, 1962).

THE OLD WORKING CLASS

Michael Harrington

In recent years the American working class has been called conservative, militant, reactionary, progressive, authoritarian, social democratic and, the unkindest cut of all, nonexistent. Except for the last, all the labels fit. The labor movement—I sharpen the focus on the organized section of the working class—contains more blacks than any other institution in American society, as well as more young whites attracted by the populist racism of George Wallace. Notwithstanding its tendencies toward ethnocentrism and antiintellectualism, the labor movement has provided a decisive political impetus for whatever democratic planning there is in America. The organized workers are, in short, no one thing; they are a varied, dynamic, contradictory mass whose position in society can drive its members toward a practical social idealism, an antisocial corporatism, or any one of the complicated variants between those extremes.

I believe that the American workers have been a crucial force behind every social gain of the past two generations, and in domestic politics their unions constitute an American kind of de facto social democracy. Perhaps the exigencies of the future will deepen the best impulses within the labor movement, and I am on the side of those within it who are fighting for such a development. But my partisanship does not make me an apologist. Precisely because I am concerned and involved, I cannot afford to gloss over tendencies that run counter to my hopes. I must try to understand the past and present of the working class with as much candor as possible if I am to help those struggling to create its future. In these pages I will try to do that by way of a broad overview of the organized and organizable working class. Insofar as I deal with history, it will be in order to understand the current position of the unions and the various futures it could make possible. But before that can be attempted, I must define a vexing term: the working class. There are serious scholars who argue that it no longer exists in America. My conclusion, however, will be that there is not simply one working class in America but two—an old working class still quite vital and a new working class being created by political and economic evolution.

It is an extraordinary thing that those who argue there is no working class in the United States can be found at the most disparate points of the political spectrum. Herbert Marcuse, who had a notable influence on the New Left youth of the 1960s, writes that " 'the people,' previously the ferment of social change, have 'moved up' to become the ferment of social cohesion." Paul Sweezy and the late Paul Baran, sympathizers first with Russian, then with Chinese Communism, argued that the organized workers in the United States have been "integrated into

SOURCE: *Dissent,* Winter 1972, pp. 146–158.

the system as consumers and ideologically conditioned members of the society."
Arthur Schlesinger, Jr., an activist liberal, says

> that the lines of division in our politics have fundamentally altered. The
> issues are no longer social or economic so much as they are cultural
> and moral. It is no longer the common men against the boss as much
> as it is the rational against the indignant, the planner against the spoiler,
> the humanist against the uneducated, the young against the old.

Perhaps the most emphatic statement of the theme comes from Clark Kerr, a
brilliant, pragmatic technocrat. He holds that "the working class not only tends
to disappear as a class-conscious and recognizable element in society; it needs to
disappear if modern industrial society is to operate with full effectiveness." High
technology, he continues, requires consensus and cooperation and therefore cannot tolerate class conflict over basic principles. So even though there are obvious
differences between industrialists and file clerks, there are not "any clear class
lines to divide them—only infinite gradations."

I disagree with those, from the authoritarian Left to the democratic Center,
who think that the American working class does not exist (the Right, which I
will not consider here, tends to have a vulgar Marxist, or paranoid, version of
the power of organized labor). To use Marx's famous distinction, the working
class in this country is not simply a class "in itself"—a mass sharing "a common
situation and common interests"—but it is a class "for itself" and the "interests
which it defends . . . [are] class interests."

First of all, consider the "old" working classes: the primarily blue-collar workers who do physical labor in the industrial economy. It has renewed itself in the
last quarter of a century and become a greater force in American politics than
at any time in the nation's history.

The total nonagricultural labor force in 1969 numbered 77.902 million men
and women. Of these, 48.993 million were "production and nonsupervisory workers on private payrolls," with the 14.647 million in manufacturing the largest
single component. Another 12.591 million were employed by federal, state, and
local government, and many of them held down such blue-collar and organizable
jobs as sanitation man or postman. There were 20.210 million union members
mainly concentrated in machinery, transportation equipment, contract construction, and transportation services.

Among the unorganized one would find the working poor, who numbered close
to 4 million in 1969 according to the government's optimistic definition of poverty. An almost equal number of the "near poor" (who include more whites and
tend more to live in families headed by a male than do the poor themselves)
were largely outside the unions. Those neither poor nor union members are most
numerous in wholesale and retail trade, in finance, insurance, real estate, and the
service industries. A good number of these are, of course, white-collar workers,
and not a few of them receive wage increases from anti-union employers whenever organized labor in the industry, or the area, makes a gain.

This working class, both organized and unorganized, has a "common situation
and common interests," experienced first and foremost in the reality that it does
not have enough money. In 1969 the Bureau of Labor Statistics computed a
"modest" budget for an urban family of four at $9,076, an amount in excess of

the income of well over half the families in the United States. The trade unionists, most of whom are among the better-off members of the "old" working class, do not achieve this standard: they are neither poor nor affluent but in-between and distinctly deprived. In September of 1969 the "average production worker" took home $102.44 for a full week's work and manufacturing workers, most of whom were organized, only received $106.75. Moreover, since these figures were computed, the cost of living has gone up by almost 20 percent and the real wage of the workers has slightly decreased.

Even if one upgrades all of these numbers because of the enormous increase in the number of working wives—18 million of them in 1969, double the figure for 1960—who add an average of 25 percent to their family income, the total still falls short of the government's modest budget. The "modest" standard, it must be emphasized, lives up to its name: it allows for a two-year-old used car and a new suit every four years. In addition to this deficiency in income, most of the union members are employed in manufacturing, construction, and transportation, i.e., in jobs with little intrinsic interest and, in the case of an assembly line in an auto plant, a dehumanizing routine. They are paid not as individuals but as members of a class: after the age of 25, the worker's income does not normally vary with increasing experience, as does that of professional and managerial employees, but usually rises as part of a negotiated group settlement. Indeed, the very fact of being paid a wage by the hour emphasizes another determinant of working-class existence, the vulnerability of the job to the vagaries of the business cycle, the ever-present possibility of being laid off.

Every governmental projection indicates a substantial increase during the next decade in the number of Americans who live under such conditions. The only category of industrial workers that will be in both absolute and relative decline over that period is that of the nonfarm laborers, which is supposed to fall from 3.6 to 3.5 million. But the number of operatives and craftsmen will increase, and the unions that were created because of the common interest of this great mass are certain to grow in the foreseeable future into the largest membership organizations in the society. In 1980, then, the "old" working class will be larger than ever before in American history.

How is it that such a massive social phenomenon and such obvious trends have been ignored, or declared nonexistent, by many observers? In part, as Penn Kemble has argued, the vantage point of intellectual perception has changed radically during the past 30 years. The social critics of the 1960s and early '70s are relatively affluent compared to the marginality and even joblessness they had experienced during the Depression. This change in their own class position may have made them less sensitive to the daily struggles of less favored people. At the crudest this indifference could be rationalized by confusing the relative decline in fanufacturing jobs—they accounted for 39.3 percent of nonagricultural employment in 1919 and only for 28.8 percent in 1969—with an absolute decrease in the number of workers and a consequent loss of political and social power. This error was sometimes abetted by a failure to explore the fine print in the governmental definitions in which, to take one pertinent example, laundry workers, garage repairmen, and dishwashers in the service industries are not classified as blue collar.

Somewhat more subtly, there were those who acknowledged the existence of the traditional working class but argued that it had become co-opted by the society and therefore lost its distinctive character. But that, as we have just seen, is a misleading simplification. It may be that the workers, as Sweezy and Baran argue, want to be "integrated into the society as consumers," but it is surely of greater moment that the structure of injustice will not allow them, as a rule, even a "modest" income.

Still, the most sophisticated revision of the idea of the working class is based upon a very real, and momentous, shift in class structure (a shift that is also, as will be seen, the key to the emergence of a "new" working class). It is argued that economic classes defined by property relationships—entrepreneurs owning factories, shopkeepers their little businesses, farmers and peasants their plots of land, and workers possessing only their labor power to sell—have become obsolete. The joint stock company, Ralf Dahrendorf holds, separated ownership and control and thereby obviated a theory of class determined by property or the lack of it. He concludes that in the advanced economies authority, not ownership, is central to the formation of social class. And Alain Touraine writes, "it is anachronistic to depict social armies confronting each other. As we pass from societies of accumulation to programmed societies, relationships of power become increasingly more important than opposition between social groups."

These theories are usually developed with the comment that Marx, fixated as he was upon a primitive model of capitalism, was unaware of such changes. I will deal with this historical error in a footnote, since it is not central to the main line of this analysis.[1] For even granting that there have been profound transformations in the structure of the advanced economies, some of them unforeseen by even so perspicacious a thinker as Marx, what is it that makes the workers I have just described more likely to join unions than any group in society? What predisposes them toward a certain political point of view? The answer, I believe, is embarrassingly old-fashioned. These workers derive their livelihoods almost exclusively from the sale of their labor power on an anonymous, and uncertain, labor market and it is quite easy to distinguish them from their "fellow employees" who are corporation presidents or managers. There is a social chasm between these groups, not the infinite gradations postulated by Clark Kerr.

To begin with, in the upper reaches of the society property is not quite so passé as the notion of a clear-cut "separation" of ownership and control suggests. A 1967 *Fortune* survey revealed that 30 percent of the 500 largest industrial concerns "are clearly controlled by identifiable individuals or by family groups." And, as that survey pointed out, absolute numbers can be more revealing than percentages when one deals with the holdings of the executive officer of a multi-billion-dollar corporation. The board chairman of General Motors at that time "only" owned 0.017 percent of the enterprise over which he presided—but that little fraction was worth $3.917 million. The chairman of Chrysler, with a mere 0.117 percent of his company's stock, had a $2.380 million interest in the business.

More generally, the nonowning managers at the top of the society accumulate wealth. They often enjoy special stock deals and other arrangements: in 1971 the *Wall Street Journal* reported that the biggest part of executive pay in the auto industry was a bonus based on the size of profits. So it is that these managers must be counted among the golden elite, the 6½ percent of the American consumer units which, in December 1962 (there has been no downward redistribution since), had incomes of $50,000 a year or more and owned 57 percent of the wealth of the society. At stake here is not simply the annual pay but, in

Herman Miller's definition of wealth, "the sum total of equity in a home or business, liquid assets, investment assets, the value of automobiles owned and miscellaneous assets held in trust, loans to individuals, oil royalties, etc." By that standard, the "nonowning" managers own quite a bit.

The middle levels of management, particularly in the modern corporations, are not so easy to define and will be discussed at greater length in the section on the "new" working class. Now it is enough to note that this labor market is not anonymous, its salaries are not determined on a class basis, as in the case of workers, and it is less subject to the ups and downs of the business cycle. Some of the halcyon notions of the security of these strata were rudely dispelled by the recent Nixon recession, yet no one should have any trouble in distinguishing it from the lot of the wage workers.

So there is a distinct and identifiable universe of the working class even after one has taken into account the tremendous changes in class structure since Marx. The pay is better now, the boom-and-bust rhythm has been attenuated, the famous built-in stabilizers, such as unemployment insurance, are at work. Yet there are crucial elements of working-class life—relative deprivation, the impersonality of the work process, greater susceptibility to layoffs than experienced by other groups in the society, group wages—which remain and are the objective determinants of the class itself. Perhaps one of the best statements of this reality was made in the study of the English affluent worker carried out under the direction of John H. Goldthorpe and David Lockwood.

This project subjected the thesis of the *embourgeoisement* of the working class in that country to a careful empirical examination. It concluded that in England this cooptation simply had not taken place:

> A factory worker can double his living standards and still remain a man who sells his labour to an employer in return for wages; he can work at a control panel rather than on an assembly line without changing his subordinate position in the organization of production; he can live in his own house in a "middle class" estate or suburb and still remain little involved in white collar social worlds.

English data cannot, of course merely be imported to America and applied to the quite different variant of capitalism that exists here. Yet the objective indices show that in the United States as in England the worker is not an integrated participant in affluence but a member of a quite distinct stratum. And this stratum, for the most part, is neither poor nor modestly well off, indeed is better off than ever before—yet still quite deprived. But these statistics are of little political and intellectual significance if they simply describe unrelated facts about an inert mass. One has to come to the second part of Marx's famous distinction: Is the "old" working class a class "for itself," does it act collectively from a consciousness of its position in society?

A preliminary warning: If one looks for a "European"-type class consciousness in the United States—something like the attitude of that Frenchman, who when T. S. Eliot accidentally jostled him, responded, "Me, I am a proletarian exploited by the capitalist class"—it cannot be found. It is not even necessary for my purposes that a majority of the workers use the term, working class, to describe their position in society. (When asked to locate themselves on a three-class scale of upper, middle, and lower, the overwhelming majority of Americans, including the members of the AFL–CIO, will say that they are middle-class; but on a five-class scale, on which the working class is in between the poor and the middle class, many more will identify themselves as working class.) I am not in search of a rhetoric but want to describe how workers behave politically in order to maximize goals which go beyond their immediate self-interest, or even the narrow advantage of their craft and skill, and which have to do with the needs of the entire class and through it of the nation itself.

There are two major lines of argument, sometimes convergent, which hold that, even though there may be objective determinants of class in America, there has either never been or cannot now be any significant mass consciousness of that fact, moving workers to political or social action. On the one hand, it is said that the exceptional historical character of the national experience prevented the development of such a consciousness. On the other hand, it is claimed that the recent evolution of the American economy has produced a consensus in which interest groups compete over the details of the distribution of wealth but classes no longer contest more basic questions of the very mode of allocation itself.

The theory that America has always been immune from the class struggle is the generalization of a profound half-truth.[2] A country without a feudal past, possessing a vast continent to be settled once genocide had been committed against the Indians, and populated by successive waves of immigrants from the most varied European backgrounds, must differ in a number of crucial ways from the nation-states of the Old World where capitalism first emerged. Lenin wrote of America (and Britain) that there were "exceptionally favorable conditions, in comparison with other countries, for the deep-going and widespread development of capitalism."

Morris Hilquit, theorist of American socialism in the first third of the century, also talked of the "exceptional position" of America with its vast land mass, its prosperous agriculture, its tendency to make wage labor seem only a "temporary condition." But once we grant the apparent uniqueness of American capitalism, is it indeed true that class consciousness failed to play an important, much less a decisive, role in the nation's history? I think not. The conditions we describe as "American exceptionalism" slowed the emergence of that consciousness and even made its anticapitalism seem formally procapitalist. It did not, however, stop social class from becoming the most important single determinant in our political life.

Moreover, the chief factor inhibiting and distorting working-class self-consciousness was not, as is widely thought, the wealth of the society. Werner Sombart's famous remark that socialism in America ran aground "on shoals of roast beef and apple pie" was made in 1906 and has survived as a myth until this day. But, in a history of American labor (edited by that patriarch of the nonclass interpretation, J. R. Commons), Don Lescohier described as follows the two decades prior to World War I:

> Undergoing the vicissitudes of repeated periods of unemployment, experiencing in many occupations a less rapid rise of wages than living costs, [the wage earners] could see that while some groups, like the building mechanics, had made distinct progress, other groups, like the iron and steel workers, employees in meat packing plants, cotton mills,

saw mills, tobacco and clothing factories had not held their own against the rapidly rising cost of living.

Indeed, if one compares Germany and the United States between 1890 and 1914, the workers experienced steadily a relative rise in their living standards in the country that produced a mass social democratic movement rather than in the one that did not. But if it was not prosperity that prevented the development of a socialist class consciousness in America, what was it? Selig Perlman provided part of the answer in his seminal *Theory of The Labor Movement:*

> American labor remains the most heterogeneous laboring class in existence—ethnically, religiously and culturally. With a working class of such composition, to make socialism or communism the official "ism" of the movement would mean, even if other conditions permitted it, deliberately driving the Catholics, who are perhaps a majority in the American Federation of Labor, out of the labor movement, since with them an irreconcilable opposition to socialism is a matter of religious principle. Consequently, the only acceptable "consciousness" for American labor as a whole is "job consciousness" with a limited objective of "wage and job control." . . .

Perlman was right: heterogeneity made it impossible to organize the great mass of the newly arriving European workers until the '30s and acted, in a thousand different ways, to impede consciousness of membership in a single and united class. Yet Perlman was wrong: even in the '20s when he wrote, and much more so later on, the workers were constantly forced by the exigencies of their class situation to go beyond "wage and job control" and raise class issues about the organization of the entire society. Strangely enough, many scholars failed to take note of this significant phenomenon. For they had adopted, even when they were antisocialist, the criteria of the left wing of the Socialist party: that class consciousness must necessarily and exclusively take the form of allegiance to a socialist or worker's party. That party alliance did not come about; class consciousness did.

So by the early 1920s the majority of the AFL rebelled against Gompers's hostility to social legislation, adopted an approach very much like the one embodied in the socialist proposals that had been rejected during the 1890s, and embarked upon a course that led to an alliance with the Socialist party in the Conference for Progressive Political Action and support for the La Follette campaign in 1924. In 1920 the AFL was in favor of public ownership of the utilities, organization of cooperatives, and workmen's compensation. The railroad men were for the nationalization of their industry, and the Chicago Federation of Labor was in favor of a labor party. The AFL, as Phillip Taft has written of the period, "found itself, against its wishes, propelled into more active political participation." These developments did not, for the reasons Perlman described among others, take place in the guise of a socialist class consciousness. But they were a clear indication that workers were being driven to consider not simply their jobs but the society as a whole.

The class-conscious movement of the '20s did not succeed and in the latter half of the decade there was a reversion to Gomper's "voluntarist" philosophy.

But the reason for this reversal involved a trend that was to prepare the way for the great explosion of working-class militancy in the '30s. With immigration severely restricted after World War I, the expanding economy of the mid-1920s recruited its new workers from the farm and thus tipped the national demographic balance from rural to urban. The initial impact of this progressive turn of events was conservative. Ordinarily, one would have expected the unions to have grown and bettered their wages and working conditions during prosperity, but the influx of farmers, who could be satisfied by cheap wages and were suspicious of group action, depressed the labor market. The war and postwar militancy had driven the average weekly wage in manufacture up to $26.30 in 1920, but in 1921 wages dropped to $22.18 and in 1929 they had only reached $25.03, more than a dollar below the level of 1920.

Still, two momentous events had taken place in the '20s. The American working class was no longer a port of entry for millions of the foreign-born and was becoming, for the first time in its history, homogeneous; and labor was now part of a new urban majority. Once the discrepancy between low wages and high productivity in the '20s helped bring about the Great Depression, these developments were of enormous importance. They helped promote the organization of industrial workers in the CIO and were a major reason why a vast political movement based on class became a crucial feature of politics in the '30s. Richard Hofstadter, one of the few scholars to recognize the importance of this fact, wrote, "The demands of a large and powerful labor movement combined with the interests of the unemployed, gave the New Deal a social democratic tinge that had never before been present in American reform movements."

For all the dramatic struggles of the 1930s, it is clear in retrospect that the working class was not in a revolutionary mood. This point must be stressed because many scholarly critics of the notion of a class struggle in the U.S. have unwittingly adopted, not simply a Marxian definition of the concept, but a "romantic" Marxian definition. For Raymond Aron, a seminal theorist of the notion of "industrial society" (i.e., of consensus capitalism), the class struggle only exists where there is a "fight to the death" between workers and capitalists which eventuates in violence.

Such an idea can indeed be found in The Communist Manifesto, for it is a corollary of Marx's youthful error of supposing that society was fast polarizing into only two classes. But the mature Marx did not hold this view and defined the class struggle in a far more subtle and complex fashion which can also serve as an excellent guide to the reality of the American 1930s—and '70s. In his famous Inaugural Address to the International Workingmen's Association, Marx spoke of a campaign to restrict the working day to ten hours in England as "a struggle between the blind rule of supply and demand, which is the political economy of the middle class, and the social control of production through intelligence and foresight, which is the political economy of the working class."[3]

The kind of class struggle envisioned in The Manifesto did not emerge in the America of the 1930s or since; the kind analyzed in the Inaugural Address has. Given the obvious exigencies of the situation, the workers were committed as a class—and with the elections of 1936, organized as a class—to win full-employment policies requiring that the government manage the economy. But if the American workers thus committed themselves to "the social control of production through intelligence and foresight, which is the political economy of the working class," they did not call this policy "socialist." It was not simply that the historic factors identified by Perlman were at work. Beyond that, as Leon Samson has argued in a fascinating book, Americanism had become a kind of "substitutive socialism." In this country, as distrinct from Europe, bourgeois ideology itself stressed equality, classlessness, and the opportunity to share in wealth.

So in the '30s there emerged a mass political movement based upon class institutions (the unions) which demanded, not simply narrow legislation related to the needs of this or that trade or craft, but a mode of planned social organization that would give priority to the value of full employment. Since it involved significant modifications of capitalist society as it had existed until then in the United States, this idea met with violent resistance, both physical and ideological, from most employers. They recognized that, even though the worker insisted upon his loyalty to the American ideal, he was reading it in terms of his own class needs.

Thus I would argue that, for all of its truly exceptional characteristics, American capitalism eventually forced its working class to become conscious of itself and to act as a major factor in political life. The theorists of industrial, or post-industrial, society might even grant this historical case. And they would add that in the period after World War II changes in capitalist society led to the virtual disappearance of that class struggle.

Raymond Aron was an early advocate of this view. Economic conflicts over wages and hours, he said, are quite real.

> It is pure hypocrisy to think that they are always resolved in an equitable fashion, pure hypocrisy to deny a struggle over the division of the national income. But it does not thereby happen that, on the strictly economic plane, the group of workers and the group of capitalists oppose one another in a fight to the death, each one having an *essential* interest opposed to the other. The common interest of both, within the framework of the system [*cadre du régime*] is the prosperity of the enterprise and of the economy; it is growth whose necessary conditions correspond simultaneously to the interests of the managers and the employees.

Daniel Bell transposed Aron's thesis for America. There was, he said in the 1950s, an end of ideology. At certain points in his writing that phrase referred to the disappearance of grandiose simplifications about society, a happy event from any point of view. But at other points it announced a controversial trend: the disappearance from Western political life of debate and conflict over fundamental questions, a fading away of the very notion that there should or could be alternative forms of social organization. There was, Bell said,

> a rough consensus among intellectuals on political issues: the acceptance of the Welfare State; the desirability of decentralized power; a system of mixed economy and of political pluralism. . . . [And] the workers, whose grievances were once the driving energy for social change, are more satisfied with the society than the intellectuals. The workers have not achieved utopia but their expectations were less than those of the intellectuals and their gains correspondingly larger.

In a much more recent statement of this theme Bell wrote that the secret of Western society was "productivity." "Economic life could be a non zero-sum game; everyone could end up a winner, though with differential gains." But hardly had the end of ideology been proclaimed than the most tumultuous ideological decade in recent history began—the 1960s. There was a veritable explosion of ideology in the institutions of mass higher education in the advanced economies. And the workers, most dramatically in France and Italy, but in America too, kept challenging the differential distribution of gains in strike after strike.

Was this merely a case of groups struggling bitterly over the terms of a consensus? Or, to take Aron's criterion of the most crucial precondition for the existence of a social class, was there a consciousness on the part of those American workers that "their class has a unique destiny and that it cannot fulfill its vocation except by transforming the totality [ensemble] of the social organization"? If the question is posed in this way, so reminiscent of both the early Marx and the early Lukacs, then there was no class struggle in America. Yet it can be demonstrated that American labor was by now more than a mere interest group. Its class consciousness lies somewhere between the polar extremes of revolutionary transformation and interest politics.

There is, for instance, no question that the intrapersonal culture of the working class has been largely subverted by such changes in class structure as the movement of workers to the suburbs or the achievement of limited access to the consumption-oriented (and rigged) society. As Bennet Berger has documented, it is only in the old working-class neighborhoods, usually ethnic in character, that one finds a face-to-face and daily sense of a common class plight. The old coal-mining towns of Appalachia would be the most obvious example of the vanishing conditions under which social class pervades all aspects of life. But even in looking back, it is wrong to romanticize such working-class neighborhoods or to attribute to them, in Serge Mallet's phrase, a "pseudo-globalness." For instance, the Italian workers who were jammed together in New York before and after World War I were more loyal to their village in the old country, and to the *padroni* who exploited them here, than to their class.

Still, it seems obvious today, in contrast to a generation or two ago, that the worker does not enter a class community when he leaves the factory but rather participates more and more in the nonclass world of consumption. That has its positive side, as Herbert Gans discovered in his study of Levittown. The suburbanized worker, he learned, was not homogenized by the experience as much as critics of the '50s had thought. He became less localistic and suspicious, more inclined to participate in civic and political life. But, I would add, in becoming more of a "citizen" he became less of a worker.

Yet, even as there were trends making the impact of classlessness pervasive in the daily life of the individual worker, the labor movement was moving into politics in a much more profound way than in the 1930s. By the end of the '60s, the AFL–CIO, the Auto Workers, and the Teamsters all supported an ongoing political apparatus which, in terms of money, lobbying, campaign workers, and the like, was a major factor in the United States. As David Greenstone documents in his book *Labor in American Politics,* "the emergence of organized labor as a major, nationwide electoral organization of the national Democratic Party was the most important change in the *structure* of the American party system during the last quarter of a century."

This signified the organization of a class, not merely an interest group. An interest group, as Greenstone points out, has very specific demands and avoids committing itself to a single party or a broad social program out of fear that it will compromise its narrow goals. Big corporations, which tend to be Republican, usually maintain a "Democratic" vice-president to insure access to the White House no matter what. But the unions increasingly have become an organized component of the Democratic party. As Greenstone points out, they could have made a classic interest-group deal in the '60s. If the AFL–CIO had agreed to let Everett Dirksen's Congressional override of the Supreme Court's one man/one vote rule go through, Dirksen would have permitted the repeal of the federal enabling clause for state "right to work" laws. Such action on the latter issue would have meant the successful culmination of a trade union campaign of more than two decades' duration. Yet labor maximized its long-range political program by standing fast on one man/one vote rather than giving priority to its short-range organizational goals.

The unions thus became a class political force, even if in a fairly undramatic way. There was little rhetoric of class war. Yet the very appearance of national health insurance as a political issue is primarily the result of a campaign waged for years by George Meany and Walter Reuther. Even in the area of race, where so many observers tend to pit blacks against the unions, labor is the most integrated single institution in U.S. society and has done more to raise the living standards of black Americans than any force, except the federal government. Part of the confusion over this momentus trend stems from a reliance on polling data in most academic accounts of the labor movement. It is precisely the characteristic of an opinion poll that it reaches a man or woman as he or she is isolated and poses questions in a kind of political and social vacuum. It is therefore admirably suited to reflect the privatized area of a worker's mind but what it omits—as elections do not—is the effect of his participation in a workaday world, his membership in a class.

It is a failure to confront this complex reality that makes Derek Bok and John T. Dunlop miss the significance of trade union political action in their study of *Labor and the American Community*. They point out that, as recorded in the opinion polls, the workers have been giving decreasing support to union political action, and that their unions have become more and more political. The polls, I would suggest, do capture some private elements of workers' responses which in recent years have become more marked. But the elections reveal the much more significant fact that by and large those same workers vote massively in national elections for the Democratic candidates endorsed by their union. What Bok and Dunlop miss, then, is the class political attitude of the workers which is not at all the same as, and sometimes even contradicts, the sum totals of their private views. In 1968, for instance, the polls indicated significant support for George Wallace among young white workers in the North during the early fall. Yet when election day came, most of those same workers voted for Hubert Humphrey. Most of them had not changed their personal prejudices in the process, but they had understood that the exigencies of their class situation demanded they vote for a full-employment economy rather than against blacks— i.e., for Humphrey, not Wallace.

This kind of collectivism is far from the romantic Marxian consciousness as defined by Aron, but it is distinctive and clearly goes beyond narrow organizational interests. Moreover, there are a good many indications that the unions will be forced to be even more political in the coming period.

It is now apparent, even to its sophisticated devotees, that the free market is utterly incapable of allocating the resources of a technological society in a rational fashion. In 1971 Daniel Bell, who only a decade earlier had talked of the end of ideology, wrote,

> It seems clear to me that, today, we in America are moving away from a society based on a private enterprise market system toward one in which the most important economic decisions will be made at the political level, in terms of consciously defined "goals" and "priorities." In the past there was an unspoken consensus and the public philosophy did not need to be articulated. And this was a strength, for articulation often invites trials for force when implicit differences are made manifest. Today, however, there is a visible change from market to non-market political decision making.

This marks, Bell concludes, "a movement away from governance by political economy to governance by political philosophy."

It is on the basis of this analysis that Bell has been writing about a "post-industrial" society in which the decisive "new men" are the

> scientists, the mathematicians, the economists and the engineers of the new computer technology. . . . The leadership of the new society will rest, not with business or corporations as we have known them (for a good deal of production will be routinized) but with the research corporation, the industrial laboratories, the experimental stations and the universities.

But which values will determine the priorities of these new men? Bell and John Kenneth Galbraith, whose "educational-scientific estate" is another name for the "new men," assume that these educated and generally liberal administrators of power will be able to pursue their own goals. That hope has been around for years and was brilliantly formulated by Thorstein Veblen in his essay collection *The Engineers and the Price System,* which dates back to 1919. The problem is that, from Veblen's day to this, the corporations have been profit-maximizers— more and more sophisticated in their definition of profit, to be sure—and have placed their own interests above those of the society or of the engineers who work for them. The automobile companies, to take a dramatic recent example, have been fighting auto safety and pollution controls for years.

It is at this point that the politics of the American working class become crucial. For if it is indeed true that economic decisions will be increasingly made by a political rather than a market process; if the question is how to manage the economy rather than whether to do so, then what mass force is there in society to fight for social values? Some "new men" might join a progressive political coalition in their off-duty hours but, under present conditions, their working lives will be dominated by corporate values that oppose, or at least would severely limit, any restriction on the company's freedom of action. Moreover, the corporations tend to favor reactionary Keynesianism, in which the economy is stimulated by incentives to capital rather than through the meeting of human needs, which is social Keynesianism. The largest and most effective force in the society with a commitment to that kind of progressive Keynesianism is the trade union movement.

In August 1971, when Richard Nixon tacitly admitted the bankruptcy of *laissez-faire* ideas which had created an ingenious recession-inflation, labor reacted in characteristic fashion. Nixon had proposed a federal job cut and a retreat from welfare reform, strict wage controls, vague price controls, and no limit on profits, dividends, and other forms of upper-class compensation. He further proposed an investment tax credit on machinery produced by American companies, a measure that might give business a $5 billion benefit (which would have to be added to the better than $3 billion a year earlier offered by the President in the form of accelerated depreciation for the corporations).

The AFL–CIO Executive Council responded:

> Instead of extending the helping hand of the federal government to the poor, the unemployed, the financially strapped states and cities, and to the inflation-plagued consumer, the President decided to further enrich big corporations and banks. . . . Mr. Nixon's program is based on the infamous "trickle down" theory. It would give huge sums of money belonging to the people of the United States to big corporations. He would do this at the expense of the poor, the state and local governments and their employees and wage and salary earners.

The AFL–CIO was here articulating what Marx called "the political economy of the working class" as it applies in a post-Keynesian society. This response is rooted in the class position of the members of the labor movement. They stand to gain from redistributionist federal policies favoring those either subaffluent or poor; they are opposed to a management of the economy that maximizes the interests of corporations. The difference between these two versions of Keynesianism is, I would suggest, both profound and systematic. Which one of them prevails will determine much about the shape of the future.

When Irving Louis Horowitz asks skeptically why the "interest-determined demands of the working class are somehow instinctively and intuitively more progressive than those of other sectors," he overlooks the union's stand on such an issue. It is the result, not of instinct or intuition, but of class position. For there is a working class "for itself" with a political consciousness that goes far beyond "job consciousness" and expresses itself in social reformism toward the society as a whole. This class consciousness is not revolutionary but, in practical and programmatic terms, it is remarkably similar to that found among the social democrats of Europe—even when it is sometimes couched in an antisocialistic rhetoric. It is not based on that "world apart" of intrapersonal class values which existed at an earlier stage of capitalism. It might be more accurately described, to use a term employed by the British students of the affluent worker, as an "instrumental collectivism.". . .

NOTES

1. In *The Communist Manifesto* Marx unquestionably thought society was polarizing into a giant working class and a tiny bourgeoisie and held to a rather simplistic, property-determined theory of social class. But as early as 1856, Marx, whom Dahrendorf charges with not having understood the importance of the joint stock company, wrote,

"It cannot be denied that the application of the joint stock company to industry characterizes a new epoch in the economic life of modern nations." (Marx-Engels, *Werke* [hereafter *MEW*], Dietz Verlag, Berlin, 1953, XII, p. 33.) In a famous letter to Engels in 1858 in which he outlined *Das Kapital,* he indicated that the culmination of his analysis—which was never written—would deal with "stock capital as the most developed form [of capitalism] with all the contradictions." (*MEW,* XXIX, p. 312.)

In the third volume of *Das Kapital,* Marx did refer briefly to the separation of ownership and control, and Engels added a note when he published the volume after Marx's death saying that this trend had become even more important. In the revised edition of his famous popularization of Marxism, *Anti-Duhring,* Engels was even more emphatic on this count. (*MEW,* XX, p. 617.) Moreover in the posthumously published *Theories of Surplus Value,* Marx not only discussed the appearance of new middle strata linked to the phenomenon of the corporation but saw them as an inevitable outcome of the capitalist dynamic itself. (*MEW,* XXVI: Pt. 1, p. 190.) Why, then, did Marx fail to include this material in his own theory of class? The answer is found on the last page of Volume III of *Das Kapital.* It constitutes only the second page of Marx's discussion of classes and it concludes: "Here the manuscript breaks off." But even though death prevented Marx from formally and systematically revising the simplifications and errors of the *Manifesto,* it is clear that he understood that the class structure of his own time was being profoundly modified by the separation of ownership and control. Much of what Dahrendorf, and others, present as a critique of Marx is thus only Marxian common sense.

2. What follows is a summary of a much more detailed, and documented, analysis to be found in my *Socialism* (New York: Saturday Review Press, 1972).

3. Those who wished to downgrade this speech usually argue that Marx was making pragmatic political concessions to the British trade unionists who were so important to him in the First International. But, as I document at length in my book *Socialism,* the tactic of the Inaugural was central to the politics to Marx and Engels from the late '50s to the time of their respective deaths. There was a brief period during and after the Paris Commune when responding to Bakuninist critics on their left and the vilifiers of the Commune on their Right, they seemed to turn back to the language and mood of the *Manifesto.* But that was only an episode. It is, however, important to note that there is one basic oversimplification in the Inaugural. As early as the mid-1850s, in his analysis of the "imperial socialism" of Napoleon III, Marx had understood that the conservatives and reactionaries could use collectivist methods to serve their own purposes. (*MEW,* XII, pp. 24, 27, 33.) This notion was deepened, particularly by Engels, in response to Bismarckian "socialism" and led to the theory of "state socialism" in which government intervenes on behalf of the bourgeoisie. So a more comprehensive Marxian development of the formulation in the Inaugural would emphasize that the "intelligence and foresight" would have to be exercised by and for the workers, not by and for Bonapartists, Bismarckians, fascists, Stalinists, Maoists, etc.

ALIENATION AND FREEDOM IN PERSPECTIVE

Robert Blauner

. . . In the complex and diversified manufacturing sector of an advanced industrial society, at least three major kinds of blue-collar factory work exist at the same time: the traditional manual skill associated with craft technology; the routine low-skilled manual operations associated with machine and assembly-line technologies; and the "non-manual" responsibility called forth by continuous-process technology.[1] Although craft skill will continue to play a significant role, the shift from skill to responsibility is the most important historical trend in the evolution of blue-collar work. The relative decline of unskilled, standardized jobs is, in the long run, a positive development;[2] however, a considerable amount of the routine work that negates the dignity of the worker will very likely persist in the foreseeable future.

TECHNOLOGY, FREEDOM, AND THE WORKER'S SOUP

Of the several dimensions of alienation, the impact of technology is greatest with respect to powerlessness, since the character of the machine system largely determines the degree of control the factory employee exerts over his socio-technical environment and the range and limitations of his freedom in the work situation. In general, the long-run developments in this area parallel the historical evolution in blue-collar work. The interconnection between traditional manual skill and control is so intimate that theoretical distinctions between the two concepts become blurred: the very definition of traditional skill imples control over tools, materials, and pace of work. It is therefore no surprise that printers and other workers in craft technologies command a variety and degree of freedom unrivaled in the blue-collar world.

Machine technology generally reduces the control of the employee over his work process. Workers are rarely able to choose their own methods of work, since these decisions have been incorporated into the machines' very design and functioning. In the textile industry, pace and output are determined by the machine system and the organization of tasks; for the most part, operatives simply respond to the rhythms and exigencies of the technical system instead of initiating activity and exerting control.[3] In the assembly-line technology of the automobile industry, the worker's control is reduced to a minimal level. The

SOURCE: *Alienation and Freedom: The Factory Worker and His Industry* (Chicago: University of Chicago Press, 1967), pp. 169–182.

conveyor-belt apparatus dictates most movements of the operative and pre-empts many of his potential choices and decisions.

An apparently trivial situation, the homely "case of the worker's soup," strikingly illustrates how a continuous-process technology restores the personal freedoms of the employee. This incident also points out the disparity in atmosphere between assembly-line and automated work environments. When asked about the possibilities of setting his own work pace, a chemical operator mentioned that the men often warm up a can of soup on a hot plate within the automated control room where they are stationed. Suppose this soup is on the stove, ready to eat, just at the time that's officially scheduled for the operator's round of instrument readings, an activity that takes about thirty minutes. "You can eat the soup first and do the work later, or you can take the readings earlier than scheduled, in order to have the soup when it's hot," reported this operator. In other words, the nature of production work in an automated technology makes it possible for the employee to satisfy personal and social needs when he feels like it, because he can carry out his job tasks according to his own rhythm. The automobile assembly-line worker who gets a craving for a bowl of soup is in an entirely different situation. He must wait for his allotted relief time, when another worker takes his place on the line, and if he still wants soup at that time he will probably drink it hurriedly on his return from the lavatory. Ironically but fittingly, his will be the "automated" soup, purchased from a commercial vending machine, since there is no room and no time for hot plates and cans of soup on an automotive conveyer belt.

If we shift from this consideration of long-run historical developments to look at the broad range of industrial environments today, it appears that only a minority of blue-collar workers are as controlled and dominated by technology or supervision as are automobile and textile workers. It is likely that most workers have jobs that permit them to set their own work pace, at least within limits— although adequate evidence on this point is lacking, unfortunately. Because of enlightened personnel policies and because an affluent society can afford a relaxed atmosphere at the point of production, most workers are free from intensive pressures on the job. Among all the factory employees in the Roper study, only 24 per cent said they had to work too fast. And because of prosperity, a more employee-oriented management, and the policing function of labor unions, the great majority of workers today are free from close and arbitrary supervision, a means of control that was quite prevalent a generation or two ago.

On the other hand, one aspect of control over the immediate work process is generally lacking in factory work: the freedom to choose the techniques and methods of doing the job. Predetermination of these decisions by engineers, foremen, and time-study men is the norm in mass-production industry. Probably only craftsmen and the few blue-collar operators in the new automated industries have much opportunity to introduce their own ideas in the course of their work. . . .

Inherent in the idea of responsibility as the worker's job requirement is a degree of control over that area of the work process that is his domain. A long-run decline in powerlessness is therefore to be expected because of the character of automated technology and the nature of manual work in highly mechanized systems. But the unusual degree of freedom in industrial chemical plants is not simply a consequence of these factors. The economic expansion and general prosperity of the industry contribute much to the relaxed atmosphere on the job.

Therefore automated industrial technology will not automatically guarantee freedom and control, since some automated firms and industries will be under economic stress in that far distant future when automation will be the dominant technology. In addition, automated technologies will take many forms, and variations within automated industries will result in different modes and levels of freedom.

DIVISION OF LABOR AND MEANING IN WORK

Along with the progressive mechanization of technology, another important historical trend in industrial development has been the increasing subdivision of labor within more and more rationalized systems of work organization. This has intensified the alienation of meaninglessness, making it more difficult for manual workers to find purpose and function in their work. There are hopeful signs in continuous-process plants, however, that automation is reversing this long-run development also.

Meaninglessness is rare in craft industries, because the products are unique rather than standardized and because the division of labor remains on the elementary level of craft specialization. Even the unskilled laborer shoveling cement on a building site is making a contribution toward the construction of a particular and tangible structure. His work is organized by the building problems of the individual site, and therefore he develops a task-completion orientation rather than a cyclical-repetitive approach to the job. In addition, craftsmen tend to work on large parts of the product: linotype operators set the type for all the pages of a book or magazine; hand compositors work on the whole page.

The increasing division of labor characteristic of both machine and assembly-line industries tends to undermine the "substantive rationality" natural to the craft organization of work. Product standardization in the mass-production industries means that work involves a repetitive cycle rather than a succession of distinctive tasks. Work organization further limits the employee to one segment of the product and a small scope of the process involved in its manufacture. Textile operatives, for example, are confined to one room in the mill, which contains a department carrying out only one process of the dozens required for the completion of the product, and in that room they generally perform only one or two of the total number of productive tasks. In automobile assembly, the proportion of product worked upon and the scope of operations becomes even more minute. And the operative's sense of purpose and function is reduced to a minimum when he attaches steering columns all day long and has nothing to do with any part of the automobile besides his own restricted specialty. It is highly ironic, and also tragic, that workers are confined to the most limited task assignments in the very industry where they know the most about the product and the processes because of the *expertise* gained working on their own cars.

Fortunately, however, fractionization of work does not continue to increase in a "straight-line" fashion as technology develops higher and higher levels of mechanization. The most characteristic feature of automation is its transfer of focus from an individual job to the process of production. The perspective of the worker is shifted from his own individual tasks to a broader series of operations that includes the work of other employees. Since automated processes are integrated and continuous rather than divided in the way that labor is divided, the responsibility of one employee for his share of a plant's process is inevitably linked to the responsibility of other workers.

Since the decentralized subplants that make up a continuous-process factory manufacture different products and since automated technology has reduced the number of workers necessary for each process, each man's job assignments and responsibilities differ from those of his workmates. Therefore each operator senses that he is contributing a unique function to the processing of his department's product, even though the product is standardized and remains the same from day to day. The unique function of each operator is enmeshed in a network of interdependent relations with the functions of others. And responsibility as a job requirement demands thinking in terms of the collective whole rather than the individual part. For all these reasons, automation results in a widening of the worker's scope of operations[4] and provides new avenues for meaning and purpose in work.

There is little meaninglessness in craft production because each craftsman makes a contribution to a unique *product*. In continuous-process production there is little alienation of this type because each operator contributes a unique *function* in the processing of a standardized product. Meaninglessness is most intensified on the automobile assembly line because both the product and the function of the individual worker is so highly standardized. Whereas the conveyer belt represents an extreme in this situation, as well as many others, the alienation of meaninglessness is probably more widespread and serious than that of powerlessness among the general labor force today, since the elaborate division of labor within the typical factory makes it difficult for most employees to relate their jobs to the larger purposes and goals of the enterprise.

TECHNOLOGY, TIME PERSPECTIVE, AND INVOLVEMENT

In the course of industrial development, there has probably been a tendency for manual work to become inherently less engrossing and for instrumental, external considerations to gain in importance over intrinsic task satisfactions. It is difficult for the manual worker to identify with the standardized products of mass-production industries or to become deeply involved in their manufacture. Therefore, like meaninglessness, self-estrangement in the work process tends to be a more common state among factory workers today than the alienation of powerlessness. But it is a mistake to view self-alienation simply as a generalized predicament of the factory worker in modern society, since its intensity depends on the specific conditions of industrial technology and the division of labor.

The nature of an industry's technology and its division of labor determine the rhythm of the manual worker's job and the characteristic orientation toward time that he experiences in the course of his work. They thus influence the degree to which the worker can become involved and engrossed in work activity and the degree to which he is likely to be detached or alienated from his immediate tasks. Craft technology and traditional manual skill create an unique-task work rhythm in which there is involvement in the present situation on the basis of images of the future completion of the product or task. The skilled worker must be emotionally engaged in the immediate activity of molding raw materials and solving problems of construction; craft work does not permit the barter of present-time gratifications for the future rewards. On the other hand, the unskilled routine jobs in the standardized machine and assembly-line industries foster a repetitive-cycle work rhythm, a detachment from present tasks, and a concern with the future cessation of the activity itself, rather than the completion of specific tasks.[5] Since the intrinsic activity of the work in these industries tends to result in monotony rather than any immediate gratifications, the meaning of the job is largely found in instrumental future-time rewards: wages, fringe benefits, and, when present, economic security.

Continuous-process technology and the work of monitoring automatic equipment results in still another rhythm, one that is new and unique in factory settings. It is the variety and unpredictability of the "calm-and-crisis" mode of time experience that is probably most liberating. There are periods of routine activity when such tasks as instrument-reading and patrolling are carried out, periods of waiting and relaxing when the routine work is done and operations are smooth, and also periods of intense activity when emergency breakdowns must be controlled. In the calm situations there is probably much detachment and monotony, coupled with a habituated attention to the potential occurrence of something extraordinary; however, in the crisis periods, total involvement in the immediate present results.

Continuous-process technology offers more scope for self-actualization than machine and assembly-line technologies. The nature of the work encourages a scientific, technical orientation and the changing character of the technology results in opportunities for learning and personal development for a considerable section of the blue-collar labor force. In contrast, work in machine and assembly-line industries is rarely complicated by problems and difficulties that might challenge the worker's capacities and shake him out of his routine and thus offers little potential for personal development.

The effect of these technological variations on involvement in work can be seen when employees in each of these industries are asked whether their jobs are interesting or monotonous. The great majority of all factory workers consider their jobs interesting; the significant point is the pattern that relative differences in monotony take. As we advance up the scale of industrial development, the proportion of workers who find their jobs dull increases from a scant 4 per cent in the printing industry, to 18 per cent in the textile industry, and to 34 per cent in the automobile industry (and to 61 per cent of those unskilled auto workers concentrated on the assembly line). But in the chemical industry, only 11 per cent complain of monotony, which suggests that automation may be checking the long-run trend toward detachment and self-alienation in factory work.

INDUSTRIAL STRUCTURE, SOCIAL ALIENATION, AND PERSONALITY

The historical development of mechanized technology and rationalized work organization has influenced social alienation as well as powerlessness, meaninglessness, and self-estrangement, because these trends have affected industrial social structure. Different technologies result in variations in the occupational distribution of the industrial labor force, in the economic cost structures of the company, and in the size and layout of the factory. These factors, in turn, affect the degree of integration and cohesion in an industry and the extent to which factory workers feel a sense of belonging in an industrial community. Because of variations in industrial social structure, industries differ in their modes of social control and sources of worker discipline, and distinctive social types and personalities are produced that reflect the specific conditions of their industrial environment.

Craft industries are usually highly integrated on the basis of the traditions and norms of the various occupational specialties, and social alienation is low because of the skilled worker's loyalty to, and identification with, his particular craft and trade union. Skilled printers, like workers in the building trades and other craftsmen, are relatively independent of their companies, since the market demand for their skills gives them mobility in an industrial structure made up of large numbers of potential employers. The occupational structure and economic organization of craft industries thus make the work force autonomous from management, rather than integrated with it or alienated from it. This autonomy is expressed in the skilled craftsman's characteristic (and characterological) resentment of close supervision. Since the management control structure has little effective power and since craft technology is too undeveloped to be coercive, the locus of social control in these work settings is the journeyman's own internalization of occupational standards of work excellence and norms of "a fair day's work." Work discipline in craft industries is therefore essentially self-discipline. The industrial environment produces a social personality characterized by an orientation to craftsmanship and quality performance, a strong sense of individualism and autonomy, and a solid acceptance of citizenship in the larger society. Satisfied with his occupational function, the craftsman typically has a highly developed feeling of self-esteem and a sense of self-worth and is therefore ready to participate in the social and political institutions of the community as well as those of his craft.

Because machine industries have low-skilled labor forces, occupational groups have less identity and autonomy. Therefore they rarely provide a basis for social integration. The unskilled worker in these industries is more dependent on his employer, and the company thus tends to be the central institution in the industrial community. A characteristic of machine industries that usually contributes to social integration is the large number of female employees. Male workers feel that their status is higher and that they are recognized as more important than the women. They have somewhat increased chances for promotion into the minority of jobs with skill or responsibility. Women, who tend to be more satisfied than men with the prevailing unskilled routine jobs, "cushion" the occupational floor in machine industries, raising the ceiling slightly for the men who might otherwise be frustrated in low positions.

In southern textiles, unique historical and geographical factors have been critical in producing a social structure that is more cohesive and highly integrated than most machine industries. With the mills located principally in small towns and villages, the industrial community centered around the factory is almost identical with the local community itself. Southern textile towns are traditional societies that are highly integrated, and commitment to mill employment seems to follow naturally from the strong loyalties to family, church, and locality. Social control is thus centered in the folkways of the community and the paternalistic domination of management. Factory discipline is not based on the internalized motivation characteristic of printers but stems from a number of largely external sources. These include a mechanized technology, and subdivided work organization that is more coercive than that of the craft industries and the rather close supervision of foreman and other management representatives. Of course social control is also rooted in the tendency of the tradition-oriented textile worker to accept management authority and the industrial staus quo. The typical social personality produced by this industrial environment is almost diametrically opposed to that of the craftsman. In addition to submissive attitudes toward authority, the textile worker tends to have little autonomy or individuation and to have a low level of aspiration, which includes an indifferent attitude to the meaningfulness of his work. The low estimate of self-worth and the absorption in the relatively narrow confines of kinship and church counter any expression of citizenship and participation in larger social worlds.

Two consequences of assembly-line technology and work organization, the "massified" occupational distribution and extremely large factories, are the critical elements underlying the social structure of the automobile industry. The mass of workers are at a uniform level of low skill, and the majority of men in assembly plants are paid almost exactly the same rate. The relative lack of occupational differentiation by skill, status, or responsibility creates an industrial "mass society" in which there are almost no realistic possibilities of advancement. The industry therefore lacks a built-in reward system for reaffirming its norms and integrating the worker into a community based on loyalty to the company. Social alienation is further intensified because automobile workers are low skilled, without strong occupational identity, and loyalty to an independent craft is not possible for most employees.

In addition, the technology and elaborate division of labor require a large physical plant and a sizable work force. As a rule, the larger the factory, the more tenuous is the employee's sense of identification with the enterprise and the greater the social and sympathetic distance between him and management. The automobile assembly plant stands at the apex of the historical development toward larger and larger factories: the proportion of workers employed in plants with more than 1,000 persons is 21 per cent in printing, 25 per cent in textiles, and 82 per cent in the transportation equipment industries. Automobile production may be the ideal example of an industry where large plants and firms have most contributed to the extreme development of an impersonal work atmosphere and to the breakdown of sympathetic communication and identification between employees and managment.

In these circumstances, social control rests on consensus and more on the power of management to enforce compliance to the rule system of the factory, a power sometimes effectively countervailed by the strong labor union, which has a legitimate mandate to protect certain interests of the workers. The compelling rhythms of the conveyer-belt technology and the worker's instrumental concern for his weekly pay check are more important to him than internalized standards of quality performance or an identification with organizational goals in providing the discipline that gets work done in an orderly fashion. The social personality of the auto worker, a product of metropolitan residence and exposure to large, impersonal bureaucracies, is expressed in a characteristic attitude of cynicism toward authority and institutional systems, and a volatility revealed in aggressive response to infringements on personal rights and occasional militant collective action. Lacking meaningful work and occupational function, the automobile worker's dignity lies in his peculiarly individualistic freedom from organizational commitments.

AUTOMATION AND SOCIAL INTEGRATION

Social alienation is widespread in the automobile industry because of the marked anomic tendencies inherent in its technology and work organization. In the chemical industry, on the other hand, continuous-process technology and more favorable economic conditions result in a social structure with a high degree of consensus between workers and management and an integrated industrial community in which employees experience a sense of belonging and membership. Social alienation is absent because of the combined effect of a number of factors: of first importance are the balanced skill distribution and the differentiated occupational structure that markedly contrast with the non-stratified structure in automotive plants.

Continuous-process technology results in a wide variety of occupational categories, and it requires workers at all levels of skill and responsibility. Because oil refineries and chemical plants produce an assortment of products and by-products, there are many different processes taking place in individual plant buildings, each of which has a work crew composed of slightly different job positions. Unskilled laborers are needed, as are large numbers of process operators at moderate, as well as high, levels of responsibility, and skilled maintenance craftsmen are also in demand. Such a status system is a socially integrating force, since it provides many high positions to which employees many aspire, and the successful workers most exemplify the values and standards of the company. When possibilities for greater rewards of higher pay and status exist, workers are motivated to perform well and internalize the goals of the enterprise.

Secondly, automation reverses another long-run trend, that of increasing factory size, and results also in a distinctive change in plant layout in these industries. A reduction in the number of employees in a plant operation is due partly to automation itself and partly to the campanies' conscious decentralization policies. (Chemical and oil firms seem to prefer many medium-sized plants rather than a few giant operations.) More importantly, the decentralization principle is applied to a single factory. In steel mills, automobile assembly plants, textile mills, and print shops, the departments that carry out the various stages of the production process all exist under the same roof—so that there is, in essence, only one plant. But though chemical plants and oil refineries are spread out over a large terrain, they are decentralized into a large number of individual buildings or subplants that are spatially separated from each other. In each of these a different product is made or a particular process is carried out by a crew of operators who have collective responsibility for the total operation, as well as individual responsibilities for certain parts of it. These "Balkanized" units and the work teams attached to them serve as centers of employee loyalty and identification and give work in the continuous-process industries a cohesive "small plant" atmosphere, even though the employer is actually a large national corporation. These small work teams are an effective source of work discipline. Men perform up to standard because they do not want to let down their workmates or their department. Collective control by the working crew will probably become more important in many industries besides continuous-process ones, since team responsibility is the natural outgrowth of the integrated process inherent in automated technology per se.

Informal work groups are even more important to the worker and more central a factor in over all morale in machine and assembly-line technologies because the unskilled, repetitive jobs lack intrinsic gratifications and make social satisfactions more imperative. Unfortunately, cohesive work groups are a problematic outcome in these technologies, because, unlike process production, they do not naturally result in team operations or collective responsibility. In many simple machine and light-assembly industries, individual employees work very close to others who do similar or identical jobs, and informal cliques are formed which maintain norms of production and provide a sense of belonging and cohesion. In the textile industry, however, workers with multimachine assignments are spread out at great distances in very large rooms, so that no working groups can be formed. Similarly, automobile assembly production, with its serial operations, places each worker next to a different set of workers, so that stable groups with clear and distinct identities do not easily form.

A third factor contributing to social integration in the continuous-process industries is the changed character of automated work. The difference in the nature of work performed by production workers and managers has been one of the most significant factors underlying class conflict within the factory. But with automation, the work of the blue-collar process operators becomes very similar to that of the white-collar staff—it is clean, includes record-keeping and other clerical tasks, and involves responsibility. Thus automation may eliminate the "innate" hostility of men who work with their hands toward "pencil-pushers" and administrators. And, conversely, white-collar employees will probably gain an enhanced understanding of, and respect for, the work of blue-collar men, since the office staff's contact with the plant and its production problems increases in automated firms, due to the greater need for checking and consultation.

The cohesive social structure in the continuous-process industries is further supported by the economic basis of automated production. As industrial technology becomes more mechanized, the cost structure of the enterprise changes. Since the investment in expensive machinery rises sharply in automated industries and the number of production workers declines, the proportion of total cost that is capital equipment increases and the proportion of labor cost decreases. A capital-intensive cost structure means that heightened efficiency, increased output, and higher profits can more easily be attained through exploitation of technology rather than the exploitation of the worker. The hard-pressed textile firms and to a lesser extent the automobile assembly plants, with their relatively low levels of mechanization and high labor costs, attempt to remain competitive by getting as much as possible out of each worker. The cost structure furthers the tendency to use the workers as "means," as commodities in the classic Marxist sense. The economic base of automated technology allows a more enlightened management to view the workers as human beings, as partners in a collective enterprise, who, because of their responsibility for expensive machinery and processes, must be considered in terms of their own needs and rights.

In addition to the structural economic relations that result from the nature of automated production, contingent economic conditions have also contributed greatly to social integration. Heavy chemicals has been a highly prosperous growth industry. Economic prosperity has permitted large chemical companies to provide their employees with a regularity of employment and long-range job security that is not possible in less stable industries. Since security of employment is the fundamental precondition of a worker's commitment to his company and industry, economics is therefore basic to the cohesion and consensus in chemicals. A second precondition of employee loyalty and identification is an opportunity to advance and improve one's status. The long-term growth in the industry has brought with it the expansion of plants and labor force, making advancement, as well as permanent employment, a meaningful reality. Economic prosperity has furthered social integration in still another way: it has permitted a relaxed atmosphere on the job and co-operative rather than strained and conflict-laden relations between workers and supervisors. In direct contrast, the economic fluctuations in the automobile industry mean that irregular employment is common, a fact that profoundly militates against an atmosphere of consensus and good will.

Due to all these factors, the social personality of the chemical worker tends toward that of the new middle class, the white-collar employee in bureaucratic industry. As a new industry whose important growth has been in the period of the large-scale corporation, heavy chemicals has been able to provide its blue-collar workers with the career employment (permanency, regular promotions, company benefits) that has generally been the fate only of white-collar people. The automated operator's work—light, clean, involving the use of symbols, and resulting in regular contact with engineers, salesmen, and supervisors—is also somewhat similar to that of the office employee. And his mentality is not far different; he identifies with his company and orients himself toward security. Like the white-collar man, this security comes from his status as an employee, from his dependence on the benevolent and prosperous company, rather than his own independence. Generally lukewarm to unions and loyal to his employer, the blue-collar in the continuous-process industries may be a worker "organization-man" in the making.

Of course the high degree of consensus and cohesion in the chemical industry is not typical. Nor is the situation in automobile assembly, where social alienation is so extreme, characteristic of the average manufacturing establishment. On the whole, social alienation is not as widespread in American industry as meaninglessness and self-estrangement are. The majority of blue-collar workers are committed to their roles as producers, and are loyal (although within limits)[6] to their employers. This is supported by the findings in the Roper study that 73 per cent consider their company as good or better than any other place to work in their industry; only 17 per cent said other companies were better, and 10 per cent were undecided. Although the development of technology through the assembly line has reduced the cohesion of industrial social structure, other long-term trends have probably lessened the social alienation of factory workers that was so prevalent in the early period of industrialization. Modern bureaucratic organization is based on universalistic standards of justice and fair treatment, and its system of rules has enhanced the normative integration of industry. The long period of economic prosperity and its concomitants—steady employment, higher wages, better living standards, and promotion opportunities—have profoundly contributed to the secular decline in the worker's class consciousness and militancy, a development that reflects the growing consensus between employees and employers and the increase in the worker's feeling that he has a stake in industry. . . .

NOTES

1. These types correspond exactly with the three stages in the evolution of manual work that Alan Touraine has distinguished at the Paris Renault Automotive Works. *L'evolution du travail ouvrier aux usines Renault* (Paris: Centre National de la Recherche Scientifique, 1955).

2. Only in terms of the nature of manual work, of course; the loss of jobs resulting from these technological changes is a more serious matter to the individual worker than any historical improvement in the dignity of labor.

3. On the whole, powerlessness increases with growing mechanization within this group of industries. In the less-developed shoe and apparel industries workers operate individual machines, and they usually are able, therefore, to control both the pace at which they work and the quantity of their output. Since they can stop and start their own machines, they are also relatively free to leave their work stations for brief periods.

4. James Bright, *Automation and Management* (Cambridge: Harvard University Press, 1958), pp. 183–184.

5. The difference in time orientation between craft and machine-assembly tasks corresponds closely to Hannah Arendt's distinction between work and labor. *The Human Condition* (Chicago: University of Chicago Press, 1958).

6. Loyalty to the company does not preclude persistent loyalty to labor unions and occasional opinions that the interest of these organizations may conflict, as the proponents of the "dual loyalty" thesis have pointed out. Compare Ross Stagner, "Dual Allegiance as a Problem in Modern Society," *Personnel Psychology*, VII (1954); Lois Dean, "Union Activity and Dual Loyalty," *Industrial and Labor Relations Review*, VII (1954); and Theodore Purcell, *The Worker Speaks His Mind on Company and Union* (Cambridge: Harvard University Press, 1954), pp. 248–262.

ALIENATED WORKER, ALIENATED CONSUMER

Andre Gorz

. . . As Marx had foreseen, monopoly capitalism found itself faced with the problem of shaping subjects for the objects to be marketed; not of adjusting supply to demand, but demand to supply.

Is has solved this problem by conditioning individuals to suit the most profitable production—not only in their individual needs but equally in their perception of the world (their conception of the State, society, civilization, coexistence with other societies and civilizations, etc.). In order to harness society for purposes of private accumulation, on the level of individual consumption as well as of public consumption (government spending), it has made every effort to extend its dictatorship to all aspects and every sphere of private life, to become the master of individuals in their work, their leisure, their home, in the schools, in the information available to them, in the way in which they reproduce their labor power, in their relationships with other human beings. By the extension of its dictatorship to culture, to private life, to local and national institutions, monopoly capitalism has finally appeared in its true light: as a system which requires production for the sake of production, i.e., accumulation for the sake of accumulation, a system which requires a society of compulsory consumption. And also, to be sure, a system which requires a type of individual susceptible to the pressures designed to make him a passive consumer: mass individuals on whom the system can impose purposes, desires, and wishes by which to manipulate them.

But if we limit our analysis to these aspects of "affluent capitalism" we remain on the surface only of the phenomenon. Its root is in the capitalist relationships of production. In truth, the "alienated consumer" is an "individual who reflects in his need for consumption his alienation as an agent of production." The alienated consumer is one and the same as the manual, intellectual, or white collar worker who is cut off from his fellow workers made passive by the military discipline of the factory, cut off from his product, ordered to sell his time, to execute with docility a pre-fabricated task, without worrying about the purposes of his work. The passive and "massified" consumer required by capitalist production in order to subordinate consumption is not created by capitalism altogether by means of advertising, fashion, and "human relations," as is often asserted; on the contrary, capitalism *already* creates him within the relationships of production and the work situation by cutting off the producer from his product; and, what is more, by cutting the worker off from his work, by turning this

SOURCE: *Strategy for Labor,* (Boston: Beacon Press, 1967), pp. 70–73.

work against him as a certain pre-determined and alien quantity of time and trouble which awaits the worker at his job and requires his active passivity.

It is because the worker is not "at home" in "his" work, because this work, negated as a creative activity, is a calamity, a pure *means* of satisfying needs, that the individual's active and creative needs are amputated, and he no longer finds his sphere of sovereignty except in non-work, that is to say in the satisfaction of passive needs, in consumption, and in domestic life.[1]

On the basis of this prior pre-conditioning, monopoly capitalism can play on the passive and individual needs of consumption, can purpose ever more complicated and sophisticated modes of satisfaction, develop the need to escape, sell means of forgetting, of distracting oneself from the pressures of industrial organization, means of dreaming that one is human—because there is no chance of actually becoming such—by the acquisition of prefabricated symbols of humanity. And the farther capitalism advances on this road, the more it deadens an already mass-produced and mutilated humanity by means of satisfactions which, while they leave the fundamental dissatisfaction intact, distract one from it; and the more it hopes that these men, preoccupied with ways of escaping and forgetting, will forget to challenge the basis of the whole system, namely the alienation of labor. Capitalism civilizes consumption and leisure in order not to have to civilize social relationships, the relationships of production and of work; it alienates individuals in their work, thereby enabling it to alienate them all the better in their consumption; and inversely, it alienates them in consumption in order to alienate them better in their work.

It is impossible to break out of this vicious circle by maintaining labor struggles on the quantitative level of demands for greater consumption; and inversely it is impossible to challenge the neocapitalist model of consumption (except by invoking very abstractly one or another scale of spiritual values, teeming with medieval and primitivist nostalgia) without attacking the root of "spiritual poverty," namely the alienation of labor.

This task is evidently not simple. The subordination of consumption to production, of all aspects of life to monopoly accumulation, does not provoke a spontaneous revolt. There may even seem to be a circularity: the priorities of the neo-capitalist model of consumption correspond to real needs within the present relationships of production and work, and it may seem impossible to challenge the former until the latter have been transformed.

This circularity is nevertheless more apparent than real. Because the point is not, as Christian ideologists sometimes assert, to begin by reducing the immediate satisfactions which the "consumers' society" promises to alienated workers, and to promise them instead truer satisfactions in the future. The question of the purpose of work, of the model of society, and of consumption, should not be put in the form of an alternative between "frivolous opulence" and "virtuous austerity" but, with reference to immediate demands themselves, in terms of essentially *political* options for the future.

One of the first goals of a political alternative will be to break down the wall which separates the producer from his product and which puts the worker, as mystified consumer, in contradiction with himself as alienated producer. The workers' immediate demands concerning wages, hours, quotas, and qualifications provide the unions, and above all the factory-based sections of the labor parties, with the opportunity to raise the problem of the social and individual utility of the products to which the work is subservient, the question of the value (or worth-lessness) of planned innovations, of the real quality of the product, of the orientation which production ought to have in view of felt needs and of the existing scientific and technical potentialities. . . .

NOTE

1. I have been paraphrasing Marx: "What constitutes the alienation of labor? First, that the work is *external* to the worker, that it is not part of his nature; and that, consequently, he does not fulfill himself in his work but denies himself, has a feeling of misery rather than well-being, does not develop freely his mental and physical energies but is physically exhausted and mentally debased. The worker therefore feels himself at home only during his leisure time, whereas at work he feels homeless. His work is not voluntary but imposed, *forced labor*. It is not satisfaction of a need, but only a *means* for satisfying other needs. . . .

"We arrive at the result that man (the worker) feels himself to be freely active only in his animal functions—eating, drinking and procreating, or at most also in his dwelling and in personal adornment—while in his human functions he is reduced to an animal. The animal becomes human and the human becomes animal.

"Eating, drinking and procreating are of course also genuine human functions. But abstractly considered, apart from the environment of other human activities, and turned into final and sole ends, they are animal functions."—"Economic and Philosophical Manuscripts," translated by T. B. Bottomore, in Erich Fromm, *Marx's Concept of Man* (Ungar, 1961), pp. 98–99.

AFFLUENCE AND THE WORKERS' WORK WORLD

John H. Goldthorpe
David Lockwood
Frank Bechhofer
Jennifer Platt

. . . [L]eaving aside for the moment the matter of class identity, little qualitative change at all may have occurred in the *class situation* of the affluent worker— in the sense, that is, of the position he holds within the social organisation of production and the constraints and life-chances that he consequently experiences. The workers [in this study] were still men who gained their living through placing their labour power at the disposal of an employer and receiving payment for particular amounts of work done. Indeed, the way in which they had typically become affluent was in effect by devaluing the possibilities of non-economic rewards in employment and by working in jobs that offered a relatively high level of pay in return for a corresponding level of stress and deprivation: in other words, by being prepared to experience their work *as labour and as little else.*

Moreover, we are unable to accept the view that this cost of working-class affluence, as illustrated in our findings, must necessarily be diminished as a result of current 'modernising' tendencies in industrial technology and administration. On the basis of our own investigation and of a now substantial body of other evidence, we would seriously question the idea that these developments automatically transform the nature of industrial work and relationships to the extent that such categories as 'labour' and 'labour force' become no longer applicable.[1] To begin with, the 'objective' consequences of technological progress by no means all run in the same direction of making work less taxing and more intrinsically rewarding, or of lessening functional and status differences between managers and managed: as we have noted, contrary effects to these may well be produced as, for example, through the requirement of shiftworking or by the yet further reduction of career mobility from shop-floor to management grades. Furthermore, the response of rank-and-file workers to greater opportunities for participation in the social life or the affairs of the enterprise, whether resulting from changes in technology or from management policy, need not and will not be invariably positive. Again as our study would indicate, where employees' central life interests are not located in their work, and where work is defined in almost exclusively instrumental terms,

SOURCE: *The Affluent Worker in the Class Structure* (Cambridge: Cambridge University Press, 1969), pp. 82–84, 179–187.

little further involvement in the activities and relationships of work may be sought beyond the minimum implied by the employment contract itself.

To generalise from our findings, therefore, we would maintain that so far at least as the world of work is concerned, the thesis of working-class *embourgoisement* can have little relevance to present day British society. Whatever changes may have been taking place in the sphere of consumption, in the sphere of production a fairly distinctive working class can still be readily identified, even when attention is concentrated on progressive industrial sectors and modern establishments. Moreover, in so far as this last statement might appear in need of qualification, this, we would suggest, is primarily the result of ongoing changes in industry that are affecting *nonmanual* rather than manual workers and are bringing some of the former closer to the position of the latter rather than *vice versa*—for example, the growing scale of units of administration, the spread of office mechanisation and even automation, the increasing recruitment of men destined for senior posts direct from institutions of higher education, and so on. As a result of these various rationalising tendencies, a stratum of white-collar workers has now obviously emerged whose members are dissociated from decision-making or control functions, perform entirely routine and generally unrewarding tasks, and have little more opportunity for career mobility than their blue-collar counterparts.[2]

Even then, the significance of this development, especially in blurring lines of class division in industry, should not be exaggerated. It must be remembered that the new white-collar labour force contains a high proportion of women workers whose employment at a subordinate level improves the chances of male workers occupying higher grade positions. And secondly, it would appear from recent research that the rationalisation of white-collar work does not in fact produce factory conditions in the office nor alienated employees to the extent that has sometimes been supposed. In other words, it is important that the thesis of the white-collar worker becoming 'proletarian' should be regarded as critically as that of the manual worker becoming middle-class. At all events, as we have sought to show [in our work] fairly marked contrasts still remain between the work experience, expectations and aspirations of most samples of white-collar workers that have thus far been studied and those of the affluent manual workers who were represented in our own enquiry. . . .

In turning now to the second possible interpretation of the new working class —that based on the idea of alienation—it may be remarked at the outset that in this case problems of empirical assessment are particularly great. To begin with, 'alienation', as used in this connection, is not a specifically sociological concept: it is rather a notion expressive of a certain human and social philosophy which often figures crucially in a rhetoric of revolution. It is not intended to be tested against fact. Furthermore, as we have earlier implied, some ambiguity exists as to whether alienation in this usage is to be understood as a *latent* or a *manifest* condition. According to writers such as, say, Marcuse or Gorz, alienation is displayed on a wide scale among the working classes of neo-capitalist societies in the form primarily of compulsive and escapist consumption; numbed by the abundant satisfaction of their 'false' needs and in other ways systematically manipulated, the masses exist in a state of generally acquiescent, if occasionally uneasy or fractious, servitude. On the other hand, though, a writer such as Mallet is concerned to argue that within advanced capitalism long-term changes are occurring which give rise to an actual *awareness* of alienation, at least on the part of certain groups of workers; and in this case the emergence of some new form of radical class consciousness and associated socio-political action is foreseen. Thus, while these two versions of 'alienation' are not necessarily incompatible, it is important to try to distinguish which emphasis is predominant in any argument that is being examined, since, as will be seen, rather different sets of issues tend to be raised.

As regards, firstly, the idea of latent alienation, it may be said that this offers an undoubtedly persuasive means of summing up many of the salient findings that we have reported on the attitudes and behaviour of the workers we studied. For example, the overriding concern they display with increasing their standards of domestic consumption, the extent to which their future objectives are defined in terms of such standards, their home-centred and typically privatised style of life—all these are features which could be regarded as aptly exemplifying, to use Gorz's words, 'une civilisation de al consommation individuelle': a form of society, that is, in which 'l'individu est sollicité de s'évader de sa condition de producteur social, de se reconstituer un microcosme *privé* dont il jouirait et sur lequel il règnerait en souverain solitaire'.[3] Moreover, the fact that our respondents' own images of the social order were rarely structured in terms of class oppositions or status hierarchies, and the prevalence rather of largely destructured 'money' models, would appear to show quite strikingly the extent to which the 'civilisation of individual consumers' was indeed represented in their social consciousness—inhibiting their awareness of the inequalities of power and forms of exploitation upon which the existing order rests. Finally, and most crucially, the idea of alienation appears closely applicable to our respondents' experience of their work and to the meaning and place that work typically held in their social lives. In this respect, indeed, Marx's original characterisation of 'alienated labour' can stand as a not greatly exaggerated account of our major conclusions:

> . . . work is *external* to the worker . . . it is not part of his nature . . . ; consequently, he does not fulfiill himself in his work but denies himself, has a feeling of misery rather than well-being, does not develop freely his mental and physical energies but is physically exhausted and mentally debased. The worker, therefore, feels himself at home only during his leisure time, whereas at work he feels homeless. His work is not voluntary but imposed, *forced labour*. It is not the satisfaction of a need, but only a *means* for satisfying other needs.[4]

It could, then, certainly be claimed that the alienated worker (in the above sense) is, at all events, far more readily recognisable in our research data than the worker 'on the move towards new middle-class values and middle-class existence'. However, while this is so, it is also the case that there are a number of respects in which the findings of our study do not fall so neatly into line with the 'latent alienation' thesis, and that we thus remain sceptical concerning certain of its underlying assumptions.

One such assumption, for instance, is that alienation, as seen in a preoccupation with 'false' consumer needs, derives fundamentally from the work situation; from the nature, that is, of work-tasks and relationships. As Gorz puts it, in a passage we earlier quoted in full:

It is precisely because the worker is not 'at home' in 'his' work; because, denied him as creative active function, this work is a calamity, a *means* solely of satisfying needs, that the individual is stripped of his creative, active needs and can find his own power only in the sphere of non-work— the satisfaction of the passive needs of personal consumption and domestic life . . .[5]

Or, in the words of an Italian socialist writer, Bruno Trentin: 'the "alienated consumer" is the person who, in his consumer needs, reflects his alienation as an agent of production'.[6]

In this way, therefore, the neo-Marxist position comes close to that of largely non-Marxist industrial sociologists who have taken employees' immediate experience of work within a given form of technical organisation as critically determining their industrial attitudes and behaviour at all levels and, in some cases, as also shaping their more general sociopolitical orientations. But, as we have argued at length elsewhere, such a position is not one which accords well with the findings of our own—or of a now increasing number of other—investigations. Specifically, it may be objected that there is in fact no direct and uniform association between immediate, shop-floor work experience and employee attitudes and behaviour that are of wider reference. This is so because the effects of technologically determined conditions of work are always *mediated* through the meanings that men give to their work and through their own definitions of their work situation, and because these meanings and definitions in turn *vary* with the particular sets of wants and expectations that men bring to their employment. Thus, among the workers we studied, no systematic relationship was to be found between the degree to which their work might be considered as objectively 'alienating' and, say, the strength of their attachment to their jobs, the nature of their relationships with workmates, or their stance in regard to their employing organisation.[7]

Consequently, it becomes difficult to see the instrumental attitudes and behaviour that our respondents in the main displayed as being primarily and basically the effect of their—often significantly differing—tasks and roles within the organisation of production. Rather, their propensity to accept work as essentially a means to extrinsic ends would seem better understood as something that to an important degree existed independently of, and prior to, their involvement in their present work situations. This latter interpretation, moreover, is strongly confirmed by a fact that we earlier emphasised: namely, that many of our respondents, and especially of those in routine, semi-skilled jobs, had previously performed work of an intrinsically more rewarding or at least less 'alienating' character, although no doubt in return for appreciably lower earnings than they currently enjoyed.[8] Thus, if we consider the assemblers in our sample—as representing the popular archetype of 'alienated labour'—we find that 10% had previously been employed *chiefly* in nonmanual jobs, 13% as skilled craftsmen, and another 16% in various forms of relatively skilled manual work; further, only 19% had *never* held a job more skilled than their present one, and as many as 58% had at some stage been in either nonmanual or craft employment. At the same time, 76% of these men referred to the level of pay as a reason for staying in their present jobs, and in the case of 31% this was the only reason offered.[9]

For some proportion of the workers we studied, therefore, exactly the reverse of the argument advanced by the theorists of alienation would appear to apply. Rather than an overriding concern with consumption standards reflecting alienation in work, it could be claimed that precisely such a concern constituted the motivation for these men to take, and to retain, work of a particularly unrewarding and stressful kind which offered high pay in compensation for its inherent deprivations.[10] It might indeed still be held that to devalue work rewards in this way for the sake of increasing consumer power is itself symptomatic of alienation —perhaps even of alienation in an extreme form. But in this case, of course, the idea of work as being invariably the prime source of alienation has to be abandoned and its origins must be sought elsewhere; specifically, in whatever social-structural or cultural conditions generate "consumption-mindedness" of the degree in question.

In this regard, furthermore, we may take up one other doubt about the bases of the alienation thesis. As a secondary factor to the nature of work in maintaining the working class in a state of latent alienation, the influence of advertising and of the media of mass communication generally has regularly been cited.[11] This claim, we may note, would seem to endow media effects with a much greater potency than has thus far been demonstrated by empirical research;[12] but, quite apart from this, it is obviously inadequate in itself to explain why *some* workers should be far more motivated to force up their consumption standards than others—even to the point of sacrificing their working lives. Since the mass media are in their very nature a potential source of influence on all members of the "mass" society, what is required is some account of how individuals and groups are *differentially* exposed and responsive to the models of consumption that the media present. We have ourselves already advanced a number of relevant hypotheses, together with some supporting evidence, which attach importance to such factors as life-cycle phase, local community structure, and geographical, residential and social mobility; factors, that is, which seem likely to determine the extent to which media influences will be countered or unopposed or even reinforced by *interpersonal* influences. However, there is obviously still a serious lack of investigation in this field. *If* giving priority to "the passive needs of personal and domestic life" is to be taken as constitutive of alienation, then, one would suggest, serious analysis calls for the development of a new empirical sociology of consumption rather than for the refurbishing of an old philosophical anthropology of production.

Finally, though, the point may be underlined that to label attitudes to work and consumption, such as those which our respondents displayed, as "alienation" (leaving aside all questions of their source) is in effect to make a form of social diagnosis which in the end cannot be rejected by force of logic or evidence and which, by the same token, others are in no way constrained to accept. For our own part, we would simply observe that it is not to us self-evident why one should regard our respondents' concern for decent, comfortable houses, for labour-saving devices, and even for such leisure goods as television sets and cars, as manifesting the force of "false" needs; of needs, that is, which are "superimposed upon the individual by particular social interests in his repression."[13] It would be equally possible to consider the amenities and possessions for which the couples in our sample were striving as representing something like the minimum material basis on which they and their children might be able to develop a more individuated style of life, with a wider range of choices, than has hitherto been possible for the mass of the manual labour force. And in particular, given the harsh dilemma that our respondents frequently faced between more inherently rewarding work and greater economic resources with which to carry through their family projects—a dilemma largely avoided by those in more advantageous class positions—we would not be inclined to speak *de haut en bas* of "stunted mass-produced humanity," "made-to-measure consumers" or "sublimated slaves."[14]

The second version of the alienation thesis that we have alluded to envisages that under certain conditions, currently being created by the development of capitalist society, working-class alienation will in fact become manifest and will express itself in forms of class action of a radical kind. As we have earlier remarked, an argument on these lines has perhaps been worked out most fully by Serge Mallet.[15] For Mallet, it will be recalled, the crucial development is the increasing importance within western economies of technologically advanced, capital-intensive plants in which production operations are of a highly integrated character. In such plants, Mallet contends, the close interdependence of managements and employees and the solidarity which tends to grow up between different groups of employee favour the emergence of a new trade unionism of a syndicalist type, capable, in the long term, of revitalising the working-class movement.

An initial observation which may be made on this analysis is that it again reveals a preoccupation with the nature of work-tasks and -roles and of work environment as the determinants of socio-political perspectives. Mallet, in fact, almost entirely neglects the out-plant lives of the members of the new working class with which he is concerned. His grounds for doing so, which he makes no attempt to substantiate, consist essentially of a version of the "dual social identity" thesis which we have earlier referred to: "La classe ouvrière a effectivement cessé de vivre à part . . . L'ouvrier cesse de se sentir tel lorsqu'il sort de l'usine."[16] Thus, he claims, it is only by studying the workers in question "en tant que producteurs" that the distinctive characteristics of their class situation can be understood.

The ways in which this argument might be called into doubt, both logically and empirically, should by now be evident enough.[17] However, even if we leave these aside, there remains our basic objection to the general approach which Mallet adopts: namely, that the wider social and social-psychological implications of a given type of work environment are to a significant degree *indeterminate* so long as the orientations to work of the employees involved are not also specified. In our own investigation, we were not able to study workers under extremely advanced technological conditions. But we were able to show that across several contrasting work environments, ranging from small-batch machine production to process production, a broad *similarity* in many aspects of workers' attitudes and behaviour was the notable feature: a similarity which could be seen as deriving from a shared orientation to work of a markedly instrumental kind. Moreover, it may be added that the process workers in our sample—the group, that is, working within the most integrated production system—were, if anything, less concerned than men in other groups with possibilities for "participation" in plant or in work affairs generally. For example, the process workers contained the lowest proportion of trade unionists who believed that the unions should try to get workers a share in management (22%); the lowest proportion of "regular" or "occasional" attenders at union branch meetings (0%); and the lowest proportion of men reporting that they consulted their shop stewards "very often" or "a good deal" (17%). Further, they also revealed the lowest level of participation in work-based clubs and societies—only 4% being classed as regular attenders—and the lowest proportion (34%) attracted by the idea of promotion.[18]

Thus, what one is led to conclude, and other more extensive research than our own now bears this out, is that a production system which is highly integrated in a technical or functional sense does not in any automatic way tend to produce a high degree of social integration of employees in the plant—either in the manner envisaged by Mallet or in that suggested by Blauner and other writers previously considered.[19] For one thing, it would seem probable that automated or process production systems may, in fact, in certain respects inhibit social integration;[20] but, more importantly, the possibilities for, and constraints upon, the organisation of social relationships which such systems entail must be seen simply as setting limits to patterns that are actually determined by wider social-structural and cultural influences. On this basis, it could well be argued that the emergent forms of worker action and labour relations described by Mallet in the enterprises he studied are far more a "French" phenomenon—a product, say, of French trade union structure and ideology, of French styles of management, of the pattern of French economic development and so on—than they are a phenomenon of technologically advanced plants *per se*.

Lastly, in regard to Mallet, we may note that the findings of our own enquiry do appear consistent with a possibility which he considered, but then discounted, as an alternative to the idea that syndicalism at plant level will lead on to a new stage in the "global" class struggle. That is, the possibility that workers in modern, high-productivity enterprises will adopt an increasingly particularistic approach to industrial relations, thus giving rise to a new "corporatism" and the consolidation of a new labour aristocracy. Certainly among the workers we studied there was a general appreciation of the extent to which their individual prosperity depended upon the economic fortunes of the firms in which they were presently employed. The majority revealed a preparedness for "teamwork" and "accommodation" in their attitudes towards their firms, even while being eager to press for as large a share in the proceeds of such co-operation as they could possibly get.[21] Moreover, if it is accepted, as Mallet apparently does accept, that the typical goals and aspirations of the new working class are for secure and rising incomes and higher living standards, then it is difficult to see why such a stance *vis-à-vis* employers is not a largely rational one. At all events, the point can scarcely be evaded that even in enterprises where a concern with increasing worker participation and control develops, this need not be oriented towards class, as opposed to sectional objectives, nor need it entail any commitment to radical change in the wider economic or social order. Rather than representing alienation made manifest, *syndicalisme gestionnaire* could be simply an advanced form of instrumental collectivism.

It will, then, by now be evident that, in our view, interpretations of the new working class in terms of alienation, whether this is seen as a latent or a manifest state, give rise to a variety of doubts and objections. In so far as such interpretations are open to critical examination from a sociological standpoint, they reveal weaknesses of both an analytical and empirical kind. Basically, we would argue, these weaknesses stem from the insistence of alienation theorists on the crucial significance of the nature of work activity and relationships to any understanding of working-class social being and consciousness. This insistence stands in direct contrast with (and has sometimes served as a useful corrective to) the tendency of adherents of the *embourgeoisement* thesis to concentrate their attention on consumption and domestic life, and to leave almost entirely out of account the worker as producer. However, as against both these emphases, we would maintain that the relative importance of these two different areas of social life and experience to the understanding of working-class perspectives and modes of action is not an issue to be decided *a priori:* it is rather, a central one for sociological enquiry. . . .

NOTES

1. Briefly, the relevant findings could be said to show that the development of automated (including continuous flow) productions systems (i) has very little variable effects on skill levels and 'mixes' within industrial plants; (ii) may give rise to new forms of strain and monotony in work—e.g., ones associated with continuous concentrated attention; (iii) *may* increase operators' feelings of lacking control over, and of being divorced from, the production process; (iv) *may* prevent work group formation through dispersing men widely over large areas of plant; (v) tends to increase shift-working substantially. The work of Naville is of particular significance in this respect. See, for example, P. Naville, "The Structure of Employment and Automation," *International Social Science Bulletin,* vol. 10, No. 1 (1958) and *L'Automation et le Travail Humaine* (Paris, 1961); W. A. Faunce, "Automation and the Automobile Worker," *American Sociological Review,* vol. 18 (August 1958); B. Karsh, "Work and Automation," in Howard Boone Jacobson and Joseph S. Roucek (eds.), *Automation and Society* (New York, 1959); Ronald Gross, "The Future of Toil," in Shostak and Gomberg (eds.), *Blue-Collar World;* and P. Blumberg, *Industrial Democracy: The Sociology of Participation* (London, 1968), pp. 53–64.
2. It is in this context, we would believe, that evidence of an instrumental approach to their employment among white-collar employees must be understood. See, for example, Weir and Mercer, 'Orientations to Work among White-Collar Workers'. Proceedings of the Social Science Research Council Conference on Social Stratification and Industrial Relations (January 1969). We would, however, regard such findings as indicating an aspect of 'normative convergence', rather than implying the elimination of all significant differences in the experience and meaning of work between manual and nonmanual grades.
3. *Stratégie Ouvrière et Néocapitalisme* (Paris, 1964), p. 66.
4. Karl Marx, 'Alienated Labour' in 'Economic and Philosophical Manuscripts of 1844', trans. T. B. Bottomore, *Karl Marx: Early Writings* (London, 1963).
5. See Goldthorpe et al., *The Affluent Worker in the Class Structure,* pp. 16–17.
6. From *Tendenze del Capitalisma italiano* (Rome, 1962). Quoted in Gorz, 'Work and Consumption', in Anderson and Blackburn (eds.), *Toward Socialism,* p. 348. Cf. Marcuse, *One-Dimensional Man,* p. 8. See IAB, chaps. 2, 3, 4.
7. Goldthorpe et al., *The Affluent Worker: Industrial Attitudes and Behavior* (IAB) (Cambridge, 1968), chaps. 2, 3, 4.
8. See Goldthorpe et al., *Affluent Worker in the Class Structure,* pp. 55–57; also IAB, pp. 32–36.
9. See IAB, pp. 27–36, and also John Goldthorpe, "Attitudes and Behaviour of Car Assembly Workers; a Deviant Case and a Theoretical Critique", *British Journal of Sociology,* vol. 17, No. 3 (September 1966).
10. Such a pattern of behaviour should not, moreover, be thought of as particularly unusual. See, for example, the research reports cited in *IAB,* p. 33, n. 2; p. 39, n. 2; p. 61, n. 1; also Ingham, 'Organisational Size, Orientation to Work and Industrial Behaviour.' It should be added here that the main way in which alienation theorists differ

from industrial sociologists who have emphasised the implications of technology is that the former also see as a crucial factor in the work situation the nature of property relationships. Thus, they might reply to our argument above that within capitalist society all wage labour is basically alienating and that therefore choice between different types of work, in the way we are concerned with, is largely illusory. Such a claim means denying the validity or importance of the mass of empirical research which shows that certain types of work-task and -role are regularly experienced as less depriving and as more inherently rewarding than others. A real difficulty in trying to explore the neo-Marxian theory of alienation, by means of empirical research, is in fact that of knowing exactly what connection is being presumed between the nature of work-tasks and -roles on the one hand and the bases of industrial authority on the other.

11. See, for example, Gorz, *Stratégie Ouvrière et Néocapitalisme*, pp. 58–69, 111–118; Marcuse, *One Dimensional Man*, pp. 4–9, and 'Liberation from the Affluent Society', in David Cooper (ed.), *The Dialectics of Liberation* (London, 1968).

12. See the reviews provided in Joseph T. Klapper, *The Effects of Mass Communication* (Glencoe, 1957), and Denis McQuail, *Towards a Sociology of Mass Communications* (London, 1969).

13. Marcuse, *One-Dimensional Man*, p. 5. Perhaps Marcuse and like thinkers, as well as prophets of *embourgeoisement*, need to be reminded that 'a washing machine is a washing machine is a washing machine'.

14. In further investigating the undoubtedly negative aspects of an instrumental orientation to work and a privatised out-of-work life, a more heuristically valuable notion than 'alienation' might be that of 'identity'. See, for example, the insightful comments in Thomas Luckmann and Peter Berger, 'Social Mobility and Personal Identity', *European Journal of Sociology*, vol. 5, no. 2 (1964), and also in Luckmann, *Das Problem der Religion in der modernen Gesellschaft* (Freiburg, 1963).

15. See, Goldthorpe et al., *Affluented Worker in the Class Structure*, pp. 18–19.

16. *La Nouvelle Classe Ouvrière* (Paris, 1963), p. 9.

17. It is particularly remarkable that Mallet should have been led to an acceptance of the 'dual society identity' view on the basis of French data and experience. For a more detailed and considered discussion of the matter, including some critical comment on Mallet, see Jean-Marie Rainville, *Condition Ouvrière et Intégration Sociale* (Paris, 1967).

18. See *IAB*, pp. 90–92, 98–109, 119–120. While the number of process workers we interviewed was decidedly small ($N = 23$) it is important to remember that these men were the élite of the Laporte production employees; i.e. the highest paid, chiefly on account of their seniority and of the responsibility entailed in their jobs. Thus they would appear to be a specially appropriate sample to consider in the present connection.

19. See in particular the detailed report by Friedrich Fürstenberg, 'Structural Changes in the Working Class: a situational study of workers in the Western German chemical industry' in J. A. Jackson (ed.), *Sociology Studies I: Social Stratification* (Cambridge, 1968). In a variety of ways, Fürstenberg's findings reveal interesting similarities with our own as reported in this and previous publications.

20. Goldthorpe et al., *Affluent Worker in the Class Structure*, pp. 40–41.

21. See IAB, pp. 72–89.

WORKING-CLASS AUTHORITARIANISM

Seymour Martin Lipset

The gradual realization that extremist and intolerant movements in modern society are more likely to be based on the lower classes than on the middle and upper classes has posed a tragic dilemma for those intellectuals of the democratic left who once believed the proletariat necessarily to be a force for liberty, racial equality, and social progress. The Socialist Italian novelist Ignazio Silone has asserted that "the myth of the liberating power of the proletariat has dissolved along with that other myth of progress. The recent examples of the Nazi labor unions, like those of Salazar and Peron . . . have at last convinced of this even those who were reluctant to admit it on the sole grounds of the totalitarian degeneration of Communism. . . ."

. . . At first glance the facts of political history may seem to contradict this. Since their beginnings in the nineteenth century, workers' organizations and parties have been a major force in extending political democracy, and in waging progressive political and economic battles. Before 1914, the classic division between the working-class left parties and the economically privileged right was not based solely upon such issues as redistribution of income, status, and educational opportunities, but also rested upon civil liberties and international policy. The workers, judged by the policies of their parties, were often the backbone of the fight for greater political democracy, religious freedom, minority rights, and international peace, while the parties backed by the conservative middle and upper classes in much of Europe tended to favor more extremist political forms, to resist the extension of the suffrage, to back the established church, and to support jingoistic foreign policies.

Events since 1914 have gradually eroded these patterns. In some nations work-in-class groups have proved to be the most nationalistic sector of the population. In some they have been in the forefront of the struggle against equal rights for minority groups, and have sought to limit immigration or to impose racial standards in countries with open immigration. The conclusion of the anti-fascist era and the emergence of the cold war have shown that the struggle for freedom is not a simple variant of the economic class struggle. The threat to freedom posed by the Communist movement is as great as that once posed by Fascism and Nazism, and Communism, in all countries where it is strong, is supported mainly by the lower levels of the working class, or the rural population.[1] No other party has been as thoroughly and completely the party of the working class and the

SOURCE: *Political Man* (Garden City, N.Y.: Anchor Books, Doubleday, 1963), pp. 87, 89–92, 114–116.

poor. Socialist parties, past and present, secured much more support from the middle classes than the Communists have.

Some socialists and liberals have suggested that this proves nothing about authoritarian tendencies in the working class, since the Communist party often masquerades as a party seeking to fulfill the classic Western-democratic ideals of liberty, equality, and fraternity. They argue that most Communist supporters, particularly the less educated, are deceived into thinking that the Communists are simply more militant and efficient socialists. I would suggest, however, the alternative hypothesis that, rather than being a source of strain, the intransigent and intolerant aspects of Communist ideology attract members from that large stratum with low incomes, low-status occupations, and low education, which in modern industrial societies has meant largely, though not exclusively, the working class.

The social situation of the lower strata, particularly in poorer countries with low levels of education, predisposes them to view politics as black and white, good and evil. Consequently, other things being equal, they should be more likely than other strata to prefer extremist movements which suggest easy and quick solutions to social problems and have a rigid outlook.

The "authoritarianism" of any social stratum or class is highly relative, of course, and often modified by organizational commitments to democracy and by individual cross-pressures. The lower class in any given country may be more authoritarian than the upper classes, but on an "absolute" scale all the classes in that country may be less authoritarian than any class in another country. In a country like Britain, where norms of tolerance are well developed and widespread in every social stratum, even the lowest class may be less authoritarian and more "sophisticated" than the most highly educated stratum in an underdeveloped country, where immediate problems and crises impinge on every class and short-term solutions may be sought by all groups.[2]

Commitments to democratic procedures and ideals by the principal organizations to which low-status individuals belong may also influence these individuals' actual political behavior more than their underlying personal values, no matter how authoritarian.[3] A working class which has developed an early (prior to the Communists) loyalty to democratic political and trade-union movements which have successfully fought for social and economic rights will not easily change its allegiance.

Commitments to other values or institutions by individuals (cross-pressures) may also override the most established predispositions. For example, a French, Italian, or German Catholic worker who is strongly anticapitalist may still vote for a relatively conservative party in France, Italy, or Germany, because his ties to Catholicism are stronger than his resentments about his class status; a worker strongly inclined toward authoritarian ideas may defend democratic institutions against fascist attack because of his links to anti-fascist working-class parties and unions. Conversely, those who are not inclined toward extremist politics may back an extremist party because of certain aspects of its program and political role. Many persons supported the Communists in 1936 and 1943 as an anti-fascist internationalist party.

The specific propensity of given social strata to support either extremist or democratic political parties, then, cannot be predicted from a knowledge of their psychological predispositions or from attitudes inferred from survey data.[4] Both evidence and theory suggest, however, that the lower strata are relatively more authoritarian, that (again, other things being equal) they will be more attracted to an extremist movement than to a moderate and democratic one, and that, once recruited, they will not be alienated by its lack of democracy, while more educated or sophisticated supporters will tend to drop away. . . .[5]

MAKING OF AN AUTHORITARIAN

To sum up, the lower-class individual is likely to have been exposed to punishment, lack of love, and a general atmosphere of tension and aggression since early childhood—all experiences which tend to produce deep-rooted hostilities expressed by ethnic prejudice, political authoritarianism, and chiliastic transvaluational religion. His educational attainment is less than that of men with higher socioeconomic status, and his association as a child with others of similar background not only fails to stimulate his intellectual interests but also creates an atmosphere which prevents his educational experience from increasing his general social sophistication and his understanding of different groups and ideas. Leaving school relatively early, he is surrounded on the job by others with a similarly restricted cultural, educational, and family background. Little external influence impinges on his limited environment. From early childhood, he has sought immediate gratifications, rather than engaged in activities which might have long-term rewards. The logic of both his adult employment and his family situation reinforces this limited time perspective. As the sociologist C. C. North has put it, isolation from heterogeneous environments, characteristic of low status, operates to "limit the source of information, to retard the development of efficiency in judgment and reasoning abilities, and to confine the attention to more trivial interests in life."[6]

All of these characteristics produce a tendency to view politics and personal relationships in black-and-white terms, a desire for immediate action, an impatience with talk and discussion, a lack of interest in organizations which have a long-range perspective, and a readiness to follow leaders who offer a demonological interpretation of the evil forces (either religious or political) which are conspiring against him.[7]

It is interesting that Lenin saw the character of the lower classes, and the tasks of those who would lead them, in somewhat these terms. He specified as the chief task of the Communist parties the leadership of the broad masses, who are "slumbering, apathetic, hidebound, inert, and dormant." These masses, said Lenin, must be aligned for the "final and decisive battle" (a term reminiscent of Armageddon) by the party which alone can present an uncompromising and unified view of the world, and an immediate program for drastic change. In contrast to "effective" Communist leadership, Lenin pointed to the democratic parties and their leadership as "vacillating, wavering, unstable" elements—a characterization that is probably valid for any political group lacking ultimate certainty in its program and willing to grant legitimacy to opposition groups.[8]

The political outcome of these predispositions, however, is not determined by the multiplicity of factors involved. Isolation, a punishing childhood, economic and occupational insecurities, and a lack of sophistication are conducive to withdrawal, or even apathy, and to strong mobilization of hostility. The same underlying factors which predispose individuals toward support of extremist movements under certain conditions may result in total withdrawal from political activity and concern under other conditions. In "normal" periods, apathy is most frequent among such individuals, but they can be activated by a crisis, especially if it is accompanied by strong millennial appeals. . . .[9]

NOTES

1. The sources of variation in Communist strength from country to country have already been discussed in chap. 2, [of *Political Man*] in relation to the level and speed of economic development.

2. See Richard Hoggart, *The Uses of Literacy* (London: Chatto Windus, 1957), pp. 78–79 and 146–148, for a discussion of the acceptance of norms of tolerance by the British working class. Prothro and Levon Melikian, in "The California Public Opinion Scale in an Authoritarian Cluture," *Public Opinion Quarterly,* vol. 17 (1953). pp. 353–363, have shown, in a study of 130 students at the American University in Lebanon, that they exhibited the same association between authoritarianism and economic radicalism as is found among workers in America. A survey in 1951–1952 of 1,800 Puerto Rican adults, representative of the entire rural population, found that 84 per cent were "somewhat authoritarian," as compared to 46 per cent for a comparable U.S. population. See Henry Wells, "Ideology and Leadership in Puerto Rican Politics," *American Political Science Review,* vol. 49 (1955), pp. 22–40.

3. The southern Democrats were the most staunch opponents of McCarthy and his tactics, not because of any deep opposition to undemocratic methods but rather because of an organizational commitment to the Democratic party.

4. For a detailed discussion of the fallacy of attempting to suggest that political behavior is a necessary function of political attitudes or psychological traits, see Nathan Glazer and S. M. Lipset, "The Polls on Communism and Conformity, in Daniel Bell (ed.), *The New American Right* (New York: Criterion Books, 1955), pp. 141–166.

5. The term "extremist" is used to refer to the attitudes and predispositions of individuals (or of groups, where a statistical aggregate of individual attitudes, and not group characteristics, as such are of concern). The term "authoritarian" has too many associations with studies of attitudes to be safely used to refer also to types of social organizations.

6. C. C. North, *Social Differentiation* (Chapel Hill: University of North Carolina Press, 1926), p. 247.

7. Most of these characteristics have been mentioned by child psychologists as typical of adolescent attitudes and perspectives. Werner Cohn, in an article on Jehovah's Witnesses considers youth movements as a prototype of all such "proletarian" movements. Both "adolescence fixation and anomie are causal conditions" of their development (p. 297), and all such organizations have an "aura of social estrangement" (p. 282). See Werner Cohn, "Jehovah's Witnesses as a Proletarian Movement," *The American Scholar,* vol. 24 (1955), pp. 281–299.

8. The quotes from Lenin are in his *Left Wing Communism: An Infantile Disorder* (New York: International Publishers, 1940), pp. 74–75. Lenin's point, made in another context, in his pamphlet, *What Is to Be Done?* that workers left to themselves would never develop socialist or class consciousness, and that they would remain on the level economic "day to day" consciousness, unless an organized group of revolutionary

intellectuals brought them a broader vision, is similar to the generalizations presented here concerning the inherent limited time perspective of the lower strata.

9. Various American studies indicate that those lower-class individuals who are nonvoters, and who have little political interest, tend to reject the democratic norms of tolerance. See Samuel A. Stouffer, *Communism, Conformity and Civil Liberties* (New York: Doubleday, 1955), and G. M. Connelly and H. H. Field, "The Non-Voter, Who He Is and What He Thinks," *Public Opinion Quarterly,* vol. 8 (1944), p. 182. Studies of the behavior of the unemployed in countries in which extremist movements were weak, such as the United States and Britain, indicate that apathy was their characteristic political response. See E. W. Bakke, *Citizens Without Work* (New Haven: Yale University Press, 1940), pp. 46–70. On the other hand, German data suggest a high correlation between working-class unemployment and support of Communists, and the middle-class unemployment and support of Nazis. In France, Italy, and Finland today, those who have been unemployed tend to back the large Communist parties of those countries. See chap. 7 and Erik Allardt, *Social Struktur och Politisk Aktivitet* (Helsingfors: Söderstrom Förlagsaktiebolag, 1956), pp. 84–85.

WORKING-CLASS AUTHORITARIANISM: A CRITIQUE

Seymour Michael Miller
Frank Riessman

DEMOCRACY—FORM AND SUBSTANCE

. . . Lipset's definition of political liberalism or non-economic democracy seems to include the following: (1) civil liberties for political dissidents (2) civil rights for ethnic and racial minorities; (3) internationalist foreign policy; (4) liberal immigrant legislation; (5) support of a multi-party system; (6) an eschewal of black-and-white thinking; (7) a willingness to compromise and to be gradualist; (8) renunciation of chiliastic, millennial hopes; (9) refusal to engage in extremist thinking and to support extremist political movements.

This yardstick—a complex compound of political values and mechanisms, social attitudes and intellectual orientations—is employed by Lipset to compare the working class and the middle class. Lubell has criticized Lipset's criteria in the following way: "His norm of democratic non-extremist man seems limited to people who share the ideals of New Deal liberals." While we personally feel that the world would be a better place in which to live if these ideals were more widely held, we would hesitate to conclude that those who do not share them are necessarily non-democratic or authoritarian.

Another issue in Lipset's analysis of political liberalism is his insistence that economic and social democracy are no longer linked with political liberalism, although historically they were closely tied. Yet Lipset himself, in a very interesting chapter,[1] has argued that political democracy is likely to flourish only where economic (and social) equalitarianism exist. As Lipset acknowledges, workers are strongly in favour of economic equalitarianism; thus they may be contributing to the furtherance of political democracy.

The evidence that Lipset adduces to support the notion that workers do not support democratic political institutions is fragmentary, consisting mainly of Stouffer's political tolerance scale and of responses in West Germany to the question, "Do you think that it would be better if there were one party, several parties or no party?" (A similar question with similar results—relative low choice of the multi-party alternative by workers—was employed in a number of nations, Lipset informs us.) A number of issues are involved, however, in the interpretation of this question and its results.

It is a poor question since "better" for what or for whom may have varying

SOURCE: *British Journal of Sociology*, September 1961, pp. 264–267, 269–272.

referents among respondents. The question may be interpreted by some respondents as a question about general views of political systems, by others in terms of their critical feelings about what is currently occurring in a nation. Since these two interpretations may be class-linked rather than randomly distributed, the results may be unclear.

Sometimes Lipset seems to be saying that the working class is basically and preponderantly authoritarian; at other times, the argument is that it is more authoritarian than the middle class. In the present instance, working-class strata do not have a high relative or absolute support of the multi-party system. Comparison of the two classes is difficult, however, because the "no opinion" responses are particularly high among working-class groups. If we take favourable attitudes towards the "one-party" or "no-party" alternatives as better indicators of possible authoritarianism (than the non-selection of the multi-party system choice) then it appears that these choices are minority positions within the working class. (Among semi-skilled workers, 35 per cent favour either an one-party or no-party situation; among unskilled workers, 38 per cent, and among skilled workers, 27 per cent, roughly the same percentage found among small business men and lower white-collar groups.)

An additional problem in the Lipset conceptualization is that many shades of opinion may exist between pro-democratic and pro-authoritarian attitudes. Lipset seems, here in the discussion of multi-parties and elsewhere, to imply a dichotomous variable—a democratic or anti-democratic (authoritarian) attitude. One can be abstractly (and perhaps with extremist zeal) pro-democratic to the extent that it is the overriding political value, as Lipset seems to imply when he concludes his book with the contention that ". . . democracy is not only or even primarily a means . . . it is the good society itself in operation" (p. 404). An intermediate attitude might be favourable to democracy but concerned with certain operational problems. Through varying shades we can move to the extremist position that democracy does not meet the psychological needs of men and the political requirements of an effective State. Not to hold the 100 per cent pro-democratic position first mentioned is not necessarily to hold the 100 percent anti-democratic position, Moreover, criticism of a democratic practice or a lack of confidence in certain democratic means may not imply the embracing of authoritarianism.

More basic to Lipset's conceptualization of democracy is its non-pluralistic quality. Lipset seems to see democracy as necessarily involving certain institutions. But these institutional modes, like multi-party systems, are only means to the achievement of democratic practice. Schumpter, whom Lipset acknowledges as strongly influencing his views of democracy, has well stated the problem:

> Beyond "direct democracy" lies an infinite wealth of possible forms in which the "people" may partake in the business of ruling or influence or control those who actually do the ruling. None of these forms, particularly none of the workable ones, has any obvious or exclusive title to being described as Government by the People if these words are to be taken in their natural sense.[2]

Criticism of or doubt about the practice of multi-party systems or other democratic institutions may indicate the need for the imaginative development of new approaches and practices rather than serving as an indication of anti-democratic attitudes.[3] Our political tastes also tend to favour a multi-party system (and other traditional democratic practices) but we are not convinced that they are the only or most effective way of going about achieving democracy and functioning government, *both* of which are important.

Indeed, there seems to be a disquieting tension between present forms of democracy and effective government. One cannot have unalloyed feelings about the performance of some democratic institutions. Although many liberal intellectuals seem to be strongly of the mind that the present procedures of democracy are necessary for the effective execution of *their* professional role and for the general welfare, this view may be an example of black-and-white, extremist thinking which ignores the dysfunctions which may be occurring.[4] A sociology of knowledge analysis of the liberal concern with certain democratic procedures may reveal a simplistic, dogmatically held set of attitudes rather than the "complex and gradualistic" orientation which Lipset believes to be integral to the democratic temper.

The other major data bearing on support of democratic institutional forms are drawn from Stouffer's political tolerance study.[5] The results of this study are generally depressing to all democrats. We hesitate therefore to add the further depressing comment of Bordua that "We might . . . hypothesize that Stouffer's community leaders [and the middle class generally] are more tolerant precisely because they are less punitive rather than because they are committed to civil liberties."[6] (Material in parentheses added.) Workers' less tolerant attitudes may be more of a general acceptance of punitive measures against deviants than a specific disavowal of civil liberties. (Remember that in the United States communists were painted as criminals not dissidents.) We have long felt[7] that the lack of concern with important aspects of civil liberties is one of the factors which encourage *some* workers to be interested in movements of extreme left and right.[8] We agree here partially with Lipset but believe that he has gone too far with the data in packaging the complex mix of workers' attitudes into an authoritarian gladstone bag.

Another aspect of the anti-democratic outlook of workers is the tendency of workers, according to Lipset, to see issues in black-and-white, good-and-evil terms. We think that there is some validity in this contention, but one disturbing element in completely accepting the black-and-white interpretation is the large percentage of "don't knows," "uncertain" among workers on opinion polls, particularly among the low-educated group with whom Lipset is primarily concerned. The admission of uncertainty or non-interest does not seem to support an interpretation of a dogmatic, flat view of the world.

Further, low turnout of workers in elections is unlikely to be assoiated with a sharply divided world view. If the working class tended ". . . to view politics in terms of sharp dichotomy, in black and white terms, would this not encourage their participation in political affairs? If one "knows" what is right and wrong, and who is good and evil, decision making becomes easier. The worker will not be subject to the confusion that arises from a complex perspective."[9]

THE PSYCHODYNAMIC UNDERTONE

While Lipset emphasizes that the causes of the alleged working-class authoritarianism are primarily lack of education, economic insecurity, and a homogeneous environment, he nevertheless introduces personality variables as important contributing factors. "To sum up, the lower-class individual is likely to have been exposed to punishment, lack of love, and a general atmosphere of tension and aggression since early childhood—all experiences which tend to produce deep-rooted hostilities expressed by ethnic prejudice, political authoritarianism and chiliastic transvaluational religion."[10]

Lipset's interpretation of the importance of early-life experiences is based on familiar conceptualizations for which evidence is scanty and contradictory explanations available.[11] For example, Lipset cites the child-rearing evidence summarized by Bronfenbrenner[12] in support of his authoritarian thesis. Lipset notes that Bronfenbrenner reports, in a comprehensive review of the many child-rearing studies, that physical punishment is utilized far more frequently by the working class as a discipline technique, while the middle class uses reasoning, isolation and love-oriented techniques of discipline. Lipset goes on to state that "a further link between such child-rearing practices and adult hostility and authoritarianism is suggested by the finding of two studies in Boston and Detroit that physical punishments for aggression, characteristic of the working class, tend to increase rather than decrease aggressive behavior."[13]

A careful analysis of the Boston data, however, reveals that this interpretation may be somewhat misleading. Sears, Maccoby and Levin[14] in reporting the Boston data state that while aggressive behaviour shows a *slight* positive correlation with punishment and with high permissiveness, the child's aggression is relatively low except in the group where both high permissiveness and high punishment are *combined*.[15]

High permissiveness is more characteristic of the middle class and high punitiveness is more typical of the lower class. Thus each class has child-rearing patterns mildly conducive to the continuance of aggression. High aggressive behaviour in the child, however, is a product of high permissiveness and high punitiveness operating together and this combination is not distinctly characteristic of either class.

With regard to the Detroit study conducted by Miller and Swanson,[16] it should be noted that while the authors indicate the negative consequences of corporal punishment, which is more frequent in the working class, they also note the negative effects of the psychological forms of discipline, which are characteristic of the middle class. Most significant however, is the fact that Miller and Swanson point out that it is mixed discipline (a combination of physical and psychological forms of discipline) which is most effective. They state that boys trained in this manner are more "realistic," "are neither uncontrolled nor overly constricted," and "are not excessively direct or indirect in their expression of aggression."[17] Their data indicate that this mixed form of discipline occurs more frequently in the working class.[18]

THE SOCIAL EXPLANATION

Lipset argues that the homogeneity of the working-class environment is a major reason for the limited perspectives and simplistic thinking of workers. Elsewhere, however, in a most penetrating and useful article, centering on the importance of cross-pressures, he asserts that:

> The lower-income groups in most stratified societies are exposed to strong upper-class influences through the press, radio, schools, churches, etc.; the existing system has many traditional claims to legitimacy which influence even the lower classes. Yet the lower classes are also exposed to influences favouring reformist or radical voting from their class organizations and from their own life experience. *They are thus placed in a situation of conflicting information and opposing group pressures.* Members of the upper classes, on the other hand, are seldom exposed to much working-class propaganda or group pressure; they live in a relatively "homogeneous political environment" where all influences point in one political direction. This may be one reason for the generally observed class difference in voting turnout [i.e. the upper classes with less cross-pressures are more likely to vote], . . . a crude index of the political homogeneity of the social environment of various social categories. . . . tended to support the notion of greater homogeneity of political environment for the upper classes. . . .[19] (Parenthetical material and italics added.)

Faced with the fact that workers and their unions frequently have liberal positions on non-economic issues, Lipset contends that these positive positions arise from the leadership of the working-class organizations. To a considerable extent this is true, but in the face of cross-pressures there is unlikely to be a blind following of the leadership. Possibly leaders are able to attract some workers to the liberal position on the value level.[20]

In essence, Lipset's underlying approach is well expressed in his statement: 'A leftist intellectual should not be upset to learn that poverty, insecurity, and ignorance do not produce as "decent" people as do wealth, security, and knowledge.'[21] Here Lipset indicates which variables, namely, poverty, insecurity, and lack of education, are crucial in the formation of working-class values and character structure. More than that, he indicates the direction in which these factors supposedly mould values.

We would not deny that all three are significant variables, but we would question the simplicity of Lipset's implication as to how they function and we wonder whether other variables may not be equally decisive in affecting attitudes and behaviour. To be specific: there may be conditions of working-class existence, such as removal from competitiveness and status concern, the concentration in workplaces, extended family structures, which produce many co-operative, democratic trends. Poverty and insecurity do no necessarily and inevitably produce less 'decent' values. Under certain conditions they can lead to the development of solidaristic, warm feelings. Similarly, wealth, security, and knowledge can lead to tolerant and democratic values under some conditions. Under other conditions, as we know, they may lead to smugness, elitism, intellectualism, and coldness. Many other variables in addition to wealth, education, and security are decisive in the formation of liberal and democratic values.[22]

AN ALTERNATIVE VIEW

We have no counter interpretation of the evidence which is as parsimonious as Lipset's view, for at times the Lipset analysis seems to imply a black-and-white, good-and-evil contrast between the middle class and working class.[23] The former is pro-democratic in attitudes and behaviour, the latter anti-democratic in attitudes and frequently in behaviour. While many middle-class individuals dramatically support liberal positions in many nations today, many others have had or do have an anti-democratic outlook with strong authoritarian overtones. Many fascist and illiberal movements, for example, have had important middle-class support.[24] In Lipset's own analysis of McCarthyism,[25] to cite only one illustration, he has given considerable attention to the illiberal 'status politics' of the middle class.

The sad and complex truth seems to be that no class has a monopoly on pro- or anti-democratic attitudes. *Neither class, we believe, is psychologically authoritarian, but both classes have values which could be turned in the direction of political authoritarianism under certain conditions.*

Among the pro-democratic attitudes of workers not mentioned by Lipset would seem to be their frequent anti-elitist, outspoken, co-operative, underdog and informality orientations, as well as their acceptance of leadership with the accompanying delegation of authority.

Among the anti-democratic attitudes of the middle class ignored by Lipset are its frequent conventionalism, competitiveness, status concern, fear of authority, over-intellectualism, and snobbery.

In our interpretation, workers possess a number of traits which have authoritarian potential: the desire for strong leadership and definite structure; anti-intellectualism; a punitive ('tough') attitude towards violation of the law, etc. While these attitudes might lead to or might be manipulated in an authoritarian direction, their major source and meaning derives from the traditionalism and concrete, result-oriented pragmatism which we feel characterize American workers.[26]

These traits may look like certain brands of authoritarianism and may in fact be linked with authoritarianism under certain conditions. It is doubtful, however, that genotypically they have the same roots as authoritarianism. Nor need they inevitably operate in an authoritarian direction. They can become authoritarian and anti-democratic, but this is a potential, rather than a perpetual actuality.

NOTES

1. Chap. 2, 'Economic Development and Democracy' of *Political Man*.
2. Joseph Schumpeter, *Capitalism, Socialism and Democracy* (New York: Harper & Brothers, 1950), p. 247.
3. The rise of controversy mainly within a political party rather than between political parties indicates that important changes are taking place in multi-party government. 'The Stalemate Society' is a derisive term that has been employed to describe the inaction which frequently results from this situation.
4. The defects of the practice of progressive education—a programme early and widely rejected by workers—indicate the ritualistic concern with democracy and the uncon- cern for over-all goals which sometimes plague the abstract middle-class ideologue of democracy.

5. Samuel A. Stouffer, *Communism, Conformity and Civil Liberties* (New York: Double-day, 1955).

6. David Joseph Bordua, *Authoritarianism and Intolerance, A Study of High School Students,* unpublished Ph.D. thesis, Department of Social Relations, Harvard University, 1956, p. 228.

7. Frank Riessman, *Workers' Attitudes Towards Participation and Leadership,* unpublished Ph.D dissertation, Columbia University, 1955.

8. Bordua offers an intriguing finding concerning the determinants of intolerance and authoritarianism. If religion is held constant, class differences in political tolerance and authoritarianism are insignificant. The working class in the Boston area is high on intolerance and authoritarianism because it has more Catholics than the middle class. If this finding is replicated in studies in other parts of the United States, it raises some questions about the factors involved in high scores on intolerance and authoritarianism tests. Bordua, *Authoritarianism,* p. 109.

   The attractions of the extreme left in certain situations may be, as Almond points out, its effectiveness rather than, as Lipset contends, its simplistic character. Gabriel Almond, review of *Political Man,* in *American Sociological Review,* vol. 25 (October 1960), pp. 753–754.

9. Harry Brill, 'Lipset on Political Participation and Civil Liberties,' undergraduate seminar paper, Department of Sociology and Anthropology, Brooklyn College, May, 1960, p. 6. This paper will be published in the Berkeley sociology journal.

10. P. 120. The fundamentalist religious orientation of many (Protestant) workers which Lipset interprets as resulting from the 'same underlying characteristics' as those which lead to 'allegiance to authoritarian political movements' can be differently explained. A good deal of this fundamentalist movement is away from or perhaps against the middle-class and upper-class-oriented Protestant churches, which are largely unsympathetic to working-class adherents. Moreover, while the bulk of the adherents of fundamentalist churches may be workers, the bulk of workers are not in fundamentalist churches.

11. We deal with these interpretations in a series of papers. Most interesting in this connection is our 'A Critique of the Non-Deferred Gratification Image of the Workers', forthcoming. Fred Strodtbeck has made a somewhat similar point in questioning the frequent assertion that the female-dominated broken home leads to compulsive masculinity among lower-class children. Review of Robert F. Winch, *Mate-Selection: A Study of Complementary Needs,* in *American Sociological Review,* vol. 24 (June, 1959), p. 438.

12. Urie Bronfenbrenner, 'Socialization and Social Class Through Time and Space,' in E. E. Maccoby, T. M. Newcomb, and E. L. Hartley (eds.), *Readings in Social Psychology* (New York: Henry Holt, 1958), p. 419.

13. P. 114.

14. Robert Sears, Eleanor E. Maccoby, and Harry Levin, 'The Socialization of Aggression', in Maccoby, Newcomb, and Hartley, (eds.), *Social Psychology,* pp. 350–359.

15. The discussion of punishment here includes physical as well as non-physical punishment.

16. Daniel R. Miller and Guy E. Swanson, *Inner Conflict and Defense* (New York: Henry Holt, 1960).

17. *Ibid.,* p. 399.

18. *Ibid.,* p. 426. In a reanalysis of the data of the Gluecks' study of Youth in the Cambridge-Somerville Area near Boston, it was found that lower-class youth who were prejudiced against minorities had not had a more disturbed early family life than lower-class youth who were unprejudiced. It is suggested that family pathology may be important in the etiology of middle-class prejudice though not of lower-class. These

results raise some question about early-life experience, prejudice and authoritarianism. William Cord, Joan McCord and Alan Howard, "Early Familial Experiences and Bigotry," *American Sociological Review*, vol. 25 (October 1960), pp. 717–722.

19. Seymour M. Lipset et al., "The Psychology of Voting: An Analysis of Political Behavior," in Gardner Lindzey (ed.), *Handbook of Social Psychology* (Cambridge, Mass.: Addison-Wesley, 1954), pp. 1133–1134. Cf. Brill, 'Political Participation,' pp. 3–5. Lipset closely restates this position in *Political Man*, pp. 205–206.

20. Since middle-class individuals are more likely to join groups than are workers, it may be that the former's liberal positions are also somewhat or occasionally influenced by their leaders.

21. Seymour Martin Lipset, "Reply to Lahav," *American Sociological Review*, vol. 25 (February 1960), pp. 90–91.

22. Lipset does at times, as indicated earlier, declare that other factors are important, that personal attitudes and orientations do not determine political behaviour. He generally cites in this connection the nature of working-class organizations which usually lead workers to behave more democratically than their personalities. When one considers both working-class and middle-class attitudes and behaviour, it is clear that the analysis is much too limited. Despite the sophisticated disclaimers, the tenor of Lipset's thinking seems to be the role of personality and class position in political choice. Cf. 'Reply to Lahav,' p. 91.

23. We regret the necessity of criticizing the middle class, since such derogation has already become a well-established and fashionable industry in the United States. But in the context of the Lipset discussion it seems unavoidable to raise some questions about the middle-class attitudes with which workers' attitudes are explicitly or implicitly compared.

24. A very provocative analysis citing illustrations of middle-class support of certain forms of fascism will be found in ' "Fascism"—Left, Right, and Center,' chap. 5 of *Political Man*. American examples of middle-class devotion to extremism are cited in C. Vann Woodward, 'The Populist Heritage and the Intellectual,' *American Scholar*, vol. 29 (Winter 1959–1960), p. 69.

25. Seymour Martin Lipset, 'The Sources of the "Radical Right," ' in Daniel Bell (ed.), *The New American Rights* (New York: Criterion Books, 1955), pp. 166–233. For a critical assessment of the point of view presented in this book, which largely ignores the importance of working-class support of McCarthyism, see the review of the book by S. M. Miller in *Public Opinion Quarterly*, vol. 20 (Autumn 1956), pp. 611–613.

26. We have attempted to develop a more cohesive analysis of workers in 'The Working-Class Subculture: a New View,' presented at the 1960 meetings of the American Sociological Association.

B.   The New Worker:
A New Revolutionary Vanguard?

INTRODUCTION

One of the new themes in the current debate on the working class has centered on the emergence and growing importance of "educated labor" in the work force of the "post-industrial society." Does "educated labor" represent an emergent social class or stratum with revolutionary potential or is it merely a skilled stratum whose concern for maintaining its "professional status" serves to differentiate it from the larger body of the working class in a continually evolving capitalist society? The first three selections elaborate the concept of the "new working class," while the last reflects a critical attitude toward this concept.

Denitch, in "Is There a 'New Working Class'?", explicitly links the discontent of both students and the more highly educated younger members of the work force to the limited availability of creative and self-fulfilling work opportunities. Student discontent is "only a harbinger of the discontent of a new and growing class" characterized by relatively high levels of skill and intellectual development but little opportunity for participation in decision making. Denitch warns, however, that this new working class can become a significant force for institutional change "only in alliance with sections of the old working class."

Touraine's focus in "New Classes, New Conflicts," is on the relationship of the new strata of technician-employees to a "new dominant class" of technocrats and bureaucrats. Effective opposition to the social domination of the latter cannot be expected from "marginal social elements." It must come from "those who possess scientific and technical competence" but lack power. For Touraine the old themes of class, power, and conflict remain valid tools of social analysis but are reinterpreted within the framework of alienation and bureaucratic domination rather than the more traditional Marxian concept of capital-labor exploitation.

173

The selection from the HEW report, *Work in America,* focuses on the work attitudes of the young. Perhaps the chief impact of the relatively high educational attainments of young workers is to raise expectations associated with work more rapidly than the economy can meet them. The work attitudes of the young reflect not a rejection of the work ethic *per se* but "a shift away from their willingness to take on meaningless work in authoritarian settings that offers only extrinsic rewards." The challenge to managerial authority which results from these attitudes is not confined to young workers; it is only one aspect of the questioning of traditional authority throughout society.

Aronowitz, while writing from a radical perspective, denies the emergence of a new class in contemporary capitalism and treats technicians as "merely a differently trained stratum of the industrial working class." He also questions the extent to which the higher educational attainments of the work force as a whole are rooted in the requirements of new technology and suggests some alternative explanations of this phenomenon.

IS THERE A "NEW WORKING CLASS"? A BRIEF NOTE ON A LARGE QUESTION

Bogdan Denitch

Mass university education, in the advanced industrial countries, is leading to a shift in the function and character of university-educated personnel. From an elite education for sons of notables preparing to assume leading roles, there is a turn to vocational training and, also, to an imprecise rite of passage designated to prepare technicians and white-collar workers for a bureaucratized economy. This trend has reduced many of the old-style professionals to paid employees of institutions. The process has advanced farthest in the United States, though a number of factors make awareness of it clearer in France and some East European countries. It is important to distinguish between the effect of *mass* university education, primarily a post-World War II phenomenon, and the older discontent of *unemployed* university graduates centered on status demands and often associated with right-wing movements.

The post-World War II expansion of universities has coincided with a growing demand for university graduates. Relatively high salaries and social mobility obtained through university education disguise their real loss of power and status. Students of working-class or lower-middle-class origin tend to accept the university environment, since for them it does represent a major chance for social advance. But with them, too, promise evoked by higher education clashes with the result, which is often work-compartmentalized to a degree that an older generation of university graduates would find unrecognizable. Two results follow. Leaving the university after graduation comes to seem increasingly unattractive, since meaningful work *in terms of their own education,* particularly for students of the social sciences and humanities, is hard to find. And a fertile ground is created for hostility toward a society that seems incapable of assuring satisfying work even to university graduates.

This discontent is most clearly articulated in the social sciences and humanities, where the training one gets—the ability to critically analyze institutions and ideologies—has little relationship to the work one will end up doing. For what can one do today with an undergraduate degree in the social sciences or the humanities? The better-situated students in those disciplines increasingly accept the fact that their undergraduate degree is only a prerequisite for entering graduate schools. Yet, while graduate school postpones entry into the job market, it also increases the gap between the training one gets and the work one will do; not all graduate students, after all, choose academic careers.

SOURCE: *Dissent,* July–August 1970, pp. 351–355.

This change in the role of universities reflects new needs of the economy: needs for increasing numbers of salaried people with technical and bureaucratic skills who will be dependent on institutions in which they hold no power. It is a process that can be observed in advanced industrialized societies, both East and West. Whole generations trained to think in terms of societal issues are offered roles as powerless, if well-paid, employees. Those with specific skills find their work compartmentalized and routinized. The shift in the authority of engineers and skilled scientists in industry also reduces them to a *new* highly-trained working class.[1]

One root of student discontent lies in this shift of role. Students increasingly resent the fact that modern society seems incapable of providing meaningful work and participation in decision-making. Far from temporary, the wave of student radicalism is neither localized in respect to political issues (an end to the Vietnam War might not reduce student rebellion in the U.S.) nor centered on the organization of universities. Nor is it in essence rooted in a conflict of generations. It represents instead the inchoate early struggles of "a class in the process of becoming," mostly unaware of its own needs and acting archaically or irrationally. Students have sometimes been called neo-Luddites. We should remember that the Luddites were an anachronistic expression of a then *new* working class in the process of being formed out of the old crafts; they were striking out in a socially irrelevant way at symbols of their *new* status marking the end of their old role. I would like to suggest in a crude parallel that the direction of student discontent toward the universities is analogous. Not the university but their own new position in society is a major cause of student alienation, just as not the machine but the new social organization of work changed the role of the old craftsmen.

Student discontent is, in my view, only a harbinger of the discontent of a new and growing class. This discontent will probably reach students in the technical sciences later than those in the social sciences, if only because the latter have been trained to generalize ideas and societal issues. For those from the technical sciences a recognition of their real status may come only at work, where they will be joining portions of the old industrial working class whose skills and training also move them toward the creation of a new group of highly-skilled technicians.

The process, which makes unskilled and semi-skilled workers less powerful, makes many skilled workers more important. They are harder to train and replace. Because of their strategic position small groups of highly-skilled workers can often paralyze entire plants. Workers in process-flow industry who maintain the ever more complex machinery, skilled workers in communication industries, IBM, electronics and even in some of the old trades—tool- and die-makers, plant electricians, and certain branches of the building trades—begin to converge with the technicians and younger engineers into a new working class. For them, too, the gap between capabilities and decision-making becomes increasingly less rational, for often they are as competent to make day-to-day decisions as the foremen and management. Their skills are a key to modern production, and not the often archaic skills of the managers and owners.[2]

The rationality of factory organization and the legitimacy of discipline are threatened when they seem based not on superior knowledge but on institutional power alone. In all the modern industrial societies, power, after all, remains in the hands of the old elites. It was always more difficult to be a foreman or supervisor, to exercise authority over highly-skilled workers than over the unskilled, particularly when the skill of the workers and their knowledge of the work process was greater than that of lower-level management. A traditional way of handling this problem in such trades as printing, tool- and diemaking, etc., has been to have "working foremen" who were members of the union and organizers of tasks rather than managers of men. In many countries the highly skilled workers have developed a great deal of control over the work pace and process, eliminating lower management entirely. Thus the immediate authority faced by the worker was half-voluntary, subject to his democratic organization and therefore legitimate. With the new working class, however, the skills of the workers, whether utilized or not, are so often superior to those of the lower, middle and sometimes even higher management that authority derives from the organizational structure alone; it is neither reasonable nor legitimate.

A new working class, indispensable to modern economies, has a potential social weight greater than its actual numbers, which, in any case, are growing. Seemingly divergent strands—massive discontent among students in most industrial societies—a decrease in the independence of professionals, the "proletarianization" of many technicians and engineers, the increasing militancy of strategically-placed groups of skilled workers (particularly in Western Europe) are interconnected. They represent an early phase in the developing consciousness of a stratum in modern industrial societies which can be described as a "new working class." While this term has been used in the United States,[3] it is generally counterposed to the more traditional stress on the working class as agency for social change. There is peculiar continuity between the New Left attempt to identify the young intelligentsia as the major group potentially committed to radical social change and the decades-old liberal stress on middle-class liberals as the active political element. Both agree that the traditional working class is passive and will remain so. I say, however, that the new working class must help transform the labor movement and can become a significant social force only in alliance with sections of the old working class.

In France in 1968 and Italy in 1970, the most militant strikers came from areas with the most advanced technology and the highest proportion of highly skilled or educated workers in electronics, chemistry, auto, aircraft, as well as from previously passive "middle-class" professions—teaching and journalism. Characteristic of these strikers is a stress on democracy at the point of production rather than mere traditional wage demands. Strikers of this kind indicate that relatively high wages do not succeed in buying off discontent. A sense of powerlessness is not sufficient for revolt; but a sense of powerlessness at work combined with a feeling of power as a social group provides an impetus toward organized militancy. This militancy expresses itself not only in regard to wages and working conditions but also in regard to problems of control in the work process. The demand for some form of worker's control increasingly characterizes the strikes in Europe— and it is raised by the most skilled workers and technicians, more often than not against the desire of the union leaders and parties of the Left.

This has profound implications for any analysis of student rebellions and "middle-class" discontent, but even more for the trade-union and socialist movements. For the latter understanding and relating to this process is a matter of life and death. In Western Europe both the Social Democratic and Communist parties find that their bases of strength remain in the old working class, and these not only shrink numerically but become strategically less important. In

France it was the previously Catholic trade unions (CFTU) rather than the Communist-led CGT that repeatedly took that initiative in strikes and alone related sympathetically to the students during May 1968. The CFTU's primary strength is in industries where the new rather than the old working class predominates.

A major dividing line between Marxist and non-Marxist radicals has always been the insistence of Marxists that forces for social transformation had to exist in the society itself. Subjective desires of would-be revolutionists could never be enough. Around this issue center most of the polemics between Marx and Bakunin; it is the issue that led Kautsky to attack the Bolsheviks as neo-Jacobins. On the whole question of just how central is the presence of objective historical forces are waged bitter polemics between Guevarists and Marxists in Latin America.

In a way, both New Left utopianism and the increasingly reformism of the mass working-class parties in Western Europe are based on the same analysis of the role of the old working class. Each sees the industrial working class as passive and, if anything, conservative. They reach a pessimistic view of the possibilities for social change deriving from the action of the industrial working class, and therefore become either de-facto liberal reformers or seek a different agency for social change. A theory of social change based on revolt of both the external colonies and internal marginal groups—either as yet unsocialized, as in the case of the students, or economically marginal, as in the case of the sub-proletariat—may sound extremely "radical." But, implicitly, it rejects the view that *conscious and voluntary* action of the *majority* in its own name and interests is either a possible or, for that matter, desirable way to achieve a socialist society. Its central view is that at least in the advanced industrialized countries, "socialism" can and should be imposed by marginal revolutionary minorities on a generally reactionary majority—and particularly against the desires of a working class seen as the core of this reaction.

Two views are common in the New Left: first, a profound pessimism about the possibilities of mobilizing mass support, which sees the working class as bought off by the consumer-oriented society or even racist and reactionary; second, a view of student revolt as the symptom of a generational revolt rather than a reflection of major social shifts. These analyses combine to give the New Left an unreal, temporary, marginal character—to fixate it as a form of kamikaze radicalism without hope of producing major social change, yet determined to make the (necessarily only moral) gesture.

What underlines the relevance of the growing layer of technically and intellectually trained workers is that they are also to be found in the one-party "socialisms" of Eastern Europe where massive growth of the universities has an even more explosive potential—unless, of course, we assume an infinite capacity of those regimes to absorb and buy off their university-trained cadres. The irrationality and inefficiency, not to speak of the brutality, of the Eastern European societies is more "pure" than that of the welfare capitalism of the West. This is perhaps the reason why the demands there are so much clearer at this time: democratization of major institutions (the government, mass organizations and party) or a multiparty system, and self-management or workers' control of enterprises. Few of the oppositionists use New Left rhetoric, and if some small circles of intellectuals may have absorbed the "new and modern" view that the working class is reactionary and coopted, it is an illusion that no regime dares have. In Prague in 1968 workers called for workers' councils and a real say in day-to-day decisions over production, while intellectuals centered on intellectual freedoms. The reluctance of the Prague liberals to introduce workers' councils may go a long way to explain the relative indifference to the early phase of the Russian occupation by the same workers who, through massive slowdown, continued the struggle long after many intellectuals had left the country or had become silent.

Demands for workers' control or workers' councils are of course not new. They are to be found in early Marx, in Bakunin, Proudhon, and Kropotkin. They were present in the writings of some Bolsheviks and Rosa Luxemburg. Workers' control was not only central to the demands of the Workers' Opposition in the early Bolshevik period; it was the instinctive response of the working class in Spain at the opening of the Civil War. However, it is also true that most of the European Left parties, including Communist after the victory of Stalin, have borrowed heavily from the Jacobin tradition of revolutionary centralism. Though centralism was viewed not as antithetical to democracy but as an instrumental against local, entrenched power, it did lead to neglect of the content and day-to-day organization of power. Nationalization of the means of production was seen by the Left primarily as depriving the old ruling classes of its economic power, but not as fundamentally changing work relations inside the newly nationalized industry. Today, renewed demands for workers' control reflect not only dissatisfaction of the workers in the nationalized industries of both Western and Eastern Europe with the old authoritarian structures. The changing character of the work force and mode of production further creates an ever larger pool of workers who believe that they are capable of running the industry and at least those social organizations most relevant to their day-to-day lives. A working though imperfect model of workers' control and decentralization in Yugoslavia gives the discussion some reality.

The fleshing-out of demands to control one's community and work place can give radical intellectuals a focus. It also forms a platform from which the utopian and elitist views current in so much of the student New Left can be confronted. Democratic socialist critics of the irrational and putschist rhetoric of the student radicals have too often criticized them in the name of old platforms and unexciting vistas of endless drudgery for the demands developed in a different era. Today a new meaning can be given to demands to extend democracy to all aspects of social and political life—and the technical skills and education of the new working class equip it to challenge the monopoly of expertise of the old elites.

NOTES

1. The most cogent discussion of the theories of the new working class is to be found in Serge Mallet, *La Nouvelle Classe Ouvrière* (Paris: Seuil, 1969).
2. This is even more striking in Eastern Europe where the political "skills" of the managers of nationalized enterprises are, if anything, more anachronistic than the training of their opposite numbers in the West. E.g., recent studies in Poland and Yugoslavia show that most managers who have a university degree tend to have a general law or economics degree.
3. See Richard Flacks, "The Revolt of the Young Intelligentsia: Revolutionary Class Consciousness in Post Scarcity America," in *Revolution Reconsidered* (New York: Free Press); and Michael Harrington, "Whatever Happened to Socialism," *Harper's,* February 1970.

NEW CLASSES, NEW CONFLICTS

Alain Touraine

A new kind of society is being born. If we want to define it by its technology, by its "production forces," let's call it the programmed society. If we choose to name it from the nature of its ruling class, we'll call it technocratic society.

In social analysis and in practice, the notion of social class has been too intimately bound up with the social organization of the era of capitalist industrialization for that notion not to be profoundly questioned in any consideration of a society in which the creation of knowledge, the systems governing production, distribution, and information, and the network of political and economic decisions form a social and economic organization profoundly different from the nineteenth century. Must we abandon the idea that the class struggle holds a central place in sociological analysis? Many have been tempted to answer affirmatively simply because the analytical tools inherited from an earlier period are clearly unable to explain the new situation. Our plan moves in the opposite direction. It will affirm the fundamental importance of class situations, conflicts, and movements in the programmed society. This plan can only be realized if we detach ourselves as completely as possible from historically defined images and ideas and become involved in a radical renewal of social analysis. One could attempt to adapt the old ideas to new situations, but such an exercise would be futile because it takes no account of social practice. If we wish to retain the useful idea of social class and free it from any particular historical experience and interpretation, we must begin, not with a definition, but with critical analysis of the themes of social class and class society as they have come to us, especially in Europe. We must set out, not from a new abstraction, but from the examination of a concrete representation of social organization.

. . . If property was the criterion of membership in the former dominant classes, the new dominant class is defined by knowledge and a certain level of education. The question is whether there exists a superior level of education with characteristics distinct from those of lower levels, the acquisition of which creates a system of social selection and the possession of which acts as a symbol of membership in the higher class. The more advanced levels within the educational systems become progressively more specialized—but only up to a point. Beyond that point, the tendency is reversed and education concentrates on the acquisition of general methods of analysis. Analogously, lower functionaries do not specialize; middle management is more and more specialized according to rank; at the top, officials enjoy great horizontal mobility. On the other hand, the education of the

SOURCE: *The Post-Industrial Society* (New York: Random House, 1971), pp. 27–28, 51–69.

top level tends to be independent of any specialized body of professors and is largely provided for by members of the elite whose own education has guaranteed their success; top management officials play an important role in deciding what is taught at the Ecole Nationale d'Administration. Education tends also to be transformed into a mechanism of initiation into a particular social group and to take on a symbolic character, most often represented by attendance at a particular school or university. Entrance examinations take the place of final examinations, which indicates the relative importance of recruitment programs as opposed to the communication of knowledge.

In this way, a new aristocracy is created along with a consciousness of the separation between it and the middle echelons of the hierarchy. Between the staff and the manager, the civil administrator and the director, sometimes between even the highly placed research worker and the "boss," a separation is established and marked by many signs, including sometimes significant differences in income. A hierarchical continuity among bureaucrats and technocrats may appear to exist but it is a rare case when the members of a great organization cannot recognize the line that separates them.

Technocracy is also a meritocracy which regulates entrance into its ranks by controlling credentials. This phenomenon is perhaps more accentuated in France than in other countries, for French technocracy has been able to impose itself on the traditional State structures and the prestige which the "great schools"[1] and professional bodies have been able to preserve. The same tendency is manifest in all industrial countries, including the United States where many great universities are almost transformed into large professional training schools, recruiting by competitive examination.

Once in the managerial category, one never leaves it. Many technocrats certainly see their positions improve or worsen, depending on whether the governmental administration is favorable to them or not. But they have great job security and their income is safe even if they are "unattached." In this way, a social group is formed. It is certainly not homogeneous but has a definite self-consciousness, adopts certain behavior patterns, and exercises considerable control over recruitment.

The technocracy is a social category because it is defined by its management of the massive economic and political structures which direct development. It conceives society simply as the totality of the social means needed to mobilize this development. It is a dominant class because, in proclaiming identification with development and social progress, it identifies the interests of society with those of the great organizations which, vast and impersonal as they are, are nonetheless centers for particular interests.

Technocratic ideology may be liberal or authoritarian—these variations are of the greatest importance—but it consistently denies social conflict, though willingly recognizing the existence of tensions and competing strategies. These conflicts do exist, rooted in the accumulation and concentration of decision-making power and knowledge. Technocratic organizations wrap themselves in secrecy and distrust public information and debate. They aggressively build their own power, impose more and more rigid social integration on their members, and manipulate the channels of production and consumption. They are centers of power that create new forms of inequality and privilege. On the global level, we speak of central and peripheral nations, a de facto distinction between the rulers and the subjects.

Similarly, within a particular nation, there is a growing separation between the central and ruling elements within the great organizations and a new *plebs* which is subject to change beyond its control, to publicity campaigns and propaganda, and to the disorganization of its earlier social structures.

It is more difficult to define those whose interests are opposed to those of the technocrats. In a market capitalism, the wage-earners are the dominated class because they are subject in the labor market to the power of those who hold capital. In the programmed society, directed by the machinery of growth, the dominated class is no longer defined in terms of property, but by its dependence on the mechanisms of engineered change and hence on the instruments of social and cultural integration. One's trade, one's directly productive work, is not in direct opposition to capital; it is personal and collective identity in opposition to manipulation. This may seem abstract, in the sense that man is no longer involved simply in his occupational role. He is involved as worker, but also as consumer and as an inhabitant, in a word as an alien subjected to a decision-making system operated in the name of the collectivity.

This is why the role formerly played by attachment to one's trade is today played by attachment to one's *space*. The worker is not defending himself simply as a worker, but more broadly as a member of a community, attached to a way of life, to bonds of family and friends, to a culture. There was a time when the appeal to history and geography was raised by the new dominant classes, the conquering bourgeoise, which believed in evolution and progress and was attached to the formation of great national unities and great channels of trade. Today, the dominant class relies on the economy and sometimes on the social sciences, which offer it the categories that best define its developmental and programming action. History and geography, attachment to tradition and to the soil, have become the style of thought and feeling of those who resist transplantation. Sometimes, they resist blindly, but sometimes they demand that industry move to the manpower and not always the other way around, that the entire territory be harnessed instead of only favoring the great industrial concentrations. Regional consciousness and the defense of local liberties are the principal foundation of resistance to technocracy.

The defense of the city, illustrated by Henri Lefebvre, plays an increasingly important analogous role. The urban milieu, a diversified location of social exchanges, tends to explode. Residential sections become diversified and more and more clearly stratified. The rapid growth of cities leads to the construction of dwelling units which answer the elementary need for shelter of workers but are bereft of autonomous social life. To the degree that society more rapidly modifies its environment and its own material conditions, the importance of the destruction of ecological balances and the conditions of habitability makes itself felt more and more. At the same time as the most pathological forms of capitalism disorganize social space by delivering it over to speculation, technocratic power, wrapped up in its plan for growth, resistant to negotiation and new information, destroys the capacity of society to transform its life-forms, to imagine a new kind of space, and to develop new forms of social relations and cultural activities. Social struggles can no longer remain limited to the domain of labor and business, because the hold of economic power over social life is more general than ever and reaches every aspect of personal life and collective activities.

Bureaucracy is the label we give to opacity within the economic organization.

Only complex organization of technical and human means makes progress possible in production and productivity. Each of these organized systems has a certain inertia, because of routine and from the need to stabilize the relations among the various parts of the whole. Each system realizes that the more complex an organization is, the more necessity there is to devote an important part of its resources to the treatment of its internal problems. In the same way, a complex machine can function only part of the time and resetting, repairs, and maintenance create a wide gap between theoretical and real production. This does not, however, keep a modern machine from having a greater return than an older one.

Internal functional demands may be transformed into an autonomous system with its own rules and relationships. For example, if there must be a hierarchy of functions, professional activity can still be disrupted by an overriding concern for career-building, pointless multiplication of the signs of social rank, or technically unjustified expansion of the hierarchical ladder. Like the government service, the university and the health services, the industrial world knows the problem of W. H. Whyte, Jr.'s "organization man,"[2] a mixture of conformism and opportunism, sometimes mixed with a concern for good "human relations" which gets in the way of difficult decisions.

Dahrendorf, following Renner, defined bureaucrats as a "service class" (*Dienstklasse*). But this definition is not well adapted to the new situation we have to describe. It fits better an older system of organization, the State structure (the Prussian *Beamtentum*), and the civil-service officials whom the French fear and mock.

This rigidly hierarchical, military type of bureaucracy, in which each person is defined by the delegation of authority he has received, belongs essentially to the past even when it manages to survive. Each administrative reform strikes a blow against it and it seems particularly ineffective when production tasks are assigned to it, as is the case with many public services. The inertia of a modern bureaucracy does not result from its rigidity but from its complexity and the interrelations woven among services, bureaus, and functions. While definite orders are deformed to an absurd degree as they descend through the hierarchy, there are endless conferences designed to insure respect for the interests of the participants and the slowing down of the whole organization.

Resistance comes, not any longer from the inertia of the base which lacks initiative, but from the defense mechanisms of the big and little wheels in all the parts of the organization chart; it comes from the formation of classes, alliances, coalitions, and schools of thought which throw the system into confusion. They transform the system into a patchwork of baronies and fenced-in hunting preserves. This is how it is with bureaucrats: adept at change, agents of progress beyond doubt, but also often careerists, vain, distrustful, absorbed in their subtle stratagems and their desire to reinforce their own importance by holding back information, by fostering their own prestige in every way possible, and by defending the internal demands of the organization in opposition to its external purposes.

We must retain one important idea from Dahrendorf's analysis. The bureaucrats do not make up the whole of the "new middle class," nor even the whole of the intermediary levels of a great organization. Beside them there exist increasingly important masses of *employees* and *technicians* whose power, in terms of negotiation, authority, and influence, is weak or non-existent. We are not thinking of the new "proletariat," the employees whose tasks are as repetitive, monotonous, and restrictive as those of assembly-line workers. Rather, we are thinking of relatively advanced groups: technical workers, designers, higher ranking office workers, and technical assistants who do not take part in the bureaucratic game and who are more directly exposed to its consequences than the traditional workers, who are relatively protected by the weakness of their involvement and their great numbers at the base of the organization charts. These technician-employees represent the principal focus of resistance to the bureaucracy, while the immense mass of "clients" of the administrations represent a quasi-group which gives its protests concrete expression only with great difficulty.

This analysis seems to us to explain better the observable extension in France of the collective presentation of grievances by these middle-level professional categories than overly general ideas about their revolutionary capacities. The technicians are not taking over the place of the skilled workers at the head of the class struggle. Certainly, as a new social category begins to become conscious of its situation, it is easy to resurrect doctrines or an extremist vocabulary which directly question the principles of social organization. The collective energy of the technicians is much more directed toward redress within their organizations and pro-test against the bureaucracy, as well as the defense of employment status and careers. The forms of these efforts are often new and their strength is felt to the degree that economic circumstances and the short supply of technicians on the market give this group considerable power at the bargaining table—but the inspiration is not revolutionary.

On the level of *technical execution,* the most striking fact is the rapidity of change. Engineers, research centers, and laboratories are intent on accelerating the "obsolescence" of the techniques in use. The life expectancy of machines, procedures, and formulations is continually being shortened. It is difficult to measure how much waste is created in this way. Many observers, however, have noted that important expenditures for equipment (calculators, for example) are made without careful study of operating costs, simply because a new machine is a symbol of modernity. The gadget craze is not restricted to individuals; it is equally widespread in business and administration.

Technicists form a category with little chance of transforming itself into a social class, for two reasons: they are dispersed and, above all, they succeed at their excesses only if they are also technocrats or bureaucrats. We do not, as a result, include them in a list of the new social classes.

Technicism reveals itself best by its incapacity to grasp the whole picture of the problems an organization poses. The complexity of a social system is broken down by recourse to rules which are often nothing but rituals. For a long time, the critics of the so-called scientific organization of work have demonstrated the errors resulting from the reduction of human work to a succession of elementary movements and of the worker psychology to an impoverished image of *homo oeconomicus.* Both factories and administrations are aware of the rigidity of this technicism against which the skilled workers rebel especially.

One category of victims possesses a particular importance. The obsolescence of techniques is accompanied by the obsolescence of skills. A more and more numerous category of obsolete workers is formed, men forty or forty-five years old—sometimes even, in areas where techniques evolve quickly, thirty or thirty-five years old—newly created half-pay workers, the second part of whose active life is a long decline cut up by unexpected unemployment or sudden ruin. The "old"—these obsolete workers as much as the retired—are more and more precisely a new proletariat, as rejected and exploited by progress as others were by property.

The young can find themselves in a similar situation to the degree that their training either does not correspond to the needs of the economy or is underemployed when the labor market is unfavorable to them. What we too easily call the lack of adaptation of certain groups of workers is rather the sign of a social system in which training and employment are not organized so that technical and economic evolution produces the maximum professional and personal advantage for all and in which individuals are not protected by sufficient powers of social intervention.

These conflicts are all of the same nature. They predicate opposition between managers driven by the desire to increase production and adapt themselves to the imperatives of power and individuals who act less as workers defending their wages than as persons and groups seeking to maintain their sense of personal life. What these wage-earner/consumers seek is *security,* that is, a predictable and organizable future which will allow them to make plans and to count on the fruits of efforts they have willingly made.

The principal opposition between these two great classes or groups of classes does not result from the fact that one possesses wealth or property and the other does not. It comes about because the dominant classes dispose of knowledge and control *information.* Work comes to be less and less defined as a personal contribution and more as a role within a system of communications and social relations. The one who controls exerts influence on the systems of social relations in the name of their needs; the one who is controlled constantly affirms his existence, not as member of an organization, element of the production process, or subject of a State, but as an autonomous unit whose personality does not coincide with any of his roles. This is the reason—in our eyes justified—why the idea of *alienation* is so widespread. We are leaving a society of exploitation and entering a society of alienation.

What dominates our type of society is not the internal contradictions of the various social systems but the contradictions between the needs of these social systems and the needs of individuals. This can be interpreted in moral terms, which has aroused scant sociological interest because there is nothing more confused than the defense of individualism against the social machinery; it is easy to move beyond this kind of interpretation. As Galbraith has vigorously reminded us,[3] economic progress depends more and more not only on the quantity of available labor and capital but on the ability to innovate, to accept change, and to utilize every work capability.

A mechanical conception of society runs up against the resistance of individuals and groups who, out of hostility to being manipulated, limit their production and adopt a passive attitude toward organizations and decisions in which they do not participate. This was the case with Taylorism.[4] In a society which is progressively more tertiary—one in which the treatment of information plays the same central role that the treatment of natural resources played at the beginning of industrialization—the most serious form of waste is the lack of participation in decision-making. It is symptomatic that all studies demonstrate that the first condition of such participation is information. This observation, however, has more profound consequences than many are willing to face. Being informed means more than merely knowing what is taking place. It means being familiar with the background, reasons, and methods which lead to a decision and not merely with the reasons alleged to justify it. This is why unions or consultation committees ask to see the balance sheet of a firm, and to know the sources of the various categories of its revenue. Information is necessary to make decisions.

The central importance of this problem is underlined by the difficulties involved in any attempt to solve it. This is not simply because those who possess the information resist sharing it and prefer to retreat behind pseudosociological statements. The difficulties are also due to the fact that access to information presupposes a new attitude toward claims and grievances, acceptance of economic rationality, rejection of the idea that society is entirely dominated by conflict among private interests, recourse to experts whose relations with those responsible for action are difficult, etc. Seeking information is an expression of an active social politics. Lack of information (hence of participation in the systems of decision and organization) defines alienation. The alienated individual or group is not only the one left on the sidelines, subject to control or deprived of influence; it also includes the one who loses his personal identity and is defined only by his role in the system of exchanges and organization. It includes the consumer pushed by advertising and credit to sacrifice his economic security for the sake of goods whose distribution is justified by the interests of the producer rather than by the satisfaction of real needs. It includes as well the worker who is subject to systems of organization whose over-all efficiency does not balance their exorbitant human cost. As class conflict over property loses its importance and explosiveness by being localized and institutionalized, the new conflicts focus on the direction of society as a whole and arouse defense of self-determination.

We have just defined the principal social conflicts of programmed societies. The experience of societies characterized by capitalist industrialization is that those groups most subject to social domination are not necessarily the ones who most actively lead the fight. The further removed they are from the centers of power, the more exploited they are and the more their struggle is limited to the defense of the material conditions of existence, and it is difficult to move them to the offensive. Such responsibility must be borne not only by groups whose capacity to resist is greater—intellectuals or skilled workers with a higher standard of living and education or a stronger position in the labor market—but also by those who participate more directly in the central mechanics of economic progress.

The struggle is not led by marginal social elements who can only rise up for brief periods or support offensive action with their mass, but by central social elements who, in their opposition to those who hold power, use the instruments of production which their opponents claim to control. This used to be the role of the skilled workers; today, it is the role of those who possess scientific and technical competence. They are closely connected with the great organizations but their identity is not defined by their hierarchical authority in them. Often they even enjoy great independence from the organizations that utilize their services. They are agents of development, for their work is defined by the creation, diffusion, or application of rational knowledge; they are not technocrats, because their function is defined as *service*, not as production. . . .

NOTES

1. Engineers, high civil servants, economic experts, army officers, and a large part of Scientists are trained in France not in the universities but in schools, highly selective, and generally considered professionally superior to the universities. The most important ones are the Ecole Nationale d'Administration, the Ecole Polytechnique, and the Ecole Normale Supérieure.
2. William H. Whyte, Jr., *The Organization Man* (New York: Simon & Schuster, 1956).
3. John Kenneth Galbraith, *The Affluent Society* (New York: Houghton Mifflin, 1958).
4. Fréderic Winslow Taylor and his followers relied mostly on individual wage incentives to foster workers' willingness to increase production.

   The Bedaux system was between the wars one of the most widespread systems of job study. Every job was characterized by a certain proportion of activity and rest. The criteria on which such a proportion was established were secret and were never supported by scientific studies.

THE YOUNG WORKER

Special Task Force, Department
of
Health, Education and
Welfare

THE YOUNG WORKER—
CHALLENGING THE
WORK ETHIC?

More than any other group, it appears that young people have taken the lead in demanding better working conditions. Out of a workforce of more than 85 million, 22½ million are under the age of 30. As noted earlier, these young workers are more affluent and better educated than their parents were at their age. Factually, that is nearly all that can be generalized about this group. But it is asserted by such authors as Kenneth Keniston, Theodore Roszak, Charles Reich, and others, that great numbers of young people in this age group are members of a counter-culture. The President's Commission on Campus Unrest wrote that this subculture "found its identity in a rejection of the work ethic, materialism, and conventional social norms and pieties." Many writers have stressed the alleged revolt against work, "a new 'anti-work ethic' . . . a new, deep-seated rejection by the young of the traditional American faith in hard work."[1] But empirical findings do not always support the impressionistic commentaries.

It is commonly agreed that there is a difference between the in-mode behavior of youth and their real attitudes. Many young people do wear beads, listen to rock music, and occasionally smoke pot, but few actually live in communes (and these few may be working very hard), and even fewer are so alienated that they are unwilling to play a productive role in society. Daniel Yankelovich conducted national attitudes studies of college students from 1968 to 1971 and found that two-thirds of college students profess mainstream views in general.[2] But their feelings in particular about work (and private business) are even more affirmative:

—79% believe that commitment to a meaningful career is a very important part of a person's life.

—85% feel business is entitled to make a profit.

—75% believe it is morally wrong to collect welfare when you can work.

—Only 30% would welcome less emphasis on working hard.

SOURCE: *Work in America*, Report of Special Task Force to Secretary of Health, Education, and Welfare, Subcommittee on Employment Manpower, and Poverty (Washington, D.C.: Government Printing Office, 1973).

While student feelings about work itself are generally high, Yankelovich found that attitudes towards authority are changing rapidly. In 1968 over half (56% of all students indicated that they did not mind the future prospect of being "bossed around" on the job. By 1971 only one out of three students (36%) saw themselves willingly submitting to such authority. Equally important, while 86% of these students still believe that society needs some legally based authority to prevent chaos, they nevertheless see a distinction between this necessity and an authoritarian work setting.

Rising Expectations

Yankelovich also found a shift in student opinion on the issue that "hard work will always pay off" from a 69% affirmation in 1968 to a 39% affirmation in 1971. This certainly was, in part, indicative of the conditions in the job market for college graduates in 1971. But more basically, we believe, it highlights a paradox inherent in a populace with increasing educational achievement. Along with the mass media, education and its credentials are raising expectations faster than the economic system can meet them. Much of what is interpreted as anti-work attitudes on the part of youth, then, may be their appraisal of the kinds of jobs that are open to them.

The following case study of a young woman who is a recent college graduate illustrates the gap between expectations and reality:

> I didn't go to school for four years to type. I'm bored; continuously humiliated. They sent me to Xerox school for three hours. . . . I realize that I sound cocky, but after you've been in the academic world, after you've had your own class (as a student teacher) and made your own plans, and someone tries to teach you to push a button—you get pretty mad. They even gave me a goldplated plaque to show I've learned how to use the machine.[3]

The problem is compounded by the number of students who are leaving school with advanced degrees, like the young Chicago lawyer in the following case:

> You can't wait to get out and get a job that will let you do something that's really important. . . . You think you're one of the elite. Then you go to a place like the Loop and there are all these lawyers, accountants, etc., and you realize that you're just a lawyer. No, not even a lawyer—an employee; you have to check in at nine and leave at five. I had lots of those jobs—summers—where you punch in and punch out. You think it's going to be different but it isn't. You're in the rut like everybody else.[4]

Today's youth are expecting a great deal of intrinsic reward from work. Yankelovich found that students rank the opportunity to "make a contribution," "job challenge," and the chance to find "self-expression" at the top of the list of influences on their career choice. A 1960 survey of over 400,000 high school students was repeated for a representative sample in 1970, and the findings showed a marked shift from the students valuing job security and opportunity for promotion in 1960 to valuing "freedom to make my own decisions" and "work that seems important to me" in 1970.[5]

Many of these student findings were replicated in the Survey of Working Conditions sample of young workers. For example, it seems as true of young workers as it is of students that they expect a great deal of fulfillment from work. But the Survey findings show that young workers are not deriving a great deal of satisfaction from the work they are doing. Less than a quarter of young workers reply "very often" when asked the question, "How often do you feel you leave work with a good feeling that you have done something particularly well?"

PERCENTAGE ANSWERING

AGE GROUP	"VERY OFTEN"
Under 20	23
21–29	25
30–44	38
45–64	43
65 and over	53

Other findings document that young workers place more importance on the value of interesting work and their ability to grow on the job than do their elders. They also place less importance than do older workers on such extrinsic factors as security and whether or not they are asked to do excessive amounts of work. But the Survey documents a significant gap between the expectations or values of the young workers and what they actually experience on the job. Young workers rate their jobs lower than do older workers on how well their jobs actually live up to the factors they most sought in work. For example, the young value challenging work highly but say that the work they are doing has a low level of challenging.

It has also been found that a much higher percentage of younger than older workers feel that management emphasizes the *quantity* more than the *quality* of their work. Furthermore, it is shown that this adversely affects the satisfaction of younger workers. Such findings contradict the viewpoint that there is a weakening of the "moral fiber" of youth.[6]

Many young union members are challenging some basic assumptions about "a fair day's work for a fair day's pay." In the past, unions concerned themselves with establishing what a fair day's pay would be, while the employer's prerogative was to determine what constitutes a fair day's work. Young workers are now challenging both unions and management by demanding a voice in the setting of both standards, as the following case illustrates:

> Three young workers, aged twenty and twenty-one, were hired to clean offices at night. One evening the foreman caught one of the young janitors (who went to school during the day) doing his homework; another was reading the paper and the third was asleep with his feet up on a desk. The foreman exploded and gave them a written warning. The workers filed a grievance protesting the warnings: "We cleaned

all the offices in five hours by really hustling and who the hell should get upset because we then did our own thing." One young worker said, "At school during study period I get my studies done in less than the hour and no one bugs me when I do other things for the rest of the time. We cleaned all those offices in five hours instead of eight. What more do they want?"

The union steward said he tried hard to understand what they were saying: "But the company has the right to expect eight hours work for eight hours pay. I finally got the kids to understand by taking them outside and telling them that if they got the work finished in five hours, then the company would either give them more work, or get rid of one of them. They're spacing it out nicely now and everyone's happy," he said, satisfied to have settled the grievance within the understood rules.[7]

The author of this study writes that the young workers were far from satisfied with the agreement. They wanted the union to establish what had to be done and how much they would be paid to do it, and then they wanted the same freedom that professionals have to decide how to operate within the time and work frame allotted.

In summary, we interpret these various findings not as demonstrating a shift away from valuing work *per se* among young people, but as a shift away from their willingness to take on meaningless work in authoritarian settings that offers only extrinsic rewards. We agree with Willis Harman that:

The shape of the future will no more be patterned after the hippie movement and the Youth Revolution than the Industrial Age could have been inferred from the "New Age" values of the Anabaptists.[8]

New Values

A mistake is made, however, if one believes that the new attitudes toward authority and the meaning of work are limited to hippies. Judson Gooding writes that young managers, both graduates of business schools and executive trainees, "reflect the passionate concerns of youth in the 1970's—for individuality, openness, humanism, concern and change—and they are determined to be heard."[9]

Some young people are rejecting the corporate or bureaucratic worlds, while not rejecting work or the concept of work or profit. Gooding tells of one young former executive who quit his job with a major corporation because

You felt like a small dog. Working there was dehumanizing and the struggle to get to the top didn't seem worth it. They made no effort to encourage your participation. The decisions were made in those rooms with closed doors. . . . The serious error they made with me was not giving me a glimpse of the big picture from time to time, so I could go back to my little detail, understanding how it related to the whole.[10]

This young man has now organized his own small business and designed his own job. As the publisher of a counter-culture newspaper, he might be considered a radical in his beliefs and life style, yet he says "profit is not an evil." Of course, many young workers do question the *use* of profits, especially those profits that they feel are made at the expense of society or the environment. Some businesses themselves are adopting this same attitude.

It may be useful to analyze the views of today's youth not in terms of their parents' values but in terms of the beliefs of their grandparents. Today's youth believe in independence, freedom, and risk—in short, they may have the entrepreneurial spirit of early capitalism. Certainly they are more attracted to small and growing companies, to small businesses and to handicrafts, than to the bureaucracy, be it privately or publicly owned. (The declining opportunity for such small-scale endeavors . . . probably contributes to both the job dissatisfaction of the young and their apparent lack of commitment to the kinds of jobs that are available.) On the other hand, their parents share a managerial ethic that reflects the need for security, order, and dependence that is born of hard times. Of course, this is being a bit unfair to the older generation and a bit over-generous with our youth, but it serves to get us away from the simplistic thinking that the "Protestant ethic has been abandoned." Who in America ever had the Protestant ethic and when? Did we have it in the thirties? Did the poor people or even middle-class people ever have it? It is argued by Sebastian deGrazia that the Protestant ethic was never more than a myth engendered by the owner and managerial classes to motivate the lower working class—a myth which the latter never fully accepted.[11] Clearly, it is difficult to measure the past allegiance of a populace to an ideology.

But we *can* measure the impact of the present work environment on youth's motivation to work. For example, the Survey of Working Conditions found that youth seem to have a lower attachment to work than their elders on the same job. There are several reasons other than a change in the work ethic why this might be so. *First,* as we have already posited, young people have high expectations generated by their greater education. *Second,* their affluence makes them less tolerant of unrewarding jobs. *Third,* many new workers, particularly women, are voluntary workers. They are more demanding because they don't *have* to take a job. *Fourth,* all authority in our society is being challenged—professional athletes challenge owners, journalists challenge editors, consumers challenge manufacturers, the moral authority of religion, nation, and elders is challenged. *Fifth,* many former students are demanding what they achieved in part on their campuses a few years ago—a voice in setting the goals of the organization. The lecture has been *passé* for several years on many campuses—in colloquia and in seminars students challenge teachers. Managers are now facing the products of this progressive education. (One wonders what will happen when the children of today's open classroom, who have been taught to set their own goals and plan their own schedules, enter the workforce.)[12] *Sixth,* young blue-collar workers, who have grown up in an environment in which equality is called for in all institutions, are demanding the same rights and expressing the same values as university graduates. *Seventh,* there is growing professionalism among many young white-collar workers. They now have loyalty to their peer group or to their task or discipline, where once they had loyalty to their work organization.

In sum, it does not appear that young workers have a lower commitment to work than their elders. The problem lies in the interaction between work itself and the changing social character of today's generation, and in the failure of decision makers in business, labor, and government to recognize this fact.

The young worker is in revolt not against work but against the authoritarian system developed by industrial engineers who felt that "the worker was stupid, overly emotional . . . insecure and afraid of responsibility."[13] This viewpoint is summed up in Frederick Taylor's classic dictum to the worker:

> For success, then, let me give one simple piece of advice beyond all others. Every day, year in and year out, each man should ask himself, over and over again, two questions. First, "What is the name of the man I am now working for?" and having answered this definitely, then, "What does this man want me to do, right now?"

The simplistic authoritarianism in this statement would appear ludicrous to the young worker who is not the uneducated and irresponsible person on whom Taylor's system was premised. Yet, many in industry continue to support a system of motivation that was created in an era when people were willing to be motivated by the stick. As an alternative to this approach, many personnel managers have offered the carrot as a motivator, only to find that young people also fail to respond to this approach.

From our reading of what youth wants, it appears that under current policies, employers may not be able to motivate young workers at all. Instead, employers must create conditions in which the worker can motivate himself. This concept is not as strange as it seems. From biographies of artists, athletes, and successful businessmen, one finds invariably that these people set goals for *themselves*. The most rewarding race is probably one that one runs against oneself. Young people seem to realize this. They talk less positively than do their elders about competition with others. But they do talk about self-actualization and other "private" values. Yankelovich found that 40% of students—an increasing percentage—do not believe that "competition encourages excellence," and 80% would welcome more emphasis in the society on self-expression.

Compared to previous generations, the young person of today wants to measure his improvement against a standard he sets for himself. (Clearly, there is much more inner-direction than David Riesman would have predicted two decades ago.) The problem with the way work is organized today is that it will not allow the worker to realize his own goals. Because of the legacy of Taylorism, organizations set a fixed standard for the worker, but they often do not tell him clearly why that standard was set or how it was set. More often than not, the standard is inappropriate for the worker. And, in a strange contradiction to the philosophy of efficient management, the organization seldom gives the worker the wherewithal to achieve the standard. It is as if the runner did not know where the finish line was; the rules make it a race that no worker can win.

It is problematic whether the intolerance among young workers of such poor management signals temporary or enduring changes in the work ethic. More important is how management and society will reckon with the new emphasis that the workplace should lose its authoritarian aura and become a setting for satisfying and self-actualizing activity.

NOTES

1. *Economist,* April 30, 1972.
2. Daniel Yankelovich, *The Changing Values on Campus,* 1972.
3. Joyce Starr, "Adaptation to the Working World," 1972.
4. *Ibid.*
5. *Project Talent: Progress in Education, a Sample Survey,* American Institutes for Research, 1971.
6. Harold Sheppard and Neal Herrick, *Where Have All the Robots Gone?,* 1972.
7. John Haynes, "The New Workers: A Report," 1970.
8. Sidney Harman, "Responsibilities of Businessmen," 1972.
9. Judson Gooding, "The Accelerated Generation Moves Into Management," 1971.
10. *Ibid.*
11. Sebastian deGrazia, *Of Time, Work and Leisure,* 1962.
12. See chap. 5 for a further discussion of this point.
13. Quoted in Paul Campanis, "You Are What You Work At," 1972.

DOES THE UNITED STATES HAVE A NEW WORKING CLASS?

Stanley Aronowitz

The dramatic rise of student radicalism in the past decade, together with the development of new worker militancy in all advanced industrial countries, has put Marxists once more on the offensive in the prolonged ideological debate about the revolutionary potential of the underlying population of advanced industrial societies and of the working class in particular. Events of the past two years have belied the forecasts of "end of ideology" theorists who confidently proclaimed the era of working-class integration into advanced capitalist society at the close of the 1950's. Not only has ideological ferment spread throughout student ranks, but wildcat movements against both union and corporate hierarchies have mushroomed in Great Britain, France, Italy, and, more recently, in the United States. Most widely discussed and novel, perhaps, is some evidence of the emergence of a significant political force within working-class ranks: the professional, technical, and scientific workers, within both industry and the university. Among Marxists, this has led to much attention and controversy about a new working class. In this context, can the United States be said to have developed a new working class of that type? . . .

CRITICISMS OF THE THEORY

To anticipate in brief the criticisms of the theory, they reduce themselves to the following:

1. There is no new "class" in contemporay capitalist society. The emergence of the technicians as important elements in the work force is undeniable. But the decline of skills as technology advances, the rise in the general level of education for the whole working class, and the erosion of professionalism by these tendencies has made more apparent the fact that the technicians are merely a differently trained stratum of the industrial working class. The only sense in which the term New Working Class has meaning is by reference to the new generation of workers —not so much by the material processes of production. Yet the rise in the general

SOURCE: G. Fischer (ed.), *The Revival of American Socialism* (New York: Oxford University Press, 1971), pp. 199–216.

education level for this new generation *narrows* the differences between various strata of the working class, rather than making the distinction between technicians and manual workers more sharp.

2. The New Working-Class theorists have tended to overstate the extent of changes within material production. Thus they exaggerate the qualitative aspects of the position of the technicians.

3. The New Working-Class theory does not distinguish sharply enough the technocrats who do control production, but cannot be construed as a new working class, and the technicians who are an important stratum of the working class. This constitutes an all-important distinction.

4. There is not enough attention paid to the origins of occupationally based strata. Does the assignment of highly trained workers in the labor force correspond to new material requirements? Or is it bureaucratically determined? In turn, the question of the role of education in the development of the forces of production is inadequately examined. There seems to be a too-easy assumption that the rise of the qualifications for certain categories of labor is required by new technology. In short, New Working-Class theory has a sociology, but not a political economy.

5. It is doubtful that the tendencies described by Mallet can be universally applied. This is less a criticism of the New Working-Class theory than of those who have attempted to apply the theses to this country. In any case, the role and political significance of technicians must be examined specifically in every context.

The rest of the paper develops the five criticisms just stated and applies them to the United States.

There are several issues left unresolved by Denitch and Oppenheimer as well as the major European writers who advance the New Working-Class thesis. The first issue is the confusion inherent in the term, New Working Class. For Veblen, and implicitly in the work of Serge Mallet, the term refers to the group of technicians within modern industry who actually control elements of the production process, if not the corporate hierarchy itself. In fact, the patterns of domination inherent in corporate organization are presumed to be in conflict with the creative performance of technical work, and beyond production, the development of technology. It is our contention that, with the exception of the most advanced industries in technological terms, the preponderance of American industries do not conform to the notion of the centrality of the working technician within the production process. The leading industries of American capitalism have centralized both knowledge and power within the portion of technicians and scientists who are, at the same time, middle- or upper-level corporate managers.

The use of the concept of the New Working Class to embrace all college-trained workers departs sharply from its most precise importance. In modern industry, the question is whether a section of managers who actually control some processes of the work can be radicalized by making an alliance with the rest of the work force.

This point brings out a second confusion. It appears to me untenable to affix the term "new class" to the rising proportion of mental to physical workers in the labor force as a whole. The rise of the so-called white-collar strata, particularly the technicians, is more complex than the presumed development of technology. The rise of the university-trained worker has sources beyond the changes in material production, although this aspect of the problem has great significance for revolutionary strategy. From the point of view of numerical growth, the service, corporate, and public bureaucracies account for most of the new jobs for university and technically trained workers. Here several issues need clarification. First, the shift from manufacturing employment to nonproductive jobs in the Marxian sense is a consequence of important economic changes since World War II rather than of significant technical developments. The most important of these is the key role occupied by the state in the political economy, particularly its role as investor and consumer of commodities and regulator of relations within and between classes. Second, the expansion of the service and welfare sectors, especially the distributive industries and health and education, are only qualitatively new developments in relation to the economy. But within these industries technology has not changed so radically that new qualifications for the work force are called into existence.

Especially in the United States, the problem of the relations of technological change to occupational stratification and corporate organization is rarely addressed by proponents of the New Working-Class theory. We will argue that the growth of the state bureaucracies is socially unnecessary and is related more to the requirements of capitalist domination than the development of the productive forces. If anything, work within these bureaucracies has become less complex than within the production sphere. The simplification of tasks is facilitated both by the computerization of many administrative functions and by the rationalization of these functions. No development corresponding to the integrative aspects of continuous flow operations in the oil and chemical industry is widespread within government and corporate offices which, on the contrary, seem to proliferate personnel and functions in an extraordinary irrational pattern.

A further problem with the concept of the New Working Class as it is used in contemporary literature is the ambiguity of the way in which "class" is employed. If the managerial technicians are to be construed as a class, then Victor Fey's concept of *"the wage earning middle class"*[1] seems more appropriate than identifying this group with the working class. Another way of viewing this group is to comprehend it simply as a stratum of the familiar managerial or professional servant class which includes all corporate managers, university presidents and key professors, politicians and other high government officials. This group shares the outlook of the ruling class and serves its interest by running the machinery of government and the coporations, but does not control the fundamental decision-making.

KNOWLEDGE AS A PRODUCTIVE FORCE

It is important to take account of the increase in size and importance of the stratum of college-trained mental workers both in the sphere of material production and in the various bureaucracies. This stratum can only be construed as a class if the model advanced by modern sociologists such as Dahrendorf, Lipset, and others of the pluralistic theories of class is adopted. This is not the place to argue once more the Marxian theory of class, according to which class position is determined by the relationship of the workers to the means of production. There is no dispute that the social weight of university-trained workers in the labor force has increased. In the manufacturing industries they are growing in numbers at twice the rate of any other stratum of workers. In the public, corporate, and service bureaucracies their development has been similarly dramatic. But there is not enough evidence that they share different interests or, in the long run, will develop a different outlook than other strata of wage workers.

Further, the appearance of the university-trained worker is the result of the general rise of the educational level of the whole working class, as much as it depends on changes within industry. Although these developments have historically been closely related, it may be that the rise of mass higher education is only partially a function of the technological requirements of modern industry. The configuration of occupational strata, of credentials and qualifications, is as much a function of social domination as it is of industrial progress. The U.S. labor force is one of the most highly stratified in the capitalist world. Minute stratification is a function of both specialization and the general division of labor and of the impact of trade-union and professional organizations which have assisted corporations to impose complex divisions within the working class.

Mass higher education arose as much from the need of capitalism to prolong the withdrawal of youth from the labor force after the 1950's due to economic stagnation as it did from the need to provide a highly trained labor force for industry. If Marx's thesis that the tendency of modern industry to reduce skills is true, then it would be erroneous to ascribe the development of the university solely in terms of either material production or the rise of the public sector. Higher education and all schooling now has a broad social function in relation to the distribution of the labor force.

It would be well, at this point, to enter a caveat to the general proposition that knowledge has, in fact, become the decisive productive force in United States capitalism. More accurate is to recognize that U.S. capitalism is characterized by extreme unevenness in the development of both the economy and its technological base. The extent to which machinery has replaced human labor varies widely from industry to industry. In general, in comparison to other capitalist countries, this country's forces of production are retarded in consumer goods industry.[2]

The relatively low proportion of technical and scientific workers to semi-skilled and unskilled production workers is illustrated in the textile industry, where this group constitutes less than 3 per cent of the work force, automobiles, where the percentage is well below 10 per cent, and transportation, where technicians constitute about 3.5 per cent of all workers in the industry. In these industries operatives constitute well over 50 per cent of all workers.

Even in some basic industries, particularly fabricated metals and primary metals, it would be dangerous to overstate the extent of the emergence of the importance of the technical workers. In the basic-steel industry technicians constitute about 6 per cent of the labor force, while the proportion is somewhat larger in metals fabrication. The composition in the pulp and paper industry is somewhat similar, except the growth of the technical labor force is projected to increase by 50 per cent by 1975 due to the rapid technology development of the industry.

The low proportion of technical workers reflects the fact that consumer goods industries have experienced little technological change in the past decade. Most of them are still operating in phase two of industrial capitalism, that is, the period of specialization and rationalization epitomized by the assembly line. The division of labor during the mechanization era was rather minute. Technical processes have not kept pace with industrial expansion. The slow rate of technical development and change in these industries can be attributed to the pre-eminence of the war economy in the post-war period.

The key industries in the defense sector, electronics and chemicals, have become leading industries in the American economy, both economically and technologically. Supported by public funds, these industries have been the beneficiaries of tremendous research operations. Ever more the massive development of new weaponry with its concentration on nuclear power and electronic and chemical components has placed these industries at the center of the third industrial revolution. In the third phase of industrial capitalism, automation and computerization reintegrate the labor force under the hegemony of those who are the possessors of the knowledge required to develop and operate new processes. If Marx's prediction of the transformation of the forces of production contained in his *Grundrisse* has been fulfilled in contemporary industrial society at all, its primary expression is in chemicals, oils, and electronics. Marx wrote:

> As large-scale industry develops, the creation of real wealth depends less and less upon labor time and the quantity of labor expended and more upon the might of the machines set in motion during labor time. The powerful effectiveness of the machines bears no relationship to the labor time which it cost to produce them. Their power, rather derives from the general level of science and the progress of technology . . . neither the actual labor expended by man, nor the length of time during which he works, is the great pillar of production and wealth.[3]

According to Marx, labor under the new technology is relegated to the role of bystander and watcher and the concept of productive labor becomes transformed from the application of brute labor power to the production of knowledge. Those institutions involved in the production of knowledge (the universities and the technical schools as well as private corporations) are as much a part of the production system as the factory. The schools now become knowledge factories, not only for the production of managerial elites, but for the production of a large segment of the working class. But to the extent that scientific research is conducted by the universities they also participate in the development of technology and are essential to the changes in the character of large-scale industry, particularly in the war sector of the economy.

TECHNICIAN VERSUS TECHNOCRAT

The New Working-Class theory bases itself on the assumption that the traditional industrial proletariat is gradually diminishing to the point of approaching political insignificance,"[4] and being replaced by a stratum of highly trained technicians who perform their productive labor as research, quality control, and organization. In short the character of productive work, it is claimed, has decisively shifted in advanced industrial society to mental rather than physical labor in consequence of the widespread introduction of automation and cybernation into dominant sectors of the American economy.

The strategic implications of this thesis for socialist strategy are evident. The new working class, by virtue of its broader understanding of the production process and its centrality to it, is in a position to challenge the patterns of decision-making by capitalist managers and expose thereby the true despotism of capital. The struggle for workers' control, over the pace and direction of investment, as well as the hierarchial organization of the production process itself, constitutes a crucial transitional demand for exposing the inherent conflict of labor and capital in the modern era. The growing conflict between the broader understanding and control by the technical worker over the production process on one hand and his decreased autonomy in determining the direction of investment and other crucial management decisions constitutes the basis for the potential power of the technical worker in becoming a lever for social transformation.

Here the distinction between the technocrat and the technician is essential. The growing importance of a scientifically trained technocratic elite within United States capitalism is commensurate with the appearance of industries which rely on scientific knowledge for their development. The technocrats are intimately involved in the dominant power system. Often they are the heart of the management stratum. This group is not to be confused with the technical workers who possess knowledge but are bereft of power. Indeed, it is the conflict between their greater knowledge and centrality to the production process and their powerlessness which constitutes their revolutionary potential. Technicians have merely become a more important element of the working class. They share the propertylessness and alienation of any other industrial worker. Often the technical worker in the advanced industries replaces the old blue-collar foreman on the production line. The rising qualifications for leading positions in many industries may be a consequence of the rising technical requirements of production. Supervision in the automatic factory carries the requirement that it be of a wider scope. But the fact that an engineer occupies a foreman's role, or that it is technicians rather than craftsmen who are responsible for quality control in a chemical plant, simply comprehends the fact that the similar occupations require a higher level of educational preparation than in more traditional industries. The function of the supervisor remains the same. Plant organization and hierarchy has relegated him to roughly the same position as his predecessor, the manual workers.

THE PROLETARIANIZATION OF TECHNICIANS

In some industries, the research function is more closely integrated into the production process. The 25 per cent of the work force in chemicals and oils engaged in intellectual labor is largely employed in development activities. But it would be mistaken to draw too broad conclusions from this limited phenomenon. In manufacturing industries as a whole, the decline of the old industrial working class is neither precipitous nor is the rise of the technical worker dramatic. The projected growth of technical, professional, and scientific workers between 1960 and 1975 in manufacturing is only 3.4 per cent and the decline of semi-skilled and skilled workers is only 1.3 per cent. The real change has been the longterm disappearance of the unskilled laborer who has given way to the semi-skilled worker.

Moreover, the relatively slow growth of the technical stratum in manufacturing industries shows no signs of great acceleration. Fundamentally, the New Working-Class theory relies on rapid technical development within the framework of capitalism. There are several reasons why this has not happened. First, the assumption is made of a large surplus of capital which can be invested in technological change in the wake of the sharp curtailment of opportunities for capital investment in the world market. In fact, rapid technological change has occurred in western Europe in precisely those industries where U.S. investment has lagged, the consumer goods sector. The division of labor in world capitalism has forced the United States to become the chief military power, thus limiting its development in other sectors. Second, the reindustrialization on an advanced technological level of U.S. industry seems beyond the present financial capacity of corporations in both the competitive and the monopoly sector. One reason for the deteriorated position of U.S. capital is the inflationary spiral which has afflicted the U.S. economy since 1965. Another is the pre-eminence of investment in western Europe by multi-national corporations controlled by U.S.-based groups.

There are exceptions to the general rule of technological stagnation. It appears that investment plans in the steel industry indicate some expansion of capacity on the basis of new technologies. But the limits to the widespread application of this technology appear as the recession cycle reappears as a regular feature of capitalist stagnation. Another limit is indicated by the amortization problem in computerization of steel processes. The rule of thumb, five-year amortization, seems difficult to realize.

More profoundly, the rising productivity of labor in all mechanical industries since World War II has not resulted in the permanent disemployment of the labor force. Instead, the rise of the public sector, corresponding to the critical role played by the state within the corporate capitalist system, the expansion of retail and other services, and the stabilization of the permanent army at more than 3 million men combined in the 1950's and 1960's successfully to absorb new labor force entrants and re-employ those displaced by technological change, product displacement, and industrial stagnation.

But the short-term prospects for the U.S. economy indicate that the education system has overproduced technical workers in comparison to the pace of technological change within manufacturing industry and the growth of over-all economic activity. The overproduction of technicians has been apparent for some time. Apart from scientifically trained personnel, the glut on the labor market has been apparent among liberal arts and social science fields. Since education and health are not merely ancillary services to manufacturing industries but are industries themselves with a vital role in maintaining capitalist stability, the rise of the public sector was a critical factor in preventing a more apparent surplus of college-trained workers. The dramatic growth of education and health services, together with the rapid increase in corporate and state administrative bureaucracies, accounted for a greater number of trained technicians than the manufacturing industry during the past two decades. Twenty-eight per cent of employees in public administration are categorized as professional and technical workers. Since this sector accounts for about 15 per cent of the total labor force, or about 11 million workers, nearly 4 million college-trained workers are employed in these jobs.

By 1975 there will be more than 3 million health workers, about 1 million of them professionals and technical workers. The rise of the "new working class" therefore is more apparent in the public service sector than in the production of commodities. But in what sense is this stratum really a "new" working class?

The technicians, including engineers, scientists and non-professional technical workers, have found their work to be rationalized and atomized along the lines of the old divisions of labor, rather than sharing in decision-making or participating globally in control over the production process.

A good example of the relatively low level of skill and responsibility assigned to scientific workers is the communications industry, a major component of electronics. On one hand, professional and technical workers constitute about one-third of the labor force in giant plants such as the Western Electric factory in Kearny, New Jersey, or the nearby International Telegraph and Telephone plant in Clifton. But work is organized along mechanical lines. The assembly-line model predominates over integrative patterns of work assignment. Engineers complain bitterly that they are "overtrained" for the complexity of their tasks. Scientists holding managerial posts are virtually the only persons occupying strategic positions with research and production spheres. Knowledge in the factory is concentrated in few hands, rather than diffused among the highly trained work force.

The proletarianization of technicians is not merely the result of their growing numerical importance within advanced industries. It is also a consequence of the relatively low skill required for the performance of their tasks. Gorz recognizes this development.

> The technical or scientific worker in automated industry is consigned to permanent unemployment. As far as his individual tasks go, and hence, as far as his level of consciousness allows, he tends to transfer his interest from his purely individual work to his social function and from his purely individual role in production to the social significance and purpose of management.[5]

The tendency of labor in automated industries is to polarization. Contrary to commonly held belief, the technocrats and not the technicians monopolize both knowledge and power at the work place.

The technician has less autonomy than the skilled worker of fifty years ago, or even many skilled workers in service and technically retarded industries. His degree of control over the production process compares to that of the semi-skilled worker on the assembly line. His qualifications do not match the nature of his labor.

Self-consciousness among technicians employed by large corporations of their position in the corporation no longer corresponds to nineteenth-century professionalism. The metal worker is simply a production worker or low-level supervisor analogous in function and stratification to the industrial proletariat and foremen of the mechanical phase. An indication of a changed consciousness can be measured by the examples of technical unionism—particularly the slow growth of the professional and technical divisions of the electrical and auto workers' unions, and the dramatic rise of public employee's unions corresponding to the growth of the state in the political economy.

EDUCATION OR TRAINING?

The strongest argument for the idea of the New Working Class is that the present and future generations of workers have qualitatively higher educational qualifications than previous generations. We have seen that higher education does not imply greater application of knowledge to the world of work. On one hand, different skills are required by automated industries and the state bureaucracies than the older industries. These skills may be broadly defined as technical and administrative in contrast to mechanical skills of the old journeymen. On the other hand, the level of education possessed by most workers is greater than that required by their jobs.

The contradiction between the rising level of education of larger numbers of workers and the restricted scope of their labor is a form of the conflict between the advance in the forces of production and the fetters put upon them by the old relations of production. The development of the capacity of human labor to transform nature in the service of man and to abolish itself has reached the point where it strains to break out of the confining bourgeois social relations. It is not so much the qualitatively new means of production which have created the crisis, but the level and the scale of knowledge possessed by human labor. This is the heart of the New Working-Class thesis and seems to me its valid core.

There are limits to the idea of the rising general level of education. It involves the distinction between education and training. Education in America has been deteriorating for many decades while training has been broadly disseminated among the underlying population. The proliferation of community colleges and technical schools during the 1950's was fostered by the government to meet a particular cold war need to overcome the shortage of technical and scientific labor for the new means of production in the military sector. The social and political requirements fulfilled by the expansion of higher education facilities were related more to the fact that the rising productivity of labor made early entrance into the labor force unnecessary. The rise of mass higher education became an important means of disguising the rate of employment and simultaneously providing the equivalent of "work" for millions of young people.

The emphasis of the community colleges, second-level state colleges, and the technical institutes is training in a specific task. It is generally acknowledged that the liberal arts curriculum in most of these schools is less than useless. It appears designed, albeit unconsciously in many instances, to discourage interest among students in the arts and humanities. Social science is either taught in the most boring and oppressive manner, or is oriented toward practical tasks in industry. Students having become disillusioned with the broad objects of education in primary and secondary schools, regard their college experience as a *means* to obtaining the necessary credentials or limited training required by industry or public bureaucracies as prerequisites for employment.

The vocational emphasis of higher education is virtually universal in institutions not specifically mandated to produce managerial, scientific, or educational elites. The instrumental philosophy ensconced in most college curricula is matched by the view of education as a "useful tool" by most students. If school has become a way to stay out of the army, a way to obtain a credential, a method of overcoming the isolation most individuals experience in urban life and finding a new community, then the concept of education as knowledge is clearly peripheral, if not irrelevant, to the university experience.

Yet, the hero of a recent Hollywood film, *Getting Straight,* asks a college president exorcized by student radicalism, "If you didn't want them to protest, why did you give them library cards?" The national student strike of May 1970, ostensibly called to protest the entrance of U.S. troops into Cambodia and to protest the killing of four students at Kent State University in Ohio by national guardsmen, was a reflection of a much deeper challenge to capitalist institutions, particularly the higher education factories. Students were not only protesting the particular acts of violence perpetrated by the national administration and its military arms, but were expressing their dissatisfaction with American culture, their protest against the poverty of student life, against the instrumental character of technocratic education. The student movement over the past decade represents the crisis of bourgeois ideology, particularly the breakdown of the socialization of the new generation of workers into the routines of industrial labor. To a large degree, this dissatisfaction has generated a deep chasm between the old liberal values transmitted by culture itself and the growing authoritarian character of all social institutions.

EFFECTS OF THE YOUTH REVOLT

The restiveness of the youth and the collapse of universally accepted values constitutes a massive social challenge to the capitalist order. Not that this generation of workers has opted for an alternative politics or a new set of values. The situation is in flux. Some young people have chosen to remove themselves from the "straight" world; others have decided to live in communes within urban areas, but are forced to participate in the world of work. The majority of this generation still lives within the confines of industrial routine, whether manifested within the university, the plant, or the state bureaucracy. But explosions are becoming more frequent. These are not only manifested in the form of political protest or in the impulse to unionize among college-trained workers. They appear in the increasing difficulty reported by corporations in recruiting young college graduates for managerial and administrative jobs. This phenomenon has become deeply disturbing to the corporations. They recognize that some of the most brilliant students in the elite universities are no longer directed to careers within industrial or scientific establishments. Students enter the world of work out of need rather than desire. Work is viewed as labor by an increasing number of highly skilled workers who "live" increasingly after their work day has ended —who create a privatized existence outside the work place like their manual worker counterparts.

There are differences between the activities of manual and college-trained workers. The college-trained worker watches television less often, does not spend so much time in his home, does not have the same kinds of social outlets available to manual workers, such as social clubs built around taverns, union halls, or nationality organizations. In many ways, college-trained workers possess fewer social contacts. Unlike manual workers these do not depend on family and the job, but may be based on school contacts, civic activities, or interests. It is not uncommon for these workers to join ski clubs, bridge groups, encounter groups (a sign of their social isolation), and political organizations of various kinds. These "outside" activities are as likely to form their primary social relationships as the job.

The formation of an extramural life outside the job inevitably leads to a weakening of the corporate hold on the individual. Of course, there are still many companies who retain their "family" character. Companies such as IBM attempt to involve their managers and their administrators in a full social life based on the work place. The corporate man has not disappeared; it simply was a phenomenon of the forties and fifties which has been losing ground for at least a decade. The disappearance of the ethos of organization man within the present generation of workers is an implicit anti-capitalist critique. More important, it reveals the deep-seated desire for individual and collective autonomy among young workers.

Thus far, the most visible signs of the youth revolt have been in the form of refusal. There are few signs of a concerted attempt among young workers in skilled and semi-skilled occupations to direct their efforts to challenging the institutions in terms of an attempt to wrest control from the corporate hierarchies, although the fight for student power in the university raged simultaneously with the anti-war protests in the 1960's and the recent May 1970 strike.

Yet the objective conditions for a challenge to the restricted character of mental labor within corporate and state institutions exist. Large numbers of students who have participated in the general denouncement by their generation of bourgeois values now work in research and administrative institutions. These workplaces resemble factories and have reproduced the specialization of tasks characteristic of industrial plants.

If the first impulse of the new generation of skilled mental workers has been to retreat to their own personal lives because they have refused to be incorporated by the bureaucracies, it may not be too long before they recognize privatization as no solution. The next step in some cases has been unionization rather than the demand for control over their own work. It is likely that many mental workers will relive the experiences of their manual workers counterparts of previous periods. Faced with increasingly frustrating and meaningless work, but also with fixed salaries in the face of the inflationary economy, they have begun to organize around their immediate economic needs. It would be an error to regard this development as just another trade-union movement. The advance from the organization man (or its state counterpart the "public servant") to recognition that they are just another group of workers with ordinary working-class demands is a qualitative advance for the mental workers.

A BUREAUCRATIC PROFESSIONALISM

The response of the state and corporate bureaucracies to the proletarianization of the professions has been to encourage professionalism. One example of this has been the demand by government and corporations that job-seekers possess academic credentials far in excess of job requirements. In part, the demand for credentials is a necessary consequence of the overproduction of intellectual and technical labor in the past decade. On the other hand, it represents the effort to reassert the hierarchy of status which was indigenous to the old professionalism. The professional associations have reinforced this tendency. Thus, the struggle against professionalism is a key question of the New Working Class since occupational and professional differentiation bureaucratically rather than technologically determined is a major weapon in the hands of the ruling class for dividing workers.

The unionization of the new generation of mental workers is proceeding in fits and starts. At this juncture it appears that the unions of government employees are acquiescent to the efforts of the bureaucracies to enforce rigid occupational differentiation. Thus the extreme unevenness of the situation is producing, at the same time, an impulse to organization among these workers and a growing tendency toward reaction by their unions. Even the unions have had to take note of their new constituency. Teachers', municipal, and federal workers' unions are not cut from whole cloth. Some of the union leaders have had to pay obeisance to the broad anti-war sentiment of their memberships. But this rhetorical moderate leftism has not prevented the same leaders from becoming virtual allies of city politicians. It is no secret, for example, that many local leaders of the huge State, County, and Municipal Workers' Union are close advisers and political lieutenants of liberal mayors in several large cities, such as New York, San Francisco, and Philadelphia. This alliance has meant that public employee unions have been rendered harmless on everyday job conditions and have tended to support the maintenance of professional qualifications and standards.

THE VANGUARD UNDER STATE
MONOPOLY CAPITALISM

Th New Working-Class theory cannot be denied as a broad generalization of the inherent tendencies in advanced capitalist countries to create a broad stratum of technically and scientifically trained workers whose interests are similar to the old manual workers. But some assert their vanguard role in the "long march through institutions" because they represent the new productive forces whose development is most fettered by existing social relations. Instead, it appears that to the extent that the new productive forces are emerging, the whole working class shares in the rise of educational attainment. If the new means of production can be developed by capitalism throughout the whole of industrial production, the question of the New Working Class becomes moot. Nor is it necessarily true that only the college-trained stratum of the workers will raise qualitative demands, or lead the way toward workers' control struggles. As the achievement of higher and technical education becomes the property of the entire generation of new workers, the characteristics of the current mental workers will be more apparent in the rest of the population.

In any case, the concept of vanguard is rather ambiguous in the period of state monopoly capitalism. The integration of the state with the underlying production of commodities on one hand and the narrowing of the distinctions between mental and physical labor on the other are broad trends which defy the uniqueness of the concept of professions or the special role of scientists, engineers, and technicians. In short, the "new working class" is nothing but this generation and future generations of workers. They will demand, more and more, control over the production of society and autonomy in their own work and lives.

The impetus for this development is as much rooted in the general breakdown of social institutions as it is in the dissonance between qualifications and work. One of the major weaknesses of all New Working-Class theory, except in the writing of Gorz, is the mechanistic framework of its analysis: the theory fails to integrate the crisis of institutions and ideologies, within the superstructure, with the observed changes within the base of society. Mallet does not understand the automony of superstructure as an important analytic clue to the development of a new consciousness among young, educated workers. The revolt against the technical bureaucracy is more than a function of the critical role of technicians within the most advanced industries and universities. In the United States it is also a consequence of the conflict between the old values of freedom and autonomy and the centralization of all institutions of daily life.

The bourgeoisie has lost claim to its own values. The separation of values from the institutions supposed to embody them can, in the long run, be traced to the underlying irrationality of production relations and the thwarting of initiative by the technical bureaucracy. There is no doubt that the struggle of the corporate bourgeoisie to limit the objects of education represents their recognition of the dissonance between knowledge and the interests of the social system of domination. In the United States the fissure penetrates all social layers, even the sons and daughters of the bourgeoisie. The only recourse left to the corporations is to use violence as a method of rule. The increasing tendency among young students and workers is to a global criticism of capitalism rather than a sectoral critique of particular aspects of it. Yet while the New Working-Class theory has a critique of the work place, it is *not* equally prepared to extend its critique to society as a whole. Thus, it tends to syndicalism rather than revolutionary Marxism.

In sum, the idea of the New Working Class is, at best, confusing. At worst it is misleading. In the first place, we have shown that its alleged predominance in the sphere of material production is overstated when applied to U.S. capitalism and the U.S. labor force as a whole. Second, an examination of material production reveals that few industries employ technical and scientific personnel as controllers of the labor process. In those industries where advanced technologies have become pervasive, a tiny stratum of the labor force, the technocrats, exercises power over the production process. But this group is no different from the corporate managers as a whole and cannot be drawn into the working class.

The answer to our main question, then, is: the United States does *not* have a New Working Class.

NOTES

1. Victor Fey, "Les Classes Moyennes Salariées," in *En Partant du "Capital,"* edited by the author (Paris: Anthropos, 1968), pp. 97–115.
2. See Seymour Melman, *Our Depleted Society* (New York: Harcourt, Brace & World, 1965).
3. Quoted in Michael Harrington, *The Accidental Century* (New York: Macmillan, 1965),

pp. 266–268, from Karl Marx, *Grundrisse der Kritik der Politischen Ökonomie* (Berlin: Dietz, 1953), pp. 592, 593.

4. Paul Piccone, "Students' Protest, Class Structure, and Ideology," *Telos,* vol. 2, No. 1 (Spring 1969), p. 113.

5. André Gorz, "Capitalist Relations of Production and the Socially Necessary Labour Force," *International Socialist Journal,* Vol. 2, No. 10 (1964), pp. 415–429.

V.   STUDENTS, EDUCATION, AND THE WORKING CLASS

INTRODUCTION

Education has played an increasingly important role in advanced industrial societies. In some theories of "postindustrial" society, education replaces capital as the strategic factor of production, signaling the decline of labor-capital conflict and the traditional class relationships of a capitalist society. The radical perspective, however, insists that educational institutions, rather than undermining class stratification, reinforce the class structure. Thus, in the radical analysis education reproduces class inequalities, while in the liberal view education reduces economic inequality. More recently, the liberal perspective has been shaken by the so-called "meritocracy debate," a subject we shall turn to in a subsequent chapter. In this section we are concerned with recent critical literature on education focusing on the way educational institutions function to service the needs of business and government and simultaneously reproduce existing class inequalities.

The problem of the "uncredentialled" in a society which increasingly relies on academic degrees and diplomas as job-screening devices is discussed by Berg in the selection from *Education and Jobs: The Great Training Robbery*. The overemphasis on academic credentials in determining access to limit employment opportunities reinforces the barriers to the economic advancement of the lower strata of the population. Under these circumstances, class distinctions are reinforced and the liberal assumptions about the consequences of equality of opportunity become questionable.

Lasch and Genovese turn their attention to some of the sources for tensions within the university by examining the relationship of the university to the changing labor requirements of advanced capitalism. They argue in "The Education and the University We Need Now" that students (youth) increasingly represent an "economically superfluous" group which cannot be absorbed in useful and rewarding work under existing economic institutions. Hence the need for the "custodial" function of prolonged, compulsory schooling and its attendant problems. These problems cannot be resolved, according to Lasch and Genovese, except by changing the class structure of neocapitalism.

In the selection "Unequal Education and the Reproduction of the Hierarchical Division of Labor," Bowles discusses the variety of mechanisms through which educational institutions transmit class inequalities from one generation to the next and document the continuing close relationship between parents' class position and children's educational fates. Schools, he argues, were never designed to reduce inequalities but have been used primarily to "meet the needs of capitalist employers for a disciplined and skilled work force." The distribution of resources is seen linked to the distribution of economic and political power in the society at large.

Finally, Jencks and Riesman distinguish between the goals of "more mobility" and "more equality" as consequences of the liberal commitment to equality of opportunity. They argue that what the United States needs is not increased status competition but greater equality of result. They are skeptical that the extension of higher education to new social strata will contribute significantly to the development of an egalitarian society.

Thus, in each of these selections liberals as well as radicals are beginning to explore more fully the relationship of education to capitalist class relationships.

THE GREAT TRAINING ROBBERY:
EDUCATION, CLASS BARRIERS,
AND THE LIBERAL CREED

Ivar Berg

. . . The defenders of the educational establishment point out that things could be worse and that critics have overstated their case. Education, they assert, produces thoughtful citizens and material well-being; the economic benefits to the society are accordingly stressed and linked, by assertion, to social welfare. But surely, in a discussion of education, the definition of social welfare must go beyond aggregated tallies of material benefits to include the matter of education's role in the distribution of social product. And when the issues are thus joined, the defense is less compelling.

Educational credentials have become the new property in America. Our nation, which has attempted to make the transmission of real and personal property difficult, has contrived to replace it with an inheritable set of values concerning degrees and diplomas which will most certainly reinforce the formidable class barriers that remain, even without the right within families to pass benefices from parents to their children.

As a number of my colleagues have suggested, employers can derive benefits from the employment of better-educated workers that outweigh the pathological correlates of "excessive" education; after all, the intent was only to open up the narrower economic issues. But the use of educational credentials as a screening device effectively consigns large numbers of people, especially young people, to a social limbo defined by low-skill, no-opportunity jobs in the "peripheral labor market."[1]

Barriers against greater mobility are not made less imposing by public policies that reinforce the access to formal education of middle- and upper-income youngsters through subsidy and subsidy-like arrangements. Today, tax-supported and tax-assisted universities are full of nutant spirits from families whose incomes are well above those of the average taxpayers. The personal advantages to those who hold academic credentials are sufficiently well known that the majority of Americans do not even pause to question the TV spots or subway posters that warn of the lifetime hazards facing "dropouts."

If the barriers to mobility are not fully visible to the disinherited, poverty warriors have been armed with weapons to subdue the poor in skirmishes against

SOURCE: *Education and Jobs: The Great Training Robbery* (New York: Praeger, 1970), pp. 185–194.

the "disadvantaged" which have distracted attention from a much-needed war against poverty. Substantial funds from that war chest have been consumed by educational mercenaries who campaign against the personal—which is to say educational—deficiencies of the youthful poor. Foot-long ads addressed to "educational technologies" offer grand salaries and extensive benefits to induce men and women (many of those who respond are public-school teachers) to enroll in the legions who will train impoverished youths in encampments across the land, financed by profitable cost-plus contracts.[2]

During the life of the office of Economic Opportunity and the thousand community-action programs it spawned, unemployment rates among the nation's less educated have dropped; black workers had an unemployment rate of 6.8 per cent in 1968—"the lowest," according to the Department of Labor, "since 1953."[3] But it is not at all clear what portion of this gain—modest as it is—is attributable to the war against poverty. The Labor Department's estimate that "the sharp Vietnam buildup began, largely unexpectedly, at the very time the economy was already being propelled toward full employment by surging civilian demand" must be balanced against its own statement that "in the two years after mid-1965, increased defense expenditures generated a total of 1.8 million jobs—some 700,000 in the Armed Forces and about a million in private industry."[4] Whatever can be said in favor of our wars, it is unsettling that they are among the significant mergers of our time.

The quality of public education available to the poor and near-poor is almost uniformly low, a fact that contributes increasingly to the visibility of the barrier between the haves and the have-nots. For the have-nots, especially black Americans, there is a special pain in all this, for they are underrepresented in the policy-making councils that have decreed the frightful mess in urban education and the segregated style of American living and learning, but they are over-represented among those who suffer the penalties in foxholes overseas and rat-holes at home.

At least as sharp a pain must afflict some thoughtful liberals in America. For them formal education has been the equilibrating mechanism in a progressing industrial democracy that has been relatively free of class conflict. It was the liberal who helped to sell America on education and who saw in education the means by which merit might ultimately conquer unearned privilege. He must now acknowledge that he is the defender of a most dubious faith. For while he struggles from the edges of hard-earned privilege to help the poor, he must live off these privileges in the education of his own children.

Consider, in this context, that over one third of all schoolage children in New York City, many of them the sons and daughters of earnest liberals, attend private and parochial schools.[5] It is at least ideologically convenient for the parents of these children to champion the cause of the neighborhood school and the decentralization of desperately sick urban public-school programs. The serious question of whether this makes educational and political sense may be effectively begged in favor of a willingness to "allow others" the control *they* have over their children's school experience.[6]

The position that such reforms will reverse educational inequities does put a good face on their ruggedly individualistic pursuit of their own narrow self-interest; it may be doubted whether the ragged individuals thereby left to fend for themselves will necessarily benefit from this quaint version of egalitarianism. The middle-class children of liberal and conservative parents in silk-stocking districts are doubly blessed, of course, with relatively good public schools and a self-serving ideology about the seemingly neutral principle of the neighborhood school that has now become an article of faith for many inner-city dwellers. These desperate people have gained the ideological support—and sometimes the financial support—of progressive whites, many of whom are masters at converting liberal principles into a tasteful though distracting pragmatism. Since the logics in defense of urban educational reforms are presented only less delectably by Southern politicians, the long-run advantages of such tinkering will unquestionably depend in part on the success of reformers in demonstrating that they do not mean simply to raise the hopes of their repressed protagonists. Such a demonstration must take account of the credentials barriers and the employment levels that help to sustain them; again, the education-employment nexus becomes strategically important.

SOME GENERAL CONCLUSIONS

The results of the present study do not give much weight to the economic argument in its detail, although it would be foolish to deny that education is involved in the nation's capacity to produce goods and services. . . . Let us state, however, that they (the results of the Berg study) give grounds for doubting that it is useful to regard education in America within a simplified framework in which a person's *years of schooling* are taken as a significant measure; schools are too diverse and people too differentiated to permit the routine and automatic confusion of the morals, motives, and capabilities of the licensed with their licenses. The experience with marriages in Western society may illustrate the point.

Another general conclusion from the data must be that we could profitably and sensibly redirect our educational investments in order to improve primary and secondary public education. It is consistent with the observations in preceding chapters that America should be doing a far better job in assuring that *all* of her people reach adult life with twelve years of quality training and education. Employers, for example, indicate that their educational requirements reflect their dissatisfaction with what public education is accomplishing. Added expenditures for higher education, which already constitutes 34 per cent of direct educational outlays, is not likely to change all this.

Within the educational establishment there is further room for redirection.

> The missing link in education is development research as it is practiced in industry. . . . Though there is great need for more basic research in education, there is an immediate demand for more extensive developmental work which will evaluate and apply the findings of research and demonstrate their practical worth. At present only 10 to 12 per cent of the funds expended on educational research and development are devoted to development.[7]

It would also be desirable from all points of view if those who failed to take full advantage of their educational opportunities in their youth had a second chance, after discovering themselves and developing the attitudes that serve the learning process, in a system of adult education. Under present circumstances, life-long consequences stem from decisions made by, for, and against youths. And it may be questioned whether a citizen should suffer all his life with the disabilities that come of having been exposed, for example, to a poor grade-school experience, where "functional illiteracy" paves the way for disenchantment, delinquency, or deprivation.

Education needs to be reformed in America by striking a balance between "too much" for some and "not enough" for others. The tendency on the part of employers to raise educational requirements *without careful assessments of their needs, in both the short and the long run,* can benefit neither managers nor the system they extol.

This purposeless credential consciousness further handicaps education, especially higher education, in the pursuit of its promise to liberate people and to help preserve for a society its better traditions and commitments. This part of our cultural heritage is already in danger of being obscured by a growing materialism, stifled by know-nothing "status politics" and radical rightism, and weakened by the radical, disenchanted Left.

There is no escaping the fact that in America the political and social wellbeing of the individual are bound up with his economic opportunities. It is therefore a matter of great moment to the society whether the economic argument in favor of education takes far more account of the complexities involved in measuring the relationships among abilities, educational achievements, and job requirements. The efforts presented in the present volume give abundant support to the position that the issues involved in these relationships have not been adequately joined and that a more differentiated line of analysis needs to be considered in framing public policy toward education. Policies calculated to generate job opportunities for a growing population would seem to deserve higher priority than those designed to rationalize, by their stress on education, the considerable difficulties imposed on those without academic credentials.

At the same time, the data give reason for concern about the personal wellbeing of the growing numbers who do not find that their investments in education are earning them the rewards they were taught to anticipate. The political consequences of latent discontent are not necessarily less threatening to democratic institutions than those of the noisier versions of American disaffection.

Finally, it is appropriate to call attention to the role of the American academic community in the processes by which credentials have come to loom so significantly in the lives of their fellow citizens. A Columbia University colleague has put one major aspect of the matter well:

> Is it not dangerously presumptuous to insist, despite our lack of understanding about the contribution of college schooling to occupational performance, that nevertheless, all professionals must pay a toll to the schools and the teachers? University administrators and college professors have been put into a position that all too closely resembles the old robber barons on the Rhine. They exact not just coin from those who wish passage to professional employment but also the more valuable asset, time—four to eight years of students' lives. . . .

> For those who want to do more than pass through to a career . . . college has much to offer for its cost. The offering takes the form of

perspectives, understanding, and insights rather than lucrative techniques and productive skills. . . . [However] not all persons find such an education to their taste or in their interests; some may wish to pursue a career as immediately as possible, postponing until later, or doing without, the contribution education might make to their lives. At present, choice is denied. Entrance to a career is through college, where schooling all too often is masked as education. Would not the colleges, teachers, students, and those who look forward to professional careers be better served if other entry ways were open, available, and used.[8]

It is by no means clear that Professor Kuhn's questions are easily answered, but they deserve the attention of educators who manage to sluice gates that determine so substantially the directions of the nation's manpower flows.

Another major aspect of academics' role in credential-making catches them up in the apparatuses that maintain the status quo with respect to the distribution of America's wealth. Data presented earlier call attention to the "class bias" that attends the economics of education, a development that exacerbates the increasingly conservative implications of education in America.

The significance of this development gains additional force in a study of "the methodology for estimating the benefits and costs of higher education for a state, and . . . the relationships of these benefits and costs to legislative policy," by Professors Hansen and Weisbord, of the University of Wisconsin.[9] Using data on the California system of higher education, the authors, distinguished students of the economics of education, report:

Public subsidies for higher education in California tend to go disproportionately to students from relatively high-income families and are received in quite different amounts by people even within given income classes. Almost 40 per cent of the student-age population receives no subsidy whatsoever, while a relatively small group receives very substantial subsidies. Whether this pattern of subsidy distribution is consistent with the social objective of equality of educational opportunity is certainly open to question.[10]

The academic community may, of course, uphold high standards for admission to their institutions, both public and private on the basis of hallowed academic principles. The fact is, however, that the "educationally disadvantaged" students will *not* receive credentials for the well-paying jobs in the economy to which high academic standards and degrees stand in problematic relation.

Perhaps the academic community owes it to the losers to re-examine the talents and capabilities of the considerable population groups to which current educational measures, tests, and examinations do not attend. Perhaps such a charge relates to the matter of "relevance," about which more is said than done on America's comfortable campuses these days. One's own experiences as an educator are not heartening, but pessimism in respect to reforms that would be responsive to the needs of losers is a most inappropriately self-serving emotion for the innumerable subsidized tenants of America's academic mansions.

NOTES

1. See Dean Morse, *The Peripheral Worker* (New York: Columbia University Press, 1969).
2. See Ivar Berg and Marcia Freedman, "Job Corps: A Business Bonanza," *Christianity and Crisis,* May 31, 1965.
3. *Manpower Report of the President* (Washington, D.C.: U.S. Government Printing Office, 1969), p. 23. White unemployment rates were 3.2 per cent. *Ibid.,* p. 44.
4. *Ibid.,* p. 25.
5. David Rogers, *110 Livingston Street* (New York: Random House, 1968), pp. 56, 59.
6. Private-school parents, of course, may point out that their control over their children's school experience is limited to choice of school—not by any means an unlimited choice at that—since the demand for private-school services has fostered a certain indifference reminiscent of the public-school pathologies in large cities.
7. *Innovation in Education: New Directions for the American School* (New York:, 1968), p. 30.
8. James W. Kuhn, "The Misuse of Education: The Problem of Schooling for Employment," speech presented at the inauguration of Dr. Gordon C. Bjork as President of Linfield College, McMinnville, Oregon, May 20, 1969.
9. W. Lee Hansen and Burton A. Weisbrod, *Benefits, Costs and Finance of Public Higher Education* (Chicago: Markham, 1969), p. vii.
10. *Ibid.,* p. 84.

THE EDUCATION AND THE UNIVERSITY
WE NEED NOW

Christopher C. Lasch
Eugene D. Genovese

A peculiar feature of neocapitalism in America is the presence of large groups which are excluded from production and which, because they are economically superfluous, must be kept in places of detention. The most important of these groups are the blacks and others of the new poor, young people, and women. By considering these latter groups as superfluous people we can discover the way in which old institutions, like the school and the family, have taken on new functions of custody and detention. We are thus brought face to face with the crisis of American society in one of its most acute forms: for it is precisely those institutions that are breaking apart under the revolt of their subordinate members —students, young people generally, and, increasingly, women. These elements currently form the most militant sections of the white Left.

For young people—and, as higher education becomes compulsory for all, this category includes almost everyone between the ages of, say, thirteen and twenty-two or even twenty-five or twenty-six—the condition of being excluded from useful work is historically new. Formerly young people entered the labor force in large numbers. The gradual achievement of universal eduation, like many other reforms that appear now only to have hastened the coming of the "technetronic society," was wrested from the ruling class in the face of determined opposition. The struggle for universal education was part of the struggle of disfranchised groups and classes to free themselves. Thus free schools went hand in hand with efforts to eradicate child labor. Feminism contributed a second source of pressure for democratizing the schools.

These struggles, however, might not have succeeded if capitalism had not out-lived its early dependence on child labor and female labor (on unskilled labor in general) at the same time as it was generating a growing need for highly trained technicians and professionals. These developments had the effect of rendering the industrial labor of women and children superfluous, for the first time in history. Together with the unions' monopoly of a shrinking labor market, the changed situation made it both feasible and desirable to exclude women and children from the working force. Both the family and the school were profoundly altered as a result.

In the case of the schools, these changes, together with an already existing

SOURCE: *New York Review of Books,* October 9, 1969, pp. 21–24.

tendency to make the schools into a total educational environment (a tendency that goes back as far as the seventeeth century), spelled the slow death of the medieval concept of education, which left the pupil free of supervision outside school hours. In the nineteenth and twentieth centuries this concept, already feeble in the secondary schools, disappeared even from higher education and gave rise to the phenomenon of the university *in loco parentis:* the residential college with its close supervision of all aspects of students' lives.

The segregation of the young in a state of prolonged adolescence means that they are kept in a subordinate and dependent condition (not merely unemployed but unemployable) at a time when they are physically mature and would formerly have qualified for adult status. This fact underlies the peculiarly generational character of the student revolt. It also tends to create a subculture of youth, although this "youth culture" is partly synthetic, created by the corporations and their propaganda agencies for purposes of commercial exploitation—for although the young are unemployable, they command impressive spending power. Young people are thus the victims not only of institutional segregation and low status, but of cynical propaganda that glorifies youth and tries to convince them that they have the best of everything. The official glorification of youth in the twentieth century closely resembles the nineteenth-century glorification of womanhood, which was cynically designed to keep women in a subordinate position, but which many women internalized, just as many young people today internalize the glorification of youth and remain permanently adolescents, emotionally, intellectually, and—not least—politically.

The problem of youth can no more be solved within bourgeois society than any of the other problems with which it is faced, because the solution requires a fundamental reorganization of education, and this in turn depends on a reorganization of the entire economy. What needs to be done is precisely what neocapitalist society cannot do without commiting suicide: destroy the custodial function, of schools; dissociate education from the process of providing qualifications for work, so far as this is possible, and where it is not, recognize more frankly the character of education as apprenticeship while seeking to improve apprenticeship itself; and, finally, provide acceptable alternatives to formal schooling, both for young people and—equally important—for adults.

Technical training should be shifted from the university to a new system of secondary schools, thereby releasing the university from its custodial responsibilities and freeing it for serious intellectual work. Graduation from the new technical academies or colleges, which students would enter at thirteen or fourteen and from which they would emerge at eighteen or nineteen, should qualify them for most work now open only to holders of a college degree. The object of such schools should be, not to offer the traditional rounded education—which in any case has become a hollow pretense even in the university—but to train scientific generalists, people qualified for technical work but capable of critical and independent thought and, in particular, aware of the philosophical and social implications of scientific work and of modern technology.

In a humane and rational system of secondary education, specialization would not be allowed to interfere with the more basic objective, now neglected at every level of the school system, of relating specific scientific knowledge to general scientific knowledge and science itself to human experience generally. By sacrificing its pretensions to classical education, the technical college would be in a better position than the university to capitalize on students' hunger for "relevance" by offering, for example, instruction in the scientific understanding of society instead of burdening students with required courses in the humanities which seem "irrelevant" to most students for many good reasons along with many bad ones.

The technical school, by retreating not only from the absurd pretense to offer a complete classical training but also from the present swollen conception of the school as the sum of a person's education, would make it possible for young people to enter the adult world at eighteen or nineteen. It would also be organized in such a way as to free them, while they are still in school, from compulsory full-time instruction, leaving them with time for games, jobs, reading, and the cultivation of the inner life. The possibility of attending a university and pursuing scholarly work should always remain open to those who are interested in and qualified for such work, while the years of technical schooling and apprenticeship should provide time and space in which young people can change their minds about the direction they wish to take.

One of the first priorities of a new social order is variety, a greatly extended spectrum of choices. Higher education, in various forms, needs to be made widely available to adults, while young people, on the other hand, should be exempted from compulsory schooling and provided with other means of qualifying for work. Even today, much technical training takes place on the job itself—tacit proof that prolonged academic training is far from indispensable, even for many highly skilled jobs. A recent study by the sociologist Ivar Berg (*Trans-action,* March 1969) suggests that in many cases there is no correlation at all between education and industrial efficiency, and that academic credentials are usually more important in getting jobs than in actually doing them. This helps to explain why so many students, both in the high schools and in the universities, experience education as an arbitrary confinement and as something "irrelevant" not only to the search for truth but even to qualification for honest employment.

It also helps to explain why disaffected students, both in secondary schools and in the universities, tend to be concentrated in the humanities and social sciences. In the scientific and technical disciplines, academic training still bears a discernible relationship to work and is often indispensable to the process of qualification. Students in these fields know that their futures depend on mastering an exacting discipline.

What many employers value, however, is not academic training itself but the academic degree, and a large number of students, knowing this, naturally gravitate to subjects which, since they are irrelevant to employment in any case, at least have the advantage of being relatively undemanding. The erosion of academic standards in the humanities and social sciences reflects, among other things, the school's attempt to provide job training that is irrational even on its own terms; and the restoration of academic standards, accordingly, would directly challenge prevailing arrangements by exposing some of the more glaring absurdities of compulsory education and by making it more difficult than it has been for schools to serve merely as places of detention and custody.

American capitalism nevertheless demands prolonged compulsory schooling, even when it does not directly qualify people for employment, because if prolonged schooling ceased to be compulsory, society would have to find something useful and rewarding for young people to do. Any efforts to desanctify education and to provide a more rational and flexible system of apprenticeship will be fiercely resisted by the ruling bureaucracies. That is why a new system will not be adopted until it becomes the goal not simply of student movements but of the working classes as well. The object of educational reform has to be seen not merely as a way of freeing youth from compulsory mis-education (in Paul Goodman's phrase) but as humanizing apprenticeship—a necessary step in the self-emancipation of the working class and particularly of its intellectual and technical strata. Educational reform, in other words, has to be seen as a class question.

Not that young people themselves constitute a social class, as some of the spokesmen of the student movement have claimed. To call them a class obscures what is precisely one of the most interesting conclusions to emerge from an analysis of youth, women, blacks, and other groups that exist for the most part outside the system of industrial production and therefore outside the class structure to which that system gives rise. The questions now being raised by these groups are not class questions in any strict sense—and this is the heart of the matter—they are class questions in the broad sense that they cannot be resolved except by changing the class structure of American society—that is, by putting an end to the hegemony of the bourgeoisie. The problems of youth cannot be dealt with except by restructuring an educational system geared to the needs of the bourgeoisie, the reform of which the bourgeoisie will resist with all its force. Educational reform cannot be regarded, therefore, as a matter of peculiar concern to students. The entire working class and large sections of the middle class have a stake in changing the system, and it will not be changed except through their joint efforts.

The current turmoil in the universities shows how urgently radical change is needed and yet how far radicals are from understanding what needs to be done. The changes in production that have made young people superfluous and transformed the secondary school beyond recognition have altered the institutional function of the university. The university no longer serves as an exclusive club for the children of the ruling class and a few privileged souls co-opted from below. It still retains the old functions: it trains professionals and high functionaries of the traditional type, and more important, it trains the managerial elite and performs direct and vital services for the corporations and the government. But its most striking function today—apart from the custodial function it shares increasingly with the secondary schools—is that of training an army of intellectual workers on which the corporate system depends. In the last twenty-five years the university has become, in a special sense of the term, a working-class institution. It trains intellectual and technical workers in the special skills needed to run the industrial and governmental bureaucracies and to carry out all the commands of the managerial elite. Higher education has become another form of industrial apprenticeship.

These developments have had a disastrous effect on the traditional concept of higher education as a quest for meaning, order, and intellectual synthesis demanding, in the university, an atmosphere of unrestricted inquiry and freedom from outside interference. Traditionally the universities enjoyed a high degree of autonomy compared with other institutions of ruling-class control, and this permitted them, on occasion, even to become centers of opposition to the ruling class. The new trade-school function of the universities, superimposed on their traditional ruling-class functions, tends to make higher education another form of production.

The traditional functions themselves, moreover, have changed their character. Instead of training men of general culture who govern society through the elaboration of a unified world-view that makes sense of experience and to which all activities can be related, the university now trains men who govern through the application of specialized skills to the solution of technical problems. It also carries on government-financed research that will be directly useful to the corporations and to government, particularly the military. These activities further erode the autonomy of the university, which remains a ruling-class institution as well as a trade school, but in a new sense. No longer is the university viewed as a place in which to raise philosophical questions about the very premises of the society it serves.

All these developments greatly complicate the problems confronting the Left. Because it needs a radical intelligentsia, which can no longer be trained elsewhere, the Left has an immediate stake in the survival of the university as a partially autonomous institution. In fighting to preserve and extend the university's autonomy, however, the Left faces at the outset the grim fact that much of the ground on which it must fight has already been lost. Yet the same historical changes that have led to this result simultaneously present radicals with an unprecedented opportunity to train a new kind of working-class intellectual and to raise the cultural level of the working class as a whole. If higher education has become a form of apprenticeship, the Left can use its tactical leverage in the university to humanize the conditions of apprenticeship—that is, to provide the working class and the "new middle class" with the means of their own emancipation.

The ruling class wishes to use the universities, much as it wishes to use the school system as a whole, to train intellectual workers to do their jobs competently, to find compensation for powerlessness in a culture of consumption, and to mind their own business in matters of state. The Left has the power—provided it overcomes its neo-Luddism and begins to take itself seriously in the academic world—to organize a broad coalition of forces within the university community and eventually, one hopes, in American society itself, for the purpose of providing students with the means of becoming not merely intellectual workers but workers who can think and question and thereby defend their own class interests against those who would keep them docile and passive.

This does not mean providing students with courses in guerrilla warfare and the crimes of American imperialism. It implies something more positive and more serious: the restoration of the unity of learning. Science and engineering must become once again a branch of philosophy, a means not simply of solving predefined problems but of raising questions about the ends of human life. The arts and humanities must be rescued from their present degraded, essentially ornamental position and established on an equal footing with science, as studies that make their own contribution to the understanding of the objective world. Unless these things are done, the working class and the American people as a whole will have no defense against a technological anti-culture that perpetrates one atrocity after another against people of other nations while it ruins its own environment and increasingly reduces its citizens to insecurity and anxiety. What is required, therefore, is not more curricular reforms designed to provide a sugar coating of the humanities and "general education" for industrial apprenticeship, but a reform of apprenticeship itself, in the form of a general attack on the instrumental conception of culture.

The issue, reduced to its simplest terms, is the issue between an enlightened and a degraded working class. But since that issue is now bound up with the survival of the university as a semi-autonomous institution and, indeed, with the survival of all that is valuable in Western culture, academic radicals are in a position to find strong allies among many liberals and conservatives both on university faculties and among the students. An alliance to reform the university, in turn, would provide radical intellectuals with a political setting in which to carry on the more strictly cultural struggle to convince liberals and conservatives that the culture they value cannot be preserved without a fundamental reform of American society itself.

UNEQUAL EDUCATION AND THE REPRODUCTION OF THE HIERARCHICAL DIVISION OF LABOR

Samuel Bowles

The ideological defense of modern capitalist society rests heavily on the assertion that the equalizing effects of education can counter the disequalizing forces inherent in the free market system. That educational systems in capitalist societies have been highly unequal is generally admitted and widely condemned. Yet educational inequalities are taken as passing phenomena, holdovers from an earlier, less enlightened era, which are rapidly being eliminated.

The record of educational history in the U.S., and scrutiny of the present state of our colleges and schools, lend little support to this comforting optimism. Rather, the available data suggest an alternative interpretation. In what follows I will argue (1) that schools have evolved in the U.S. not as part of a pursuit of equality, but rather to meet the needs of capitalist employers for a disciplined and skilled labor force, and to provide a mechanism for social control in the interests of political stability; (2) that as the economic importance of skilled and well educated labor has grown, inequalities in the school system have become increasingly important in reproducing the class structure from one generation to the next; (3) that the U.S. school system is pervaded by class inequalities, which have shown little sign of diminishing over the last half century; and (4) that the evidently unequal control over school boards and other decision-making bodies in education does not provide a sufficient explanation of the persistence and pervasiveness of inequalities in the school system. Although the unequal distribution of political power serves to maintain inequalities in education, their origins are to be found outside the political sphere, in the class structure itself and in the class subcultures typical of capitalist societies. Thus unequal education has its roots in the very class structure which it serves to legitimize and reproduce. Inequalities in education are a part of the web of capitalist society, and likely to persist as long as capitalism survives.

SOURCE: R. C. Edwards, M. Reich, and T. E. Weisskopf (eds.), *The Capitalist System* (Englewood Cliffs, N.J.: Prentice-Hall, 1972), pp. 219–299.

THE EVOLUTION OF CAPITALISM
AND THE RISE OF MASS
EDUCATION

In colonial America, and in most precapitalist societies of the past, the basic productive unit was the family. For the vast majority of male adults, work was self-directed, and was performed without direct supervision. Though constrained by poverty, ill health, the low level of technological development, and occasional interferences by the political authorities, a man had considerable leeway in choosing his working hours, what to produce, and how to produce it. While great inequalities in wealth, political power, and other aspects of status normally existed, differences in the degree of autonomy in work were relatively minor, particularly when compared with what was to come.

Transmitting the necessary productive skills to the children as they grew up proved to be a simple task, not because the work was devoid of skill, but because the quite substantial skills required were virtually unchanging from generation to generation, and because the transition to the world of work did not require that the child adapt to a wholly new set of social relationships. The child learned the concrete skills and adapted to the social relations of production through learning by doing within the family. Preparation for life in the larger community was facilitated by the child's experience with the extended family, which shaded off without distinct boundaries, through uncles and fourth cousins, into the community. Children learned early how to deal with complex relationships among adults other than their parents, and children other than their brothers and sisters.[1]

It was not required that children learn a complex set of political principles or ideologies, as political participation was limited and political authority unchallenged, at least in normal times. The only major socializing institution outside the family was the church, which sought to inculcate the accepted spiritual values and attitudes. In addition, a small number of children learned craft skills outside the family, as apprentices. The role of schools tended to be narrowly vocational, restricted to preparation of children for a career in the church or the still inconsequential state bureaucracy. The curriculum of the few universities reflected the aristocratic penchant for conspicuous intellectual consumption.

The extension of capitalist production, and particularly the factory system, undermined the role of the family as the major unit of both socialization and production. Small peasant farmers were driven off the land or competed out of business. Cottage industry was destroyed. Ownership of the means of production became heavily concentrated in the hands of landlords and capitalists. Workers relinquished control over their labor in return for wages or salaries. Increasingly, production was carried on in large organizations in which a small management group directed the work activities of the entire labor force. The social relations of production—the authority structure, the prescribed types of behavior and response characteristic of the workplace—became increasingly distinct from those of the family.

The divorce of the worker from control over production—from control over his own labor—is particularly important in understanding the role of schooling in capitalist societies. The resulting hierarchical social division of labor—between controllers and controlled—is a crucial aspect of the class structure of capitalist societies, and will be seen to be an important barrier to the achievement of social class equality in schooling.

Rapid economic change in the capitalist period led to frequent shifts of the occupational distribution of the labor force, and constant changes in the skill requirements for jobs. The productive skills of the father were no longer adequate for the needs of the son during his lifetime. Skill training within the family became increasingly inappropriate.

And the family itself was changing. Increased geographic mobility of labor and the necessity for children to work outside the family spelled the demise of the extended family and greatly weakened even the nuclear family. Meanwhile, the authority of the church was questioned by the spread of secular rationalist thinking and the rise of powerful competing groups.

While undermining the main institutions of socialization, the rise of the capitalist system was accompanied by urbanization, labor migration, the spread of democratic ideologies, and a host of other developments which created an environment—both social and intellectual—which would ultimately challenge the political order.

An institutional crisis was at hand. The outcome, in virtually all capitalist countries, was the rise of mass education. In the U.S., the many advantages of schooling as a socialization process were quickly perceived. The early proponents of the rapid expansion of schooling argued that education could perform many of the socialization functions which earlier had been centered in the family and to a lesser extent, in the church. An ideal preparation for factory work was found in the social relations of the school: specifically, in its emphasis on discipline, punctuality, acceptance of authority outside the family, and individual accountability for one's work. The social relations of the school would replicate the social relations of the workplace, and thus help young people adapt to the social division of labor. Schools would further lead people to accept the authority of the state and its agents—the teachers—at a young age, in part by fostering the illusion of the benevolence of the government in its relations with citizens. Moreover, because schooling would ostensibly be open to all, one's position in the social division of labor could be portrayed as the result not of birth, but of one's own efforts and talents. And if the children's everyday experiences with the structure of schooling were insufficient to inculcate the correct views and attitudes, the curriculum itself would be made to embody the bourgeois ideology. Where precapitalist social institutions—particularly the church—remained strong or threatened the capitalist hegemony, schools sometimes served as a modernizing counter-institution.

The movement for public elementary and secondary education in the U.S. originated in the 19th century in states dominated by the burgeoning industrial capitalist class, most notably in Massachusetts. It spread rapidly to all parts of the country except the South. The fact that some working people's movements had demanded free instruction should not obscure the basically coercive nature of the extension of schooling. In many parts of the country, schools were literally imposed upon the workers.

The evolution of the economy in the 19th century gave rise to new socialization needs and continued to spur the growth of education. Agriculture continued to lose ground to manufacturing; simple manufacturing gave way to production involving complex interrelated processes; an increasing fraction of the labor force was employed in producing services rather than goods. Employers in the most rapidly growing sectors of the economy began to require more than obedience and punctuality in their workers; a change in motivational outlook was required. The new structure of production provided little built-in motivation. There were fewer jobs like farming and piece-rate work in manufacturing in which material reward was tied directly to effort. As work roles became more complicated and interrelated, the evaluation of the individual worker's performance became increasingly difficult. Employers began to look for workers who had internalized the production-related values of the firms' managers.

The continued expansion of education was pressed by many who saw schooling as a means of producing these new forms of motivation and discipline. Others, frightened by the growing labor militancy after the Civil War, found new urgency in the social control arguments popular among the proponents of education in the antebellum period.

A system of class stratification developed within this rapidly expanding educational system. Children of the social elite normally attended private schools. Because working class children tended to leave school early, the class composition of the public high schools was distinctly more elite than the public primary schools. And university education, catering mostly to the children of upper-class families, ceased to be merely training for teaching or the divinity and became important in gaining access to the pinnacles of the business world.

Around the turn of the present century, large numbers of working class and particularly immigrant children began attending high schools. At the same time, a system of class stratification developed within secondary education. The older democratic ideology of the common school—that the same curriculum should be offered to all children—gave way to the "progressive" insistence that education should be tailored to the "needs of the child." In the interests of providing an education relevant to the later life of the students, vocational schools and tracks were developed for the children of working families. The academic curriculum was preserved for those who would later have the opportunity to make use of book learning, either in college or in white-collar employment. This and other educational reforms of the progressive education movement reflected an implicit assumption of the immutability of the class structure.

The frankness with which students were channeled into curriculum tracks, on the basis of their social class background, raised serious doubts concerning the "openness" of the class structure. The relation between social class and a child's chances of promotion or tracking assignments was disguised—though not mitigated much—by another "progressive" reform: "objective" educational testing. Particularly after World War I, the capitulation of the schools to business values and concepts of efficiency led to the increased use of intelligence and scholastic achievement testing as an ostensibly unbiased means of measuring the product of schooling and classifying students. The complementary growth of the guidance counseling profession allowed much of the channeling to proceed from the students' "own" well-counselled-choices, thus adding an apparent element of voluntarism to the system.

The class stratification of education during this period had proceeded hand in hand with the stratification of the labor force. As large bureaucratic corporations and public agencies employed an increasing fraction of all workers, a complicated segmentation of the labor force evolved, reflecting the hierarchical structure of the social relations of production.

The social division of labor had become a finely articulated system of work relations dominated at the top by a small group with control over work processes and a high degree of personal autonomy in their work activities, and proceeding by finely differentiated stages down the chain of bureaucratic command to workers who labored more as extensions of the machinery than as autonomous human beings.

One's status, income, and personal autonomy came to depend in great measure on one's place in the hierarchy of work relations. And in turn, positions in the social division of labor came to be associated with educational credentials reflecting the number of years of schooling and the quality of education received. The increasing importance of schooling as a mechanism for allocating children to positions in the class structure, played a major part in legitimizing the structure itself. But at the same time, it undermined the simple process which in the past had preserved the position and privilege of the upper class families from generation to generation. In short, it undermined the processes serving to reproduce the social division of labor.

In pre-capitalist societies, direct inheritance of occupational position is common. Even in the early capitalist economy, prior to the segmentation of the labor force on the basis of differential skills and education, the class structure was reproduced generation after generation simply through the inheritance of physical capital by the offspring of the capitalist class. Now that the social division of labor is differentiated by types of competence and educational credentials as well as by the ownership of capital, the problem of inheritance is not nearly as simple. The crucial complication arises because education and skills are embedded in human beings, and—unlike physical capital—these assets cannot be passed on to one's children at death. In an advanced capitalist society in which education and skills play an important role in the hierarchy of production, then, laws guaranteeing inheritance are not enough to reproduce the social division of labor from generation to generation. Skills and educational credentials must somehow be passed on within the family. It is a fundamental theme of this paper that schools play an important part in reproducing and legitimizing this modern form of class structure.

CLASS INEQUALITIES IN U.S. SCHOOLS

Unequal schooling reproduces the hierarchical social division of labor. Children whose parents occupy positions at the top of the occupational hierarchy receive more years of schooling than working class children. Both the amount and the content of their education greatly facilitate their movement into positions similar to their parents'.

Because of the relative ease of measurement, inequalities in years of schooling are particularly evident. If we define social class standing by the income, occupation, and educational level of the parents, a child from the 90th percentile in the class distribution may expect on the average to achieve over four and a half more years of schooling than a child from the 10th percentile. As can be seen in Table 1, social class inequalities in the number of years of schooling received arise in part because a disproportionate number of children from poorer families do not complete high school. Table 2 indicates that these inequalities are exacer-

TABLE 1   Percentage of Male Children Aged 16–17 Enrolled in Public School, and Percentage at Less Than the Modal Grade Level, by Parent's Education and Income, 1960*

	PERCENT OF MALE CHILDREN AGED 16–17 ENROLLED IN PUBLIC SCHOOL	PERCENT OF THOSE ENROLLED WHO ARE BELOW THE MODAL LEVEL
1. Parent's education less than 8 years Family income:		
less than $3,000	66.1	47.4
$3,000–4,999	71.3	35.7
$5,000–6,999	75.5	28.3
$7,000 and over	77.1	21.8
2. Parent's education 8–11 years Family income:		
less than $3,000	78.6	25.0
$3,000–4,999	82.9	20.9
$5,000–6,999	84.9	16.9
$7,000 and over	86.1	13.0
3. Parent's education 12 years or more Family income:		
less than $3,000	89.5	13.4
$3,000–4,999	90.7	12.4
$5,000–6,999	92.1	9.7
$7,000 and over	94.2	6.9

SOURCE: Bureau of the Census, Census of Population, 1960, Vol. PC-(2)5A, Table 5.
* Family income for 12 months preceding October 1965.
According to Bureau of the Census definitions, for 16-year-olds 9th grade or less and for 17-year-olds 10th grade or less are below the modal level. Father's education is indicated if father is present; otherwise mother's education is indicated.

bated by social class inequalities in college attendance among those children who did graduate from high school: even among those who had graduated from high school, children of families earning less than $3,000 per year were over six times as likely *not* to attend college as were the children of families earning over $15,000.

Inequalities in schooling are not simply a matter of differences in years of schooling attained. Differences in the internal structure of schools themselves and in the content of schooling reflect the differences in the social class compositions of the student bodies. The social relations of the educational process ordinarily mirror the social relations of the work roles into which most students are likely to move. Differences in rules, expected modes of behavior, and opportunities for choice are most glaring when we compare levels of schooling. Note the wide range of choice over curriculum, life style, and allocation of time afforded to college students, compared with the obedience and respect for authority expected in high school. Differentiation occurs also within each level of schooling. One needs only to compare the social relations of a junior college with those of an elite four-year

TABLE 2   College Attendance in 1967 among
High School Graduates, by Family Income*

FAMILY INCOME	PERCENT WHO DID NOT ATTEND COLLEGE
Total	53.1
under $3,000	80.2
$3,000 to $3,999	67.7
$4,000 to $5,999	63.7
$6,000 to $7,499	58.9
$7,500 to $9,999	49.0
$10,000 to $14,999	38.7
$15,000 and over	13.3

* Refers to individuals who were high school seniors in
October 1965 and who subsequently graduated from high
school. Source: U.S. Department of Commerce, Bureau
of the Census, *Current Population Report*, Series P-20, No.
185, July 11, 1969, p. 6. College attendance refers to both
two- and four-year institutions.

college, or those of a working class high school with those of a wealthy suburban
high school, for verification of this point.

The differential socialization patterns in schools attended by students of different social classes do not arise by accident. Rather, they stem from the fact that
the educational objectives and expectations of both parents and teachers, and the
responsiveness of students to various patterns of teaching and control, differ for
students of different social classes. Further, class inequalities in school socialization patterns are reinforced by the inequalities in financial resources. The paucity
of financial support for the education of children from working class families not
only leaves more resources to be devoted to the children of those with commanding roles in the economy; it forces upon the teachers and school administrators
in the working class schools a type of social relations which fairly closely mirrors
that of the factory. Thus financial considerations in poorly supported working
class schools militate against small intimate classes, against a multiplicity of elec-
tive courses and specialized teachers (except disciplinary personnel), and preclude
the amounts of free time for the teachers and free space required for a more
open, flexible educational environment. The lack of financial support all but
requires that students be treated as raw materials on a production line; it places
a high premium on obedience and punctuality; there are few opportunities for
independent, creative work or individualized attention by teachers. The well-
financed schools attended by the children of the rich can offer much greater
opportunities for the development of the capacity for sustained independent work
and the other characteristics required for adequate job performance in the upper
levels of the occupational hierarchy.

While much of the inequality in U.S. education exists between schools, even
within a given school different children receive different educations. Class stratification within schools is achieved through tracking, differential participation in
extracurricular activities, and in the attitudes of teachers and particularly guidance
personnel who expect working class children to do poorly, to terminate schooling
early, and to end up in jobs similar to their parents'.

Not surprisingly, the results of schooling differ greatly for children of different social classes. The differing educational objectives implicit in the social relations of schools attended by children of different social classes has already been mentioned. Less important but more easily measured are differences in scholastic achievement. If we measure the output of schooling by scores on nationally standardized achievement tests, children whose parents were themselves highly educated outperform the children of parents with less education by a wide margin. A recent study revealed, for example, that among white high school seniors, those students whose parents were in the top education decile were on the average well over three grade levels ahead of those whose parents were in the bottom decile.[2] While a good part of this discrepancy is the result of unequal treatment in school and unequal educational resources, it will be suggested below that much of it is related to differences in the early socialization and home environment of the children.

Given the great social class differences in scholastic achievement, class inequalities in college attendance are to be expected. Thus one might be tempted to argue that the data in Table 2 are simply a reflection of unequal scholastic achievement in high school and do not reflect any *additional* social class inequalities peculiar to the process of college admission. This view is unsupported by the available data, some of which are presented in Table 3. Access to a college educa-

T A B L E 3 **Probability of College Entry for a Male Who Has Reached Grade 11***

| | | SOCIOECONOMIC QUARTILES† | | | |
		Low 1	2	3	High 4
Ability Quartiles†	Low 1	.06	.12	.13	.26
	2	.13	.15	.29	.36
	3	.25	.34	.45	.65
	High 4	.48	.70	.73	.87

* Based on a large sample of U.S. high school students as reported in John C. Flannagan and William W. Cooley, *Project TALENT, One-Year Follow-Up Studies,* Cooperative Research Project No. 2333, School of Education, University of Pittsburgh, 1966.

† The socioeconomic index is a composite measure including family income, father's occupation and education, mother's education, etc. The ability scale is a composite of tests measuring general academic aptitude.

tion is highly unequal, even for children of the same measured "academic ability."

The social class inequalities in our school system and the role they play in the reproduction of the social division of labor are too evident to be denied. Defenders of the educational system are forced back on the assertion that things are getting better; the inequalities of the past were far worse. Yet the available historical evidence lends little support to the idea that our schools are on the road to equality of educational opportunity. For example, data from a recent U.S. Census survey reported in Table 4 indicate that graduation from college has become increasingly dependent on one's class background. This is true despite the fact that the probability of high school graduation is becoming increasingly equal across social classes. On balance, the available data suggest that the number of years of schooling which the average child attains depends at least as much now upon the social class standing of his father as it did fifty years ago.[3]

TABLE 4   Among Sons Who Had Reached High School, Percentage Who Graduated from College, by Son's Age and Father's Level of Education

Son's Age in 1962	Likely Dates of College Graduation*	Less Than 8 Years	FATHER'S EDUCATION					
			Some High School		High School Graduate		Some College or More	
			Percent Graduating	Ratio to <8	Percent Graduating	Ratio to <8	Percent Graduating	Ratio to <8
25–34	1950–1959	07.6	17.4	2.29	25.6	3.37	51.9	6.83
35–44	1940–1949	08.6	11.9	1.38	25.3	2.94	53.9	6.27
45–54	1930–1939	07.7	09.8	1.27	15.1	1.96	36.9	4.79
55–64	1920–1929	08.9	09.8	1.10	19.2	2.16	29.8	3.35

* Assuming college graduation at age 22.
SOURCE: Based on U.S. Census data as reported in William G. Spady, "Educational Mobility and Access: Growth and Paradoxes." *American Journal of Sociology*, vol. 73, No. 3 (November 1967).

The argument that our "egalitarian" education compensates for inequalities generated elsewhere in the capitalist system is patently fallacious. But the discrepancy between the ideology and the reality of the U.S. school system is far greater than would appear from a passing glance at the above data. In the first place, if education is to compensate for the social class immobility due to the inheritance of wealth and privilege, education must be structured so that the poor child receives not less, not even the same, but *more* than equal benefits from education. The school must compensate for the other disadvantages which the lower-class child suffers. Thus the liberal assertion that education compensates for inequalities in inherited wealth and privilege is falsified not so much by the extent of the social class inequalities in the school system as by their very existence, or, more correctly, by the absence of compensatory inequalities.

Second, considering the problem of inequality of income at a given moment, a similar argument applies. In a capitalist economy, the increasing importance of schooling in the economy will increase income inequality even in the absence of social class inequalities in quality and quantity of schooling. This is so simply because the labor force becomes differentiated by type of skill or schooling, and inequalities in labor earnings therefore contribute to total income inequality, augmenting the inequalities due to the concentration of capital. The disequalizing tendency will of course be intensified if the owners of capital also acquire a disproportionate amount of those types of education and training which confer access to high-paying jobs.

CLASS CULTURE AND CLASS POWER

The pervasive and persistent inequalities in U.S. education would seem to refute an interpretation of education which asserts its egalitarian functions. But the facts of inequality do not by themselves suggest an alternate explanation. Indeed, they pose serious problems of interpretation. If the costs of education borne by students and their families were very high, or if nepotism were rampant, or if formal segregation of pupils by social class were practiced, or educational decisions were made by a select few whom we might call the power elite, it would not be difficult to explain the continued inequalities in U.S. education. The problem of interpretation, however, is to reconcile the above empirical findings with the facts of our society as we perceive them: public and virtually tuition-free education at all levels, few legal instruments for the direct implementation of class segregation, a limited role for "contacts" or nepotism in the achievement of high status or income, a commitment (at the rhetorical level at least) to equality of educational opportunity, and a system of control of education which if not particularly democratic, extends far beyond anything resembling a power elite. The attempt to reconcile these apparently discrepant facts leads us back to a consideration of the social division of labor, the associated class cultures, and the exercise of class power.

The social division of labor based on the hierarchial structure of production gives rise to distinct class subcultures. The values, personality traits, and expectations characteristic of each subculture are transmitted from generation to generation through class differences in family socialization and complementary differences in the type and amount of schooling ordinarily attained by children of various class positions. These class differences in schooling are maintained in large measure through the capacity of the upper class to control the basic principles of school finance, pupil evaluation and educational objectives.

The social relations of production characteristic of advanced capitalist societies (and many socialist societies) are most clearly illustrated in the bureaucracy and hierarchy of the modern corporation. Occupational roles in the capitalist economy may be grouped according to the degree of independence and control exercised by the person holding the job. There is some evidence that the personality attributes associated with the adequate performance of jobs in occupational categories defined in this broad way differ considerably, some apparently requiring independence and internal discipline, and others emphasizing such traits as obedience, predictability, and willingness to subject oneself to external control.

These personality attributes are developed primarily at a young age, both in the family and, to a lesser extent, in secondary socialization institutions such as schools. Because people tend to marry within their own class (in part because spouses often meet in our class segregated schools), both parents are likely to have a similar set of these fundamental personality traits. Thus children of parents occupying a given position in the occupational hierarchy grow up in homes where child-rearing methods and perhaps even the physical surroundings tend to develop personality characteristics appropriate to adequate job performance in the occupational roles of the parents. The children of managers and professionals are taught self-reliance within a broad set of constraints; the children of production line workers are taught obedience.

While this relation between parents' class position and child's personality attributes operates primarily in the home, it is reinforced by schools and other social institutions. Thus, to take an example introduced earlier, the authoritarian social relations of working class high schools complement the discipline-oriented early socialization patterns experienced by working class children. The relatively greater freedom of wealthy suburban schools extends and formalizes the early independence training characteristic of upper-class families.

The operation of the labor market translates differences in class culture into income inequalities and occupational hierarchies. The personality traits, values, and expectations characteristic of different class cultures play a major role in determining an individual's success in gaining a high income or prestigious occupation. The apparent contribution of schooling to occupational success and higher income seems to be explained primarily by the personality characteristics of those who have higher educational attainments. Although the rewards to intellectual capacities are quite limited in the labor market (except for a small number of high level jobs), mental abilities are important in getting ahead in school. Grades, the probability of continuing to higher levels of schooling, and a host of other school success variables, are positively correlated with "objective" measures of intellectual capacities. Partly for this reason, one's experience in school reinforces the belief that promotion and rewards are distributed fairly. The close relationship between the amount of education attained and later occupational success thus provides a meritocratic appearance to mask the mechanisms which reproduce the class system from generation to generation.

Positions of control in the productive hierarchy tend to be associated with positions of political influence. Given the disproportionate share of political power held by the upper class and their capacity to determine the accepted patterns of behavior and procedures, to define the national interest, and in general to control the ideological and institutional context in which educational decisions are made, it is not surprising to find that resources are allocated unequally among school tracks, between schools serving different classes, and between levels of schooling. The same configuration of power results in curricula, methods of instruction, and criteria of selection and promotion which confer benefits disproportionately on the children of the upper class.

The power of the upper class exists in its capacity to define and maintain a set of rules of operation or decision criteria—"rules of the game"—which, though often seemingly innocuous and sometimes even egalitarian in their ostensible intent, have the effect of maintaining the unequal system.

The operation of two prominent examples of these "rules of the game" will serve to illustrate the point. The first important principle is that excellence in schooling should be rewarded. Given the capacity of the upper class to define excellence in terms on which upper-class children tend to excel (for example, scholastic achievement), adherence to this principle yields inegalitarian outcomes (for example, unequal access to higher education) while maintaining the appearance of fair treatment. Thus the principle of rewarding excellence serves to legitimize the unequal consequences of schooling by associating success with competence. At the same time, the institution of objectively administered tests of performance serves to allow a limited amount of upward mobility among exceptional children of the lower class, thus providing further legitimation of the operations of the social system by giving some credence to the myth of widespread mobility.

The second example is the principle that elementary and secondary schooling should be financed in very large measure from local revenues. This principle is supported on the grounds that it is necessary to preserve political liberty. Given the degree of residential segregation by income level, the effect of this principle is to produce an unequal distribution of school resources among children of different classes. Towns with a large tax base can spend large sums for the education of their disproportionately upper-class children even without suffering a higher than average tax rate. Because the main resource inequalities in schooling thus exist between rather than within school districts, and because there is no effective mechanism for redistribution of school funds among school districts, poor families lack a viable political strategy for correcting the inequality.

The above rules of the game—rewarding "excellence" and financing schools locally—illustrate the complementarity between the political and economic power of the upper class. Thus it appears that the consequences of an unequal distribution of political power among classes complement the results of class culture in maintaining an educational system which has thus far been capable of transmitting status from generation to generation, and capable in addition of political survival in the formally democratic and egalitarian environment of the contemporary United States.

NOTES

1. This account draws upon two important historical studies: P. Aries, *Centuries of Childhood* (New York: Random House, 1970); and B. Bailyn, *Education in the Forming of American Society* (New York: Random House, 1960).
2. Calculation based on data in James S. Coleman, *et al., Equality of Educational Opportunity,* vol. 2 (Washington, D.C.: U.S. Dept of Health, Education & Welfare, Office of Education, 1966), and methods described in S. Bowles, "Schooling and Inequality from Generation to Generation," mimeo, 1971.
3. See P. M. Blau and O. D. Duncan, *The American Occupational Structure* (New York: Wiley, 1967). More recent data do not contradict the evidence of no trend towards equality. A 1967 Census survey, the most recent available, shows that among high school graduates in 1965, the probability of college attendance for those whose parents had attended college has continued to rise relative to the probability of college attendance for those whose parents had attended less than eight years of school. See U.S. Bureau of the Census, *Current Population Reports,* Series P-20, No. 185, July 11, 1969.

MOBILITY OR EQUALITY?

Christopher Jencks
David Riesman

MOBILITY OR EQUALITY?

If neither financial aid nor de-emphasizing academic competence promises much change in the outcome of competition between the advantaged and the disadvantaged, what does? One answer is that reform must come in the area where the previous section located the major cause of current disparity: the subjective attitudes of the competitors rather than the objective characteristics of the competition. Reformers must somehow deal with the fact that, popular mythology to the contrary notwithstanding, the poor outsider is not usually "hungrier" than the rich insider and is not usually willing to make greater sacrifices to achieve the same objective. On the contrary, it is the children of the upper-middle classes who are most likely to be "hooked" on power and privilege, or at least on the kind of work that leads to privilege, and who are most willing to do what must be done to feed this addiction.

Schools and colleges do sometimes make an effort to alter this pattern. A suburban school, for example, will sometimes try to persuade an upper-middle class family not to push its subnormal son toward college, and will try to counsel the child into a less demanding career. But parents usually take such advice very badly, and many schools are reluctant even to offer it. At the opposite end of the spectrum teachers and counselors usually make some effort to push their most talented students into college preparatory curricula and then into college itself, even if the child comes from a family where this is not expected.

Yet it seems clear that none of these efforts to prod from the outside has much effect: even dull children of the upper-middle class usually go to college anyway, and the adept children of the lower class, unless notably athletic or brilliant, still drop out in large numbers. In part, no doubt, this reflects the fact that the school itself is often half-hearted in its devotion to academic values. A well-spoken middle-class child who "just can't learn" still seems "nice" to his teacher, while a more sullen and less controlled working-class child who does equally good work may seem like a "troublemaker."[1] So the former is pushed into a program that will allow him to attend an unselective college, while the latter is given a hard time, made even more rebellious, and often eventually pushed out on the street. These non-academic standards of merit almost inevitably tend to favor

SOURCE: *The Academic Revolution* (Garden City, N.Y.: Doubleday, Anchor Books, 1969), pp. 146–154.

237

the middle-class student over the upwardly mobile, though we have occasionally seen the opposite sort of bias too.

Yet the heart of the problem is not, we think, in the educational system. So long as the distribution of power and privilege among adults remains radically unequal, and so long as some children are raised by adults at the bottom while others are raised by adults at the top, the children will more often than not turn out unequal. In part this may be because parents with time, money, and the respect of their fellows can do a better job raising their children than the parents who lack those things. But the real point is that children raised in different circumstances necessarily have different hopes, expectations, and compulsions. We suspect that these differences account for more of the class variation in college chances than all other differences combined.

Such differences can be eradicated. America could commit itself, for example, to a kibbutz-like system of child rearing, in which all children would be raised communally and biological ancestry would count for relatively little. In its most extreme form such a system could virtually equalize life chances, making every child's future dependent on his genes. We do not think, however, that such a proposal would win much popular support in America, even among those whose children would presumably benefit. Rightly or wrongly, most Americans are convinced that children need to have someone around who is unconditionally and passionately devoted to them, someone who will love them not in the collective way that a good preschool teacher loves her charges but in the individual way that parents love their children. The experience of the kibbutzim suggests that this premise is probably oversimple and perhaps wrong, but it is not likely to be abandoned for that reason.

Failing such radical measures, what can we realistically hope to do? We suggested earlier that the rate of intergenerational turnover in the best-educated sixth of American men had fallen over the past generation from 62.2 to 60.6 per cent. This is hardly a significant difference. Yet the past generation has seen quite significant changes both in the relationship of college costs to incomes and in the devices colleges use to attract and select students. This suggests that mobility rates are not greatly affected by these variables. Reforms of the kind we have discussed—in the college financing, school atmosphere, and the like—might conceivably raise the turnover rate in the educational elite to 65 per cent but even that is problematic.

Nor are we convinced that efforts to go beyond these modest limits would be particularly desirable unless they were accompanied by more fundamental changes in the character of American society. If adult wealth and power remain as unequally distributed as they now are, and if child rearing remains family based, increasing the rate of social mobility substantially above its present level could be a formula for misery. A mobile, fluid society in which men move up and down is simultaneously a competitive, insecure, and invidious society. The more we have of the one, the more we will have of the other.

This truth is often forgotten—nowhere more often, indeed, than in higher education. But it is fundamental. If, for example, colleges attracted as many applicants from the lower strata as they now do from the upper strata, the admissions scramble would become even more hectic than it is. There would be no more room at the top of the academic system, because the amount of room at the top is by definition limited. The "best" colleges are "best" precisely because they are competitive and exclusive. If they got more applicants they would not expand appreciably to accommodate demand, for that would jeopardize their elite standing. They would raise standards even further than they have already done, making it even harder for those who now apply (including the already upwardly mobile) to get in. Most professors would no doubt welcome such a development, on the ground that it was another step toward "a really first-rate student body." Corporate recruiters and professional schools would probably also be pleased, since it would facilitate their efforts to sift and screen talent. But if we were right at the outset when we suggested that downward mobility is usually more painful than blocked upward mobility, such a change might not do much for the sum total of human happiness.

Suppose, for example, that Yale must choose between two applicants. One is an obviously gifted boy from the wrong side of the tracks in Bridgeport. The other is a competent but unremarkable youngster whose father went to Yale and now practices medicine in New York. All right-thinking people assume that Yale should choose the first boy over the second. We agree. Nonetheless, this decision almost certainly causes more individual misery than the alternative. If the Bridgeport boy is refused a place at Yale and goes to the University of Connecticut (where he still has a fair chance of discovering a new world) or even to the University of Bridgeport (where this is conceivable if less likely), he will be disappointed but seldom shattered. The University of Connecticut is a smaller step up than Yale, but it may in fact more nearly fit his temperament if not his talents. The New Yorker who fails to make Yale and winds up at the University of Connecticut, on the other hand, will very likely feel himself branded a failure. Connecticut may suit his talent, but probably not his temperament. The verdict will seem doubly harsh for being just. The rejected Bridgeport boy can blame his fate on snobbery and feel it is not his fault but "the system." The New Yorker has no such defense.

In stressing the price of meritocracy we are not arguing for its abandonment. Efforts to accommodate the upwardly mobile have always been a crucial ingredient in economic growth. While it is in one sense true that the relative amount of room at the top is fixed so long as the distribution of wealth and influence is fixed, it is also true that the absolute amount of room is not fixed. Efforts to expand the amount of room at the top may come to nothing in relative terms, but they ensure that the absolute size of the system will keep growing. Incomes are constantly rising, unskilled jobs are being replaced by more skilled ones, and all this makes people feel they are better off even if their relative position is unchanged. In good part these changes take place because talented individuals insist on carving out new niches for themselves. The old elite is paid off—its income keeps rising and its influence declines slowly if at all—but upwardly mobile individuals create new parallel elites that share in the ever-larger pie. In a sense this means that the old elites are downwardly mobile, for their relative position is no longer unchallenged. But it is precisely their effort to maintain their old status, while somehow accommodating the more gifted and insistent outsiders, which forces expansion all along the line. If opportunities for upward mobility and the fear of downward mobility diminish, this kind of pressure for expanding and upgrading the over-all system diminishes correspondingly. Indeed, expansion may slow down or stop altogether. Contrary to what many people think, growth is not automatic; it is strenuous and sometimes painful. It is much easier for those who are already well off just to let things go on as they are. Complacent elites that feel their position secure tend to do just that. It is the hot breath of the upwardly mobile that keeps them running—though conscience plays a role too.

Nonetheless, there is a point of diminishing returns beyond which the advantages of meritocracy and mobility to society as a whole may no longer offset their disadvantages to individuals who fail to meet the test. We know no way of telling when a given society has reached that point. Viewed from the top there is always a shortage of talent, and hence an argument for encouraging still more youngsters to compete for elite jobs and life styles, even though no more can make it than in the past. From the bottom, too, there always seems to be a shortage of opportunity, and hence a reason for being even more ruthless in weeding out incompetents who owe their privileges mainly to their ancestry. Both views are correct, and one of the great virtues of meritocratic competition is that it fuses them in such a way as to keep the system as a whole expanding. Nonetheless, there seems to be something basically perverse and sadistic in trying to make society any more competitive and status conscious than it already is. If, to revert to our earlier example, there are talented boys who do not want to go to Yale and mediocre ones who do, is any useful purpose really served by recruiting the former and excluding the latter? It is one thing to say that men who want a given thing that is in short supply should be judged on their merits in deciding who gets it. It is something else to say that the demand for such goodies (and insofar as B.A.s are certificates of competitive rank, they are among them) should be deliberately intensified.

What all this suggests is that further efforts to increase mobility may be not only fruitless but undesirable. What America most needs is not more mobility but more equality. So long as American life is premised on dramatic inequalities of wealth and power, *no* system for allocating social roles will be very satisfactory. Genes may be somewhat better than parental status, but damning a man for having a low IQ is not in the end much better than damning him for having a black skin or a working-class accent. Furthermore, unless discrepancies in parental influence and life styles are reduced, the possibility of increasing mobility is in fact remote. Only if the elite knew that downward mobility could not involve falling very far would it be willing to tolerate the probability that its children would do less well than itself. And only if its influence were relatively limited could it be forced to tolerate such developments.

Whether education makes people more or less equal has not been much debated in recent years, though Jefferson and other pre-industrial political philosophers were much concerned with it. Yet it is in some ways the central political question posed by the academic revolution. Our tentative answer to it is that elites based on knowledge are likely to be somewhat larger, somewhat less exclusive, somewhat less powerful, and somewhat more responsible than elites based on property. And while the accumulators of property probably work as hard as the accumulators of knowledge in the first upwardly mobile generation, the children and grandchildren of property are less likely to keep at it than the children of expertise. Still, all this seems to be a difference of degree, not of kind. If, for example, we revert to income distribution as a measure of equality, it seems clear that the spread of education has not brought anything like a revolution. Yet it could be argued that the modest redistribution of income away from the top 5 per cent and toward the middle classes, that took place during the Depression and World War II was in some way casually related to the enormous jump in the median educational attainment of the young during the 1920s and 1930s. Conversely, it could be claimed that the stability of income distribution since World War II reflected the relatively slow rise in median attainment since then. If this hypothesis were correct—and we must emphasize that we are rather skeptical—it would provide a strong argument for attempts to make higher education as nearly universal as secondary education became a generation ago.[2]

Whatever the effects of education on the social structure, we find very little evidence that colleges are committed to reducing the intellectual inequalities among men and some evidence that they tend to increase them. A relatively small number of established institutions dominate American society, and colleges are understandably concerned with educating the men who seem likely to control these institutions. They may educate others because they cannot get their hands on the future elite, because they are not entirely sure who the future elite will be, or because it is politically expedient to mix students who will control established institutions with students who will merely work for and around them. But despite all these complications and the ideological noise that accompanies them, the basic fact is that future leaders are likely to get more attention than future followers. Americans are virtually unanimous that potential doctors, for example, both need and deserve more expensive education than potential hospital orderlies (or even potential nurses); that prospective corporation executives require more expensive education than prospective assembly line foremen; and that future legislators ought to get a more expensive education than future voters. Nor is there any real opposition from the academic profession itself, which has rarely had the public schools' bias against ability grouping, honors programs, and other devices for giving promising students special attention. (Neither has the academic profession shared the school teachers' commitment to equality within its own ranks; professors rarely oppose merit pay, for instance, whereas school teachers mostly do.)

Not even the critics of higher education seem to oppose this pattern of recognizing and accentuating inequality. There are, it is true, some who advocate a redistribution of educational resources. But their aim is almost always to increase social mobility rather than to make America a more classless society. They have no objection to spending more on future doctors than on future orderlies. They simply object to a system that spends more on the sons of *past* doctors than on the sons of *past* orderlies. If given a "fair chance," they say, more children from poor families would be able to rise into the next generation's elite. They also argue that it is dangerous to try to decide too early who has the ability to become a doctor. If resources are concentrated on those who show promise of joining the future elite while they are still young, the much discussed "late bloomer" will never bloom at all. But by accepting the basic premise that people with a bright future need a better education than those with a dim future, such critics also accept the present degree of stratification in society and end up in arguments over statistical correlations and cost-benefit ratios.[3]

The more radical critics of higher education seem equally unconcerned about inequalities in the distribution of educational effort. Many are so allergic to the form and content of American education that they believe in the moral superiority of dropouts. For them, the young man who stays in school longest and gets the most intensive training is the most victimized rather than the most favored member of his generation. From this perspective the problem is not that "good" students get more and better education than "poor" ones, but that the good students seem to have a monopoly on the good jobs, while the poor students are condemned to poor jobs and low incomes. While radical critics would almost all like to see a more egalitarian society, they usually propose to achieve it by ignoring differences in individual competence rather than by reducing them.[4]

Our own guess is that universal higher education will diminish the economic or social differences among classes a little but not much. It must be remembered, however, that the universalization of college is also an attempt to spread what have traditionally been thought of as upper-middle class customs and concerns to people whose rank in the economic and occupational spectrum will remain lower-middle. In a superficial sense this effort is plainly succeeding. Even with far from universal higher education, many of those who have not been to college feel defensive and try to adopt the collegiate style. How deep this adaptation goes is problematic, however. We suggested at the outset that a great deal of what happens to undergraduates is anticipatory socialization. If a student realizes that he is not going to find a place in the upper-middle range of the social spectrum, his assimilation of upper-middle culture may slow down or stop altogether. Furthermore, even if most students keep assimilating what we have called upper-middle class attitudes in college, they will retain mainly those that their adult life re-enforces. A college graduate whose income remains below the national average, for example, and whose occupational status makes him feel inferior to the majority of Americans, is likely to have great difficulty maintaining the kind of self-confidence and self-respect that often seem to undergird upper-middle class ideals. If that is the case, it may be theoretically impossible for many aspects of upper-middle class behavior to spread to the whole society. Those on or near the bottom may, simply by dint of their position and regardless of education, need their own special style to protect them from the consequences of their situation.

Another reason for doubt about universal higher education's chances of spreading upper-middle class values is the growth of predominantly lower-middle and working-class commuter colleges which seem to do comparatively little to alter the habits and attitudes students bring to them. These colleges enroll many of their students only part time; they create almost no social community outside the classroom; and they encourage students to regard higher learning as a commodity, acquired in the same impersonal ways as groceries or lingerie. In some of these colleges, especially the two-year ones, the faculty does not even try to change the customs and concerns of its students, and the students themselves come without expecting such a change to take place. Together, such students and teachers may conspire to make college no more than a continuation of secondary school. Academic standards may be higher, "homework" assignments may be longer, but the basic pattern of authority and passivity can remain unchanged. Such a college may (and should) transmit technical skills and thus help the students move into professional jobs, and it may in this way also encourage them to move into a new subculture. But only in this indirect sense is it likely to affect students' view of themselves or of society. As the demand for higher education becomes more widespread and the tax burden climbs, politicians will be increasingly tempted to channel as many students as possible into these presumptively (though not always actually) cheap public commuter colleges.

This means that universal higher education, while in some ways helping to blur class differences, may also legitimize and freeze them by giving all sorts of youngsters the outward parity of the B.A. Our over-all feeling is that homogenization is proceeding faster than differentiation, but this is a very tentative and impressionistic judgment. Our feeling rests primarily on our sense that at the faculty level all but the junior colleges are caught up in the academic revolution. Yet the relative similarity of adult objectives at different colleges may not matter as much as we think. The student culture is a prism giving faculty pressures different meanings from one campus to another. From a student's viewpoint a public commuter college is a very different milieu from a private residential college, and the fact that the faculty say the same sorts of things may be relatively unimportant compared to the fact that most of a student's classmates hear what the faculty say in different ways on different campuses. We think that colleges have more in common than their constituencies do, and tend to make their constituencies more alike, but this would be hard to prove quantitatively.[5]

Be that as it may, it is at least clear that universal higher education and the academic revolution will not contribute to the emergence of an egalitarian, classless society in the same relatively clear-cut way that they contribute to the emergence of a non-sectarian, ethnically homogenized, nationally organized, and in some ways sexually undifferentiated one.

NOTES

1. For evidence that somewhat similar nonacademic biases are also at work in colleges, see Julius Davis, "What College Teachers Value in Students," *College Board Review* (Spring 1965), pp. 15–18.
2. Another approach to measuring the effects of education on income distribution is to look at the distribution *within* groups of any given attainment. A few random calculations suggest that the income distribution among college graduates is considerably more equitable than among elementary school dropouts. What this means is by no means entirely clear.
3. Cost-benefit analysis need not, of course, support the status quo in all its aspects. See André Danière, "Cost-Benefit Analysis of Federal Programs of Financial Aid to College Students," Cambridge, mimeographed, 1967. But an economic analysis of educational "outputs" which assumes that present income differentials represent real differences in productivity and which allocates educational resources on this premise can hardly be expected to imply the need for radical changes in income differentials.
4. There are exceptions: men who care enough to work with any student because he is there, often out of some religious commitment, and other men whose idiosyncratic values lead them to concentrate their efforts on students who are athletic, charming, wealthy, pretty, or whatever. But the student who counted on any of these things to get him attention or help would usually be disappointed.
5. For a review of literature that draws this conclusion among others, see Philip E. Jacob, *Changing Values in College: An Exploratory Study of the Impact of College Teaching,* New York, Harper, 1957.

VI. RACE, POVERTY, AND CLASS: THE LABOR MARKET AND CAPITALISM

INTRODUCTION

The emergence of the civil rights movement and violent eruptions in urban centers in the sixties focused attention on the persistence of poverty within affluence and shattered the illusion that the United States was moving toward social and economic equality. Liberal responses based on traditional approaches to the explanation of inequality and poverty were responsible for the implementation of various programs to resolve the resulting tensions: "antipoverty programs," job training programs, welfare assistance, increased investment in ghetto education, antidiscrimination legislation, and so on all celebrated in the slogan, "The Great Society."

The failure of these programs to achieve any significant amelioration of poverty and inequality stimulated a creative radical reevaluation of the nature of class and racial inequality and of the sources of division within the working class. One of the results has been a shift in focus away from the traditional white-collar–blue-collar distinction to the dichotomy between "primary" and "secondary" workers.

The readings are divided into two parts. The first two selections by Leftwich and Tobin exemplify the use of traditional tools of economic analysis (both micro and macro) to explain inequalities in economic reward and appropriate policies to reduce them. The remaining selections (by Harrison, Watchel, and Tabb) offer new constructs emerging from the new radical responses.

In the selection, "Income Distribution and the Market," Leftwich's exposition of marginal productivity theory provides the framework for regarding income inequality as primarily reflecting differences in the productivity of the "resources" which workers offer on the labor market. The reduction of inequality can rely chiefly on measures designed to increase the productivity of low-income groups (extension of education, removal of barriers to mobility in the labor market). Such measures, according to Leftwich, can be accomplished within the framework of the price system and the free enterprise economy. In his article, "On Improving the Economic Status of the Negro," Tobin focuses on the macroeconomic policies required to reduce racial differences in economic status. The major prerequisite for the attainment of this goal is a "tight labor market," a condition readily achieved through appropriate fiscal and monetary policies. The primary obstacles to racial economic equality are not existing political and

246

economic institutions, but irrational fears of excessive inflation and balance-of-payments deficits.

The "dual labor market" theory has become a central element in the new radical interpretation of persistent class inequality and poverty. The main aspects of the dual labor market approach in its various forms are presented by Harrison in "The Theory of the Dual Economy." This approach may be summarized as follows. There is a sharp segmentation in the labor market separating the "periphery" of the working class from its central "core." The characteristics of jobs in these two sectors or markets differ markedly. "In the primary labor market, the attributes of jobs and the behavioral traits of workers interact (e.g., by mutual reinforcement) to produce a structure characterized by high productivity, non-poverty wages and employment stability." The secondary labor market encompasses jobs and workers distinguished from those in the "core" sectors by low productivity, poverty wages, and employment instability. There is considerable intrasector worker mobility but little movement between sectors.

The boundary between the sectors is perpetuated by differences in technology ("modern" versus "primitive"), market structure ("oligopoly" versus "competition"), the importance of on-the-job training, and in personality characteristics reinforced by differing socializing institutions (school and family) and work experiences.

Watchel, in the selection, "Capitalism and Poverty in America: Paradox or Contradiction?", incorporates the theory of labor market segmentation into a broader radical interpretation of existing inequality and poverty. This radical perspective regards poverty and inequality as functionally related to "the basic system defining institutions of capitalism: labor markets, class and the state." Poverty and inequality, therefore, cannot be corrected by "manipulating some personal attribute of the individual" (a basic assumption of much public policy and social research), but only by changing basic capitalist institutions.

In "Race Relations Models and Social Change," Tabb deals explicitly with the relationship between race and class. In his view, the social and economic position of blacks is best explained by their simultaneous status as an "internal colony" (relative to white society as a whole) and as a "marginal working class." The beneficiaries are seen as including both a white "labor aristocracy" and a dominant business class confronting a divided working class.

INCOME DISTRIBUTION AND THE MARKET

Richard Leftwich

INDIVIDUAL INCOME DETERMINATION

The generally accepted principles of individual income determination and of income distribution are provided by marginal productivity theory. These principles have been met in previous chapters [of Leftwich's book] but we shall draw them together and summarize them in this section. A distinction will be made among conditions of pure competition, both in product markets and in resource markets—monopoly in product markets, and monopsony in resource markets. First we shall note certain criticisms levied against marginal productivity theory; then we shall discuss its role in the determination of individual incomes.

Criticisms of Marginal Productivity Theory

Marginal productivity theory is sometimes criticized on two counts. In the first place, some refuse to accept it because they believe it attempts to justify or approve the existing income distribution—and they do not like the existing distribution. However, observation of how a free enterprise economy does in fact distribute income in no sense constitutes justification or approval of that distribution. If marginal productivity principles furnish the best available explanation of income determination and income distribution in a free enterprise economy, we should understand their operations whether or not we like their results. A clear understanding of how distribution occurs necessarily precedes any intelligent modification of it.

The second criticism is more serious. Some maintain that marginal productivity is not an adequate basis for income determination and distribution theory— that there is no close correlation between the remunerations received by resource owners and the values of marginal product or the marginal revenue products of the resources which they own. If these critics are correct, and can produce the evidence substantiating their criticisms, then marginal productivity must go by the board—as must most of the rest of the marginal analysis of economic activity. To date the necessary evidence has not been forthcoming and marginal productivity continues to occupy the center of distribution theory.

SOURCE: *The Price System and Resource Allocation* (New York: Holt, Rinehart & Winston, Fourth Edition, 1973), pp. 307–309, 311, 313–317, 322–325.

Income Determination

The principles of income determination where pure competition prevails, both in product markets and in resource markets, were developed in another chapter. The owner of a given resource is paid a price per unit for the units employed equal to the value of marginal product of the resource. However, the price of the resource is not determined by any single employer or by any single resource owner. It is determined by the interactions of all buyers and all sellers in the market for the resource.

If for some reason the price of a resource should be less than the value of its marginal product, a shortage will occur. Employers want more of it at that price than resource owners are willing to place on the market. Employers, bidding against each other for the available supply, will drive the price up until the shortage disappears and each is hiring (or buying) that quantity of the resource at which its value of marginal product equals its price.

A price high enough to create a surplus of the resource will set forces in motion to eliminate the surplus. Employers take only those quantities sufficient to equate its value of marginal product to its price. Resource owners undercut each other's prices to secure employment for their unemployed units. As price drops, employment expands. The undercutting continues until employers are willing to take the quantities that resource owners want to place on the market.

Where some degree of monopoly[1] exists in product markets, the foregoing principles will be altered to some extent. Monopolistic firms employ those quantities of the resource at which its marginal revenue product is equal to its price. Thus the price per unit received by owners of the resource is less than its value of marginal product, and the resource is exploited monopolistically.

Some degree of monopsony in the purchase of a given resource will cause it to be paid still less than its marginal revenue product. The monopsonist, faced with a resource supply curve sloping upward to the right, employs that quantity of the resource at which its marginal revenue product is equal to its marginal resource cost. Marginal resource cost is greater than the price paid for the resource. Monopsonistic exploitation of the resource occurs to the extent that its marginal revenue product exceeds its price. If the resource purchaser is also a monopolist, marginal revenue product of the resource in turn will be less than its value of marginal product, and the resource will be exploited monopolistically as well as monopsonistically.

An individual's income per unit of time is the sum of the amounts earned per unit of time by the various resources which he owns. If he owns a single kind of resource, his income will be equal to the number of units placed in employment multiplied by the price per unit which he receives for it. If he owns several kinds of resources, the income from each can be computed in the same manner. These can be totaled to determine his entire income. . . .

CAUSES OF INCOME DIFFERENCES

With reference to the determinants of individual[2] incomes, it becomes clear that differences in incomes, arise from two basic sources: (1) differences in the kinds and quantities of resources owned by different individuals, and (2) differences in prices paid in different employments for units of any given resource. The former are the more fundamental. The latter arise from various types of interference with the price system in the performance of its functions and from any resource immobility which may occur. . . .

In this section we shall consider, first, differences in kinds and quantities of labor resources owned by different individuals. Next, differences in capital resources owned will be discussed. Last, we shall examine the effects on income distribution of certain interferences with the price mechanism.

Differences in Labor Resources Owned

The labor classification of resources is composed of many different kinds and qualities of labor. These have one common characteristic—they are human. Any single kind of labor is a combination or complex of both inherited and acquired characteristics. The acquired part of a man's labor power is sometimes referred to as human capital; however, separation of innate ability from the results of investment in the human agent, if we were able to accomplish it, would be of little value to us.

Labor can be subclassified horizontally and vertically into many largely separate resource groups. Vertical subclassification involves grading workers according to skill levels from the lowest kind of undifferentiated manual labor to the highest professional levels. Horizontal subclassification divides workers of a certain skill level into the various occupations requiring that particular degree of skill. An example would be the division of skilled construction workers into groups—carpenters, bricklayers, plumbers, and the like. Vertical mobility of labor refers to the possibility of moving upward through the vertical skill levels. Horizontal mobility means the ability to move sideways among groups at a particular skill level.

HORIZONTAL DIFFERENCES IN LABOR RESOURCES. At any specific horizontal level, individuals may receive different incomes because of differences in demand and supply conditions for the kinds of labor which they own. A large demand for a certain kind of labor relative to the supply of it available will make its marginal revenue product and its price high. On the same skill level, a small demand for another kind of labor relative to the supply available will make its marginal revenue product and its price low. The difference in prices tends to cause differences in incomes for owners of the two kinds of labor. Suppose, for example, that initially bricklayers and carpenters earn approximately equal incomes. A shift in consumer tastes occurs from wood construction to brick construction in residential units. The incomes of bricklayers will increase while those of carpenters will decrease because of the altered conditions of demand for them. Over a long period of time horizontal mobility between the two groups tends to decrease the income differences thus arising.

Quantitative differences in the amount of work performed by individuals owning the same kind of labor resource may lead to income differences. Some occupations afford considerable leeway for individual choice of the number of hours to be worked per week or per month. Examples include independent professional men such as physicians, lawyers, and certified public accountants, along with independent proprietors such as farmers, plumbing contractors, and garage owners. In other occupations, hours of work are beyond the control of the individual. Yet in different employments of the same resource, differences in age, physical endurance, institutional restrictions, custom, and so on, can lead to differences in hours worked and to income differences among owners of the resource.

Within a particular labor resource group, qualitative differences or differences in the abilities of the owners of the resource often create income differences. Wide variations occur in public evaluation of different dentists, or physicians, or lawyers, or automobile mechanics. Consequently, within any one group, variations in prices paid for services and in quantities of services which can be sold to the public will lead to income differences. Usually a correlation exists between the ages of the members of a resource group and their incomes. Quality tends to improve with accumulated experience. Data reported by Friedman and Kuznets suggest, for example, that incomes of physicians tend to be highest between the tenth and twenty-fifth years of practice, and incomes of lawyers tend to be highest between the twentieth and thirty-fifth years of practice.[3]

VERTICAL DIFFERENCES IN LABOR RESOURCES. The different vertical strata themselves represent differences in labor resources owned and give rise to major labor income differences. Entry into high-level occupations such as the professions or the ranks of business executives is much more difficult than is entry into manual occupations. The relative scarcity of labor at top levels results from two basic factors. First, individuals with the physical and mental characteristics necessary for performance of high-level work are limited in number. Second, given the necessary physical and mental characteristics, many lack the opportunities for training and the necessary environment for movement into high-level positions. Thus limited vertical mobility keeps resource supplies low relative to demands for them at the top levels and it keeps resource supplies abundant relative to demands for them at the low levels.

Differences in labor resources owned because of differences in innate physical and mental charactristics of individuals are accidents of birth. The individual has nothing to do with choosing them. Nevertheless they account partly for restricted vertical mobility and for income differences. The opportunities of moving toward top positions and relatively large incomes are considerably enhanced by the inheritance of a strong physical constitution and a superior intellect; however, these by no means ensure that individuals so endowed will make the most of their opportunities.

Opportunities for training tend to be more widely avaliable to individuals born into wealthy families than to those born into families in the lower-income groups. Some of the higher-paying professions require long and expensive university training programs—often beyond the reach of the latter groups. The medical profession is a case in point. However, the advantages that the wealthy have should not be over-emphasized. Every day we see individuals who have had the initial ability, the drive, and the determination necessary to overcome economic obstacles thrown in the way of vertical mobility.

Differences in social inheritance constitute another cause of differences in labor resources owned. These will be closely correlated with differences in material inheritance. Frequently, individuals born on the wrong side of the tracks face family and community attitudes that sharply curtail their opportunities and their desires for vertical mobility. Others, more fortunately situated, acquire the training necessary to be highly productive and to obtain large incomes because it is expected of them by the social groups in which they move. Their social position alone, apart from the training induced by it, may be quite effective in facilitating vertical mobility.

Differences in Capital Resources Owned

In addition to inequalities in labor incomes, large differences occur in individual incomes from differences in capital ownership. Different individuals own varying quantities of capital—corporation or other business assets, farm land, oil wells, and property of various other forms. We shall examine the fundamental causes of inequalities in capital holdings.

MATERIAL INHERITANCE. Differences in the amounts of capital inherited or received as gifts by different individuals create large differences in incomes. The institution of private property on which free enterprise rests usually is coupled with inheritance laws allowing large holdings of accumulated property rights to be passed on from generation to generation. The individual fortunate enough to have selected a wealthy father inherits large capital holdings, his resources contribute much to the productive process, and he is rewarded accordingly. The son of the southern sharecropper, who may be of equal innate intelligence, inherits no capital, contributes less to the productive process, and receives correspondingly a lower income.

FORTUITOUS CIRCUMSTANCES. Chance, luck, or other fortuitous circumstances beyond the control of individuals constitute a further cause of differences in capital holdings. The discovery of oil, uranium, or gold on an otherwise mediocre piece of land brings about a large appreciation in its value or its ability to yield income to its owner. Unforeseen shifts in consumer demand increase the values of certain capital holdings while decreasing the values of others. National emergencies such as war lead to changes in valuations of particular kinds of property and, hence, to different incomes from capital. Dalton cites an example of the stockholders in a concern which made mourning weeds. As the casualty lists grew during World War I, their capital holdings appreciated in value.[4] Fortuitous circumstances can work in reverse, also, but even so their effects operate to create differences in the ownership of capital.

PROPENSITIES TO ACCUMULATE. Differing psychological propensities to accumulate and differing abilities to accumulate lead to differences in capital ownership among individuals. On the psychological side a number of factors influence the will to accumulate. Stories circulate of individuals determined to make a fortune before attainment of a certain age. Accumulation sometimes occurs for purposes of security and luxury in later life. It sometimes occurs from the desire to make one's children secure. The power and the prestige accompanying wealth provide the motivating force in some cases. To others, accumulation and manipulation of capital holdings is a gigantic game—the activity involved is fascinating to them. Whatever the motives, some individuals have them and others do not. In some instances the will to accumulate may be negative and the opposite of accumulation occurs.

The ability of an individual to accumulate depends largely upon his original holdings of both labor resources and capital resources. The higher the original income the easier saving and accumulation tend to be. The individual possessing much initially in the way of labor resources is likely to accumulate capital with his income from labor—he invests in stocks and bonds, real estate, a cattle ranch, or other property. Or the individual possessing substantial quantities of capital initially—and the ability to manage it—receives an income sufficient to allow saving and investment in additional capital. In the process of accumulation, labor resources and capital resources of an individual augment each other in providing the income from which further accumulation can be accomplished. . . .

A GREATER MEASURE OF EQUALITY

For various reasons—economic, ethical, and social—many people favor some mitigation of income differences. The causes of differences should furnish the clues for measures leading toward their mitigation—if movement toward greater equality is thought by society to be desirable. Thus equalizing measures may be (and are) attempted via the price system or they may be (and are) attempted through redistribution of resources among resource owners. We shall consider each of these in turn.

Via Administered Prices

Equalizing measures attempted via the price system are likely to miss their mark except in monopsonistic cases. Where competitive and monopolistic conditions prevail in product markets and where competitive conditions prevail in the purchase of a given resource, the equilibrium price of the resource tends to be equal to its value of marginal product or its marginal revenue product, as the case may be. Additionally, the resource tends to be so allocated that its price is the same in its alternative employments. Successful administered price increases are likely to result in unemployment and malallocation of the resource and this in turn contributes toward greater rather than smaller income differences. . . . Administered resource prices in monopsony cases can offset monopsonistic exploitation of a resource by increasing both its price and its level of employment.

Via Redistribution of Resources

The major part of any movement toward greater income equality must consist of redistribution of resources among resource owners, since here is the major cause of income differences. Redistributive measures can take two forms: (1) redistribution of labor resources, and (2) redistribution of capital resources.

LABOR RESOURCES. Labor resources can be redistributed through measures designed to increase vertical mobility. Greater vertical mobility will increase labor supplies in the top vocational levels and decrease labor supplies in the lower levels. Greater supplies at the top will decrease values of marginal product or marginal revenue products and consequently will reduce the top incomes. Smaller supplies at the lower levels will increase values of marginal product or marginal revenue products, thereby increasing incomes at the lower occupational levels. The transfers from lower to higher occupations will mitigate income differences and will increase net national product in the process.

At least three methods of increasing vertical mobility can be suggested. First, there are possibilities of providing greater equality in educational and training opportunities for capable individuals. Second, to the extent that differences in capital ownership are reduced, greater equality in the economic opportunities for development of high-grade labor resources will tend to occur. Third, measures may be taken to reduce those barriers to entry established by associations of resource owners in many skilled occupations.[5]

Measures to increase horizontal mobility also can serve to decrease income differences. These include the operation of employment exchanges, perhaps some subsidization of movement, vocational guidance, adult education and retraining programs, and other measures of a similar nature. The argument here is really one for better allocation of labor resources, both among alternative jobs within a given labor resource category, and among the labor resource categories themselves. Greater horizontal mobility, as well as greater vertical mobility, will increase net national product at the same time that it decreases income differences.

CAPITAL RESOURCES. Redistribution of capital resources meets considerable opposition in a free enterprise economy. Many vociferous advocates of movement toward greater income equality will protest vigorously measures designed to redistribute capital ownership—and these are the measures which will contribute most toward that objective. The opposition centers around the rights of private property ownership and stems from a strong presumption that the right to own property includes the right to accumulate it and to pass it on to one's heirs.

Nevertheless, if income differences are to be mitigated, some means of providing greater equality in capital accumulation and capital holdings among individuals must be employed. The economy's system of taxation may move in this direction. In the United States, for example, the personal income tax, the capital gains tax, and estate and gift taxes—both federal and state—already operate in an equalizing manner.

The personal income tax by its progressive nature serves to reduce income differences directly and in so doing it reduces differences in abilities to accumulate capital. But the personal income tax alone cannot be expected to eliminate those differences without seriously impairing incentives for efficient employment of resources and for reallocation of resources from less productive to more productive employments.

The capital gains tax constitutes either a loophole for escaping a part of the personal income tax, or a plug for a loophole in the personal income tax, depending upon one's definition of income. The capital gains tax is applied to realized appreciation and depreciation in the value of capital assets. Those who can convert a part of their income from capital resources into the form of capital gains have that part of their remuneration taxed as capital gains at a rate ordinarily below the personal income tax rate. For them the capital gains tax provides a loophole through which personal income taxes can be escaped. On the other hand, if certain capital gains would escape taxation altogether under the personal income tax, but are covered by the capital gains tax, the latter can be considered a supplement to the personal income tax. In either case the capital gains tax allows some remuneration from capital resources to be taxed at rates below the personal income tax rates and, if differences in opportunities to accumulate capital are to be mitigated, it must be revised to prevent individuals from taking undue advantage of its lower rates.

Estate and gift taxes will play the major roles in any tax system designed to reduce differences in capital ownership. The estate taxes in such a system would border on the confiscatory side above some maximum amount in order to prevent the transmission of accumulated capital resources from generation to generation. Gift taxes would operate largely to plug estate tax loopholes. They would be designed to prevent transmission of estates by means of gifts from the original owner to heirs prior to the death of the original owner.

REDISTRIBUTION AND THE PRICE SYSTEM. Redistribution of labor resource and capital resource holdings can be accomplished within the framework of the price system and the free enterprise economic system if movement toward greater income equality is thought by society to be desirable. Redistribution measures such as those sketched out above need not seriously affect the operation of the price mechanism. In fact, the price mechanism can act as a positive force assisting the measures to reach the desired objectives. Some of the fundamental measures— educational opportunities, progressive income taxes, gift and estate taxes—are already in existence, although their effectiveness could be increased greatly. Redistribution measures can be thought of as rules of the free enterprise game —along with a stable monetary system, monopoly control measures, and other rules of economic conduct.

NOTES

1. Again we use the term to refer to all cases in which the firm faces a downward sloping product demand curve. They include cases of pure monopoly, oligopoly, and monopolistic competition.
2. The term *individual* will be used throughout the rest of the chapter to refer to a spending unit regardless of its size or composition.
3. Milton Friedman and Simon Kuznets, *Income from Independent Professional Practice* (New York: National Bureau of Economic Research, 1945), pp. 237–260.
4. Hugh Dalton, *The Inequality of Incomes* (London: Routledge & Kegan Paul, 1925), p. 273.
5. An example of such a barrier is provided by the professional association which controls licensing standards when prospective entrants must be licensed in order to practice the profession.

ON IMPROVING THE ECONOMIC
STATUS OF THE NEGRO

James Tobin

I start from the presumption that integration of Negroes into the American society and economy can be accomplished within existing political and economic institutions. I understand the impatience of those who think otherwise, but I see nothing incompatible between our peculiar mixture of private enterprise and government, on the one hand, and the liberation and integration of the Negro, on the other. Indeed the present position of the Negro is an aberration from the principles of our society, rather than a requirement of its functioning. Therefore, my suggestions are directed to the aim of mobilizing existing powers of government to bring Negroes into full participation in the main stream of American economic life.

The economic plight of individuals, Negroes and whites alike, can always be attributed to specific handicaps and circumstances: discrimination, immobility, lack of education and experience, ill health, weak motivation, poor neighborhood, large family size, burdensome family responsibilities. Such diagnoses suggest a host of specific remedies, some in the domain of civil rights, others in the war on poverty. Important as these remedies are, there is a danger that the diagnoses are myopic. They explain why certain individuals rather than others suffer from the economic maladies of the time. They do not explain why the overall incidence of the maladies varies dramatically from time to time—for example, why personal attributes which seemed to doom a man to unemployment in 1932 or even in 1954 or 1961 did not so handicap him in 1944 or 1951 or 1956.

Public health measures to improve the environment are often more productive in conquering disease than a succession of individual treatments. Malaria was conquered by oiling and draining swamps, not by quinine. The analogy holds for economic maladies. Unless the global incidence of these misfortunes can be diminished, every individual problem successfully solved will be replaced by a similar problem somewhere else. That is why an economist is led to emphasize the importance of the overall economic climate.

Over the decades, general economic progress has been the major factor in the gradual conquest of poverty. Recently some observers, J. K. Galbraith and Michael Harrington most eloquently, have contended that this process no longer operates. The economy may prosper and labor may become steadily more productive as in the past, but "the other America" will be stranded. Prosperity and progress have already eliminated almost all the easy cases of poverty, leaving a hard

SOURCE: *Daedalus,* Fall 1965, pp. 485–493, 497–498.

core beyond the reach of national economic trends. There may be something to the "backwash" thesis as far as whites are concerned.[1] But it definitely does not apply to Negroes. Too many of them are poor. It cannot be true that half of a race of twenty million human beings are victims of specific disabilities which insulate them from the national economic climate. It cannt be true, and it is not. Locke Anderson has shown that the pace of Negro economic progress is peculiarly sensitive to general economic growth. He estimates that if nationwide per capita personal income is stationary, nonwhite median family income falls by 5 percent per year, while if national per capita income grows 5 percent, nonwhite income grows nearly 7.5 percent.[2]

National prosperity and economic growth are still powerful engines for improving the economic status of Negroes. They are not doing enough and they are not doing it fast enough. There is ample room for a focused attack on the specific sources of Negro poverty. But a favorable overall economic climate is a necessary condition for the global success—as distinguished from success in individual cases—of specific efforts to remedy the handicaps associated with Negro poverty.

THE IMPORTANCE OF A TIGHT LABOR MARKET

But isn't the present overall economic climate favorable? Isn't the economy enjoying an upswing of unprecedented length, setting new records almost every month in production, employment, profits, and income? Yes, but expansion and new records should be routine in an economy with growing population, capital equipment, and productivity. The fact is that the economy has not operated with reasonably full utilization of its manpower and plant capacity since 1957. Even now, after four and one-half years of uninterrupted expansion, the economy has not regained the ground lost in the recessions of 1958 and 1960. The current expansion has whittled away at unemployment, reducing it from 6.5 to 7 percent to 4.5 to 5 percent. It has diminished idle plant capacity correspondingly. The rest of the gains since 1960 in employment, production, and income have just offset the normal growth of population, capacity, and productivity.

The magnitude of America's poverty problem already reflects the failure of the economy in the second postwar decade to match its performance in the first.[3] Had the 1947–56 rate of growth of median family income been maintained since 1957, and had unemployment been steadily limited to 4 percent, it is estimated that the fraction of the population with poverty incomes in 1963 would have been 16.6 percent instead of 18.5 percent.[4] The educational qualifications of the labor force have continued to improve. The principal of racial equality, in employment as in other activities, has gained ground both in law and in the national conscience. If, despite all this, dropouts, inequalities in educational attainment, and discrimination in employment seem more serious today rather than less, the reason is that the overall economic climate has not been favorable after all.

The most important dimension of the overall economic climate is the tightness of the labor market. In a tight labor market unemployment is low and short in duration, and job vacancies are plentiful. People who stand at the end of the hiring line and the top of the layoff list have the most to gain from a tight labor market. It is not surprising that the position of Negroes relative to that of whites improves in a tight labor market and declines in a slack market. Unemployment itself is only one way in which a slack labor market hurts Negroes and other disadvantaged groups, and the gains from reduction in unemployment are by no means confined to the employment of persons counted as unemployed.[5] A tight labor market means not just jobs, but better jobs, longer hours, higher wages. Because of the heavy demands for labor during the second world war and its economic aftermath, Negroes made dramatic relative gains between 1940 and 1950. Unfortunately this momentum has not been maintained, and the blame falls largely on the weakness of the labor markets since 1957.[6]

The shortage of jobs has hit Negro men particularly hard and thus has contributed mightily to the ordeal of the Negro family, which is in turn the cumulative source of so many other social disorders. The unemployment rate of Negro men is more sensitive than that of Negro women to the national rate. Since 1949 Negro women have gained in median income relative to white women, but Negro men have lost ground to white males.[7] In a society which stresses bread-winning as the expected role of the mature male and occupational achievement as his proper goal, failure to find and to keep work is devastating to the man's self-respect and family status. Matriarchy is in any case a strong tradition in Negro society, and the man's role is further downgraded when the family must and can depend on the woman for its livelihood. It is very important to increase the proportion of Negro children who grow up in stable families with two parents. Without a strong labor market it will be extremely difficult to do so.

UNEMPLOYMENT. It is well known that Negro unemployment rates are multiples of the general unemployment rate. This fact reflects both the lesser skills, seniority, and experience of Negroes and employers' discrimination against Negroes. These conditions are a deplorable reflection on American society, but as long as they exist Negroes suffer much more than others from a general increase in unemployment and gain much more from a general reduction. A rule of thumb is that changes in the nonwhite unemployment rate are twice those in the white rate. The rule works both ways. Nonwhite unemployment went from 4.1 percent in 1953, a tight labor market year, to 12.5 percent in 1961, while the white rate rose from 2.3 percent to 6 percent. Since then, the Negro rate has declined by 2.4 percent, the white rate by 1.2.

Even the Negro teenage unemployment rate shows some sensitivity to general economic conditions. Recession increased it from 15 percent in 1955–56 to 25 percent in 1958. It decreased to 22 percent in 1960 but rose to 28 percent in 1963; since then it has declined somewhat. Teenage unemployment is abnormally high now, relative to that of other age groups, because the wave of postwar babies is coming into the labor market. Most of them, especially the Negroes, are crowding the end of the hiring line. But their prospects for getting jobs are no less dependent on general labor market conditions.

PART-TIME WORK. Persons who are involuntarily forced to work part time instead of full time are not counted as unemployed, but their number goes up and down with the unemployment rate. Just as Negroes bear a disproportionate share of unemployment, they bear more than their share of involuntary part-time unemployment.[8] A tight labor market will not only employ more Negroes; it will also give more of those who are employed full-time jobs. In both respects, it will reduce disparities between whites and Negroes.

LABOR-FORCE PARTICIPATION.   In a tight market, of which a low unemployment rate is a barometer, the labor force itself is larger. Job opportunities draw into the labor force individuals who, simply because the prospects were dim, did not previously regard themselves as seeking work and were therefore not enumerated as unemployed. For the economy as a whole, it appears that an expansion of job opportunities enough to reduce unemployment by one worker will bring another worker into the labor force.

This phenomenon is important for many Negro families. Statistically, their poverty now appears to be due more often to the lack of a breadwinner in the labor force than to unemployment.[9] But in a tight labor market many members of these families, including families now on public assistance, would be drawn into employment. Labor-force participation rates are roughly 2 percent lower for nonwhite men than for white men, and the disparity increases in years of slack labor markets.[10] The story is different for women. Negro women have always been in the labor force to a much greater extent than white women. A real improvement in the economic status of Negro men and in the stability of Negro families would probably lead to a reduction in labor-force participation by Negro women. But for teenagers, participation rates for Negroes are not so high as for whites; and for women twenty to twenty-four they are about the same. These relatively low rates are undoubtedly due less to voluntary choice than to the same lack of job opportunities that produces phenomenally high unemployments for young Negro women.

DURATION OF UNEMPLOYMENT.   In a tight labor market, such unemployment as does exist is likely to be of short duration. Short-term unemployment is less damaging to the economic welfare of the unemployed. More will have earned and fewer will have exhausted private and public unemployment benefits. In 1953 when the overall unemployment rate was 2.9 percent, only 4 percent of the unemployed were out of work for longer than twenty-six weeks and only 11 percent for longer than fifteen weeks. In contrast, the unemployment rate in 1961 was 6.7 percent; and of the unemployed in that year, 17 percent were out of work for longer than twenty-six weeks and 32 percent for longer than fifteen weeks. Between the first quarter of 1964 and the first quarter of 1965, overall unemployment fell 11 percent, while unemployment extending beyond half a year was lowered by 22 percent.

As Rashi Fein points out elsewhere . . . , one more dimension of society's inequity to the Negro is that an unemployed Negro is more likely to stay unemployed than an unemployed white. But his figures also show that Negroes share in the reduction of long-term unemployment accompanying economic expansion.

MIGRATION FROM AGRICULTURE.   A tight labor market draws the surplus rural population to higher paying non-agricultural jobs. Southern Negroes are a large part of this surplus rural population. Migration is the only hope for improving their lot, or their children's. In spite of the vast migration of past decades, there are still about 775,000 Negroes, 11 percent of the Negro labor force of the country, who depend on the land for their living and that of their families.[11] Almost a half million live in the South, and almost all of them are poor.

Migration from agriculture and from the South is the Negroes' historic path toward economic improvement and equality. It is a smooth path for Negroes and for the urban communities to which they move only if there is a strong demand for labor in towns and cities North and South. In the 1940's the number of Negro farmers and farm laborers in the nation fell by 450,000 and one and a half million Negroes (net) left the South. This was the great decade of Negro economic advance. In the 1950's the same occupational and geographical migration continued undiminished. The movement to higher income occupations and locations should have raised the relative economic status of Negroes. But in the 1950's Negroes were moving into increasing weak job markets. Too often disguised unemployment in the countryside was simply transformed into enumerated unemployment, and rural poverty into urban poverty.[12]

QUALITY OF JOBS. In a slack labor market, employers can pick and choose, both in recruiting and in promoting. They exaggerate the skill, education, and experience requirements of their jobs. They use diplomas or color or personal histories as convenient screening devices. In a tight market, they are forced to be realistic, to tailor job specifications to the available supply, and to give on-the-job training. They recruit and train applicants who they would otherwise screen out, and they upgrade employees whom they would in slack times consign to low-wage, low-skill, and part-time jobs.

Wartime and other experience shows that job requirements are adjustable and that men and women are trainable. It is only in slack times that people worry about a mismatch between supposedly rigid occupational requirements and supposedly unchangeable qualifications of the labor force. As already noted, the relative status of Negroes improves in a tight labor market not only in respect to unemployment, but also in respect to wages and occupations.

CYCLICAL FLUCTUATION. Sustaining a high demand for labor is important. The in-and-out status of the Negro in the business cycle damages his long-term position because periodic unemployment robs him of experience and seniority.

RESTRICTIVE PRACTICES. A slack labor market probably accentuates the discriminatory and protectionist proclivities of certain crafts and unions. When jobs are scarce, opening the door to Negroes is a real threat. Of course prosperity will not automatically dissolve the barriers, but it will make it more difficult to oppose efforts to do so.

I conclude that the single most important step the nation could take to improve the economic position of the Negro is to operate the economy steadily at a low rate of unemployment. We cannot expect to restore the labor market conditions of the second world war, and we do not need to. In the years 1951–53, unemployment was roughly 3 percent, teenage unemployment around 7 percent, Negro unemployment about 4.5 percent, long-term unemployment negligible. In the years 1955–57, general unemployment was roughly 4 percent, and the other measures correspondingly higher. Four percent is the official target of the Kennedy-Johnson administration. It has not been achieved since 1957. Reaching and maintaining 4 percent would be a tremendous improvement over the performance of the last eight years. But we should not stop there; the society and the Negro can benefit immensely from tightening the labor market still further, to 3.5 or 3 percent unemployment. The administration itself has never defined 4 percent as anything other than an "interim" target.

WHY DON'T WE HAVE A TIGHT LABOR MARKET?

We know how to operate the economy so that there is a tight labor market. By fiscal and monetary measures the federal government can control aggregate spending in the economy. The government could choose to control it so that unemployment *averaged* 3.5 or 3 percent instead of remaining over 4.5 percent except at occasional business cycle peaks. Moreover, recent experience here and abroad shows that we can probably narrow the amplitude of fluctuations around whatever average we select as a target.

Some observers have cynically concluded that a society like ours can achieve full employment only in wartime. But aside from conscription into the armed services, government action creates jobs in wartime by exactly the same mechanism as in peacetime—the government spends more money and stimulates private firms and citizens to spend more too. It is the *amount* of spending, not its purpose, that does the trick. Public or private spending to go to the moon, build schools, or conquer poverty can be just as effective in reducing unemployment as spending to build airplanes and submarines—if there is enough of it. There may be more political constraints and ideological inhibitions in peacetime, but the same techniques of economic policy are available if we want badly enough to use them. The two main reasons we do not take this relatively simple way out are two obsessive fears, inflation and balance of payments deficits.

Running the economy with a tight labor market would mean a somewhat faster upward creep in the price level. The disadvantages of this are, in my view, exaggerated and are scarcely commensurable with the real economic and social gains of higher output and employment. Moreover, there are ways of protecting "widows and orphans" against erosion in the purchasing power of their savings. But fear of inflation is strong both in the U.S. financial establishment and in the public at large. The vast comfortable white middle class who are never touched by unemployment prefer to safeguard the purchasing power of their life insurance and pension rights than to expand opportunities for the disadvantaged and unemployed.

The fear of inflation would operate anyway, but it is accentuated by U.S. difficulties with its international balance of payments. These difficulties have seriously constrained and hampered U.S. fiscal and monetary policy in recent years. Any rise in prices might enlarge the deficit. An aggressively expansionary monetary policy, lowering interest rates, might push money out of the country.

In the final analysis what we fear is that we might not be able to defend the parity of the dollar with gold, that is, to sell gold at thirty-five dollars an ounce to any government that wants to buy. So great is the gold mystique that this objective has come to occupy a niche in the hierarchy of U.S. goals second only to the military defense of the country, and not always to that. It is not fanciful to link the plight of Negro teenagers in Harlem to the monetary whims of General de Gaulle. But it is only our own attachment to "the dollar" as an abstraction which makes us cringe before the European appetite for gold.

This topic is too charged with technical complexities, real and imagined, and with confused emotions to be discussed adequately here. I will confine myself to three points. First, the United States is the last country in the world which needs to hold back its own economy to balance its international accounts. To let the tail wag the dog is not in the interests of the rest of the world, so much of which depends on us for trade and capital, any more than in our own.

Second, forces are at work to restore balance to American international accounts—the increased competitiveness of our exports and the income from the large investments our firms and citizens have made overseas since the war. Meanwhile we can finance deficits by gold reserves and lines of credit at the International Monetary Fund and at foreign central banks. Ultimately we have one foolproof line of defense—letting the dollar depreciate relative to foreign currencies. The world would not end. The sun would rise the next day. American products would be more competitive in world markets. Neither God nor the Constitution fixed the gold value of the dollar. The United States would not be the first country to let its currency depreciate. Nor would it be the first time for the United States—not until we stopped "saving" the dollar and the gold standard in 1933 did our recovery from the Great Depression begin.

Third, those who oppose taking such risks argue that the dollar today occupies a unique position as international money, that the world as a whole has an interest, which we cannot ignore, in the stability of the gold value of the dollar. If so, we can reasonably ask the rest of the world, especially our European friends, to share the burdens which guaranteeing this stability imposes upon us.

This has been an excursion into general economic policy. But the connection between gold and the plight of the Negro is no less real for being subtle. We are paying much too high a social price for avoiding creeping inflation and for protecting our gold stock and "the dollar." But it will not be easy to alter these national priorities. The interests of the unemployed, the poor, and the Negroes are under-represented in the comfortable consensus which supports and confines the current policy.

Another approach, which can be pursued simultaneously, is to diminish the conflicts among these competing objectives, in particular to reduce the degree of inflation associated with low levels of unemployment. This can be done in two ways. One way is to improve the mobility of labor and other resources to occupations, locations, and industries where bottlenecks would otherwise lead to wage and price increases. This is where many specific programs, such as the training and retraining of manpower and policies to improve the technical functioning of labor markets, come into their own.

A second task is to break down the barriers to competition which now restrict the entry of labor and enterprise into certain occupations and industries. These lead to wage- and price-increasing bottlenecks even when resources are not really short. Many barriers are created by public policy itself, in response to the vested interests concerned. Many reflect concentration of economic power in unions and in industry. These barriers represent another way in which the advantaged and the employed purchase their standards of living and their security at the expense of unprivileged minorities.

In the best of circumstances, structural reforms of these kinds will be slow and gradual. They will encounter determined economic and political resistance from special interests which are powerful in Congress and state legislatures. Moreover, Congressmen and legislators represent places rather than people and are likely to oppose, not facilitate, the increased geographical mobility which is required. It is no accident that our manpower programs do not include relocation allowances.

INCREASING THE EARNING CAPACITY OF NEGROES

Given the proper overall economic climate, in particular a steady tight labor market, the Negro's economic condition can be expected to improve, indeed to improve dramatically. But not fast enough. Not as fast as his aspirations or as the aspirations he has taught the rest of us to have for him. What else can be done? This question is being answered in detail by experts elsewhere. I shall confine myself to a few comments and suggestions that occur to a general economist.

Even in a tight labor market, the Negro's relative status will suffer both from current discrimination and from his lower earning capacity, the result of inferior acquired skill. In a real sense both factors reflect discrimination, since the Negro's handicaps in earning capacity are the residue of decades of discrimination in education and employment. Nevertheless for both analysis and policy it is useful to distinguish the two.

Discrimination means that the Negro is denied access to certain markets where he might sell his labor, and to certain markets where he might purchase goods and services. Elementary application of "supply and demand" makes it clear that these restrictions are bound to result in his selling his labor for less and buying his livelihood for more than if these barriers did not exist. If Negro women can be clerks only in certain stores, those storekeepers will not need to pay them so much as they pay whites. If Negroes can live only in certain houses, the prices and rents they have to pay will be high for the quality of accommodation provided.

Successful elimination of discrimination is not only important in itself but will also have substantial economic benefits. Since residential segregation is the key to so much else and so difficult to eliminate by legal fiat alone, the power of the purse should be unstintingly used. I see no reason that the expenditure of funds for this purpose should be confined to new construction. Why not establish private or semi-public revolving funds to purchase, for resale or rental on a desegregated basis, strategically located existing structures as they become available?

The effects of past discrimination will take much longer to eradicate. The sins against the fathers are visited on the children. They are deprived of the intellectual and social capital which in our society is supposed to be transmitted in the family and the home. We have only begun to realize how difficult it is to make up for this deprivation by formal schooling, even when we try. And we have only begun to try, after accepting all too long the notion that schools should acquiesce in, even reinforce, inequalities in home backgrounds rather than overcome them.

Upgrading the earning capacity of Negroes will be difficult, but the economic effects are easy to analyze. Economists have long held that the way to reduce disparities in earned incomes is to eliminate disparities in earning capacities. If college-trained people earn more money than those who left school after eight years, the remedy is to send a larger proportion of young people to college. If machine operators earn more than ditchdiggers, the remedy is to give more people the capacity and opportunity to be machine operators. These changes in relative supplies reduce the disparity both by competing down the pay in the favored line of work and by raising the pay in the less remunerative line. When there are only a few people left in the population whose capacities are confined to garbage-collecting, it will be a high-paid calling. The same is true of domestic service and all kinds of menial work.

This classical economic strategy will be hampered if discrimination, union barriers, and the like stand in the way. It will not help to increase the supply of Negro plumbers if the local unions and contractors will not let them join. But experience also shows that barriers give way more easily when the pressures of unsatisfied demand and supply pile up.

It should therefore be the task of educational and manpower policy to engineer over the next two decades a massive change in the relative supplies of people of different educational and professional attainments and degrees of skill and training. It must be a more rapid change than has occurred in the past two decades, because that has not been fast enough to alter income differentials. We should try particularly to increase supplies in those fields where salaries and wages are already high and rising. In this process we should be very skeptical of self-serving arguments and calculations—that an increase in supply in this or that profession would be bound to reduce quality, or that there are some mechanical relations of "need" to population or to Gross National Product that cannot be exceeded.

Such a policy would be appropriate to the "war on poverty" even if there were no racial problem. Indeed, our objective is to raise the earning capacities of low-income whites as well as of Negroes. But Negroes have the most to gain, and even those who because of age or irreversible environmental handicaps must inevitably be left behind will benefit by reduction in the number of whites and other Negroes who are competing with them. . . .

CONCLUSION

By far the most powerful factor determining the economic status of Negroes is the overall state of the U.S. economy. A vigorously expanding economy with a steadily tight labor market will rapidly raise the position of the Negro, both absolutely and relatively. Favored by such a climate, the host of specific measures to eliminate discrimination, improve education and training, provide housing, and strengthen the family can yield substantial additional results. In a less beneficent economic climate, where jobs are short rather than men, the wars against racial inequality and poverty will be uphill battles, and some highly touted weapons may turn out to be dangerously futile.

The forces of the marketplace, the incentives of private self-interest, the pressures of supply and demand—these can be powerful allies or stubborn opponents. Properly harnessed, they quietly and impersonally accomplish objectives which may elude detailed legislation and administration. To harness them to the cause of the American Negro is entirely possible. It requires simply that the federal government dedicate its fiscal and monetary policies more wholeheartedly and singlemindedly to achieving and maintaining genuinely full employment. The obstacles are not technical or economic. One obstacle is a general lack of understanding that unemployment and related evils are remediable by national fiscal and monetary measures. The other is the high priority now given to competing financial objectives.

In this area, as in others, the administration has disarmed its conservative opposition by meeting it halfway, and no influential political voices challenge the tacit compromise from the "Left." Negro rights movements have so far taken no interest in national fiscal and monetary policy. No doubt gold, the federal budget, and the actions of the Federal Reserve System seem remote from the day-to-day firing line of the movements. Direct local actions to redress specific grievances and to battle visible enemies are absorbing and dramatic. They have concrete observable results. But the use of national political influence on behalf of the goals of the Employment Act of 1946 is equally important. It would fill a political vacuum, and its potential long-run pay-off is very high.

The goal of racial equality suggests that the federal government should provide more stimulus to the economy. Fortunately, it also suggests constructive ways to give the stimulus. We can kill two birds with one stone. The economy needs additional spending in general; the wars on poverty and racial inequality need additional spending of particular kinds. The needed spending falls into two categories: government programs to diminish economic inequalities by building up the earning capacities of the poor and their children, and humane public assistance to citizens who temporarily or permanently lack the capacity to earn a decent living for themselves and their families. In both categories the nation, its conscience aroused by the plight of the Negro, has the chance to make reforms which will benefit the whole society.

NOTES

1. As Locke Anderson shows, one would expect advances in median income to run into diminishing returns in reducing the number of people below some fixed poverty-level income. W. H. Locke Anderson, "Trickling Down: The Relationship between Economic Growth and the Extent of Poverty Among American Families," *Quarterly Journal of Economics*, vol. 78 (November 1964), pp. 511–524. However, for the the economy as a whole, estimates by Lowell Gallaway suggest that advances in median income still result in a substantial reduction in the fraction of the population below poverty-level incomes. "The Foundation of the War on Poverty," *American Economic Review*, vol. 55 (March 1965), pp. 122–131.

2. Anderson, "Trickling Down," Table 4, p. 522.

3. This point, and others made in this section, have been eloquently argued by Harry G. Johnson, "Unemployment and Poverty," unpublished paper presented at West Virginia University Conference on Poverty Amidst Affluence, May 5, 1965.

4. Gallaway, "War on Poverty." Gallaway used the definitions of poverty originally suggested by the Council of Economic Advisers in its 1964 Economic Report, that is: incomes below $3000 a year for families and below $1500 a year for single individuals. The Social Security Administration has refined these measures to take better account of family size and of income in kind available to farmers. Mollie Orshansky, "Counting the Poor: Another Look at the Poverty Profile," *Social Security Bulletin*, Vol. 28 (January 1965), pp. 3–29. These refinements change the composition of the "poor" but affect very little their total number; it is doubtful they would alter Gallaway's results.

5. Gallaway, "War on Poverty," shows that postwar experience suggests that, other things equal, every point by which unemployment is diminished lowers the national incidence of poverty by .5 percent of itself. And this does not include the effects of the accompanying increase in median family income, which would be of the order of 3 percent and reduce the poverty fraction another 1.8 percent.

6. For lack of comparable nationwide income data, the only way to gauge the progress of Negroes relative to whites over long periods of time is to compare their distributions among occupations. A measure of the occupational position of a group can be constructed from decennial Census data by weighting the proportions of the group in each occupation by the average income of the occupation. The ratio of this measure for Negroes to the same measure for whites is an index of the relative occupational position of Negroes. Such calculations were originally made by Gary Becker, *The Economics of Discrimination* (Chicago, 1957). They have recently been refined and brought up to date by Dale Hiestand, *Economic Growth and Employment Opportunities for Minorities* (New York, 1964), p. 53. Hiestand's results are as follows: Occupational position of Negroes relative to whites:

	1910	1920	1930	1940	1950	1960
Male	78.0	78.1	78.2	77.5	81.4	82.1
Female	78.0	71.3	74.8	76.8	81.6	84.3

The figures show that Negro men lost ground in the Great Depression, that they gained sharply in the nineteen forties, and that their progress almost ceased in the nineteen fifties. Negro women show a rising secular trend since the nineteen twenties, but their gains too were greater in the tight labor markets of the nineteen forties than in the nineteen thirties or nineteen fifties.

Several cautions should be borne in mind in interpreting these figures: (1) Much of the relative occupational progress of Negroes is due to massive migration from agriculture to occupations of much higher average income. When the overall relative index nevertheless does not move, as in the nineteen fifties, the position of Negroes in the non-agricultural occupations has declined. (2) Since the figures include unemployed as well as employed persons and Negroes are more sensitive to unemployment, the occupational index understates their progress when unemployment declined (1940–50) and overstates it when unemployment rose (1930–40 and 1950–60). (3) Within any Census occupational category, Negroes earn less than whites. So the absolute level of the index overstates the Negro's relative position. Moreover, this overstatement is probably greater in Census years of relatively slack labor markets, like 1940 and 1960, than in other years.

The finding that labor market conditions arrested the progress of Negro men is confirmed by income and unemployment data analyzed by Alan B. Batchelder, "Decline in the Relative Income of Negro Men," *Quarterly Journal of Economics,* vol. 78 (November 1964), pp. 525–548.

7. Differences between Negro men and women with respect to unemployment and income progress are reported and analyzed by Alan Batchelder, *ibid.*

8. Figures are given in other papers in this volume [*Daedalus*]: see, for example, the articles by Rashi Fein and Daniel Patrick Moynihan.

9. In 34 percent of poor Negro families, the head is not in the labor force; in 6 percent, the head is unemployed. These figures relate to the Social Security Administration's "economy-level" poverty index. Mollie Orshansky, "Poverty Profile."

10. See *Manpower Report of the President,* March 1964, Table A-3, p. 197.

11. Hiestand, *Economic Growth,* Table I, pp. 7–9.

12. Batchelder, *op. cit.,* shows that the incomes of Negro men declined relative to those of white men in every region of the country. For the country as a whole, nevertheless, the median income of Negro men stayed close to half that of white men. The reason is that migration from the South, where the Negro-white income ratio is particularly low, just offset the declines in the regional ratios.

THE THEORY OF THE DUAL ECONOMY

Bennett Harrison

POVERTY, DISCRIMINATION, AND UNEMPLOYMENT

Neoclassical explanations of unemployment and underemployment have, until very recently, been oriented almost entirely toward analysis of labor supply. During the 1950s, discussions of "structural unemployment" turned on the premise that certain kinds of labor (distinguished by ethnic origin, education, or location) were unable to respond "normally" when effective demand for goods and services is translated into derived demand for labor. Then,

> . . . as aggregate demand lowered unemployment and the structural hypothesis became less tenable as an explanation of high unemployment, the manpower training programs gradually shifted character and became anti-poverty programs . . . They readily harmonized with the early puritan ethic of the war on poverty. Poverty was to be eliminated by raising everyone's marginal product to the level where [they] would be able to earn an acceptable income. Education and training programs were to be the principal means for raising marginal products . . . increasing workers' human capital could eliminate poverty. . . .[1]

The author of the previous statement, Lester Thurow, is one of the most prominent members of the "human capital" school. His assessment is shared by Thomas Ribich, whose analysis of the relationship between education and poverty begins with the proposition that "a major presumption of the war on poverty is that education and training are especially effective ways to bring people out of poverty.[2]

But investments in the human capital of ghetto workers have not eliminated poverty. The results of recent quantitative studies demonstrate a fundamental flaw in the conventional wisdom, and call for a revision of the current orthodoxy which asserts that poverty is a function of inadequate human capital.[3]

A few neoclassical economists have attempted a modest revision, according to which minority underemployment is explained by the "market imperfection" of racial discrimination.[4] These theorists have been criticized for attributing unrealistically calculated, marginalist decision-making behavior to discriminating employers, and for their inability or unwillingness to recognize that discrimination

SOURCE: H. L. Sheppard, B. Harrison, and W. J. Spring, *The Political Economy of Public Service Employment* (Lexington, Mass.: Lexington Books, D. C. Heath, 1972), pp. 41–57, 61–63.

by employers takes place within the larger context of institutional racism throughout the economy.[5] Limited though they may be, however, the neoclassical studies are at least addressed to the "demand side" of the problem.

Gary Becker's analysis of discrimination is founded on the notion that every employer has his price for hiring blacks. "For each employer, for each job, there is a crucial wage differential which would make the hiring of a white and an equally qualified Negro a matter of indifference to him. This crucial wage differential, expressed as a ratio of the white wage, Becker call the 'discrimination coefficient.' "[6] The market acts so as to cause the available supply of blacks to be hired by employers with relatively low discrimination coefficients. The observed differential between black and white pay is the discrimination coefficient of the employer on the margin, the employer of blacks who is most prejudiced against them. For Becker, in other words, discrimination takes place at the point of job entry. Thurow's approach is similar in placing the focus of discrimination within the firm which pays Negroes a wage discounted to take into account the employer's "psychic cost" of integrating his workforce.

For Barbara Bergmann, on the other hand, the focus is on those employers who will not hire blacks at any wage. This is the "crowding hypothesis":

> The most important feature of an economy in which discrimination is practiced is the simple fact that some jobs are open to Negroes and some are not. The jobs open to Negroes are not a random selection, even allowing for Negroes' relatively lower education. They tend to be predominantly low in status, and to be concentrated very heavily in a few occupations. Following Donald Dewey, we might call this a "racial division of labor. . . ." Another major difference with the view of this paper is the identification of the villain of the piece. For Thurow, he is the man who hires Negroes and pays them low wages. Under the crowdedness hypothesis . . . the villain is the entrepreneur who will not hire Negroes, perhaps on behalf of or under pressure from his white workers. The entrepreneur who does hire Negroes acts towards them the way he is presumed to act towards any other factor of production: he pays them the price for which he can get them. The fact that the price for Negro labor is a lower price than he need pay white workers is attributable not to the entrepreneur who hires Negroes, but to the entrepreneur who refuses to do so, and so crowds them into the janitorships at low pay.[7]

Arrow's analysis is similar to Bergmann's in emphasizing the significance of "corner" (i.e., either-or) solutions to the intrafirm (or intrashop) labor allocation decision.

The emphasis in this paper will also be on minority workers, especially blacks, and we, too, will often speak of racial discrimination. But this study will also show that lower-class whites—those who still live in the central city poverty areas and "ghettos"—receive returns to their human capital which are substantially lower than the returns received by whites who have "escaped" the ghetto. Our analysis, in other words, leads us to hypothesize the existence of *class* as well as *race* discrimination.

Bradley Schiller has succeeded in making a quantitative distinction between the effects of class discrimination (with "class" defined by income stratum) and racial discrimination, as these are manifested through restricted access to educational and occupational opportunities.[8] Schiller estimates that, if working sons in black families enrolled in the Aid to Families with Dependent Children program could convert their inherited status (defined by parental occupation and education) and their own years of schooling into occupational status at the same "rate" that poor (i.e., AFDC-enrolled) *white* sons do, they would gain 3.32 occupational status points (on an ordinal scale of 0-100). This is, therefore, a kind of measure of the extent of racial discrimination, holding "class" constant.

If poor white sons could convert *their* inherited status and their own education into occupational status at the same "rate" that *non-poor* white sons do, they would gain 2.74 status points. This is Schiller's measure of class discrimination, holding race constant.

Finally, if poor black sons could convert their inherited status and their own schooling into occupational status at the same "rate" that non-poor white sons do, they would gain 5.66 status points. This is a measure of the *joint* effects of racial and class discrimination.

These findings require us to ask whether common structural characteristics of the economic system underlie both white and black poverty. If such is the case, then neither appeals to racial justice nor coercive antidiscrimination policies will be sufficient to eliminate poverty. As Barry Bluestone observes:

> While particular individuals now denied high-wage jobs may benefit from a removal of market barriers, low-wage jobs will still exist. At best, increased mobility will distribute workers more "fairly" over the existing sets of jobs. . . . Some black workers will exchange places with some white workers in the occupational hierarchy and some women will replace men, but increased mobility will *not,* in general, increase the number of high-wage jobs or reduce the number of jobs at poverty wages.[9]

This important proposition has received some support from Ms. Bergmann's study of the income effects of occupational "crowding." Without any compensating increase in the stock of jobs in the economy, the elimination of occupational discrimination by race would (according to the Bergmann equations) cause a 6-9 percent reduction in the incomes of white men lacking an eighth grade diploma—a group which constitutes 14 percent of all adult white men in the United States. The displacement of white women would be even greater. For both sexes, the conflict becomes greater the less substitutable we assume whites and nonwhites to be in production.[10] These calculations imply that the ofttimes vocal opposition of lower-class white ethnic groups to government programs designed to expand job opportunities for black is—in an economy such as ours—not without some reason.

Confronting the facts of class conflict and continued poverty in the United States, even after a decade in which "the federal government directed between $140 and $170 billion in aid to the poor,"[11] a small, but growing, number of young economists have begun to develop an alternative theory—what David Gordon (after Thomas Kuhn) calls a new "paradigm"[12]—to explain these phenomena.

Some of this new research to which I have alluded has grown out of what began as fairly pedestrian evaluations of various training and education programs connected with the federal "war on poverty." These studies frequently showed that training programs had little positive effect on the work situation of the poor. Enrollees in such programs typically earned no higher wages after graduation than before undertaking training. Many refused to take the programs seriously at all, remaining in them for short periods of time, earning small training stipends, and then dropping out. In fact, many enrollees told evaluators frankly that they thought of the manpower training system in the same way they thought of any other form of low-wage, marginal activity: as a temporary source of income, a place to go for short periods of time to supplement family income. They entertained little hope or expectation of actually acquiring decent permanent employment as a result of their participation in the program.

At about the same time, other researchers discovered an important flaw in the conventional wisdom about welfare recipients. It was popularly held that there exists in the economy a large, permanent "welfare class," consisting of individuals and families who themselves remain on the relief rolls for long periods of time and who not infrequently raise their children to become similarly dependent on public assistance. The researchers found, instead, that people tended to move on and off the welfare rolls, over and over again, in a fashion reminiscent of the behavior of the manpower trainees. The analogy was reinforced by the publication in 1967 of the Bureau of Labor Statistics' Minimum Urban Family Budgets, which showed clearly that families in even the richest states whose incomes derived entirely from welfare would be "enjoying" a seriously deficient standard of living. High turnover and low rates of income seemed to characterize both of our major antipoverty programs.

Anecdotal accounts of the extent to which the urban poor are forced to depend for part of their livelihood on illegal or other "irregular" activities have been available at least since the publication of the autobiographies of Claude Brown, Eldridge Cleaver, and Malcolm X.[13] Gradually, economists and sociologists began to realize that these activities were themselves organized into "markets," and that—given the unalterable constraints of the twenty-four hour day—ghetto workers might logically be assumed to allocate part of their labor time to "work" in the irregular market at the expense of time spent in other forms of incoming-bearing activity. When the structure of this "market" was explored, it was quickly found to be characterized by high turnover, unstable participation, and (after accounting for the high risks involved) relatively low average "wages." The similarity to the training and welfare "markets" was unmistakable—and quite dramatic.

Even before these discoveries were made, a few scholars had documented the existence and magnitude of "working poverty." In 1966, more than 7.3 million men and women in America were labor force participants and yet were poor.[14] In 1968, 1.3 million family heads worked thirty-five hours per week, fifty weeks a year, but still earned less than $3,500, the official poverty line then; 1.6 million part-time working family heads were also poor.[15] In terms of the much higher (but hardly luxurious) BLS Minimum Urban Family Budget, the incidence of working poverty was considerably greater: perhaps a third of all American families and 40 percent of the labor force had incomes in 1967 which fell below the BLS' "minimum" budget standard. And in 1970, 4.7 million full-time male and 6.6 million full-time female workers earned less than the $1.60 per hour "minimum" wage.[16] These workers occupied a class of jobs which bore precisely the characteristics found to be associated with the above-mentioned non-labor market activities: low pay and high turnover. Moreover, evaluations of government institutions designed to place low-income workers into "good" jobs concluded that these placement programs were succeeding only in recirculating the poor among the very low-paying, unstable jobs which they already held.

Thus, a substantial number of seemingly disparate work activities and public programs were found to share certain important commonalities. Could these interrelationships be systematic? And if so, how did these various poverty income level activities relate to the conventional American mode of family support: non-poverty wage labor? These are some of the questions that have led to the development of the germ of a new labor market theory, often referred to as the "theory of the dual economy" or the "theory of labor market segmentation."[17]

THE "CORE" OF THE ECONOMY

Dual market analysts believe the economy to be stratified into what Barry Bluestone calls a "core" and a "periphery" (see Figure 1). The division is

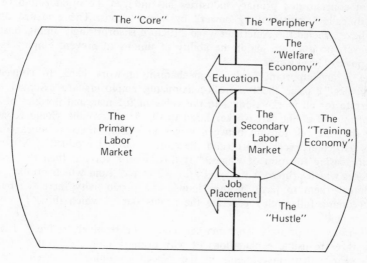

Figure 1.   The Dual Economy.

functional and not simply semantic; workers, employers, and even the under-lying technologies in the two strata behave very differently in important qualitative ways. The central institution of the "core" has been called the "primary labor market," and this is the part of the core which we shall study here.[18] In the primary labor market, the attributes of jobs and the behavioral traits of workers interact (e.g., by mutual reinforcement) to produce a structure characterized by high productivity, non-poverty wages, and employment stability.

The high productivity of primary labor is a function not only of the knowledge and skills (i.e., the "human capital") of the workers, but also (and perhaps more fundamentally) of the capital equipment with which they generally work. The market power of the typical primary firm, and the relatively high degree of profitability which is the usual corollary of such power, enable the employer to invest in modern capital equipment (frequently embodying "leading edge" technologies), to maintain that equipment, and to replace it when necessary. The same factors make it possible for such firms to invest in the "human capital" of their employees, so that the equipment will be used efficiently. While this is, of course, an ideal construct, it does seem to be broadly descriptive of the technical conditions of production in the leading, highly concentrated industries in the American economy, and provides a plausible, albeit partial, explanation of the relatively high average productivity of the core of the American labor force.[19]

Primary employers typically pay non-poverty wages. This may be partly explained by the aforementioned high average and marginal productivity of core labor, but most dual market theorists prefer a more institutional explanation. The very economic power which underlies the profits which enable primary employers to make productivity-enhancing investments also permits them to pass along a share of wage (and other cost) increases to their customers. In other words, their oligopoly position *permits* them to maintain non-poverty wage levels without seriously eroding their profit margins. At the same time, the economic power of concentrated primary industries has induced the organization of what Galbraith calls "countervailing power" by labor unions. The evidence on how unions have affected the American wage structure is surprisingly ambiguous; there is, however, no question about the ability of unions to prevent employers from paying poverty-level wages.

There is an important feedback mechanism at work here. In conventional ("neoclassical") price theory, profit-maximizing employers are assumed to pay a wage rate for all workers equal to the value of the marginal product of labor: the contribution of the last worker hired to the firm's revenue. Some economists believe that the relationship between wages and productivity is more complex, that, in particular, work effort (and therefore measured productivity) may well be an increasing function of wages.[20] If this view is correct, then the relatively high wages which primary employers are able to pay (and which primary unions "encourage" them to pay) in turn induce the productivity increases by labor which (coming full circle) generate the profits out of which those non-poverty wages are paid.

Workers in the primary labor market tend to be relatively stable.[21] There are at least three plausible explanations of why primary employers value workforce stability. First, their investments in the "specific training" of their workers—training highly specific to the particular conditions of this particular firm (or plant) and not easily transferred to other work environments—represents a "sunk cost" which they naturally wish to recoup. Workers who quit before repaying this investment in the form of contributions to output must be replaced, and the replacements must then be trained anew. In the primary labor market, turnover is *obviously* expensive and therefore undesirable from the point of view of the employer.

A second and somewhat more controversial explanation has to do with the development within large firms of what Doeringer and Piore call the "internal labor market." [22] During the 1950s, economists discovered that large corporations had developed internal capital "markets" in the form of large pools of retained earnings, the existence of which helped to insulate them from the periodic increases in the external cost of capital (and as it turns out, from government anti-inflationary monetary policy as well).[23] With large stocks of internal capital, firms could engage in long-run capacity expansion plans without having to concern themselves with changes in interest rates. During normal times, investment capital could be borrowed as usual. When interest rates rose, perhaps through government policy designed to slow down corporate investment in new plant and equipment, the firm could turn to its internal capital "market," thereby enabling the "plan" to continue. Doeringer and Piore believe that a similar process has now developed within large corporations with respect to labor as well as capital. Firms can go into the external labor market at times when conditions, such as excess supply, favor the firm in the wage-bargaining process: an obvious example is the extent to which corporations flood college campuses at graduation time each year. Since the employer-employee relation in the core of the economy is often characterized by the use of fairly long-term contracts, firms can then retain (or "hoard") this relatively cheaply-bought labor against those times when external labor is more expensive. Such internal labor markets are, therefore, institutional manifestations of the employers' desire for workforce stability.

A third explanation of firms' demand for stability is derived from the work of Kenneth Arrow, who observed that most of what workers learn about the equipment and systems with which they work is probably really learned "on-the job"; it is "learning by doing."[24] The more complex the job, i.e., the more intricate or subtle the technology and the equipment, the longer it takes the average worker to "learn" the job and to reach the point where—for all practical purposes—he has obtained his peak of efficiency. The concept is illustrated by Figure 2, where the typical "learning curve" is represented by a logistic. How-

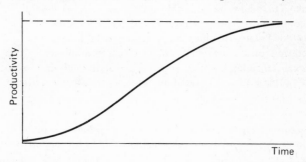

Figure 2.   Hypothetical Learning Curves in the Primary Labor Market.

ever "productivity" is measured, the question is: for any given job, how long does it take the average worker to reach his or her maximum efficiency? Is the concept of an asymptotic maximum (a limit to individual) efficiency meaningful for that job? If so, is the average learning period three weeks, three months, or three years? Consider the contrast between keypunch operators and computer operators. Both are very nearly unskilled or at best semi-skilled jobs; student computer operators are often trained by their colleges in a week. Any upper limit to the potential productivity of a computer operator is undoubtedly quite "high," so varied are the technical possibilities for performing the highly discretionary tasks associated with this job, e.g., filing, classifying, and retrieving tapes, learning to take advantage of the capabilities of a system with respect to the batching of "jobs," discovering and accommodating oneself to the idiosyncracies of one's fellow operators. Contrast this with keypunch operators who—like clerk-typists—tend increasingly to be organized into large work pools and whose maximum efficiency is essentially determined by their physical dexterity and the capacity of their machines. Once such workers reach their maximum punching, or typing, speed, continued tenure is unlikely to lead to significant improvements (and may very well lead to the opposite, as the job becomes "routine"). An even more dramatic contrast exists between the clerk-typist and the executive secretary. The latter may literally never "peak out"; he or she has to learn not only the mechanics of the job, but is also continually in the process of acquiring such subtle skills as the ability to locate his or her boss' business (and perhaps even extra-business) associates at any hour of the day at any of their favorite haunts. Clearly, it is to the employer's advantage to retain an employee whose capacity for improvement has not been exhausted.

At the same time, workers in most primary jobs seem to *want* to remain in those jobs, at least for a noticeably longer period than is the case for what we will later call "secondary workers." This is admittedly somewhat vague; while the threshold between "primary" and "secondary" wages seems to have been quantitatively identified—at from $2.25 to $3.50 per hour—very little quantitative work has yet to be performed on the tenure variable. The jobs pay relatively well, and employers, as we have seen, encourage the workers to stay. This stability of the workforce feeds back into the wage-bargaining process. Stable workers are more easily organized, and unions generally prefer to organize stable rather than unstable workers, perhaps because of the obvious consequences for strike funds, etc. To the extent that this unionization is successful, it reinforces the maintenance of non-poverty wages (as described earlier), which, in turn, induces the continued stability which, in turn, supports unionization, ad infinitum.

Efficient operation of the primary labor market requires the development of certain behavioral attitudes on the part of workers and employers, attitudes which it is the purpose of such social institutions as the educational system to inculcate. Herbert Gintis writes that:

> Economists have long noted the relationship between the level of schooling in workers and their earnings. . . . Almost no attempt has been made, however, to determine the mechanism by which education affects earnings or productivity. In the absence of any direct evidence, it is commonly assumed that the main effect of schooling is to raise the level of cognitive development of students and that it is this increase which explains the relationship between schooling and earnings. This view of the schooling-earnings linkage has provided the conceptual framework for studies which seek to "control" for the quality of schooling through the use of variables such as scores on achievement tests and I.Q.

The objective of this paper is to demonstrate that this interpretation is fundamentally incorrect.[25]

Instead, Gintis believes that "schools affect earnings" by creating an internal "social structure" whose "authority, motivational, and interpersonal relations" are designed to replicate "those of the factory and office." One of the most important instruments of this social development process is the grading system which, quite apart from (and beyond) its ostensible function of measuring cognitive ability, affords "independent reward to the development of traits necessary to adequate job performance."[26] Samuel Bowles has uncovered evidence that eighteenth and nineteenth century manufacturers consciously supported public education as a means of teaching young people, at public expense, discipline, punctuality, acceptance of outside authority, and individual accountability—behavioural traits crucial for the efficient operation of the factory system.[27]

Taken alone, there is nothing either novel or obviously pathological about these observations. Schools prepare students—behaviorally as well as technically —for the "world of work"; every manpower training agent and antipoverty warrior takes this for granted. The problem, according to Gintis, is that society and its individual members pay a very high price for the "pre-vocational training" which schools provide for primary employers. "The economic productivity of schooling is due primarily to the inculcation of personality characteristics which may be generally agreed to be inhibiting of personal development." Gintis analyzes a rich body of data on "649 upper-ability senior high school males (National Merit Scholarship Finalists)" who were scored on five achievement variables (e.g., scientific performance, humanities comprehension) and sixty-five personality variables, and a second group of 114 high school seniors "of varying ability." The measures of achievement were then correlated with the measures of personality. Gintis found that "schooling is conducive to the development of [those] traits . . . requisite for adequate job functioning in production characterized by bureaucratic order and hierarchical control." Personality traits such as perseverance, self-control, suppression of aggression, and deferred gratification were positively correlated with achievement scores. But the data also showed that "students are uniformly penalized for creativity, autonomy, initiative, tolerance for ambiguity, and independence, even after correcting for achievement.[28] From these results, and from the inference that "successful" students and workers even in the core of the economy must have learned to suppress their most creative and deeply human personality traits in order to *be* successful. Gintis concludes that "The economic productivity of schooling must be measured against an opportunity cost reflected in the development of an alienated and repressed labor force."[29]

THE "PERIPHERY" OF THE ECONOMY

The so-called "periphery" of the American economy is assumed to consist of at least four "segments," the manpower characteristics of which are remarkably similar to one another (Figure 1). Mobility among these segments seems to take place regularly, while, by contrast, workers in the peripheral stratum are able to move into the core of the economy only very infrequently.

The "Secondary Labor Market"

Research—much of it concerned with the study of ghetto labor markets[30]—has indicated the existence of a class of jobs which contrast sharply with the primary labor market along each of the three dimensions we have discussed.

Secondary workers tend to display relatively low average and marginal productivity. Until recently, one explanation for this was the dearth of "human capital," particularly formal education of at least average quality, possessed by these workers. While this continues to provide a partial explanation, it is becoming increasingly less convincing as even ghetto blacks gradually close the education gap between themselves and the average American. By 1970, the gap between the median schooling of young whites and blacks had fallen to less than half a year, as the figures in Table 1 show.

TABLE 1   **Median Years of Schooling, for Blacks and Whites, by Age**

	MEDIAN YEARS OF SCHOOL COMPLETED	
Age	Blacks	Whites
20–21 years	12.4	12.8
22–24	12.3	12.7
25–29	12.2	12.6
30–34	12.0	12.5

SOURCE: U.S. Department of Commerce, Bureau of the Census, *Current Population Reports*, Series P-23, No. 38 (BLS Report No. 394), "The Social and Economic Status of Negroes in the United States, 1970," Washington, D.C., July 1971, Table 65.

In any case, the importance of formal education in determining worker productivity is itself now in some doubt, as we have seen. Probably more important is the absence of economic power in this segment of the periphery of the economy. With little or no oligopolistic market control, and with small profit margins, secondary firms tend to use more antiquated capital, which, of course, tends to diminish productivity. Finally, the jobs themselves often do not *require* skills of any great consequence, involving instead the kind of routine unskilled tasks which attract (and at the same time reinforce the life styles of) casual laborers.

Workers in the secondary labor market receive, and firms in this stratum of the economy pay, very low wages. During the period July 1968 to June 1969, 37 percent of the black and 51 percent of the Puerto Rican male household heads living in Harlem and working at least thirty-five hours a week, fifty weeks a year averaged less than $100 per week in earnings. Nationally, in 1966, 36.3 percent of all employees working in nursing homes and related facilities earned less than $1.60 per hour, the legal minimum wage. For employees of laundry and cleaning services, fertilizer manufacturers, eating and drinking places, gasoline service stations, and retail food stores, the 1966 percentages were 75.4 percent, 41.7 percent, 79.4 percent, 66.7 percent, and 47.6 percent.[31] Annual wage income is the product of an average wage *rate* and the number of hours, days or weeks during the year in which a person works. The instability of secondary labor (discussed shortly) drives down the duration of work, while the economic structure of the peripheral firm causes it to pay a low wage rate. Taken together, these factors guarantee that workers will be forced to subsist on a poverty-level income—to the extent that they rely for income entirely on what they can earn in the secondary labor market. Low productivity contributes to the explanation of these low wages, but so does the lack of market power among peripheral employers. Moreover (as indicated earlier), dual labor market theorists believe that these factors are interdependent; the marginal firm, by paying low wages and by not providing its workers with adequate complementary capital, discourages its labor force from taking those actions or developing those attitudes which would lead to increased productivity which, if capitalized, could increase the firm's capacity to pay higher wages. The lack of economic power which characterizes peripheral firms (as reflected, for example, in the relatively high elasticity of their output demand curves) also makes it impossible for them to raise wages and other input costs without eroding profit margins, perhaps to the shut-down point. Finally, the low wages found in the secondary labor market are partly the result of the relative simplicity of the technologies in secondary industries; since skill requirements are minimal, the opportunity cost of secondary labor is low, given the large pool of readily available substitutable workers out "on the street."

While the primary labor market is characterized by a mutual employer-employee "taste" for stability, both firms and workers in the secondary labor market seem to benefit from unstable workforce behavior. That secondary labor is significantly more unstable than primary labor is incontestable. Hall, for example, writes:

> Some groups exhibit what seems to be pathological instability in holding jobs. Changing from one low-paying, unpleasant job to another, often several times a year, is the typical pattern of some workers. The resulting unemployment can hardly be said to be the outcome of a normal process of career advancement. The true problem of hard-core unemployment is that a certain fraction of the labor force accounts for a disproportionate share of unemployment because they drift from one unsatisfactory job to another, spending the time between jobs either unemployed or out of the labor force [where they go when they drop out of the labor force will be discussed later]. The most compact evidence in favor of the hypothesis that such a group exists is provided by the data on the number of spells of unemployment experienced by the labor force. Among those who were unemployed at some time in 1968, 69 percent had only one spell of unemployment, 15 percent had two spells and 16 percent had three or more. Now the overall unemployment rate in 1968 was 3.6 percent. Suppose that the average person changing jobs required one month to find a satisfactory new job. Then the average duration between spells of unemployment would be about twenty-seven months. In order to have two, much less three, spells of unemployment in the same twelve months, an individual could hardly be making normal changes in jobs, even if it is true that the normal person changes jobs every twenty-eight months. Yet almost a third of those unemployed at all in 1968, more than three million individuals, had two or more spells. The existence of this group is surely a matter of social concern.[32]

In their studies of the hard-core unemployed in St. Louis, Edward Kalachek and his colleagues concluded that "the relatively high rates of unemployment experienced by St. Louis Negroes appear to be more the result of frequent job changes than of the inability to find employment. . . . Job stability develops and unemployment experiences diminish among older workers with dependents. . . . For our sample, however, the stabilizing influence of age was not discernible until respondents were in their early 30's."[33] The researchers tested for differential work attitudes and values between the young blacks who were their principal object of study and control groups of other workers.

> A number of respondents, particularly young men in the fifteen to eighteen years of age category, admitted to engaging in nonlegitimate "hustles." . . . Still like other younger members of the study population, [such individuals] clearly see the value of jobs and education. . . . The high quit rates of young Negroes appear due not to a deviant value system, but to the frustration of low-wage-paying jobs. . . . Younger workers appear less willing or able to accept poverty level wages when they perceive the value system of the "American Dream" to be promising more.[34]

Secondary employers have several reasons for placing a low value on turnover, in sharp contrast to their fellows in the primary labor market. They can, as a rule, neither afford nor do their technologies require them to invest heavily in "specific training." Instead, they tend to rely on the "general training" (e.g., literacy, basic arithmetic) provided socially. With minimal investment in their current labor force, and given the ready availability of substitute labor outside the firm, such employers are at the very least indifferent to the rate of turnover. Moreover, these firms lack the size and wealth necessary for the development of internal labor markets. Nor have they any reason to want to develop such institutions; since their skill requirements are minimal, they are unlikely to encounter periods where the labor they need is scarce and therefore expensive to recruit through conventional ("external") labor markets. Finally, everything we have hypothesized about the technology of secondary industries implies that the typical job is easily and quickly learned, so that learning curves probably look more like that depicted in Figure 3 than that shown in Figure 2. We have already discussed some of the implications of the shape of this function. It may be added at this point that to keep a worker employed for an extended period usually requires the granting of raises in pay and various employee benefits. Moreover, there is a definite correlation between labor force stability and the probability of that force being organized. It follows that employers who already have little to lose (in terms of foregone output) by discouraging long tenure of specific workers will have still other rational reasons for discounting stability.

Workers, for their part, seem similarly to have a rational preference for instability in the secondary labor market. The jobs are boring, and do not pay well. Employers seem not to mind—and perhaps even to encourage—casual attitudes toward work. The penalities for poor industrial discipline are generally not severe. Doeringer's studies of antipoverty programs in Boston led him to conclude about the job placement system for ghetto workers that it was seldom

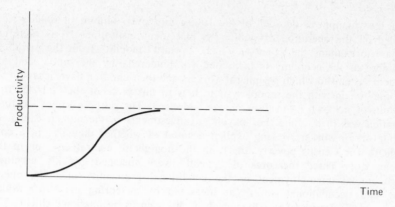

Figure 3. Hypothetical Learning Curves in the Secondary
Labor Market.

able to refer its clients to jobs paying more than they were earning before—
"only $2.00 an hour or less." This lack of upward mobility in the placement
system contributes to the poor work habits and weak job attachment of the
"hard-to-employ": "The availability of alternative low-wage job opportunities
and the unattractiveness of such low-wage work interact to discourage the formation of strong ties to particular employers." That low wages are the principal
motivating factor seems to be confirmed by the finding that, "for wage rates
higher than the 'prevailing' ghetto wage, disadvantaged workers are more likely
to be stable employees than other workers." These relationships between tenure
and wage rates were found to be at best only weakly related to the educational
attainment of the workers.[35] And, of course, this entirely rational instability
frustrates union organization so that there is no pressure for change, e.g., improvement in wages and working conditions—pressure which has been institutionalized
in the core of the economy.

Thus, where primary employers and employees interact in an institutional
setting characterized by high productivity, non-poverty level wages and high
workforce stability, the firms and work forces in the secondary labor market
tend to organize themselves into production systems displaying low productivity,
poverty level wages and low stability (high turnover). It is interesting to observe
that what appears to be "subemployment" or "underemployment" from the
conventional perspective of an essentially unified economy is now seen to be
the normal mode of employment in a backwater of that economy, a sector cut
off from the mainstream. . . .

INTERSECTORAL MOBILITY

This chapter began with references to the elaborate mythology which has
developed in America, according to which generations of immigrants were
allegedly able to lift themselves out of poverty through education and training.

During the "manpower decade" of the 1960s, moreover, billions of dollars were expended on the operation of public job placement institutions. It is therefore important to examine the extent to which "upward" mobility from the periphery to the core of the economy is facilitated (or hindered) by the school and job placement systems to which peripheral workers and their children have access.

We may begin with the school system; it is to this piece of the "puzzle" that the results of my own basic research are addressed. The purpose of my doctoral dissertation was to estimate the "payoff" to investments in the human capital of nonwhite urban workers, taking explicit account of whether they live in a core city ghetto (or Census poverty area), in the non-ghetto central city, or in the suburban ring. Three measures of "payoff" were specified: weekly earnings, average annual unemployment or the conditional probability of being unemployed, and occupational status (as measured by a scoring procedure which assigns an ordinal rank of 0–100 to each of 308 Census occupational titles). The policy variables of interest were years of school completed and participation in any of five formal training programs; all were given dummy variables specifications to permit tests for nonlinearity. Control variables specified both additively and interactively included age, sex, race, and industry group in which the person works (the latter serves also as a proxy for the complementary capital with which the person works).

The primary sample studied consisted of over 11,000 micro household interviews from the twelve largest SMSA's in the country, drawn from (even more extensive) interviews conducted in March 1966 and March 1967 by the Bureau of the Census for the Office of Economic Opportunity. These data files are referred to as the *Survey of Economic Opportunity*.

Additional samples studied (using somewhat different models) were drawn from the nearly 40,000 household interviews from the eight cities (ten ghettos) in the *1966 Urban Employment Survey*. These are Department of Labor materials.

Multivariate regression analysis showed (1) that ghetto nonwhites lag significantly behind even ghetto whites in terms of economic welfare; (2) that the economic welfare of urban nonwhites is relatively insensitive to variations in intrametropolitan residential location, although the economic welfare of whites increases substantially with the "move" from ghetto to non-ghetto central city to suburbs; and (3) that the returns to education for ghetto nonwhites are significant in terms of improved occupational status, nominal in terms of higher wages, and statistically insignificant in terms of reduced probabilities of unemployment (the number of trainees in the samples was insufficient to permit confident inference about the impact of training programs on the welfare of ghetto residents). Taken together, this third set of findings assigns a quantitative dimension to the concept of underemployment which has heretofore been unavailable in studies of poverty, discrimination, urban, and labor economics.

That the white-nonwhite welfare differentials (i.e., the differences in earnings, unemployment and occupational status) remain—even among samples of similarly-educated individuals living in the same urban neighborhoods—suggests the need for a major reorientation in both our intellectual and policy approaches to poverty. Specifically, we must shift our emphasis away from exclusive concentration on the alleged "defects" of the poor themselves toward the investigation of defects in the market system which constrains the poor from realizing their potential.

These studies compel us to conclude that the public education system does not—by itself, at any rate—promote the kind of intersectoral mobility for the peripheral worker which he or she has been led to expect. What effect *does* education have, then, particularly on ghetto blacks? For a small number, it probably does provide access to primary jobs. But the expectation certainly is otherwise. It follows that, with blacks crowded disporportionately into the secondary labor market, increasing educational investments *ceteris paribus* may only increase the effective supply of secondary labor, which might then drive black wages down even further.

Two different explanations of this insufficiency of education may be proposed. From the point of view of conventional liberal theory (i.e., a racially discriminating, but structurally integrated economy), a "market imperfection" (discrimination) is preventing the education system from functioning in its "normal capacity." In a nondiscriminating economy, those ghetto workers who made the effort to "lift themselves up" by investments in their own "human capital" *would* be rewarded with higher incomes, fewer unemployment "spells," and higher status jobs.[36]

Bowles and Gintis, on the other hand, would argue that the "normal capacity" or true social function of the education system is not so much to develop job skills as to socialize young people to the roles they are most likely to play as adult workers, given their (and their parents') place in the class structure. By this interpretation, the low returns to education received by the urban poor of both races and particularly by blacks are not the result of improper or inadequate functioning of the ghetto schools. Quite the contrary; those schools are performing precisely the function they are "intended" to perform. Their indulgence of irregular behavior (within the classroom and in terms of class attendance) prepares their students for the peripheral lifestyle which the majority of them will probably be forced to adopt. The stifling of creativity and imagination reported so often by such educational critics as Edgar Friedenberg, Ivan Illich, Jonathan Kozol, and Christopher Jencks conditions ghetto children to accept the uncreative, routine kind of unskilled work which most of them will be required to perform after they "graduate." Most important of all, the failure of ghetto schoolteachers and education programs to acquaint their students with primary lifestyles, and the tendency of teachers and guidance counsellors to "steer" their students into secondary jobs,[37] have the latent function of frustrating the development among lower-class youth of aspirations which might become socially destabilizing. That such aspirations are often formed anyway, and that the kind of schooling we are analyzing has not succeeded completely in preventing social tension, is due not so much to the inability of the schools to train productive workers because of discrimination as to the fact that the educational system does not operate in a vacuum. Other forces, over which the schools have little or no control (e.g., mass communication, the emergence of black pride and, in some places, volatile black nationalism) have—by this theory—interfered with the "normal function" of the schools. That function, to repeat, is to prepare lower-class students for secondary social and economic roles. . . .

NOTES

1. Lester Thurow, "Raising Incomes Through Manpower Training Programs," in Anthony H. Pascal (ed.), *Contributions to the Analysis of Urban Problems* (Santa Monica, Calif.: RAND Corporation, August 1968), Document No. P-3868, pp. 91–92.
2. Thomas I. Ribich, *Education and Poverty* (Washington, D.C.: Brookings Institution, 1968), p. 1.
3. Cf. Bennett Harrison, *Education, Training, and the Urban Ghetto* (Baltimore: Johns Hopkins Press, 1972), and Randall Weiss, "The Effect of Education on the Earnings of Blacks and Whites," *Review of Economics and Statistics,* May 1970.
4. Cf. Kenneth J. Arrow, *Some Models of Racial Discrimination in the Labor Market* (Santa Monica, Calif.: RAND Corporation, February 1971), Document No. RM-6253-RC; Gary S. Becker, *The Economics of Discrimination* (Chicago: University of Chicago Press, 1957); Barbara R. Bergmann, "The Effect on White Incomes of Discrimination in Employment," *Journal of Political Economy,* March/April 1971; Anne O. Krueger, "The Economics of Discrimination," *Journal of Political Economy,* October 1963; and Lester C. Thurow, *Poverty and Discrimination* (Washington, D.C.: Brookings Institution, 1969).
5. Cf. Raymond Franklin and Michael Tanzer, "Traditional Microeconomic Analysis of Racial Discrimination: A Critical View and Alternative Approach," in David Mermelstein (ed.), *Economics: Mainstream Readings and Radical Critiques* (New York: Random House, 1970); Michael Reich, "Economic Theories of Racism," in David M. Gordon (ed.), *Problems in Political Economy: An Urban Perspective* (Lexington, Mass.: D. C. Heath, 1971); and David P. Taylor, "Discrimination and Occupational Wage Differences in the Market for Unskilled Labor," *Industrial and Labor Relations Review,* April 1968.
6. Bergmann, "Effect on White Incomes," p. 308.
7. *Ibid.,* pp. 295, 310.
8. Bradley R. Schiller, "Class Discrimination vs. Racial Discrimination," *The Review of Economics and Statistics,* August 1971.
9. Barry Bluestone, "The Tripartite Economy: Labor Markets and the Working Poor," *Poverty and Human Resources,* July/August 1970, pp. 23–24.
10. Bergmann, "Effect on White Incomes," pp. 303–304.
11. Bluestone, "Tripartite Economy," p. 15.
12. David M. Gordon, *Theories of Poverty and Underemployment* (Lexington, Mass.: Heath-Lexington Books, 1972). Gordon builds upon an excellent history of science by Thomas S. Kuhn, *The Structure of Scientific Revolutions* (Chicago: University of Chicago Press, 1962).
13. Claude Brown, *Manchild in the Promised Land* (New York: Signet, 1965); Eldridge Cleaver, *Post-Prison Writings and Speeches* (New York: A Ramparts Book, Random House, 1969); *The Autobiography of Malcolm X* (New York: Grove Press, 1966).
14. Harold L. Sheppard, *The Nature of the Job Problem and the Role of New Public Service Employment* (Kalamazoo, Mich.: The W.E. Upjohn Institute, January 1969), p. 4.
15. U.S. Department of Labor, *1970 Manpower Report of the President* (Washington, D.C.: U.S. Government Printing Office, 1970), pp. 121–122. Barry Bluestone notes that the Census Bureau's sexist designation of families with working wives and unemployed husbands as "families with an unemployed head of household," tends to understate the number of working poor household heads.
16. Estimated from distributions in U.S. Bureau of the Census, *Current Population Reports,* Series P-60, No. 80, "Income in 1970 of Families and Persons in the U.S.," Government Printing Office, Washington, D.C., October 4, 1971.

17. For a good working bibliography on economic dualism in the American context, see the references cited in Gordon, *Theories of Poverty and Underemployment;* and in Bennett Harrison, "Human Capital, Black Poverty, and 'Radical' Economics," *Industrial Relations,* October 1971.

18. Some of the other interlocking institutions in the core include the schools that prepare people to work in the primary labor market, the financial intermediaries which fund the activities of primary employers, and the federal government which serves as a Keynesian "regular," of aggregate demand and—more recently—as guarantor of demand through direct contracts. See Robert Averitt, *The Dual Economy* (New York: W. W. Norton, 1968); John Kenneth Galbraith, *The New Industrial State* (Boston: Houghton Mifflin, 1967); and Herbert Gintis, "Repressive Schooling as Productive Schooling," in Gordon, *Problems in Political Economy.* We shall have more to say about the role of the education system at the end of this section.

19. According to Michael Tanzer, "the degree of discrimination against Negroes of either sex is highly correlated with the job structure of the industry. Specifically, the greater the proportion of total jobs in an industry which are laborer jobs, the greater the proportion of Negroes found in the industry as a whole and in each occupational job category separately." Franklin and Tanzer, "Traditional Microeconomic Analysis of Racial Discrimination," p. 120n. In other words, labor-intensive industries tend to employ nonwhites both aggregatively and in many different positions, while capital-intensive industries are less likely to do either.

20. Cf. Harvey Leibenstein, *Economic Backwardness and Economic Growth* (New York: Wiley-Science Editions, 1963), pp. 62–69. This is one of the earliest discussions of "the interesting possibility that the energy level of a tenant or worker rises as his income rises." At a more aggregative level, a recent United Nations study developed "social profiles" for developing countries, composed of indicators of nutrition, education, health, housing, and leisure. The researchers found that "those developing countries which had a favorable social profile in the early 1950's also tended to show more rapid economic growth in the following ten years." Salvatore Schiavo-Campo and Hans W. Singer, *Perspectives of Economic Development* (Boston: Houghton Mifflin, 1970), pp. 76–78. It is not at all uncharacteristic of the dual labor market theory that some of its roots are to be found in studies of the "Third World."

21. "The most important characteristic distinguishing jobs in the primary sector from those in the secondary sector appears to be the behavioral requirements which they impose upon the work force, particularly that of employment stability." Michael J. Piore, "The Dual Labor Market: Theory and Implications," in Gordon, *Problems in Political Economy,* p. 91.

22. Peter B. Doeringer and Michael J. Piore, *Internal Labor Markets and Manpower Analysis* (Lexington, Mass.: D. C. Heath, 1971).

23. John R. Meyer and Edwin Kuh, *The Investment Decision* (Cambridge: Harvard University Press, 1957). See also Galbraith, *The New Industrial State,* and Robin Marris, *The Economic Theory of Managerial Capitalism* (New York: The Free Press, 1964).

24. Kenneth Arrow, "The Economic Implications of Learning-by-Doing," *Review of Economic Studies,* June 1962.

25. Herbert Gintis, "Education, Technology, and the Characteristics of Worker Productivity," *American Economic Review/Proceedings,* May 1971, p. 266.

26. *Ibid.,* p. 267.

27. Samuel Bowles, "Unequal Education and the Reproduction of the Social Division of Labor," in Richard Edwards, Michael Reich, and Thomas Weisskopf (eds.), *The Capitalist System* (Englewood Cliffs, N.J.: Prentice-Hall, 1972).

28. Gintis, "Education, Technology, and the Characteristics of Worker Productivity," pp. 273–274.

29. *Ibid.*, p. 267. Bowles has posited a theory which integrates Gintis' conception of the function of schooling with the model of labor market segmentation and the findings on class discrimination. According to this theory, schools "reproduce" (i.e., preserve) class cultures from generation to generation. Labor markets then "translate" these differences in class culture into income inequalities and occupational hierarchies which in turn determine which schools the children of workers will be able to attend. See Bowles, "Unequal Education." We shall make use of this theory later, in the discussion of the role of public education as an instrument of mobility between the core and the periphery of the economy.

30. Cf. Peter B. Doeringer, with Penny Feldman, David M. Gordon, Michael J. Piore, and Michael Reich, *Low-Income Labor Markets and Urban Manpower Programs*, Department of Economics, Harvard University, January 1969, mimeographed; Thomas Vietorisz and Bennett Harrison, *The Economic Development of Harlem* (New York: Praeger, 1970); and other references cited in Gordon and Harrison (see note 17).

31. Bluestone, "Tripartite Economy," p. 25.

32. Robert E. Hall, "Why is Unemployment So High at Full Employment?" *Brookings Papers on Economic Activity*, No. 3 (Washington, D.C.: Brookings Institution, 1970), pp. 389–390.

33. Edward D. Kalachek and John M. Goering (eds.), *Transportation and Central City Unemployment*, Institute for Urban and Regional Studies, Washington University, Working Paper INS 5, March 1970, p. 8.

34. *Ibid.*, pp. 8–9.

35. Peter B. Doeringer, "Ghetto Labor Markets—Problems and Programs," Program on Regional and Urban Economics, Discussion Paper No. 35, Harvard University, May 1968, mimeographed, pp. 10–11.

36. For example, Glazer and Moynihan assume that public education would help to improve the employment status of blacks if only the "serious obstacles to the ability to make use of a free educational system to advance into higher occupations" could be removed. Moreover, "there is little question where [these obstacles] must be found: in the home and family and community." Nathan Glazer and Daniel P. Moynihan, *Beyond the Melting Pot* (Cambridge: Harvard University Press, 1963), pp. 49–50. Herman Miller, Chief Economist of the Census Bureau, has written that "it is entirely possible and indeed likely that productivity potentials of nonwhites have been raised, as suggested by the theory that correlates increases in years of schooling with additions to human capital, but [that] these potentials may not have materialized, owing to discrimination." Herman P. Miller, "Does Education Pay Off?", in Selma J. Mushkin (ed.), *Economics of Higher Education* (Washington, D.C.: U.S. Department of Health, Education, and Welfare, 1962), p. 132.

37. I refer here to the common practice of advising lower-class students that they will be unable to obtain work in certain occupations and should therefore concentrate on other "traditional" positions. When such advice is taken, it amounts to self-fulfilling prophecy. It is important to note that not all the students in a predominantly lower-class school are treated this way. Many schools use an internal "tracking" system, in which students with "promise" are placed in substantially separate curriculums from those with less or no "promise." "Placement in these curriculums may determine the student's entire future life [and] it is known . . . that even very able boys from working-class homes who fail to make really good grades in the seventh and eighth grades are seldom advised to take a college preparatory course. This is not equally true of

boys from white-collar homes." Patricia Cayo Sexton, "Education and Income: Senior High Schools," in Gordon, *Problems in Political Economy*, pp. 201–202. Lee Webb is currently attempting to explore the relationship between this fascinating internal segmentation of education "markets" and the labor market segmentation described in the text.

CAPITALISM AND POVERTY IN AMERICA: PARADOX OR CONTRADICTION?

Howard M. Wachtel

The apparent *paradox* of "poverty amid affluence" has consumed the attention of many social scientists during the last decade. Books were written with that title, grant proposals took this as their theme, and hardly an article was written on poverty without these words, in some form, figuring in a set of erudite conclusions. But is the coexistence of poverty and affluence *paradoxical*—a condition that seems "absurd but may actually be true in fact" (to borrow a definition from *Webster's*)—or is it contradictory in the dialectical sense? Poverty as a contradiction of capitalism implies that there is some logical and necessary relationship between the basic system-defining institutions of capitalism and one of its consequences—poverty. The question posed in this paper is whether poverty and inequality are *necessary functional* aspects of capitalism or merely aberrational defects which can be remedied by marginal adjustments.

Poverty amid capitalist affluence should not necessarily surprise us. The very process through which capitalist affluence emerges create, as well, its opposite— capitalist poverty. This is a useful way to understand the differences between orthodox economists and reformist politicians on the one hand, who view poverty and other societal problems as some accidental (paradoxical) occurrence which can be corrected by dealing with its surface manifestations, and on the other hand radical political economists, who see poverty as emerging from the contradictions of capitalism and propose doing something about capitalism itself as the only way to deal with its surface manifestations.

The contradictions within capitalism that generate conditions of poverty and inequality are *antagonistic,* thereby giving rise to the sort of conflicts we have witnessed during the 1960s. The trajectory of change arising from that conflict (both in a quantitative and a qualitative sense) is a crucial part of a dialectical analysis of society (Mao Tse-tung, pp. 337–345.) However, this topic deserves at least a paper in itself and can only follow logically from an exposition of the radical paradigm and its application to poverty and inequality such as is presented in this paper.

The objective of this paper is to sketch an emerging radical paradigm and

SOURCE: *Monthly Review,* June 1972, pp. 51–61.
In preparing this paper, I have benefited from the comments of R. Muller, P. Sweezy, R. Simon, G. Peabody, R. England, J. Weaver, H. Aylesworth, B. Harrison, S. Bowles, and the participants in the American University Union for Radical Political Economics Discussion Group.

apply it to the existence of poverty and inequality in America.[1] Moreover, what T. Kuhn (pp. 148–150) calls the "incommensurability of paradigms" inhibits proponents of competing paradigms from making "contact with each others' viewpoint."[2] There is disagreement over the questions which must be investigated, the conceptual categories of the paradigm, the functional relationships among the categories of the paradigm, the methodology employed in the analysis, and the techniques of empirical verification.[3]

THE FUNCTIONS OF POVERTY AND INEQUALITY

Poverty and inequality have an important role to play in capitalism; these conditions are by no means entirely dysfunctional.[4] First, extreme wage and income inequality is necessary to induce workers to perform alienating work for external rather than internal rewards, under job conditions they do not control. (R. Edwards and A. MacEwan, pp. 354–355.) Second, the existence of a poverty underclass (a lumpenproletariat) serves as a warning to the non-poor that their fate could be much worse, thereby mitigating labor militancy by dividing labor along status lines. Third, to the extent that the poor form a "reserve army of the unemployed," wages are depressed, some unions are weakened, and labor's ability to obtain a greater share of income generated in production is diminished. Fourth, the *non-poor's* real income is substantially increased by poverty (especially that of the working poor), since commodities and services can be obtained at lower prices so long as wages are depressed by the existence of the poor and capital retains its power to extract profits. In this way, we all benefit from the existence of poverty, though usually one only hears of the direct beneficiaries of poverty—slumlords, exploiting factory owners, and the like. In large part, the tenacity of poverty in the face of "wars" against it can be explained by these important functional attributes of poverty in a capitalist society.

This does not mean that the social system as we know it today could not survive without the *precise amount of poverty and degree of inequality* we presently have. Rather, *functionalism,* as used here, means that things work better for the dominant class when there is a substantial degree of inequality and poverty. We could perhaps reduce poverty and inequality somewhat—the marginal adjustment sought by orthodox social scientists and politicians—without producing substantive *qualitative change*. In fact, a *small amount* of cross-class mobility is important in legitimating existing power relationships and in stabilizing the social system. However, at some point *quantitative* reductions in poverty and inequality would result in a *qualitative* change in the system as we know it today. To the extent that stratification within the working class militates against class unity and class consciousness, the poverty subclass in the short-term *manifests* more of a functional rather than an antagonistic relationship with respect to capitalism. The dominance of the functional over the antagonistic relationship, however, need not prevail for all time. The *manifest* functional attribute of poverty conceals but does not nullify the underlying contradictions of capitalism, which can become antagonistic as the poor become liberated from their subordinance to capitalism.

CLASS, INEQUALITY AND POVERTY

In this paper, I isolate three basic *system-defining* institutions of capitalism to analyze their effect on poverty and inequality: class relationships, labor markets, and the state (R. Edwards and A. MacEwan, p. 353.) We start our analysis of the causes of poverty and inequality with a discussion of class, defined in terms of one's relationship to the means of production—"the way in which the means of production [are] owned and . . . the social relations between men which [result] from their connections with the process of production." (M. Dobb, 1947, p. 7.) [5] For purposes of analyzing income distribution, it is sufficient to treat classes in a purely objective sense—as a category defined by the relations of production.

If an individual possesses both labor and capital, his/her chances of being poor or in a low-income percentile are substantially less than if only labor is possessed. For individuals earning incomes under $10,000, nearly all income comes from labor. However, for individuals earning between $20,000 and $50,000 (in 1966), only slightly more than half comes from labor, while for individuals with incomes between $50,000 and $100,000, only a third comes from labor. And if you are super-rich—earning in excess of $100,000—only 15 percent comes from wage and salary earnings, while two thirds is derived from returns to capital and capital gains (the balance is composed of "small business" income). (F. Ackerman et al., p. 27.)

More important than the magnitude of capital income is its unequal distribution in our economy and its monopolization by one class. Were we to socialize the ownership of capital and redistribute its returns, we could alleviate the purely financial aspect of low incomes. A direct transfer of income that would bring every family up to the Bureau of Labor Statistics' "Moderate But Adequate" living standard in 1966 (roughly $9,100) would have required $119 billion. (D. Light, p. 47.) This amounts to about 20 percent of total income, slightly *less* than the proportion of personal income derived from ownership of capital!

LABOR MARKETS, INEQUALITY, AND POVERTY

Since very few capitalists are poor, an analysis of the labor market is an important means of understanding the causes of poverty. This proposition is as old as Thomas Aquinas: "Because they are poor they become wage-earners, and because they are wage-earners they are poor." (Quoted in E. Mandel, p. 320.) Contrary to the view fostered by the media, nearly every poor person is or has been connected with the labor market in some way. First, there are enormous numbers of working poor—individuals who earn their poverty by working full-time, all year around, enabling us to purchase commodities and services at lower prices, thereby raising the real standard of living for the non-poor. In 1968, there were two and one-quarter million families (nearly 10 million individuals) with a head working full-time, full-year, and earning less than the government's parsimonious poverty income. (B. Bluestone, 1971, p. 10.)

A second significant proportion of the poor is attached to the labor force but is not employed full-time. Some of these individuals suffer intermittent periods of short-term employment and short-term unemployment, while others work for substantial periods of time and then suffer periods of long-term unemployment forming a group euphemistically called "the hard-core unemployed."

A third significant portion of the poor is handicapped in the labor market as a result of an occupational disability or poor health. However, these occupational disabilities are themselves often related to a person's earlier status in the labor force. There are greater occupational hazards and risks of poor health in low-wage jobs. In 1966, nearly *one sixth* of the labor force was disabled for a period longer than *six months*. As a consequence of disability, many households with disabled heads are poor—about 50 percent in 1966. (President's Commission on Income Maintenance, pp. 139–142.)

A fourth category of the poor is not presently attached to the labor market— retired workers, the prison population, members of the military, the fully handi- capped, and those on other forms of public assistance (principally women with dependent children). Though these individuals are not presently attached to the labor force, in nearly all instances their low income is determined by the labor- market status they occupied during their participation in the labor force.

The next question is: How do labor markets function to yield differential probabilities of becoming poor for those subject to their functioning? The emerg- ing radical analysis views labor markets as stratified, consisting of more or less permanent divisions within the working class.[6] The degree of labor market stratification has differed in different times and places and has had important implications for cyclical and secular movements in class consciousness. (D. Gordon, 1971b, pp. 112–138.) We may note, at this juncture, the particular quality of this proposition: the division of society into classes and then into strata within classes, which yields a state of both conflict between and division within classes. This contrasts with the harmonious, frictionless, and equilibrating propositions of orthodox theory, in which individuals are atomized, and their behavior is not influenced by their class or status positions. (See P. Sweezy; M. Zweig, 1971.)

The particular way in which labor becomes stratified is a complex process which has taken on different forms in different historical epochs. Certainly, a starting point is the system of learning provided by capitalist society in its broadest context: learning in schools, in the family, and through one's social network of friends and acquaintances. While orthodox economists have focused almost exclusively on the acquisition of "human capital" through formal educa- tion, on the degree of "rationality" of the human capital investment decision, and on the rate of return to that human capital, radicals have focused their atten- tion on the primary role of formal education in reproducing the class structure intergenerationally and in perpetuating stratification in the labor market. (S. Bowles, 1971.) [7] Class differences in "family socialization and complementary differences in the type and amount of schooling" transmit class status intergen- erationally (Bowles, 1971, p. 29) with this resultant manifestation in the labor market:

> The operation of the labor market translates differences in class culture into income inequalities and occupational hierarchies. The per- sonality traits, values, and expectations characteristic of different class cultures play a major role in determining an individual's success in

gaining a high income or prestigious occupation. The apparent contribution of schooling to occupational success and higher income seems to be explained primarily by the personality characteristics of those who have higher educational attainments. (Bowles, 1971, pp. 33–34.)

For this purpose, schools have developed an intricate set of mechanisms to influence personality development which, in turn, have interacted with affective traits acquired through the family and the individual's social network (one's circle of friends, acquaintances, and occupational associates). As evidence of the importance of affective traits acquired through schooling, H. Gintis (1970, pp. 268–271) has shown that these are more important than cognitive ability in predicting rates of return to schooling. Bowles (1971, p. 1) has summarized this analysis as follows:

> Schools have evolved in the United States not as part of a pursuit of equality, but rather to meet the needs of capitalist employers for a disciplined and skilled labor force, and to provide a mechanism for social control in the interest of political stability.

A second view of the source of stratification in the labor market is that associated with the *dual labor-market* theory developed during the 1960s. The essential source of stratification in this model emanates from the interaction between the characteristics of jobs and individual personality traits. The labor market is seen as dichotomized into a primary and a secondary sector in which the primary sector offers high wages, good working conditions, employment stability, and job security; while the secondary sector offers the reverse. (M. Piore, 1968, p. 2; and 1970, pp. 55–60.)

D. Gordon (1971b, pp. 112–137), in an extremely important contribution, has placed the dual labor-market theory into the context of the general radical paradigm. In his view, the degree of labor-market stratification is closely related historically to the relative power of capital and labor. Employers will always attempt to stratify labor markets for purposes of control and to satisfy what he calls a "hierarchy fetishism." (D. Gordon, 1971b, p. 131.) The jobs in the secondary sector will be filled largely with black and brown (and one might add red) workers, teenagers, and women for three reasons: first, ease with which employers can identify these groups; second, the resignation of these groups to their jobs in the secondary sector; and third, the advantages this affords to employers in dividing workers along racist, sexist, and age lines—prejudices deeply engrained in American society. (M. Reich, 1971; M. Goldberg.)

Consequently, while Piore places his emphasis on the "culture of poverty" embodied in a set of individual personality traits as the major determinant of access to the primary sector, Gordon shows that these traits are carefully nurtured by capitalist institutions in order to maximize capital's power over labor. At this point, his argument intersects with the earlier argument concerning the role of education and the family in producing the affective traits which prepare workers for their place in the labor market.

A third view of stratification in the labor market places primary emphasis on the structure of the industries and local labor markets in which the individuals are employed. (H. Wachtel and C. Betsey; B. Bluestone, 1970; B. Harrison,

1972b.) The dominant forces that determine an individual's status in the labor force lie outside his or her control and are embodied in a set of industry and local labor-market characteristics in which the individual is involved—capital-labor ratios, political power of the industry and locality, degree of market concentration, power of the trade union, profit rates, the industry's association with the state, industrial base of the local labor market, rate of growth of the local labor market, etc. Bluestone (1970, pp. 24–26) sees the economy divided into three sectors, which leads him to dub it the *tripartite economy*. The *core economy* is dominated by those industries "which comprise the muscle of American economic and political power," primarily found in durable manufacturing, construction, and some extractive industries; the *peripheral economy* is primarily agricultural, non-durable manufacturing, retail trade, and subprofessional services; and the *irregular economy* represents "monetized activity which is not included in the national income accounts," concentrated primarily in the ghetto.[8]

At the risk of drawing overly sharp distinctions, we can discern three fairly distinct views on the question of labor market stratification, with the difference among these positions being defined in terms of the aspect of the labor market which provides the primary source of stratification. The three positions can be summarized in terms of the aspect singled out for primary attention: formal education and the family (Bowles, 1971; Gintis, 1971); job characteristics interacting with personality traits (Piore; Gordon, 1971b); and industrial and local labor-market structures (Wachtel-Betsey; Bluestone, 1970; Harrison, 1972b). At this juncture, a synthesizing of these separately developed positions is in order.

The class status and labor market status of the family heavily influence the individual's acquisition of some quantity of formal education, the quality of formal education, the social network in which the individual will operate, expectations about future class and labor-market status, and the affective personality traits acquired (which are themselves produced by the interaction of schools, the family and the social network). In this connection, the analysis would have to be differentiated along race and sex lines. The characteristics of jobs available are, in part, determined by the structure of the industry and the local labor market in which the jobs are located. Given a set of personal characteristics (education, affective traits, etc.), the individual's wage earnings are heavily influenced by the structure of the industry and the structure of the local labor market. In sum, the aspect isolated for analysis reflects different phases in one overall process, encompassing an individual's entire life. The acquisition of affective traits through the family and schools (as a function of the parent's class and social status) begins to set the limits on the range of labor-force opportunities which become increasingly narrowed as one enters an occupation (dual labor-market theory) and an industry in a particular local market (tripartite labor-market theory). Two parallel systems of stratification interact—one involving individuals and occupations, the other industrial structure.

One observation is immediately apparent: there are very few elements of labor-market status that lie within the individual's control, even though virtually all public policy and social research take as their premise that low income can be corrected by manipulating some personal attribute of the individual.[9]

THE STATE, INEQUALITY, AND POVERTY

The state, especially in the present monopoly capitalist phase of American society, reinforces the power relationships emerging from the interaction of class antagonisms and the operation of labor markets. The state, as used in this discussion, embraces not only the elected government (at all levels) but the administrative bureaucracies, the military and domestic police forces, and the judiciary. (R. Miliband, chap. 3.)[10] Contemporary radicals are not the only ones who see the state as operating to reinforce class dominance. None other than Adam Smith (p. 674) noted in his *Wealth of Nations* that "civil government, so far as it is instituted for the security of property, is in reality instituted for the defense of the rich against the poor, or for those who have some property against those who have none at all."

S. Michelson (pp. 77–79) has argued persuasively that, in considering the redistributive aspects of public policy, one must first treat the influence of the state in establishing the pre-tax, pre-expenditure income distribution in the first instance. The totality of government activity must be investigated, not just those programs directly related to poverty and income distribution. (H. Wachtel, 1971 p. 9.) The two most widely cited studies of the redistributive effects of government taxation and expenditure fail to come to grips with these questions. (W. Gillespie; and Tax Foundation.) Moreover, by distributing the benefits of public goods (primarily defense) on a per capita basis, they obtain results that are downright foolish. Gillespie (p. 160) goes so far as to say that expenditures for national defense "nearly fulfill a true 'social want' because equal amounts of them are consumed (or are available for consumption) by all."

Public programs specifically designed for the poor have not attained their stated objectives. Elsewhere I have argued in detail that (Wachtel, 1971, pp. 9–16):

(1) The state reinforces the unequalizing tendencies of the market, even though liberals for the past 40 years have been attempting to bring about precisely the opposite result.

(2) Programs to aid the poor have perhaps had some slight impact in the short run, but over time have either atrophied, become anemic in their impact, or distorted in their purpose.

(3) Only those public programs that are compatible with the system-defining characteristics of monopoly capitalism will see the light of day in the first instance and will survive to suffer the fate in point two above.

These observations can be illustrated by examining three of the premier public programs to aid the poor: the social security program, the farm program, and contemporary manpower training programs.

The social security system is class-biased in favor of capital in its tax structure (only wages and salaries are taxed while income from capital is not taxed); regressive in its tax incidence (individuals earning between $4,000 and $5,000 in 1967 paid an effective rate of 9.3 percent, while individuals earning over $25,000 paid only 1.5 percent) (J. Pechman et al., p. 307);[11] and is class-biased in its payout structure (individuals are restricted to the amount of wage and salary earnings they can accumulate before losing benefits, while unlimited amounts of capital income can be accumulated without penalty). Moreover, since poor people die at an earlier age because of their exclusion from private markets for health care (S. Kelman), they obtain less benefits than a comparable higher-income person.[12]

The farm program has promoted the corporate concentration of agriculture by subsidizing technological change through a variety of complex mechanisms and by *decapitalizing* the small independent farmer. The system is class-biased in that owners of farms are paid not to produce, but the farm workers who are displaced by this process and by technological change receive nothing. In addition, farm subsidies are notorious for their inequitable distribution. (Watchel, 1971, p. 12.)

The manpower training programs started in the 1960s have increasingly taken on the character of training subsidies for large corporations, as evidenced by the increasing trend towards on-the-job training at the expense of institutional training, the growth of the JOBS program, and the scandalously low wages received by trainees for their efforts. The General Accounting Office (p. 1) has concluded that manpower training programs have served "primarily to reimburse employers for [training] which they would have conducted even without the government's financial assistance." Wage rates received by trainees have been very low (in many cases just at or below the minimum wage) and reveal almost no change from the wage rates received by trainees before training. (S. Levitan and G. Mangum, pp. 51 and 206.)

Two prominent students of American welfare have concluded that the primary purpose of welfare programs historically and at present has been to furnish low-wage workers to employers and to persuade welfare recipients that even the most onerous job is preferable to the stigma of welfare. (F. Piven and R. Cloward.) A measure of our immunization against such obvious conditions is the little-noticed admission in the *1968 Manpower Report of the President* that "Public Assistance often serves as a form of wage supplementation for the low-paid, partially employed workers." (Quoted in B. Harrison, 1972a, p. 22.)[13]

SUMMING UP

The evidence presented in this paper supports the proposition that poverty and inequality are a contradiction of capitalism—a logical consequence of the proper functioning of the capitalist institutions of class, labor markets, and the state. Beyond any marginal adjustments, these system-defining institutions of capitalism must be challenged to make any fundamental changes in the life of the low-income populations in America.

The orthodox analysis, by way of contrast, views poverty as the result of some *individual failure* which can be corrected by an *individual adaptation*. The roots of this view lie deep in the ideology of capitalism; virtually all research and social policy since the industrial revolution are based on this proposition: poorhouses (prisons), work farms (Job Corps centers), outdoor relief (the WIN program), the Speenhamland System (income maintenance). (See B. Coll; R. Bremner.) The modern variant is the application of human capital theory to poverty, where low incomes are seen as resulting from an inadequacy in the individual's human capital which can be corrected simply by augumenting the stock of human capital through more formal education, manpower training, and the like. (Watchel, 1–9.) Once again, as in the Elizabethan Poor Laws, the poor are blamed for their own condition, and the solution is supposed to lie in finding that manipulable attribute of the individual which will permit the correction of the condition.

The orthodox research of the 1960s has told us nothing about the *causes of poverty,* which are to be found in the basic system-defining institutions of capitalism: labor markets, class, and the state. This research has merely provided estimates of the differential importance of various individual characteristics associated with the poor. It is quite consistent with the proposition that the poor are poor because of some individual failure, and it has received widespread acceptance and support precisely because it has been conveniently supportive of existing economic arrangements and the prevailing ideology.

NOTES

1. Because of space limitations, I will sketch only the bare outlines of the analysis and will provide substantial references to buttress the arguments of the paper.
2. This is an especially difficult task for the overwhelming majority of economists trained only in the orthodox tradition who have not had their "noses . . . rubbed . . . against radical economics. . . ." (M. Bronfenbrenner, p. 765)
3. For an introduction to Kuhn's methodology and its application to economics, see *Union for Radical Political Economics,* especially pp. 1–66.
4. For purposes of this paper I am interested both in poverty (low income in some absolute sense) and inequality (low income in some relative sense). Another approach to the functional aspects of poverty is taken by H. Gans.
5. Within the past several months, the important insights provided by a class analysis have begun to take root even among some of the more prestigious journalists. B. Nossiter (p. D1) laments the absence of academic research on power and argues that "Marxist theory offers a useful entry point." N. von Hoffman (p. B1) notes the opportunities lost in understanding contemporary American capitalism by not having any Marxists in Washington and by the absence of a "Marxist regularly appearing before congressional committees."
6. C. Kerr provided an earlier analysis of stratified ("balkanized" in his terminology) labor markets, but the analysis was never pursued thereafter. Taussig's "non-competing groups" is also a precursor to contemporary theories of stratification.
7. Bowles (1972) and Gintis (1970) view the contradictions in education and the creation of a "new working class" of educated labor as important factors of change emerging in American society.
8. Harrison (1972a) synthesizes the dual labor market and tripartite economy theories in examining the economic behavior of ghetto residents. He finds that the structural characteristics of welfare, training programs, hustling, and jobs in the secondary (or peripheral) sector are functionally quite similar.
9. My own empirical analysis (Wachtel-Betsey), corroborated by Bluestone's work-in-progress, indicates that industry structure is an important determinant of an individual's wage, overshadowing individual human capital variables.
10. For an interesting critique of Miliband, see I. Balbus.
11. These calculations are based on the assumption that employer taxes are shifted "backward" to the employee. J. Brittain's empirical work supports this contention.

297   CAPITALISM AND POVERTY IN AMERICA

12. Inabel Lindsay, Dean of Howard University's School of Social Studies, suggests that benefits should be paid to blacks at an earlier age "since fewer blacks—in view of their higher mortality and lower longevity—receive full benefit from past contributions." ("Early Social Security. . . .")

13. Mandel (p. 337) has generalized this observation: "The State, by guaranteeing to the wage-earners certain services which they do not have to purchase with their money wage, . . . plays the role of central cashier for the bourgeoisie, *paying part of wages in collective form so as to socialize certain needs.*" (Emphasis in original.)

REFERENCES

F. Ackerman, H. Birnbaum, J. Wetzler, and A. Zimbalist, "Income Distribution in the United States," *Review of Radical Political Economics,* Summer 1971, 3, 20–43.

I. Balbus, "Ruling Elite Theory vs. Marxist Class Analysis," *Monthly Review,* May 1971, 23, 36–46.

B. Bluestone, "Economic Theory, Economic Reality, and the Fate of the Poor," mimeo, 1971.

———, "The Tripartite Economy: Labor Markets and the Working Poor," *Poverty and Human Resources,* July–August 1970, 5, 15–35.

S. Bowles, "Contradictions in U.S. Higher Education," in J. Weaver (ed.), *Political Economy: Radical Versus Orthodox Approaches* (Boston: Allyn and Bacon, 1973), pp. 165–205.

———, "Unequal Education and the Reproduction of the Social Division of Labor," *Review of Radical Political Economics,* Fall/Winter 1971, 3, 1–30.

R. H. Bremner, *From the Depths, The Discovery of Poverty in the United States* (New York, 1967).

J. Brittain, "The Incidence of Social Security Payroll Taxes," *American Economic Review,* March 1971, 61, 110–125.

M. Bronfenbrenner, "Radical Economics in America," *Journal of Economic Literature,* September 1970, 8, 747–766.

B. D. Coll, *Perspectives in Public Welfare: A History,* Washington, 1969.

M. Dobb, "The Economic Basis of Class Conflict," in M. Dobb, *On Economic Theory and Socialism* (New York, 1955), pp. 93–103.

———, *Studies in the Development of Capitalism* (New York, 1947). "Early Social Security Suggested for Blacks," *Washington Post,* September 3, 1971.

R. C. Edwards and A. MacEwan, "A Radical Approach to Economics: Basis for a New Curriculum," *American Economic Review,* May 1970, 60, 352–363.

H. Gans, "The Uses of Poverty," *Social Policy,* July/August 1971, pp. 20–24. General Accounting Office, *Improvements Needed in Contracting for On-The-Job Training Under the Manpower Development and Training Act of 1962,* Washington, D.C., 1968.

W. I. Gillespie, "Effect of Public Expenditures on the Distribution of Income," in R. A. Musgrave (ed.), *Essays in Fiscal Federalism* (Washington, D.C., 1965), pp. 122–186.

H. Gintis, "Education, Technology, and the Characteristics of Worker Productivity," *American Economic Review,* May 1971, 61, 266–279.

———, "New Working Class and Revolutionary Youth: A Theoretical Synthesis and a Program for the Future," *Review of Radical Political Economics,* Summer 1970, 2, 43–73.

M. P. Goldberg, "The Economic Exploitation of Women," *Review of Radical Political Economics,* Spring 1970, 2, 35–47.

D. M. Gordon *a*, "Class and the Economics of Crime," *Review of Radical Political Economics*, Summer 1971, *3*, 51–75.

———, *b*, "Economic Theories of Poverty and Underemployment," mimeo, 1971.

B. Harrison *a*, "The Dual Economy and Public Service Employment," in B. Harrison, H. L. Sheppard, and W. Spring (eds.), *Public Service Employment and National Manpower Policy* (Kalamazoo, 1972).

———, *b*, *Education, Training, and the Urban Ghetto* (Baltimore, 1972).

———, "Human Capital, Black Poverty, and 'Radical' Economics," *Industrial Relations*, October 1971, *10*, 277–286.

B. Horvat, *An Essay on Yugoslav Society* (White Plains, 1969).

S. Kelman, "Toward the Political Economy of Medical Care," *Inquiry*, September, 1971, *8*, 30–38.

C. Kerr, "The Balkanization of Labor Markets," in E. W. Bakke (ed.), *Labor Mobility and Economic Opportunity* (Cambridge, 1954), pp. 92–110.

T. S. Kuhn, *The Structure of Scientific Revolutions*, second ed. (Chicago, 1970).

S. Levitan and G. L. Mangum, *Federal Training and Work Programs in the Sixties* (Ann Arbor, 1969).

D. Light, "Income Distribution: The First Stage in the Consideration of Poverty," *Review of Radical Political Economics*, Summer 1971, *3*, 44–50.

E. Mandel, *Marxist Economic Theory*, vol. 1 (New York, 1968).

Mao Tse-tung, "On Contradiction," in *Selected Works of Mao Tse-Tung* (Peking, 1967), pp. 311–347.

S. Michelson, "The Economics of Real Income Distribution," *Review of Radical Political Economics*, Spring 1970, *2*, 75–86.

S. M. Miller and P. Roby, *The Future of Inequality* (New York, 1970).

R. Miliband, *The State in Capitalist Society* (New York, 1970).

B. D. Nossiter, "Owning the Management and Managing the Owners," *Washington Post*, August 12, 1971, p. D1.

J. A. Pechman, H. J. Aaron, and M. K. Taussig, *Social Security: Perspectives for Reform* (Washington, D.C., 1968).

M. J. Piore, "Public and Private Responsibilities in On-The-Job Training of Disadvantaged Workers," M.I.T. Working Paper, 1968.

———, "Jobs and Training," in S. H. Beer and R. E. Barringer (eds.), *The State and the Poor*, (Cambridge, 1970), pp. 53–83.

F. F. Piven and R. A. Cloward, *Regulating the Poor, The Functions of Public Welfare*, (New York, 1971).

President's Commission on Income Maintenance Programs, *Background Papers*, Washington, D.C., 1970.

M. Reich, "The Economics of Racism," in D. M. Gordon (ed.), *Problems in Political Economy: An Urban Perspective* (Lexington, 1971), pp. 107–113.

A. Smith, *The Wealth of Nations* (New York, 1937).

P. M. Sweezy, "Toward a Critique of Economics," *Review of Radical Political Economics*, July 1971, *3*, 59–66.

Tax Foundation, Inc., *Tax Burden and Benefits of Government Expenditures by Income Class*, 1961 and 1965 (New York, 1967).

Union for Radical Political Economics, *On Radical Paradigms in Economics* (Ann Arbor, 1971).

N. von Hoffman, "Nixon Isn't a Very Good Marxist," *Washington Post*, August 13, 1971, p. B1.

H. M. Wachtel and C. Betsey, "Employment at Low Wages," *Review of Economics and Statistics*, forthcoming.

H. M. Wachtel, "Looking at Poverty from a Radical Perspective," *Review of Radical Political Economics,* Summer, 1971, *3,* 1–19.

M. Zweig, "Black Capitalism and the Ownership of Property in Harlem," mimeo, 1970.

————, "Bourgeois and Radical Paradigms in Economics," *Review of Radical Political Economics,* July 1971, *3,* 43–58.

RACE RELATIONS MODELS AND SOCIAL CHANGE

William Tabb

THE GHETTO AS COLONY

. . . The key relationships which must be demonstrated before the colonial analogy can be accepted are the existence between two distinct and clearly separate groups of a superior-inferior status relationship encompassing both (1) economic control and exploitation, and (2) political dependence and subjugation. If these can be demonstrated to exist, then the case can be made that the ghetto must break the shackles imposed by colonial exploitation for meaningful long-range improvement to take place.

In defining colonialism, militants argue that the spatial separation of colony and colonial power is secondary to the existence of control of the ghetto from the outside through political and economic domination by white society. An historical comparison of the forms which colonialism has taken, and a description of the place of blacks in the American economy, make clear that internal colonialism is an apt description of the exploitation of blacks in our society.

The vast majority of colonies were established by Western powers over technologically less advanced peoples of Asia, Africa, and Latin America. Military supremacy, combined with judicious bribing of local leaders and a generous sprinkling of Christian missionaries, enabled an outside power to dominate an area spatially separate from the ruling state. In some colonies there was extensive settlement by Europeans. If the territory was relatively unpopulated (Canada, Australia, New Zealand, and the United States), a policy of genocide and exchanging land for beads allowed the settlers to gain control. When their numbers and strength grew, the settlers could demand independence from the mother country. Nationhood was usually followed by a continuing economic relationship, but on better terms than the colony had enjoyed before it became independent. In some of the cases where European settlement was large but still a small minority of the total population, often a long and bloody struggle for independence resulted. Algeria is a case in point.

The black experience in America was somewhat different. Here the colonized were brought to the "mother" country to be enslaved and exploited. Internal colonialism thus involves the conquest and subjugation of a people and their physical removal to the ruling state. The command of the resources of the captive people (their labor power) followed. One can find parallel cases in the

SOURCE: *Social Problems*, Spring 1971, pp. 433–441.

histories of ancient Egypt, Greece, and Rome. In these nations slaves were also brought to the mother country to be exploited, to do the dirty work of these "great societies." The grandeur of the mother country was built on the backs of the exploited slaves.

In the United States an important part of the capital accumulated in the early nineteenth century also came from slave labor. North (1961) suggests that the timing and place of an economy's development is determined by the success of its export sector and the disposition of the income received by the export sector. He argues that in the key years in which capital accumulation took place, "it was the growth of the cotton textile industry and the demand for cotton which was decisive. The vicissitudes of the cotton trade were the most important influence upon the varying rates of growth in the economy during the period" (1961:67). That New England merchants, through their control over the foreign trade and commerce of the country, and over insurance and shipping, did much of the actual accumulating should not be allowed to obscure this point. Cotton was the strategic variable. It paid for our imports, and "the demand for western foodstuffs and northeastern services and manufacturers was basically dependent upon the income received from the cotton trade." (North: 1961:67). This is not an attempt to single out one factor as providing the "key" to development; but as cotton was the "carrier" industry inducing economic growth, so slavery was the basis of cotton production. Often the terrible burden of slavery is acknowledged, but rarely is the contribution of slave labor to the capital accumulation process seen as the very sizable factor in American development that it truly was.

To bring the story quickly to the present, the relevant question is: did the freeing of the slaves make a structurally significant difference in the colonial relationship? A comparison between the black ghetto as a colony within the United States today and the typical ex-colony which has gained its nominal political independence yet remains in neo-colonial subjugation suggests that in both instances formal freedom is not to be equated with real freedom.

Introductory chapters of a standard development textbook present a description of the typical less-developed country: low per capita income, high birth rate, a small, weak middle class, low rates of increase in labor productivity, in capital formation, and in domestic savings, as well as a small monetized market. The economy of such a country is heavily dependent on external markets, where its few basic exports face an inelastic demand (i.e., a demand which is relatively constant regardless of price and so expanding total output may not mean higher earnings.) The international demonstration effect (the desire to consume the products which are seen generally available in the wealthier nations) works to increase the quantity of foreign goods imported to the underdeveloped country, putting pressure on their balance of payments since the value of imports exceeds the value of exports. Much of the small modern sector of the underdeveloped economy is owned by outsiders. Local entrepreneurship is limited, and in the absence of intergovernmental transfers, things might be still worse.

The economic relations of the ghetto to white America closely parallel those between third world nations and the industrially advanced countries. The ghetto are for the most part unskilled. Businesses lack capital and managerial know-how. Local markets are limited. The incidence of credit default is high. Little saving takes place in the ghetto, and what is saved is usually not invested locally. Goods also has a relatively low per capita income and a high birth rate. Its residents and services tend to be "imported" for the most part, only the simplest and the most labor-intensive are produced locally. The ghetto is dependent on one basic export—its unskilled labor power. Aggregate demand for this export does not increase to match the growth of the ghetto labor force and unemployment is prevalent. Cultural imperialism is also part of the relationship; ghetto schools traditionally teach the history of the "Mother Country" as if blacks had no part in its development, as if blacks had no identity of their own, no culture, no origins worthy of mention in the chronicles of the world's nations and peoples. The dominant culture is constantly held up as good, desirable, worthy of emulation. The destruction of the indigenous culture is an important weapon in creating dependence and reinforcing control.

Consumer goods are advertised 24 hours a day on radio and television; ghetto residents are constantly reminded of the availability of goods and services which they cannot afford to buy. Welfare payments and other governmental transfers are needed to help pay for the ghetto's requirements. Welfare, however, only reinforces the dependency relationship, reinforces the psychology of inferiority, keeping body barely together even as it gnaws at the soul, sapping militancy and independence. (It should also be said in this context that the welfare rights movement shows both a greater reservoir of strength and a political awareness of the role of welfare in attempting to perpetuate inequality.) Local businesses are owned, in large numbers, by non-residents, many of whom are white. Marginal, low-profit businesses are more likely to be owned by blacks; larger, more profitable ones are owned by whites (Heilbrun, 1970; Zweig, 1970). Important jobs in the local public economy (teachers, policemen, and postmen) are held by white outsiders. These "disparities" are not lost on area residents, many of whom see the ownership patterns, the direction and nature of capital flows, as both systematic and endemic to a system of colonialism.

It has been suggested that the distortion of the local economy caused by outside ownership can be compared to the creation of underdevelopment in external colonies through processes described by Frank (1967). In this light, the dishonest practices of ghetto merchants (Caplovitz, 1967; Sturdivant, 1969) and the crippling effects on ghetto residents (Grier and Cobbs, 1968; Clark, 1965) can be seen not as unfortunate occurrences which come about through "unfair dealings" by greedy individuals, but rather as the direct result of the unequal power relations between the internal colony and the white mother-country.

The conclusion has been drawn from the colonial model that attention should be centered on attempting to create community control over the local public economy, to encourage black ownership in the private sector, and in some cases to promote collectivization of the local economy. These political and economic programs may be seen as attempts to achieve black power. This phrase, greeted only a few years back with great horror by many whites and also some blacks, has been accepted, accommodated, and increasingly, it is charged, used by the same forces which have long controlled the destiny of the black ghettos to impose the equivalent of neo-colonialism. The objective of indirect rule can be detected in statements such as the following by Jacob Javits, . . . addressing the United States Chamber of Commerce in 1968. "American business has found that it must develop host country management and new forms of joint ownership in establishing plants in the fiercely nationalistic less-developed countries, (so too) this same kind of enlightened partnership will produce the best results in the slums of our own country." It is not only the desire to continue to do business which leads to a willingness to accept blacks as junior partners; long-range self-interest dictates such a policy on even more basic grounds of self-interest. For example, the final report from a conference for corporate executives held at the Graduate School of Business at Columbia University in January 1964 stresses that "practical businessmen must recognize that this (ghetto rebellion) is a deep-seated economic problem that threatens every business, perhaps even our business system" (Ginsberg, 1964:87). Since that meeting the corporate house organs and business community journals have been flooded with articles stressing the need for corporate involvement.

The rationale for this new found interest has not gone unnoticed by blacks, who have placed "black capitalism" and "corporate involvement" in the context of neo-colonialism. Allen (1969:187–8), for example, writes:

> . . . any black capitalist or managerial class must act, in effect, as the tacit representative of the white corporations which are sponsoring that class. The task of this class is to ease corporate penetration of the black communities and facilitate corporate planning and programming of the markets and human resources in those communities. This process occurs regardless of the personal motivations of the individuals involved, because it stems from the nature of the corporate economy itself and the dependent status of the fledgling, black capitalist-managerial class.

Increasingly even the acquiring of political control of city hall in predominantly black urban areas is a "hollow prize," since the local tax base just cannot support the programs needed by the central cities. The "independent" local political administration is dependent on "foreign aid" from the external mother country. Hence the total independence of a black nation would mean even greater poverty for blacks who would have their labor power and little else. Independence based on community control would have a less extreme, but essentially similar result, perpetuating division within the working class.

Such an analysis also suggests that black power need not finally be measured by its ability to establish black autonomy from white society. Black control over the black community brings benefits only if it is within the context of an ability to enforce demands for the transfer of significant resources. Effectiveness in this area necessitates alliances with other groups to pressure for common goals. The questions of alliance with whom and for what have generally been answered: coalition with the labor movement to redistribute resources to the working class and low income people, away from corporations and all those enjoying "unearned" income. (See Rustin, 1966). While this answer appears in accord with some strands of Marxian theory, it is an answer which has been repeatedly rejected by most white workers and their union leadership.

Blauner (1969:393) has argued that the utility of the colonial analogy depends upon the distinction between "colonization as a process and colonialism as a social, economic, and political system" arguing that "Important as are economic factors, the power of race and racism cannot be sufficiently explained through class analysis." (1969:394) Blauner (1969:396) stresses the "common *process* of social oppression" which he sums up in his discussion of "the colonization complex."

Blauner's distinction makes the colonial analogy a more acceptable one. At the same time it points in the direction of a wider theory of exploitation in which colonization as a process can be seen as a method of class subjugation in which part of the working class—black Americans, and indeed Mexican Americans, Puerto Ricans, and others are separated out as a distinct group from the rest of the working class to serve the function of a pariah group creating division in the working class and perpetuating division within the working class.

The reasons an alliance has been difficult to forge must be investigated in more detail in terms of the objective relations between white and black workers in the historic development of American capitalism.

BLACKS AS A MARGINAL WORKING CLASS

Marxists have long recognized that some segments of the working class enjoy privileges and material gain at the expense of other workers. (Thompson, 1964; Hammonds, 1928). Engels saw the small minority of skilled artisans in the England of 1844 as forming "an aristocracy among the working class" (a phrase appearing in the introduction of the 1892 edition of *The Conditions of the Working Class in England in 1844*). Lenin in the eighth chapter of *Imperialism* suggests that at least some segments of the working class benefit from the exploitation of colonial labor.

The marginal working class, Leggett (1968:14) has written, "refers to a sub-community of workers who belong to a subordinate ethical or racial group which is unusually proletarianized and highly segregated. Workmen of this type fill many manual roles in heavy industry and face an inordinant amount of economic insecurity. This is evidenced by their large concentration in marginal occupational positions, their lack of formal education, and finally and most obviously, their high rate of unemployment." The isolation of the blacks is in many respects similar to that of other workers who are forced to form their own separate communities. Kerr and Siegel (1954:191) describe the coal town and the logging camp as ghetto-like, worlds unto themselves, in which a sense of group solidarity develops. "These communities," they write, "have their own codes, myths, heroes, and social standards. There are few neutrals in them to mediate the conflicts and dilute the mass . . . all the members of each of these groups have the same grievances." The strike for the isolated mining town is "a kind of colonial revolt against far removed authority, an outlet for accumulated tensions, and a substitute for occupational and social mobility." (Kerr and Siegel 1954:192). The ghetto rebellion can be described in similar terms.

The extent to which the capitalist class is able to isolate segments of the working class from each other strengthens its position. By creating a marginal working class of blacks and giving white workers a relatively more privileged position, it strengthens its control. If one group of workers are able to command higher pay, to exclude others from work, and if the other group or groups of workers are limited in their employment opportunities to the worst jobs and lowest pay, then a marginal working class has been created which benefits the labor aristocracy and to an even greater extent the capitalist class. The marginal working class produces goods which are generally available below the cost which would have been obtained if they had received wages closer to those paid to the labor aristocracy which had used its bargaining position to its own advantage. Thus Hobsbawn suggests, "The aristocracy of labor arises when the economic circumstances of capitalism make it possible to grant significant concessions to the proletariat, while certain strata manage, by means of their special scarcity, skill, strategic position, organizational strength, etc., to establish notably better conditions for themselves than the rest" (1970:50). In just such a manner has black labor generally been excluded from equal status, to the benefit of white society—capitalist and worker alike.

From the time black slaves were free to sell their labor as a commodity, they came to serve both as a reserve army and as a pool of labor ready of necessity to do the "dirty work" for the society at low wages. In the first role they served as an equilibrating factor in the economy. In periods of labor shortage blacks have made important gains, but with economic downturns they have been systematically displaced. Thus the jobs that blacks were recruited for in the labor shortages of World War I and the prosperity of the twenties were taken away in the Depression. Ross (1967:15) writes: "There was widespread invasion of Negro jobs by unemployed whites, often with the assistance of employers, unions, and lawmakers. Municipal licensing ordinances were reviewed in the South in order to drive Negroes out of barbering, plumbing, and other new occupations Negroes had entered during recent years." In the second role they were restricted to the most menial, physically exhausting, and alienating labor which the white society offered. Furthermore, this allowed white society to enjoy a profusion of goods and services at prices much lower than if these commodities had been produced at prevailing white worker wages. Thus blacks served in part as the classic Marxian reserve army and also as a "non-competing group," to borrow a term from another 19th century student, John Cairnes.

Therefore, it is important to see that the position of blacks in the society is primarily a result of their position as a marginal working class. Under American capitalism someone has always played this role. Traditionally immigrant groups have served as the structural equivalent of the blacks, as a white marginal working class. In England, until the arrival of great numbers of Pakistanis in recent years, the Irish were the major occupants of this position.

In the United States institutionalized discrimination contributes to particular forms of poverty among blacks and enhances the privileges of many whites. Discrimination is the medium—in the context of U.S. economic and social history—by which a special kind of poverty and a special kind of labor reserve is maintained.

"As in the case of white poverty, Negro poverty—more clearly seen because of its extreme character—is a function of the industrial and economic structure. Elimination of discrimination will not eliminate such major sources of poverty as unemployment, casual and intermittent jobs and low-paid occupations" (Magdoff, 1965:75–6). It is within this structural framework that the place of blacks as a marginal working class becomes clearer. It is not only that blacks are often at the end of the hiring line, but also that to some extent they are standing in a different line.

> The manpower problems of the urban ghetto appear best defined in terms of a dual labor market: a *primary* market offering relatively high-paying, stable employment, with good working conditions, chances

of advancement and equitable administration of work rules; and a *secondary* market, to which the urban poor are confined, decidedly less attractive in all of these respects and in direct competition with welfare and crime for the attachment of the potential labor force (Piore, 1968:—23).

RACE, CLASS AND SOCIAL CHANGE

The possibilities for change on a class basis are constrained by forces largely beyond the control of black Americans. Obstacles include not merely material benefits whites receive from the exploitation of blacks, but important "psychic income" as well. Whites gain in relative status if blacks are held down. Fear of blacks is an integral accompaniment to these feelings of superiority.

Whites are made to feel better off than the blacks and so less prone to demand better pay and working conditions; on the other hand, if they become militant they can be replaced by blacks who will work for less. This factor is most relevant in low wage unskilled and semi-skilled employment. An economic system based on individual competition breeds a social system based on relative income and status. One fears moving down the status hierarchy and so fears those below trying to move up. The degree to which the individual aspires to move up leads him to identify with the group above him.

> The net result of all this is that each status group has a deep-rooted psychological need to compensate for feelings of inferiority and envy toward those above by feelings of superiority and contempt for those below. It thus happens that a special pariah group at the bottom acts as a kind of lightning rod for the frustrations and hostilities of all the higher groups, the more so the nearer they are to the bottom. It may even be said that the very existence of the pariah group is a kind of harmonizer and stabilizer of the social structure—so long as the pariahs play their role passively and resignedly. (Baran and Sweezy, 1970:309).

Thus the gains from racism often appear to outweigh the material losses. White workers' subjective calculations on the matter are not made without pressures of employers who encourage racism as well as union officials who do the same partly out of fear of new leadership groups emerging, and partly out of the recognition that if the employer can exploit black workers less he may seek to exploit whites more. It seems also that both workers and their union leaders are heavily conditioned by the "scarcity consciousness" bred during the Great Depression and sustained in each downturn. The supply of union workers is to be kept down.

If the costs and benefits of present racist arrangements to white workers are crucial determinants of the future of race relations, it is not the only key. The costs of perpetuating racism and the repression which accompanies this policy will be determined largely by the militancy of blacks and their white supporters. The climate will be further tempered by the type and number of jobs the economy generates. A slack labor market means more competition and racial tensions. A growing economy has greater potential to bring benefits to all and so minimize both race and class conflicts.

Another important factor is the apparent trend toward bifurcation within the black community. On the one hand, the black middle-class seems to have significantly expanded. The 1970 Census data should allow confirmation of this growth. Some commentators even speak of an emerging black "silent majority" (Hamilton, 1970). On the other hand, in the hard core urban poverty area conditions appear to be getting worse. The use of averages for all non-whites masks these counter trends. It may well be that even as more blacks reach middle-class status, the black underclass will become both objectively worse off and more volatile (Brimmer, 1970 and Hacker, 1970). The middle-class blacks assuming positions in the wider society will be increasingly called upon to keep the lid on things by whites and at the same time will be under pressure from below to identify with the continuing black struggle, or be denounced as oreos (like the cookie, black on the outside, white on the inside). Identity questions and the political dilemma of the black middle-class are likely therefore to intensify. Some significant degree of job integration may be possible for the middle-class black but for the vast majority of ghetto blacks, integration can only have less and less meaning, given population trends and the persistence of housing segregation. The recent employment gains of middle-class blacks have for the most part been outside the ghetto. Unlike the other black bourgeois who lived off of the larger black community, the additions to the black middle-class more and more work in the white world. Attempts to strengthen the traditionally small black entrepreneurial class which is seen as crucial by some policy makers if community stability is to be achieved in ghetto areas, have, in spite of much publicity, not been overly successful.

Even programs of "Black Capitalism," which promise to "give them a piece of the action," as President Nixon often phrased it during the last presidential campaign, are little heard of these days. The reason is evident in government statistics. There are not many profitable honest business opportunities available in the ghetto. As the minority group program of the Small Business Administration expanded in recent years, the default rate also climbed to unacceptable rates and the program has been downgraded. Similarly job creation in the private sector has been quietly shelved as the economy has moved downward. Programs to redistribute even relatively insignificant resources to black urban poor have been interpreted as race legislation and resisted by conservatives both in and out of Congress. It is the failure of liberal solutions which is startling when contrasted with the last decade's War on Poverty and Great Society rhetoric. The failure of these approaches to date has not led to searching for more basic reforms of existing economic and social institutions. The pessimism which seems to affect a large part of those academics actively engaged in policy research seems to be well founded—the inaction of government officials except selectively in the area of law enforcement is difficult to ignore.

How matters will develop in this area in the longer run is more difficult to envisage. A number of factors seem to be important. First, there is the question of the type of structural transformation the economy will undergo in the next decade. The rate at which unskilled low-paying jobs decrease as a proportion of total employment, the rate of increase in jobs requiring significant amounts of education, and the progress blacks make in educational attainment certainly provide one key. The growth of the number of educated blacks in white collar positions of high relative status may create resentment on the part of white blue collar workers whose relative position in the status hierarchy is diminished. They may react, especially as their numbers diminish through slower growth rates in blue collar occupations, especially in the skilled trades, by excluding the less educated blacks who cannot hope for white collar jobs but who are objectively qualified to enter these trades. The manner in which demand and supply in different occupations reach equilibrium may become more artificial as, for example, blacks become more heavily represented in government jobs and continue to be excluded from construction work. Second, the overall stability and rate of growth of the economy cannot but help influence black progress and white acceptance of black gains. White workers secure in their own positions and enjoying increases in real wages more willingly accept black gains. Also in terms of government expenditures for minority poor, spending more out of greatly expanded resources may be accompanied by a lighter tax burden, especially if war expenditures are also contained. On the other hand, a mild downturn such as the one now current accentuates racial conflicts as the competition for resources intensifies. Paradoxically, a severe downturn which was clearly induced by the Government's unwillingness to regulate the economy might lead to the imposition of social controls and government intervention and planning which would be in the interests of both the white working-class and minority groups. The potential for movement in this direction is certainly greater than in the 1930's. All of this is of course speculation. The point is that we have reached the situation in which we come to realize that our policy choices in this area are more and more conditioned by constraints originating elsewhere in the economy.

REFERENCES

Allen, Robert L.
  1969   *Black Awakening in Capitalist America.* New York: Doubleday, pp. 187–188.
Baran, Paul A. and Paul M. Sweezy
  1970   "Monopoly capitalism and race relations," in David Mermelstein (ed.), *Economics: Mainstream Readings and Radical Critiques.* New York: Random House.
Blauner, Robert
  1969   "Internal colonialism and ghetto revolts." Social Problems (Spring).
Boggs, James
  1968   *Manifesto for a Black Revolutionary Party.* Philadelphia: Pacesetters.
Brimmer, Andrew F.
  1970   "Economic progress of Negroes in the United States: The deepening schism." Presented at the Founders' Day Convocation at Tuskegee Institute. Mimeo.
Caplovitz, David
  1967   *The Poor Pay More.* New York: The Free Press.
Clark, Kenneth B.
  1965   *Dark Ghetto.* New York: Harper & Row.
Frank, Andre Gunter
  1967   *Capitalism and Underdevelopment in Latin America.* New York: Monthly Review Press.

Ginsberg, Eli (ed.)
1964   *The Negro Challenge to the Business Community.* New York: McGraw-Hill.
Grier, William H. and Price M. Cobbs
1968   *Black Rage.* New York: Bantam Books.
Hacker, Andrew
1970   "The violent black minority." *New York Times Magazine,* May 10.
Hamilton, Charles V.
1970   "The silent black majority." *New York Times Magazine,* May 10.
Hammond, J. L. and Barbara
1928   *Town Laborer, 1760–1832, The New Civilization.* London: Longmans Green.
Heilburn, James
1970   "Jobs in Harlem: A statistical analysis." Regional Science Association Papers.
Henderson, William L. and Larry C. Ledebur
1970   *Economic Disparity: Problems and Strategies for Black America.* New York: The Free Press.
Hobsbawm, Eric
1970   "Lenin and the 'aristocracy of labor'," in Paul M. Sweezy and Harry Magdoff, *Lenin Today.* New York: Monthly Review, p. 50.
Javits, Jacob
1968   "Remarks to the 56th annual meeting of the United States Chamber of Commerce," in United States, *Congressional Record,* 90th Congress, 2nd Session, May 7.
Kerr, Clark and Abraham Siegel
1954   "The interindustry propensity to strike—An international comparison," in Arthur Komhauser, Robert Dubin, and Arthur M. Rose (eds.), *Industrial Conflict.* New York: McGraw-Hill.
Leggett, John C.
1968   *Class, Race and Labor.* New York: Oxford University Press.
Magdoff, Harry
1965   "Problems of United States capitalism," in Ralph Miliband and John Saville, *The Socialist Register 1965.* New York: Monthly Review Press, pp. 75–76.
Meranto, Philip (ed.)
1970   *The Kerner Report Revisited.* University of Illinois: Institute of Government and Public Affairs, June.
North, Douglass C.
1961   *The Economic Growth of the United States, 1790–1860.* Englewood Cliffs, N.J.: Prentice-Hall.
Parenti, Michael
1970   "The possibilities for political change," in Philip Meranto (ed.), *The Kerner Commission Revisited.* Urbana: University of Illinois, Institute of Government and Public Affairs.
Piore, Michael J.
1968   "Public and private responsibility in on-the-job training of disadvantaged workers." Department of Economics Working Paper, No. 23. Cambridge: M.I.T., June.
Report of the National Advisory Commission on Civil Disorders
1968   New York: Bantam Books.
Ross, Arthur M.
1967   "The Negro in the American economy," in *Employment, Race, and Poverty,* (ed.) Arthur M. Ross and Herbert Hill. New York: Harcourt, Brace & World.

Rustin, Bayard
    1966   "Black power and coalition politics." *Commentary* (September).
Sturdivant, Frederick D. (ed.)
    1969   *The Ghetto Marketplace.* New York: The Free Press.
Tabb, William K.
    1970   *The Political Economy of the Black Ghetto.* New York: W. W. Norton.
Thompson, E. P.
    1964   *The Making of the English Working Class.* New York: Pantheon Books.
United States Bureau of the Census and the Bureau of Labor Statistics
    1970   *The Social and Economic Status of Negroes in the United States, 1969.* Washington D.C.: Government Printing Office, p. 75.
Zweig, Michael
    1970   ."Black capitalism and the ownership of property in Harlem." Stony Brook Working Paper No. 16. Stony Brook: Economic Research Bureau, State University of New York, August.

VII. WORKERS AND THE "MERITOCRACY" DEBATE: GENES AND CLASS

INTRODUCTION

As we previously noted, one of the major elements of the "postindustrial" society theme is the overriding importance of education and knowledge as strategic factors of production. Therefore, increasingly, cognitive skills become prerequisites for economic success and power. Recently, some analysts have associated the capacity to acquire cognitive skills primarily with differences in genetic endowment. Under these circumstances does the liberal commitment to equality of opportunity lead paradoxically to class divisions based on inherited mental abilities? These issues have caused considerable controversy among liberals and radicals.

Are class divisions and inequalities affected substantially by differences in genetic endowments of social groups or are they primarily products of historically conditioned, changeable modes of organizing production and work processes?

One of the ablest exponents of the determining role of genetic endowment in class structure has been Richard Herrnstein, of the Harvard University psychology department. The gist of Herrnstein's "message" may be presented in the form of a syllogism which he formulates as follows:

(1) If differences in mental abilities are inherited, and

(2) If success requires these abilities, and

(3) If earnings and prestige depend on success,

(4) Then social standing (which reflects earnings and prestige) will to some extent be based on inherited differences among people.

Herrnstein's challenge to both liberals and radicals is that the removal of social and economic barriers to education and access to high-level jobs will produce a class-divided society based on "meritocratic" principles, a society in which mental "ability" (largely inherited) governs the distribution of income, prestige, and power. The selections below include liberal and radical reactions to this argument, as well as Herrnstein's response to some of his critics.

Deutsch and Edsall, arguing from an "environmentalist" perspective, question the adequacy of Herrnstein's evidence and reproach him for understating the full effect of differences in environmental conditions in determining differences in I.Q. They also note that even if Herrnstein's syllogism is correct it would help to explain only the rank order of different occupational strata in modern society,

312

not the magnitude of differences in their rewards. The latter "can be controlled to a considerable extent by the organized desires of society." Thus different societies differ markedly in the extent of income and status inequalities of occupations.

In "I.Q. in the U.S. Class Structure," Bowles and Gintis subject to critical scrutiny an undisputed assumption of both liberal "environmentalists" and proponents of the determining role of genetic endowment in socioeconomic inequality: "that I.Q. is of basic importance to economic success." For Bowles and Gintis, the debate on the degree of heritability of I.Q. is largely irrelevant to an explanation of the intergenerational reproduction of class and occupational inequality. Their article presents empirical support for the position that the independent contribution of I.Q. to the achievement of "economic success" (a combined measure of an individual's income and the social prestige of his occupation) is substantially less than the impact of class background and education. The influence of the latter on economic success operates primarily not through the creation of cognitive skills but through the creation of appropriate personality traits ("motivation, orientation to authority, discipline, internalization of work norms"). However, although a family's position in the class structure is reproduced largely independently of its intellectual skills, the recent emphasis on intelligence as the basis for economic achievement "serves to legitimize an authoritarian, hierarchical, stratified, and unequal economic system of production, and to reconcile the individual to his or her objective position within this system."

THE MERITOCRACY SCARE

Karl W. Deutsch
Thomas Edsall

"Thanks be to Ammon," said the Senior Temple Priest to the young novice, "that our hieroglyphic writing is so difficult that only a few men are intelligent enough to learn to read and write. And thanks be to Ammon that we have learned to measure the average number of hieroglyphics learned by the young scholars in our temple schools. We can now compare the number of hieroglyphs by which a boy exceeds or falls short of the average number of hieroglyphs mastered by his age group. Thus the Archpriest in charge of Temple Studies can compute the hieroglyphic quotient—which the Phoenician traders call H.Q. for short—for every boy in our school; and from this H.Q. we can foretell a boy's chances for a career in the priesthood: whether he will become a member of the priestly caste, commanding the secret arts of reading and writing, or whether he will be cast out from here and put among the menials to drag stones to the site of the next pyramid."

"But it is not true, oh venerable one," said the novice, "that the children of the temple priests are encouraged from infancy to pay attention to hieroglyphics? They see them on their toys and in their nurseries, and their fathers and mothers praise them for anything they learn. Besides, their fathers and mothers feed them fish which stimulates their mental powers."

"My son," thundered the Senior Priest, "you have listened to the evil counsels of the levelers and pyramid destroyers who rave about making all men equal. Some are driven by sentimentality or by envy of their betters, but they all disregard the hard evidence of science. If all boys lived in the same homes, had the same food and toys and got the same encouragement, the smartest boys would still learn hieroglyphs faster and become the priests, and the slower learners would again have to dig ditches and drag stones. Moreover, the smart boys would beget smart boys who would again win in the examinations and the dull boys again would have dull children who would fail."

The prototypes of our imaginary temple priest and his novice are preserved only as mummies in museums—but their social philosophy still marches on. Richard Herrnstein, chairman of the Harvard University psychology department, has revived the ancient arguments, and so have researchers such as Arthur R. Jensen, William Shockley and others. Of all these, Herrnstein's argument has developed most clearly the proposition that the more we succeed in eliminating all social barriers to education and to promotions to top level jobs according to

SOURCE: *Society*, September/October 1972, pp. 71–73, 77–79.

merit, the more profoundly society will become divided into hereditary castes or classes, based on innate biological differences in mental endowment. Essentially, Herrnstein advances [four] propositions:

1. The I.Q. measures a relatively general mental capacity of each individual, reaching well beyond not only the particular test items but also well beyond the entire subculture of the middle-class oriented school systems of white populations in the highly indutrialized regions of Western Europe and North America.

2. This I.Q. is directly and completely relevant for competence, success and leadership in practical life, and hence for the acquisition of income, social status and superior class position.

3. This I.Q. is hereditary to a large degree.

4. If environmental determinants of the I.Q. (which he sees as already relatively weak) were to be made wholly equal, hereditary differences in I.Q. would produce hereditary classes or castes, based on real merit in job performance, which in turn would be based on inherited differences in intelligence; the class system would thus become deepened by strengthening its already existing association with superior or inferior biological endowment.

All the foregoing points are proved by hard scientific facts which strongly suggest that the aims of liberals and egalitarians are quite misleading; apart from these ill-advised hopes, our society is already moving toward a "growing meritocracy" and "the biological stratification of society would surely go on whether we had tests to gauge it on or not." Herrnstein himself sums up . . . :

> The message is so clear that it can be made in the form of a syllogism:
> If differences in mental abilities are inherited, and
> If success requires those abilities, and
> If earnings and prestige depend on success,
> Then social standing (which reflects earnings and prestige) will be based to some extent on inherited differences among people.

Envisioned as the end product of his syllogism is a class society "with ever greater innate separation between the top and the bottom," precisely as a necessary result of any greater equality of opportunity for the masses of our population. As barriers of social, cultural and economic discrimination are successfully removed, and as society becomes richer and more complex, says Herrnstein:

> There will be precipitated out of the mass of humanity a low capacity (intellectual and otherwise) residue that may be unable to master the common occupations . . . and are most likely to be born to parents who have similarly failed. . . . The troubles . . . that the syllogism explains, have already caught the attention of alert social scientists, like Edward Banfield, whose book *The Unheavenly City* describes the increasingly chronic lower class in America's central cities. . . . What is most troubling about this prospect is that the growth of a virtually hereditary meritocracy will arise out of the successful realization of contemporary political and social goals.

Herrnstein does not say that contemporary liberal and equalitarian aspirations and policies are undesirable or misguided. He merely suggests that they will have troubling and unexpected results—namely, a hereditary stratified society and thus apparently the opposite of the liberal goal of greater social equality and openness. In fact, however, if his predictions were correct, most people would conclude that efforts toward greater equality of opportunity would be self-defeating, and as practical persons they might be inclined to reduce their support for them. Herrnstein does not explicitly connect race with the hereditary differences in I.Q. However, when he refers to the "increasingly chronic lower class in America's central cities" which has "already caught the attention of alert social scientists," people are likely to think of blacks, even if no such thought ever crossed Herrnstein's mind.

For its explicit statements and the implications likely to be derived from them, Herrnstein's thesis must be carefully and critically examined. It is our view that his syllogism is false, both in its inner structure and in its overall design.

First, there is a basic limitation in his evidence. The chief studies he cites for the allegedly minor effect of the environment on the observed I.Q. are based on cases in which the range of environmental differences was seriously restricted. Lewis Terman's 1,500 manifestly gifted children came overwhelmingly from the white professional and middle classes. The 122 pairs of identical twins in the four studies were white, and they were placed into foster homes chosen by social agencies in an effort to make them similar. In how many of these 112 pairs were the twins separated by the full range of environmental and social contrasts found even within the white community, from "upper-upper" class in the home of one twin to "lower-lower" class in the home of the other? It seems likely that in no case was one twin raised in a white middle-class home and the other in a black ghetto slum, ravaged by poverty and unemployment.

For the same reason, however, it seems clear that the studies cited by Herrnstein offer no adequate evidence on the effect of the full range of environmental conditions—and particularly not on the full downward effect of unfavorable conditions—which exist among slums and suburbs, black and white, functional illiterates and fourth-generation college families in the United States. In particular, the 15 percent spread between the average observed I.Q.'s of white and black children, reported by Herrnstein, seems well within the 20 percent spread in average I.Q.'s that can be accounted for by environmental conditions, according to Herrnstein's own argument.

Apart from this basic weakness in regard to evidence, Herrnstein's sociological prospect seems inherently self-contradictory. Herrnstein's notion that "there will be *precipitated out* of the mass of humanity a low capacity (intellectual *and otherwise*) residue . . . born to parents who have similarly failed" (italics supplied) seems to imply a significant degree of social segregation and assortative mating, so that persons of similar low I.Q. heredity would mainly have to marry among each other.

It also seems to imply that most of the other characteristics that attract people into mutual love and marriage are also hereditary and linked to the I.Q. As Herrnstein sees it, vigor, beauty, strength, kindness, patience, sensitivity, perceptiveness and other characteristics of human behavior and personality would not cut across any supposedly hereditary I.Q. distribution and would not dilute or largely nullify its effects for most families in the course of a few generations. If any such hereditary effects existed, a considerable degree of formal or informal segregation in social contacts and in the choice of marriage partners would be essential if the social effects of the heredity assumed by Herrnstein were to persist over time.

But this assumption implicit in Herrnstein's argument conflicts with his assumption of equality of environmental conditions and education opportunity. The more marked would be the segregation of "the increasingly chronic lower class in America's central cities," the less one could pretend that educational opportunities for their children had become equal, since these opportunities depend on home and neighborhood, and food and care, both parental and in infancy. at least as much as they do on formal schooling.

Herrnstein's image of an open society is a caricature; it is an utterly competitive society in which all doors are locked and can be opened by no other key than success in competition.

In Herrnstein's world, no one does any work for its own sake or for the sake of other people, nor does anyone choose a job because he likes to do it. If ditch-digging carried the highest external rewards, says Herrnstein, the ablest individuals would compete for ditchdiggers' jobs. All work and all jobs are seen as strictly instrumental, as means for the procurement of income, power and prestige. It is a joyless rat-race where people do not enjoy the work they do, and where even their external rewards are only valuable to them insofar as they put their gains ahead of other people. It is a world from which what Veblen called the "instinct of workmanship" is absent, and greed, fear and envy reign supreme. Is this a world for which the most intelligent of the children of mankind should strive?

In reality, people often gain a sense of success and achievement from developing powers that they did not previously have, and they often measure their success against space, time, nature or their own past rather than only against their fellows. Herrnstein states that "ability . . . expresses itself in labor only for gain," such as "material wealth . . . social and political influence or relief from threat."

By his exclusive stress on the competitive aspect of human behavior, Herrnstein fails to deal with the fact that different societies differ widely in the extent of the gap which they have maintained between the incomes of different occupations and professions. In the United States the gap between the income of successful professionals and the federal minimum wage has shrunk since the 1930s from a factor of ten to a factor of seven or less. The Gini index of income inequality in France in 1962 was 52 percent, nearly twice as much as what it was then in Israel, Norway and Denmark, yet all four societies were functioning. The extent of income and status inequality is changeable. It varies among countries. It has changed in the past and it can change again.

The emotional tone of Herrnstein's presentation is designed to evoke the image of a radically class-divided future society with a vast distance in income, comfort and well-being separating a meritocratic elite from the eternal failures huddled in the central cities, and this difference maintained forever by biology. Omitted is the fact that even if his syllogism were correct, the difference would be one of only rank order—who is slightly ahead of whom else—and not necessarily by any large amount of the actual distance in income and living conditions among the different ranks.

Consider a population whose genetically constituted I.Q.'s range from 50 to 150. If, however, the same population were exposed to widely varying environmental influences, then unfavorable environmental conditions would drop the lowest group from 50 to 40 while favorable conditions would boost the observable I.Q. of the most gifted to 180, corresponding in each case to the 20 percent influence of environment in Herrnstein's model. The range of observed I.Q.'s would be from 40 to 180, that is, a full 140 points. This would correspond to the situation which, according to Herrnstein, now prevails.

If complete environmental equality could be established, and if the environment were uniformly unfavorable, then the range of observed I.Q.'s would shrink to 80 points, from 40 at the bottom to 120 at the top. If the environment were uniformly favorable, the range would be somewhat larger, from 60 to 180 points, but still smaller than the present 140 range.

Finally, if environment were uniform but relatively neutral, observed I.Q.'s would range from 50 to 150, or 100 points. In every case, however, a uniform environment would make the range of observed I.Q.'s smaller than it is now. Even if the society should not choose to reduce the inequality of rewards for different kinds of jobs, uniform conditions for the development of everyone's I.Q. would make society somewhat more equal than it is now, and not more unequal, as Herrnstein says.

A similar consideration applies to the size of Herrnstein's envisioned hereditary caste of low I.Q. failures at the bottom. A uniform environment could increase their relative numbers only if it were unfavorable. If the uniform environmental conditions were favorable or even merely neutral, they would reduce substantially the number of low I.Q. individuals in a society—a number now swelled by those whose observed I.Q. has been depressed by unfavorable environmental influences.

Nor does Herrnstein pay any attention to the meaning of material differences at different levels of social wealth. Much of modern economics is based on the principal of declining marginal utility, which says that the more we have of any particular good, the less valuable to us will be any further units of it. For example, Bedouins may fight for a water hole in the desert but in American offices there is little bloodshed for access to the water cooler. A family that has no automobile may bitterly envy the one-car family next door. If the poorer family had one car, they might still envy, though less bitterly, their two-car neighbors. But if the poorer family had two cars and the neighbors four, they might pity them for their parking problem.

Differences in rewards, in short, can be controlled to a considerable extent by organized desires of society. Societies with very different differences between top and bottom rewards have all proved viable, notwithstanding Wilfredo Pareto's opposite predictions; and the meaning of the remaining differences may depend to a considerable extent on how much people have already.

But the rest of Herrnstein's syllogism is by no means perfect. Indeed, it is quite inappropriate. A syllogism is deterministic by its nature. It says, if a implies b, and if a is certain, then b is certain. It represents a yes-or-no type of reasoning that fails to say "how much." To answer the questions "how much" and "how soon"—which are questions of both science and practical life—we must use the language of probability. Throughout most of the natural and social sciences, probabilistic models have long replaced syllogisms. It is a little surprising to see a syllogism return, like a ghost from the grave. What happens to that ghost if we translate its assertions into the language of probability?

Converting Herrnstein's syllogism into a probabilistic model cuts down the likelihood of a son's social standing being predictable from the father's I.Q. to less than 8 percent or to 10 percent if both father and mother were recruited from the small 150 I.Q. population. . . . In the third generation, even if true breeding were maintained throughout, the influence of the great-grandparents' I.Q. on their grandchild's social standing would be about 5 percent.

How do such calculations compare with some real life data? A study by Morris Janowitz of over 3,300 West German respondents in 1955 compared their social class with that of their father's. It showed that 51 percent of the upper-middle-class persons in 1955 were children of fathers who had themselves been members of the upper-middle class in 1939. During the same period, however, the proportion of upper-middle-class positions in the sample had expanded by more than one-half, from 3 percent to 4.6 percent of the total, so that it was somewhat easier by 1955 to enter the somewhat expanded upper-middle-class. German society between 1939 and 1955 had undergone a whole series of dramatic shake-ups, and yet the relative closure of the upper-middle class had remained above 50 percent. In an American sample of over 1,300 persons, 36 percent upper-middle-class fathers were reported having adult children in the upper-middle class.

If we compare these actual figures about two contemporary industrial societies with the frequency with which high I.Q. fathers would get into the upper-middle class themselves, and once arrived there, would produce children who again would be members of the upper-middle class, it would seem to follow from our probabilistic model that a society that truly equalized all environmental factors influencing the manifest I.Q. would have a much more open professional stratum, and hence would be a much more open society, than the societies in which we live today—that is, 13 percent or about one-eighth of the highly gifted fathers would be likely to have children in the upper-middle class. Compared to the actual 35 percent of such fathers in the American sample, and 51 percent in the German sample studied by Janowitz, a society with a uniformly fair environment would be almost three times as open as the American society and nearly four times as open as the German society of the 1950s. Herrnstein's prediction of an increasingly stratified society as the supposed result of greater fairness in the environment seems therefore quite false.

All these calculations only deal with the question of who would get into the competitively sought top jobs or top professions. They say nothing about the extent and direction in which these professions would change nor about the remaining differences in the economic and status rewards that might remain attached to each of them.

"Technological advance," says Herrnstein, "changes the market place for I.Q. . . . It is more than likely that some of those put out of the old jobs will not have the I.Q. for the new ones. Technological unemployment is not just a matter of . . . 'retraining' if the jobs created are beyond the native capacity of the newly unemployed."

Herrnstein is right in one important point. Performance is not entirely relative to culture. Insofar as—but only insofar as—the I.Q. measures any general capacities for attention, accuracy, speed and reliability of responses, it measures something that is important in many cultures now and that will be important in all cultures where large numbers of people must keep themselves alive in any moderately difficult environment.

But Herrnstein's argument goes far beyond this valid point. Accuracy and attention are widely needed and will be needed in the future. But extremely competitive hierarchies and caste societies are not based on any such long-lasting necessity.

First of all, jobs are not produced by blind nature or a mindless market place alone. Jobs can be designed, and are being designed often, by industrial engineers who give professional thought to alternative possibilities in designing man-machine systems. If we should allow our technology to design permanently a job structure that makes a substantial portion of our population unemployable, unhappy and oppressed, our I.Q. would be low indeed.

Secondly, and in actual fact, the current trends of economic and technological development in industrial countries do not necessarily all point in this direction. It is true that many jobs today make specific minimum demands, if they are to be done well. Often, however, these job thresholds are much lower than the median I.Q. found among people who held such jobs in 1945 or presumably among those who are holding them today. The large amount of variation around the average I.Q., which Herrnstein himself reports, bears this out. Thus the average I.Q. among truck drivers reported in the study he cites was about 88 but the actual range of I.Q.'s among the truck drivers tested varied from 16 to 149.

EMPATHY NEEDED

One major trend in modern technology has been to push many of these minimum job thresholds downward—contrary to Herrnstein's suggestion that the progress of technology would push these thresholds up. Cashiers in retail stores used to be experienced people good at doing quick additions and subtractions; modern cash registers permit high school girls to do the job at supermarket checkout counters.

The "computer visionaries" whose views Herrnstein casts aside so lightly may have a more specific suggestion to contribute. Computers can mechanize many numerical calculations; they can help to mechanize reaction speeds and steadiness of repetitive surveillance; indeed they can perhaps mechanize many of the operations, performance of which is now measured as part of the I.Q. But it is much harder for computers to mechanize empathy and sympathy, patience and care, responsiveness and love. There is no evidence that the need for these qualities will decline in the job structure of the foreseeable future and there is some evidence that the need for these types of behavior will increase.

In all advanced industrial countries, employment in the service sector is growing faster than employment in agriculture, mining or manufactures. Even so, many services have remained underdeveloped or neglected.

These trends toward a larger service sector will not lead us back toward a comfortable middle class surrounded by numerous servants, but they may lead us toward a society in which the care and maintenance of homes and gardens, streets and cities, parks and beaches, will be a matter for a whole array of new industries creating well-paid and well-respected jobs for a wide range of human talents. Even more important may become the care of infants and children, so as to cut down the many hours of virtual imprisonment of mothers of young children with their offspring, while providing also during their hours away from home the children with the individual attention, the mental stimulation, and the emotional support they need. Something similar may apply to medical and convalescent care and to the care of the old.

Throughout history, crucial job thresholds have been lowered. The more stupidly a job is organized, the more intelligent a person may have to be to do it. Reading and writing hieroglyphics quickly may have indeed required a high I.Q. Alphabetic writing made literacy vastly easier and more accessible.

Society, in its evolution, not only has the power to make jobs easier through technology but it also has the power to make needed skills more widespread, and potentially almost universal through education and acculturation.

Changes in the level of education and general culture are concealed by the I.Q. for which the same number 100 has to designate the mid-point of the scale wherever that mid-point might be. A test score that would have got us an I.Q. of 100 in 1918 would not get us a score of 100 today; more likely it would place us somewhere between 80 and 90. The median I.Q. of our children and our grandchildren may well be correspondingly higher.

This secular rise in the mid-point of the I.Q. scale reflects, of course, in considerable part the spread of education throughout our population. As this mid-point rises, however, it will carry a larger number of our population across the entrance threshold of an increasing range of jobs, even if our job structure should remain exactly what it is. In fact, the two processes may come to work together: technological change may make many jobs easier to perform while education may qualify more people to perform them.

In sum, the society of the future may be wealthier in economic goods, more powerful in technology, but above all more fluid in its job and social structures. It should be more able to design and redesign its own character instead of accepting it as unchangingly ordained by biology or fate.

The trends toward greater openness, equality and brotherhood, to which we have pointed, do not constitute necessities but opportunities. Even so, they seem to us more promising, more probable and more powerful than the points which Dr. Herrnstein stressed. They can prove decisive, if we learn to act on them.

I.Q.: MEASUREMENT OF RACE AND CLASS?

Richard Herrnstein
Karl W. Deutsch
Thomas B. Edsall

[HERRNSTEIN:]

The criticism by Karl W. Deutsch and Thomas Edsall . . . of my article in the *Atlantic* magazine ("I.Q.,"/September 1971) calls for response. My theory hinges on an argument in the form of a syllogism:

(1) If differences in mental abilities are inherited, and

(2) If success requires those abilities, and

(3) If earnings and prestige depend on success,

(4) Then social standing (which reflects earnings and prestige) will be based to some extent on inherited differences among people.

Let us start with what the syllogism does *not* say. First, it does not say, imply, or insinuate anything about racial, ethnic, or sex differences in mental abilities, nor about the origin—whether in upbringing or the genes—of such differences as may show up in empirical studies. In my article, I explicitly took an agnostic stand on group—as distinguished from social class—differences in inherited mental ability. Second, the syllogism does not say that right now, in America or anyplace else, society is either perfectly meritocratic or stratified primarily by genetic differences between the classes.

Now, what does the syllogism say, and why did I choose to say it in public? The syllogism says that social classes will be genetically distinct insofar as the criteria for class membership are themselves genetic. Moreover, it says that mental capacities qualify as such criteria, since they contribute to social standing and are substantially (at least 50%) heritable. It follows, for example, that equality of opportunity—while no doubt desirable on grounds both moral and practical—could lead to an increasingly genetic gap between the social classes.

Nothing in Deutsch and Edsall's criticisms affects any part of this argument. However, since they do manage to make almost all the common mistakes (and a few uncommon ones) provoked by this tender subject, it may be useful to sample further.

1) They assert that crucial studies of inheritance focus on middle and upper class families, and hence underestimate the negative impact of the environment on, for example, lower class families, which, in turn, overestimates the genetic factor. Specifically, they say, Terman's study of gifted children (which, incidentally, contributed *no* data to the estimate of heritability and is therefore

SOURCE: *Society*, May/June 1973, pp. 5–6.

irrelevant to this issue) used a sample that "came overwhelmingly from the white professional and middle classes." In fact, about one-third of Terman's gifted children came from families earning less than skilled workers at that time. Many came from the minor business and clerical stratum and below. While the sample was disproportionately drawn from the higher classes, in absolute composition it was far from "overwhelmingly" overprivileged.

To substantiate their criticism further, they say that the 122 pairs of identical twins who had been separated in infancy or childhood and grew up nevertheless to have an 85% correlation in I.Q. had been placed in similar environments by foster agencies, which caused the high correlation. As far as I (or any other commentator) can tell from the published accounts of these twin studies, this assertion is without foundation. Deutsch and Edsall ask rhetorically, "In how many of these 122 pairs were the twins separated by the full range of environmental and social contrasts found even within the white community, from 'upper-upper' class in the home of one to 'lower-lower' class in the home of the other?" The answer, for the largest of the four twin studies making up the 122 pairs, is that the distribution of children into foster homes was *random*.

Not just in the foregoing study, but in general there is remarkably little impact of the gross indices of the social class of foster parents on their wards' I.Q.'s. In fact, adopted children, separated from their mothers within two weeks of birth, grow up with a higher correlation between their I.Q.'s and their natural parents' education or occupational level than with their foster parents' education or occupational level. This is not to say that foster parents can contribute nothing to children's mental capacity, but merely that class factors do not account for the I.Q. correlations among natural kinfolk. It is foolish, as well as wrong, to suppose that the study of the genetic component of mental capacity has overlooked the possible role of social factors. On the contrary, it has been much on our minds.

2) As Deutsch and Edsall point out, the tendency for I.Q. to run in families is enhanced if marriage unites people with similar I.Q.'s. Then, for some unstated reason, the authors deny any substantial degree of "assortative mating," as it is called. However, according to the most recent comprehensive estimates, the I.Q. correlation between spouses is considerable, slightly higher than the correlation between natural siblings growing up together—that is, someplace above 50%.

3) Messrs. Deutsch and Edsall believe I am insensible to the pleasures of work, depicting me as crassly materialistic instead. On the contrary, I am quite sure that, for example, many vaudevillians loved their calling. Even so, it did not keep the more successful of them from switching over to radio and motion pictures when the audience switched, taking their rewards with them. My argument does not assume that no one "chooses a job because he likes to do it." Rather, it assumes only that society's rewards—from gratitude to cash—have an important effect on the flow of labor. The inherent qualities of work combine with society's rewards to give a gradient of net gain. The gradient expresses a social consensus on the relative values of different lines of work.

4) At several points in their article, my critics perform some numerical computations to underscore their arguments. Their arithmetic is relentlessly incompetent. I advise non-experts to ignore all their sentences with numbers in them, or to consult a quantitative geneticist. Let us consider a couple of instances.

a) Deutsch and Edsall feel that a heritability of .8 is not all that important, for there is .2 left for the environment. "Consider," they say, "a population whose genetically constituted I.Q.'s range from 50 to 150. If the same population were exposed to widely varying environmental influences, then unfavorable environmental conditions would drop the lowest group from 50 to 40 while favorable conditions would boost the observable I.Q. of the most gifted to 180, corresponding in each case to the 20 percent influence of environment in Herrnstein's model. The range of observed I.Q.'s would be from 40 to 180, that is, a full 140 points." They go on in this vein, taking 20% of the I.Q. itself as the measure of environmental effect. However, the .8 and .2 *do not* concern proportions of the I.Q., but proportions of the variability of I.Q. Thus, to say that I.Q. has a heritability of .8 means that 80% of the observed variance is accounted for by variations in the genes. The remaining 20% is accounted for by variations in *everything else*— the social and cultural environment, the physical environment, prenatal influences, the expertise with which the test was administered and how the testee felt that day, imperfections in the test itself, and so on. How much of the 20% is of the sort that can be altered by design, we cannot say. However, let us suppose that we could wipe out all of this non-genetic variation, leaving only the 80% variation due to the genes. My critics' arithmetic would even then be wholly inappropriate, for there would be a 20% reduction in the *variance* of I.Q., not in its *range*. In other words, right now the standard deviation of I.Q. (which is the technical measure of its variability) is about 16 points—which means that between I.Q. 84 and 116 falls about 70% of the population. If *all* non-genetic variations—from prenatal illness to family attitudes to incompetent testers—were blotted out, the standard deviation would contract to 14.3 and 70% of the population would still fall between 85.7 and 114.3.

b) Deutsch and Edsall continually confuse the correlation between individual parents and their children with heritability: "the bright 150 I.Q. men and women must have chosen marriage partners whose average I.Q. cannot have been much above 126. This, of course, is still a good deal higher than the national average of 100, but this limited degree of assortative mating reduces the actual heritability of the I.Q. of the offspring of these brilliant fathers or mothers and their merely bright spouses to a more modest .6. This compares with a reported heritability of .5 between any parent and child in the general population." In fact, a simple polygenic trait (involving several genes) that has a heritability of 100% and for which there is no assortative mating will show a parent-child correlation of .5 because either parent contributes only 50% of his or her offspring's genes. The heritability is a ratio between the genetic variance of a trait and its total variance, not the correlation between individual parents and their children. It can be mathematically proved that this biologically useful index estimates the correlation between a person's genetic endowment for a trait (the genotype) and his realized amount of it (the phenotype) by the following formula: correlation $= \sqrt{\text{heritability}}$. For the I.Q., with a heritability of .8, the correlation between phenotype and geneotype is in the vicinity of .9, whether one takes assortative mating to be high or low.

5) I noted in my article that one corollary of the syllogism concerns technological change. If automation should superannuate jobs requiring low I.Q.'s more rapidly than those requiring high ones, then I.Q. will become an increasingly important factor in employment and social standing. As I understand it, Deutsch and Edsall do not object to this conditional proposition, but rather to the possibility that automation may be drifting in the indicated direction. They note, no

doubt correctly, that automation has eased many jobs that used to be intellectually demanding. I am willing to agree that cash registers have lowered the average intellectual caliber of cashiers in stores. But, at the same time, the net effect of automation on the job market as a whole has unquestionably been in the other direction. At least since the turn of the century, the labor market has been shifting away from the low I.Q. jobs towards the high ones. The sharply decreasing proportion of farm workers and blue-collar laborers in the labor force shows that intellectual requirements are becoming more widespread. It is a commonplace that education is increasingly important for occupational success—which Deutsch and Edsall do not dispute—but they do not recognize the implication of this. Educational success is itself highly dependent on the mental capacities measured in I.Q. tests. The growing importance of education betrays the growing role of mental ability in our economic life.

So much for details, Deutsch and Edsall's criticisms were not, after all, directed at the substance of my argument, but at the forbidden conclusions I arrive at— such as that social manipulation of schools, political systems, economic practices and the other instruments of liberal reform are not likely to create an egalitarian society, or that equalization of opportunity may easily have the paradoxical effect of making social-status separations more dependent on genetic differences between people and their families. We may choose to go ahead with liberal reform and equalization anyway, but these conclusions, and the others not reviewed here, stand unscathed, still unsettling and still based on unrefuted fact.

[DEUTSCH AND EDSALL:]

Professor Herrnstein's letter fails to meet the main points of our criticism. He repeats his thesis "equality of opportunity . . . could lead to an increasingly genetic gap between the social classes," and he defends his method of syllogistic reasoning which makes such an outcome not merely possible but almost certain.

We claimed that Professor Herrnstein's method here is inappropriate and his conclusion false. His syllogism represents limited probabilities as if they were certainties. Differences in mental abilities may be *partly* inherited; success requires *in part* such abilities; earnings and prestige *in part* depend on success; and social standing reflects *in part* earnings and prestige. Multiplying these four "in part" probabilities suggests that social standing may be related *in very limited part*— only by a weak probability—to inherited differences. Dr. Herrnstein in his letter continues to omit and ignore the italicized qualifications of his argument. It remains absolute and hence misleading.

He persists in the same error with regard to long-term class divisions. Social classes, as the word is ordinarily used, imply some heritability and stability of class positions across several generations. Dr. Herrnstein does say that a regressing toward the mean tends to move the average I.Q. of children closer to the middle than the average I.Q. of their parents. Over three or four generations, therefore, the expectable hereditary advantage or handicap of the grandchildren or great-grandchildren will be greatly reduced. This point destroys much of Dr. Herrnstein's picture of a stable genetically based class society—but he ignores it.

Our third point was that technology may tend to loosen, not tighten, the link between social privilege and power and any one inheritable trait. Technology has made an increasing part of social and cultural arrangements discretionary. In many countries, people can change a larger portion of human affairs than they could in the past. But Dr. Herrnstein treats the social order and the class system as given and unchanging.

With regard to his argument about numbers, in the article he linked the factor of heritability to the range of I.Q.'s and to the expectable I.Q. of a given child as follows:

> Heritability is first and foremost the measure of breeding true, useful for predicting how much of some trait the average offspring in a given family will have. For example, to predict the I.Q. of the average offspring in a family:
>
> (1) Average the parents' I.Q.'s.
> (2) Subtract 100 from the result.
> (3) Multiply the result of (2) by .8 (the heritability).
> (4) Add the result of (3) to 100.
>
> Thus, given a mother and father each with I.Q.'s of 120, their average child will have an I.Q. of 116. Some of their children will be brighter and some duller, but the larger the family, the more nearly will the average converge onto 116. With parents averaging an I.Q. of 80, the average child will have an I.Q. of 84.

In his letter, he seems to have changed his mind and says: "The heritability is a ratio between the genetic variance of a trait and its total variance, not the correlation between individual parents and their children." Perhaps our offense in Mr. Herrnstein's eyes consists in treating seriously his argument as he had formulated it for popular consumption.

The heart of the matter remains Professor Herrnstein's misrepresentation of limited and sequentially diminishing probabilities as if they were certainties. His may be an effective way of popularizing a dogma, but a poor way of picturing reality and the findings of science.

I.Q. IN THE U.S. CLASS STRUCTURE

Samuel Bowles
Herbert Gintis

INTRODUCTION

The 1960s and early 1970s have witnessed a sustained political assault against economic inequality in the United States. Blacks, women, welfare recipients, and young rank-and-file workers brought the issue of inequality into the streets, forced it onto the front pages, and thrown it into the legislature and the courts. The dominant response of the privileged has been concern, tempered by a hardy optimism that social programs could be devised to reduce inequality, alleviate social distress, and bring the nation back from the brink of chaos. This optimism has been at once a reflection of and rooted in a pervasive body of liberal thought, as codified in modern mainstream economics and sociology. At the core of this conventional wisdom in the social sciences is the conviction that in the advanced capitalist system of the United States, significant progress toward equality of economic opportunity can be achieved through a combination of enlightened persuasion and social reforms, particularly in the sphere of education and vocational training.

The disappointing results of the War on Poverty, the apparent lack of impact of compensatory education, and in a larger sense the persistence of poverty and racism in the United States have dented the optimism of the liberal social scientist and the liberal policy maker alike. The massive and well-documented failure of the social reformers of the 1960s invited a conservative reaction, most notably in the resurgence of the genetic interpretation of I.Q. Sensing the opportunity afforded by the liberal debacle, Arthur Jensen began his celebrated article on the heritability of I.Q. with "Compensatory education has been tried, and apparently it has failed." In the debate that has ensued, an interpretation of the role of I.Q. in the class structure has been elaborated: the poor are poor because they are intellectually incompetent; their incompetence is particularly intractable because it is rooted in the genetic structure inherited from their poor and also intellectually deficient parents.[1] An explanation of the intergenerational reproduction of the class structure is thus found in the heritability of I.Q. The idea is not new: an earlier wave of genetic interpretations of economic and ethnic inequality followed in the wake of the purportedly egalitarian but largely unsuccessful educational reforms of the Progressive Era.[2]

The revival of the debate on the genetic interpretation of economic inequality

SOURCE: *Social Policy,* November/December 1972, January/February 1973, pp. 65–82, 93–95.

is thus firmly rooted in the fundamental social struggles of the past decade. Yet the debate has been curiously superficial. "The most important thing . . . that we can know about a man," says Louis Wirth, "is what he takes for granted, and the most elemental and important facts about a society are those that are seldom debated and generally regarded as settled."[3] This essay questions the undisputed assumption underlying both sides of the recently revised I.Q. controversy: that I.Q. is of basic importance to economic success.

Amid a hundred-page statistical barrage relating to the genetic and environmental components of intelligence, the initiator of the most recent exchange[4] saw fit to devote only three sparse and ambiguous pages to this issue. Later advocates of the "genetic school"[5] have considered this "elemental fact," if anything, less necessary of support. Nor has their choice of battleground proved injudicious: to our knowledge not one of their environmentalist critics has taken the economic importance of I.Q. any less for granted.[6]

We shall begin this essay with a brief review of the I.Q. controversy itself, paying special attention to the social consequences of intelligence differentials among races and social classes. This review inspires one highly perplexing question: why have American social scientists so consistently refused to question the actual role of intelligence in occupational success and income determination, in spite of the fact that the empirical data necessary for such an endeavor are well known?

In the third section we shall summarize the results of several years of empirical research into the economic importance of I.Q.[7] Our findings, based for the most part on widely available published data, document the fact that I.Q. is not an important cause of economic success; nor is the inheritance of I.Q. the reason why rich kids grow up to be rich and poor kids tend to stay poor. The intense debate on the heritability of I.Q. is thus largely irrelevant to an understanding of poverty, wealth, and inequality of opportunity in the United States.

These results give rise to a host of novel questions—novel in the sense that they would never be asked were the importance of I.Q. "taken for granted." We shall deal with some of these in succeeding sections of this essay. First, if the social function of I.Q. distinctions is not status attainment or transmission, what *is* their function? We shall argue in section four that the emphasis on intelligence as the basis for economic success serves to legitimize an authoritarian, hierarchical, stratified, and unequal economic system of production, and to reconcile the individual to his or her objective position within this system. Legitimation is enhanced merely when people *believe* in the intrinsic importance of I.Q. This belief is facilitated by the strong associations among all the economically desirable attributes—social class, education, cognitive skills, occupational status, and income—and is integrated into a pervasive ideological perspective. Second, if I.Q. is not a major determinant of social class structure, what is? What are the criteria for admission to a particular social stratum, and what are the sources of intergenerational status transmission? We shall argue in section five that access to an occupational status is contingent upon a pattern of noncognitive personality traits (motivation, orientation to authority, discipline, internalization of work norms), as well as a complex of personal attributes including sex, race, age, and educational credentials through which the individual aids in legitimating and stablizing the structure of authority in the modern enterprise itself. Thus, primarily because of the central economic role of the school system, the generation of adequate cognitive skills becomes a spin-off, a by-product of a stratification mechanism grounded in the supply, demand, production, and certification of these noncognitive personal attributes. . . . [This section is not included. For a formulation of these themes see the articles by Bowles and Harrison, pp. 233–236, 273–278.]

THE I.Q. CONTROVERSY

The argument that differences in genetic endowments are of central and increasing importance in the stratification systems of advanced technological societies has been advanced, in similar forms, by a number of contemporary researchers.[8] At the heart of this argument lies the venerable thesis that I.Q., as measured by tests such as the Stanford-Binet, is largely inherited via genetic transmission, rather than molded through environmental influences.*

This thesis bears a short elucidation. That I.Q. is highly heritable is merely to say that individuals with similar genes will exhibit similar I.Q.'s *independent* of differences in the social environments they might experience during their mental development. The main support of the genetic school is several studies of individuals with precisely the same genes (identical twins) raised in different environments (i.e., separated at birth and reared in families with different social statuses). Their I.Q.'s tend to be fairly similar.[9] In addition, there are studies of individuals with no common genes (unrelated individuals) raised in the same environment (e.g., the same family) as well as studies of individuals with varying genetic similarities (e.g., fraternal twins, siblings, fathers and sons, aunts and nieces) and varying environments (e.g., siblings raised apart, cousins raised in their respective homes). The difference in I.Q.'s for these groups is roughly conformable to the genetic inheritance model suggested by the identical twin and unrelated individual studies.[10]

As Eysenck suggests, while geneticists will quibble over the exact magnitude of heritability of I.Q., nearly all will agree heritability exists and is significant.[11] Environmentalists, while emphasizing the paucity and unrepresentativeness of the data, have presented rather weak evidence for their own position and have made little dent in the genetic position.[12] Unable to attack the central proposition of the genetic school, environmentalists have emphasized that it bears no important social implications. They have claimed that, although raised in the context of the economic and educational deprivation of Blacks in the United States, the genetic theory says nothing about the "necessary" degree of racial inequality or the limits of compensatory education. First, environmentalists deny that there is any evidence that the I.Q. difference between Blacks and whites (amounting to about fifteen I.Q. points) is genetic in origin,† and second, they deny that any estimate

---

* By I.Q. we mean—here and throughout this essay—those cognitive capacities that are measured on I.Q. tests. We have avoided the use of the word "intelligence" as in its common usage it ordinarily connotes a broader range of capacities.

† Does the fact that a large component of the differences in I.Q. among whites is genetic mean that a similar component of the differences in I.Q. between Blacks and whites is determined by the former's inferior gene pool? Clearly not. First of all, the degree of heritability is an *average,* even among whites. For any two individuals, and a *fortiori,* any two groups of individuals, observed I.Q. differences may be due to any pro-

of heritability tells us much about the capacity of "enriched environments" to lessen I.Q. differentials, either within or between racial groups.*

---

portion of genes and environment—it is required only that they average properly over the entire population. For instance, *all* of the difference in I.Q. between identical twins is environmental, and presumably a great deal of the difference between adopted brothers is genetic. Similarly we cannot say whether the average difference in I.Q. between Irish and Puerto Ricans is genetic or environmental. In the case of Blacks, however, the genetic school's inference is even more tenuous. Richard J. Light and Paul V. Smith ("Social Allocation Models of Intelligence: A Methodological Inquiry." *Harvard Educational Review,* 39 No. 3 [August 1969]), have shown that even accepting Jensen's estimates of the heritability of I.Q., the Black-white I.Q. difference could easily be explained by the average environmental differences between the races. Recourse to further experimental investigations will not resolve this issue, for the "conceptual experiments" that would determine the genetic component of Black-white differences cannot be performed. Could we take a pair of Black identical twins and place them in random environments? Clearly not. Placing a Black child in a white home in an overtly racist society will not provide the same "environment" as placing a white child in that house. Similarly looking at the difference in I.Q.'s of unrelated Black and white children raised in the same home (whether Black or white, or mixed) will not tell us the extent of genetic differences, since such children cannot be treated equally, and environmental differences must continue to persist (of course, if in these cases, differences in I.Q. disappear, the environmentalist case would be supported. But if they do not, no inference can be made).

* Most environmentalists do not dispute Jensen's assertion that existing large-scale compensatory programs have produced dismal results. (See Jensen, "How Much Can We Boost I.Q.," and, for example, Harvey Averch et al., *How Effective is Schooling? A Critical Review and Synthesis of Research Findings* (Santa Monica: RAND Corporation, 1972). But this does not bear on the genetic hypothesis. As Jensen himself notes, the degree of genetic transmission of any trait depends on the various alternative environments that individuals experience. Jensen's estimates of heritability rest *squarely* on the existing array of educational processes and technologies. Any introduction of new social processes of mental development will change the average unstandardized level of I.Q., as well as its degree of heritability. For instance, the almost perfect heritability of height is well documented. Yet the average heights of Americans have risen dramatically over the years, due clearly to change in the overall environment. Similarly, whatever the heritability of I.Q., the average unstandardized test scores rose 83 percent between 1917 and 1943. See Jencks, *Inequality.*

But compensatory programs are obviously an attempt to change the total array of environments open to children through "educational innovation." While existing large-scale programs appear to have failed to produce significant gains in scholastic achievement, many more innovative small-scale programs have succeeded. See Carl Bereiter, "The Future of Individual Differences," *Harvard Educational Review,* Reprint Series No. 2 (1969), pp. 162–170; Charles E. Silberman, *Crisis in the Classroom* (New York: Random House, 1970); Averch, *How Effective Is Schooling?* Moreover, even accepting the genetic position should not hinder us from seeking new environmental innovation—indeed it should spur us to further creative activities in this direction. Thus, the initial thrust of the genetic school can be at least partially repulsed: there is no reliable evidence either that long-term contact of Blacks with existing white environments would not close the Black-white I.Q. gap, or that innovative compensatory programs (i.e., programs unlike existing white childrearing or education environments) might not attenuate or eliminate I.Q. differences that are indeed genetic.

But the environmentalists' defense strategy has been costly. First, plausible, if not logical, inference now lies on the side of the genetic school, and it's up to environmentalists to "put up or shut up" as to feasible environmental enrichment programs. Second, in their egalitarian zeal vis-à-vis racial differences, the environmentalists have sacrificed the modern liberal intepretation of social stratification. The modern liberal approach is to attribute social class differences to "unequal opportunity." That is, while the criteria for economic success are objective and achievement-oriented, the failures and successes of parents are passed onto their children via distinct learning and cultural environments. Thus the achievement of a more equal society merely requires that all youth be afforded the educational and other social conditions of the best and most successful.[13] But by focusing on the environmental differences *between* races, they implicitly accept that intelligence differences among whites of differing social class background are rooted in differences in genetic endowments. Indeed the genetic school's data comes precisely from observed differences in the I.Q. of whites across socioeconomic levels! The fundamental tenet of modern liberal social policy—that "progressive social welfare measures" can gradually reduce and eliminate social class differences, cultures of poverty and affluence, and inequalities of opportunity—seems to be undercut. Thus the "classical liberal" attitude,[14] which emphasizes that social classes sort themselves out on the basis of innate individual capacity to cope successfully in the social environment, and hence tend to reproduce themselves from generation to generation, is restored.[15]

The vigor of reaction in face of Jensen's argument indicates the liberals' agreement that I.Q. is a basic social determinant (at least ideally) of occupational status and intergenerational mobility. In Jensen's words, "psychologists' concept of the 'intelligence demands' of an occupation . . . is very much like the general public's concept of the prestige or social standing' of an occupation, and both are closely related to an independent measure of . . . occupational status."[16] Jensen continues, quoting O. D. Duncan: ". . . 'intelligence' . . . is not essentially different from that of achievement or status in the occupational sphere . . . what we now *mean* by intelligence is something like the probability of acceptable performance (given the opportunity) in occupations varying in social status."[17] Moreover, Jensen argues that the purported trend toward intelligence's being an increasing requirement for occupational status will continue.[18] This emphasis on the role of intelligence in explaining social stratification is set even more clearly by Carl Bereiter in the same issue of the *Harvard Educational Review:* "The prospect is of a meritocratic caste system, based . . . on the natural consequences of inherited differences in intellectual potential. . . . It would tend to persist even though everyone at all levels of the hierarchy considered it a bad thing."[19] Something like death and taxes.

Jensen et al. cannot be accused of employing an overly complicated social theory. Jensen's reason for the "inevitable" association of status and intelligence is that society "rewards talent and merit," and Herrnstein adds that society recognizes "the importance and scarcity of intellectual ability."[20] Moreover, the association of intelligence and social class is due to the "screening process,"[21] via education and occupation, whereby each generation is further refined into social strata on the basis of I.Q. Finally, adds Herrnstein, "new gains of wealth . . . will increase the I.Q. gap between upper and lower classes, making the social ladder even steeper for those left at the bottom."[22] Herrnstein celebrates the genetic school's crowning achievement by turning liberal social policy directly against itself, noting that the heritability of intelligence and hence the increasing pervasiveness of social stratification will increase, the more "progressive" our social policies: "the growth of a virtually hereditary meritocracy will arise out of the successful realization of contemporary political and social goals . . . as the environment becomes more favorable for the development of intelligence, its heritability will increase. . . ." [23] Similarly, the more we break down discriminatory and ascriptive criteria for hiring, the stronger will become the link between I.Q. and occupational success, and the development of modern technology can only quicken the process.[24]

Few will be surprised that such statements are made by the "conservative" genetic school. But why, amid a spirited liberal counterattack in which the minutest details of the genetic hypothesis are contested and scathingly criticized, is the validity of the genetic school's description of the social function of intelligence blandly accepted? The widespread agreement among participants in the debate that I.Q. is an important determinant of economic success can hardly be explained by compelling empirical evidence adduced in support of the position. Quite the contrary. As we will show in the next section, the available data point strongly to the unimportance of I.Q. in getting ahead economically. In Section IV we shall argue that the actual function of I.Q. testing and its associated ideology is that of legitimizing the stratification system, rather than generating it. The treatment of I.Q. in many strands of liberal sociology and economics merely reflects its actual function in social life: the legitimization and rationalization of the existing social relations of production.

THE IMPORTANCE OF I.Q.

The most immediate support for the I.Q. theory of social stratification—which we will call I.Q.-ism—flows from the strong association of I.Q. and economic success. This is illustrated in Table 1, which exhibits the probability of achieving any particular decile in the economic success distribution for an individual whose adult I.Q. lies in a specified decile.

The data, most of which was collected by the U.S. Census Current Population Survey in 1962, refer to "non-Negro" males, aged 25 to 34, from nonfarm background in the experienced labor force. We have chosen this population because it represents the dominant labor force and the group into which minority groups and women would have to integrate to realize the liberal idea of equal opportunity, and hence to whose statistical associations these groups would become subject. The data relating to childhood I.Q. and adult I.Q. are from a 1966 survey of veterans by the National Opinion Research Center and the California Guidance Study.[25] The quality of the data preclude any claims to absolute precision in our estimation. Yet our main propositions remain supported, even making allowance for substantive degrees of error. We must emphasize, however, that the validity of our basic propositions does not depend on our particular data set. While we believe our data base to be the most representative and careful construction from available sources, we have checked our results against several data bases, including Jencks, Hauser, Lutterman, and Sewell, Conlisk, Griliches and Mason, and

T A B L E 1*   **Probability of Attainment of Different Levels of Economic Success for Individuals of Differing Levels of Adult I.Q., by Deciles**

| | | ADULT I.Q. BY DECILES | | | | | | | | |
ECONOMIC SUCCESS BY DECILES	y x 10	9	8	7	6	5	4	3	2	1
10	30.9	19.8	14.4	10.9	8.2	6.1	4.4	3.0	1.7	0.6
9	19.2	16.9	14.5	12.4	10.5	8.7	7.0	5.4	3.6	1.7
8	13.8	14.5	13.7	12.6	11.4	10.1	8.7	7.1	5.3	2.8
7	10.3	12.4	12.6	12.3	11.7	11.0	10.0	8.7	7.0	4.1
6	7.7	10.4	11.4	11.7	11.8	11.5	11.0	10.1	8.7	5.7
5	5.7	8.7	10.1	11.0	11.5	11.8	11.7	11.4	10.4	7.7
4	4.1	7.0	8.7	10.0	11.0	11.7	12.3	12.6	12.4	10.3
3	2.8	5.3	7.1	8.7	10.1	11.4	12.6	13.7	14.5	13.8
2	1.7	3.6	5.4	7.0	8.7	10.5	12.4	14.5	16.9	19.2
1	0.6	1.7	3.0	4.4	6.1	8.2	10.9	14.4	19.8	30.9

* Table 1 corresponds to a correlation coefficient r = .52.[25a]
Example of use: For an individual in the 85th percentile in Adult I.Q. (x = 9), the probability of attaining between the 20th and 30th percentile in Economic Success is 5.3 percent (the entry in column 9, row 3).

Duncan and Featherman.[26] When corrections are made for measurement error and restriction of range (see Bowles[27] and Jencks), statistical analysis of each of these data bases strongly supports all of our major propositions.

The interpretation of Table 1 is straightforward. The entries in the table are calculated directly from the simple correlation coefficient between our variables Adult I.Q. and Economic Success. In addition to reporting the correlation coefficient, we have described these data in tabular form as in Table 1 to illustrate the meaning of the correlation coefficient in terms of the differing probability of economic success for people at various positions in the distribution of I.Q.'s. We cannot stress too strongly that while the correlation coefficients in this and later tables are estimated from the indicated data, the entries in the table represent nothing more than a simple translation of their correlations, using assumptions that—though virtually universally employed in this kind of research—substantially simplify the complexity of the actual data. Now, turning to the table, we can see, for example, that a correlation between these two variables of .52 implies that an individual whose adult I.Q. lies in the top 10 percent of the population has a probability of 30.9 percent of ending up in the top tenth of the population in economic success, and a probability of 0.6 percent of ending up in the bottom tenth. Since an individual chosen at random will have a probability of 10 percent of ending up in any decile of economic success, we can conclude that being in the top decile in I.Q. renders an individual (white male) 3.09 times as likely to be in the top economic success decile, and .06 times as likely to end up in the bottom, as would be predicted by chance. Each of the remaining entries in Table 1 can be interpreted correspondingly.

Yet tables 2 and 3, which exhibit the corresponding probabilities of economic success given number of years of schooling and level of socioeconomic background,[27a] show that this statistical support is surely misleading: even stronger associations appear between years of schooling and economic success, as well

TABLE 2* **Probability of Attainment of Different Levels of Economic Success for Individuals of Differing Levels of Education, by Deciles**

ECONOMIC SUCCESS BY DECILES	YEARS OF SCHOOLING BY DECILES									
y	x 10	9	8	7	6	5	4	3	2	1
10	37.6	22.3	14.6	9.8	6.6	4.3	2.6	1.4	0.6	0.1
9	20.9	19.5	16.2	13.1	10.3	7.9	5.7	3.8	2.1	0.6
8	13.5	16.1	15.3	13.8	12.0	10.1	8.0	5.9	3.7	1.4
7	9.1	13.0	13.8	13.6	12.8	11.6	10.0	8.0	5.6	2.5
6	6.1	10.2	12.0	12.8	12.9	12.5	11.6	10.1	7.8	4.0
5	4.0	7.8	10.1	11.6	12.5	12.9	12.8	12.0	10.2	6.1
4	2.5	5.6	8.0	10.0	11.6	12.8	13.6	13.8	13.0	9.1
3	1.4	3.7	5.9	8.0	10.1	12.0	13.8	15.3	16.1	13.5
2	0.6	2.1	3.8	5.7	7.9	10.3	13.1	16.2	19.5	20.9
1	0.1	0.6	1.4	2.6	4.3	6.6	9.8	14.6	22.3	37.6

* Table 2 corresponds to a correlation coefficient $r = .63$.

Example of use: For an individual in the 85th percentile in Education $(x = 9)$, the probability of attaining between the 20th and 30th percentiles in Economic Success $(y = 3)$ is 3.7 percent (the entry in column 9, row 3).

as between social background and economic success. For example, being in the top decile in years of schooling renders an individual 3.76 times as likely to be at the top of the economic heap, and .01 times as likely to be at the bottom, while the corresponding ratios are 3.26 and .04 for social background. It is thus quite possible to draw from aggregate statistics, equally cogently, both an "educational attainment theory" of social stratification and a "socioeconomic background" theory. Clearly there are logical errors in all such facile inferences.

Of course, the I.Q. proponent will argue that there is no real problem here: the association of social class background and economic success follows from the importance of I.Q. to economic success, and the fact that individuals of higher class background have higher I.Q. Similarly one may argue that the association of education and economic success follows from the fact that education simply picks out and develops the talents of intelligent individuals. The problem is that equally cogent arguments can be given for the primacy of either education or social class, and the corresponding subordinateness of the others. The above figures are equally compatible with all three interpretations.

In this section we shall show that all three factors (I.Q., social class background, and education) contribute independently to economic success, but that I.Q. is by far the least important. Specifically we will demonstrate the truth of the following three propositions, which constitute the empirical basis of our thesis concerning the unimportance of I.Q. in generating the class structure.

First, although higher I.Q.'s and economic success tend to go together, higher I.Q.'s are not an important cause of economic success. The statistical association between adult I.Q. and economic success, while substantial, derives largely from the common association of both of these variables with social class background and level of schooling. Thus to appraise the economic importance of I.Q., we must focus attention on family and school.

Second, although higher levels of schooling and economic success likewise tend to go together, the intellectual abilities developed or certified in school make little causal contribution to getting ahead economically. Thus only a minor portion of the substantial statistical association between schooling and economic success can be accounted for by the school's role in producing or screening cognitive skills. The predominant economic function of schools must therefore involve the accreditation of individuals, as well as the production and selection of personality traits and other personal attributes rewarded by the economic system. Our third proposition asserts a parallel result with respect to the effect of social class background.

Third, the fact that economic success tends to run in the family arises almost completely independently from any genetic inheritance of I.Q. Thus, while one's economic status tends to resemble that of one's parents, only a minor portion of this association can be attributed to social class differences in childhood I.Q., and a virtually negligible portion to social class differences in genetic endowments, even accepting the Jansen estimates of heritability. Thus a perfect equalization of I.Q.'s across social classes would reduce the integenerational transmission of economic status by a negligible amount. We conclude that a family's position in the class structure is reproduced primarily by mechanisms operating independently of the inheritance, production, and certification of intellectual skills.

Our statistical technique for the demonstration of these propositions will be that of linear regression analysis. This technique allows us to derive numerical estimates of the independent contribution of each of the separate but correlated

TABLE 3* **Probability of Attainment of Different Levels of Economic Success for Individuals of Differing Levels of Social Class Background**

ECONOMIC SUCCESS BY DECILES		SOCIAL CLASS BACKGROUND BY DECILES									
	y x	10	9	8	7	6	5	4	3	2	1
	10	32.6	20.4	14.5	10.7	7.8	5.7	3.9	2.5	1.4	0.4
	9	19.7	17.5	14.9	12.6	10.5	8.5	6.7	5.0	3.2	1.3
	8	13.8	14.9	14.1	12.9	11.6	10.1	8.6	6.9	4.9	2.4
	7	10.0	12.5	12.9	12.6	12.0	11.1	10.0	8.5	6.7	3.7
	6	7.3	10.4	11.5	12.0	12.0	11.7	11.1	10.1	8.5	5.3
	5	5.3	8.5	10.1	11.1	11.7	12.0	12.0	11.5	10.4	7.3
	4	3.7	6.7	8.5	10.0	11.1	12.0	12.6	12.9	12.5	10.0
	3	2.4	4.9	6.9	8.6	10.1	11.6	12.9	14.1	14.9	13.8
	2	1.3	3.2	5.0	6.7	8.5	10.5	12.6	14.9	17.5	19.7
	1	0.4	1.4	2.5	3.9	5.7	7.8	10.7	14.5	20.4	32.6

* Table 3 corresponds to a correlation coefficient $r = .55$.
Example of use: For an individual in the 85th percentile in Social Class $(x = 9)$, the probability of attaining between the 20th and the 30th percentile in Economic Success $(y = 3)$ is 4.9 percent (the entry in column 9, row 3).

influences (social class background, childhood I.Q., years of schooling, adult I.Q.) on economic success, by answering the question: what is the magnitude of the association between any one of these influences among individuals who are equal on some or all the others? Equivalently it answers the question: what are the probabilities of attaining particular deciles in economic success among individuals who are in the same decile in some or all of the above influences but one, and in varying deciles in this one variable alone?

The I.Q. argument is based on the assumption that social background and education are related to economic success *because* they are associated with higher adult cognitive skills. Table 4 shows this to be essentially incorrect. This table, by exhibiting the relation between adult I.Q. and economic success among individuals with the same social class background and level of schooling, shows that the I.Q.-economic success association exhibited in Table 1 is largely a by-product of these more basic social influences. That is, for a given level of social background and schooling, differences in adult I.Q. add very little to our ability to predict eventual economic success. Thus, for example, an individual with an average number of years of schooling and an average socioeconomic family background, but with a level of cognitive skill to place him in the top decile of the I.Q. distribution, has a probability of 14.1 percent of attaining the highest economic success decile. This figure may be compared with 10 percent, the analogous probability for an individual with average levels of I.Q. as well as schooling and social background. Our first proposition—that the relation between I.Q. and economic success is not causal, but rather operates largely through the effects of the correlated variables, years of schooling and social class background —is thus strongly supported.* We are thus led to focus directly on the role of

T A B L E 4* **Differential Probabilities of Attaining Economic Success for Individuals of Equal Levels of Education and Social Class Background, but Differing Levels of Adult I.Q.**

				ADULT I.Q. BY DECILES						
y	x 10	9	8	7	6	5	4	3	2	1
10	14.1	12.3	11.4	10.7	10.1	9.6	9.0	8.5	7.8	6.6
9	12.4	11.4	10.9	10.5	10.2	9.8	9.5	9.1	8.6	7.7
8	11.4	10.9	10.6	10.4	10.2	9.9	9.7	9.4	9.1	8.4
7	10.7	10.5	10.4	10.3	10.1	10.0	9.9	9.7	9.5	9.0
6	10.1	10.2	10.2	10.1	10.1	10.1	10.0	9.9	9.8	9.5
5	9.5	9.8	9.9	10.0	10.1	10.1	10.1	10.2	10.2	10.1
4	9.0	9.5	9.7	9.9	10.0	10.1	10.3	10.4	10.5	10.7
3	8.4	9.1	9.4	9.7	9.9	10.2	10.4	10.6	10.9	11.4
2	7.7	8.6	9.1	9.5	9.8	10.2	10.5	10.9	11.4	12.4
1	6.6	7.8	8.5	9.0	9.6	10.1	10.7	11.4	12.3	14.1

(left axis label: ECONOMIC SUCCESS BY DECILES)

* Table 4 corresponds to a standardized regression coefficient $\beta = .13$. Example of use: Suppose two individuals have the same levels of Education and Social Class Background, but one is in the 85th percentile in Adult I.Q. ($x = 9$), while the other is in the 15th decile in Adult I.Q. ($x = 2$). Then the first individual is $10.9/9.1 = 1.2$ times as likely as the second to attain the 8th decile in Economic Success (column 9, row 8, divided by column 2, row 8).

social class background and schooling in promoting economic success.

Turning first to schooling, the argument of the I.Q. proponents is that the

* This is not to say that I.Q. is never an important criteria of success. We do not contend that extremely low or high I.Q.'s are irrelevant to economic failure or success. Nor do

strong association between level of schooling and economic success exhibited in Table 2 [see page 335] is due to the fact that economic success depends on cognitive capacities, and schooling both selects individuals with high intellectual ability for further training and then develops this ability into concrete adult cognitive skills. Table 5 shows this view to be false. This table exhibits the effect of schooling on chances for economic success, for individuals who have the same adult I.Q. Comparing Table 5 with Table 2, we see that cognitive differences account for a negligible part of schooling's influence on economic success: individuals with similar levels of adult I.Q. but differing levels of schooling have substantially different chances of economic success. Indeed the similarity of tables 2 and 5 demonstrates the validity of our second proposition— that schooling affects chances of economic success predominantly by the non-cognitive traits which it generates, or on the basis of which it selects individuals for higher education.[28]

The next step in our argument is to show that the relationship between social background and economic success operates almost entirely independently of in-

T A B L E 5*   **Differential Probabilities of Attaining Economic Success for Individuals of Equal Adult I.Q. but Differing Levels of Education**

		YEARS OF SCHOOLING BY DECILES								
ECONOMIC SUCCESS BY DECILES	y x. 10	9	8	7	6	5	4	3	2	1
10	33.2	20.6	14.6	10.6	7.7	5.5	3.8	2.4	1.3	0.4
9	19.9	17.8	15.1	12.7	10.5	8.5	6.6	4.8	3.1	1.2
8	13.8	15.0	14.2	13.0	11.6	10.1	8.5	6.8	4.8	2.3
7	9.9	12.6	13.0	12.7	12.1	11.2	10.0	8.5	6.6	3.5
6	7.2	10.4	11.6	12.1	12.1	11.8	11.2	10.1	8.4	5.1
5	5.1	8.4	10.1	11.2	11.8	12.1	12.1	11.6	10.4	7.2
4	3.5	6.6	8.5	10.0	11.2	12.1	12.7	13.0	12.6	9.9
3	2.3	4.8	6.8	8.5	10.1	11.6	13.0	14.2	15.0	13.8
2	1.2	3.1	4.8	6.6	8.5	10.5	12.7	15.1	17.8	19.9
1	0.4	1.3	2.4	3.8	5.5	7.7	10.6	14.6	20.6	33.2

* Table 5 corresponds to a standardized regression coefficient $\beta = .56$.
   Example of use: Suppose two individuals have the same Adult I.Q., but one is in the 9th decile in Level of Education ($x = 9$), while the other is in the 2nd decile ($x = 2$). Then the first individual is $15.0/4.8 = 3.12$ times as likely as the second to attain the 8th decile in Economic Success (column 9, row 8, divided by column 2, row 8).

dividual differences in I.Q. Whereas Table 3 exhibits the total effect of social class on an individual's economic success, Table 6 exhibits the same effect among individuals with the same childhood I.Q. Clearly these tables are nearly identical. That is, even were all social class differences in I.Q. eliminated, a similar pattern of social class intergenerational immobility would result.[29] Our third proposition is thus supported: the intergenerational transmission of social and economic status operates primarily via noncognitive mechanisms, despite the fact that the school

we deny that for some individuals or for some jobs, cognitive skills are economically important. Rather, we assert that for the vast majority of workers and jobs, selection, assessed job adequacy, and promotion are based on attributes other than I.Q.

T A B L E 6* **Differential Probabilities of Attaining Economic Success for Individuals of Equal Early I.Q. but Differing Levels of Social Class Background**

		SOCIAL CLASS BACKGROUND BY DECILES								
y	x 10	9	8	7	6	5	4	3	2	1
10	27.7	18.5	14.1	11.1	8.8	6.9	5.3	3.9	2.5	1.1
9	18.2	15.8	13.8	12.1	10.5	9.0	7.6	6.1	4.5	2.4
8	13.7	13.8	13.0	12.1	11.1	10.1	8.9	7.6	6.1	3.7
7	10.7	12.0	12.1	11.8	11.3	10.7	9.9	8.9	7.5	5.0
6	8.4	10.5	11.1	11.3	11.3	11.1	10.7	10.0	9.0	6.6
5	6.6	9.0	10.0	10.7	11.1	11.3	11.3	11.1	10.5	8.4
4	5.0	7.5	8.9	9.9	10.7	11.3	11.8	12.1	12.0	10.7
3	3.7	6.1	7.6	8.9	10.1	11.1	12.1	13.0	13.8	13.7
2	2.4	4.5	6.1	7.6	9.0	10.5	12.1	13.8	15.8	18.2
1	1.1	2.5	3.9	5.3	6.9	8.8	11.1	14.1	18.5	27.7

(left axis label: ECONOMIC SUCCESS BY DECILES)

* Table 6 corresponds to a standardized regression coefficient $\beta = .46$.
Example of use: Suppose two individuals have the same Childhood I.Q., but one is in the 9th decile in Social Background, while the other is in the 2nd decile. Then the first is $18.5/2.5 = 7.4$ times as likely as the second to attain the top decile in Economic Success (column 9, row 10, divided by column 2, row 10).

system rewards higher I.Q.—the attribute significantly associated with higher social class background.

The unimportance of the specifically genetic mechanism operating via I.Q. in the intergenerational reproduction of economic inequality is even more striking. Table 7 exhibits the degree of association between social class background and economic success that can be attributed to the genetic inheritance of I.Q. alone. This table assumes that all direct influences of socioeconomic background upon economic success have been eliminated, and that the noncognitive components of schooling's contribution to economic success are eliminated as well (the perfect meritocracy based on intellectual ability). On the other hand, it assumes Jensen's estimate for the degree of heritability of I.Q. A glance at Table 7 shows that the resulting level of intergenerational inequality in this highly hypothetical example would be negligible.

The unimportance of I.Q. in explaining the relation between social class background and economic success, and the unimportance of cognitive achievement in explaining the contribution of schooling to economic success, together with our previously derived observation that most of the association between I.Q. and economic success can be accounted for by the common association of these variables with education and social class, support our major assertion: I.Q. is not an important intrinsic criterion for economic success. Our data thus hardly lend credence to Duncan's assertion that " 'intelligence' . . . is not essentially different from that of achievement or status in the occupational sphere,"[30] nor to Jensen's belief in the "inevitable" association of status and intelligence, based on society's "rewarding talent and merit,"[31] nor to Herrnstein's dismal prognostication of a "virtually hereditary meritocracy" as the fruit of successful liberal reform in an advanced industrial society.[32]

I.Q. AND THE LEGITIMATION OF THE HIERARCHICAL DIVISION OF LABOR

A Preview

We have disputed the view that I.Q. is an important causal antecedent of economic success. Yet I.Q. clearly plays an important role in the U.S. stratification system. In this section we shall argue that the set of beliefs surrounding I.Q. betrays its true function—that of legitimating the social institutions underpinning the stratification system itself.

T A B L E 7*   **The Genetic Component of Intergenerational Status Transmission, Assuming the Jensen Heritability Coefficient, and Assuming Education Operates Via Cognitive Mechanisms Alone**

		SOCIAL CLASS BACKGROUND BY DECILES								
y	x 10	9	8	7	6	5	4	3	2	1
10	10.6	10.3	10.2	10.1	10.0	10.0	9.9	9.8	9.7	9.4
9	10.4	10.2	10.1	10.1	10.0	10.0	9.9	9.9	9.8	9.6
8	10.2	10.1	10.1	10.1	10.0	10.0	9.9	9.9	9.9	9.8
7	10.1	10.1	10.1	10.0	10.0	10.0	10.0	9.9	9.9	9.9
6	10.0	10.0	10.0	10.0	10.0	10.0	10.0	10.0	10.0	10.0
5	10.0	10.0	10.0	10.0	10.0	10.0	10.0	10.0	10.0	10.0
4	9.9	9.9	9.9	10.0	10.0	10.0	10.0	10.1	10.1	10.1
3	9.8	9.9	9.9	9.9	10.0	10.0	10.1	10.1	10.1	10.2
2	9.6	9.8	9.9	9.9	10.0	10.0	10.1	10.1	10.2	10.4
1	9.4	9.7	9.8	9.9	10.0	10.0	10.1	10.2	10.3	10.6

(Row stub, read vertically: ECONOMIC SUCCESS BY DECILES)

* Table 7 corresponds to .02 standard deviations difference in Economic Success per standard deviation difference in Social Class Background, in a causal model assuming Social Class Background affects Early I.Q. only via genetic transmission, and assuming Economic Success is directly affected only by cognitive variables.
   Example of use: For an individual in the 85th percentile in Social Class Background $(x = 9)$, the probability of attaining between the 20th and 30th percentiles in Economic Success $(y = 3)$, assuming only genetic and cognitive mechanisms, is 10.1 percent (the entry in column 9, row 8).

Were the I.Q. ideology correct, understanding the ramifications of cognitive differences would require our focusing on the technical relations of production in an advanced technological economy. Its failure, however, bids us scrutinize a different aspect of production—its social relations. By the "social relations of production" we mean the system of rights and responsibilities, duties, and rewards, that governs the interaction of all individuals involved in organized productive activity.[33] In the following section we shall argue that the social relations of production determine the major attributes of the U.S. stratification system.[34] Here, however, we shall confine ourselves to the proposition that the I.Q. ideology is a major factor in legitimating these social relations in the consciousness of workers.

The social relations of production in different societies are quite diverse: they lay the basis for such divergent stratification systems as communal-reciprocity, caste, feudal serf, slave, community-collective, and wage labor of capitalist and state socialist varieties. In advanced capitalist society the stratification system is based on what we term the hierarchical division of labor, characterized by power and control emanating from the top downward through a finely graded bureaucratic order.[35] The distribution of economic reward and social privilege in the United States is an expression of the hierarchical division of labor within the enterprise.

In this section, then, we shall show that the I.Q. ideology serves to legitimate the hierarchical division of labor. First, we argue that such legitimation is necessary because capitalist production is "totalitarian" in a way only vaguely adumbrated in other social spheres—family, interpersonal relations, law, and politics. Indeed history exhibits periodic onslaughts upon the hierarchical of labor and its acceptance is always problematic. Second, we argue that the I.Q. ideology is conducive to a general technocratic and meritocratic view of the stratification system that tends to legitimate these social relations, as well as its characteristic means of allocating individuals to various levels of the hierarchy. Third, we argue that the I.Q. ideology operates to reconcile workers to their eventual economic positions primarily via the schooling experience, with its putative objectivity, meritocratic orientation, and technical efficiency in supplying the cognitive needs of the labor force. Fourth, we shall argue that the use of both formal education and the I.Q. ideology was not merely a historical accident, but arose through conscious policies of capitalists and their intellectual servants to perform the functions indicated above.

THE NEED FOR LEGITIMACY

If one takes for granted the basic economic organization of society, its members need only to be equipped with adequate cognitive and operational skills to fulfill work requirements, and provided with a reward structure motivating individuals to acquire and supply these skills. U.S. capitalism accomplishes the first of these requirements through family, school, and on-the-job training, and the second through a wage structure patterned after the job hierarchy.

But the social relations of production cannot be taken for granted. The bedrock of the capitalist economy is the legally sanctioned power of the directors of an enterprise to organize production, to determine the rules that regulate worker's productive activities, and to hire and fire accordingly, with only moderate restriction by workers' organizations and government regulations. But this power cannot be taken for granted, and can be exercised forcefully against violent opposition only sporadically. Violence alone, observe Lasswell and Kaplan, is inadequate as a stable basis for the possession and exercise of power, and they appropriately quote Rousseau: "The strongest man is never strong enough to be always master, unless he transforms his power into right, and obedience into duty." Where the assent of the less favored cannot be secured by power alone, it must be part of a total process whereby the existing structure of work roles and their allocation among individuals are seen as ethically acceptable and even technically necessary.

In some social systems the norms that govern the economic system are quite similar to those governing other major social spheres. Thus in feudal society the authority of the lord of the manor is not essentially different from that of the political monarch, the church hierarchy, or the family patriarch, and the ideology of "natural estates" suffuses all social activity. No special normative order is required for the economic system. But in capitalist soicety, to make the hierarchical division of labor appear just is no easy task, for the totalitarian organization of the enterprise clashes sharply with the ideals of equality, democracy, and participation that pervade the political and legal spheres. Thus the economic enterprise as a political dictatorship and a social caste system requires special legitimation, and the mechanisms used to place individuals in unequal (and unequally rewarding) positions require special justification.

Indeed the history of U.S. labor is studded with revolts against the hierarchical division of labor, particularly prior to the full development of formal education and the I.Q. ideology in the early twentieth century.[36]

In 1844 the Lynn, Mass., shoe workers, losing control over their craft and their labor in the face of the rising factory system, wrote in their "Declaration of Independence": Whereas, our employers have robbed us of certain rights . . . we feel bound to rise unitedly in our strength and burst asunder as Freemen ought the shackles and fetters with which they have long been chaining and binding us, by an unjust and unchristian use of power . . . which the possession of capital and superior knowledge furnishes.[37] The ideology of the dispossessed farmer in the 1880s and 1890s or of the bankrupted small shopkeeper after the turn of the century is little different. That these radical thrusts against the hierarchical division of labor have by and large been deflected into more managebale wage or status demands bespeaks the power of the capitalist system to legitimize its changing structure, but in no way suggests that the perpetuation of the capitalist relations of production was ever a foregone conclusion.[38]

The Thrust of Legitimation: I.Q., Technocracy, and Meritocracy

We may isolate several related aspects of the social relations of production that are legitimized in part by the I.Q. ideology. To begin there are the overall characteristics of work in advanced U.S. capitalism: bureaucratic organization, hierarchical lines of authority, job fragmentation, and unequal reward. It is highly essential that the individual accept, and indeed come to see as natural, these undemocratic and unequal aspects of the workaday world.

Moreover, the mode of allocating individuals to these various positions in U.S. capitalism is characterized by intense competition in the educational system followed by individual assessment and choice by employers. Here again the major problem is that this "allocation mechanism" must appear egalitarian in process and just in outcome, parallel to the formal principle of "equality of all before the law" in a democratic juridicial system based on freedom of contract.

While these two areas refer to the legitimation of capitalism as a social system, they have their counterpart in the individual's personal life. Thus, just as individuals must come to accept the overall social relations of production, workers must respect the authority and competence of their own "superiors" to direct their activities, and justify their own authority (however extensive) over others. Similarly, just as the overall system of role allocation must be legitimized, so individuals must assent to the justness of their own personal position, and the mechanisms through which this position has been attained. That workers be resigned to their position in production is perhaps adequate; that they be reconciled is even preferable.

The contribution of I.Q.-ism to the legitimation of these social relations is based on a view of society that asserts the efficiency and technological necessity of modern industrial organization, and is buttressed by evidence of the similarity of production and work in such otherwise divergent social systems as the United States and the Soviet Union. In this view large-scale production is a requirement of advanced technology, and the hierarchical division of labor is the only effective means of coordinating the highly complex and interdependent parts of the large-scale productive system. Thus bureaucratic order is awarded the status of an "evolutionary universal"; in the words of Talcott Parsons: "Buraucracy . . . is the most effective large-scale administrative organization that man has invented, and there is no direct substitute for it."[39]

The hallmark of the "technocratic perspective" is its reduction of a complex web of social relations in production to a few rules of technological efficacy— whence its easy integration with the similarly technocratic view of social stratification inherent in the I.Q. ideology. In this view the hierarchical division of labor arises from its natural superiority in the coordination of collective activity and in the nurturing of expertise in the control of complex production processes. In order to motivate the most able individuals to undertake the necessary training and preparation for high level occupational roles, salaries and status must be closely associated with one's level in the work hierarchy. Thus Davis and Moore, in their highly influential "functional theory of stratification," locate the "determinants of differential reward" in "differential functional importance" and "differential scarcity of personnel." "Social inequality," they conclude, "is thus an unconsciously evolved device by which societies insure that the most important positions are conscientiously filled by the most qualified persons."[40] Herrnstein is a little more concrete: "If virutally anyone is smart enough to be a ditch digger, and only half the people are smart enough to be engineers, then society is, in effect, husbanding its intellectual resources by holding engineers in greater esteem and paying them more."[41]

This perspective, technocratic in its justification of the hierarchical division of labor, leads smoothly to a meritocratic view of the process of matching individuals to jobs. An efficient and impersonal bureaucracy assesses the individual purely in terms of his or her expected contribution to production. The main determinants of an individual's expected job fitness are seen as those cognitive and psycho-motor capacities relevant to the worker's technical ability to do the job. The technocratic view of production and the meritocratic view of job allocation yield an important corollary, to which we will later return. Namely, there is always a strong tendency in an efficient industrial order to abjure caste, class, sex, color, and ethnic origins in occupational placement. This tendency will be particularly strong in a capitalist economy, where competitive pressures constrain employers to hire on the basis of strict efficiency criteria.[42]

The technocratic view of production, along with the meritocratic view of hiring, provides the strongest form of legitimation of work organization and social stratification in capitalist society. Not only is the notion that the hierarchical division of labor is "technically necessary" (albeit politically totalitarian) strongly reinforced,

but also the view that job allocation is just and egalitarian (albeit severely unequal) is ultimately justified as objective, efficient, and necessary. Moreover, the
individual's reconciliation with his or her own position in the hierarchy of production appears all but complete: the legitimacy of the authority of superiors
no less than that of the individual's own objective position flows not from
social contrivance but from Science and Reason.

That this view does not strain the credulity of well-paid intellectuals is perhaps not surprising.[43] Nor would the technocratic/meritocratic perspective be of
much use in legitimizing the hierarchical division of labor were its adherents to
be counted only among the university elite and the technical and professional
experts. But such is not the case. Despite the extensive evidence that I.Q. is not
an important determinant of individual occupational achievement . . . and despite
the fact that few occupations place cognitive requirements on job entry, the
crucial importance of I.Q. in personal success has captured the public mind.
Numerous attitude surveys exhibit this fact. In a national sample of high school
students, for example, "intelligence" ranks second only to "good health" in importance as a desirable personal attribute.[44] Similarly a large majority chose
"intelligence" along with "hard work" as the most important requirements of
success in life. The public concern over the Coleman Report findings about
scholastic achievement and the furor over the I.Q. debate are merely indications
of the pervasiveness of the I.Q. ideology.

This popular acceptance, we shall argue, is due to the unique role of the
educational system.

Education and Legitimation

To understand the widespread acceptance of the view that economic success
is predicated on intellectual achievement we must look beyond the workplace, for
the I.Q. ideology does not conform to most workers' everyday experience on the
job. Rather, the strength of this view derives in large measure from the interaction between schooling, cognitive achievement, and economic success. I.Q.-ism
legitimates the hierarchical division of labor not directly, but primarily through its
relationship with the educational system.

We can summarize the relationships as follows. First, the distribution of
rewards by the school is seen as being based on objectively measured cognitive
achievement, and is therefore fair. Second, schools are seen as being primarily
oriented toward the production of cognitive skills. Third, higher levels of schooling are seen as a major, perhaps the strongest, determinant of economic success,
and quite reasonably so, given the strong association of these two variables exhibited in Table 2. It is concluded, thus, that high I.Q.'s are acquired in a fair
and open competition in school and in addition are a major determinant of success.
The conclusion is based on the belief that the relationship between level of
schooling and degree of economic success derives largely from the contribution
of school to an individual's cognitive skills. Given the organization and stated
objectives of schools it is easy to see how people would come to accept this
belief. We have shown in Tables 2 and 5 that it is largely without empirical
support.

The linking of intelligence to economic success indirectly via the educational system strengthens rather than weakens the legitimation process. First, day-to-day contact of parents and children with the competitive, cognitively oriented school environment, with clear connections to the economy, buttresses in a very immediate and concrete way the technocratic perspective on economic organization, to a degree that a sporadic and impersonal testing process divorced from the school environment could not aspire. Second, by rendering the outcome (educational attainment) dependent not only on ability but also on motivation, drive to achieve, perseverance, and sacrifice, the status allocation mechanism acquires heightened legitimacy. Moreover, personal attributes are tested and developed over a long period of time, thus enhancing the apparent objectivity and achievement orientation of the stratification system. Third, by gradually "cooling out" individuals at different educational levels, the student's aspirations are relatively painlessly brought into line with his probable occupational status. By the time most students terminate schooling they have validated for themselves their inability or unwillingness to be a success at the next highest level. Through competition, success, and defeat in the classroom, the individual is reconciled to his or her social position.[45]

The statistical results of the previous section fit in well with our description of the role of education in the legitimation process. The I.Q. ideology better legitimates the hierarchical division of labor the stronger are the statistical associations of I.Q. with level of schooling and economic success, and the weaker are the causal relations. Weak causal relationships are also necessary for the efficient operation of the job allocation process. I.Q. is in fact *not* a crucial determinant of job adequacy; the placement of workers solely, or even largely, on the basis of cognitive abilities would seriously inhibit the efficient allocation of workers to occupational slots. Thus there must be strong statistical association of I.Q. with economic success, but little economic reward for having a higher I.Q. in the absence of other traits normally associated with high I.Q.[46] Similarly there must be a strong statistical association between I.Q. and school success (grades), but enough individual variation to render "hard work" or good behavior important.[47] Again there must be a strong statistical association between school success and final level of education attainment, but enough individual variation to allow any "sufficiently motivated" student to achieve higher educational levels. Lastly there must be a strong association between level of education and economic success, but enough individual variation to reward "achievement motivation" and to allow for the multitude of personal attributes of differential value in educational and occupational performance.[48] All of these conditions appear to be satisfied.

The History of Legitimation: I.Q., Education, and Eugenics

The relationship between schooling, I.Q., and the stratification system is therefore by no means technologically determined within the framework of capitalist economic institutions. Nor did it arise accidentally. Rather, a growing body of historical research indicates that it grew out of a more or less conscious and coordinated attempt to generate a disciplined industrial labor force and to legitimate the rapid hierarchization of the division of labor around the turn of the century.[49]

This research strongly contests the dominant "liberal-technocratic" analysis of education. This "technocratic" view of schooling, economic success, and the requisites of job functioning supplies an elegant and logically coherent (if not empirically accurate) explanation of the historical rise of mass education in the process of industrial development. Because modern industry, irrespective of its political and institutional framework, consists in the application of increasingly complex and cognitively demanding operational technologies, these cognitive demands require an increasing level of cognitive competence on the part of the labor force as a whole. Thus the expansion of educational opportunity becomes a requisite of modern economic growth.[50] Formal education, by extending to the masses what had been throughout history the privilege of the few, opens the superior levels in the production hierarchy to all with the ability and willingness to attain such competencies. Hence the observed association between education and economic success reflects the achievement of a fundamentally egalitarian school system in promoting cognitive development.

Quite apart from the erroneous view that the determinants of job adequacy in modern industry are primarily cognitive, this interpretation of the rise of universal education in the United States finds little support in the historical record. Mass education made its beginning in cities and towns where the dominant industries required little skill—and far less cognitive ability—among the work force. The towns in which the skill-using industries located were the followers, not the leaders, in the process of mid-nineteenth-century educational reform and expansion.[51] Likewise in the late nineteenth-century rural West and South the expansion of schooling was associated, not with the application of modern technology of mechanization to farming, but with the extension of the wage labor system to agricultural employment.[52] Even the rise of the land-grant colleges—those institutions that in the popular wisdom were most finely attuned to producing the technical skills required in the modernizing agricultural sectors—cannot be explained by the cognitive needs of the economy, for during their first thirty or so years of operation they offered hardly any instruction in agricultural sciences.[53]

Thus the growth of the modern educational system did not originate with the rising cognitive requirements of the economy. Rather, the birth and early development of universal education was sparked by the critical need of a burgeoning capitalist order for a stable work force and citizenry reconciled, if not inured, to the wage labor system. Order, docility, discipline, sobriety, and humility—attributes required by the new social relation of production—were admitted by all concerned as the social benefits of schooling.[54] The popular view of the economy as a technical system would await Frederick Taylor and his scientific management movement; the Social Darwinist emphasis on intelligence appeared only in the "scientific genetics" of Binet and Terman. The integration of the I.Q. ideology into educational theory and practice had to await basic turn-of-the-century developments in the industrial order itself.

The most important of these developments was the birth of the modern corporation, with its relentless pressure toward uniformity and objectivity in the staffing of ever more finely graded hierarchical positions. The rationalistic efficiency orientation of bureaucratic order was quickly take over by a growing educational system.[55] Taylorism in the classroom meant competition, hierarchy, uniformity, and, above all, individual accountability by means of objective testing.

A second related source of educational change emanating from the economy was the changing nature of the work force. Work on the family farm or in the artisan shop continued to give way to employment in large-scale enterprises. And millions of immigrants swelled the ranks of the new working class. The unAmerican undomesticated character of this transformed work force was quickly revealed in a new labor militancy (of which Sacco and Vanzetti are merely the shadow in folk history) and a skyrocketing public welfare burden.

The accommodation of the educational system to these new economic realities was by no means a placid process. Modern education was constructed on the ripidly disintegrating and chaotic foundations of the old common school. Geared to the small town, serving native American Protestant stock, and based on the proliferation of the one-room schoolhouse, the common school was scarcely up to supplying the exploding labor needs of the new corporate order. Dramatic was its failure to deal effectively with the seething urban agglomeration of European immigrants of rural and peasant origin.[56] As large numbers of working-class and particularly immigrant children began attending high schools, the older democratic ideology of the common school—that the same curriculum should be offered to all children—gave way to the "Progressive" insistence that education should be tailored to the "needs of the child." In the interests of providing an education relevant to the later life of the students, vocational schools and tracks were developed for the children of working families. The academic curriculum was preserved for those who would later have the opportunity to make use of book learning either in college or in white-collar employment.

The frankness with which students were channeled into curriculum tracks on the basis of their race, ethnicity, or social class background raised serious doubts concerning the "openness" of the social class structure. The relation between social class and a child's chances of promotion or tracking assignments was disguised—though not mitigated much—by another "progressive" reform: "objective" educational testing. Particularly after World War I the increased use of intelligence and scholastic achievement testing offered an ostensibly unbiased means of measuring the product of schooling and stratifying students.[57] The complementary growth of the guidance counseling profession allowed much of the channeling to proceed from the students' own well counseled choices, thus adding an apparent element of voluntarism to the system.

If the rhetoric of the educational response to the economic changes after the turn of the century was "progressive," much of its content and consciousness was supplied by the new science of "evolutionary genetics," in the form of the prestigious and influential Eugenics Movement.[58] Of course, as Karier notes, "The nativism, racism, elitism and social class bias which were so much a part of the testing and Eugenics Movement in America were, in a broader sense, part of the Zeitgeist which was America." Yet its solid grounding in Mendel's Law, Darwin, and the sophisticated statistical methodologies of Pearson, Thurstone, and Thorndike lent it the air of scientific rigor previously accorded only to the Newtonian sciences.

The leitmotiv of the testing movement was the uniting constitutional character of human excellence, as rooted in genetic endowment. Moral character, intelligence, and social worth were inextricably connected and biologically rooted. In the words of the eminent psychologist Edward L. Thorndike, "to him that a superior intellect is given also on the average a superior character."[59] A glance at the new immigrant communities, the Black rural ghettos, and the "breeding" of the upper classes could not but confirm this opinion in the popular mind. Statistical information came quickly from that architect of the still popular Stanford-Binet intelligence test—Lewis M. Terman—who confirmed the association of I.Q. and occupational status. Study after study, moreover, exhibited the low intelligence of "wards of the state" and social deviants.

That a school system geared toward moral development and toward domesticating a labor force for the rising corporate order might readily embrace standardization and testing—to the benefit of the leaders as well as the led—goes without saying. Thus it is not surprising that, while the idealistic Progressives worked in vain for a humanistic, more egalitarian education,[60] the bureaucratization and test orientation of the school system proceeded smoothly, well-oiled by seed money from the Carnegie Corporation and other large private foundations, articulated by social scientists at prestigious schools of education[61] and readily implemented by business-controlled local school boards.[62]

The success of the "cult of efficiency" in education, while obviously secured through the political power of private and public corporate elites, would have appeared unthinkable outside the framework of a burgeoning corporate order within which the "system problem" of a stable labor force demanded new and creative institutional mechanisms. Only a strong labor movement dedicated to construction of a qualitatively different social order could have prevented this, or a functionary equivalent, outcome.

We conclude that the present relation of schooling, I.Q., and economic success orginated quite consciously as part of an attempt to administer and legitimate a new economic order based on the hierarchical division of labor. We reject the notion that the school system does or has ever functioned primarily to produce cognitive skills made scarce and hence valuable by the continuing modernization of the economy.

Our analysis of the contemporary structure of labor rewards, as well as our historical analysis, suggests that cognitive ability is not a particularly scarce good, and hence bears little independent reward. This conclusion will hardly be news to employers: a cotton manufacturer wrote to Horace Mann, then Secretary of the Massachusetts Board of Education, in 1841:

> I have never considered mere knowledge . . . as the only advantage derived from a good Common School education. . . . (Workers with more education possess) a higher and better state of morals, are more orderly and respectful in their deportment, and more ready to comply with the wholesome and necessary regulations of an establishment. . . . In times of agitation, on account of some change in regulations or wages, I have always looked to the most intelligent, best educated and the most moral for support. The ignorant and uneducated I have generally found the most turbulent and troublesome, acting under the impulse of excited passion and jealousy.[63]

Adequate cognitive skills, we conclude, are generated as a byproduct of the current structure of family life and schooling. This highly functional mechanism for the production and stratification of labor has acquired its present form in the pursuit of objectives quite remote from the production of intellectual skills. . . .

NOTES

1. The most explicit statement of the genetic interpretation of intergenerational immobility is Richard Herrnstein, "IQ," *Atlantic Monthly,* September 1971, pp. 43–64.

2. Michael Katz notes the historical tendency of genetic interpretations of social inequality to gain popularity following the failure of educational reform movements. Michael Katz, *The Irony of Early School Reform* (Cambridge: Harvard University Press, 1968). On the rise of the genetic interpretation of inequality toward the end of the Progressive Era, see Clarence J. Karier, "Testing for Order and Control in the Corporate Liberal State," *Educational Theory,* 22, No. 2 (Spring 1972).

3. Louis Wirth, Preface, in Karl Mannheim, *Ideology and Utopia: An Introduction of the Sociology of Knowledge* (New York: Harcourt, Brace & World, 1936), pp. x-xxx.

4. Arthur R. Jensen, "How Much Can We Boost IQ and Scholastic Achievement?" *Harvard Educational Review,* Reprint Series No. 2, 1969, pp. 126–134.

5. For example, H. J. Eysenck, *The IQ Argument* (New York: Library Press, 1971), and Herrnstein, "IQ."

6. For a representative sampling of criticism, see the issues of the *Harvard Educational Review* that followed the Jensen article.

7. Our work in this area is reported in Herbert Gintis, "Alienation and Power: Toward a Radical Welfare Economics," Ph.D. dissertation, Harvard University, 1969, Gintis, "Education and the Characteristics of Worker Productivity," *American Economic Review,* 61 (May 1971), 266–279; Samuel Bowles, "Schooling and Inequality from Generation to Generation," *Journal of Political Economy,* May-June 1972; Bowles, "The Genetic Inheritance of IQ and the Intergenerational Reproduction of Economic Inequality," Harvard Institute for Economic Research, September 1972.

8. Jensen, "How Much Can We Boost IQ?"; Carl Bereiter, "The Future of Individual Differences," *Harvard Educational Review,* Reprint Series No. 2, 1969, pp. 162–170; Herrnstein, "IQ"; Eysenck, *IQ Argument.*

9. Arthur R. Jensen, "Estimation of the Limits of Heritability of Traits by Comparison of Monzygotic and Dizygotic Twins," *Proceedings of the National Academy of Science,* 58 (1967), 149–157.

10. Jensen, "How Much Can We Boost IQ?"; Christopher Jencks et al., *Inequality: A Reassessment of the Effects of Family and Schooling in America* (New York: Basic Books, 1972).

11. Eysenck, *IQ Argument,* p. 9.

12. Jerome S. Kagan, "Inadequate Evidence and Illogical Conclusions," *Harvard Educational Review,* Reprint Series No. 2, 1969, pp. 126–134; J. McV. Hunt, "Has Compensatory Education Failed? Has It Been Attempted?" *Harvard Educational Review,* Reprint Series No. 2, 1969, pp. 130–152.

13. James S. Coleman et al., *Equality of Educational Opportunity* (Washington, D.C.: Government Printing Office, 1966).

14. For example, Edward A. Ross, *Social Control* (New York: Macmillian, 1924); Louis M. Terman, "The Conservation of Talent," *School and Society,* 19, No. 483 (March 1924); Joseph Schumpeter, *Imperialism and Social Classes* (New York: Kelly, 1951).

15. This is not meant to imply that all liberal social theorists hold the I.Q. ideology. David McClelland, *The Achieving Society* (Princeton: Van Nostrand, 1967), and Oscar Lewis, "The Culture of Poverty," *Scientific American,* 215 (October 1966): 16–25, among others, explicity reject I.Q. as an important determinant of social stratification.

16. Jensen, "Estimation of the Limits of Heritability," p. 14.

17. Otis Dudley Duncan, "Properties and Characteristics of the Socioeconomic Index," in Albert J. Reiss (ed.), *Occupations and Social Status* (New York: The Free Press, 1961), p. 142.

18. Jensen, "Estimation of the Limits of Heritability," p. 19.

19. Bereiter, "Future of Individual Differences," p. 166.

20. Herrnstein, "IQ," p. 51.

21. Jensen, "How Much Can We Boost IQ," p. 75.

22. Herrnstein, "IQ," p. 63.

23. *Ibid.*

24. *Ibid.*

25. See Peter Blau and Otis Dudley Duncan, *The American Occupational Structure* (New York: John Wiley, 1967); Otis Dudley Duncan, David L. Featherman, and Beverly Duncan, *Socioeconomic Background and Occupational Achievement: Extensions of a Basic Model,* Final Report Project No. 5-0074 (EO-191), Contract No. OE-5-85-072 Washington, D.C.: U.S. Department of Health, Education, and Welfare, Office of Education, Bureau of Research, 1968); Bowles, "Schooling and Inequality from Generation to Generation"; and Bowles, "The Genetic Inheritance of IQ," for a complete description. Similar calculations for other age groups yield results consistent with our three main empirical propositions.

25a A further word is in order on Tables 1 through 7. Most popular discussions of the relation of I.Q. and economic success (e.g., Jensen, *"How Much Can We Boost IQ"*; Herrnstein, "IQ"; Jencks, *Inequality*) present statistical material in terms of "correlation coefficients" and "contribution to explained variance." We believe that these technical expressions convey little information to the reader not thoroughly initiated in their use and interpretation. The concept of differential probability embodied in Table 1 through 7, we feel, is operationally more accessible to the reader, and dramatically reveals the patterns of mobility and causality only implicit in summary statistics of the correlation variety.

Let us repeat, Tables 1 through 7 have *not* been constructed by directly observing the decile position of individuals on each of the various variables and recording the percentages in each cell of the relevant table. This approach is impossible for two reasons. First, such statistics are simply unavailable on the individual level. As we have noted, our statistical base embraces the findings of several distinct data sources, no single one of which includes all the variables used in our analysis. Second, for certain technical reasons (e.g., errors in variables and restrictions of range), correction factors must be applied to the raw data before they can be used for analysis. These general issues are discussed in Jencks, *Inequality,* and with respect to our data, in Bowles, "The Genetic inheritance of IQ and the Intergenerational Reproduction of Economic Inequality," and Gintis, "Education and the Characteristics of Worker Productivity."

Tables 1 through 7 are constructed by making explicit certain assumptions that are only implicit, but absolutely necessary to the correlational arguments of Jensen and others. These assumptions include the linearity of the relations among all variables and the approximate normality of their joint probability distribution. Our statistical technique, then, is standard linear regression analysis, with correlations, regression coefficients, and path coefficients represented in their (mathematically equivalent) tabular form.

26. Jencks, *Inequality;* Robert Hauser, Kenneth G. Lutterman, and William H. Sewell, Socioeconomic Background and the Earnings of High School Graduates," unpublished manuscript, University of Wisconsin, August 1971; John Conlisk, "A Bit of Evidence on the Income-Education-Ability Interaction," *Journal of Human Resources,* 6 (Summer 1971) 358-362; Zvi Griliches and William M. Mason, "Education, Income, and Ability," *Journal of Political Economy,* 80, No. 3 (May-June 1972); Otis Dudley Duncan and David L. Featherman, "Psychological and Cultural Factors in the Process of Occupational Achievement," Population Studies Center, University of Michigan, 1971.

27. Bowles, "Genetic Inheritance of IQ."

27a In Table 3, as throughout this paper, socioeconomic background is measured as a weighted sum of parental income, father's occupational status, and father's income, where the weights are chosen so as to produce the maximum multiple correlation with economic success.

28. For a more extensive treatment of this point, using data from nine independent samples, see Gintis, "Education and the Characteristics of Worker Productivity."

29. For a more extensive demonstration of this proposition, see Bowles, "Genetic Inheritance of IQ."

30. Duncan, "Properties and Characteristics of the Socio-economic Index."

31. Jensen, "Estimation of the Limits of Heritability," p. 73.

32. Herrnstein, "IQ," p. 63.

33. For an explication of the social relations of production, see Andre Gorz, "Capitalist Relations of Production and the Socially Necessary Labor Force," in Arthur Lothstein (ed.), *All We Are Saying . . .* (New York: G. P. Putnam's, 1970), and Herbert Gintis, "Power and Alienation," in James Weaver (ed.), *Readings in Political Economy* Boston: Allyn & Bacon, forthcoming).

34. See Bowles, "Unequal Education and the Reproduction of the Social Division of Labor," *Review of Radical Political Economy,* 3 (Fall-Winter 1971); Bowles, "Contradictions in U.S. Higher Education," in James Weaver (ed.), *Readings in Political Economy* (Boston: Allyn & Bacon, forthcoming), for an explanation of the connection between the social relations of production and the stratification system.

35. On the origins and functions of the hierarchical division of labor, see Stephen Marglin, "What Do Bosses Do?" unpublished manuscript, Department of Economics, Harvard University, 1971; Richard C. Edwards, "Alienation and Inequality: Capitalist Relations of Production in a Bureaucratic Enterprise," Ph.D. dissertation, Harvard University, July 1972; Max Weber, *From Max Weber: Essays in Sociology* (New York: Oxford University Press, 1946); Chester I. Barnard, *The Functions of the Executive* (Cambridge: Harvard University Press, 1938). A similar hierarchy in production occurs in state socialist countries.

36. We are presently witnessing a revival of such revolts with the partial breakdown of this ideology. See Judson Gooding, "Blue Collar Blues on the Assembly Line," *Fortune,* July 1970; Gooding, "The Fraying White Collar," *Fortune,* December 1970.

37. Quoted in Norman Ware, *The Industrial Worker: 1840–1860* (New York, 1964), p. 42.

38. For contemporary discussions of the feasibility of significant alternatives to the hierarchical division of labor, see Paul Blumberg, *Industrial Democracy* (New York: Schocken Books, 1969); Carole Pateman, *Participation and Democratic Theory* (Cambridge: Cambridge University Press, 1970); Murray Bookchin, *Post-Scarcity Anarchism (Berkeley*: Ramparts Press, 1971); Gintis, "Power and Alienation."

39. Talcott Parsons, "Evolutionary Universals in Society," *American Sociological Review,* 29, No. 3 (June 1964), 507.

40. K. Davis and W. E. Moore, "Some Principles of Stratification," in R. Bendix and S. M. Lipset (eds.), *Class, Status and Power* (New York: The Free Press, 1966).

41. Herrnstein, "IQ," p. 51.

42. For a statement of this position, see Milton Friedman, *Capitalism and Freedom* (Chicago: University of Chicago Press, 1962).

43. Jensen reports that a panel of "experts" determined that higher status jobs "require" higher I.Q. See Jensen, "How Much Can We Boost IQ."

44. O. G. Brim et al., *American Beliefs and Attitudes about Intelligence* (New York: Russell Sage Foundation, 1969).

45. See Burton R. Clark, "The 'Cooling Out' Function in Higher Education," *American Journal of Sociology,* 65, No. 6 (May 1960); Paul Lauter and Florence Howe, "The Schools Are Rigged for Failure," *New York Review of Books,* June 20, 1970.

46. See tables 1 and 4.

47. See Gintis, "Education and Characteristics of Worker Productivity"; Edwards, "Alienation and Inequality."

48. See Bowles, "Unequal Education and the Reproduction of the Social Division of Labor."

49. For an extensive bibliography of this research, see Herbert Gintis, "Toward a Political Economy of Education: A Radical Critique of Ivan Illich's *Deschooling Society*," *Harvard Educational Review*, 42, No. 1 (February 1972); Bowles, "Unequal Education and the Reproduction of the Social Division of Labor"; Colin Greer, *The Great School Legend* (New York: Basic Books, 1972).

50. See Frank Tracy Carleton, *Economic Influences upon Educational Progress in the U.S., 1820–1850* (Madison: University of Wisconsin Press, 1908); Theodore W. Schultz, "Capital Formation by Education," *Journal of Political Economy*, 68 (December 1960) 571–583. This ideology is discussed in its several variations in Samuel Bowles and Herbert Gintis, "The ideology of Progressive School Reform," in Henry Rosemont and Walter Feinberg (eds.), *Work, Technology, and Education: Essays in the Intellectual Foundations of Education* (Urbana: University of Illinois Press, forthcoming), and Greer, *Great School Legend*.

51. See David Bruck, "The Schools of Lowell," honors thesis, Harvard University, 1971. In his study of cotton mill workers in Lowell in the 1840s, Hal Luft ("The Industrial Worker in Lowell," Unpublished manuscript, Harvard University, 1972) revealed no relationship whatever between worker literacy and their physical productivity. Bowles's as yet unpublished study (jointly with Alexander Field) of nineteenth-century educational expansion in Massachusetts found that the leading towns were those with cotton industries and large concentrations of foreign-born workers.

52. This is the conclusion of Robert Muchele and James Medoff ("Education and the Agrarian Order," unpublished manuscript, Harvard University, January 1972), based on a statistical study of U.S. census data. Their study sharply contradicts the interpretation of Douglas North in *The Economic Growth of the U.S., 1790–1860* (New York, 1961).

53. See William Lazonick, "The Integration of Higher Education into Agricultural Production in the U.S.," unpublished manuscript, Harvard University, 1972.

54. Bowles, "Unequal Education and the Reproduction of the Social Division of Labor," develops this argument in more detail. This perspective on the use of education is supported by a growing number of historical studies. See Bruck, "Schools of Lowell," and Katz, *Irony of Early School Reform*.

55. R. Callahan, *Education and the Cult of Efficiency* (Chicago: University of Chicago Press, 1962).

56. See Marvin Lazerson, *Origins of the Urban School* (Cambridge: Harvard University Press, 1971).

57. See Callahan, *Education and the Cult of Efficiency;* David K. Cohen and Marvin Lazerson, "Education and the Corporate Order," *Socialist Revolution,* March 1972; and Lawrence Cremin, *The Transformation of the School* (New York: Alfred A. Knopf, 1964).

58. For a short review of this movement and its relation to the development of the U.S. stratification system, see Karier, "Testing for Order and Control in the Corporate Liberal State."

59. Edward C. Thorndike, "Intelligence and Its Uses," *Harper's,* 140 (January 1920).

60. Cremin, *Transformation of the School.*

61. Karier, "Testing for Order and Control in the Corporate Liberal State."

62. George S. Counts, "The Social Composition of Boards of Education," *Review and Elementary School Journal,* Supplementary Education Monographs, No. 33 (1927); Calahan, *Education and the Cult of Efficiency.*

63. Quoted in Katz, *Irony of Early School Reform,* p. 88.

VIII. WORKING WOMEN AND THE FAMILY: SEX, CLASS, AND CAPITALISM

INTRODUCTION

The strategic role of working women is increasingly apparent in the development of modern industrial society. No theory of the working class can be complete without an examination of the particular tensions and conflicts faced by women within the structure of advanced capitalism. These tensions and conflicts are intimately connected with the changing role of women in the family and workplace. How has woman's special function in the family affected her position in the economy, and how has her changing position in the economy influenced family relationships? A discussion of these questions links the analysis of sexual stratification to the modern debate on the working class. These readings examine the sources of women's oppression and offer explanations for the emergence of the Women's Liberation movement.

In "The Economics of Women's Liberation," Bergmann presents a nonradical approach to sexual discrimination. Women's inferior and in some areas declining economic status, documented by Bergmann, results from systematic occupational segregation, with the beneficiaries male workers rather than employers as a class. Psychological factors (the psychic rewards of "keeping women in their place") rather than financial considerations of employers are the primary sources of sexual discrimination. These psychological factors have been reinforced by women's low expectations of themselves, which help rationalize employers' attitudes. Therefore, attitudinal changes on the part of both women and employers rather than fundamental changes in capitalist institutions are required for Women's Liberation.

The remaining selections present a more radical perspective on these issues. In "The Political Economy of Women's Liberation," Benston traces women's inferior status to their economic role in a capitalist economy. Since women's economic function is defined primarily within the context of the family, they are mainly concerned with consumption (use-value), a lower status activity, rather than production (exchange-value). Benston contends that "full equality in job opportunity is probably impossible without freedom from housework, and the industrialization of housework is unlikely unless women are leaving the home for jobs." In "More on the Political Economy of Women's Liberation," the Rowntrees criticize Benston's emphasis on women as houseworkers. They place greater stress on the growing importance of women in the labor force, and the discrimination they face in the workplace.

354

Harris and Silverman, in "Notes on Women in Advanced Industrial Capitalism," explore more fully the relationship between conflicts within the family and work situation to an emerging consciousness of sexual stratification. In their view, these conflicts are related to a crisis in the belief system of contemporary capitalism and to objective changes in the forces of production. The instability in the belief system has special significance for socializing institutions such as the family and is rooted in the contradiction of advanced industrial capitalism. Their argument suggests, furthermore, that women from the "new working class" strata (educated labor) are initially more likely to identify with the women's movement than those from the "traditional" working class. The conflicts over sexual stratification are seen as intimately connected with the institutional characteristics of advanced industrial capitalism.

THE ECONOMICS OF WOMEN'S LIBERATION

Barbara Bergmann

It will take a lot of changes if equal participation in the American economy for women is to become a reality. In the feminists' vision of a better future there would be, with few exceptions, no "men's occupations" and "women's occupations": women would get equal pay for equal work; they would do less unpaid work at home, and men would do more. I want to consider two sets of issues concerning the postliberation world. First, I shall explore the nature and strength of the economic forces blocking the way to the development of a world in which women would have (and would take advantage of) equal opportunities for paid work. Second, I shall try to describe some of the changes in economic and social arrangements which a more equal participation of women in the economy and a more equal participation of men in the home would entail.

WHAT'S BLOCKING WOMEN'S LIBERATION?

Aside from inertia, there are four factors which have been alleged to be at work to keep things as they are: (1) discrimination against women in employment and promotion due to male prejudice or malevolence; (2) inferior job performance by women; (3) the disinclination of many women to enter into what they view as men's roles; and (4) the profits to be made by business from keeping women in their present roles. Not all of these factors are of equal importance, as we shall see.

When we speak of employer prejudice against women we generally do not mean feelings of hatred or a desire to refrain from association with them. After all, most men are very glad to have a woman secretary right outside their office door. The most important manifestation of employer prejudice against women is a desire to restrict them to spheres which are viewed as proper for them. Everybody knows which jobs are "fit" for women: domestic and light factory work for the least educated ones; clerical and retail sales work for the high-school graduates and even some of the college graduates; and teaching, nursing, and social work for those with professional inclinations. We must look to the future researches of psychologists and sociologists to tell us why human beings enjoy enforcing and conforming to occupational segregation along sex (and racial) lines, and how the occupations "belonging" to each group are selected.

SOURCE: *Challenge,* May/June 1973, pp. 11-17. (updated statistical data supplied by the author)

But the enjoyment is clearly there. In Aldous Huxley's *Brave New World*—a novel truly remarkable for the number of ominous tendencies to which it correctly called attention—each occupation is performed by genetically identical persons in identical uniforms. Huxley was satirizing not only the misuse of science and the inhumanity of the drive for efficiency but also the strong human liking for castes in economic life.

The economist Victor R. Fuchs of the National Bureau of Economic Research, who is one of the pioneers in research on women's role in the labor market, finds occupational segregation by sex to be far more extreme than occupational segregation by race. In a 1970 study he says, ". . . one of the most striking findings is how few occupations employ large numbers of both sexes. Most men work in occupations that employ very few women and a significant fraction of women work in occupations that employ very few men." Fuchs attributes occupational segregation and the low pay for women it entails largely to the conditioning of women by society to avoid certain fields. A later study, by Malcolm Cohen of the University of Michigan, attributes most of the pay differences between men and women to "barriers to the entry of women into employment in higher paying jobs."

Up to now, the relative importance of discrimination in filling these high paying jobs and the relative importance of women's failure to compete for them in explaining occupational segregation by sex have not really been carefully measured by anyone. In the end, it may prove statistically impossible to separate out the precise importance of the various factors. However there is considerable evidence that discrimination is far from a negligible factor. Much of the evidence is anecdotal, but no less real for being so.

The economic results of occupational segregation for women are low wages. Women are relegated for the most part to those occupations in which experience adds very little to the status and productivity of the worker as she advances in age. After a year or two a secretary is about as good as she will ever be, while her junior executive boss, who may have the same formal education as she, continues to gain in confidence, knowledge and technical competence, and of course makes commensurate advances in pay.

Since the boundaries separating the men's occupational preserve from the women's are economically speaking artificial and not easily changed, the women's preserve may tend to get overcrowded, especially if the proportion of women in the labor force increases. This is exactly what has been occurring. Between 1950 and 1970, the number of men working increased by 15 percent, while the number of women working increased by 70 percent (see Table 1).

Into what kind of jobs did these women go? Because of employer discrimination and their own limited horizons, millions of them went into the traditional women's preserve—clerical work. In that 20-year period, there was a very great increase in the number of women clerical workers; they more than doubled their numbers. About one quarter of women workers were in the clerical category in 1950, and by 1970 more than one in three working women were clerical workers. There was no change in the nature of the economy to require such a dramatic upsurge in clerical employment. On the contrary, computerization tends to reduce the demand for clerks. These extra women were absorbed through the classic mechanism of a flexible economy—clerks lost ground in pay, and took on lower-priority work. That clerical jobs of the type filled by

T A B L E 1   **Employed Persons by Major Occupation Group and Sex, and Wage Changes, 1950–1970***

MAJOR OCCUPATION GROUP	EMPLOYED PERSONS (thousands) 1950	1970	EMPLOYMENT CHANGE 1950–70 (%)	AVERAGE ANNUAL RATE OF GROWTH OF WAGES† (%)
Men				
Professional & Technical Workers	2,696	6,890	+155.6	5.0
Managers, Officials and Proprietors	5,439	6,896	+ 26.8	4.9
Clerical Workers	3,035	3,497	+ 15.2	4.5
Sales Workers	2,379	2,724	+ 14.5	4.3
Craftsmen & Foreman	7,482	9,737	+ 30.1	4.1
Operatives	8,810	9,539	+ 8.3	4.0
Nonfarm Laborers	3,435	3,499	+ 1.9	4.5
Private Household Workers	125	26	− 79.2	—
Other Service Workers	2,560	3,185	+ 24.4	4.2
Farm Workers	6,196	2,692	− 56.6	—
Total Men	42,156	48,686	+ 15.3	4.7
Women				
Professional & Technical Workers	1,794	4,431	+147.0	5.1
Managers, Officials and Proprietors	990	1,301	+ 31.4	3.9
Clerical Workers	4,597	10,337	+124.9	3.5
Sales workers	1,443	1,990	+ 37.9	4.7
Craftsmen & Foreman	188	290	+ 54.3	—
Operatives	3,336	4,272	+ 28.1	3.7
Nonfarm Laborers	84	115	+ 36.9	—
Private Household Workers	1,758	1,559	− 11.3	3.6
Other Service Workers	2,092	4,954	+136.8	5.0
Farm Workers	1,212	472	− 61.1	—
Total Women	17,493	29,722	+ 69.6	4.1

* SOURCES: U.S. Bureau of the Census, *Statistical Abstract of the United States, 1970* (91st edition), Washington, D.C., 1970, p. 225; and U.S. Bureau of the Census, Current Population Reprints, Series P-60, No. 69, "Income Growth Rates in 1939 to 1968 for Persons by Occupation and Industry Groups, for the United States," Government Printing Office, Washington, D.C., 1970, Tables 19–20.

† Compound rate of growth in wage or salary income of year-round full-time workers, 1955–1968.

women became relatively overcrowded is shown by the fact that, during this period, wage rates in this relatively poorly paid occupation lagged still farther behind all other occupational groups for men and women (see last column of Table 1).

Interestingly, some progress apparently was made in the professional and technical group and the service worker group during the fifties and sixties. Women increased their representation in these occupations substantially, yet enjoyed better than average increases in pay rates. I take this as evidence of expanding demand for women in these fields, possibly involving some desegregation of employment in the particular jobs which make up these two large occupational groups.

Allegations concerning women's inferior job performance center on the lower commitment of some women to the labor market. Many women do leave jobs for prolonged periods to give birth to and take care of babies, or to follow their husbands to another city. At any given age they have less work experience, on the average, than men of the same age. A great deal has been made of women's relative lack of experience, but the truth is that in the kinds of jobs women are mostly consigned to, experience counts for very little in terms of skill or pay.

Women have been quitting jobs at a higher rate than men (the latest figures, for 1968, show quit rates of 2.6 percent per month for women in manufacturing and 2.2 percent for men. But calculations by Professor Isabel Sawhill of Goucher College indicate that about half of the gap in quit rates is due to the fact that women are heavily employed in the kinds of occupations in which *men and women* tend to quit more often, whereas men are heavily employed in the kinds of jobs in which stability of employment is rewarded.

Unfortunately, the women dropouts give all women a bad name in the labor market. Unless the liberationists can succeed in making maternity leaves of more than three weeks unfashionable (as the bearing of three or more children has recently become unfashionable), the women who do want equality with men are going to continue to suffer guilt by association. There will also have to be a decrease in the propensity of men to accept a job in another city without consideration of the effect on their wives' careers.

We come finally to the allegation, usually made by radicals out to discredit capitalism, that women's subjection is all a capitalist plot. Who benefits financially from maintenance of the *status quo?* The most obvious beneficiaries of prejudice against women are male workers in those occupations in which women are not allowed to compete. This lack of competition raises pay and in certain circumstances may reduce unemployment in an occupation largely reserved for males. Of course, wives who have a stay-at-home ideology also gain when women are excluded from their husbands' occupations. This undoubtedly accounts for some of the social pressure against women's liberation.

It is not the male workers or their wives who do the discriminating, however. The employers of the male workers (almost entirely males themselves) are the ones who do the actual discriminating, although of course they are cheered on in their discriminatory ways by their male employees. The employers actually tend to lose financially, since profits are lowered when cheap female help is spurned in favor of high-priced male help. Thus, good strategy for the women's movement would be to fight against the exclusion of women from "men's jobs" and leave the equal-pay-for-equal-work battle until the former fight was won, by which time the pay issue might have solved itself. Whatever losses there are to discriminating employers are in all probability not very large. However, profits to discriminating employers from discriminatory hiring cannot possibly be an important roadblock in the way of nondiscriminatory treatment for women.

Will capitalism collapse if women don't stay home and spend their time purchasing consumer goods? In fact, women who stay home are a poorer market for capitalist enterprise's products than women who go to work. Women who stay at home bake cakes and make dresses. Women who go to work patronize bakeries and dress shops more. A woman who leaves the home for a job will undoubtedly spend less time thinking about and seeking the detergent that will leave her clothes whiter than white, but she will probably buy the same amount of detergent, unless she starts patronizing a commercial laundry, in which case it will be the laundry that buys the detergent. Some nonworking women do make a career out of shopping and spend a great deal of money on items of doubtful utility, but the spending tendencies of most of these women would probably not be significantly reformed if they went to work. It is true that they would have to spend more dollars per hour, but they and their spendthrift male counterparts would have plenty of hours left, as we shall see.

To sum up, discrimination against women is an important factor in keeping women segregated by occupation and earning low pay. This discrimination does not by and large serve the economic ends of those who do the discriminating, although it does benefit male employees. The financial gains to those who do the discriminating are low or negative. The major cause served is psychological (it feels so good to have women in their "place"). The cavalier attitudes and low expectations of many women themselves concerning their paid work are also probably important, and may help to rationalize some employer taboos against hiring women for occupations (such as executive) in which a considerable investment in on-the-job training by the employer is called for. In short, for the post-liberation world to arrive, women's attitudes must be liberated, employers' attitudes must be liberated; but we may be able to do without a revolution which overthrows capitalism.

WHAT WOULD THE POSTLIBERATION ECONOMY LOOK LIKE

The success of the women's liberation movement would mean a radical reduction in the division of labor by sex, both inside and outside the home. It is difficult to imagine a "women's liberation" which did not include greater participation and success for women in the economy. Some of the ideologues of the movement have emphasized that postliberation woman should not adopt the aggressive habits of preliberation man, but it is difficult to envision success for women in the economic spheres from which they have been hitherto excluded without at least some movement in that direction.

The economic consequences of those changes in habit of both women and men which would constitute "women's liberation" would be enormous. We can assume it would be customary for all women who are not students to do paid work outside the home and for all men to do as much unpaid work inside the home as women will do. Both in paid employment and in unpaid work at home there would be an end to the stereotyping of occupations and tasks as suited for men or for women only.

One obvious consequence would be a large increase in the size of the labor force in paid work. If women had participated in the labor force to the degree that men of their age group did in 1970, the labor force would have been 30 percent larger than it was (see Table 2). Certainly, a rapid growth of the labor force by anything like that extent would create grave problems of digestion for the economy, but the change in habits and the growth of the labor force are both likely to be gradual.

T A B L E 2   **Female Labor Force, Current and "Postliberation" Basis (thousands)**

AGE GROUP	CURRENT FEMALE LABOR FORCE	FEMALE PARTICIPATION RATE	MALE PARTICIPATION RATE	"POST-LIBERATION" FEMALE LABOR FORCE
16–17	1,268	33.2	43.1	1,645
18–19	1,914	53.0	66.1	2,387
20–24	4,929	57.7	86.9	7,423
25–54	18,192	49.9	95.8	34,926
55–59	2,554	49.0	89.3	4,655
60–64	1,607	36.0	74.3	3,317
65–69	662	17.7	40.1	1,500
70 & Over	396	5.5	18.1	1,303
Total	31,523			57,156

Based on data of September 1970. SOURCE: U.S. Bureau of Labor Statistics, Employment and Earnings, October 1970. Postliberation increase in women working = 81.3%; postliberation increase in total labor force = 29.9%.

Gradual or not, any important increase in the size of the labor supply tends to create downward pressures on wage rates, and to raise profits. I would expect, however, that the increase in the number of persons on the labor market would be at least partially balanced by a fall in the number of hours worked, so that the labor supply in terms of person-hours might increase a great deal less than 30 percent. If the fall in the workweek just balanced the increase in persons working, we would have a 31-hour workweek (for both men and women, of course). This might work out to five six-hour days per week or to four eight-hour days. Quite obviously, both working men and working women would have more time than they now do to enjoy the pleasures of domestic life; and those wives who changed over from full-time housewifery to "full-time work" would experience less of a wrench than they would have to under the present 40-hours-per-week regime in paid work.

One of the most dramatic effects of women's liberation would be the change in the size and pay of occupations from which women had been excluded or had excluded themselves. Assuming, for example, that the number of places in medical schools will in the future be responsive to the number of qualified applicants, the number of physicians might in time double, and the income of physicians would surely come down at least relatively. The benefits to nonphysicians in terms of better services and cheaper health care are quite obvious. The financial losses to the present members of the medical profession (and their stay-at-home wives) are also obvious, but even they might enjoy the shorter workweek and lower patient load.

After a discussion of women as physicians it is only fair to discuss women as streetcleaners. The Soviet Union is always held up as a horrible example of what happens when women's liberation is tried, we have all seen the pictures of elderly women, scarves tied around their heads, sweeping the streets in the Moscow winter. These pictures and their captions are supposed to make us feel sorry for these women in a way we would not feel sorry for male streetcleaners. But I don't think we should shrink from the notion of streetcleaning as an occupation appropriate to the physically fit of both sexes. Streetcleaning is probably healthier and more interesting than clerical work; and when these jobs are well paid, they are much sought after.

Professor Estelle James of Stony Brook made some calculations of the effect on wage rates that a relaxation of occupational segregation by sex would entail. She assumed that women would compete on an equal footing with men of the same educational achievement. Occupations having similar requirements in terms of education, intelligence, skill, and experience would not have different pay scales, as they now do, depending on whether they are in the men's or women's preserve. Occupations previously reserved for women, which currently command low pay, would shrink in size as the rate of pay in them rose. Women would shift to those occupations previously reserved for men, which would increase in size, and which would experience a fall in pay. For example, in jobs held by those with a high-school diploma or better, she estimates that previously male occupations would increase in size by almost 15 percent and that wage rates in these occupations would decrease by about 15 percent. Employment in previously female occupations would be cut about 35 percent, and the pay would increase about 55 percent. Let me hasten to add that the decreases in wage rates projected for men would in actuality be translated in most cases into low or zero rates of increase, because the transition would occur only gradually and would be mitigated by increases in productivity. Despite this fact, Professor James' calculations suggest that women's liberation would bring a radical change in the lineup of occupational wage rates.

One of the benefits of the achievement of women's liberation would be a reduction in the incidence of poverty. One-third of poverty families are those the Census Bureau defines as "headed by women." When a man leaves his family or dies, the family loses the worker who was discriminated against least. The low pay of most of the jobs open to women means that when the woman goes out to work she has a poor chance of earning an income above the poverty level. The boring nature of many of these jobs, plus the lack of incentive that the low pay entails, induces many women who have lost their husbands through separation or death to languish at home on welfare payments. Thus, in the United States, discrimination against women combined with a high incidence of marital instability has helped to increase the incidence of poverty. We have estimated that about two-thirds of the poverty among black and/or female-headed families in which the head of the family works is due to discrimination.

The achievement of women's liberation obviously involves changed distribution of work in the home. Arrangements may be made for outside paid help in cooking, dishwashing, shopping, child care, and cleaning chores, but family members are still going to have to do a considerable amount of unpaid domestic work. Norton Dodge's monumental study *Women in the Soviet Economy* shows that Soviet men have taken over some of the housework, but probably far from a fair share of it. Russian men who work an eight-hour day spend an average of one and a half hours a day on household chores, whereas women who work an eight-hour day spend three and seven-tenths hours a day on such chores.

In the United States, one effect of greater participation in paid employment for women might very well be an increase in the popularity of communal living arrangements. In addition to the virtue of broadening the companionship of the family circle, such arrangements take advantage of economies of scale in meal preparation and child care.

But all of this is, so far as I can see, grossly unlikely. If the current level of interest in women's liberation were to continue for decades, then the transformations I have been describing would occur. But that is a very big "if." In the meantime, individual women who want to do work other than full-time unpaid domestic labor will just have to go on bucking the prejudice of employers, fighting their own laziness and sense of insufficiency, and nagging their husbands to help them with the dishes.

THE POLITICAL ECONOMY OF WOMEN'S LIBERATION

Margaret Benston

The "woman question" is generally ignored in analyses of the class structure of society. This is so because, on the one hand, classes are generally defined by their relation to the means of production and, on the other hand, women are not supposed to have any unique relation to the means of production. The category seems instead to cut across all classes; one speaks of working-class women, middle-class women, etc. The status of women is clearly inferior to that of men,[1] but analysis of this condition usually falls into discussing socialization, psychology, interpersonal relations, or the role of marriage as a social institution.[2] Are these, however, the primary factors? In arguing that the roots of the secondary status of women are in fact economic, it can be shown that women as a group do indeed have a definite relation to the means of production and that this is different from that of men. The personal and psychological factors then follow from this special relation to production, and a change in the latter will be a necessary (but not sufficient) condition for changing the former.[3] If this special relation of women to production is accepted, the analysis of the situation of women fits naturally into a class analysis of society.

The starting point for discussion of classes in a capitalist society is the distinction between those who own the means of production and those who sell their labor power for a wage. As Ernest Mandel says:

> The proletarian condition is, in a nutshell, the lack of access to the means of production or means of subsistence which, in a society of generalized commodity production, forces the proletarian to sell his labor power. In exchange for this labor power he receives a wage which then enables him to acquire the means of consumption necessary for satisfying his own needs and those of his family.

> This is the structural definition of wage earner, the proletarian. From it necessarily flows a certain relationship to his work, to the products of his work, and to his overall situation in society, which can be summarized by the catchword alienation. But there does not follow from this structural definition any necessary conclusions as to the level of his consumption . . . the extent of his needs, or the degree to which he can satisfy them.[4]

SOURCE: *Monthly Review,* September 1969, pp. 13–24.

We lack a corresponding structural definition of women. What is needed first is not a complete examination of the symptoms of the secondary status of women, but instead a statement of the material conditions in capitalist (and other) societies which define the group "women." Upon these conditions are built the specific superstructures which we know. An interesting passage from Mandel points the way to such a definition:

> The commodity . . . is a product created to be exchanged on the market, as opposed to one which has been made for direct consumption. *Every commodity must have both a use-value and an exchange-value.*
>
> It must have a use-value or else nobody would buy it. . . . A commodity without a use-value to anyone would consequently be unsalable, would constitute useless production, would have no exchange-value precisely because it had no use-value.
>
> On the other hand, every product which has use-value does not necessarily have exchange-value. It has an exchange-value only to the extent that the society itself, in which the commodity is produced, is founded on exchange, is a society where exchange is a common practice. . . .
>
> In capitalist society, commodity production, the production of exchange-values, has reached its greatest development. It is the first society in human history where the major part of production consists of commodities. It is not true, however, that all production under capitalism is commodity production. Two classes of products still remain simple use-value.
>
> The first group consists of all things produced by the peasantry for its own consumption, everything directly consumed on the farms where it is produced. . . .
>
> The second group of products in capitalist society which are not commodities but remain simple use-value consists of all things produced in the home. Despite the fact that considerable human labor goes into this type of household production, it still remains a production of use-values and not of commodities. Every time a soup is made or a button sewn on a garment, it constitutes production, but it is not production for the market.
>
> The appearance of commodity production and its subsequent regularization and generalization have radically transformed the way men labor and how they organize society.[5]

What Mandel may not have noticed is that his last paragraph is precisely correct. The appearance of commodity production has indeed transformed the way that *men* labor. As he points out, most household labor in capitalist society (and in the existing socialist societies, for that matter) remains in the pre-market stage. This is the work which is reserved for women and it is in this fact that we can find the basis for a definition of women.

In sheer quantity, household labor, including child care, constitutes a huge amount of socially necessary production. Nevertheless, in a society based on commodity production, it is not usually considered "real work" since it is outside of trade and the market place. It is pre-capitalist in a very real sense. This assignment of household work as the function of a special category "women" means that this group *does* stand in a different relation to production than the group "men." We will tentatively define women, then, as that group of people who are responsible for the production of simple use-values in those activities associated with the home and family.

Since men carry no responsibility for such production, the difference between the two groups lies here. Notice that women are not excluded from commodity production. Their participation in wage labor occurs but, as a group, they have no structural responsibility in this area and such participation is ordinarily regarded as transient. Men, on the other hand, are responsible for commodity production; they are not, in principle, given any role in household labor. For example, when they do participate in household production, it is regarded as more than simply exceptional; it is demoralizing, emasculating, even harmful to health. (A story on the front page of the *Vancouver Sun* in January 1969 reported that men in Britain were having their health endangered because they had to do too much housework!)

The material basis for the inferior status of women is to be found in just this definition of women. In a society in which money determines value, women are a group who work outside the money economy. Their work is not worth money, is therefore valueless, is therefore not even real work. And women themselves, who do this valueless work, can hardly be expected to be worth as much as men, who work for money. In structural terms, the closest thing to the condition of women is the condition of others who are or were also outside of commodity production, i.e., serfs and peasants.

In her recent paper on women, Juliet Mitchell introduces the subject as follows: "In advanced industrial society, women's work is only marginal to the total economy. Yet it is through work that man changes natural conditions and thereby produces society. Until there is a revolution in production, the labor situation will prescribe women's situation within the world of men."[6] The statement of the marginality of women's work is an unanalyzed recognition that the work women do is *different* from the work that men do. Such work is not marginal, however; it is just not wage labor and so is not counted. She even says later in the same article, "Domestic labor, even today, is enormous if quantified in terms of productive labor." She gives some figures to illustrate: In Sweden, 2,340 million hours a year are spent by women in housework compared with 1,290 million hours spent by women in industry. And the Chase Manhattan Bank estimates a woman's overall work week at 99.6 hours.

However, Mitchell gives little emphasis to the basic economic factors (in fact she condemns most Marxists for being "overly economist") and moves on hastily to superstructural factors, because she notices that "the advent of industrialization has not so far freed women." What she fails to see is that no society has thus far industrialized housework. Engels points out that the "first premise for the emancipation of women is the reintroduction of the entire female sex into public industry. . . . And this has become possible not only as a result of modern large-scale industry, which not only permits the participation of women in production in large numbers, but actually calls for it and, moreover, strives to convert private domestic work also into a public industry."[7] And later in the same passage: "Here we see already that the emancipation of women and their equality with men are impossible and must remain so as long as women are excluded from socially productive work and restricted to housework, which is private." What Mitchell has not taken into account is that the problem is not simply one of getting women into *existing* industrial production but the more complex one of converting private production of household work into public production.

For most North Americans, domestic work as "public production" brings immediate images of Brave New World or of a vast institution—a cross between a home for orphans and an army barracks—where we would all be forced to live. For this reason, it is probably just as well to outline here, schematically and simplistically, the nature of industrialization.

A pre-industrial production unit is one in which production is small-scale and reduplicative; i.e., there are a great number of little units, each complete and just like all the others. Ordinarily such production units are in some way kin-based and they are multi-purpose, fulfilling religious, recreational, educational, and sexual functions along with the economic function. In such a situation, desirable attributes of an individual, those which give prestige, are judged by more than purely economic criteria: for example, among approved character traits are proper behavior to kin or readiness to fulfill obligations.

Such production is originally not for exchange. But if exchange of commodities becomes important enough, then increased efficiency of production becomes necessary. Such efficiency is provided by the transition to industrialized production which involves the elimination of the kin-based production unit. A large-scale, non-reduplicative production unit is substituted which has only one function, the economic one, and where prestige or status is attained by economic skills. Production is rationalized, made vastly more efficient, and becomes more and more public—part of an integrated social network. An enormous expansion of man's productive potential takes place. Under capitalism such social productive forces are utilized almost exclusively for private profit. These can be thought of as *capitalized* forms of production.

If we apply the above to housework and child rearing, it is evident that each family, each household, constitutes an individual production unit, a pre-industrial entity, in the same way that peasant farmers or cottage weavers constitute pre-industrial production units. The main features are clear, with the reduplicative, kin-based, private nature of the work being the most important. (It is interesting to notice the other features: the multi-purpose functions of the family, the fact that desirable attributes for women do not center on economic prowess, etc.) The rationalization of production effected by a transition to large-scale production has not taken place in this area.

Industrialization is, in itself, a great force for human good; exploitation and dehumanization go with capitalism and not necessarily with industrialization. To advocate the conversion of private domestic labor into a public industry under capitalism is quite a different thing from advocating such conversion in a socialist society. In the latter case the forces of production would operate for human welfare, not private profit, and the result should be liberation, not dehumanization. In this case we can speak of *socialized* forms of production.

These definitions are not meant to be technical but rather to differentiate between two important aspects of industrialization. Thus the fear of the barracks-like result of introducing housekeeping into the public economy is most realistic under capitalism. With socialized production and the removal of the profit motive and its attendant alienated labor, there is no reason why, *in an industrialized society,* industrialization of housework should not result in better production, i.e., better food, more comfortable surroundings, more intelligent and loving child-care, etc., than in the present nuclear family.

The argument is often advanced that, under neocapitalism, the work in the home has been much reduced. Even if this is true, it is not structurally relevant. Except for the very rich, who can hire someone to do it, there is for most women, an irreducible minimum of necessary labor involved in caring for home, husband, and children. For a married woman without children this irreducible minimum of work probably takes fifteen to twenty hours a week, for a woman with small children the minimum is probably seventy or eighty hours a week.[8] (There is some resistance to regarding child-rearing as a job. That labor is involved, i.e., the production of use-value, can be clearly seen when exchange-value is also involved—when the work is done by baby sitters, nurses, child-care centers, or teachers. An economist has already pointed out the paradox that if a man marries his housekeeper, he reduces the national income, since the money he gives her is no longer counted as wages.) The reduction of housework to the minimums given is also expensive; for low-income families more labor is required. In any case, household work remains structurally the same—a matter of private production.

One function of the family, the one taught to us in school and the one which is popularly accepted, is the satisfaction of emotional needs: the needs for closeness, community, and warm secure relationships. This society provides few other ways of satisfying such needs; for example, work relationships or friendships are not expected to be nearly as important as a man-woman-with-children relationship. Even other ties of kinship are increasingly secondary. This function of the family is important in stabilizing it so that it can fulfill the second, purely economic, function discussed above. The wage-earner, the husband-father, whose earnings support himself, also "pays for" the labor done by the mother-wife and supports the children. The crucial importance of this second function of the family can be seen when the family unit breaks down in divorce. The continuation of the economic function is the major concern where children are involved; the man must continue to pay for the labor of the woman. His wage is very often insufficient to enable him to support a second family. In this case his emotional needs are sacrificed to the necessity to support his ex-wife and children. That is, when there is a conflict the economic function of the family very often takes precedence over the emotional one. And this in a society which teaches that the major function of the family is the satisfaction of emotional needs.[9]

As an economic unit, the nuclear family is a valuable stabilizing force in capitalist society. Since the production which is done in the home is paid for by the husband-father's earnings, his ability to withhold his labor from the market is much reduced. Even his flexibility in changing jobs is limited. The woman, denied an active place in the market, has little control over the conditions that govern her life. Her economic dependence is reflected in emotional dependence, passivity, and other "typical" female personality traits. She is conservative, fearful, supportive of the status quo.

Furthermore, the structure of this family is such that it is an ideal consumption unit. But this fact, which is widely noted in Women's Liberation literature, should not be taken to mean that this is its primary function. If the above analysis is correct, the family should be seen primarily as a production unit for housework and child-rearing. *Everyone* in capitalist society is a consumer; the structure of the family simply means that it is particularly well suited to encourage consumption. Women in particular *are* good consumers; this follows naturally from their responsibility for matters in the home. Also, the inferior status of women, their general lack of a strong sense of worth and identity, make them more exploitable than men and hence better consumers.

The history of women in the industrialized sector of the economy has depended simply on the labor needs of that sector. Women function as a massive reserve army of labor. When labor is scarce (early industrialization, the two world wars, etc.) then women form an important part of the labor force. When there is less demand for labor (as now under neocapitalism) women become a surplus labor force—but one for which their husbands and not society are economically responsible. The "cult of the home" makes its reappearance during times of labor surplus and is used to channel women out of the market economy. This is realtively easy since the pervading ideology ensures that no one, man or woman, takes women's participation in the labor force very seriously. Women's real work, we are taught, is in the home; this holds whether or not they are married, single, or the heads of households.

At all times household work is the responsibility of women. When they are working outside the home they must somehow manage to get both outside job and housework done (or they supervise a substitute for the housework). Women, particularly married women with children, who work outside the home simply do two jobs; their participation in the labor force is only allowed if they continue to fulfill their first responsibility in the home. This is particularly evident in countries like Russia and those in Eastern Europe where expanded opportunities for women in the labor force have not brought about a corresponding expansion in their liberty. Equal access to jobs outside the home, while one of the preconditions for women's liberation, will not in itself be sufficient to give equality for women; as long as work in the home remains a matter of private production and is the responsibility of women, they will simply carry a double work-load.

A second prerequisite for women's liberation which follows from the above analysis is the conversion of the work now done in the home as private production into work to be done in the public economy.[10] To be more specific, this means that child-rearing should no longer be the responsibility solely of the parents. Society must begin to take responsibility for children; the economic dependence of women and children on the husband-father must be ended. The other work that goes on in the home must also be changed—communal eating places and laundries for example. When such work is moved into the public sector, then the material basis for discrimination against women will be gone.

These are only preconditions. The idea of the inferior status of women is deeply rooted in the society and will take a great deal of effort to eradicate. But once the structures which produce and support that idea are changed then, and only then, can we hope to make progress. It is possible, for example, that a change to communal eating places would simply mean that women are moved from a home kitchen to a communal one. This *would* be an advance, to be sure, particularly in a socialist society where work would not have the inherently exploitative nature it does now. Once women are freed from private production in the home, it will probably be very difficult to maintain for any long period of time a rigid definition of jobs by sex. This illustrates the interrelation between the two preconditions given above: true equality in job opportunity is probably impossible without freedom from housework, and the industrialization of housework is unlikely unless women are leaving the home for jobs.

The changes in production necessary to get women out of the home might seem to be, in theory, possible under capitalism. One of the sources of women's liberation movements may be the fact that alternative capitalized forms of home production now exist. Day care is available, even if inadequate and perhaps expensive; convenience foods, home delivery of meals, and take-out meals are widespread; laundries and cleaners offer bulk rates. However, cost usually prohibits a complete dependence on such facilities, and they are not available everywhere, even in North America. These should probably then be regarded as embryonic forms rather than completed structures. However, they clearly stand as alternatives to the present system of getting such work done. Particularly in North America, where the growth of "service industries" is important in maintaining the growth of the economy, the contradictions between these alternatives and the need to keep women in the home will grow.

The need to keep women in the home arises from two major aspects of the present system. First, the amount of unpaid labor performed by women is very large and very profitable to those who own the means of production. To pay women for their work, even at minimum wage scales, would imply a massive redistribution of wealth. At present, the support of a family is a hidden tax on the wage earner—his wage buys the labor power of two people. And second, there is the problem of whether the economy can expand enough to put all women to work as a part of the normally employed labor force. The war economy has been adequate to draw women partially into the economy but not adequate to establish a need for all or most of them. If it is argued that the jobs created by the industrialization of housework will create this need, then one can counter by pointing to (1) the strong economic forces operating for the status quo and against capitalization discussed above, and (2) in fact that the present service industries, which somewhat counter these forces, have not been able to keep up with the growth of the labor force as presently constituted. The present trends in the service industries simply create "underemployment" in the home; they do not create new jobs for women. So long as this situation exists, women remain a very convenient and elastic part of the industrial reserve army. Their incorporation into the labor force on terms of equality—which would create pressure for capitalization of housework—is possible only with an economic expansion so far achieved by neocapitalism only under conditions of full-scale war mobilization.

In addition, such structural changes imply the complete breakdown of the present nuclear family. The stabilizing consuming functions of the family, plus the ability of the cult of the home to keep women out of the labor market, serve neocapitalism too well to be easily dispensed with. And, on a less fundamental level, even if these necessary changes in the nature of household production were achieved under capitalism it would have the unpleasant consequence of including *all* human relations in the cash nexus. The atomization and isolation of people in Western society is already sufficiently advanced to make it doubtful if such complete psychic isolation could be tolerated. It is likely in fact that one of the major negative emotional responses to women's liberation movements may be exactly such a fear. If this is the case, then possible alternatives—cooperatives, the kibbutz, etc.—can be cited to show that psychic needs for community and warmth can in fact be better satisfied if other structures are substituted for the nuclear family.

At best the change to capitalization of housework would only give women the same limited freedom given most men in capitalist society. This does not mean, however, that women should wait to demand freedom from discrimination. There *is* a material basis for women's status; we are not merely discriminated against, we are exploited. At present, our unpaid labor in the home is necessary if the entire system is to function. Pressure created by women who challenge their role will reduce the effectiveness of this exploitation. In addition, such challenges will impede the functioning of the family and may make the channeling of women out of the labor force less effective. All of these will hopefully make quicker the transition to a society in which the necessary structural changes in production can actually be made. That such a transition will require a revolution I have no doubt; our task is to make sure that revolutionary changes in the society do in fact end women's oppression.

NOTES

1. Marlene Dixon, "Secondary Social Status of Women." (Available from U.S. Voice of Women's Liberation Movement, 1940 Bissell, Chicago, Illinois 60614.)
2. The biological argument is, of course, the first one used, but it is not usually taken seriously by socialist writers. Margaret Mead's *Sex and Temperament* is an early statement of the importance of culture instead of biology.
3. This applies to the group or category as a whole. Women as individuals can and do free themselves from their socialization to a great degree (and they can even come to terms with the economic situation in favorable cases), but the majority of women have no chance to do so.
4. Ernest Mandel, "Workers Under Neocapitalism," paper delivered at Simon Fraser University. (Available through the Department of Political Science, Sociology and Anthropology, Simon Fraser University, Burnaby, B.C., Canada.)
5. Ernest Mandel, *An Introduction to Marxist Economic Theory* (New York: Merit Publishers, 1967), pp. 10–11.
6. Juliet Mitchell, "Women: The Longest Revolution," *New Left Review,* December 1966.
7. Frederick Engels, *Origin of the Family, Private Property and the State* (Moscow: Progress Publishers, 1968), chap. 9, p. 158. The anthropological evidence known to Engels indicated primitive woman's dominance over man. Modern anthropology disputes this dominance but provides evidence for a more nearly equal position of women in the matrilineal societies used by Engels as examples. The arguments in this work of Engels do not require the former dominance of women but merely their former equality, and so the conclusions remain unchanged.
8. Such figures can easily be estimated. For example, a married woman without children

is expected each week to cook and wash up (10 hours), clean house (4 hours), do laundry (1 hour), and shop for food (1 hour). The figures are *minimum* times required each week for such work. The total, 16 hours, is probaly unrealistically low; even so, it is close to half of a regular work week. A mother with young children must spend at least six or seven days a week working close to 12 hours.

9. For evidence of such teaching, see any high school text on the family.

10. This is stated clearly by early Marxist writers besides Engels. Relevant quotes from Engels have been given in the text; those from Lenin are included in the Appendix. [not included in this book]

MORE ON THE POLITICAL ECONOMY OF WOMEN'S LIBERATION

Mickey Rowntree
John Rowntree

In the September 1969 issue of *Monthly Review* there is an article by Margaret Benston on "The Political Economy of Women's Liberation." She defines women as "that group of people who are responsible for the production of simple use-values in those activities associated with the home and family." Further, they are "denied an active place in the market" and "remain a very convenient and elastic part of the industrial reserve army." While agreeing with Benston's analysis of women's role in the home, we feel that the changing sex composition of the labor force since the Second World War belies her emphasis on women as house-workers, which minimizes their role as wage laborers.

In the United States in 1940, only about 1 in 4 women (14 years and over) were in the labor force, 1 in 10 mothers worked, and about 1 in 12 women (18–24 years old) were still in school. By 1968, almost 2 in 5 women (16 years and over) were in the labor force, 2 in 5 mothers worked, and more than 1 in 5 women (18–24 years) were still in school.[1] Rather than excluding women from the labor force, monopoly capitalism has increasingly drawn women out of the home and into the market. Between 1947 and 1968 the labor force participation rate for men in both civilian and military employment fell from 86.8 percent to 81.2 percent (reflecting longer schooling and earlier retirement), while that for women rose from 31.8 percent to 41.6 percent. This marked increase in the proportion of women working occurred while the proportion of adult women in school increased dramatically; for 18–24 year-olds, women in school increased from 9.9 percent in 1950 to 22.1 percent in 1967, and now exceeds the proportion of 18–24 year-old men who were in school in 1950, 20.1 percent. During the same period, 1950–1968, the percentage of women not in the labor force because they were "keeping house" fell from about 60 percent of women to less than 50 percent. In July 1969, there were 47,681,000 males (93.4 percent of the total) 20 to 64 years old in the total labor force, while there were 25,807,000 females (48.1 percent) 20 to 64 years old in the total labor force and 25,810,000 females not in the labor force because they were "keeping house."

It is difficult to treat women simpy as unpaid producers of use-values in the home when more than two fifths of them are in the labor force. (Only three fourths of men are in the *civilian* labor force.) Only 28.1 percent of the civilian

SOURCE: *Monthly Review*, January 1970, pp. 26–32.

labor force in 1947, women were 37.1 percent in 1968. In April 1969, while women accounted for only 20 percent of employment in transportation and utilities and only 28 percent of manufacturing workers, they were 39 percent of wholesale and retail trade workers, 43 percent of total government employees, 51 percent of workers in finance, insurance, and real estate, and 54 percent of service workers. Not only are women crucial members of the labor force, but the home is ceasing to provide them with a shelter from the imperatives of the market. The Department of Labor says that 90 percent of girls today will work some time in their lives.[2]

If the system needs to keep women in the home, as Benston says, then it is failing badly at meeting this need. Benston also suggests that one of the sources of the women's liberation movements may be the development of embryonic capitalized forms of home production which are freeing women to demand equality in work, pay, and status. Looking further for clues to the recent upsurge of interest in the problems of women, perhaps we should look not just at the home and not just at the work place, but at the contradiction between women's role in the one and the other. Women have been doing unpaid labor in the home for a very long time; this by itself is an unlikely source of women's discontent. Further, we argue that higher unemployment rates, lower wages, and unequal job opportunities for women are the results of the contradiction between women's cultural role and women as free wage-laborers.

In this society the father's family role is a market one, that of "provider." This role is compatible with his role as free wage-worker. But the mother's culturally defined role is a nonmarket one, the practical day-to-day care of children. While men can comfort themselves with the thought that "at least I'm providing for my family," working women fear that "I'm neglecting the children, too." As a result, women experience all the alienation faced by any worker under capitalism, face a conflict rather than a reinforcement of cultural values, and are not even financially rewarded for their discomfort.

To be treated equally as a free wage-worker requires equal cultural freedom to enter into the wage relation. But women do not enter the market with the same cultural freedom as men. Men face lower unemployment rates than women. Women's role as mother contributes to this difference. Further, labor-market segmentation is exacerbated by the fact that men face conscription into the armed forces, so that the draft creates a relative labor shortage of male workers. From 1947 to 1962, when the armed forces averaged about two and a half million men, the yearly male unemployment rates averaged 4.6 percent, or only about 0.6 percent lower than the 5.2 percent for women during the same period. Since 1962, however, when the military averaged more than three million men, the male unemployment rate was only 3.83 percent, or about 1.67 percent lower than the 5.5 percent for women. Because they face the draft, men receive the "bonus" of lower unemployment rates. Furthermore, the typical work experience of women is to enter the labor market twice as many times as men do—once before they have children and once after the children are old enough to allow mothers to return to work. In recent years almost half of the unemployed women are "re-entering the labor force." In July 1969, the percentage of those women who were unemployed by reason of "losing the last job," was approximately 37, or close to their proportion of the total labor force; on the other hand, of persons unemployed by reason of "re-entering the labor force," women outnumbered men by 2.2 times. Finally, since the "provider" role is the father's, mobility is largely determined by his job opportunities, not the mother's; thus, the woman in two-worker families bears disproportionately any unemployment burden involved in mobility. Thus, the higher unemployment rates faced by women, while not independent of "discrimination," are largely due to the fact that women, in their role as mother in the nuclear family, enter the labor market on different terms than do men. The "natural market forces" do the rest.

The median income of women workers is only about 60 percent of the median income of men workers. There is no doubt some truth in the businessman's explanation of this difference, that women do have absentee rates two to four times higher than men's and the job tenure of women is about half that of men (2.8 years vs. 5.2 years).[3] It is the mother, not the father, who leaves the labor force to have children and then stays home from work when they need care. These factors entail more outlay for overtime and more frequent training of workers, adding to the costs of hiring women. Contributing to the lower median incomes of women are the facts that women are predominantly white-collar workers (about 60 percent of women workers), are relatively non-unionized (a situation made difficult to remedy due to low job tenure), have been competing with a rapidly expanding supply of women workers, and face some overt discrimination. In any case it is clear that, given women's conflict between rearing children and working, employers tend to hire women at jobs where training costs are relatively low and absenteeism is not costly.

Equal access to jobs outside the home, one of Benston's preconditions for women's liberation, will require that men and women become equally free of non-market norms of behavior. Perhaps the increasing discontent among women is due to the rapid proletarianization of women who are facing a market which expresses the contradiction between the non-market norms of motherhood and the market norms of free wage labor. If women were to attain equal pay and if parents were to share the practical child-care responsibilities, the contradiction between the nuclear family and free wage-labor under capitalism would become clear as employers turned from married to single workers because of their greater reliability and job tenure. Of course, as associates who agree that the emancipation of women requires, in addition to equality, the industrialization of housework and the socialization of child-rearing, we can struggle for the abolition of both the nuclear family and capitalism. But it should be clear that capitalism itself is undermining the nuclear family as mothers become workers. (Currently, in any month, alomst 40 percent of mothers with children under eighteen are in the labor force.)

Lastly, we believe the data call into question Benston's statement that "no one, man or woman, takes women's participation in the labor force very seriously." The three fifths of working women who are married and contributing to family income probably take it very seriously. The dramatic recruitment of women into the labor force since the Second World War and the concomitant increasing exploitation of family labor have been largely responsible for the spread of the "middle-class life style." The U.S. Department of Labor aptly summarizes the situation as of March 1967:

Nearly half of all women 18 to 64 years of age work in any one month. About 3 out of 5 of these women are married and living with their husbands. Almost all of these wives contribute to family income. It is often the wife's earnings that raise family income above poverty levels. In other families the wife's contribution raises the family's income from low- to middle-income levels. In fact, it is at the middle-income level that the largest proportion of wives are in the labor force.

There were 42.6 million husband-wife families in the United States in March 1967. In 15 million of these families, the wife was in the paid labor force. In the husband-wife families where the wife was an earner, the median family income in 1966 was $9,246 a year. In those families where the wife did not work, the median family income was $7,128.

The likelihood of escaping poverty is much greater among husband-wife families when the wife is an earner than when she is not. Nearly 5 million husband-wife families had incomes of less than $3,000 in 1966. Only 5 percent of all husband-wife families fell into this income group when the wife was in the paid labor force; 15 percent, when she was not.

An income of about $7,000 in 1966 dollars is considered a modest but adequate income for an urban family of four. Twenty-nine percent of all husband-wife families had incomes below this mark when the wife was a worker; 49 percent, when she was not.

The higher the annual family income (up to $15,000), the greater is the likelihood that the wife is in the labor force. The labor force participation of wives in March 1967 was lowest (13 percent) in families with 1966 incomes of less that $2,000, and highest (53 percent) in families with incomes of $12,000 to $14,999.

Just how much do working wives contribute to family income? According to a study made by the Bureau of Labor Statistics, the median percent of family income in 1966 accounted for by the wife's earnings was 22.2 percent. However, when the wife worked full time year round, it was 36.8 percent.[4]

These data speak for themselves. The maintenance of the family's standard of living, and in many cases the avoidance of poverty, is now substantially dependent upon not one but two income earners. This is an irreversible process. Women's participation in wage labor can no longer be regarded as "transient." The time is past when women can go home again.

NOTES

1. Unless otherwise noted, all calculations are derived from *Historical Statistics of the United States, the Statistical Abstract of the United States,* 1968 and 1969, and *Employment and Earnings,* vol. 16, No. 2, August 1969. For working mothers, see U.S. Department of Labor, Women's Bureau, Leaflet 37, "Who Are the Working Mothers?", 1967.
2. Reported in the *San Francisco Chronicle,* September 15, 1969.
3. V. C. Perella, "Women and the Labor Force," *Monthly Labor Review,* February 1968, p. 9; H. R. Hamel, "Job Tenure of Workers, January 1966," *Monthly Labor Review,* January 1967, Special Labor Force report, p. 31.
4. U.S. Department of Labor, Women's Bureau, "Working Wives—Their Contribution to Family Income," December 1968.

NOTES ON WOMEN IN ADVANCED CAPITALISM

Alice Harris
Bertram Silverman

Social conflicts in contemporary capitalism reflect various stages of historical change. Some conflicts are indicators of newly emerging patterns of social relations while others are struggles over still unresolved problems. The workers', student, Black, and women's movements contain elements of both the past and the future. Social scientists often search for leading indicators of social change. The transformation of Western civilization during the early phase of the industrial Revolution was first reflected in certain strategic economic sectors rather than in sharp discontinuities in the overall growth rates. The women's movement that has emerged in the late 1960s, it will be argued, is such a leading indicator of underlying social and economic forces that are transforming advanced capitalist society.

Many historical turning points have opened new perceptions of social reality. These transitions have produced tensions in existing patterns of social relationships. Groups previously too inarticulate and submerged to impress us with their presence find their voice and force us to reinterpret our historical experience and thus reorder our social consciousness.

One of the tasks of social analysis is to bring our social consciousness into greater accordance with changing social reality. Social movements and conflicts are the raw materials for such analysis. But numbers alone are not decisive. The women's movement may only represent a fraction of its potential constituency, but it reflects major tensions latent and manifest within our social system.[1]

Yet the discovery of women as an important force for historical change is not the most important aspect of social analysis. Marx did not discover the proletariat, nor was he the first to understand its significance for the transformation of industrial capitalism. His major contribution was to develop a theory of working-class evolution as part of a systematic model of capitalist development. To understand the role of women it is necessary to do for sexual stratification what Marx did for class stratification: to integrate the role of women in contemporary capitalist society as part of a framework for understanding the dynamics of modern capitalism. What follows are some notes toward that goal.

Despite the recent outpouring of literature about women, most studies have

SOURCE: *Social Policy,* July/August 1973, pp. 16–22.

not related the growing tensions over sexual stratification to structural changes of late capitalism. The books that have become household words such as Betty Friedan's *The Feminine Mystique,* Germaine Greer's *The Female Eunuch,* and Kate Millett's *Sexual Politics* are part of the women's movement. They are not explanations of its sources. But the popular literature does reveal, perhaps because it so often repeats, the focus of much discontent. It points to the ways in which women feel insolated from each other, and it picks up the boring and meaningless qualities of their lives. It reflects what seems to be a social identity crisis in terms of sexual relationships and images as well as in the roles that women perform. This crisis emerges in the tension between family and work roles; tensions that the literature explains by pointing to the structure of the family and the nature of the work world and of educational institutions.[2] For example, Viola Klein and Alva Myrdal argue in *Women's Two Roles* that

> It has become evident . . . that the increasing employment of women in all the advanced countries of the West has been a long-term development extending over many years, and not merely a temporary stop-gap due to the emergencies of war, or other sudden calamities. But . . . there has been no fundamental re-organization of our society such as would make this development beneficial to all concerned.[3]

The few attempts by Marxist analysts to deal with the family have concentrated primarily on the earlier phases of capitalist development. Evelyn Reed, for example, like Engels, sees the emerging nuclear family as the product of a newly property-conscious society. Because the family circumscribes women's role, it becomes the source of women's failure either to aspire or to achieve outside its limits. In a recent paper Angela Davis examined the ways in which early capitalism removed women from the sphere of commodity production and assigned them to dependent family roles.[4]

But those who have explored the contemporary women's movement, Marxists among them, have failed to account for the impact on the family of changing forces of production in late capitalism. Margaret Benston, for example, attributes women's inferior status to their exclusion from commodity production.[5] She ignores both the socialization functions of women within families and the changing nature of these functions to complement a changing economic structure.[6] Her framework cannot explain why women have become increasingly dissatisfied with their traditional roles. Similarly families may serve different functions for different social classes in different periods of time. As some strata of the working class become more affluent, the role of the family in relation to its children and in relation to the community alters. Women are called upon to serve new functions. Explanations, like that offered by Shulamith Firestone in the *Dialectic of Sex,* which ignores changes in class factors over time, obscure these distinctions.

Attempts to explain the present movement thus fall prey to two difficulties. They tend to isolate women from their social class and ethnic context, assuming that women qua women have class interests and therefore can develop consciousness without reference to the discrete conditions of their lives. They argue from the theoretical perspective of an industrial society, neglecting concurrent changes in production and consumption that are creating new contradictions in our political economy.

In that respect Juliet Mitchell's *Women's Estate,* which points to the contradiction between ideology and the present social relations of women in families and at work, is important. In an attempt "to come up with some Marxist answers" to feminist questions, Mitchell concludes that the women's liberation movement is a result of two contradictions: "there is the contradiction between their position in production and an ideology that virtually excludes them from it," and then there is "the family itself which contains the contradictions of its ideology (which stabilizes it) and of its economic function (which changes it)."[7]

Ideas about what women are supposed to do have not caught up with what women in fact do in contemporary families. To understand adequately why not, we need to ask a series of questions: What has been the impact of recent changes in the forces of production on existing institutional arrangements within capitalism? How do changes in productive forces particularly affect women from different classes and ethnic groups? Is the women's movement a reflection of the developing contradictions in the social relations of late capitalism?

CHANGES IN THE FORCES OF PRODUCTION

Although Marx had little to say on the subject of women, his approach to social conflict does provide a fruitful framework for the analysis of women's discontent. Marx's omission is due to the lower priority of the issue during his lifetime. Until World War II the central conflict of the capitalist mode of production was overwhelmingly expressed in the worker-capitalist relationship; specifically, the male's relationship to the means of production. Although the subordination of women was an integral part of the social structure of capitalism, it was not the primary source of conflict.

More recently the manifestations of social conflict have undergone significant changes. The continued expansion of productive capacity, reflected in higher levels of labor productivity, has provided the resources that enable late capitalism to contain and modify the labor-capital conflict. But this has not eliminated social conflicts associated with contradictions inherent in the private control, organization, and direction of the productive forces and the economic surplus.[8] In part tensions over sexual stratification are more recent manifestations of the conflict between social and private control over productive resources.

The progressive development of the productive forces creates the real potential for a postscarcity economy. The reduced proportion of the labor force necessary to fulfill our basic needs is one visible indicator of this possibility. Marx's vision that labor could become life's principal need rather than merely a means to life is consistent with our technological progress.[9] Such a trend would reduce the need for incentives based on the "carrot" of unequal material rewards and status and the "whip" of hierarchical power and economic insecurity. Moreover, advances in the forces of production produce the skills, education, and culture necessary to collective participation in and social control of the economy. But these are only potentials.[10]

Social conflicts in contemporary capitalism as a result of policies designed to contain the potentials inherent in a postscarcity economy. Early in the present century the traditional class structure and its distribution system began to encounter difficulty in absorbing the continuing expansion of the economic surplus. The anticipated results were economic stagnation and intensified labor-capital conflict.[11] The institutional responses to these problems were gradually developed in this country and reached their fruition during the Great Depression and World War II. Essentially an elaborate corporate bureaucratic superstructure was created to plan, control, and manipulate consumer needs and to reduce labor-capital conflict.[12]

As a result mass education, modern communications, and technology have reinforced the privatization manifested in ever increasing specialization, credentialism, inequality, and bureaucratic domination. The repressive work environment has been reproduced in the white-collar milieu and social participation in decision making has been inhibited. The hierarchical ordering of society for purposes of personal gain is not inherent in the logic of industrialization but in the way industrialization is institutionalized. It is the mode of organization that determines the material resources and power and creates the needs, values, and goals of society.

Although expanding labor productivity has reduced for many the most serious abuses of the distribution system, it has not fundamentally altered the capitalist mode of organization. State and corporate planning and control have helped reduce and contain class conflict. Though significant, these modifications in economic organization have not altered the private direction and control of productive resources. But they have influenced the manifestations of social conflict in ways that have special significance for the development of the women's movement.

There have been several recent attempts to present various new definitions and constructs of late capitalism. The most prominent were, first, David Riesman's *The Lonely Crowd,* then John Kenneth Galbraith's *The Affluent Society,* more recently *The New Industrial State,* and now Daniel Bell's *The Coming of Post-Industrial Society.* Each attests to significant changes in the sphere of production and consumption in modern capitalism. Each in its own way identifies alternative potentials inherent in modern technology and their containment in various forms of privatization.[13] But each has tended to explain many of the various forms of privatization[14] as inherent in advanced industrialization rather than as a consequence of the continued control of economic organization for private gain and profit.

The containment of the labor-capital conflict does not mean that capitalism has been transformed. As Marcuse points out, late capitalism, through rising labor productivity, socializes some sectors of the working class into accepting their own repression. We have yet to ask how the failure to socialize the growing economic surplus reproduces or displaces the conflict to other spheres of activity.

The private appropriation of the economic surplus and its use for private gain and profit continue to create tensions within the economic structure. But since they are no longer expressed primarily through class conflict, they emerge as conflicts within the meaning system, here defined as the values that legitimize the existing distribution of power and status.[15] Although these tensions appear as a value crisis, with subjective and psychological overtones, the instability in the meaning system is rooted in objective contradictions within the economic system.

WOMEN'S ROLE

It is beyond the scope of this article to deal extensively with the effect of objective contradictions on the meaning system, but a brief outline may suggest the argument. Our economic system needs an ideology to justify repressive work, economic inequality, and the hierarchical order. The justifications are familiar: higher income is the reward for hard work; free access to resources (education) makes inequality a result of the normal distribution of talent and intelligence. Existing hierarchy is rooted in the nature of technology and the division of labor. But the conflicts between the potentials of the productive forces and their containment by the existing mode of organization are beginning to demystify these justifications.

First, the expansion of consumption and education undermines the efficacy of the "carrot" as a means to insure the acceptance of repressive work. The capitalist solution of the "paradox of thrift" produces its own paradox vis-à-vis the incentive system. Increasing consumption undermines the willingness to postpone immediate gratification. Second, the containment of the labor-capital conflict, the truce between what James O'Connor calls Big Labor and Big Business, has itself undermined the truce over income distribution that some economists had suggested exists.[16] The underclass, or secondary workers, who constitute as much as 60 percent of our inner-city labor force, is breaking the liberal myth that equality is simply a matter of access to resources or hard work.[17] Third, the growth of educated labor, both as a consequence of the requirements of the social division of labor and as a means of surplus absorption, has increased the resistance to irrational authority and reopened the question of the inherent logic of industrialization with respect to hierarchy and bureaucratic domination. Finally the externalities (social costs) of private surplus absorption are undermining community cohesion itself. There are growing doubts about whether the growth in material goods produces any significant increases in social welfare. Therefore, economic growth, one of the normative standards by which the economic system measures its rationality, is questioned.

These tensions are producing considerable instability in the meaning system that justifies the distribution of status and power. Without the illusions that effort and talent inevitably yield higher places in the hierarchy, credentials are no longer sufficient substitutes for repressive work. For that strata which has achieved relatively high levels of education and consumption, aspirations to social mobility are no longer self-evident. The weakening of the meaning system begins to pose difficult questions about the legitimacy of previously accepted social roles and status. Among some segments of our population these role conflicts are producing a serious identity crisis—a crisis that reflects a search for new definitions (norms) to define participation in the social system. The search for "authenticity" in social relationships is symptomatic of this crisis and reflects the unmasking of social roles owing to the instability of the meaning system. These tensions within the meaning system are not translated directly into conflict between labor and capital. They seem to affect three groups most seriously: youth, who are in the process of being integrated into the social system; educated labor, who are primarily responsible for its interpretation and translation; and women, who bear the primary responsibility for socializing youth.

But tensions in the meaning system do not lead inevitably to a radical critique of the economic system. On the contrary, they may provoke demands for stronger assertions of traditional values previously associated with stability. Because conflicts over social roles are not translated directly into class conflict, predictions are difficult. But while we cannot predict directions, the contradictions in the economic structure previously outlined make it probable that conflict in the meaning system will continue.

Although these conflicts sometimes find expression in the sphere of production,[18] the crisis in the meaning system is most directly experienced in socializing institutions, particularly the family and school. It is here that educated women with adequate incomes experience most directly the instability in the meaning system. These women, of course, experience the conflicts of a commodity culture in a general way. They are among its primary victims, because not only are they the major consumers in our society but also they are isolated by the products they consume. Where adequate incomes prevail, and women are both well educated and removed from their extended families, certain familiar forms of behavior become manifest. They become isolated from their peers, over-involved with their children, and concerned with justifying their daily chores.

STRATIFICATION IN TRANSITION

But more significantly women are the vehicles through whom the meaning system is translated. They confront children who begin to raise questions about their parents' values—questions that emerge directly from the inconsistencies of contemporary capitalism. The value of education for "getting ahead" is no longer self-evident. Surrounded by relative affluence, children question the aspirations toward higher status and spiraling mobility that parents would instill in them. With the leisure to respond to social problems, young people protest the costs of an economy that does not channel its surplus in socially useful directions. Daughters who aspire to careers force mothers who have always been dependent on husbands to consider the value and meaning of their own lives. Thus questions about how to socialize children bring women who have primary childrearing responsibilities very close to the value conflicts in our society. For women these questions reinforce their identity conflict and create some serious disaffection with their role within the family.

These role conflicts have been reinforced by changes in the social division of labor that have altered the function of the family and the nature of work. Objective forces have reinforced the subjective conflicts over sexual roles and stratification. Real possibilities for women's equality exist in the tendencies within late capitalism which have been contained by the privatization of the capitalist mode of production.

To understand the impact of changes in the social division of labor on sexual stratification, some broad historical distinctions need to be drawn. The evolution of the wage system, during the phase of relatively low labor productivity and therefore low consumption when capitalism faced the problem of surplus creation, required family institutions that would integrate the young into the system of commodity production of that period. Under those circumstances the family tended to have two primary characteristics. First, the family was primarily authoritarian and repressive because youth had to be placed at a relatively early age into the authoritarian conditions of work. Affective relationships were not functional. Marriages were frequently arranged and divorces were virtually nonexistent. Second, the family was a social insurance system, usually part of an extended unit where the casualties of the economic system could be helped. In its extended form the family was the basic system of cohesion in an increasingly impersonal world.

Woman's role was defined primarily in relationship to the male and she was subordinate to him and dependent on his means of livelihood. Yet her consciousness of inequality was limited because the fundamental problem of the family was not the male-female relationship but subsistence—that is, the male's relationship to the world of work, the class issue. Moreover, a woman performed recognizably useful functions. She created a considerable quantity of nonmarket goods necessary for maintaining the level of subsistence. Her exclusive concern with childbearing appeared to be an inevitable natural function. She was not yet aware that this "biological" role was socially conditioned. The overwhelming requirements of the system at large and of her family function negated any sense that she was not a valuable human being.

However, the development of the social division of labor contained the seeds for the evolution of this consciousness and with it the recognition of women's privatization. Angela Davis correctly states the contradiction, but she does not analyze the historical transformation that led women to question their social position.

> Through a dialectical inversion, it is the radical separation of the producer from nature that lays the basis for the *social* creation of women as eternally natural beings. This is to say, women are socially imprisoned within the natural roles which are no longer naturally necessary.[19]

The continued development of the social division of labor under conditions of late capitalism increasingly explodes the rationalization of women's role because her socially imprisoned roles are no longer socially necessary. What at first seems natural and needs no explanation is no longer apparent.

Recent changes in the division of labor have accelerated this process in several ways. In the first place technological advances potentially reduce our work force needs. Fewer people can now do more work than ever before. The need for children to replace their parents in the work force is decreasing. Second, changes in the kind of work performed, from manual labor to white-collar work, reduce the need for authoritarian and repressive childbearing patterns. We are all familiar with the trend toward permissive childbearing, with the movements in our schools towards "open classrooms," "interaging," and self-regulated study programs. These reflect conflicts about the need to raise repressed children. Since parts of the labor force no longer have to be prepared for such repressive roles, some mothers no longer need to instill the harsh values of an older society. For women these changes bring to the force the increasing importance of affective relationships and, therefore, raise questions concerning the subordination and dependency of their sexual roles.

A third consequence of work force and technology changes is to extend the life span of men and women, but especially of women. The incidence of death from childbirth is now statistically negligible. Because she also has fewer children, the average woman can expect to be relatively free from childbearing responsibilities from about the age of thirty-five, when the youngest child enters school.

Fourth, and last, the complexity of work and credentialism has increased to the point where the family plays a smaller and smaller role in socializing the few children it does produce. Increasingly the socializing function is taken over by educational institutions and the mass media. Since children will probably no longer do the same kind of work as their fathers, parents relinquish their attempts to train to other institutions.

SERVICE SOCIETY EMPLOYMENT

These changes not only reduce the significance of families but also specifically reduce the significance of women in them. They are common to all industrial societies. In some families women are all but free of the restraints imposed by their former outdated function. This freedom is counteracted in other families by strong ethnic ties, which impose on women socialization functions that are derived from traditional or religious cultures, or by economic constraints where relative poverty prevails. Under these circumstances families still feel the need to train their children to take their places in the old manual sector of the labor force or to instill in them aspirations toward upward mobility. For many sectors of the labor force the economic and ideological constraints of an older industrial society no longer bind women to traditional roles.

To summarize, women experience awareness of their status through two primary sources. First, the crisis in the meaning system creates tensions within the socializing institutions, particularly in the family. Second, traditional roles of women are undermined by changes in the social division of labor that alter the function of the family. These changes in objective conditions reinforce the trend to redefine women's roles and raise questions about the traditional system of sexual stratification. But the direction of these objective changes, toward the enlarged participation of women in society, is inhibited by traditional modes of social relations. Consequently, as income rises, women increasingly question at various levels of consciousness the social necessity of their so-called natural roles. For increasing numbers of women the "escape" from traditional roles has become possible through changes in the productive structure, in particular the growth of the human service sector and the emergence of what is generally referred to as "the service society."

The shift in production structure away from harsh manual labor and excessive hours as well as dissatisfaction with their roles at home has encouraged women to enter the work force.[20] But entry into the labor market creates new conflicts. For many work is seen as an extension of family roles, justified by the need to "help out" at home.[21] Yet women must continue to perform effectively all the family tasks on which a commodity culture relies. As many have noted, women are thus caught in a conflict. They work to help out at home, yet feel guilty about neglecting home and children in order to work. The tug between two jobs takes its toll in conflict within both roles; this conflict leads women in the vanguard of the contemporary movement to demand both the restructuring of families to share responsibilities and chores and the restructing of jobs to provide more time for families.

Not only does sexual stratifications create conflict within the family, but also women's functions within the family create special problems for them within the labor market. While all workers experience the contradictions of the shift in productivity, women experience them in special ways. Because their primary functions are seen as caring for their families, women are relegated to secondary positions as easily replaceable workers. There, with top positions closed to them, they are unable to compete for the status that validates the lives of many men. High wages, which have traditionally justified unpleasant or physically tiring roles, are less effective in satisfying those who left home to find gratifying roles. In addition women who are not primary breadwinners (60 percent of the women who work are presently married and living with their husbands) are more free to raise questions about the quality of their work experiences.[22]

Women's position as secondary workers intensifies the degree to which their capacities are underutilized. Men whose jobs and responsibilities do not match their educational skills complain of boredom,[23] but women in this category are far more numerous. The more highly educated a woman the greater the likelihood that she will work, no matter what her marital, or financial status. But despite high educational levels, women tend to be employed in low-paying, low-status jobs. Intermittent work, as well as prejudices against women workers, makes the education gap far wider for women than it is for white men. They are invariably paid less than their male colleagues and have far less opportunity for upgrading. The female labor force is concentrated in the low-paying service and white-collar sectors of the job market. Neither their pay nor their responsibility matches their educational skills.

Finally the costs of neglecting community needs are most apparent to those who work in the service sector. Traditional jobs for women are in the human services as teachers, nurses, social workers. This sector has expanded more rapidly than any other since World War II. As a result more and more women now joining the labor force for the first time are entering the service sector. Although women constitute only 16.8 percent of the blue-collar work force, and 37 percent of the civilian labor force, they make up 64 percent of all service workers.

Involvement in the human services such as social welfare and education, at whatever level, reveals the neglect of social needs caused by a disparity in social priorities in late capitalism. Nurses, teachers, and social workers are trained to believe that their jobs are in the interests of human welfare, but the reality they face often contradicts the education they have received. Imbued with an ideology of service, many quickly discover the realities of inequality and the self-serving nature of the bureaucratic hierarchy.[24]

The relationship between sexual stratification and work is also related to the question of social strata. For those who see work primarily as an instrument for increased consumption, the tensions previously outlined can be more easily contained. Indeed many women may work precisely to meet the increasing cost of raising children. Consequently some women who are performing new roles may consider their contribution to the family of crucial importance. For these women the traditional rewards of high wages and advancement in the hierarchy are sufficient to contain conflicts in the jobs they perform. Just as role conflicts owing to a crisis in the meaning system can lead to a search for traditional values, so women's dissatisfaction over work roles can be contained by traditional trade-union methods.

But growing numbers of women who work out of choice, who are young, relatively affluent, well educated, and have few children, are increasingly conscious of conflict in their sexual roles. In search of new roles to replace those made dysfunctional by changing economic structures, these women encounter roadblocks to equality and participation set up by the priorities of advanced capitalism. Dissatisfied at home, they question their capacities as mothers and wives. The search for jobs raises conflicts between societal goals, which validate the family, and their own needs for creative satisfaction. Demands for jobs and opportunities commensurate with their abilities lead to an awareness that such jobs exist for neither men nor women. Holding a job raises the issues of social priorities now being confronted by other groups in other ways.

Since the number of women who feel conflict over sexual roles is increasing, it is clear that the women's liberation movement has long-range implications for the society as a whole. Incremental changes directed at containing the conflict already seem to be in progress, but they indicate a tendency to undermine sexual unity by stressing class differences. An Equal Rights Amendment and HEW enforcement of an affirmative action hiring plan in universities and elsewhere both promise to open doors to job opportunity, but they do not offer to restructure jobs. To free women from the home, tax abatements have been given to working mothers for the first time, but since these benefit only those who can afford the cost of child care, the poor are excluded. Day-care centers have so far been offered in limited numbers and only to the poor.

But conflicts over sexual roles are only symptoms of a crisis that has emerged from the contradictions between the potentials of an industrial society and the institutional constraints of advanced capitalism. The women's movement has become a leading indicator of that crisis because the social relations that are determined by sexual stratification conflict with the potentials inherent in the changing productive structure. A resolution of the conflicts over sexual stratification requires a reevaluation of the goals and priorities and ultimately the economic and social organization of advanced capitalism.

NOTES

1. A parallel is the labor movement, whose importance until relatively recently could not be measured by the number of workers in labor unions.
2. See any of the recent studies of working women on this point, especially Juanita Kreps, *Sex in the Market Place* (Baltimore: Johns Hopkins Press, 1970); Valerie Kincaide Oppenheimer, *The Female Labor Force in the United States: Demographic and Economic Factors Governing Its Growth and Changing Composition,* Population Monograph No. 5 (Berkeley: University of California Press, 1970).
3. Alva Myrdal and Viola Klein, *Women's Two Roles: Home and Work* (London: Routledge & Kegan Paul, 1956), p. 184.

4. Evelyn Reed, *Problems of Women's Liberation: A Marxist Approach* (New York: Pathfinder Press, 1970); Angela Davis, "Women and Capitalism: Dialectics of Oppression," paper delivered at Society for the Philosophical Study of Dialectical Materialism, New York City, December 28, 1971.

5. Margaret Benston, "The Political Economy of Women's Liberation," *Monthly Review*, September 1969, pp. 13–27.

6. To respond, as M. and J. Rowntree have done (*Monthly Review*, January 1970, pp. 26–32), by pointing out that 42 percent of all women now work is to miss the point. Not the fact of work but the self-perceptions of working women are crucial.

7. Juliet Mitchell, *Women's Estate* (New York: Pantheon, 1971), pp. 99, 173.

8. Economic surplus is equivalent to Paul Baran's definition of potential economic surplus—that is, the difference between the output that could be produced in a given natural and technological environment with the help of employable productive resources and what might be regarded as essential consumption. Despite some methodological problems with the definition of essential consumption, Baran's concept provides the possibility of breaking with other definitions that depend upon the accepted values of the economic system. See Paul Baran, *The Political Economy of Growth* (New York: Monthly Review Press, 1967), chap. 2.

9. Marx consistently maintained this view throughout his writings. Cf. Karl Marx, *Critique of the Gotha Program*. A more traditional economist, John Maynard Keynes, predicted the advent of a postscarcity economy: "When the accumulation of wealth is no longer of high social importance, there will be great changes in the code of morals. We shall be able to rid ourselves of many of the pseudomoral principles which have hag-ridden us for two hundred years, by which we have exalted some of the most distasteful of human qualities into the position of the highest virtues. We shall be able to afford to dare to assess the money-motive at its true value. The love of money as a possession—as distinguished from the love of money as a means to the enjoyments and realities of life—will be recognised for what it is, a somewhat disgusting morbidity, one of those semi-criminal, semi pathological propensities which one hands over with a shudder to the specialists in mental disease. All kinds of social customs and economic practices, affecting the distribution of wealth and of economic rewards and penalties which we now maintain at all costs, however distasteful and unjust they may be in themselves, because they are tremendously useful in promoting the accumulation of capital, we shall then be free, at last, to discard." See "Economic Possibilities for Our Grandchildren," in *Essays in Persuasion* (New York: Harcourt Brace, 1932), pp. 369–370.

10. Herbert Marcuse defines the irrationality of the late capitalist system precisely in the containment of these potentials. See *One Dimensional Man* (Boston: Beacon, 1964).

11. The stagnation thesis, developed during the Great Depression, was a consistent response to the institutional conditions of traditional capitalism. Its most well-known spokesman was Alvin Hansen. His theory failed to take into account the institutional responses of capitalism. More recent theories such as James Duesenbury's relative income hypothesis do not adequately relate institutional changes to consumer behavior.

12. For a more detailed discussion of this development, see James Weinstein, *The Corporate Ideal in the Liberal State* (Boston: Beacon, 1968) for the response to the labor problem; Alfred D. Chandler, Jr., *Strategy and Structure: Chapters in the History of American Industrial Enterprise* (New York: Doubleday, Anchor, 1966), for the response of corporations to changing market conditions; and John Kenneth Galbraith, *The Affluent Society* (Boston: Houghton Mifflin, 1958), for a discussion of consumer manipulation, particularly his chapter on the Dependence Effect. For a

more general discussion of the problems of surplus absorption, see Paul Baran and Paul Sweezy, *Monopoly Capitalism* (New York: Monthly Review Press, 1966).

13. Cf. David Riesman's concept of false personalization, John Galbraith's social imbalance, and Daniel Bell's bureaucratic harness.

14. David Riesman defines enforced privatization as the "generic term for the restrictions —economic, ethnic, hierarchical, familial—that keep people from adequate opportunities for leisure, including friendship." See *The Lonely Crowd* (New York: Doubleday, Anchor, 1950), p. 64.

15. For a more extensive discussion of the relationship between the meaning system, social class, and inequality, see Frank Parkin, *Class Inequality and Political Order* (New York: Praeger, 1971).

16. Galbraith, *Affluent Society,* chap. 7; James O'Connor, "Inflation and the Working Class," *Socialist Revolution,* March–April 1972, pp. 33–46.

17. Tom Vietorisz, Bennett Harrison, and William Spring, *New York Times Magazine,* November 5, 1972. See also Christopher Jencks et al., *Inequality* (New York: Basic Books, 1972), and David Gordon, *Theories of Poverty and Underemployment* (Lexington, Mass.: Heath, 1972).

18. See the recent HEW report on work in the United States.

19. Davis, "Women and Capitalism," p. 22.

20. Oppenheimer, *Female Labor Force,* p. 187.

21. This despite the fact that most women who work still do so out of need. The Virginia Slims Poll, 1970, reported that 48 percent of all women who worked did so to bring in extra money. Elizabeth Koontz, on the other hand, argues that 75 percent of married women who work come from families with total incomes of less than $10,000 per year. "Not Just for Pin Money," U.S. Department of Labor, Women's Division, 1970.

22. Kreps, *Sex in the Market Place,* p. 4.

23. "Boredom on the Assembly Line," *Life,* September 1972; *New York Times,* December 22, 1972.

24. See James O'Connor, "The Fiscal Crisis of the State: Part II," *Socialist Revolution,* March–April 1970, p. 89, for an elaboration of this point.

IX. THE REGULATION OF CLASS CONFLICT: THE INTEGRATION OF LABOR IN THE CORPORATE STATE

INTRODUCTION

Radicals and liberals differ in their interpretations of the role of the state in institutionalizing class conflict. Liberal analysis suggests that Marx seriously underestimated the state's function as a regulator and mediator of class conflict. According to this approach, progressive social welfare legislation has eliminated the most serious abuses of contemporary capitalism and labor-management policies have integrated the trade union into an accepted bureaucratic legal structure. Furthermore, capitalist economic planning has reduced the possibility of major economic crises. For liberals, these trends reflect the imperatives of advanced technology and the logic of industrialization. Radicals have explained these trends as means of containing the contradictions of corporate capitalism and the potential radicalism of workers and explored their impact on recent manifestations of social conflict. The readings in this section are concerned with the impact of the state on trade unions and the regulation of inflation as a central problem of labor-capital relations.

In "Corporate Liberalism and the Modern State," Weinstein outlines a radical theory of the origin of the corporate state. According to Weinstein, the ideology of corporate liberalism had been partially worked out and tried in the United States by the end of World War I and was fostered by the leaders of the largest corporations and financial institutions. Labor policy was designed primarily for purposes of social control and the consolidation of capitalist power. In "The Capitalism of the Proletariat," Bell discusses the transformation of the labor movement from "social" to "market" unionism and the integration of unions into the corporate structure. He outlines the limits of this process and predicts the decline of the trade union movement. Finally, Bell presents a liberal perspective on the possible reemergence of unions as a social movement. In "Trade Unionism in America," Aronowitz presents a radical approach to the trade unions. Since, inevitably, collective bargaining integrates unions into state capitalism, he argues that only alternative forms of worker struggles and institutions can revitalize working-class consciousness and the movement toward worker control. The possibility of such a strategy is suggested in the growing discontent in the workplace.

State regulation of aggregate demand within a structure of union-management collective bargaining in monopolistic industries has shifted preoccupation from economic depression to the problems of inflation. In "The Control of the Wage-Price Spiral," Galbraith presents the liberal argument that wage-price controls

392

are a logical extension of capitalist planning. In "Inflation and the Working Class," O'Connor presents a radical perspective on the contradictions inherent in increased participation of the state in advanced capitalism. According to O'Connor, the modern capitalist state has increasingly socialized many of the costs of production (e.g., education, research, health, etc.) but must continue to rely on taxes to finance its expanded activities. Many of these costs and expenditures are in fact subsidies to private capital, at times allied with labor. Consequently, state expenditures tend to outrun taxes because "the state has socialized many costs of production but has not socialized profits." However, the underlying reason for the fiscal crisis is the collaboration between what O'Connor calls Big Labor and Big Capital and the state which tends to pass cost inflation on to the competitive and state sectors. These factors combine to create a fiscal crisis of the state. They also intensify labor conflict particularly in the competitive sector, which is unable to absorb the rising costs of production or pass them on to consumers. O'Connor evaluates the options open to advanced capitalism and indicates the class forces that undermine their implementation.

CORPORATE LIBERALISM AND THE MODERN STATE

James Weinstein

. . . [Our two main theses] run counter to prevailing popular opinion and to the opinion of most historians. The first is that the political ideology now dominant in the United States, and the broad programmatic outlines of the liberal state (known by such names as the New Freedom, the New Deal, the New Frontier, and the Great Society) had been worked out and, in part, tried out by the end of the First World War. The second is that the ideal of a liberal corporate social order was formulated and developed under the aegis supervision of those who then, as now, enjoyed ideological and political hegemony in the United States: the more sophisticated leaders of America's largest corporations and financial institutions.

[Our study] is not based upon a conspiracy theory of history, but it does posit a conscious and successful effort to guide and control the economic and social policies of federal, state, and municipal governments by various business groupings in their own long-range interest as they perceived it. Businessmen were not always, or even normally, the first to advocate reforms or regulation in the common interest. The original impetus for many reforms came from those at or near the bottom of the American social structure, from those who benefited least from the rapid increase in the productivity of the industrial plant of the United States and from expansion at home and abroad. But in the current century, particularly on the federal level, few reforms were enacted without the tacit approval, if not the guidance, of the large corporate interests. And, much more important, businessmen were able to harness to their own ends the desire of intellectuals and middle class reformers to bring together "thoughtful men of all classes" in "a vanguard for the building of the good community."[1] These ends were the stabilization, rationalization, and continued expansion of the existing political economy, and, subsumed under that, the circumscription of the Socialist movement with its ill-formed, but nevertheless dangerous ideas for an alternative form of social organization.

There are two essential aspects of the liberal state as it developed in the Progressive Era, one tightly and sometimes indistinguishably intertwined with the other, but both clearly different. The first was the need of many of the largest corporations to have the government (usually the federal government) intervene in economic matters to protect against irresponsible business conduct and to assure

Source: *The Corporate Ideal in the Liberal State* (Boston: Beacon Press, 1968), pp. ix–xv.

stability in marketing and financial affairs. Gabriel Kolko has examined this aspect in his *The Triumph of Conservatism*,[2] and I will deal with it only peripherally. The second was the replacement of the ideological concepts of laissez faire, or the Darwinian survival of the fittest, by an ideal of a responsible social order in which all classes could look forward to some form of recognition and sharing in the benefits of an ever-expanding economy. Such a corporate order was, of course, to be based on what banker V. Everitt Macy called "the industrial and commercial structure which is the indispensable shelter of us all."[3]

The key word in the new corporate vision of society was responsibility, although the word meant different things to different groups of men. To most middle class social reformers and social workers—men such as Frank P. Walsh of Kansas City, or Judge Ben B. Lindsey of Denver, or Walter Weyl of the *New Republic,* or Jane Addams of Hull House, responsibility meant, first of all, the responsibility of society to individual Americans or to underprivileged social classes. To the corporation executives it meant, above all, the responsibility of all classes to maintain and increase the efficiency of the existing social order. Of course some middle-class reformers, like *New Republic* editor Herbert Croly, understood that progressive democracy was "designed to serve as a counterpoise to the threat of working class revolution."[4] But even for them the promotion of reform was not an act of cynicism: they simply sought a way to be immediately effective, to have real influence. Their purpose was not only to serve as defenders of the social system, but also to improve the human condition. In the most profound sense they failed, and badly; yet they were a good deal more than simply lackeys of the capitalist class.

The confusion over what liberalism means and who liberals are is deep-seated in American society. In large part this is because of the change in the nature of liberalism from the individualism of laissez faire in the nineteenth century to the social control of corporate liberalism in the twentieth. Because the new liberalism of the Progressive Era put its emphasis on cooperation and social responsibility, as opposed to unrestrained "ruthless" competition, so long associated with businessmen in the age of the Robber Baron, many believed then and more believe now, that liberalism was in its essence anti-big business. Corporation leaders have encouraged this belief. False consciousness of the nature of American liberalism has been one of the most powerful ideological weapons that American capitalism has had in maintaining its hegemony. An intellectual tradition has grown up among liberal ideologues that embodies this false consciousness. Arthur M. Schlesinger, Jr., intellectual in residence of the Kennedys, for example, writes that "Liberalism in America has been ordinarily the movement on the part of the other sections of society to restrain the power of the business community."[5] Consistent with this assertion is the popular image of movements for regulation and social reform—the Pure Food and Drug Act, the Federal Trade Commission, workmen's compensation, social security, unemployment insurance, the poverty program—as victories of "the people" over "the interests." In one sense this is true. Even so, Schlesinger's pronouncement is misleading. It is not only historically inaccurate, but serves the interests of the large corporations by masking the manner in which they have exercised control over American politics in this century.

Both in its nineteenth and twentieth century forms, liberalism has been the political ideology of the rising, and then dominant, business groups. Changes in articulated principles have been the result of changing needs of the most dynamic and rapidly growing forms of enterprise. Thus in the days of Andrew Jackson, liberalism's main thrust was against monopoly (and Arthur Schlesinger tells us this meant it was anti-business). But more recent scholarship has shown that it was the new business class, made up of individual small entrepreneurs (as well as threatened and declining farmers and artisans), that fought state chartered monopoly. Rising entrepreneurs struggled to free business enterprise of the outmoded restrictions of special incorporation and banking laws and to end what was then an overly centralized control of credit. Their laissez faire rhetoric in opposition to "unnatural" or artificial privilege was that of the common man, but their achievements—general incorporation and free banking laws, the spread of public education and popular suffrage—created the conditions for unfettered competition and rapid industrial growth. Half a century later that competition and industrial expansion had led to the development of new forms of monopoly, grown so powerful that a relative handful of merged corporations came to dominate the American political economy. Thereafter, liberalism became the movement for state intervention to supervise corporate activity, rather than a movement for the removal of state control over private enterprise.

To achieve conditions suitable for free competition during the Age of Jackson, the rising entrepreneurs and their political representatives had to believe in, and promote, ideals of equality of opportunity, class mobility, and noninterference by the government with individual initiative (although, even then, government subsidy of such necessary common services as railroads and canals was encouraged where private capital was inadequate to do the job). At the turn of the century the new trust magnates also pressed for reform in accordance with their new political, economic, and legal needs. The nature of the ideals and the needs in the two periods were different. In the first, the principles of competition and individual efficiency underlay many proposed reforms; in the second, cooperation and *social* efficiency were increasingly important. But in each case the rising businessmen— or, at least, many of them—helped promote reforms. In both instances, business leaders sponsored institutional adjustment to their needs, and supported political ideologies that appealed to large numbers of people of different social classes in order to gain, and retain, popular support for their entrepreneurial activity. In the Progressive Era, and ever since, corporation leaders did this by adapting to their own ends the ideals of middle class social reformers, social workers, and socialists.

My main concern . . . is not with the social reformers, men and women who might be called ordinary liberals. Instead I will focus on those business leaders (and their various political and academic ideologues) who saw liberalism as a means of securing the existing social order. They succeeded because their ideology and their political economy alone was comprehensive. Radical critics of the new centralized and manipulated system of social control were disarmed and absorbed by the corporate liberals who allowed potential opponents to participate, even if not as equals, in a process of adjustments, concession, and amelioration that seemed to promise a gradual advance toward the good society for all citizens. In a formal democracy, success lay in evolving a social vision that could be shared by most articulate people outside the business community. Corporate liberalism evolved such a vision. More than that, it appealed to leaders of different social groupings and classes by granting them status and influence as spokesmen for their constituents on the condition only that they defend the framework of the existing social order.

As it developed, the new liberalism incorporated the concepts of social engineering and efficiency. The corollary was a disparagement of "irresponsible" individualism and localism. On the municipal level, as Samuel P. Hays has observed, the drama of business-led reform lay in competition between two systems of decision-making. One was based upon ward representation and traditional ideas of grass-roots involvement in the political process; the other, growing out of the rationalization of social life made possible by scientific and technological developments, required expert analysis and worked more smoothly if decisions flowed from fewer and smaller centers outward toward the rest of society. The same competition went on at the federal level, although formal changes in the political structure were more difficult to make and, therefore, less extensive. In general, however, the Progressive Era witnessed rapid strides toward centralization and a decline in importance of those institutions which were based upon local representation, most obviously in the decline of Congress and the increasing importance of the executive branch in the shaping of policy and in the initiation of legislation. As Hays concludes, this development constituted an accommodation of forces outside the business community to political trends within business and professional life.[6]

The process of developing social reform through extra-political negotiation between various social groupings went on most consistently in the early years of the century in one organization, the National Civic Federation. It is, therefore, central to this study. The National Civic Federation was primarily an organization of big businessmen, although it established the principle of tripartite (business-labor-public) representation in public affairs. Founded in 1900, it was the leading organization of politically conscious corporation leaders at least until the United States entered the First World War. I will, in addition, look at the circumstances under which small businessmen acted like big businessmen—that is, when they played the role of class-conscious political reformers, capable, if necessary, of transcending their most immediate, or apparent, interests or traditions. And I will examine the role of leaders of the major political parties during the Progressive Era (1900 to 1920), to explore their relationship to particular business groupings, but, more important, the manner in which they assimilated and translated into legislation the social and institutional principles talked about and advocated by business leaders in the Civic Federation and other organizations. In short, this book will attempt to show that liberalism in the Progressive Era—and since—was the product, consciously created, of the leaders of the giant corporations and financial institutions that emerged astride American society in the last years of the nineteenth century and the early years of the twentieth.

NOTES

1. Sidney Kaplan, "Social Engineers as Saviours: Effects of World War I on Some American Liberals," *The Journal of the History of Ideas,* XVII (June 1956), 347.
2. New York, 1963.

3. Speech to the 17th Annual Meeting of the National Civic Federation, January 22, 1917, Box 187, National Civic Federation papers, New York Public Library.
4. Kaplan, "Social Engineers," pp. 354–355.
5. Arthur M. Schlesinger, Jr., *The Age of Jackson* (Boston: Little, Brown, 1946), p. 505.
6. Samuel Hays, "The Politics of Reform in Municipal Government in the Progressive Era," *Pacific Northwest Quarterly,* LV, No. 4 (October 1964), pp. 168–169.

THE CAPITALISM OF THE PROLETARIAT

Daniel Bell

TRADE-UNIONISM, said George Bernard Shaw, is the capitalism of the proletariat. Like all such epigrams, it is a half-truth, calculated to irritate the people who believe in the other half. American trade-unionism would seem to embody Shaw's description, but in fact it only half-embodies it—at most. True, the American labor leader will mock socialism and uphold capitalism; yet he has built the most aggressive trade-union movement in the world—and one, moreover, that has larger interests than mere economic gain. Abroad, the European Marxist hears the labor leader praise the free enterprise system as the most successful method yet devised for a worker to obtain a fair, and rising share, of the country's wealth; within the United States, the American businessman listens to the labor leader denouncing him in wild and often reckless rhetoric as a greedy profiteer, monopolist, and exploiter. How reconcile these contradictions? One U.S. labor leader sought to do so in these terms: *to* your wife, he said, you talk one way; *about* your wife, you talk another. Very clever; but, one might add, another half-truth —at most.

William James once said that whenever you meet a contradiction you must make a distinction, for people use the same words but mean two different things. One way out of this seeming contradiction, therefore, is to see American trade-unionism as existing in two contexts, as a *social movement* and as an economic force (*market-unionism*), and accordingly playing a different role in each. The social movement is an *ideological* conception, shaped by intellectuals, which sees labor as part of a historical trend that challenges the established order. Market-unionism, on the other hand, is an *economic* conception, a delimiting of role and function, imposed by the realities of the specific industrial environment in which the union operates.

Any labor movement finds itself subject to all the ideological pressures of the "left," whether social, communist, or syndicalist. After all, it is in the name of the workers that these social movements proclaim their slogans; and the labor movement itself is one of the chief vehicles of social change. But in the United States, the image of trade-unionism as a social movement took a unique course, as plotted in the theory—inspired largely by the "Wisconsin school" of John R. Commons and Selig Perlman—of "Laborism." The theory argues that the trade-union movement, although fashioned ideologically, has a different source of cohesion than the radical movement, i.e., the limited, day-to-day, expectation of social improve-

SOURCE: *The End of Ideology* (New York: The Free Press, 1960), pp. 211–223.

ent. By its concentration on the specific issues at hand, it must necessarily reject
e far-flung socialist and radical ideologies; unlike them, it is both in the world
d *of* the world. In its operation, it can indeed become a force for social change,
t only by "sharing" power rather than seeking the radical transformation of
ciety. This sharing of power takes place both in the factory—through bargaining
a wages and working conditions, and sometimes on production standards—and
a society] through seeking legislation for the increased welfare of the worker.

"Laborism" is the dominant ideology, to the extent that there is one, of the
merican labor movement. In the past it has been the conservative defense of the
nions against the recriminations of the radicals; it was a rationalization of the
rely economic role of the unions. Yet, despite its theorists, even it has come
 have a political force of its own. Pale ideology though it is, it still conceives
 unionism as a social movement, and it still conceives of itself as being opposed
 the employer class as a whole. Contemporary American unionism could only
ve flourished with the aid of a favorable political—and social—climate, [and
is was] provided by the New Deal. More importantly, the Roosevelt Admini-
ration provided, through law, two extraordinary protections: first, the legal
bligation of employer to bargain collectively with unions; and second, the grant-
g of *exclusive* representation rights to a *single* union within a defined bargaining
nit. This, plus the growth of various union security devices (e.g., maintenance-
f-membership clauses, union shops, etc.) gave the unions a legal protection that
w union movements enjoyed anywhere.[1] "Laborism" is associated usually with
e New Deal and Fair Deal, and with the left wing of the Democratic party. It
lls for improved social-welfare benefits, for a tax program which falls mostly
n the wealthy, and it cries out incessantly against "monopolies."

But here lies an anomaly and the source of a contradiction: for *market-union-
m*, collective-bargaining unionism, can only exist in monopoly situations, a mon-
poly created either by the employers or by the unions. In fact, the only industries
 the United States where unionism is strong today are those where a monopoly
tuation, industry- or union-created, exists.

The reason is fairly simple. *The chief purpose of market-unionism is to elimi-
ate wages as a factor in competition.* Where an industry is only partially unionized
nd wages therefore can be utilized as a competitive lever, a union must either
npose a monopoly or go under; the erosion of the American textile unions is a
ase in point.

The pattern of monopoly follows that of the different markets. In oligopolistic
arkets, i.e., in industries dominated by a few firms, the unions eliminate wages
s a competitive factor by "pattern bargaining," that is, by imposing wage agree-
ent on all firms in the industry. While, theoretically, bargaining is still done
ith individual firms, in practice (as is seen in the case of steel) the agreement
 industrywide. In the highly competitive or small-unit-size fields, the unions have
epped in and provided a monopoly structure to the market, limiting the entry of
rms into the industry, establishing price lines, etc. This has been true most notably
n the coal industry, in the garment industry, and in the construction trades.

In coal, where the industry could not do it itself, the miners' union has enforced
 basic price floor for the entire industry. This has been done in various ways:
hrough legislative price-fixing, as in the Guffey Coal Act of the first years of the
ew Deal; outright production-restriction schemes, as in Pennsylvania, which
imit the tonnage of anthracite that can be mined in the state; by keeping the

mines open only three days a week; by staggered strikes in order to reduce coal surpluses, etc.

The garment unions have established a fixed series of price lines, or grades, for men's clothing and women's dresses, thus bringing order out of chaotic competition. By limiting the number of contractors who can sew and finish dresses for a single manufacturer, and by stopping firms from moving out of a fixed geographical area, the International Ladies' Garment Workers' Union has been able to restrict the number of firms in the industry and to police the market.

The most elaborate form of market stabilization exists in the construction trades. The power of the unions resides in the fact that they serve as a work contractor, i.e., as the labor-force recruiting agent, for the employer. Few of the firms that bid on the heavy construction work (dams, power stations, roads, factories, atomic installations, etc.) maintain a permanent labor force; nor do they know the local labor market; they rely on the union [for experienced and skilled men]. Even the small home-builder needs the union to provide stability. The major factor in the cost of each competing home contractor is the wages he must pay. In northern California alone, there are 12,000 construction firms bidding on various home constructions. The union is in no position to bargain with each single contractor. Therefore the union organizes an *employers'* association and enforces stability in the market by holding wage rates constant over a period of time.

Long ago, the construction unions and the contractors were quick to realize the monopoly advantages to be gained by mutual co-operation. Thus, on many local projects, outside contractors are kept out because the unions refuse to supply them with labor; or if they win a bid, they find themselves afflicted by strikes or slowdowns.

Often the union, as in the case of coal, can decide the fate of firms and the future of an industry. Because of competing fuels, like natural gas and oil, the demand for coal has shrunk almost a third in the last ten years. John L. Lewis and the union faced a choice. Either they could seek to restrict output and force all the firms in the industry to share the dwindling market, thus saving the marginal firms, or they could allow the marginal firms to go to the wall. In the decisive coal negotiations of 1952 the Southern coal producers, owners mostly of smaller mines, offered to meet all the union demands if Lewis would order three-day production in the industry. The large mechanized mines opposed this move since it meant higher overhead costs for unutilized equipment. Lewis, reversing a previous course, chose to line up with the large mechanized mines and their desire for continuous output. The decision meant higher wages for the men but a permanent loss of jobs in the industry. The union could accept that because of the natural attrition of an aging mine work force. Other unions could not solve the dilemma so easily.

Thus it is that a trade-union, operating in a given market environment, necessarily becomes an ally of "its" industry. Less realized is the fact that, in the evolution of the labor contract, the union becomes part of the "control system of management." He becomes, as C. Wright Mills has put it, a "manager of discontent."

It is difficult for a manager, faced with an aggressive group of union leaders across a bargaining table, to realize that the trade-union performs a vital function *for him.* All he can think of is that, because of the union, he has lost some of his power. And to a great extent this is true: he cannot fire a man at whim, promotions are on the basis of seniority, a foreman cannot make job transfers—these are performed by the union.

But in taking over these powers the union also takes over the difficult function of specifying priorities of demands, and in so doing, it not only relieves management of many political headaches but becomes a buffer between management and rank-and-file resentments. The union, particularly on the local plant level, is not a monolith but a web of interest groups which reaches far down to the lowest unit of plant organization, the work group. There interests often conflict: skilled vs. unskilled, piecework vs, hourly-paid, night-shift vs. dayshift, old vs. young. In formulating its demands, the union has to decide: should a wage increase go "across the board" (i.e., be equal for everybody) or should it be on a percentage basis in order to maintain the differentials in skill?

The second fact is that the union often takes over the task of disciplining the men, when management cannot. This is particularly true during "wildcat strikes," when the men refuse to acknowledge the authority of management but are forced back to work by the union leaders who, by the logic of a bargain, have to enforce a contract.

Managing these discontents becomes difficult not only at bargaining periods but throughout the year as well. During a time of layoffs, the question of which type of seniority is to be followed (whether by particular type of work or by a plantwide list) becomes a bread-and-butter struggle. But the major headache arises when workers, in order to keep a company competitive, and thus safeguard jobs, cut their wage rates, tighten their time assignments, and accept increased production loads. In effect, they disrupt the uniform patterns which the union has been seeking to impose throughout the industry. The problem of "my company first" is one that has plagued the United Auto Workers: should the national office seek to maintain uniform standards, and if so, to push the marginal company to the wall? Or should it protect the employment of the men by allowing them to cut wages and reduce standards? In recent years, the UAW has chosen to safeguard employment.

The question of "my company first" has its counterpart in this "my industry first" attitude of different unions. Thus the interest conflicts become raised to national levels. The teamsters oppose government favors for the railroad. The coal union seeks higher tariffs against foreign oil production and unites with the railroads—since the railroads gain a large share of their income from hauling coal—in joint lobbying ventures. The machinists, whose strength is in the aircraft industry, will lobby for more planes, while the boilermakers, who construct ships, urge a larger navy. More generally, unions will often engage in joint promotional campaigns with an industry in order to stimulate demand and save jobs. This is as true for the "socialist" Ladies' Garment Workers as for the narrow, craftminded plasterers' union. In these, as in many other instances (e.g., trucking, glass, etc.), the initiative has come from the unions, since they are more powerful and more market-conscious than any single firm.

In effect, then, the logic of market-unionism leads to a limited, uneasy partnership of union and company, or union and industry; uneasy because in many cases employers would still prefer to exercise sole power, although the more sophisticated employers know the value of such powerful allies as the union in safeguarding their interests; uneasy, too, because there is still the historic tendency of labor, acting as a social movement, to oppose the employers as a class. This tendency derives from the ideological conception of labor as the "underdog." More specifically, it has been reinforced by the political alliances, forged in the early days of the New Deal, which enabled labor to obtain legislative protection for its organizing activities. These political alliances lead necessarily to wider areas of group or class conflict: tax policy, subsidized housing, medical insurance, and the whole range of welfare measures which add up to a more or less coherent philosophy of liberal politics.

The distinction between the *social movement* and *market-unionism* is not, as might seem at first glance, a distinction between political and collective-bargaining unionism. In present-day society, the latter division no longer exists. All unions are, willy-nilly, forced into politics. The problem is what sort of politics will be played. Will the AFL-CIO simply be a political arm for market-unionism, protecting the various interest groups that are its members, or will it become part of a genuine social movement?

Some clue to the answer may be found from American labor's past. In the nineteenth century there were four main strands: fraternalism, cooperation, political action, and collective bargaining.[2] While one easily assumes that collective bargaining is the unique form of American unionism, it took nearly a half a century of debate and experiment to come to this form. United States labor was always reluctant to accept the wages system. Its early organizers sought escape in free land, money reform, and failing that, in the creation of producer co-operatives. The vast power of industry, and the openness of the political system, caused many individuals to feel that political action, rather than economic bargaining, was the easier road to better conditions. The large movement for shorter hours, for example, in the 1880's was almost entirely a political movement. But the unwillingness of the Socialists to modify their goals, and the insistence by Gompers on separate trade organization which could achieve an integral role in the market, turned American labor to its bargaining role. But, always, concurrently, there was the image of the social movement. If we apply the distinction between social movement and market-unionism to the past, we derive the following periodization:

(1) From 1860 to 1880, U.S. labor was primarily a social movement. The socialist and anarchist influences were paramount. There was a high degree of political activity, and many efforts to create labor parties. Unions built producers' co-operatives and supported many reform schemes. The extent of organization, however, was small.

(2) From 1880 to 1920, the two tendencies were in conflict: the AFL represented the narrow conception of market-unionism, while such groups as the Socialists, the IWW, and other anarcho-syndicalist elements sought to build radical labor movements. The AFL won out.

(3) From 1933 to 1940 (the period of the 1920's was one of stagnation), labor once again assumed the role of a social movement. The emerging CIO, faced by the attacks of the industrial combines, tended to take on an ideological coloration. The influx of the intellectuals, particularly the Socialists and the Communists, heightened this radical political quality. Support by the federal government gave labor an awareness of the necessity for political action. And John L. Lewis, a shrewd and dynamic labor leader, realized the possibility of welding together a new political bloc.

(4) From 1940 to 1955, labor lost this ideological flavor and concentrated,

instead, on market-unionism. There were several reasons. First, the sense of national unity created by the war. Second, the acceptance by large industry of trade-unionism, at first because of the need for uninterrupted production, later because of the realization that the unions could not be broken directly. Third, the need of the newly built unions to consolidate their collective-bargaining position in the plant. Fourth, the attack on the Communists in the unions, beginning in 1947, and the eventual elimination of their influence.

And the future? Where U.S. labor goes from here is a difficult question, for the trade-union movement is now at an impasse. The source of its difficulty lies deep in the facts of present-day American life.

1. *Union membership has reached its upper limit.* In the last seven years U.S. unions have ceased to grow. In fact, the proportion of the unionized in the work force has actually declined.[3]

Today there are roughly 16 million workers (plus another 850,000 members of Canadian affiliates) belonging to American trade-unions as against 2 million a quarter of a century ago. Measured against a labor force of 65 million persons, this is slightly under 25 per cent; seen more realistically as a proportion of the wage and salaried persons (i.e., excluding farmers, self-employed professionals, and small businessmen), the unions have organized about 30 per cent of the employee group of the society. But in organizing this 30 per cent, they have reached a saturation mark; they have organized as much of their potential as they can.

If one distinguishes between blue-collar and white-collar workers, then it is likely that about 75 per cent of the blue-collar force—factory workers, miners, railway men, building craftsmen, and laborers—belong to unions. In coal and metal mining, in railroad and construction, in public utilities, unions have organized between 80 and 90 per cent of the blue-collar force. In basic manufacturing —auto, aircraft, steel, rubber, ship, glass, paper, electrical equipment, transportation equipment—about 80 per cent of plant production workers are organized. The remaining obstacle in the unorganized units is their small size. A UAW survey, for example, showed that 97 per cent of the unorganized plants within the union's "jurisdiction" have less than fifty workers. These plants are extremely difficult to organize. The social relations within a small firm are very different from those in a large one: the identification with an employer is greater; employer counterpressure is easier; the cost to the union of reaching and servicing these places is very high and often "uneconomic," since unions, as business organizations, have their cost and efficiency problems as well. The only unorganized *industries* are oil, chemicals, and textiles. In oil and chemicals, wages are extraordinarily high because labor costs are only a slight element in total costs, and workers are organized in independent unions. In textiles, the old paternalistic and Southern mill-village pattern has been strong enough to resist unionization.

What then of the other fields? In the trade and service fields, employing about fifteen million workers, unions have only a slight foothold—in restaurants, hotels, laundries—but usually only in the metropolitan centers where other unions have been able to help organization. Most of these units are small, [thus] difficult to organize. With the expansion of the *distributive field*, general unions, such as the Teamsters, are bound to grow, particularly since the Teamster method of organization is often to organize employer associations and "blanket" the workers into the unions. But this growth will be offset by the shrinkage in the *industrial* work force.[4]

In the white-collar and office field (banks, real estate, insurance, as well as the office forces of the large industrial companies), unions have failed signally. In plants where the blue-collar force is organized, the firm usually follows the practice of granting tandem wage increases to the office workers, so that the latter have no need or incentive to join a union. In the insurance companies and in white-collar employment generally, there is a high turnover. Jobs are held by young girls, recruited directly from school, who leave for marriage after five or six years and who are reluctant to join a union. In general, white-collar workers in the U.S., for status reasons, fear to identify themselves with the dirty-handed blue-collar workers. In European and Asia countries, teachers and civil service employees may consider themselves the leaders of the working class. In the U.S. these groups seek to emphasize the differences between them.

2. *Unions have reached the limits of collective bargaining.* This may be a startling statement, but yet it is one of the most important facts tending to re-shape the American labor movement. By the "limits of collective bargaining" I mean simply the growing awareness by unions that they can obtain wage and welfare increases equal to the increases in the productivity of the country. Such a story may be an old one to unions in Europe, who are sensitive to the trade positions of their countries, but it is new in the United States.

Even the *idea* of productivity is a relatively recent one. (It is, perhaps, one of the reasons why Marx's analysis of capitalism has been proven wrong. For Marx, wealth was gained through "exploitation." Now we can see that wealth, private corporate wealth and national wealth, increases only through increases in pro-ductivity.) The turning point in American labor history, I think, came with the idea of the annual productivity wage increases. This is the conception that the workers are entitled *each year* to a wage increase above and beyond the change in the cost of living. One may argue about how much productivity has ad-vanced—whether it is 2 percent, 3 percent, or 4 percent; these are statistical questions. What is settled is the fact that each year the living standard of the worker will advance—in the case of the auto workers, about 3 per cent. (If one compounds the 3 percent increase, then the living standards will have doubled in a little over twenty-five years.) Curiously, the idea of the productivity wage increase was not a union but a corporation innovation, by General Motors. The company offered such a wage increase in return for a five-year contract, guaranteeing labor peace.

Today the idea of the productivity wage increase has spread throughout most of basic American manufacturing. In this way a strong demand factor is built into the economy, thus holding off a downturn of the business cycle. But wage rises are geared to the most productive sector of the economy, while inefficient firms, or industries which by their nature cannot increase productivity (barbers, waiters, etc.), have to match these increases. This leads to a strong inflationary impact on the economy.

Such questions aside, the importance of the productivity wage increase is that, despite the lingering rhetoric of militancy, unions have accepted the idea of limits to what can be obtained through economic bargaining. I do not mean to suggest that there will be no more bargaining. But we have here the *bureaucratization* of bargaining in the establishment of limits.[5]

3. *The rise of the salariat.* A third crucial change in the nature of the American labor movement arises from the shifting composition of the work force. Briefly put, the *proletariat* is being replaced by a *salariat,* with a consequent change in the psychology of the workers. The trend arises in part from the fact, as Colin Clark long ago noted, that with increasing productivity, greater output is being achieved with a smaller industrial work force, while the demand for new services, entertainment, recreation, and research means the spread of more and new middle-class occupations.

But we have appreciated less the changes in the work force *within* the giant manufacturing firms themselves. For with the increases in production have come increases in research, merchandising, sales and office force, etc. In the chemical industry, for example, from 1947 to 1952, production increased 50 per cent; the blue-collar force increased 3 per cent; the white-collar force by 50 per cent. In the fifteen largest corporations in the country, the salaried work force is already one-third to one-half of the hourly-paid production force. For example:

	HOURLY WORKERS	SALARIED WORKERS
du Pont	52,000	31,000
Standard Oil	30,000	27,500
Westinghouse	70,000	40,000
Ford	135,000	40,000
G.M.	360,000	130,000

The change to a "salariat" has been intensified in the 1950's by two principal developments: the enormous rise in research and development within American industry, creating a new technical class, and the expansion of automation processes which result in the upgrading of skilled workers. From 1947 to 1957, the number of professional and technical workers increased by 60 per cent, the highest growth rate of any occupational group in the post-World War II period. In the next decade, this group increased an additional 43 per cent, or two-and-a-half times as fast the the labor force as a whole. While the semi-skilled group remained almost constant over ten years (from 12.2 to 12.9 million workers), the technical and professional, the non-production worker, has increased over 50 per cent in the same period. If one excludes the service fields, the number of white-collar workers in the United States by 1956, for the first time in U.S. history, exceeded the number of blue-collar workers.[6]

These salaried groups do not speak the old language of labor. Nor can they be appealed to in the old class-conscious terms. Their rise poses a difficult problem for the leadership of the American labor movement.

4. *The loss of* élan *and the disfavor of the public.* The labor movement, in its present form, is less than twenty-five years old, and the men on top are the men who built it. But they are no longer young—the average age of the AFL-CIO executive council is in the middle sixties—and they have lost their *élan.* The organizing staffs, too, are old, and there is no longer the reservoir of young radicals to rely on for passing out leaflets at the plant sites.

But more than this, there is a crisis in union morality and public confidence. It is not simply a problem of racketeering.[7] Racketeering is shaped by the market. It has always had a hold in the small-unit construction trades, the longshoremen, and the teamsters, where the chief cost to an employer is "waiting time" and where one can therefore easily exact a toll from employers. And one finds no racketeering in the mass-production industries. Even in the fields where "shakedowns" are comon, racketeering is on a considerably smaller scale today than twenty-five years ago, when the industrial gangster flourished in the U.S. The real sickness lies in the decline of unionism as a moral vocation, the fact that so many union leaders have become money-hungry, taking on the grossest features of business society, despoiling the union treasuries for private gain. And where there has not been outright spoilation—typical of the teamster, bakery, textile, and laundry unions—one finds among union leaders an appalling arrogance and high-handedness in their relation to the rank and file, which derives from the corruption of power. Such gross manifestations of power have alienated a middle-class public which, for twenty years, was tolerant of, if not sympathetic to, unionism.

The future of any movement depends upon the character of its leaders, the strength of its traditions (the impelling force) and the sharpness of its goals (the compelling forces), and the challenges of the society of which it is a part.

Certainly the radical tradition of the labor movement has almost vanished, and of those individuals who came out of the Socialist or leftwing movement, such as Dubinsky, Potofsky, Rieve, Curran, Quill, and Reuther, only Reuther still has the drive and desire to widen labor's definition of its goals. The men at the top of labor unions today have little energy for intensive political action or a desire to take a leading political role. At the middle levels, which reflect themselves largely in the state and city rather than national scenes, many of the younger labor leaders are eager for means to enhance their status and power, and it is quite likely that these men will step into the political arena in order to gain recognition and will do so by becoming more active in the Democratic party. . . .

NOTES

1. The most succinct summary of the role of government in aiding the formation of unions can be found in two articles by Archibald Cox and John T. Dunlop in the *Harvard Law Review:* "Regulation of Collective Bargaining by the N.L.R.B.," 63 *Harvard Law Review* 380 (1950), and "The Duty to Bargain Collectively," 63 *Harvard Law Review* 1097 (1950). For a detailed discussion of United States labor law, see Millis and Brown, *From the Wagner Act to Taft-Hartley* (Chicago, 1950). For a review of the historical climate, see Derber and Young (eds.), *Labor and the Deal* (Madison, Wis., 1957).

2. The standard histories, of course, of the labor movement are those by John R. Commons and his associates on *The History of Labor in The United States.* These volumes are principally from an AFL point of view in that they see job-consciousness as the "natural" expression of the American labor movement. A variant point of view can be found in the two volumes, neglected today, by Norman Ware: *The Industrial Worker 1840–1860,* and *The Labor movement in the United States, 1860–1895.* Ware, writing in the twenties, when the AFL was at its nadir, was skeptical about its success, and he took a more favorable view of the Knights of Labor than did Selig Perlman, Commons' chief disciple. The most valuable part of Ware's books is his emphasis on industrialization and its consequences for unionization, an emphasis which is lacking in the Commons volumes.

3. The argument that union growth had reached a plateau and possible saturation was first presented in a number of articles in the Labor section of *Fortune* in 1951 and 1952 and summarized in my article "The Next American Labor Movement," *Fortune,* April 1953. This contention was disputed by Professor Irving Bernstein in an article in the *American Economic Review* in July 1954. The issues were debated at the Seventh Annual Meeting of the Industrial Relations Research Association and printed in the volume of *Proceedings* of that meeting. For a summary of my statistical evidence, see my paper on "Union Growth" in those proceedings, December 1954.
4. It is likely that many craft and industrial unions, in order to resist shrinkage, will become "general" unions taking in whatever workers are at hand. This is what John L. Lewis tried with his District 50 of the Mine Workers, and this is what Hoffa [was] doing in 1959.
5. Arthur Ross has noted "the withering away of the strike," the fact that in the U.S. and almost every country there is a secular decline in the number of strikes. This is, I suggest, a consequence of such bureaucratization and the knowledge of limits.
6. For some detailed statistics on these changes, see my two articles in the Labor section of *Fortune* magazine, April and June 1958. The basic figures on changes in the U.S. class structure can be seen in the table below.
7. Given my distinction between *market-unionism* and the *social movement,* one can say that racketeering is a pathology of market-unionism, while communism is the pathology of the social movement.

Changes in the Class Structure of the United States

	1947 (IN THOUSANDS)	1956 (IN THOUSANDS)	1947–56 (% CHANGE)
Total employed	57,843	64,928	12.2%
White-Collar Occupations			
Professional, technical, and kindred workers	3,795	6,096	60.6
Managers, officials, and proprietors	5,795	6,552	13.1
Clerical and kindred workers	7,200	8,838	22.8
Sales workers	3,395	4,111	21.1
Blue-Collar Occupations			
Craftsmen, foremen, and kindred workers	7,754	8,693	12.1
Operatives and kindred workers (semi-skilled)	12,274	12,816	4.4
Laborers, except farm and mine	3,526	3,670	4.1
Mixed Occupations			
Service workers	4,256	5,485	28.9
Private-household workers	1,731	2,124	22.7
Farm Occupations			
Farm laborers and foremen	3,125	2,889	(− 7.6)
Farmers and farm managers	4,995	3,655	(−26.8)

TRADE UNIONISM IN AMERICA

Stanley Aronowitz

. . . For most workers, trade unions remain the elementary organizations of the defense of their immediate economic interests against employers. Despite the despicable performance of labor movement leadership during the past 30 years, and especially in the last two decades—including its adherence to the imperialist policies of the succesive Democratic and Republican administrations from Truman to Nixon and its collaboration with the large corporations to discipline the workers against their own interests—blue- and white-collar workers regard their unions as their only weapon against the deterioration of working conditions and the rampant inflation responsible for recent declines in real wages.

In part, trade unions retain their legitimacy because no alternative to them exists. Workers join unions because, in most cases, maintenance of membership in a union is a condition of employment. A union bureaucracy can betray the workers' elementary economic demands for a considerable period of time. However, the last decade has been studded with examples of rank-and-file uprisings against the least responsible of the labor bureaucrats. Still, in nearly all cases of rank-and-file revolts aimed at replacing union leadership, the new group of leaders has reproduced the conditions of the old regime. In the steel, rubber, electrical, government-workers' and other important unions one can observe some differences in the style of administration, in the leadership's willingness to conduct strike struggles and in the political sophistication of the bureaucracy. But these unions are neither radical nor have they made sharp breaks from the predominant policies of the labor movement in the contemporary era.

Some radicals explain this phenomenon in a purely idealistic way. According to conventional wisdom, the weakness of the factional struggles within the unions over the past decade has been that they have been conducted without an alternative ideological perspective. The Left has been largely irrelevant to them. Therefore, if the new leadership merely recapitulates, as Marx put it, "the same old crap," we should blame our own failure to concentrate our political work within the working class. Presumably, a strong Left could have altered the kind of leadership and the program of the rank-and-file movements.

There is undoubtedly some truth in these assertions. Yet the disturbing fact is that the Communist Left was a part of the trade unions' leadership for many decades prior to 1950, after which most C.P. members and other Leftists were thrown out of many unions. In some unions there are remnants of the Left still in power. There is a tendency to explain the failure of the old Communist Left by reference to its "revisionist" policies. Such superficial explanations assume

SOURCE: *Liberation*, December 1971, pp. 22–27, 37–41.

that if only the politics of radical labor organizers had been better, the whole picture would have been qualitatively different. This will be shown not to be the case.

If the trade union remains an elementary organ of struggle, it is chiefly a force for integrating the workers into the corporate capitalist system. Trade unions have historically fought to determine the price of labor power on more favorable terms to the workers. But inherent in the labor contract is the means both to insure some benefit to the workers and to provide a stable, disciplined labor force to the employer. The union both wins rights and assumes obligations in the collective bargaining agreement.

Under contemporary monopolistic capitalism, these obligations include: (1) the promise not to strike, except under specific conditions, or at the termination of the contract: (2) a bureaucratic and hierarchical grievance procedure consisting of many steps during which the control over the grievance is systematically removed from the shop floor and from workers' control; (3) a system of management prerogatives wherein the union agrees to cede to the employer "the operation of the employer's facilities and the direction of the working forces, including the right to hire, suspend, or discharge for good cause and . . . to relieve employees from duties due to lack of work" and, (4) a "checkoff" of union dues as an automatic deduction from the workers' pay checks.

The last provision, incorporated into 98 per cent of union contracts, treats union dues as another tax on workers' wages. It is a major barrier to close relations between union leaders and the rank and file. Workers have come to regard the checkoff as another insurance premium. Since workers enjoy little participation in union affairs, except when they have an individual grievance or around contract time, the checkoff of union dues—designed originally to protect the union's financial resources—has removed a major point of contact between workers and their full-time representatives. This procedure is in sharp contrast to former times, when the shop steward or business agent was obliged to collect dues by hand. In this period, the dues collection process, however cumbersome for the officials, provided a means for workers to voice their complaints, as well as a weapon against the abuses of bureaucracy.

The modern labor agreement is the heart of class collaboration between the trade unions and the corporations. It mirrors the bureaucratic and hierarchical structure of modern industry and the state. Its provisions are enforced not merely by law, but by the joint efforts of corporate and trade-union bureaucracies. Even the most enlightened trade-union leader cannot fail to play his part as an element in the mechanisms of domination over workers' rights to spontaneously struggle against speedup or *de facto* wage cuts, either in the form of a shift in the work process or by inflationary price increases. The unions' hands are tied by law as well as by the contract.

The role of collective bargaining today is to provide a rigid institutional framework for the conduct of the class struggle. The struggle at the point of production has become regulated in the same way as have electric and telephone rates, prices of basic commodities and foreign trade. The regulatory procedure in labor relations includes government intervention in collective bargaining, the routinization of all conflict between labor and the employer on the shop floor, and the placing of equal responsibility for observing plant rules upon management and the union.

The objective of this procedure is to control labor costs as a stable factor of production in order to permit rational investment decisions by the large corporations. The longterm contract insures that labor costs will be a known factor. It guarantees labor peace for a specified period of time. The agreement enables employers to avoid the disruption characteristic of stormier periods of labor history when workers' struggles were much more spontaneous, albeit more difficult.

An important element in the labor contract is that most of the day-to-day issues expressing the conflict between worker and employer over the basic question of the division of profit are not subject to strikes. In the automobile and electrical agreements as well as a few others, the union has the right to strike over speedup, safety issues or a few other major questions, after several steps of the grievance procedure have been completed. In the main, however, most complaints about working conditions and work assignments are adjudicated in the final step of the grievance procedure by an "impartial" arbitrator selected by both the union and management. In industries where the strike weapon is a permitted option, the union leaders usually put severe pressure on the rank and file to choose the arbitration route, since strikes disrupt the good relations between the bureaucracy and management, a situation valued highly by liberal corporate officials and union leaders.

With few exceptions, particularly in textile and electrical corporations, employers regard labor leaders as their allies against the ignorant and undisciplined rank-and-file workers. This confidence has been built up over the past 35 years of industrial collective bargaining.

The trade unions serve corporate interests in America today. This is not merely the result of the conservative consciousness of the leadership. The trade unions have become an appendage of the corporations because they have taken their place as a vital institution in the corporate capitalist complex. Their role as an organ of struggle has virtually expired.

The democratic foundations of the trade unions have been undermined almost universally. The Left understood that the old craft unions were essentially purveyors of labor power. The terror and violence of craft-union leadership against the rank and file was only the most extreme expression of their monopoly over the labor force. They controlled both the supply of skilled labor and its price. Since the old unions were defined narrowly by their economic functions and by then conservative ideology, the assumption of socialists and communists who helped build industrial unions, which included the huge mass of unskilled and semi-skilled workers, was that these organizations would express broader political and social interests, if not radical ideologies.

The new industrial unions organized in the past 40 years were to be organs of rank-and-file power. The workers would have an opportunity to participate in union affairs on all levels of decision-making. On the whole, despite corruption and bureaucratic resistance to the exercise of membership control, many unions in the United States have retained the forms but not the content of democracy. It is possible to remove union leaders and replace them, but it is not possible to transcend the institutional constraints of trade unionism itself.

In most of the newer unions formed during the New Deal period within the CIO, the membership elects all union officials within the local union. Local unions consisting of a membership from a single large plant (usually those of giant corporations in the auto, electrical, steel, and rubber industries) are led by persons who rise from the rank and file. But as soon as workers become officers of these local unions, they are often made fulltime union officials (or, if not officially designated as such, the company will tolerate a *de facto* full-time officialdom within the plant, even though officers and grievance committeemen remain on the company payroll and will punch in every morning, turn out an hour's worth of work, and then proceed to take care of union business on company time).

The company once fought the idea of full-time, inplant officials. In the period of greater trade-union militancy about shop floor issues such as speedup, incentive pay rates, and health and safety conditions, the full-timer within the plant was a hindrance to the company. But the general pattern of bureaucratization of even the democratically elected in-plant officials had made them valuable allies of the company for discipline of the work force. Trade-union education programs aimed at in-plant officials teach the sanctity of the union contract. Contract administration is the heart of trade-union education. The local union is impressed with his legal and moral responsibility to enforce the contract, even if it entails taking the company's side against abuses by the rank and file.

Local union officers believe that the contract works in general for the benefit of the membership. Faced with company violations of many of its protective provisions, especially with respect to working conditions, the officer becomes committed to the procedures provided within the contract for dealing with grievances. As a guardian of both the workers and the interest of the union, the officer comes to oppose arbitrariness of management as well as the irresponsibility of the rank and filer. In the past 25 years, most local union officials, although more subject to rank-and-file pressure than the officials directly employed by the union, have developed an ambivalent position with respect to the labor process.

Matters are often complicated by the ambitions of the local officer. Since there is little genuine class-consciousness informing his activity, he tends to accept the paths of upward social movement available to him. These consist chiefly of two options: a promotion to full-time work for the union outside the plant or upgrading to a supervisory position with the company. It is not uncommon for talented officers of local unions to choose either path with impunity. Nor is it accurate to understand the ambitions of local officials in terms of "selling out" to the company or to the union. Many foremen, personnel directors or plant managers, were once militant and capable local union officials. Their promotion is a sign of recognition of their abilities by companies and trade-union bureaucracies. Rank-and-file members of the union are simultaneously angry and proud of the upgrading of a union official. More often, the membership expects such promotions, so that aspiring for union office has become an early rung in a career ladder for ambitious workers seeking to get off the line or the machine. Militants within the shop who possess a strong sense of class may condemn the phenomenon of moving up by local union officers, but it is difficult to condemn without an alternative social vision and movement which defines personal aspirations in a way different from contemporary bourgeois mores.

Trade unions have fallen victim to the same disease as the broader electoral and legislative system. Just as the major power over the state has shifted from the legislative to the executive branch of government, power over union affairs has shifted from the rank and file to the corporate leaders, the trade-union officials and the government. Trade unions are regulated by the state both in their relations with employers and in their internal operations. Moreover, the problems of union leadership have been transformed from political and social issues to the routines of contract administration and internal bureaucratic procedures such as union finances. The union leader is a business executive. His accountability is not limited to the membership—it is extended to government agencies, arbitrators, courts of law, and other institutions that play a large role in regulating the union's operations.

The contradiction between the role of the trade union as organ of struggle and integrator of the labor force is played out at every contract negotiation in major industries.

Over the past several years, the chasm between the leadership and membership has never been more exposed. During this period, a rising number of contract settlements have been rejected by the rank and file. In 1968, nearly 30 per cent of initial proposed settlements were turned down by union memberships. The rank and file has veto power, but no means of initiative in contract bargaining. In the first place, many major industries have agreements which are negotiated at the national level. There is room for local bargaining over specific shop issues, but the main lines of economic settlements are determined by full-time officials of the company and the union; many rank-and-file bargaining committees are relegated to the role of bystander, window-dressing or advisor in union bargaining. One reason for this concentration of power in full-time officials is the allegedly technical nature of collective bargaining in the modern era. Not only leaders and representatives of the local membership sit on the union's side of the bargaining table, but lawyers, insurance and pension experts, and sometimes even management consultants as well. The product of the charade which is characteristic of much collective bargaining today is a mammoth document which reads more like a corporate contract or a mortgage agreement than anything else. In fact, it is a bill of sale.

I would argue that the specialization of functions within the trade unions is only partially justified by the needs of the membership. Insurance and pension plans do require the employment of specific talents, but the overall direction of worker-employer relationships has been centralized in the hands of experts as a means of preventing the direct intervention of the rank and file. More, the domination of specialists within the collective bargaining process signals the removal of this process from the day-to-day problems of the workers. The interpretation of provisions of the agreement is beyond the intervention of the rank and file. The special language of the contract, its bulk and its purely administrative character helps perpetuate the centrality of the professional expert in the union hierarchy.

In this connection, it is no accident that the elected union official has limited power within the collective bargaining ritual (and, in a special sense, within the union itself). Few national union leaders make decisions either in direct consultation with the membership or with fellow elected officials. The hired expert, particularly the lawyer, holds increased power in union affairs because of the business-like character of labor relations, the legal constraints upon union as well as rank-and-file initiative and the specialized content of all union agreements.

But the union official is not distressed by the growing need for experts. He has employed the expert as a buffer between the officialdom and the restive rank and file. As in other institutions, experts have been used to rationalize the conservatism of the leadership in technical and legal terms, leaving the official free to remain politically viable by supporting the sentiments expressed by the membership while, at the same time, rejecting their proposed actions.

During the past decade in the auto, steel, rubber and other basic manufacturing industries, the critical issues of working-class struggle have been those related to control over the work place. The tremendous shifts in plant location, work methods, job definitions and other problems associated with investment in new equipment, expansion and changing skills required to operate new means of production, have found the union bureaucracies unprepared The reasons for trade-union impotence at the work place go beyond ideology. They are built into the sinews of the collective bargaining process.

Many important industries have national contracts between the union and the companies covering most monetary issues, including wages. In the electrical, auto and steel industries, negotiations are conducted with individual companies, but in reality there is "pattern" bargaining. A single major producer is chosen by the union and corporations to determine wage and fringe benefit settlement for the rest of the industry. All other negotiations stall until the central settlement is reached.

The national leadership of the union always poses the wage demands as the most important negotiating issues. Problems such as technological changes, work assignments, job classifications and pace of work are negotiated at the local level after the economic package has been settled. And by the time the local negotiations begin—often conducted between rank-and-file leaders and middle managers—the national union has lost interest in the contract. Its entire orientation is toward the narrowly defined "economic" side of the bargaining. Although many agreements stipulate that resumption of work will not take place before the resolution of local issues, the international representatives and top leaders of the union put enormous pressure on the membership to settle the local issues. It is at the plant level that the sell-outs take place. The local feels abandoned, but rank-and-file resentment is diverted to the failure of the shop leadership rather than the top bureaucracy because the national union has "delivered the goods."

After every national auto settlement, a myriad of local walkouts are called over work-place issues. These strikes are short-lived and usually unsuccessful in preventing the company's attack on working conditions. In the main, young workers and black workers are the spearhead in struggles against speedup. The impatience of the bureaucracy with this undisciplined action is expressed in long harangues to local leaders and the rank and file by international representatives, employees of the national union. When persuasion fails, the local is sometimes put into receivership and an administrator is sent from the head office to take over the local until the revolt is quelled and order is restored.

The conventional wisdom of today is to admit the conservative character of trade unions in the era of monopoly capitalism—their integration and subordination to the large corporations. At the same time, many radicals stress the important defensive role trade unions perform during periods when growing capitalist instability forces employers to launch an offensive against workers' living standards and working conditions. . . .

The bureaucratization of the trade unions, their integrative role within production, their conservative political ideology and their dependence on the Democratic party are not primarily the result of the consciousness of the leading actors in the rise of industrial unionism. To the extent that the Left participated in redefining the trade unions as part of the corporate system, it must now undertake a merciless critique of its own role before a new working-class strategy can be developed.

However, it is not enough to admit bureaucratic tendencies in the unions or in their Left leadership. The strategy flowing from this focus is to reform the unions from within in order to perfect their fighting ability and rank-and-file class-consciousness. This line of thinking categorically denies that the unions are mainly dependent variables within the political economy.

One of the important concepts of Marxist orthodoxy is that economic crisis is an inevitable feature of capitalist development, and that the tendency of employers will be to reduce and attack the power of trade unions during periods of declining production. The government-employer attempts to circumscribe workers' power by restricting trade-union functions will produce rank-and-file pressure, confronting the leadership with the choice of struggle against capital or their own displacement. Thus the unions become objectively progressive despite their conservative leadership.

However, strategies for rank-and-file reform ignore the bureaucracy and conservatism inherent in the present union structure and function, as well as the role of the unions in the division of labor. . . . The growth of bureaucracy and the decline of rank-and-file initiative is built into the theory and practice of collective bargaining.

Moreover, the strategy of trade-union reform ignores the fact that the last 35 years of industrial unionism has failed to effect any substantive change in the distribution of income. Trade unionism under conditions of partial unionization of the labor force cannot do more than redistribute income within the working class. Workers in heavily organized industries such as auto, rubber and steel have relatively high wages compared to workers in consumer goods industries such as garments and shoes (which have migrated to the south), retail and wholesale workers, and most categories of government and agricultural workers.

The high wages of certain categories of industrial workers depend as much on the high proportion of capital to living labor and the monopoly character of basic industries as they do on trade-union struggle. The tendency for employers in heavy industry to give in on union wage demands presupposes their ability to raise prices and productivity. In competitive industries such as light manufacturing, the unions have been transformed into stabilizers of industrial conflict in order to permit high rates of profits where no technological changes can be introduced. The result has been low wages for large numbers of blacks, Puerto Ricans and poor whites locked into these jobs.

The self-protective orientation of trade unionism conceived as demands based on industry or occupation is partially responsible for racism. Racist ideology is not only rooted in the "privileges" of white workers. On the contrary, it is based upon their economic and social insecurity and their industrial and trade-union consciousness. High wages are not the same as white-skin privelege because these are determined by the historical level of culture. Nor have the relative wage and occupational advantages of whites meant an end to their exploitation.

Since advanced capitalism requires consumerism both as ideology and as practice to preserve commodity production, its payment of high wages to large segments of the working class, and minimum income to those excluded from the labor markets, is not objectively in the workers' interest. It is a means to take care of the market, or demand, side of production.

The ability of workers to purchase a relatively large quantity of consumer goods is dependent on the forces of production, which include the scale and complexity of technology and the productivity and skill of the labor force. Technological development, in turn, is dependent on the availability of raw materials and the degree of scientific and technical knowledge in society.

The most important issue to be addressed in defining the tasks ahead is not the question of inflation, wages or general economic conditions. No matter how inequitable the distribution of income, no matter how deep the crisis, these conditions will never, by themselves, be the soil for revolutionary consciousness.

Revolutionary consciousness arises out of the conditions of alienated labor, which include economic conditions but are not limited to them. Its starting point is in the production process. It is at the point of mental and manual production, where the world of commodities is produced, that the worker experiences his exploitation. Consumption of waste production, trade-union objectives in the direction of enlarging wages and social benefits, and the division of labor into industries and sections, are all mediations which stand between the workers' existential exploitation at the work place and their ability to comprehend alienated labor as class exploitation.

Radicals have tended to address the problem of consciousness from the wrong end. We assume that racism, trade unionism or conservatism will either be dissolved by discussion and exhortation alone, or that "objective" conditions will force new understandings among workers. The notion that ideologies can be changed through ideological means or that capitalistic contradictions will change consciousness with an assist from ideological "correct lines" or education is a nonrevolutionary position: in both cases, the role of practice is ignored. Nor will workers' struggles against economic hardship necessarily raise political consciousness.

In this connection, one must reconsider the standard radical interpretation of the failure of the CIO to emerge as an important force for social change as a function of the misleadership of its officials and the opportunism of the Communist Party and other radical parties that participated in its formation. According to a recent work on the development of the CIO by Art Preis, a contemporary labor reporter writing from a Trotskyist position, the 1930s were a prerevolutionary period. Preis writes: "The first stage of awakening class consciousness was achieved, in fact, with the rise and consolidation of the CIO. The second stage will be marked by a further giant step, the formation of a new class party based on the unions." Within this interpretation, unions are the preliminary step workers must take on the way to achieving political class-consciousness—that is, the recognition by a decisive section of the working class that the solutions to its immediate problems as well as to long-run ills reside in its assumption of power over the whole society and the transformation of all social relations. The assumption is that the bonds of solidarity forged in the course of trade-union struggles can, with the proper ideological leadership within the working class and with the proper systemic crisis, produce political consciousness. Evaluations of the 1930s, therefore, find the economic crisis a necessary condition for the development of class-consciousness, but blame the Communist and Socialist policies for the failure of a significant radical force to develop among the mass of workers.

The analysis offered in the preceding section of this paper runs directly counter to this interpretation. To be sure, my discussion of the rise of industrial unionism should have made it clear that there was indeed a failure of Left leadership, that radical ideologies and organizations played virtually no independent role in the trade unions after 1935. But there is no genuine evidence that the CIO (even with a "correct" strategy on the part of the Left) could ever have become an organized expression of a new class politics in America; or that trade unionism in the era of state capitalism and imperialism can be other than a force for integrating workers. To understand the present situation, therefore, both the barriers to and the potential for the emergence of a revolutionary movement among workers—it is necessary to trace the specific dimensions of workers' consciousness as it has developed in the United States.

One hundred years ago, workers fought desperately for the right to form unions and to strike for economic and social demands. Unions arose out of the needs of workers. In the period of the expansion of American capitalism they were important means for restraining the bestiality of capital. Even into the twentieth century, long after the labor movement as a whole stopped reflecting their interests, workers fought for unions. But their hope was not to become new agents of social transformation. Industrial workers joined unions in the twentieth century seeking a share in the expansion of American capitalism, not its downfall.

Since the 1920s, the ideology of expansion has permeated working-class consciousness. On the one hand, many workers have no faith in the corporations to provide for their needs unless forced to do so by powerful organizations. On the other, Amercian expansion abroad, and the intervention of the government in the operation of the economy, has convinced workers that the frontier of economic opportunity was not closed to them. The persistence of the idea of individual mobility amidst recognition of the necessity for collective action is partially attributable to the immigrant base of a large portion of the industrial working class in the first half of the twentieth century. The comparative advantages of American capitalism to the semi-feudal agrarian societies of Europe in the early part of this century remained vital influences on workers' consciousness despite the great depression. For the minority of radical immigrant workers who didn't buy the expansionist ideology, corporations and the government reacted with consistent deportations, jail terms and attempts at demoralization.

Thus the violence of Amercian labor struggles has been a two-pronged factor in the development of working-class consciousness. On the one hand, it indicates the militancy with which workers have been prepared to conduct their struggles. But the readiness of employers and the government to use methods of severe repression to break strikes and cleanse the working class of its most militant elements has become an object lesson for workers. Working-class consciousness is suffused with the awesome power of the corporations over American life. They have sought and helped create unions which mirror the hierarchical structure of corporations and can compete with them in marshalling resources with which to bargain effectively. James Hoffa was a hero to many workers because he represented, not a challenge to the robber baron, but the labor equivalent of him. Hoffa was seen as a formidable opponent to the corporations precisely because the Teamsters were the quintessential business union.

Strikes in the United States are of longer duration than in any advanced capitalist country. Workers know that large corporations cannot be immediately crippled by walkouts and that their resources are usually ample to withstand months of labor struggle. Moreover, in some industries, employers have created strike insurance plans to protect themselves. Similarly, unions have long since developed institutional forms of strike insurance. The largest unions boast of huge strike funds. During the 1970 auto strike, however, the multimillions in the United Auto Workers' strike chest were exhausted within a few months, even though benefits never exceeded 25 dollars a week for the several hundred thousand GM workers. At the same time, thousands of workers lost their savings to pay for the strike. The companies drove home another lesson to the workers: despite unions, strikes are expensive. Although the threat of starvation is no longer an immediate deterrent to militancy, the legitimacy of labor unions among workers is reinforced by their ability to raise money and to render concrete assistance to strikers' families.

It cannot be denied that working-class militancy has generally been ambivalent in the United States. Workers here are no less anti-employer than any other working class in the world. Strikes are bloodier, conducted for longer periods and often manifest a degree of solidarity unmatched by any other group of workers. But working-class consciousness is industry-oriented, if not always job-oriented. Workers will fight their unions and the companies through wildcat strikes and other means outside the established framework of collective bargaining. But they are ideologically and culturally tied to the prevailing system of power, because until now it has shown the capacity to share its expansion with a large segment of the working class.

Black workers, women and youth have historically been excluded from these shares. But since 1919 it is not accurate to claim that black workers are not integrated at all into the industrial work force. They are excluded from unions representing skilled construction workers. But blacks constitute between one-third and two-fifths of the work force in the auto and steel industries, and smaller but significant proportions of other mass production industries. They are more militant than older white workers because they are not given the relatively easier jobs in the plants, but are forced to work in the dirtiest, lower-paid occupations. Moreover, they are under-represented within the top echelons of union leadership. At best, tokenism characterizes most union responses to the large number of black workers in the shops.

Discrimination against blacks and, to a lesser extent, young white workers, has led to the formation of caucus movements inside the unions based on the specific demands of these groups. Some black caucuses seek more union power and, at the same time, demand upgrading to better paying skilled jobs. Youth caucuses have been organized within the UAW making similar demands, but have gone further to suggest that the rigidity of industrial labor be relaxed. Some caucuses have asked that the uniform starting time of most work places be rescinded, that supervision be less severe, and that ways be found to enlarge job responsibility so that the monotony and meaninglessness of most assembly-line tasks can be eased. Young workers are groping for ways to control their own work, even though they are making piecemeal demands. Black workers are demanding liberation from the least satisfying of industrial tasks and more control over union decision-making processes.

But these are only tentative movements toward a different kind of working-class consciousness. They are still oriented toward making demands on companies and unions, and do not aim at autonomously taking control over their own lives, even their own work. Within the American working-class no significant movement or section of workers defines itself as a class and sees its mission to be the same as the liberation of society from corporate-capitalist social relations.

Such consciousness will never arise in America from abject material deprivation. The position of the U.S. in the world has become more precarious since the end of World War II, but workers are not yet convinced that American capitalism has reached a dead end. However, the consciousness that most work in our society is deadening and much of it unnecessary has permeated the minds of young people, including the new entrants into the factories and offices. The growing awareness of the need for new forms of labor manifests itself in spontaneous ways. Corporations are becoming concerned that young workers are not sufficiently disciplined to come to work on time, or even every day. The new plans for a shorter number of work days, even if they propose to retain the 40-hour work week, are not likely to catch fire in the near future. But it indicates that corporations are searching for new methods of coping with the manifest breakdown of industrial discipline among the millions of workers who have entered the labor force in the past decade and have not experienced the conservatizing influence of the depression. After all, if poverty is not really a threat for large numbers within our society, how can they be expected to endure the specialization of work functions and their repetitive character? The spectre that haunts American industry is not yet the spectre of Communism, as Marx claimed. It is the spectre of breakdown leading to a new conscious synthesis among workers.

It is the practice of trade unions and their position within the production which determine their role in the social process. The transformation of the working class from one among many competing interest groups to capitalism's revolutionary gravedigger depends on whether working-class practice can be freed from the institutions which direct its power into bargaining and participation instead of workers' control.

The trade unions are likely to remain both a deterrent to the workers' initiative and a "third party" force at the work place, objectively serving corporate interests both ideologically and in the daily life of the shop, and remaining a diminishing instrument of workers' struggles to be employed selectively by them. But the impulse to dual forms of struggle—shop committees, wildcat strikes, steward movements—may become important in the labor movements of the future.

The rise of new instruments of workers' struggle would have to reject the institutionalization of the class struggle represented by the legally sanctioned labor agreement administered by trade-union bureaucracies. Workers would have to make conscious their rejection of limitations on their freedom to take direct action to meet their elementary needs at the work place. Although many wildcat strikes are implicitly caused by issues which go beyond wage demands, these remain hidden beneath the grosser economic struggles. Labor unions are not likely to become formally committed to the ideas of workers' control over working conditions, investment decisions, and the objects of labor. On the contrary, they will remain "benefits-oriented," fighting incessantly to improve the economic position of their own membership in relation to other sections of the work force rather than relative to the employers. They will oppose workers' efforts to take direct action beyond the scope of the union agreement and to make agreements with the boss on the informal basis of power relations on the shop floor.

The forms of anti-union consciousness within the working class are confused by the fact that they partially reflect the inability of these workers to organize collectively to defend their interests on an independent basis. Trade unionism still appears as a progressive force among the mass of working poor, such as farm and hospital workers, who labor under conditions of severe degradation. At first, unionization seems to be a kind of deliverance from bondage. But after the initial upsurge has been spent, most unions fall back into patterns of class collaboration and repression. At the point when grinding poverty has been overcome and unions have settled into their conservative groove, their bureaucratic character becomes manifest to workers.

We are now in the midst of a massive reevaluation by organized industrial workers of the viability of the unions. However, it is an action critique, rather than an ideological criticism of the union's role and the legal implications of it. In the end, the spontaneous revolt will have to develop its own alternative forms of collective struggle and demands. It is still too early to predict their precise configuration in the United States. But the European experience suggests that workers' councils and committees, that is, autonomous creations of workers at the point of production, will not replace the unions immediately, but will exist side by side with them for some time.

In recent years the more liberal elements of the trade-union bureaucracy have joined with anti-war forces in opposition to the war in Vietnam. To some extent, this new surge of interest by liberal labor leaders is attributable to their recognition that no substantial sentiment for the war exists among the rank and file. Indeed, there is widespread understanding in the ranks of labor that the war has hurt labor's economic interests. The willingness of some leaders to speak out is also a belated effort by Old Leftists of the socialist and communist variety to redress their silence during the cold war years. The New Left is somewhat bemused by this new phenomenon. In some respects, the incipient coalition between anti-war activists and labor officials represents growing respect by New Leftists for the working class.

Some young radicals have even gone into plants and offices in order to become part of the workers' movement. For them, the question of the trade unions is of fundamental importance since many workers are to be found in the unions (about a quarter of the labor force, but a majority of workers in large industries and an increasing proportion of government workers), or are seeking union representation. I hope this analysis has shown that the unions have become a reactionary force in American society and that workers have come to regard them as another form of social insurance, but less and less as an instrument of their own struggle. The working poor will still choose unions as a means of escape from poverty. Even government workers and service workers can obtain temporary benefits from unionism, especially in the fight for higher wages during the period of new union organization. But the role of radicals is neither to enter the union bureaucracies (even with the slogan of "democratizing" the unions) nor to provide the ideological grist for rank-and-file insurgencies aimed at replacing incumbent leaders. I believe that militants influenced by New Left movements have an important role to play in the workers' movement. First, if the New Left has meant anything for the development of a new revolutionary movement in America, it is the politics of self-control and self-management. Consciousness about the importance of autonomy at the work place still takes the form of spontaneous refusal by workers to collaborate with the discipline of the corporation or the gradualism of the unions. Workers, even the youth and the blacks, have not achieved self-consciousness of their own needs and the obstacles to meeting them. Radicals can do more than participate in the routine of the shop and the periodic outbreaks of rank-and-file militancy. Most of all, radicals can make conscious the political and cultural side of the revolt, because it is these dimensions alone which can develop an internal cadre for new radical forms of workers' organization within the work place and in society. At present, study groups of militants could be formed to discuss the contemporary situation of workers, the war, and other general political issues. But most of all, radicals can generate discussions of alternatives to present social arrangements, new forms of life and labor, and social demands corresponding to them. The characteristic quality of Old Left agitation in the shops was its concentration on bread and butter, to the exclusion of all other problems of everyday life. The other side of the coin has been mechanically contrived attempts to link shop issues with broader political issues such as the war. Radical agitation is usually boring, or worse, fails to engage people in thinking and learning about what else is possible besides the Chinese or the Soviet models of socialism (sure losers for American workers).

Until now, radical agitation has lacked humor. It is preeminently excremental in style as well as in content. To a certain extent, the economistic, grim quality of radical participation in workers' struggles reflects the shallowness of their understanding of working-class life and a religious concept of politics. Politics for us must become a joyful activity, since, as the French sociologist Henri Lefebvre has pointed out, revolution usually takes the form of the festival (not the spectacle, as some student radicals are wont to believe).

There is no reason for workers to choose an alternative political and personal perspective if it promises nothing but more sacrifice, boring meetings and internecine warfare, on the one hand, or such sterile political goals as much radical propaganda is likely to furnish, on the other. Unless the new radicals are purveyors of enlightenment, of a new way of looking at the world, of a libertarian alternative which promises deliverance from powerlessness and bureaucracy, and the poverty of daily life for most people, then workers are justified in staying where they are. The virtue of the present is that it is familiar and can be dealt with in some way.

Will the workers follow the radicals instead of the bureaucrats? Let's hope not. The only thing radicals can do now is to speak clearly about what they actually believe. Let the workers themselves take care of strategy and tactics. When radicals cease to look upon themselves as outside the working class, they can participate in these deliberations. But then, they will have ceased to be an "outside force" in the sociological sense, even if they remain so politically for a time.

One advantage of today's young radicals in comparison to the recent past is that they share much of the same culture as young workers. The distinctions of dress, artistic tastes and even language have narrowed. The critical difference remains educational achievement, not life style. But education ought to be precisely what the radical is all about in the work place. His role is to generate thought, and when possible, theory and action. Of course, the social distinctions really disappear among government workers, many of whom share the same technical education of their more political comrades. Thus the material bases for estrangement between the politicals and others have been undermined by the homogeneous culture of the present period of American life. Radicals need to recognize their own subjectivity—that is, that they too are revolutionary subjects—and not exhibit their contempt for workers by failing to go beyond the immediate economic or political "issues" on the grounds that ordinary workers are not capable of understanding.

In the next few years, radicals have an unparalleled chance to redeem their inheritance. Millions of youth have entered the shops, government jobs and service industries. College educated people are taking jobs driving cabs or, if they are lucky, factory jobs. The New Left is merging with an important sector of workers, at least socially. This is not to claim that revolutionary consciousness is extant among young workers, or even young black workers. What is clear, however, is the disrespect youth have for the traditional work roles, for the opportunities offered by the corporations for advancement and power, for the promise of security and integration offered by the unions. The cultural revolt converges with the revolt against oppressive working and economic conditions. But it has not defined itself as a project of social transformation. That is the task of theory and education. And that is where the New Left comes in.

THE CONTROL OF THE WAGE-PRICE SPIRAL

John Kenneth Galbraith

Men of conservative temperament have long suspected that one thing leads to another. The effect of the regulation of aggregate demand on public wage and price policy admirably validates their suspicion.

The state regulates aggregate demand by providing a volume of purchasing power sufficient to employ the available labor force. A low level of unemployment is a recognized test of the success of the economy and of the proficiency of those who guide it. And this . . . is not easily achieved. The notion of employment and unemployment has little meaning in the industrial system. What is involved is a complex fitting of highly diverse qualifications to highly diverse needs. For those with the least educational qualification, there is comparatively little need. Only a very high level of aggregate demand will bring them into employment, if they can be employed at all, and by that time there will be great shortages of manpower in the higher levels of qualification.

At any reasonably high level of demand, prices and wages in the industrial system are inherently unstable. This is certainly so when demand is strong enough to begin enrolling the hard core of more or less unemployable unemployed. Then wages and prices press each other up in a continuing spiral. It is convenient, in describing this spiral, to break into it at the point where wages act on prices. But it is a continuous process and no causal significance should be attached to wage increases merely because they are the starting point.

When unemployment is small, the bargaining position of unions is, in general, strong. Members can face a strike with the assurance that they cannot be replaced. As a more practical matter they know that they will be inflicting the maximum loss of business on the employer and that after the strike is over they will promptly be recalled to work.

Employers, on their side, will deem it wise under such circumstances to grant increases in wages. The strong demand insures that the added costs of the higher wages can be passed along to the consumer or other buyer. By the time unemployment is reduced to the hard-core categories, there will usually be a shortage of some classes of production workers.[1] Higher wages will seem to be a way of holding or recruiting manpower. Collective bargaining ordinarily embraces a substantial part of the industry. This means that all or most firms are affected by the wage increase at the same time. All will thus be led to increase prices at the same time. This, together with the strong demand, eases or erases the fear that the

SOURCE: *The New Industrial State* (Boston: Houghton Mifflin, 1967), pp. 247–261.

control over prices so essential for planning will be jeopardized because some firm will not go along.

The rise of the mature corporation has added significantly to the likelihood of the spiral. The entrepreneurial corporation was presumed to maximize the profits that were allowed to it by the current state of demand. And this, we may agree, was its tendency. If the profits had previously been at a maximum and prices were then at the level that yielded this maximum, wage increases could not be passed on in the form of higher prices. One cannot improve on the most. If wage increases could not be passed on, they would have to be paid for out of earnings. And in the nature of the entrepreneurial enterprise these earnings accrued in substantial measure to the entrepreneur. Again there is the special poignancy of paying when the individual has himself to pay. The entrepreneur had reason to resist. If he did yield, the wage increase did not necessarily increase prices, since, to repeat, these were already set to yield the maximum profit.

In the mature corporation the technostructure sets prices not where they maximize profits but where they best contribute to the security of the technostructure and to the growth of the firm. This means with rare exceptions that it has latitude to increase revenues by increasing prices. Accordingly, it can pass wage increases along. It will be led to do so because a strike, implying contingencies and uncertainties beyond the control of the technostructure, is always a threat to its security. Labor conflict also cultivates attitudes that are hostile to identification and thus damaging to the motivational system. And, finally, the technostructure with which the decision on wages resides, does not itself have to pay.

The circle can now be completed. Price increases become cost increases for customers—either other industries or ultimate consumers. In either case, eventually or immediately, they raise living costs and thus become an inducement to another round of wage demands. Given regulation of demand with the goal of providing full employment, and in the absence of other steps, this spiral of wage and price increases is an organic feature of the industrial system.[2,3]

It also accords solidly with experience. That the modern large firm has the option of passing on wage increases is taken for granted. If demand and employment are high, no one ever asks whether the steel, automobile or aluminum industry can raise their prices following the conclusion of a new collective bargaining contract, but only whether they will need or choose to do so.[4] Between 1947 and 1960 there was no year in which wholesale prices of durable consumer goods as well as those of finished capital goods did not rise. Both categories are closely identified with the industrial system. The increase in the price of consumer durables during these thirteen years was about 25 per cent; for capital goods it was about 40 per cent. In agriculture and nondurable consumer goods, which are wholly or partially outside the industrial system, the price increase was much smaller and much less persistent. Price behavior in the industrial system strongly colored attitudes toward prices as a whole. "The domestic economic policy of the United States during the last years of the 1950's [was] dominated by the fear of inflation."[5]

The seemingly obvious remedy for the wage-price spiral is to regulate prices and wages by public authority. In World War II and the Korean War in the United States, demand pressed strongly the capacity of the labor force as well as that of the industrial plant. Apart from the exceptional strength of this pressure, especially in World War II, there was nothing unique about the wartime situation. Economic institutions and behavior are not drastically altered either by declared or undeclared war. During both conflicts the wage-price spiral was successfully contained by controls. In the two years of 1941 and 1942 in the United States, the wholesale price index of industrial products rose a little more than 7 points. In the following three years, with greatly increased demand and virtual full employment, but with controls in effect, the index increased only 2.4 points. Price increases for machinery, chemicals and metal products, all closely identified with the industrial system, were even less. Between 1950 and 1951, after the outbreak of the Korean War, the wholesale index of capital goods showed prices rising by 7 points; that of consumer durables rose by 5 points. The following year, after wage and price controls were imposed, each index rose by only about one point.

This experience was not, however, greatly influential. It was assumed that war had, somehow, established new conditions as well as new imperatives. These made the experience irrelevant for peacetime. All groups influentially concerned also had a strong traditional resistance to controls. On few questions, indeed, have employers, unions and professional economists been more united in ideology than in opposition to price and wage regulation.

Employers had always reacted to controls in the tradition of the entrepreneurial firm. Price control could only be for the purpose of reducing profits. Public interference with wages might be a way of reinforcing the demands of the unions. But perhaps also it might seem to be a threat to the autonomy of the technostructure. And, more generally, the mystique of freedom, embracing but presumably going beyond the freedom to make money, strongly defended the principle of free markets.

Unions had also long reacted adversely. This was a legacy of their experience with the entrepreneurial firm. That firm had a strong interest in resisting union demands. It had privileged access to newspapers, public opinion and the state. Any wage regulation, other than that establishing minimum wages, would be, it was felt, for the purpose of keeping wages down. To be dependent even on a friendly government was to lose capacity for independent action to press rightful demands.

For economists, as will be sufficiently evident, a massive intellectual vested interest was involved. As noted, nearly all teaching and technical discourse assumed markets with unfettered prices in which producers sought to maximize their return. To admit of the need for price or wage control was to destroy the determinacy of this system and the associated theoretical apparatus. Instead of revealing to students by precise and rational diagrams the prices that would maximize profits for a producer, it would be necessary to consider what price a bureaucrat might believe consistent with wage and price stability. Economics would be reduced to the level of political science. Truth has its obligations to dignity.

Besides it would not work. Here we encounter again the commitment to avarice. Only the soft-minded could suppose that government, by regulation, could thwart the primal instinct for self-enrichment.

In consequence, professional economists had accepted the inevitability of inflation at full employment or had simply evaded the issue with whatever grace they could command. "Most economists would, in normal peacetime, favor controlling inflation by . . . fiscal and monetary policies rather than by simply legislating price ceilings." "It would be nice if we could insist upon having complete price stability and maximal employment and growth . . . it may be that citizens of a modern mixed economy can find no shelters in which they can live with full security and compromise."[6]

Yet, paradoxically, all associated with the industrial system also benefit substantially from restraints on prices and wages. What is opposed in principle is desirable in practice. Uncontrolled price and cost increases are much less dangerous to the security of the technostructure than uncontrolled price reductions such as might result from price competition or be forced by a severe shrinkage of aggregate demand. Given the strong demand that induces the price and cost increases in the first place, it is possible to offset cost increases by raising prices. It is not at all easy to offset falling prices by reducing wages or other costs. Nevertheless, planning is greatly facilitated if prices and costs are stable. Inflationary price and cost increases, moving unpredictably through the system, make long-term contracts impossible and everywhere introduce an unwelcome element of randomness and error. Price stability also facilitates the management of demand. Prices being given, the way is open to persuade the customer on other points. If prices are changing, he may respond in his purchases to these. This response is unpredictable, which is to say it interferes with effective management.

If wages are rising, increases in compensation for white-collar employees and in the technostructure will also be required. This will be at a time when there are unfilled positions. There will be some resulting danger of unsettling the salary structure and inducing competition for scarce talent. Another random element thus enters and interferes with planning. The mature corporation and its technostructure therefore have good reasons for wishing to avoid the wage price spiral. And to accept restraint, since it applies to both costs and wages, is not necessarily to sacrifice earnings. Should there be sacrifice, as always in the mature corporation, it is not suffered by those who agree to it.

Thus, once again economic development shows a remarkable degree of internal consistency. The industrial system must, by its nature, be subject to external restraint on its prices. As the mature corporation evolves it can accept and even welcome such restraint.

Restraint is useful in practice also to the unions. The spiral requires that they invest much of their energies in keeping abreast of price increases. Only a small and unpredictable portion of a pay rise brings higher real income. The rest compensates for price increases. Thus with uncontrolled wages and prices, the union has a large and essentially unproductive task of merely keeping even. For the rank and file the effect is even worse. Gains are won as the result of lengthy and elaborate collective bargaining. If only for demonstration purposes there will be an occasional strike. And then these gains evaporate as prices rise. The whole process has an unpleasant aspect of legerdemain. "It makes no sense to have the boss put a nickel in wages in your pocket with one hand and take out a dime in prices with the other."[7]

Outside of the industrial system, the spiral also has adverse effects. And these sectors of the economy are important in forming public attitudes. Here are farmers, civil servants, the self-employed and the employees of small enterprises. Within the industrial system, as wages force up prices and prices force up wages, those who receive these payments remain automatically abreast. A passenger in even a very fast automobile is reasonably certain of keeping up with it. A man running alongside is not so well situated. The insiders are protected against loss of real income; the outsiders are not. More generally the individual who gets added income, as a result of a general inflationary movement, attributes it not to larger economic causes but to his own virtue and diligence. The higher prices that take it away he attributes to bad public policy. Finally, there are many categories of income recipients—municipal employees, hospital and library and like workers, pensioners of all kinds—whose incomes do not rise appreciably. Their complaint is even more acute.

Economic discussion in the fifties was not only dominated by the problem of inflation but also by efforts to shift the blame. The corporations blamed the excessive wage demands of the unions. The unions blamed the avaricious and monopolistic prices of the corporations.[8] Democrats blamed the Republican administration and Republicans the previous Democratic administration and the Congress. Some saw the spiral as a Communist plot to debauch the currency, and the Reverend Gerald L. K. Smith thoughtfully blamed the Jews.

In fact, the wage-price spiral is the functional counterpart of unemployment. The latter occurs when there is insufficient demand; the spiral operates when there is too much and also, unfortunately, when there is just enough. Both unemployment and inflation are taken by the public to be indications of failure. Here the economists reenter. Whatever their predilections, they cannot escape public attitudes. These will no more allow excuses for inflation than for unemployment. And since the system is unstable at full employment, there is no alternative to control. However regretted, it is inescapable. This even the most ardent defenders of the market have discovered when they have arrived in Washington to take a position with the Council of Economic Advisers or otherwise experience the chilling realities of responsibility. For the duration of their service, the notion of maintaining full employment without interference with markets has to be put aside. Only when they are safely back in the universities again can it be gratefully exhumed.

Since all the relevant groups affirm the importance of free markets in principle, while needing control in practice, the solution has been to impose control in practice while affirming the commitment to free markets in principle. This semantic triumph has been aided by long-standing recognition that what is not permissible in principle is often necessary in practice.

It has also been aided by the technological dynamic of the industrial system. This, with its associated use of capital, insures a progressive increase in output per worker, although in varying amounts from industry to industry. These productivity gains allow, in turn, for annual wage increases without either higher prices or reduced earnings. Given a reasonably affluent wage level—an exemption from the pressures of physical need—workers may be more content to accept a moderate wage increase with stable prices than a larger one with the prospect of partial loss from rising living costs. Since the corporation is not experiencing rising costs, it can accept stable prices as its part of the bargain. All that remains is for the state to give a clear initiative in this regulation.

This initiative was, perhaps, the most important innovation in economic policy of the administration of President John F. Kennedy. In the earliest days of the administration, it was agreed among those concerned with economic policy that some special mechanism for restraint would be required were there to be a close approach to full employment. Generalized pleas to unions and employers for restraint had been sufficiently tried; in the absence of definition, all parties identified restraint with their normal behavior. Accordingly, in September of 1961 the United Steel Workers, then engaged in contract negotiations with the steel companies, were asked by President Kennedy to hold their demands within what could be granted from productivity gains. And the steel companies were asked to keep their prices stable. The policy and the standards for its application were then detailed the following January in the annual Economic Report. "The general guide for non-inflationary wage behavior is that the rate of increase in wage rates (including fringe benefits) in each industry be equal to the trend rate of over-all productivity increases."[9] In April, 1962, after negotiating a wage contract generally consistent with these standards, the steel companies, led by the United States Steel Corporation, announced an increase in steel prices averaging six dollars a ton. Strong government pressure, strongly adverse public and business opinion and some historic Presidential invective brought a recision of the increases. Thereafter for several years the wage guideposts, as they came to be called, and the counterpart price behavior were a reasonably accepted feature of government policy. Wage negotiations were closely consistent with the guidelines. Prices of manufactured goods were stable.

Nevertheless, of the various adaptations of government policy to the planning of the industrial system, the control of wages and prices is on the least secure footing. Partly this is because the divorce of ideology from action has so far excluded any deliberate effort to devise a fully effective system of control. On occasions of public ceremony, businessmen and numerous union leaders must still proclaim their commitment to the free market. And likewise economists. It is hard to turn from these liturgical exercises to a consideration of practical measures for insuring that the guideposts will be observed. In the thirties, although the commitment of economists to the canons of sound finance was still strong, a minority accepted the implications of the Keynesian system and proceeded to work out its application to practical fiscal policy. Though radical this was not wholly disreputable. To work on methods of wage and price control is not reputable. Only after a scholar is in public office is the ban lifted. And then he is careful to speak not of control but (as frequently here) of restraint. The amenability of the corporations and unions to control—ideology to the contrary—means that it need not be very strong. But it is hard to take purely hortatory enforcement very seriously. "These guideposts . . . do not have the force of law; the scowls by the President . . . cannot solve the dilemmas of full employment and price stability."[10]

This lack of ideological sanction also leaves the danger that someone will appear in a position of responsibility for whom the liturgy of the free market is a guide to action. He will insist that there be no interference with wages and prices. Otherwise the gods of free enterprise will be not appeased. Then it will have to be learned anew that, given the imperatives of demand regulation and full employment, there will be inflation.[11]

Finally there is a serious danger—one that is evident as this is written in 1966 —that wage and price restraints will be asked to accomplish more than they are capable of doing. In a sense they do not prevent inflation. Rather they keep the wage and price spiral from producing inflationary increases in prices—increases in prices over a large range of products and unrelated to any expansion in output —when demand is at levels sufficient to provide full or nearly full employment. But demand must not be greatly in excess of this amount. If it is too high, price increases outside the industrial system, competition to fill vacancies, payments for early or preferential deliveries and the feeling of unions that they should share in high profits will act to break down the restraints. The proper remedy is higher taxes or reduced government spending to cut down on the demand. These are painful actions. The regulation of demand is politically asymmetrical: expansion is far easier than contraction. Accordingly a failure of wage and price restraints in face of excessive aggregate demand also remains a danger to this accommodation to industrial planning.

Yet, while there may be difficulties, and interim failures or retreats are possible and indeed probable, a system of wage and price restraint is inevitable in the industrial system. As noted, neither inflation nor unemployment are acceptable alternatives.[12] No other advanced industrial community, socialist, non-socialist or ideologically hostile to socialism, has found it possible to dispense with such regulation. The United States, the most developed of the industrial communities, will not be an exception.

The necessity for control arises in the apparatus of industrial planning. This planning, we have seen, replaces prices that are established by the market with prices that are established by the firm. The firm, in tacit collaboration with the other firms in the industry, has wholly sufficient power to set and maintain minimum prices. Although in Europe cartels can seek the support of the courts for this purpose, this recourse is not essential. And the firm goes on to exercise control over what is purchased at these prices. Given this management of demand for the individual product together with an effective regulation of aggregate demand, the minimum prices so set are secure. There is no serious danger that they will be broken down by competition or a failure of demand.

This price control accords protection, however, only against price reduction. It does not embrace the unions and hence does not provide any protection against concessions to them and concurrent price increases. And the remedy is beyond the scope of the individual firm. It knows that others will forswear price reductions that are disastrous for all. But it cannot count on others to resist wage increases and to forgo resultant price increases, for these, however inconvenient for planning and the economy at large, are not disastrous. The market having been abandoned in favor of planning of prices and demand, there is no hope that it will supply this last missing element of restraint. All that remains is the state. So, in the end, there is no alternative to having the state complete the structure of planning.

With minimum prices established by the firms, demand that is managed by them for specific products, demand that is managed in the aggregate by the state and maximum levels established by the state for wages and prices, the planning structure of the industrial system is effectively complete. All that remains is to insure that everyone, at all times, refer to it as an unplanned or market system.

In this connection, it is worth noting, the weakness of the present machinery for enforcing maximum prices will not, in the end, be a handicap. The entrepreneurial enterprise was subordinate to and regulated by the market. Being under the dominance of the market, it had substantial independence from the state. The power of the state to control its behavior was, accordingly, a most important question. The enterprise was free to bring to bear formidable powers of obstruction and resistance. The mature corporation, as part of a comprehensive structure of planning, has no similar independence. It identifies itself with social goals, and adapts these to its needs. It cannot easily fight that with which it is so associated. More specifically, if the state is effectively to manage demand, the public sector of the economy, as we have seen, must be relatively large. That means that the state is an important customer, and it is especially needed in developing advanced technology which would otherwise be beyond the scope of industrial planning. Under these circumstances the independence of the mature corporation is further circumscribed. It is deeply dependent on the state. It does not accordingly have the luxury of defiance. It may go far in adapting the goals of the state to its needs. But it cannot, any more than a department of government itself, pursue objectives at odds with those of the state. In numerous ways the state can deny it vital needs. And since other firms are identified with social goals and these reflect adaptation, they will tend to consider the resistance antisocial and the sanctions justified.[13] There is no chance, on this issue, of a solid front by mature corporations against the state.

NOTES

1. To be distinguished from the unfilled positions in the higher levels of qualification in the technostructure.

2. In recent years there has been a formidable dispute between economists as to whether demand pulls up prices, or costs, especially wages, push them up. Much polemical blood has also been spilled on the issue. Again something more than scientific verity is involved. If demand is the activating factor, then unemployment could be minimized and inflation could be controlled by precise regulation of demand. No questions of price and wage control arise. But if wages shove up prices and the higher prices lead to new wage demands, the plausible course is to control one or both. The cost-push thesis is also inconsistent with the doctrine of maximization, for, as noted, if a firm can respond to a wage increase by raising prices and increasing its net revenues (some rather remote theoretical contingencies apart) it could have done so before the wage increase. It did not, so it was not maximizing its revenues prior to the wage increase.

   In fact, within the industrial system, as just indicated, both strong demand and the push of costs are factors in the instability of prices at or near full employment. For a further and competent discussion of these relationships, see William G. Bowen, "Wage Behavior and the Cost-Inflation Problem" in *Labor and the National Economy*, edited by the same author (New York: Norton, 1965). An important study, affirming the cost-push thesis, to which I am much indebted is Sidney Weintraub's *Some Aspects of Wage Theory and Policy* (New York: Chilton Books, 1963).

3. It is not necessarily characteristic of the economy outside the industrial system. In agriculture, professional and other services, imported products and some raw materials, the push of wages is likely to be unimportant. Prices rise primarily in response to strong demand. Some of the past debate between economists over the comparative importance of cost-push and demand-pull inflation has been the result of different men looking at different parts of the economy.

4. This is a choice which nearly all economists concede but which cannot be reconciled in any practical way with the doctrine of profit maximization.

5. Charles L. Schultze, "Creeping Inflation—Causes and Consequences," *Business Horizons*, Summer 1960, University of Indiana. Dr. Schultze, at this writing Director of the Budget, has argued that a contributing cause of inflation during this time was unusually sharp changes in demand. These exerted an upward pull on prices in industries where the demand was increasing; and since prices rise more easily than they fall there was no compensating reduction in areas of declining demand. At the same time union demands are increased by the favorable earnings in the areas of expansion and the demands are readily conceded. This exaggerates the spiral. Cf. *Recent Inflation in the United States*, Study Paper No. 1, Joint Economic Committee, Congress of the United States, Study of Employment, Growth and Price Levels (September 1959). Also, W. G. Bowen and S. H. Masters, "Shifts in the Composition of Demand and the Inflation Problem," *American Economic Review*, LIV, No. 6 (December 1964). It will be evident that this explanation is an elaboration rather than a contradiction of the explanation offered above. Inflation occurs when demand is strong and the effect of strong demand is exaggerated by shifts in demand.

6. Paul A. Samuelson, *Economics*, Sixth Edition (New York: McGraw, 1964), pp. 386, 792.

7. A. H. Raskin, "The Squeeze of the Unions," *Atlantic Monthly*, April 1961. Reprinted in Bowen, "Wage Behavior," p. 8. He was commenting on a common attitude of steel workers.

8. See the discussion by Schultze, "Creeping Inflation."

9. *Economic Report of the President*, January 1962.

10. Samuelson, *Economics*, p. 792.

11. This tendency to divorce ideology from practical action, with the danger that innocent but devout believers will be guided by the ideology, is a more general affliction. Thus our relations with the Soviet Union are presumed, by ideology, to be marked by total conflict—the climactic confrontation between socialism and free enterprise. In fact, they have been characterized by practical accommodation on a great many matters— in Berlin, in resisting the proliferation of nuclear weapons, in awareness of the danger of war by accident, in preventing nuclear fallout, in the U.N. and in a considerable range of scientific and cultural development. In 1964 in the campaign of Senator Goldwater the policy fell into the hands of those who were guided by the liturgy of conflict rather than by the reality of accommodation.

12. I once considered it possible that, by adequate compensation, a volume of unemployment consistent with stable prices could be made socially and politically tolerable. Cf. *The Affluent Society*, pp. 298–307. This I now doubt.

13. Efforts by the steel industry—U.S. Steel in 1962 and Bethlehem in 1966—to break through current price restraints are a case in point. These efforts were a reflection of older entrepreneurial attitudes. The government on both occasions threatened use of its power as a customer—though it is less in the case of steel than in many industries. Both public and a good deal of business opinion condemned the actions as antisocial or, at a minimum, showing a poor sense of public relations. On the latter, see Richard Austin Smith, *Corporations in Crisis* (New York: Doubleday, 1963), pp. 157 *et seq.*

INFLATION AND THE WORKING CLASS

James O'Connor

THE FISCAL CRISIS OF THE STATE

. . . Our general conclusion is that the growth of capitalist production places increasing stresses and strains on the state budget. On the one hand, at least twenty-five per cent and perhaps as much as one-third of the work force is directly or indirectly employed by the state. Further, tens of thousands of doctors, welfare workers, and other self-employed and privately employed professionals and technicians use facilities provided by the state and are dependent in whole or in part on government budgets. Finally, tens of millions of men and women are dependent on the state budget as clients and recipients of state services. On the other hand, the state continues to rely on taxes—even though traditional state functions have been greatly expanded and many new functions added. In other words, private capital, at times alone and at times allied with labor, has socialized many costs and expenses of production, but has not socialized profits. In modern capitalism, state expenditures tend to outrun taxes; what people need from the state exceeds what they are willing to pay to the state.

The underlying reason for the fiscal crisis is the basic relation between Big Capital and Big Labor, who, in effect, "export" their conflicts to the competitive and state sectors of the economy. This happens in a number of different ways: first, labor and capital in the monopolistic sector support the growth of state-financed higher education, research and development activities, transportation and communications facilities, and other indirectly productive state investments. From the standpoint of Big Labor, the more costs of production are socialized, the higher will be productivity and wages in the monopolistic sector. In the words of one observer, "labor and the academic liberals joined with downtown business interests in sponsoring urban renewal; with auto manufacturers and highway contractors in supporting vast road projects; with suburban legislators in promoting state-supported higher education."[1] Second, unions and management in monopolistic industries collaborate in the introduction of labor-saving technology, which leads to an expansion of employment in both the competitive and state sectors. Labor income in state industries tends to be determined by productivity and wages in monopolistic industries. Thus, when the state "takes up the slack" by expanding state employment (as opposed to increasing welfare), costs in state industries tend to increase. More, there is a steady upward pressure on unit labor costs attributable to the growth of wages in the monopolistic sector.

SOURCE: *Socialist Revolution,* March/April 1972, pp. 33–46.

433

Third, Big Labor and Big Capital combine to socialize the *social* costs of production, the costs of ameliorating urban decay, reducing pollution and other environmental damage, and so on. Shifting these costs to taxpayers as a whole permits profits *and* wages in monopolistic industries to expand more rapidly. Fourth, reproduction costs such as medical expenses and retirement income of workers in monopolistic industries also tend to be socialized. Both Big Labor and Big Capital presently support national health insurance, the expansion of old age and survivors insurance, and similar social outlays. Monopolistic industries burdened with expensive health and medical insurance programs that labor unions have won through collective bargaining seek to shift this burden to the state. Normally, they can count on the willing collaboration of unions sensitive to membership demands for better and more comprehensive health care. Last but not least, both Big Capital and Big Labor are ardent supporters of the military budget.[2]

There is one crucial difference between the attitudes of Big Capital and Big Labor toward economic activity organized by the state. Capital normally opposes the establishment of state industry that competes with private capital. Put another way, capital opposes any program that socializes profits. Thus big business supports national health insurance and opposes socialized medicine; favors federal highway programs and opposes state-managed construction firms; agitates for enormous military budgets and the sale of state armories and other production facilities to private capital. Not only are costs of production socialized but also profits are guaranteed. In the field of health and medicine and in the system of military contracting, in particular, these guaranteed profits can reach astronomical heights, placing additional drains on the state budget.

ROLE OF TAXATION AND INFLATION

In the advanced capitalist countries, state expenditures in relation to gross national product have risen more or less steadily from the last decade of the nineteenth century to the present.[3] This has been the result of the socialization of many of the costs and expenses of production and the subsidization of profits. By and large, state expenditures have contributed to the growth of total production. Thus, the state and private sectors have expanded simultaneously. State spending has increased taxable incomes and the tax base and hence have been self-financing in whole or in part. But as the costs of the state sectors continue to rise out of proportion to productivity in the state sector, it becomes less and less possible to finance state activities from the "growth dividend." Within the framework of capitalist property relations, there are only three ways for the state to cover these rising costs: higher tax rates, inflation, or increases in productivity in state activities. [Here] we [shall] take up tax and inflationary finance.

When costs are especially unpopular among the working class as a whole, such as the costs of the war in Southeast Asia, the state falls back on inflationary finance by monetizing the public debt, that is, by borrowing from itself and forgoing real borrowing. In general, the higher the rate of interest, the more likely that the state will finance expenditures by "borrowing from itself," in essence, by arbitrarily increasing bank liabilities. When costs are relatively popular among the working class, for example, the rising costs of public education, the state will increase taxes. And when costs are unpopular among private businessmen and workers in monopolistic and state industries, such as the costs of welfare, irresistible political pressures are created to cut back expenditures.

Whatever the particular combination of tax and inflationary finance used by the state, the effect is to reduce the real wages of the work force as a whole. A hypothetical example . . . : Suppose that productivity and money wages in [monopolistic and] state industries and competitive industries are growing by three per cent and one per cent per year, respectively. Next, let us assume that inflation or taxes or both reduce money wages in all three sectors by two percentage points (under the conditions that inflation and the tax load fall proportionately on working class income). The effect will be to confine the rise in real wages in monopolistic and state industries to one per cent annually, and to *lower* real wages in competitive industries. Now let us bring in our familiar assumption that the work force is divided evenly between the three sectors, and that productivity in the state and competitive sectors rises by one per cent per year. Real wages in monopolistic and state industries thus rise slightly more than the increase in average productivity in the economy as a whole, while real wages in the competitive sector fall below average productivity increases.

It is important to stress that this entire process is triggered by the agreement between labor and capital in monopolistic industries to keep money wages in this sector in step with productivity, and the "agreement" between state workers and state administrators to keep money wages in the state sector in line with money wages in the monopolistic sector. In other words, the relations of production in the monopolistic and state sectors work to the absolute disadvantage of workers in the competitive sector. Workers in competitive industries are not only the direct victims of social oppression (and therefore economic discrimination), but also are indirect victims because they are forced to pay a share of the costs of production in monopolistic industries (e.g., taxes to finance higher education). Perhaps it is not too much to say that it is the relationship between labor and capital in the monopolistic and state sectors—enforced on labor by the power of capital—that is the basic cause of the impoverishment of workers in the competitive sector.

In the last analysis, competitive workers are materially impoverished because they are socially oppressed, the victims of racism and sexism. But the causal relationship between oppression and impoverishment runs both ways. The relative or absolute decline in real wages has the effect of reducing material standards of life, and lowering opportunities for upward mobility within the work force as a whole. Simultaneously, declining material standards force the competitive work force to rely on state services for bare survival (thus increasing costs within the state sector, and stimulating the entire mechanism again). The absence of opportunities for upward-mobility and increasing dependency on the state reinforce racist and sexist attitudes and race-typing and sex-typing of jobs. As a result bitterness and antagonism between "mainstream" workers in the monopolistic and state sectors and "peripheral" workers in the competitive sector increase. Finally, the issue of taxes and budgetary priorities becomes a central issue dividing the work force as a whole: monopolistic and state workers call for budgetary priorities in their favor. The only possible way for the work force as a whole to get what it wants is to establish an alliance against capital as a whole. But this is impractical because of the agreement between Big Capital and Big Labor that guarantees workers in the monopolistic sector their "fair share" of productivity gains in return for more than a modicum of labor peace.

RELATIONS OF PRODUCTION IN THE MONOPOLISTIC INDUSTRIES

At this point, we can see that the fiscal crisis of the state (the tendency for expenditures to outrace revenue) is at root a social crisis in the form of economic and political antagonisms that divide not only labor and capital but also the work force as a whole. The social crisis (bitterness and conflict between blacks and whites, women's liberation, welfare rights struggles) and the fiscal crisis that mirrors and enlarges the social crisis sooner or later work their way back into the arena where the big battles between labor and capital are fought—the monopolistic industries.

Despite the steady advance of money wages, real wages tend to fall behind productivity gains in the monopolistic sector. In the United States, between 1965 and 1970 productivity in manufacturing industries increased by about thirteen per cent, while real wages remained the same.[4] This fact has potentially stupendous effects on the functioning of capitalist society as a whole. On the one hand, union leaders increasingly become unable to discipline rank-and-file workers whose standard of life is threatened by inflation and taxation. On the other hand, union leaders increasingly become *unwilling* to discipline the rank-and-file. They are no longer willing to sit back and watch union membership stagnate or decline (while collaborating actively with employers in the introduction of labor-saving innovations) because they are no longer confident that the wages of union members who retain their jobs will rise in step with productivity, or even maintain themselves at an even level. In this way, inflation and heavy taxation encourage militancy on the part of both union leaders and rank-and-file.

The result is that the unions organize defensive strikes to keep *real* wages in line with productivity. If these strikes are successful (as many of them have been during 1970–1971), money wages increase more rapidly than physical productivity. This has the effect of pushing up unit labor costs, which forces monopolistic industries to raise prices to protect profit margins. Across-the-board increases in prices in the absence of commensurate rises in productivity and production are inflationary. They are especially (at least in the short run) inflationary to the degree that there is an expansion of employment and production in the competitive and state sectors, where productivity is relatively low, hence pulling down average productivity in the economy as a whole. In one sense, the "cost-push" theory of inflation is correct: the erosion of living standards by inflation forces workers to defend these standards, which in turn causes more inflation.

The entire mechanism described above is perpetuated in this way. Wage increases in the monopolistic sector spread to the state sector, increasing unit labor costs in state industries. If monopolistic industries protect profit margins by introducing more labor-saving methods of production, workers are "pushed" into the competitive sector where labor income is low. More and more workers thus come to depend on the state budget to maintain their living standards. If monopoly capital depends solely on price increases to maintain profits, inflation worsens, burdening the state with more costs and encouraging workers to demand higher money wages. In either case, taxes or inflation or both will rise, and the social crisis will deepen.

THREE OPTIONS OPEN TO THE STATE

Sooner or later, monopoly capital must face a critical dilemma. On the one hand, monopoly capital is compelled to grant increases in money wages to avoid a rupture in relations with unions and workers, even though unit labor costs and prices rise continuously. On the other hand, domestic inflation reduces foreign demand for United States products, cutting into exports and worsening the balance of trade. This is particularly serious as time goes on because foreign sales constitute a rising portion of total sales of many of the largest corporations.[5] Further, inflation pushes up interest rates, which in turn chokes off mortgage and credit-financed spending on housing and consumer durables—the two mainstays of the private economy. If prices are kept from rising, costs cut into profit margins; if prices are raised, falling demand reduces sales and profits (demand will fall particularly low if inflation is accompanied by growing unemployment).

There are three possible ways out of this dilemma—managed recession, wage-price controls and increased productivity in the private and state sectors, which would in turn require a remodeling of the relations of production throughout the society.[6] Let us consider the practicality of each of these ways in turn.

The first option is to use fiscal and monetary policy to reduce aggregate demand, increase unemployment, and weaken the bargaining power of unions in the monopolistic and state industries. The positive effect is to reduce the rate of increase of money wages, unit labor costs, and interest rages, and to slow down the growth of price inflation. One negative effect is the reduction of aggregate demand and sales. Another negative effect is the increase in the number of unemployed and under-employed workers and therefore the number of people dependent on the state. At the same time, managed recession reduces aggregate wage and profit income, lowers the tax base, cuts into tax receipts, and squeezes the budget from the revenue side. On the other hand, unemployment of labor and underutilization of productive capacity mean that state spending raises not only aggregate demand but also real output and income, and finally, the tax base and tax receipts. In other words, in a recession state expenditures help to pay for themselves and in terms of the real resources used can be virtually costless. Nevertheless, recessions create demands on the state budget at precisely the time when the ability of the state to meet these demands without recourse to large-scale deficit financing is weakened. More important, serious recession is a threat to the harmonious relations between Big Labor and Big Capital. For these reasons, no modern government could long retain power in the event that it choose to depend exclusively or mainly on the option of managed recession.

The second option is to impose wage-price controls on the monopolistic sector.[7] From the standpoint of capital in the monopolistic sector, wage and price controls have the same advantage as a managed recession: responsibility for keeping money wages down is shifted from the industries themselves to the government. A lid is placed on wages, but it is difficult for the unions to blame management. Wage-price controls have the additional advantage of reducing the risk of a downward spiral of employment, income, demand, production, and profits—a risk that is always latent in managed recessions. If the state decides on a particular volume of investment (and thus savings) needed for high employment or balance of payments equilibrium, and establishes wages and prices such that this volume of investment and savings is forthcoming, the state effectively controls the distributive shares of income and guarantees a certain level of profits.[8] On the other hand, from the standpoint of labor in the monopolistic industries, wage and price controls are anathema. The reason is that the unions are forced to bargain away their right to improve labor's share of income in return for policies designed to maintain high employment. Labor and capital in the monopolistic sector are also reluctant to agree to controls because they represent a conscious choice to give up their privileged status vis-à-vis labor and capital in the competitive sector. During the 1960s, "economists and others who have been closest to union-management negotiations tend to regard guidepost wage restraints as nonexistent or very minimal."[9]

In addition, there are two serious disadvantages of wage and price controls from the standpoint of monopoly capital. First, controls introduce an element of inflexibility in the ability of management in the monopolistic sector to mobilize and allocate capital profitably. Second, as we have suggested, wage and price controls transform antagonisms between labor and capital into conflicts between labor and the state. Controls thus open objective possibilities for alliances between workers in monopolistic and competitive industries. The real danger of wage and price controls is the potential growth of a class-conscious and unified working class.[10] How dangerous this can be for the stability of the capitalist system was illustrated by the May 1968 general strike in France, where state management of the economy in peacetime has reached unprecedented levels. Finally, from the point of view of the state administration, wage and price controls are extremely difficult to enforce: for one thing, thousands of wage rates are not determined by collective bargaining at the national level but rather at the base by local management; for another, it is difficult to win agreement on how to measure productivity; moreover, fringe costs are not subject to controls.

The third and in the long-run the only practical option available to the state is to encourage the growth of productivity in both the monopolistic and state industries (raising productivity in competitive industries is highly impractical because of the great number of firms, their small scale, and the relative absence of economic integration). Private ownership of the means of production prevents direct intervention by the state and effective direct planning of production, investment, technological priorities, prices, and so on.[11] As a result, the state is forced to put its own house in order by increasing efficiency in state industries (including facilities owned by state contractors). Immediately, a seemingly insurmountable problem confronts the state administration: goods production in the state sector is not destined for the market but rather is contracted for the state agencies. Most tangible goods produced by or for the state are unique outputs, one-of-a-kind products. Policies to increase efficiency in state industries boil down to the use of modern management techniques such as systems analysis and program budgeting. Since World War II, and particularly since 1960, the federal government in the United States has been increasingly preoccupied with the "efficiency" and "economic rationality" of its various programs, especially the military program. In the Department of Defense, "a buyer-seller scheme [attempts] to impose on a sprawling network of military units a coordination and constraint that controls economic units under private property in the market."[12] And the use of "cost-benefit" analyses of government programs is widespread in all of the federal departments.

These techniques are able to cut some of the fat from the budget, but not very much. For one thing, the very meaning of "efficiency" outside of the market-place, where there are no independent buyers and sellers, continues to be debated by economists and government officials. Moreover, as we know, in the provision of services it is difficult to raise productivity, whether the services are provided by private or state capital. Conflicting private interests also limit the ability of the state to develop programs characterized by *overall* efficiency; for example, river valley development and transportation programs must satisfy the conflicting claims of different kinds of private interests. In industries supplying military goods, the state underwrites capital investments, guarantees orders, provides needed technical help and frees private capital from economic risk and uncertainty, thus eliminating the traditional "entrepreneurial function" and virtually guaranteeing a high level of inefficiency. Government programs that aim to stabilize the social order by providing regular employment for unskilled or underemployed workers are also inefficient from the standpoint of minimizing costs and maximizing output. For example, one of the reasons that the federal government has hesitated to automate postal services is fear of the political implications of adding to unemployment.[13] Finally, in the absence of a firm *détente* with the Soviet Union with regard to the "permissible" type, number, and deployment of weapons, the Department of Defense must concentrate mainly on new weapons development, rather than on improving the efficiency of traditional weapons production and distribution. All in all, it would appear that the prospect of improving productivity in established state activities is relatively dim.

"Increased productivity" in the state sector therefore has a very special meaning. It will be recalled that the importance of state activities is that they can be in-directly productive from the standpoint of the private sector, especially monop-olistic industries. State investments of various kinds provide valuable infrastructure for private capital. It follows that "increased productivity" means less increasing efficiency in current state activities than it does *changing budgetary priorities as a whole*. Options to reduce unit labor costs in the state sector are few, but options to lower labor costs in the monopolistic sector are many, and to a degree untried. An obvious example is education and manpower development. Education and job training programs can be designed to tap more fully available manpower reserves, and to create fresh reserves, inhibiting upward pressures on wages and supplying more skilled labor to industry. Existing education programs in colleges and universities can be "rationalized" by gearing degree programs to "career goals." More "efficiency" can be cut from highway and other transportation programs by eliminating duplication of facilities and by locating new housing and industrial developments on the periphery of metropolitan areas where land and construction costs are relatively small. Still more savings could be made by developing a vast "half-way house" program for mental patients and criminal offenders. The list of new budgetary priorities is potentially endless.

Programs such as these hold out many advantages to monopoly capital (and to a lesser degree state contractors). The development of a full-scale "social industrial complex" would provide opportunities for military contractors to convert production facilities to non-military uses (as they have to a small degree in California since 1966). But because state contractors in the military field have a vested interest in the cold war and the expansion of the military establishment, most of the advantages of a social-industrial complex would accrue to the monopolistic sector. Education, training, housing, and other social programs geared to expanding productivity and financed by the state would provide fresh fields of investment for monopolistic industries. Social tensions arising from the material impoverishment of workers in competitive industries might be reduced by creating jobs for those presently unemployed and underemployed. And to the degree that social investments were organized directly under the auspices of monopolistic industries (such as new corporate-organized teaching systems sold to local school districts), the fiscal crisis of the state might be in part relieved directly.

By contrast, private capital in the competitive sector has everything to lose and little to gain from the growth of a social-industrial complex. Competitive capital in goods-producing industries requires cheap labor and a flexible, often transient labor force. Competitive capital in distribution thrives on slum housing, high rents, and high retail prices. Competitive activities in the sphere of circulation —in particular, small and exploitive credit and loan companies—also have a strong interest in maintaining the status quo. Consequently, the precondition for the success of a program of social reconstruction based on the needs and priorities of monopoly capital is the elimination of the power of small-scale capital, not only in the marketplace, but also in the arenas of local and state politics where local and regional capital in competitive industries has much influence and power.

Moreover, labor unions in the monopolistic sector potentially have a great deal to lose from the development of a social-industrial complex. The main reason is that the surplus generated within monopolistic industries that is presently distributed to workers in the form of money wages commensurate with (or in excess of) productivity would have to be appropriated by the state and plowed into programs for social reconstruction. And although social investments geared to expanding productivity in the monopolistic sector would raise productivity in the long run, during the transition period, the rate of growth of productivity would no doubt decline, affording a relatively narrow basis for wage increases in the monopolistic sector. Thus radical shifts in budgetary priorities require deep-going changes in the relations of production as a whole. And radical shifts in the structure of the tax system in favor of monopoly capital and impoverished workers in the competitive sector (for example, via the negative income tax) and against workers in monopolistic and state industries also require profound changes in the relationships between and within social classes in America.

NOTES

1. Leonard Ross, "The Myth that Things Are Getting Better, *New York Review of Books,* August 12, 1971.
2. We have confined our analysis to the relationships within and between the three sectors of the economy producing and distributing goods and services. There is another sec-

tor which is normally organized by private capital and which engages in financial activities (or circulation of capital). In America, the same families and interest groups which dominate the monopolistic industries also control the major financial institutions. The cooperation of the banks is indispensable to both the private and state sectors of the economy. For example, when the state takes over unprofitable private activities such as urban transit or puts up new infrastructure (e.g., downtown urban renewal projects), bonds must be floated to finance the purchase of investment. Amortizing these bonds over a long span of time is a very expensive proposition (as in the cases of the Chicago and New York City rapid transit systems)—expensive from the standpoint of taxpayers as a whole.

3. Richard A. Musgrave, *Fiscal Systems* (New Haven, 1969), pp. 96–98, Tables 4–1, 4–2, and 4–3; pp. 102–104, Tables 4–4, and 4–6.
4. This is a rough approximation of the relation between real wages and productivity in the monopolistic sector because many manufacturing industries are competitive. Since money wages in monopolistic industries no doubt increased more than in competitive industries, and since taxes and inflation fall more or less equally on workers in both sectors, our guess is that the disparity between productivity and real wages in monopolistic industries during this period was less than the data cited above indicate.
5. "The War and Its Impact on the Economy," *Review of the Union for Radical Political Economics,* Special Issue, August 1970.
6. Until now, monopoly capital has been able to export some of its inflation to Western Europe by establishing the dollar as the world's reserve currency. This has been very important in "solving" the dilemma outlined above. There is still another possibility, to which President Nixon gives only lip service—namely, breaking up industrial and "labor" monopolies with the aim of making the economy more competitive.
7. Actually, controls have to be placed on any sector in which money wages advance significantly more rapidly than productivity—e.g., in the construction industry in the United States.
8. A good discussion of the issue is Domenico Mario Nuti, "On Incomes Policy," *Science and Society* 33:4 (Fall–Winter 1969), p. 422.
9. E. Robert Livernash, "Wages and Benefits," in *A Review of Industrial Relations Research* (Madison: Industrial Relations Research Association, University of Wisconsin, 1970), Vol. I, p. 102.
10. Wage and price controls or incomes policies "tend to bring the crisis in the trade union movement to a head, rather than integrating it further into the State and eliminating conflict" (Ernest Mandel, "A Socialist Strategy for Western Europe," *International Socialist Journal* 2:10 [August 1965], p. 433.
11. In Britain, however, the state is remodeling the industrial relations system by encouraging the establishment of "productivity agreements" between labor and capital that give management more control over labor costs. The number of workers covered by these agreements increased from one-half million in 1966 to six million in 1969 (David Purdy, "The State and Labour: A Brief Analysis," manuscript, September 1970).
12. The economics of this arrangement are discussed in Norman V. Breckner, "Government Efficiency and the Military 'Buyer-Seller' Device," *Journal of Political Economy* 68:5 (October 1960).
13. On the other hand, the new Postal Service has negotiated an agreement with two newly combined postal unions that gives the service wide latitude in introducing automation and changing work rules.

X. THE TURN TO WORKER CONTROL: REFORM OR REVOLUTION?

INTRODUCTION

We opened the debate on the working class with the ideas of Marx, who saw in the direct control of producers over the production process the means of overcoming alienation and exploitation. It is significant that the idea of worker control has reemerged in "postindustrial" capitalism and is being given serious consideration by spokesmen for both liberal and radical thought. Why a convergence of liberal and radical thought on this theme? How do we explain the turn to worker control in the light of the theory of "embourgeoisement," the end of class conflict and predictions of the coming of a "classless society"?

In liberal analysis, the interest in worker control flows from various constructs of "postindustrial" society. It reflects an interest in resolving problems of bureaucratization and increasing the possibility of democratic participation in large-scale industrial organizations. Thus, for some liberals, the demand for worker control is a central element in the logic of modern capitalist development, and is a historically viable means of gradually reforming modern industrial societies.

Radicals, on the other hand, view the worker control movement as a strategy for rekindling working-class consciousness and as a method of confronting capitalist institutions and power. Thus, in contrast to liberals, radicals see worker control as a strategy for the revolutionary transformation of capital-labor relations and the means of realizing the socialist goal.

Jenkins' article "Industrial Democracy" documents the various forms which the movement for worker participation in management has taken recently in Western Europe, contrasting the differing philosophies underlying efforts to combat job dissatisfaction in Western Europe and the United States. In some Western European countries, trade union representatives share seats on boards of directors with private shareholders, while in others the first steps have been taken to extend decision-making power to workers on the factory floor. Both types of measures are regarded as steps to extend "industrial democracy." In the United States, according to Jenkins, authoritarian management methods and ideology are more firmly entrenched, and the granting of initiative to workers is regarded as a "management technique," not a movement toward industrial democracy. But in both Western Europe and the United States the steps taken reflect increasing worker dissatisfaction with an autocratic work environment.

In "Power to the Workers?," Dahl presents a liberal perspective on the desirability of expanding democracy to the workplace. He explores the technological,

444

organizational, and political constraints on realizing the goals of worker control and examines the possibility of "interest group management" (joint participation by consumers, workers, government, and managers) as an intermediate stage. Paradoxically, for Dahl, the old worker and his union may be important obstacles to the realization of self-management.

Gorz presents a radical position on the significance of worker control. In "A Radical Strategy for Worker Control," the movement for worker control is seen as a strategy for challenging the capitalist mode of decision making in enterprises and in society as a whole. By moving beyond the issue of wages, this strategy is aimed at undermining the integration of worker and union into the corporate state and as a vehicle for the attainment of socialism.

INDUSTRIAL DEMOCRACY

David Jenkins

A widespread movement is under way in Western Europe to combat worker alienation and job dissatisfaction through industrial democracy: the statutory granting of genuine decision-making power to workers at all levels.

The European movement goes well beyond the current American efforts to attack the authoritiarian and bureaucratic excesses of work through job enrichment, job redesign and worker participation. The reasoning behind the European and American activity is similar.

But the methods being used in the United States, although they give workers more freedom to exercise their own initiative and judgment, do not give them a real share in company decision-making, and they do not alter the basic pyramidal power structure.

Why should the European and American approaches to the common problem of work and workers be so different? What are the differences on the two sides of the Atlantic?

In Europe, industrial democracy has long since passed the stage of being merely another chic leftish philosophical cobweb spun by Continental intellectuals. It is a top-priority goal with deadly seriousness and great vigor by politicians, labor leaders and (not least) the workers themselves.

The current wave of interest in industrial democracy goes well beyond the West German system created by the co-determination legislation passed in the early nineteen-fifties.

This system, known as "Mitbestimmung" in German, gives labor and capital equality on company "supervisory boards" (somewhat comparable to American boards of directors) in the coal and steel industries and minority positions in other industries.

In the equality method, the union and the shareholders' group each names half the board members, and the resulting board then names one additional neutral member. In the minority approach, the union names a third of the board members.

This arrangement has been criticized because the formal "influence" is so remote from the day-to-day concerns of the average worker that it does little to cure his alienation.

But it is sufficiently popular that both the unions and Willy Brandt's Social Democratic party have long sought to extend the equality concept to all industries. The Social Democrats have now persuaded their coalition partners, the

SOURCE: *New York Times*, May 13, 1973.

Free Democrats, to accept an expansion of the system, and a joint program is now being drawn up.

New legislation, more or less patterned on the West German model, has gone into effect this year in the Netherlands, Sweden and Norway, giving workers seats on boards of directors or other high-level bodies that appoint and control management.

In these countries, however, there is a key difference from the German approach. The laws themselves were preceded by several years of carefully planned projects to introduce democracy directly on the factory floor, where workers are more interested in possessing power and know more about matters over which they can be given power.

A number of large and small countries—such as Shell, Philips, Norsk Hydro, Volvo and Saab—initiated these projects. They used methods superficially similar to some of the more advanced participative techniques used in America that often show remarkable results in raising productivity as well as in increasing job satisfaction.

In Europe, however, it is widely understood that such management innovations were part of a broad-based movement toward industrial democracy.

These projects have demonstrated two main points:

(1) Democratic management need not increase costs. Quite the contrary. It is found that if a company can put employes' intelligence and creativity to work, profitability is increased.

(2) In virtually every case where such methods have been tried, employes have responded enthusiastically to the chance to obtain more freedom and responsibility. Indeed, they often develop greater involvement in company matters remote from their particular jobs.

As an example, Nobo Fabrikker, a Norwegian maker of office furniture and heating elements, began an experiment in the nineteen-sixties in a single small department. It removed foremen, abolished the conventional assembly line, trained workers to perform a variety of tasks and allowed them to organize in groups to plan, assign and schedule work among themselves.

The results, in terms of both job satisfaction and productivity, were so positive that the methods have since spread through most of the company. Low-level workers have become far more interested in all phases of company operations than anyone had thought possible.

Legislation is being pushed, or at least considered, in other countries, too.

In Denmark, Premier Anker Jorgensen (a former labor leader) is urging passage of an "economic democracy" bill. It is designed to give employees more decision-making power and to create a profit-sharing fund.

In France, the program of the leftist front in the recent parliamentary elections included industrial democracy, impelling President Pompidou to promise to "limit assembly lines and to humanize working conditions." Legislation is said to be in preparation.

In Britain, the Labor party chief, Harold Wilson, recently called for "a living and real democracy in industry." He said this would make "industry much more efficient and society in general much wealthier."

In many European countries, the idea of industrial democracy is so thoroughly accepted as a practical and attainable goal that it is almost impossible to find any one who does not favor the basic principle.

A Swedish newspaper quizzing teen-agers on their vocational plans drew this definition from a 12-year-old boy: "A bad job is where others make all the decisions and you have to do what they say."

In contrast, the lack of attention being paid to industrial democracy in America can seem puzzling.

After all, the basic conditions are the same as in Europe. An increasingly affluent, well-educated and sophisticated work force is decreasingly willing to accept autocratic work environments that not only are tiresome but also can often be done away with to the great benefit of both workers and companies. The nationwide worker revolt in France in May, 1968, expressed the same basic work frustrations that appeared in the breakdown at General Motors' automated Lordstown, Ohio, plant in 1972.

Not only are the complaints similar—so are the effective cures.

Participation methods that have been used in some progressive United States companies—such as Monsanto, Corning Glass, Eaton, Texas Instruments and Syntex—demonstrate that American, no less than European workers, are eager to make more use of their judgment and latent creativity.

In fact, some of the advanced plants of General Foods and Procter & Gamble may go further in giving workers increased freedom and responsibility than any company in Europe.

Yet in America these methods are regarded only as "management techniques," not as steps on the road to industrial democracy. Most United States executives object strongly to the use of the word "democracy" to describe their companies, and they are generally appalled at the suggestion that their methods might have a connection with over-all pressures in society.

Indeed, the whole subject is so sensitive in some advanced companies that they decline to release information on their "radical" methods.

Neither are United States unions much interested in industrial democracy. Labor leaders in almost every Western European country are aggressively pushing the cause, and some (as in Britain, Sweden and France) have radically altered their positions in recent years in favor of more industrial democracy.

But there is scarcely a union official in the United States who has the slightest familiarity with, or sympathy for, any type of industrial democracy. (Exceptions are found in the United Auto Workers, where Irving Bluestone, vice president, wants to obtain more control for workers over their own jobs and eventually over management of the companies as well.)

It may well be that labor leaders in the United States are more solidly in favor of autocratic management methods than executives are.

Following a spurt of publicity on job redesign and participation projects, some union leaders have angrily protested that the methods are being consciously used to fight unionism by making workers too content (which is often quite true) and that workers rarely receive extra pay for extra productivity (also true).

However, instead of taking the initiative in gaining some control over these methods to benefit workers, as many European union leaders have done, they have simply attacked their use. It may seem strange for unions to criticize methods that make workers too content, but the world of United States labor is not an altogether rational one.

What are the reasons for the American indifference to industrial democracy? One is doubtless the brutality of American economic life, which (relative to

Europe) makes shutdowns, layoffs and other sudden disasters such great potential realities that problems of work organization can seem almost trivial by comparison.

Another reason is America's peculiar class structure, which so often isolates middle-class intellectuals and social critics from blue-collar and white-collar workers who might be able to use some shrewd social analysis applied to their problems.

One exceptionally large barrier to industrial democracy is the traditional and accepted pattern of intracompany power.

The revered ideology of free enterprise rewards the successful man not only with material gain but also with power over those below him. Managers who have been trained to believe that power over people is one of the prerequisites of success and who are trained to believe that only authoritarian companies can survive are, understandably, not especially enthusiastic about democracy.

Despite the current flurry of interest in participative management, only a tiny minority of companies are applying non-authoritarian techniques to any appreciable extent. And in some United States companies that have initiated advanced participative methods, executives have attempted—often successfully—to kill off innovations that threaten to upset the orthdox authoritarian structure.

Just now, authoritarian ideas seem dominant in the United States. A couple of years ago a prominent personnel executive remarked to me:

"The political climate in the United States has gone quite reactionary, and this is private enterprise's way of expressing the political climate. Right-wing political viewpoints correlate with right-wing management viewpoints."

While European political leaders are striving to give workers more power over their lives, the President of the United States is pointing out that the average American is like "the child in the family" who has to be told what to do. When such attitudes are in the ascendancy, can ideas of democracy, industrial or otherwise, flourish?

The popularity of industrial democracy could, of course, surge rapidly and unexpectedly (as such things tend to do in America) if the nation's politicians, social philosophers and other intellectuals should initiate a broad public discussion of the subject.

Great numbers of employes are abundantly aware of their dissatisfaction with their jobs, but scarcely anyone in the United States recognizes that large-scale improvements are possible, practicable and desirable. If people should become conscious of the very real possibilities that exist, the results could well be explosive.

Some observers feel there may be explosions of a different sort if this does not happen. Arne Derefeldt, a Swedish personnel specialist, wrote after a trip through America:

"It would greatly surprise me if the concept of industrial democracy should be given much serious attention in the United States during the nineteen-seventies. But if it isn't, then one can see, rather pessimistically, great risks for disturbances in American working life, at the latest toward the end of the decade."

POWER TO THE WORKERS?

Robert A. Dahl

The pseudo-private corporations of the United States and the pseudo-public firms of the USSR have this much in common: neither comes close to achieving "industrial democracy." As an organizing principle, hierarchy seems to have won over democratic participation.

Probably the most radical alternative to the American and Soviet methods of governing economic enterprises is the system of self-management that has been developed in Yugoslavia since 1950. Yugoslavia is the only country in the world where a serious effort has been made to translate the old dream of industrial democracy into reality—or into as much reality as dreams usually are. Let me add at once that in the government of its state apparatus, Yugoslavia is not, of course, representative democracy. The leadership has not yet permitted an opposition party to exist; as the famous cases of Djilas and Mihajlov show, merely to advocate an opposition party may land one in jail. Yet if Yugoslavia is less democratic than the United States in the government of the state, it is more democratic in the way industries are governed. In both respects, of course, it is much more democratic than the USSR.

In fact, it was after Yugoslavia broke out of the Soviet orbit that her leaders introduced social self-management[1] as a deliberate and systematic effort to shift from the orthodox, highly centralized, bureaucratic Soviet-style socialism toward a socialism that would be more democratic, liberal, humane, and decentralized. During their brief revolution in 1968, the Czechs also moved rapidly toward decentralized socialism. Beginning in June, 1968, elected councils were established within a few months in several hundred firms, including the Skoda works in Pilsen, the largest in Czechoslovakia. But after the Russians moved in, this dangerous challenge to bureaucratic socialism was suppressed and the radical idea of self-management was attacked as antisocialist; the only appropriate representative of the workers was, naturally, the party.

Although in Yugoslavia the most dramatic step toward industrial democracy and the one most relevant here was the introduction of workers' councils throughout all economic enterprises,[2] the principle of social self-management was gradually extended to include practically every kind of organized unit—local governments, rural coops, schools, hospitals, apartment houses, the post office, telephone services.[3]

It would be a gross exaggeration to say that self-management of economic enterprises in Yugoslavia is a complete or wholly satisfactory achievement of

SOURCE: *New York Review of Books,* November 19, 1970, pp. 20–24.

industrial democracy. But, in conjunction with other aspects of the Yugoslav system, about which I shall have a word to say in a moment, the workers' councils seem to have produced not only a relatively decentralized economy but a substantial amount of participation by workers in the government of industry and of work generally. To be sure, the workers' councils are by no means autonomous; here as elsewhere in Yugoslavia organized party opposition is not permitted; strikes are rare and of doubtful legality; and the special influence of the party is important. Nonetheless, it seems clear that the councils elected by the workers are very much more than a façade behind which the party and state officials actually manage an enterprise.

What happens to "property rights" in such a system? Who *owns* the factory, railroad, bank, retail firm? In this kind of system the great myth of the nineteenth century stands exposed; ownership is dissolved into its various components. What is left? A kind of ghostly penumbra around the enterprise. The enterprise is described in the constitution as "social property." But it might be closer to the mark to say that *no one owns it*. It is not, certainly, owned by the state or by shareholders. It is not owned by the workers. The point is that "property" is a bundle of rights. Once the pieces in this bundle have been parceled out, nothing exactly corresponding to the conventional meaning of ownership or property remains.

How competently would the employees of large firms in the United States manage their enterprises under such a system? Would American enterprises be as efficiently run as at present? One ought to keep in mind that even a modest decline in physical productivity could be offset by some important gains, of which the most significant would be to transform employees from corporate subjects to citizens of the enterprise. How great a gain this would be depends on how much value we (and the employees) attach to democratic participation and control, as good both intrinsically and in their consequences for self-development and human satisfaction, quite independently of other goals.

In the absence of strictly relevant experience, predictions about productivity are of course hazardous. Although one can hardly compare Yugoslavia and the United States on this matter, it is significant that the introduction of self-management in Yugoslavia was followed by a rapid rise in productivity. As to the consequences for productivity of the various less radical schemes of employee participation and consultation that have been tried out in this country and elsewhere, the evidence is inconclusive.[4]

But surely the most relevant consideration is that in the United States management is increasingly professional and therefore available for hire. In fact, the emerging practice in the American corporation is for managers and even management teams to shift about among firms. In a recent book on the American corporation, Richard Barber writes:

> . . . the old notion that a responsible official stays with his company, rising through the ranks and wearing the indelible badge of Ford or IBM or duPont, is quaint and out of tune with a world of skilled scientific business management. It is not that the new executive is any less interested in or dedicated to the success of the company that employs him; rather it is that he sees himself as a specialist whose skills and

growth are in no way necessarily associated with any particular enterprise.[5]

I don't see why a board of directors elected by the employees could not select managers as competent as those selected by a board of directors chosen by banks, insurance companies, or the managers themselves. The board of a self-governing firm might hire a management team on a term contract in the way that a board of directors of a mutual fund often does now—and also fire them if they are incompetent. If the "profit motive" is all that it has been touted to be, who would have more at stake in improving the earnings of a firm than employees, if the management were responsible to them rather than to stockholders?

Moreover, the development of professional managers sharply spotlights the old question, *Quis custodiet ipsos custodes?* As Barber points out:

> With corporate managers holding the reins of widely diversified, global firms, but conceiving of themselves essentially as professionals, what are the rules—the standards—with which these men are to be governed in their use of the immense power they possess? As well, how are those *within* the corporation—especially its multitudinous family of technocrats and middle-level executives—to be protected from encroachment on their legitimate interests?[6]

Although Barber poses the question, he offers no answer. Yet self-management is one solution too obvious to be ignored—except in a country blinded by an unthinking adherence to the absolute conception of a "private" firm "owned" by stockholders.

It is not, I think, the question of competence that raises problems for the introduction of self-management in American firms, but the possibility that on the one hand many employees of a particular firm might not wish to participate in governing it, while on the other hand many people outside the firm might not only want to participate but could make a very good case for their right to do so.

Consider the people who work in an enterprise. While many employees, particularly technicians and lower executives, would probably welcome self-management, it is very much open to doubt, unfortunately, whether blue-collar workers want to allocate any of their attention, time, and energy to governing the enterprises in which they work. Although sentimentalists on the left may find the idea too repugnant to stomach, workers and trade unions may be the greatest barriers at present to any profound reconstruction of economic enterprise in this country. Several aspects of their outlook militate against basic changes. Along with the officialdom of the trade union movement, workers are deeply ingrained with the old private property view of economic enterprise. What is perhaps more important, affluent American workers, like affluent workers in many other advanced countries and the middle class everywhere, tend to be consumption-oriented, acquisitive, privatistic, and family-centered. This orientation has little place for a passionate aspiration toward effective citizenship in the enterprise (or perhaps even in the state!). The job is viewed as an activity not intrinsically gratifying or worthwhile but rather as an instrument for gaining money which the worker and his family can spend on articles of consumption.

In so far as this is true, the modern worker has become what classical economists said he was: an economic man compelled to perform intrinsically unreward-ing, unpleasant, and even hateful labor in order to gain money to live on. So far as its intrinsic rewards are concerned, work is simply so much time lost out of one's life. The work place, then, is not a small society; it is simply a place where you put in time and labor in order to earn money.[7] The union is a necessary instrument, but it is also a crashing bore. Solidarity is a matter of sticking to-gether during bargaining and strikes in order to get better wages and working conditions, but is not animated by any desire to change the structure of power within the firm.

The result for many workers is that a chance to participate in the government of a factory or business (even during working hours) might well hold slight attrac-tion. We know, after all, that in every representative government in the world, and even in the more direct democracy of many New England towns, including my own, a great many citizens are indifferent toward their opportunities to participate. How much more true this is likely to be in the business firm: so long as the enterprise pays good wages, its affairs seem even less interesting than affairs of state. In addition to reflecting these attitudes of their constituents, trade union leaders could easily in-terpret self-management as a threat to their influence: the consequences for incum-bent leaders would at best be uncertain, and like leaders generally, most trade union leaders prefer to avoid risks.

Yet these bleak prospects are by no means the whole story. The impetus toward self-management may not come from the strata which the conventional left (old and new) has for so long courted with such meager response. It may come instead from the white-collar employees, technicians, and the executives themselves. What is more, there is a good deal of evidence to show that although participa-tion may not guarantee increased output in the conventional sense, it does generally increase the worker's satisfaction with an interest in his work. If a significant number of employees, whether white-collar or blue-collar, were to discover that participation in the affairs of their factory or firm—or that part most directly important to them—contributed to their own sense of competence and helped them to control an important part of their daily lives, then lassitude and indiffer-ence toward participation might change into interest and concern. Of course, we should not expect too much. But we should also not reject self-management because it may not measure up to the highest ideals of participation—ideals that are, after all, not met in any democratic association.

The most severe problem raised by self-management is, I believe, the existence of interests other than the employees of an enterprise: not only consumers but others who may be affected by decisions about location, employment, discrimina-tion, innovation, safety, pollution, and so on. Decisions made in the automobile industry for example, have obvious consequences for a great many persons outside the industry. Car buyers are affected by poor safety features and by planned obsolescence. Unless the industry can be induced to develop and adopt exhaust control devices, nearly all of us stand a good chance of suffering harm. . . .

How can these and other affected interests be sure that their claims will be fairly weighed in the decisions of the firm? By focusing attention on the state as the best agent of all such affected interests, this question often drives the advocate to change straight onto the horns of the old dilemma: either bureaucratic socialism or else the private property solution. Is the only alternative to the giant American corporation the highly centralized, bureaucratically run enterprise that, however much the dead weight of hierarchy violates socialism in theory, is the usual outcome of socialization in practice? It is precisely because it enables us to escape this dilemma that self-management is so hopeful an alternative. Have we then escaped the dilemma only to find it lying in wait farther down the road?

I shall not pause to argue with any reader, if there be one, who is so unworldly as to suppose that once "the workers" control an enterprise they will spontaneously act "in the interests of all." Let me simply remind this hypothetical and I hope nonexistent reader that if self-management were introduced today, tomorrow's citizens in the enterprise would be yesterday's employees. Is their moral redemption and purification so near at hand? If not, must self-management wait until workers are more virtuous than human beings have ever been heretofore? For my part it seems wiser to arrange the structure of government on the assumption that people will not always be virtuous and at times surely will be tempted to do evil, yet in a way that will produce the incentive and the opportunities to act according to their highest potential.

If we keep in mind that internal controls over the decisions of a firm can be supplemented by controls from outside, whether by the government of the state or by other economic entities, we will easily see that various affected interests might be protected in roughly three ways that are not mutually exclusive.

To begin with, in addition to workers, others whose interests would be affected by these decisions of an enterprise might be given the right to participate in decisions—to have a direct say in management, for example, through representatives on the board of directors of the firm. Thus the board of directors might consist of one-third representatives elected by employees, one-third consumer representatives, one-third delegates of federal, state, and local governments. A system of this kind might be called *interest group management*.

Now candor compels me to admit that interest group management seems much more in the American grain than self-management. It fits the American ethos and political culture, I think, to suppose that conflicting interests can and should be made to negotiate: therefore let all the parties at interest sit on the board of directors. It would be a very American thing to do. Interest group management is, then, a development much more likely than self-management. It is hard for me to see how American corporations can indefinitely fight off proposals like those most recently made by Ralph Nader for consumer or public members on their boards.

I can readily see how we may arrive incrementally at interest group management of giant firms. One of these days a group of stockholders may succeed in electing several consumers' representatives to a board of directors. Some trade union leaders might be co-opted. A federal law might compel boards to accept a few public representatives. In time, a reform-minded national administration might even push a law through Congress providing in some detail for representation of employees, consumers, and the general public on the boards of all firms over some minimum size. Since this innovation would probably be enough to deflate weak pressures for further change, the idea of self-management would be moribund.

Yet even if interest group management is more likely, it is much less desirable, in my view, than self-management. For one thing, interest group management does very little to democratize the internal environment of an enterprise. Instead, it would convert the firm into a system of rather remote delegated authority.

For there is no democratic unit within which consumer representatives, for example, could be elected and held accountable. The delegates of the affected interests doubtless would all have to be appointed in one way or another by the federal government, by organized interest groups, by professional associations. There would be the ticklish problem of what interests were to be represented and in what proportions—a problem the Guild Socialists struggled with, but never, I think, solved satisfactorily.

Since the consequences of different decisions affect different interests, have different weights, and cannot always be anticipated, what particular interests are to be on the board of management, and how are they to be chosen? Are the employees to elect a majority or only a minority? If their representatives are a majority, the representatives of other affected interests will hardly be more than an advisory council. If a minority, I fear that most people who work for large enterprises would be pretty much where they are now, remote from the responsibility for decisions.

Doubtless interest group management would be an improvement over the present arrangements, and it may be what Americans will be content with, if the corporation is to be reformed at all. Yet it is a long way from the sort of structural change that would help to reduce the powerlessness of the ordinary American employee.

Moreover, interest group management would not eliminate the need for economic and governmental controls. For example, it would be madness in any economy to allow a firm unlimited power over the price of its product or unlimited access to funds for investment. Internal decisions on such matters may be influenced by market forces, by bargaining, by a regulatory agency, or by other means; but they cannot be left wholly within the discretion of the particular enterprise. Is it not through these external controls, rather than through participation in the internal control of the firm, that the affected interests could be best represented and protected in a system of self-management?

I cannot stress too strongly the importance of external controls, both governmental and economic. I do not see how economic enterprises can be operated satisfactorily in a modern economy, capitalist, mixed, socialist, or whatever, without some strategic external controls over the firm and its profits. However much the Yugoslavs recoil from the Soviet example of bureaucratic socialism, on this point they have no doubts. Their external controls include the forces of the market and credit, norms for salaries and the allocation of revenues, and the ubiquitous presence of the well-disciplined League of Communists. A firm is forbidden by law from selling off its assets for the benefit of the employes. The central government sets minimum wage levels; local governments may increase these levels. Depreciation rates are regulated. Foreign exchange restrictions are severe.

It is worth keeping in mind, too, that the less effective the external economic controls are—the influences of the customers and suppliers on costs and prices, of suppliers of capital and credit on interest rates and terms of borrowing, of competing firms and products on the growth and prosperity of other firms—the greater must be the governmental controls. Just as the extreme limit of economic controls is the fully competitive economy (whether capitalist or socialist), so the extreme limit of governmental controls is bureaucratic socialism. The optimum combination of internal, governmental, and economic controls will not be easy to find.

Yet it seems obvious that if we place much value on democracy at the work place, our present arrangement is ludicrously far from desirable. As for alternatives, only self-management can provide anything approaching genuine democratic authority in the American business firm. Neither the present system, nor bureaucratic socialism, nor even interest group management, holds out much real hope for reconciling the imperatives of economic organization with democratic authority.

NOTES

1. "Social self-management" is the English translation of the Serbo-Croatian term used to cover the various forms of participatory authority at the lower levels. Thus the workers' councils are said to represent workers' self-management; at the municipal level (the commune) the term self-government is often used. See, e.g., *Constitution of the Socialist Federal Republic of Yugoslavia,* chap. 2, Art. 6, and chap. 5, Art. 96.
2. Every person working in an enterprise is entitled to participate in the choice of the workers' council. In an enterprise with fewer than thirty people, the council consists of everyone in the enterprise except the director; in firms with more than seventy people, they must elect a council; in firms with between thirty and seventy persons they opt for one solution or the other.

   The workers' council elects an executive body, the managing board, and the director, who is also ex officio a member of the managing board. The director has a four-year term, cannot be a member of the workers' council, and is typically a professional; thus the relationship between workers' council and directors is not unlike that between city manager and council in manager-council governments in the U.S. Members of the board are appointed for one year and cannot serve for more than two years in succession; three-quarters of the members must be production workers.
3. Readers looking for information about Yugoslavia's experience with self-management will find a brief, objective account (together with short descriptions of efforts toward industrial democracy in Sweden and the abortive movement in Czechoslovakia in 1968) in *agenour* (Brussels, November 1969), pp. 28–40. Jiri Kolaja's *Workers' Councils: The Yugoslav Experience* (New York: Praeger, 1966) is short and seemingly reliable, though somewhat out of date.

   The best critical account to come to my attention is by a Swiss sociologist, Albert Meister, *Socialisme et Autogestion, L'Experience Jougoslave* (Paris: Editions du Seuil, 1964), though it too goes barely beyond 1960. Hugh A. Clegg's *A New Approach to Industrial Democracy* (Oxford: Blackwell, 1963) and Adolf Sturmthal's *Workers' Councils* (Cambridge: Harvard, 1965) place workers' control in Yugoslavia in a comparative context of movements toward industrial democracy.

   The most perceptive treatment of citizenship and industrial democracy I know is Graham Wootton's *Workers, Unions and the State* (London: Routledge & Kegan Paul, 1966). A skeptical but not wholly unsympathetic treatment of industrial democracy from the perspective of a Swedish professor of business administration is Eric Rhenman, *Industrial Democracy and Industrial Management* (London: Tavistock, 1968).
4. See, for example, Rhenman, *Industrial Democracy and Industrial Management,* pp. 83–84.
5. *The American Corporation: Its Power, Its Money, Its Politics* (New York: Dutton, 1970), p. 97.
6. *Ibid.,* p. 98.

7. The best evidence on this point that I am aware of comes from a study of attitudes of affluent workers in Britain, not the United States. See the three volumes of *The Affluent Worker,* edited by John H. Goldthorpe, David Lockwood, Frank Bechofer, and Jennifer Platt (Cambridge: At the University Press, 1968–69), vol. 1, *Industrial Attitudes and Behavior;* vol. 2, *Political Attitudes and Behavior;* vol. 3, *In the Class Structure.* See especially vol. 3, chap. 3, "The World of Work."

A RADICAL STRATEGY FOR
WORKER CONTROL

André Gorz

. . . Quite apart from the actual capitalist exploitation of labor power, the work situation is characterized in form and in content by the oppressive subordination of labor to capital.

At no matter what level and under whose direction, workers' training tends in fact to produce men who are mutilated, stunted in knowledge and responsibility. The dream of large industry is to absorb the worker from cradle to grave (from the layette at birth to the coffin at death, with job training, housing, and organized leisure in between), so as to narrow his horizon to that of his job. It is important, to begin with, not to give the worker (and not to permit him to acquire) skills superior to those which his specialized job requires. (This is "in order to avoid problems of adaptation," as an important French industrialist candidly explained at a recent management forum.) The worker must not be permitted to understand work as an essentially creative act; for such thoughts might lead him to reflect, to take the initiative, and to make a decision, as for example the decision to go sell his labor power elsewhere.

For its repetitive tasks, whether those of clerks in the banks and insurance houses or those of solderers in electronics, industry requires passive and ignorant manpower. Recruited on leaving school (in a rural area, by preference) and trained either on the job or in the trade schools, this manpower will not acquire a trade which will give it professional antonomy and human dignity, but merely the skills required in the individual company which hires it. In this way the company exercises over its workers not only a kind of perpetual property right, but also the right to regulate qualifications, wages, hours, quotas, piecework, etc., as it sees fit.

Even for skilled workers, the production process nevertheless remains obscure. For the semi-skilled workers, the dominant contradiction is between the active, potentially creative essence of all work, and the passive condition to which they are doomed by the repetitive and pre-set tasks dictated by assembly line methods, tasks which transform them into worn-out accessories to the machine, deprived of all initiative. For the highly skilled workers, on the other hand, the dominant contradiction is between the active essence, the technical initiative required in their work, and the condition of passive performers to which the hierarchy of the enterprise nevertheless still condemns them.

SOURCE: *Strategy for Labor* (Boston: Beacon Press, 1968), pp. 35–40, 41–43, 46–47, 48–54.

With the exception of certian industries employing chiefly unskilled labor—industries which are rapidly declining in importance—the level of technical training required for the average job is rising; but along with his increasing technical responsibilty, the worker gains no correspondingly greater mastery over the conditions to which he is subjected and which determine the manner of his work (nor, of course, is there a greater mastery over the product). Responsible for his work, he is not master of the conditions under which he carries it out. The company which hires him requires of him both creativity in the execution of his task and passive, disciplined submission to the orders and standards handed down by management.

On the margin of civil society, with its formal liberties, there thus persists behind the gates of factories, a despotic, authoritarian society with the military discipline and hierarchy which demands of the workers both unconditional obedience and active participation in their own oppression. And it is only normal that this militarized society should, on suitable occasions, assert itself as the true face of capitalist society. It tends to break out of the factory walls and to invade all domains of civil life, championing the principle of authority, the suppression of thought, criticism, speech, and assembly. In its social model, the ideal man is active but limited and submissive, having extensive skills but restricting their application to the technical domain only. . . .

The oppression of the worker, the systematic mutilation of his person, the stunting of his professional and human faculties, the subordination of the nature and content of his working life to a technological evolution deliberately hidden from his powers of initiative, of control, and even of anticipation—the majority of wage demands are in fact a protest against these things. Wage demands are more often motivated by a revolt against the workers' condition itself than by a revolt against the rate of economic exploitation of labor power. These demands translate the desire to be paid as much as possible for the time being lost, the life being wasted, the liberty being alienated in working under such conditions; to be paid as much as possible not because the workers value wages (money and all it can buy) above everything else, but because, at the present stage of union activity, only the price of labor power may be disputed with management, but not control over the conditions and nature of work.

In short, even when highly paid, the worker has no choice but to sell his skin, and therefore he tries to sell it as dearly as possible. And inversely, no matter what price he receives for selling his liberty, that price will never be high enough to make up for the dead loss which he suffers in qualitative and human terms; even the highest pay will never restore to him control over his professional life and the liberty to determine his own condition.

The simple wage demand thus appears as a distortion and a mystification of a deeper demand; exclusive concentration on the pay envelope is an impasse into which the labor movement is headed. For the movement is going in precisely the direction management wants: it is abandoning to management the power of organizing the production process, the quantitative and qualitative content of working hours and of working conditions as they see fit, in exchange for bonuses to "compensate" for the increased mutilation of the working man. The movement thus accepts the fundamental criteria of the profit economy, namely that everything has a price, that money is the supreme value, that any and everything may be done to men provided they are paid. The movement is becoming increasingly "Americanized," as the European management wants it to be: the workers abandon all efforts to control and transform the relations of production, the organization of the productive process and capitalist control of the enterprise; they leave the company free to pursue its maximum profit and to reign unchallenged over society, receiving in exchange occasional large crumbs from capital's head table. The working class movement is allowing industry to produce a new mass of lobotomized proletarians whom eight hours of daily degradation and of work by the clock leaves with only a weary desire for escape, an escape which the merchants and manipulators of leisure time and culture will sell them on credit even in their homes, persuading them in the bargain that they are living in the best of all possible worlds.

In truth, if the working class wishes to preserve its potential as the ruling class, it must first of all attack the workers' condition on the job, because it is there, where the worker is most directly alienated as producer and citizen, that capitalist society can be most immediately challenged. Only by a conscious rejection of oppressive work conditions, by a conscious decision to submit these conditions to the control of the associated workers, by an unceasing effort to exercise antonomous self-determination over the conditions of labor, can the working class maintain or assert permanently the autonomy of its consciousness as a class, and the human emancipation of the worker as a supreme end.

The achievement of workers' autonomy within the productive process, writes Vittorio Foa,

> is the most important point of union strategy, [and] the point around which democracy in an industrial society revolves. The organization of labor tends toward an increasing dissociation of decision from execution: it makes the worker into a simple, docile instrument, without control over the process of production as a whole or over its external connections. This organization tends, in other words, to subordinate the worker rigidly to the profit-oriented decisions of the employer. Even the worker's desire for a fairer share of the national product is used against him, with his complicity, to transform him into a particular type of consumer; and the resulting mass consumption increases the profits of the system. However well developed the political institutions may be, the law of production tends increasingly to be independent of political democracy, independent of the rights of free thought, free press, free association, etc. Experience shows that this fundamental lack of liberty in the modern work situation is a permanent menace to public liberties.

> Some people think that this subordination of workers is an inevitable consequence of the modern organization of production, as inevitable in a socialist regime as in a capitalist one, that this signifies that all industrial society must be condemned, and that this subordination will perhaps not be overcome until the post-industrial society, when human labor has been replaced by machines. We do not believe in this inevitability; we believe that collective action can achieve democracy. Others think that oppression arises exclusively from private appropriation of the means of production, and that once public expropriation of

capital has been achieved, the workers' liberty will be automatically as-
sured. This also seems to us inexact: socialist power can expropriate the
private capitalist and create in this way the premises of workers'
liberty; but if the organization of production in the enterprise and in
the total economy remains bureaucratized with a rigid system of centralized decision making, then the workers will continue to experience
social production as an alien process and will find themselves in a
subordination in certain ways similar to that in the capitalist countries.

The problem of industrial society, with its advanced organization of
production and of labor, is the problem of the democratic organization
of the worker's condition at work, the problem of workers' self-determination of their future and of their present, their work situation, the
quantitative and qualitative content of their performance, and thus also
self-determination of the social reproduction of their labor power. At
the monopoly stage of capitalism it is no longer possible to oppose
the power of the State to that of private monopolies: the masses no
longer cling to illusions on this subject. At the monopoly stage of
capitalism, the construction of democracy must also find forms of expression which, stemming from the workers' condition, embrace it in its
entirety and thereby embrace the entire human condition.

Thus the problem of democracy in industrial society can await neither
post-industrial society nor socialism. It should be faced in the present.
And this is precisely what the highest level of union struggle is doing
today. . . .[1]

Formal recognition of the union organization and of civil liberties on the
job remains an abstract demand, incapable of mobilizing the workers as long as
it is not organically linked to the demand for concrete workers' powers over the
conditions of work. The former demands are not ends in themselves; the organization and its civil liberties have value only insofar as they permit the pursuit of
substantial workers' powers.

And these substantial powers, as we have just indicated, consist of union control over all aspects of the work situation, in order to:

1. subordinate and adapt the exigencies of the production process to the needs
of the workers;

2. narrow the sphere of management's arbitrary powers;

3. install, finally, a true workers' counter-power, capable of challenging and of
positively counterbalancing the capitalist system of decision making in the
company (and by extension in the society).

These three aspects, implied in the demand for workers' control over the
work situation, are in fact more concrete as themes for mobilization and
action than the simple wage demand which they necessarily involve. The im-
penetrability of the overall production process, the workers' ignorance of the
economic and technical decisions which determine the conditions of their activity,
force them in practice to leave the substance of their work entirely up to
managerial control. In most cases, the union now negotiates nothing but the
minimum price of labor power, leaving the employer free to exploit the labor

force as he sees fit and to dispense premiums and bonuses over which he often has sole control and which, by definition, are not contracturally negotiable.

An increase in the basic wage either has no practical effect, or may be cancelled by a number of devices, including intensification of labor (that is, the extortion of supplementary work in the same time—a speed-up), cutting various bonuses; or the introduction of new machines which make the job more complex without granting promotions and higher wages; or demoting workers on certain jobs, a demotion which may not be accompanied by a wage cut but which entails in any case a professional devaluation for the workers concerned, a halt in the development of their capacities, and the loss of autonomy in their work.

General demands for increased wages cannot, in such a situation, improve the deteriorating condition of the worker; they cannot bring about a reduction in the rate of exploitation or of profit; they cannot even measure the impact of the proposed wage increase on the rate of exploitation and of profit. But above all, in big industry, wage demands cannot adequately cover situations as diverse as those of the laborer, the semi-skilled and skilled worker, the specialist, and the technician, whose incomes vary in each case according to sex, region, city, company, and shop.

The existing great differences in working conditions and wage levels within the same industry and for the same type of work make it impossible to mobilize the working class around general and undifferentiated demands concerning the minimum and hourly rates. And in fact, the only large all-embracing workers' movements which France has known since 1954 concerned either political goals (defense of "republican liberties" or of threatened union rights) and were thus necessarily defensive protest movements which lasted only a short time, due to their lack of political outlets and of a positive program of attack; or else they were limited to the public and nationalized sectors where differences in wage levels did not exist because of the State's monopoly over employment.

This is further evidence that general and undifferentiated slogans are incapable of uniting and mobilizing a working class which itself is differentiated to an extreme; they are incapable of launching an offensive against the employers' discretionary powers over economic and technical matters, against the contradictory evolution of productivity, wages, and profits.

This is why the first task of the working class movement today is to elaborate a new strategy and new goals which will indivisibly unite wage demands, the demand for control, and the demand for self-determination by the workers of the conditions of work. The only way to unite and mobilize a differentiated working class at present is to attack the class power of the employers and of the State; and the only way to attack the class power of the employers and the State is to wrest from each employer (and from the State) a vital piece of his power of decision and control.

Concretely, the goal of this attack should not be to achieve modifications and accommodations of the workers' condition within the framework of a given management policy and a given stage in the technological development of the industry; for such a victory, besides being non-generalizable beyond the individual company, could rapidly be taken away from the workers, as rapidly as improvements in techniques and in the organization of production permit. On the contrary, the working class movement must demand permanent power to determine, by contract, all aspects of the work situation and the wage scale, so that all modifications in the productive process must be negotiated with the workers, and so that the workers can materially influence the management of the enterprise and orient it in a given direction . . .

. . . Within the framework of this battle—whose general objectives are adaptable to each particular local situation and which embraces the most varied demands and specific problems in a single class perspective—there is quite naturally another fight, namely the battle for the recognition and autonomy of the labor organization in the enterprise. The latter is not the ultimate goal; it is rather the indispensable means which gives the workers the power to challenge and to control management policy and to determine and to impose their own policy regarding working conditions; for it is at work that the workers experience the power of capital and their conflict with society most directly. If the transformation of society and the political power of the working class are to have a meaning, then the workers must master their oppressive condition at work. . . .

Of course this battle will not lead to the immediate abolition of profit; it will not give *power* to the working class; it will not result in the abolition of capitalism. Victory will only lead to new battles, to the possibility of new partial victories. And at each of its stages, above all in its first phase, the battle will end with a compromise. Its path will be beset with pitfalls. The union will have to make certain agreements with management. The union will be unable to reject management's power as a whole, to challenge capitalist policy as a whole. The union will have to "dirty its hands." With each compromise, with each agreement at the end of a battle, it will endorse the employers' power with its signature.

We must not hide or minimize these facts. The dangers in the line of action which I have just outlined are real. Why then do we prefer this line to the present tactics? Let us look more closely.

Should we reject an economic policy based on profit? Should the working class take power? Should we refuse to endorse the employers' power? Of course; that goes without saying. But the workers endorse the employers' power every day, by punching in on time, by submitting to an organization of labor over which they have no power, by collecting their wages. They thereby accept the profit system; the power of the working class remains for them a dream. Does this mean, at least, that they or the union which represents them do not dirty their hands, that they remain free to reject the whole system altogether? That may be true. But their challenge and their rejection of capitalism remain on the level of general intentions and speechmaking; the challenge is abstract, its purity is sterile. The workers lack the means to turn their rhetoric into hard facts. The power of the employer and of capital remain intact. The workers lack positive accomplishments. They end up by falling into all the traps they had hoped to avoid. . . .

The dominant tendency in large modern industry is no longer that of maximum exploitation of its workers by means such as the individual bonus and the whip. The dominant tendency (with numerous exceptions which, however, represent the past and not the future) is to "integrate the workers." The modern employer knows that the piecework system does not "pay" any more; he knows even better that in a large enterprise where fixed capital is more important than circulating capital, regularity matters more than anything else. To obtain regularity, individual output must not be stimulated too much: each increase will be followed by a decrease. Five per cent of the workers who produce double or triple the norm are less interesting than a whole shop producing one hundred per cent of the norm permanently and on the average, and this average, moreover, represents the sum of three distinct levels of effort: a third of the workers producing at eighty per cent, a third at one hundred per cent, and a final third producing at one hundred and twenty per cent of the average output, for example.

To obtain this regularity, the employer foresees the unpredictable, especially wage demands. The tactics of the "clean handed union" thus do not bother him at all. These tactics leave the employer the power which is most important to him: the power of decision and of control; the power to determine the increases to which he will be forced to consent, in order to maintain these increases within the margins which he has fixed, and to shield these margins from all effective challenge.

Thus the union falls prey to "integration" even in the demands which it advances and the concessions which it obtains. Foreseen by management's program, these demands are integrated from the beginning into the budget and encroach very little on management's policy. Nor does the union succeed in effectively challenging a planned layoff by protest movements: the cost of protest strikes is forseen in the company budget, and the layoffs will take place as planned after the "challenge" is over. In this way union action remains without a grip on the employer's decisions and on the details of his policy, precisely because union action rejects them totally; this rejection is itself one of the elements in management's policy. And this policy remains sovereign in practice. The employer keeps the initiative: it is he who constantly confronts the union with new situations of an economic, structural, technical, or organizational order, situations which affect the professional status, the careers, the lives of the workers, situations which force them to move in the direction intended by the employer's strategy. The union has no choice but to say "yes" or "no,"[2] and its "no" has no consequence, results in no visible progress in the succession of battles which the workers carry out. The same type of battle is always repeated, and the workers always return to the point of departure.

In this way the challenge remains abstract, does not become concrete, and does not progress. There is no meaningful link between its goals of reduction and suppression of exploitation, negotiation of all elements of wages, guarantee of employment and career, elevation of living standard according to needs, abolition of the dictatorship of profit, and its daily actions. The goals stand on one side and the actions on the other, and there is no progress from one to the other.

If, on the other hand, the union seizes control of the elements on the basis of which management policy is worked out, if it anticipates the employer's decisions, if at each step it presents its own alternative solution, and if it fights on that basis, then it will challenge capitalist policy more effectively than a hundred fiery speeches. The union will be in a position to exercise control over technical, productive, and professional developments, to push them in the optimum social, economic, and human direction. This means, for example, that instead of fighting *against* layoffs and reorganization plans, the union should fight *for* a plan of reorganization, reclassification, and re-employment, a plan whose every aspect is under permanent union control. Instead of fighting against new machines and the new organization of labor which these impose, it should fight over the type of machines, the process of their installation, the future organization of labor, the future job classifications, before the reorganization takes place. Instead of fighting against the intensification of exploitation, the union should fight to gain control over the program of amortization and investment to assure that the workers benefit from it.

Does the union, by acting in this way, accept the capitalist system? In a sense, it does, without a doubt; but I have already said that it also accepts the system by pretending to reject it and by enduring it. But the important thing is not to have to endure it: it must be accepted only in order to change it, to modify its bases, to counter it point by point and at each step, in order to force it to go where the workers want it to go; in short, in order to bring capitalism to a crisis and to force it to retreat to a different battlefield. And with each partial victory, with each reconversion, merger, reorganization, investment, or layoff prevented or imposed by the union, the workers' power is strengthened, the workers' level of consciousness rises; the freedom of the employers—capitalism's sphere of sovereignty—is diminished, and the essential weakness of the system is displayed: the contradiction between the logic of profit and the needs and exigencies of men.

Is this class collaboration? Unquestionably that would be the case if the union accepted the responsibilities of "cooperation" with management, if the union lost sight of its goal, which is not a little more prosperity at any price, but the emancipation of the workers and the achievement of their right to determine their own condition; it would be class collaboration if the union agreed to participate in the elaboration of policy decisions and guaranteed their execution. But precisely this participation, advocated by the *"concertistes,"*[3] must be firmly rejected. It is not a question of elaborating a neo-paternalistic company policy with management; it is a matter of opposing a union policy to that of management, of struggling for a company-, industry- and region-wide plan, a well-elaborated and coherent plan, one which demonstrates concretely the opposition between the desirable and the possible, on the one hand, and a profit-oriented reality on the other hand.

Clearly, the battle must be concluded with a settlement, a compromise. The only ones to be shocked by this would be the left wing extremists, with whom Lenin already clashed, pointing out that there are good compromises and bad compromises. Under the circumstances, compromise would be bad if the union renounced its plan and its perspectives, in order to settle for an intermediate solution. But why should it renounce its plan? The settlement which concludes the battle simply signifies that all of the plan's objectives could not be obtained: the union has reached a compromise on the basis of the employer's adoption of a substantial part of its plan; and the union exercises its control over this plan. Thus the battle ends with a partial victory, won by force, and with a "moral" victory which, in this case, is complete. For in the course of the struggle, the workers' level of consciousness has risen; they know perfectly well that all their demands are not satisfied, and they are ready for new battles. They have experienced their power; the measures which they have imposed on management go in the direction of their ultimate demands (even though they did not obtain complete satisfaction). By compromising they do not renounce their goal; on the contrary, they move closer to it. By reaching a settlement the union does not alienate its autonomy (no more than when it accepts an eight per cent raise although it had asked for twelve per cent); it does not endorse management's plan; on the contrary, it forces management to guarantee (with union control) the execution of the essentials of the union plan.

Such is the strategy which begins to establish the power of the union to negotiate all aspects of the work situation, to diminish thereby the autonomy of the employer and, by extension, the class power of management and the State. This is not an institutional union power; it is rather a positive and antagonistic power of challenge which leaves union autonomy intact. This power, once it is achieved after necessarily long and hard struggles,[4] will establish a permanent and continuous challenge to management decisions; it will permit the union to anticipate these decisions, to influence them before they are made; it will place the workers in an offensive, not a defensive position; it will elevate their level of consciousness and competence; it will deepen their knowledge of the productive process; it will force them to specify their goals, scaled according to a strategic and programmatic vision, goals which they intend to oppose to the capitalist plan on the company, industry and regional levels, and on the level even of the national economy; it will give rise to partial and local demands (which is today not the case) within the framework of an overall and coherent perspective of response ("alternative") to monopoly capitalism, a perspective which will reciprocally influence and clarify the local demands; and in this way it will stimulate a continually resurging struggle with more and more advanced goals, at a higher and higher level.

Thus, the demand for workers' power in the enterprise does not necessarily signify the development of particularism or of company "patriotism."[5] On the contrary, this demand will have a militant and mobilizing substance, a meaning and a chance of success, insofar—but insofar only—as it is conceived as a local adaptation of an overall response to the model of capitalist development. This demand requires such an overall vision to be effective on the political level (on the level of the big decisions regarding national development and economic policy), just as political action requires the support of mobilized and militant masses; it requires this vision not only in order to make progress, but also and above all in order to establish itself as a popular counter-power capable of overcoming the obstructive power of the private and public centers of decision making in a decentralized and non-bureaucratic manner.

Thus, the demand for and the exercise of workers' power, of self-determination and control, quite naturally lead to a challenge of the priorities and purposes of the capitalist model.

NOTES

1. Vittorio Foa, "I socialisti e il sindacato" and "Considerazioni sulla vertenza dei metallurgici," *Problemi del Socialismo,* March and June 1963.
2. Sometimes the union cannot even say "no" to management offers which tie its hands, destroy its autonomy, integrate it, and buy labor peace in exchange for some material advantages.

   This inability to say "no" to the worst management offers is illustrated by the agreement signed with the "Plastiques de Roubaix" company in January 1964 by the CGT, the CFTC, the General Confederation of Labor, Working Force (CGT-FO—*Confédération Générale du Travail, "Force Ouvrière"*), and the General Confederation of Permanent Employees (CGC—*Confédération Générale des Cadres*). The principal points of the agreement are:

—A productivity (not output) bonus: the benefits of productivity are distributed in equal parts among workers and management, the latter remaining master of the method of distribution (wage increase or reduction in hours);

—Profit-sharing: twenty per cent of the net profits are distributed to the employees. But management remains master of the rate of amortization and investment (and therefore of the amount of net profit). Management policy is thus entirely screened from the union (a defect which the output bonus, as we have defined it, would have avoided).

—Guaranteed monthly wages, but overtime may be demanded in exchange for working hours that have been lost due to temporary layoffs and their partial compensation.

—"Each employee, conscious that his interest is to have a smooth-running enterprise, guarantees that he will fulfill his assigned task in the prescribed conditions." Thus, no negotiation of the conditions and the organization of work, but subordination of labor to the logic of profit.

—Anti-strike clauses providing for a four-day prior notice by the union of intent to strike, followed by a labor-management conference, followed, in case the spokesmen reach no agreement, by an additional four days' notice.

—Furthermore, grievances concerning work load must be handled by "consultation" with "labor experts" under conditions "to be determined for each case separately." The union representatives are thus called on to guarantee that the workers will not eventually challenge the working conditions which management has fixed "in association" with them.

The implicit recognition of the union organization is under these conditions equivalent to a complete loss of union autonomy.

3. "*Concertistes*" are advocates of closer cooperation between labor and management. [Translators' note.]

4. The struggle of one million Italian metal workers for these goals lasted nine months, including the equivalent of 42 days of strike. During five of these nine months, the goal was to achieve measures of workers' control over management, a goal which the management tried to dissociate from the *general* wage demands which it was willing to meet.

5. This particularism at present develops precisely because a perspective which tightly links local demands to class action is lacking.

Index